Middle School 3-1
학교시험 완벽대비

1학기 전과정

적중 100 plus

영어 기출문제집

중3

천재 | 정사열

Best Collection

구성과 특징

교과서의 주요 학습 내용을 중심으로 학습 영역별 특성에 맞춰 단계별로 다양한 학습 기회를 제공하여
단원별 학습능력 평가는 물론 중간 및 기말고사 시험 등에 완벽하게 대비할 수 있도록 내용을 구성

Words & Expressions

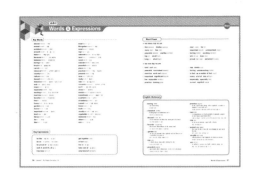

Step1	Key Words 단원별 핵심 단어 설명 및 풀이 Key Expression 단원별 핵심 숙어 및 관용어 설명 Word Power 반대 또는 비슷한 뜻 단어 배우기 English Dictionary 영어로 배우는 영어 단어
Step2	실력평가 단원별 수시평가 대비 주관식, 객관식 문제풀이
Step3	서술형 대비 학업성취도 및 수행능력평가 대비 서술형 문제풀이

Conversation

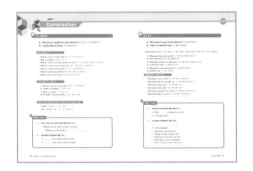

Step1	핵심 의사소통 소통에 필요한 주요 표현 방법 요약 핵심 Check 기본적인 표현 방법 및 활용능력 확인
Step2	대화문 익히기 교과서 대화문 심층 분석 및 확인
Step3	교과서 확인학습 빈칸 채우기를 통한 문장 완성 능력 확인
Step4	기본평가 시험대비 기초 학습 능력 평가
Step5	실력평가 단원별 수시평가 대비 주관식, 객관식 문제풀이
Step6	서술형 대비 학업성취도 및 수행능력평가 대비 서술형 문제풀이

Grammar

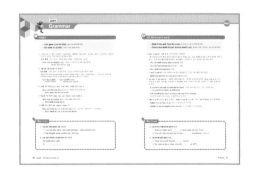

Step1	주요 문법 단원별 주요 문법 사항과 예문을 알기 쉽게 설명 핵심 Check 기본 문법사항에 대한 이해 여부 확인
Step2	기본평가 시험대비 기초 학습 능력 평가
Step3	실력평가 단원별 수시평가 대비 주관식, 객관식 문제풀이
Step4	서술형 대비 학업성취도 및 수행능력평가 대비 서술형 문제풀이

Reading

Step1	구문 분석 단원별로 제시된 문장에 대한 구문별 분석과 내용 설명 확인문제 문장에 대한 기본적인 이해와 인지능력 확인
Step2	확인학습A 빈칸 채우기를 통한 문장 완성 능력 확인
Step3	확인학습B 제시된 우리말을 영어로 완성하여 작문 능력 키우기
Step4	실력평가 단원별 수시평가 대비 주관식, 객관식 문제풀이
Step5	서술형 대비 학업성취도 및 수행능력평가 대비 서술형 문제풀이 교과서 구석구석 교과서에 나오는 기타 문장까지 완벽 학습

Composition

|영역별 핵심문제|

단어 및 어휘, 대화문, 문법, 독해 등 각 영역별 기출문제의 출제 유형을 분석하여 실전에 대비하고 연습할 수 있도록 문제를 배열

|단원별 예상문제|

기출문제를 분석한 후 새로운 시험 출제 경향을 더하여 새롭게 출제될 수 있는 문제를 포함하여 시험에 완벽하게 대비할 수 있도록 준비

|서술형 실전 및 창의사고력 문제|

학교 시험에서 점차 늘어나는 서술형 시험에 집중 대비하고 고득점을 취득하는데 만전을 기하기 위한 학습 코너

|단원별 모의고사|

영역별, 단계별 학습을 모두 마친 후 실전 연습을 위한 모의고사

교과서 파헤치기

- **단어Test1~3** 영어 단어 우리말 쓰기, 우리말을 영어 단어로 쓰기, 영영풀이에 해당하는 단어와 우리말 쓰기
- **대화문Test1~2** 대화문 빈칸 완성 및 전체 대화문 쓰기
- **본문Test1~5** 빈칸 완성, 우리말 쓰기, 문장 배열연습, 영어 작문하기 복습 등 단계별 반복 학습을 통해 교과서 지문에 대한 완벽한 습득
- **구석구석지문Test1~2** 지문 빈칸 완성 및 전문 영어로 쓰기

Contents

이책의 차례

Express Your Feelings

의사소통 기능

- 기쁨이나 슬픔에 대해 묻기
  How are you feeling?

- 기쁨 표현하기
  I'm glad to hear that.

언어 형식

- 간접의문문
  Everyone knows **what it means**.

- 관계대명사의 계속적 용법
  People also use ROFL, **which** means "Rolling On the Floor Laughing."

교과서
Words & Expressions

Key Words

- **actually** [ǽktʃuəli] 부 실제로
- **available** [əvéiləbl] 형 구할 수 있는, 이용할 수 있는
- **book** [buk] 동 예매하다, 예약하다
- **chance** [tʃæns] 명 기회, 가능성
- **conversation** [kànvərséiʃən] 명 대화
- **cupboard** [kʌ́bərd] 명 찬장
- **deliver** [dilívər] 동 전달하다
- **drone** [droun] 명 드론
- **emoji** [imóuji] 명 이모지
- **emoticon** [imóutikàn] 명 이모티콘
- **even** [íːvən] 부 심지어, ~조차
- **excited** [iksáitid] 형 흥분한, 신난
- **expression** [ikspréʃən] 명 표현
- **facial** [féiʃəl] 형 얼굴의
- **finally** [fáinəli] 부 드디어, 마침내, 마지막으로
- **form** [fɔːrm] 명 형식, 방식, 형태
- **fried** [fraid] 형 기름에 튀긴
- **funny** [fʌ́ni] 형 웃긴
- **gentleman** [dʒéntlmən] 명 신사
- **grade** [greid] 명 학년, 등급, 성적
- **guess** [ges] 동 추측하다, 짐작하다
- **healthy** [hélθi] 형 건강에 좋은
- **human** [hjúːmən] 형 인간적인, 인간의
- **invite** [inváit] 동 초대하다
- **joke** [dʒouk] 명 농담
- **laughter** [lǽftər] 명 웃음
- **letter** [létər] 명 문자, 편지
- **light** [lait] 명 빛, 등
- **lunch break** 점심시간
- **lunch menu** 점심 메뉴

- **mark** [mɑːrk] 명 기호, 표시
- **mean** [miːn] 동 의미하다
- **meaningful** [míːniŋfəl] 형 의미 있는
- **miss** [mis] 동 그리워하다
- **move** [muːv] 동 이사하다
- **nervous** [nə́ːrvəs] 형 초조한
- **popular** [pápjulər] 형 인기 있는
- **present** [préznt] 명 선물
- **promise** [prámis] 동 약속하다 명 약속
- **quite** [kwait] 부 꽤
- **represent** [rèprizént] 동 나타내다, 대표하다
- **since** [sins] 전 ~부터, ~ 이후
- **stick** [stik] 명 막대기, 나뭇가지
- **symbol** [símbəl] 명 상징
- **tear** [tiər] 명 눈물
- **text** [tekst] 명 글, 문서, 문자 메시지
- **tone** [toun] 명 어조, 말투
- **top** [tɑp] 형 맨 위의, 최고의 명 꼭대기, 정상
- **travel** [trǽvəl] 동 여행하다 명 여행
- **try** [trai] 동 먹어 보다
- **type** [taip] 동 타자 치다, 입력하다
- **various** [vέəriəs] 형 다양한
- **video chat** 화상 채팅
- **visit** [vízit] 동 방문하다
- **visually** [víʒuəli] 부 시각적으로
- **whole** [houl] 형 완전한, 전체의, 전부의
- **wonder** [wʌ́ndər] 동 궁금해 하다
- **written** [rítn] 형 글로 쓴, 글로 표현된

Key Expressions

- **a group of** 한 무리의
- **a lot** 많이
- **be worried about** ~에 대해 걱정하다
- **break wind** 방귀를 뀌다
- **can't wait for** ~을 몹시 기다리다
- **care for** ~을 좋아하다
- **grow+비교급** 점점 ~해지다
- **happier than ever** 어느 때보다 행복한
- **have fun** 즐거운 시간을 보내다

- **keep in touch** 계속해서 연락하다
- **let+목적어+동사원형** ~가 …하도록 허락하다
- **laugh out loud** 큰 소리로 웃다
- **stand for** ~을 의미하다, 상징하다
- **such as** ~와 같은
- **take a look at** ~을 보다
- **the same ~ as** ~와 같은 …
- **Why don't you+동사원형 ~?** ~하는 게 어때?
- **with+명사+형용사** … (명사)가 ~(형용사) 한 채로

Word Power

※ 서로 반대되는 뜻을 가진 어휘

- □ **popular**(인기 있는) ↔ **unpopular**(인기 없는)
- □ **available**(구할 수 있는) ↔ **unavailable**(구할 수 없는)
- □ **healthy**(건강한) ↔ **unhealthy**(건강하지 않은)

- □ **whole**(전체의) ↔ **partial**(일부분의)
- □ **nervous**(초조한) ↔ **calm**(차분한)
- □ **top**(맨 위의) ↔ **bottom**(밑바닥의)

※ 서로 비슷한 뜻을 가진 어휘

- □ **chance** : **opportunity** (기회)
- □ **book** : **reserve** (예약하다)
- □ **various** : **diverse** (다양한)

- □ **funny** : **humorous** (재미있는)
- □ **move** : **migrate** (이사하다, 이주하다)
- □ **finally** : **eventually** (마침내, 드디어)

English Dictionary

- □ **available** 구할 수 있는
  → able to be bought or used
  구입되거나 사용될 수 있는

- □ **book** 예약[예매]하다
  → to arrange to have a seat, room, performer, etc. at a particular time in the future
  미래의 특정 시간에 좌석, 방, 공연자 등을 갖도록 준비하다

- □ **conversation** 대화
  → an informal talk involving a small group of people or only two
  소수의 사람들 또는 단지 두 명의 사람들이 관여한 비공식적인 이야기

- □ **deliver** 전달하다
  → to bring goods, letter, etc, to the proper person
  적절한 사람에게 물건이나 편지 등을 가져다 주다

- □ **emoticon** 이모티콘
  → a short set of keyboard symbols that represents the facial expression used in email, etc, to show feelings
  감정을 나타내기 위해 이메일 등에 사용되는 얼굴 표정을 나타내는 일련의 짧은 키보드 기호

- □ **form** 형식, 방식
  → a type or variety of something
  어떤 것의 유형 또는 종류

- □ **gentleman** 신사
  → a man who is polite, well educated and has excellent manners
  공손하고, 교육도 잘 받고, 예의가 뛰어난 남자

- □ **guess** 추측하다
  → to give an answer to a particular question when you do not have all the facts and so cannot be certain if you are correct
  모든 사실을 가지고 있지 않아서 당신이 옳은지 확신할 수 없을 때 특정 질문에 대답을 하다

- □ **human** 인간의, 인간적인
  → being, relating to, or belonging to a person or to people as opposed to animals
  동물과는 반대로 사람 또는 사람에 관계되거나 소속되어 있는

- □ **represent** 나타내다, 대표하다
  → to be accepted as meaning a certain thing
  어떤 것을 의미하는 것으로 받아들여지다

- □ **since** ~ 이후
  → from a time in the past until a later past time or until now
  과거의 어떤 시간에서부터 나중의 과거 시간까지 또는 현재까지

- □ **symbol** 상징
  → a sign, shape, or object that is used to represent something else
  다른 무언가를 나타내기 위해 사용되는 표시, 모양, 또는 물체

- □ **tone** 어조, 말투
  → the quality of somebody's voice, especially expressing a particular emotion
  특히 특정한 감정을 표현하는 누군가의 목소리의 특질

- □ **type** 타자 치다, 입력하다
  → to write something using a computer or typewriter
  컴퓨터나 타자기를 사용하여 무언가를 쓰다

- □ **various** 다양한
  → having many different features
  다양한 특징을 가지고 있는

- □ **visually** 시각적으로
  → in a way that is connected with seeing or sight
  보는 것 또는 시력과 연결되는 식으로

- □ **written** 글로 쓴
  → involving writing rather than speaking
  말하기보다는 쓰기와 관련된

서답형

01 주어진 영어 설명에 맞게 문장의 빈칸에 알맞은 말을 쓰시오.

> You can _____ tickets at a 20 percent discount.

> <영어설명> to arrange to have a seat, room, performer, etc. at a particular time in the future

➡ _____

중요

02 다음 빈칸에 들어갈 말로 가장 적절한 것은?

> _____ is human. We laugh out loud when we hear a joke, see something funny or feel happy.

① Sadness   ② Nature
③ Love   ④ Laughter
⑤ Dialog

[03~04] 다음 설명에 해당하는 단어를 고르시오.

03

> able to be bought or used

① sale   ② facial
③ advisable   ④ possible
⑤ available

04

> an informal talk involving a small group of people or only two

① conversation   ② proverb
③ motto   ④ promise
⑤ goal

서답형

05 다음 우리말에 맞게 빈칸에 알맞은 말을 두 단어로 쓰시오.

> LOL은 '크게 소리 내어 웃기'를 상징한다.

➡ LOL _____ "Laughing Out Loud."

중요

06 빈칸에 공통으로 들어갈 말로 알맞은 것은?

> (A) The emoticon XD _____es our happy feelings more visually than ha-ha and LOL do.
> (B) The _____ started from London on time.

① fix   ② pass   ③ express
④ watch   ⑤ miss

서답형

07 다음 짝지어진 단어의 관계가 같도록 알맞은 말을 주어진 철자로 시작하여 쓰시오.

> chance : opportunity
> = eventually : f_____

중요

08 다음 빈칸 (A), (B)에 들어갈 말로 알맞게 짝지어진 것은?

> These days, people use – a "face with tears of joy." This is a small picture called an "emoji." Lots of laughing emojis are ___(A)___ to use online, so people can express their laughter in ___(B)___.

① available – a way
② banned – various ways
③ banned – a way
④ available – various ways
⑤ banned – unique ways

01 다음 빈칸에 들어갈 말을 〈보기〉에서 찾아 쓰시오. (필요하면 변형하여 쓰시오.)

┌─ 보기 ─┐
mean   since   write   work
└────────┘

"Ha-ha" is a form of _____ laughter. Everyone knows what it _____. Actually, it has been used _____ long ago. Even Shakespeare used "ha-ha" in his works.

02 〈보기〉의 단어를 활용하여 문장의 빈칸을 완성하시오.

┌─ 보기 ─┐
actual   fry   mean   face
└────────┘

(1) _____, I'm sad. I'll miss all of you.
(2) I'm glad to give him something _____.
(3) Laughing marks can represent our _____ expression and deliver our voice tone.

03 다음 우리말과 같은 표현이 되도록 문장의 빈칸을 채우시오.

(1) 다양한 웃음 표시를 사용함으로써, 우리는 친구들에게 우리가 얼마나 그들을 좋아하는지 보여줄 수 있다.
➡ By using _____ laughing marks, we can show our friends how much we care for them.

(2) 많은 웃음 이모지가 온라인에서 사용될 수 있다.
➡ Lots of laughing _____ are available to use online.

(3) 이 표현들은 상당히 빠르게 타자 칠 수 있어서 인기를 얻었다.
➡ These expressions have become popular because they can be _____ quite quickly.

04 영영풀이에 해당하는 단어를 〈보기〉에서 찾아 첫 번째 빈칸에 쓰고, 두 번째 빈칸에는 우리말 뜻을 쓰시오.

┌─ 보기 ─┐
human   guess   gentleman   tone
└────────┘

(1) _____ : to give an answer to a particular question when you do not have all the facts and so cannot be certain if you are correct: _____
(2) _____ : the quality of somebody's voice, especially expressing a particular emotion: _____
(3) _____ : being, relating to, or belonging to a person or to people as opposed to animals: _____

05 빈칸에 공통으로 알맞은 단어를 주어진 철자로 시작하여 쓰시오.

• Read the _____ carefully and then answer the questions.
• Kids also want to express emotions in their _____s using various emoticons.

➡ t_____

Conversation

① 기쁨이나 슬픔에 대해 묻기

• **How are you feeling?** 기분이 어떠니?

■ How are you feeling?은 '기분이 어떠니?'라는 뜻으로 상대방의 기쁨이나 슬픔 등의 감정에 대해 물을 때 사용하는 표현이다.
"I'm feeling … / I feel … / I am … "을 이용해서 응답한다.

기쁨이나 슬픔에 대해 물어보는 다른 표현

• How do you feel?
• Are you feeling happy[sad]?
• Are you happy[sad]?

• A: How are you feeling? 기분이 어떠니?
  B: I'm feeling really happy today. 오늘 정말 행복해.

• A: Are you happy? 너는 행복하니?
  B: Yes, I am. I'm happy. 응. 그래. 난 행복해.

• A: How are you feeling? 기분이 어떠니?
  B: Not so good. I'm not happy with the weather. It's raining too hard.
  그렇게 좋지 않아. 날씨가 마음에 들지 않아. 비가 너무 많이 내리고 있어.

핵심 Check

1. 다음 대화의 빈칸에 들어갈 알맞은 것은?

B: Yena, _____

G: I'm feeling very sad, Seho. My best friend Juhin is moving away.

① How do you do?
② What do you think about my friend?
③ Why don't you get some sleep?
④ How are you feeling?
⑤ Can you tell me about your friend, Seho?

② 기쁨 표현하기

> • **I'm glad to hear that.** 그 말을 들으니 기쁘구나.

- 'I'm (very) glad to ~'는 '~해서 (매우) 기쁘다'라는 뜻으로 'to' 뒤에는 동사원형이 온다. 이어지는 내용을 절로 쓸 때는 "I'm glad (that) ~"으로 말한다.
  - A: I'm very glad to be a 3rd grader. How about you? 3학년이 되어서 매우 기뻐. 너는 어때?
    B: I'm glad, too. 나도 기뻐.

- 기쁨을 표현할 때 다음과 같이 말할 수 있다.
  - I'm glad to+동사원형 ~.
    e.g. I'm glad to be here. 여기 와서 기뻐.

  - I'm glad (that)+주어+동사 ~.
    e.g. I'm glad that we won the game. 우리가 경기에서 이겨서 기뻐.

  - I'm delighted to+동사원형 ~.
    e.g. I'm delighted to get a present from him. 그로부터 선물을 받아서 기뻐.

- 다음과 같은 표현들은 강한 기쁨을 표현한다.
  - I feel like a million dollars. 기분이 아주 좋아.
  - I'm walking on air right now. 지금 하늘을 나는 기분이야. (기분이 매우 좋아.)
  - I couldn't be happier. 난 이보다 더 행복할 수가 없을 거야.
  - I've never been better. 이보다 더 좋을 순 없어.

핵심 Check

2. 다음 우리말에 맞도록 빈칸에 들어갈 알맞은 말을 쓰시오.

   새로운 나라로 여행할 기회를 얻게 되어 기뻐.

   = I'm _____ have a chance to travel to a new country.

   ① glad that   ② happy for
   ③ glad to   ④ nice of
   ⑤ feeling like

Step Up – Real-life Scene

I Like Their Emojis

Nari: Hi, Jiho. ❶How are you feeling?

Jiho: ❷I'm happier than ever, Nari.

Nari: I know why. ❸You did it, didn't you?

Jiho: Yes. I finally booked four tickets for the VTS concert!

Nari: Good job. Did you tell Minsu and Yujin about ❹that?

Jiho: Sure. Oh, I just got messages from them. They said they are really happy. Look.

Nari: ❺How cute! I like their emojis. They will bring light sticks and a nice camera.

Jiho: ❻I'm glad to hear that. We're going to have lots of fun!

나는 그들의 이모지가 마음에 들어

나리: 안녕, 지호. 기분이 어떠니?

지호: 어떤 때보다 행복해, 나리야.

나리: 왜 그런지 알겠다. 너 해냈구나, 그렇지?

지호: 그래. 내가 마침내 VTS 콘서트 표를 4장 예매했어!

나리: 잘했어. 민수와 유진이에게도 그것에 대해 말했니?

지호: 물론이지. 오, 그들에게서 방금 메시지를 받았어. 그 애들도 정말 기쁘다고 말했어. 봐.

나리: 정말 귀엽구나! 나는 그들의 이모지가 마음에 들어. 그 애들은 광선 막대기와 멋진 카메라를 가져올 거야.

지호: 그 말을 들으니 기쁘다. 우리는 정말 재미있을 거야!

❶ '기분이 어떠니?'라는 뜻으로 상대방의 기쁨이나 슬픔 등의 감정에 대해 물을 때 사용하는 표현이다.
❷ '비교급 than ~' 구문으로 기쁨을 표현하는 것이다. 'ever'는 비교급과 함께 '지금까지', '이제까지'의 의미로 사용된다.
❸ 'didn't you?'는 부가의문문 형태로 앞 문장의 평서문이 일반동사 긍정문일 때 부가의문문은 부정문 형태로 사용한다.
❹ that은 지시대명사로 'VTS 콘서트 표를 4장 예매한 것(booking four tickets for the VTS concert)'을 가리킨다.
❺ 감탄문으로 'How+형용사(+주어+동사)!' 형태를 사용한다. 'they are'가 생략되어 있다.
❻ 기쁨을 표현하는 말이다.

Check(√) True or False

(1) Jiho told Yujin and Minsu about booking the tickets.　　T ☐ F ☐

(2) Nari likes emojis which Jiho sent Minsu and Yujin.　　T ☐ F ☐

Start Off – Listen & Talk A 1

G: Jihun, you're moving to another country next week. How are you feeling?

B: ❶I'm excited to go to a whole new world, Yunju.

G: I'm glad to hear that. ❷I was worried about you.

B: Actually, I'm sad, too. I'll miss all of you a lot.

G: ❸Let's keep in touch online.

B: Okay. Let's have video chats often.

G: 지훈아, 너 다음 주에 다른 나라로 이사 가네. 기분이 어때?

B: 완전히 새로운 나라에 가게 되어 흥분돼, 윤주야.

G: 그 말을 들으니 기쁘구나. 나는 너를 걱정했어.

B: 사실, 슬프기도 해. 너희 모두를 많이 그리워할 거야.

G: 온라인으로 계속 연락하자.

B: 좋아. 자주 화상 채팅하자.

❶ 'I'm excited to V'는 '…해서 흥분돼'라는 의미로 기쁨의 감정을 나타내는 표현이다.
❷ 'be worried about'은 '~에 관해 걱정하다'라는 의미이다.
❸ 'keep in touch'는 '계속 연락하다'라는 의미이다.

Check(√) True or False

(3) Jihun is going to move to a new country next week.　　T ☐ F ☐

(4) Jihun and his friends will have video chats.　　T ☐ F ☐

Start Off B – Listen & Talk B

B: Yena, ❶how are you feeling?

G: ❷I'm feeling very sad, Seho. My best friend Jihun is moving away.

B: Really? I'm sorry. But don't be so sad. You two can have video chats online.

G: You're right.

B: ❸Why don't we make him a photo book as a goodbye gift?

G: Great idea. ❹I'm glad to give him something meaningful.

B: 예나야, 기분이 어떠니?
G: 아주 슬퍼, 세호야. 내 가장 친한 친구인 지훈이가 이사 간대.
B: 정말? 유감이구나. 하지만 너무 슬퍼하지 마. 너희 둘은 온라인으로 화상 채팅을 할 수 있잖아.
G: 네 말이 맞아.
B: 우리 이별 선물로 그에게 사진책을 만들어 주는 게 어때?
G: 좋은 생각이야. 그에게 뭔가 의미 있는 것을 준다니 기뻐.

❶ '기분이 어떠니?'라는 뜻으로 상대방의 기쁨이나 슬픔을 물어볼 때 사용하는 표현이다.
❷ 'I'm feeling ~.'은 'How are you feeling?'에 대한 대답으로 감정 상태를 표현할 때 사용한다.
❸ 'Why don't we+동사원형 ~?'은 제안을 할 때 사용하는 표현으로 '우리 ~하는 게 어때?'라는 의미이다.
❹ '-thing'으로 끝나는 대명사는 형용사가 뒤에서 수식한다.

Check(√) True or False

(5) Yena is feeling sad because her best friend Jihun is moving away. T ☐ F ☐

(6) Yena will give Jihun a yearbook as a goodbye gift. T ☐ F ☐

Check Yourself – Listen & Speak 1

G: Minsu, how are you feeling?

B: I'm really excited, Miso. We have a new student in our class. His name is Kim Kihun.

G: So why are you excited?

B: He was a soccer player on his school team. ❶As you know, my team needs a player.

G: I'm glad to hear that. ❷I hope he joins your team.

B: Thanks a lot.

G: 민수야, 기분이 어떠니?
B: 나 정말 신나, 미소야. 우리 반에 새 학생이 한 명 왔어. 이름은 김기훈이야.
G: 그래서 네가 왜 신나는데?
B: 그는 학교 팀 축구 선수였대. 너도 알다시피, 우리 팀은 선수가 한 명 필요하잖아.
G: 그 말을 들으니 기뻐. 그가 너희 팀에 합류하길 바랄게.
B: 고마워.

❶ As you know: 너도 알다시피, 이때의 as는 접속사로 '~이듯이'의 뜻이다.
❷ I hope (that) ~.: 나는 ~하기를 바란다.

Check(√) True or False

(7) There is a new student in the boy's class. T ☐ F ☐

(8) The new student joined the boy's team. T ☐ F ☐

📌 Get Ready 2

(1) B: You don't look happy. Are you all right?

    G: No, I'm really sad. My dog is sick. He won't eat at all.

    B: ❶That's too bad.

(2) B: It'll be a good day today! Take a look at today's lunch menu.

    G: Wow! ❷I'm glad to eat fried chicken! ❸I can't wait for lunch break.

(3) W: Good morning, Mr. Lee. How are you feeling?

    M: I'm feeling very happy this morning. ❹ Some students are helping me clean the school.

    W: I'm glad to hear that.

(4) G: You look upset. Are you all right?

    B: My mom won't ❺let me play soccer after school.

    G: Why don't you ask her one more time?

❶ 유감을 나타낼 때 사용하는 표현이다.
❷ '~해서 기쁘다'라는 의미로 기쁨을 나타낼 때 사용하는 표현이다.
❸ 'I can't wait for ~'는 '~가 무척 기다려진다'는 뜻이다.
❹ help+목적어+목적보어(동사원형/to부정사): ~가 …하는 것을 돕다
❺ '사역동사(let)+목적어+목적보어(동사원형)' 형태로 '…가 ~하도록 허락하다'는 의미이다.

📌 Start Off – Listen & Talk A 2

G: Minsu, ❶Jihun is moving to Abu Dhabi in the UAE next week. How are you feeling?

B: I'm sad. ❷I'm going to miss him a lot.

G: I'm sad, too, but I'm also happy. We can visit Abu Dhabi. He is going to invite us. He promised.

B: That's great! I'm glad to have a chance to travel to a new country.

❶ 현재진행형이 미래의 부사구(next week)와 사용될 때는 '~할 예정이다'로 해석한다.
❷ 'be going to+동사원형'은 '~할 예정이다'라는 의미이고, 여기서 miss는 '그리워하다'는 뜻이다.

📌 Fun Time

A: How are you feeling?

B: I'm nervous. ❶I forgot to bring my math homework. How are you feeling?

A: I'm nervous, too. I have a math test tomorrow. ❷I'm glad to find someone who feels the same.

B: Me, too.

❶ 'forget to+동사원형'은 '~할 것을 잊다'라는 의미이다. 'forget+V-ing(동명사)'는 '~한 것을 잊다'라는 의미이다.
❷ 'I'm glad to+동사원형'은 '~해서 기뻐'라는 의미이고, who는 관계대명사로 선행사 someone을 수식하는 형용사절을 이끈다.

📌 Express Yourself A 1

G: How are you feeling today?

B: ❶I'm really glad to get a present for my birthday.

G: What is the present?

B: It's this drone, ❷which our grandpa sent for my birthday.

G: Wow! I wonder how high it can fly.

B: Let me show you.

G: Thanks.

❶ 'I'm glad to+동사원형'에서 to부정사는 '~해서'라는 감정의 원인을 나타낸다.
❷ 콤마(comma) 뒤의 관계대명사 which는 계속적 용법으로 '접속사+대명사(and our grandpa sent it for my birthday)'로 바꾸어 사용할 수 있다.

📌 Express Yourself A 2

G: How are you feeling?

M: I'm really glad to cook my favorite food.

G: I want to know ❶what it is.

M: It's *japchae*, which is delicious and healthy.

G: I want to ❷try some.

M: Okay. Wait for 30 minutes!

❶ what it is는 간접의문문으로 know의 목적어이다.
❷ try some = try some *japchae*

● 다음 우리말과 일치하도록 빈칸에 알맞은 말을 쓰시오.

Get Ready 2

(1) **B:** You don't _____ _____. Are you all _____?

    G: No, I'm _____ sad. My dog is _____. He won't eat _____ _____.

    B: _____ _____ _____.

(2) **B:** It'll be a good day today! _____ _____ _____ at today's lunch menu.

    G: Wow! I'm _____ _____ _____ fried chicken! I _____ _____ _____ lunch break.

(3) **W:** Good morning, Mr. Lee. _____ are you _____?

    M: I'm feeling very happy this morning. Some students are _____ me _____ the school.

    W: I'm_____ _____ _____ _____.

(4) **G:** You look _____. Are you _____ _____?

    B: My mom won't _____ me _____ soccer after school.

    G: _____ _____ _____ ask her one more time?

Start Off – Listen & Talk A

1. **G:** Jihun, you're _____ to another country next week. _____ are you feeling?

    B: I'm _____ to go to a _____ new world, Yunju.

    G: I'm glad _____ _____ that. I _____ _____ _____ you.

    B: _____, I'm sad, too. I'll _____ all of you a lot.

    G: Let's _____ _____ _____ online.

    B: Okay. Let's _____ video chats often.

2. **G:** Minsu, Jihun _____ _____ to Abu Dhabi in the UAE next week. How are you feeling?

    B: I'm sad. I'm going to _____ him a lot.

    G: I'm sad, too, but I'm also happy. We can visit Abu Dhabi. He _____ _____ to _____ us. He _____.

    B: That's great! I'm _____ _____ _____ a _____ to travel to a new country.

해석

(1) **B:** 기분이 좋아 보이지 않는구나. 너 괜찮니?

    G: 아니, 나 정말 슬퍼. 내 개가 아파. 그는 아무것도 안 먹으려고 해.

    B: 정말 안됐구나.

(2) **B:** 오늘은 좋은 날이 될 거야! 오늘 점심 메뉴 좀 봐.

    G: 와! 닭튀김을 먹게 되어 기뻐! 점심시간이 무척 기다려져.

(3) **W:** 안녕하세요, 이 선생님. 기분이 어떠세요?

    M: 오늘 아침에는 기분이 아주 좋습니다. 몇몇 학생들이 학교 청소하는 것을 돕고 있어요.

    W: 그 말을 들으니 기쁘군요.

(4) **G:** 기분이 언짢아 보인다. 너 괜찮니?

    B: 엄마가 방과 후에 축구하는 것을 허락하지 않으셔.

    G: 한 번 더 말씀드려 보지 그러니?

1. **G:** 지훈아, 너 다음 주에 다른 나라로 이사가지. 기분이 어때?

    B: 완전히 새로운 나라에 가게 되어 흥분돼, 윤주야.

    G: 그 말을 들으니 기쁘구나. 나는 너를 걱정했어.

    B: 사실, 슬프기도 해. 너희 모두를 많이 그리워할 거야.

    G: 온라인으로 계속 연락하자.

    B: 좋아. 자주 화상 채팅하자.

2. **G:** 민수야, 지훈이가 다음 주에 아랍 에미리트의 아부다비로 이사 간대. 기분이 어떠니?

    B: 슬퍼. 그 애가 많이 보고 싶을 거야.

    G: 나도 슬퍼, 하지만 기쁘기도 해. 우리는 아부다비를 방문할 수 있잖아. 그가 우리를 초대할 거야. 약속했어.

    B: 그거 굉장하다! 새로운 나라로 여행할 기회를 얻게 되어 기뻐.

Start Off – Listen & Talk B

B: Yena, _____ _____ _____ _____?
G: I'm feeling very sad, Seho. My best friend Jihun is _____ _____.
B: Really? I'm _____. But _____ _____ so sad. You two can have video chats online.
G: You're right.
B: _____ _____ _____ make him a photo book _____ a goodbye gift?
G: Great idea. I'm glad to give him _____ _____.

Start Off – Speak Up – Mission

A: _____ _____ _____ feeling today?
B: I'm _____ happy. Today's lunch is great.
A: I'm _____ _____ _____ _____.

Step Up – Real-life Scene

I Like Their Emojis

Nari: Hi, Jiho. _____ are you feeling?
Jiho: I'm _____ than _____, Nari.
Nari: I know _____. You did it, _____ you?
Jiho: Yes. I finally _____ four tickets for the VTS concert!
Nari: Good job. Did you tell Minsu and Yujin _____ that?
Jiho: Sure. Oh, I just _____ _____ from them. They said they are really happy. Look.
Nari: _____ _____! I like their _____. They will _____ light _____ and a nice camera.
Jiho: _____ _____ _____ _____ _____. We're going to have lots of _____!

Fun Time

A: How are you _____?
B: I'm _____. I _____ _____ _____ my math homework. _____ _____ you feeling?
A: I'm _____, too. I have a math test tomorrow. I'm glad to find someone _____ _____ the same.
B: Me, too.

A: _____ are you feeling?
B: I'm _____. I _____ a good grade. How are you feeling?
A: I'm _____. Someone _____ my glasses.

해석

B: 예나야, 기분이 어떠니?
G: 아주 슬퍼, 세호야. 내 가장 친한 친구인 지훈이가 이사 간대.
B: 정말? 유감이구나. 하지만 너무 슬퍼하지 마. 너희 둘은 온라인으로 화상 채팅을 할 수 있잖아.
G: 네 말이 맞아.
B: 우리 이별 선물로 그에게 사진책을 만들어 주는 게 어때?
G: 좋은 생각이야. 그에게 뭔가 의미 있는 것을 준다니 기뻐.

A: 오늘 기분이 어떠니?
B: 기분이 좋아. 오늘 점심이 훌륭해.
A: 그 말을 들으니 기쁘구나.

나는 그들의 이모지가 마음에 들어
나리: 안녕, 지호. 기분이 어떠니?
지호: 어떤 때보다 행복해, 나리야.
나리: 왜 그런지 알겠다. 너 해냈구나, 그렇지?
지호: 그래. 내가 마침내 VTS 콘서트 표를 4장 예매했어!
나리: 잘했어. 민수와 유진이에게도 그것에 대해 말했니?
지호: 물론이지. 오, 그들에게서 방금 메시지를 받았어. 그 애들도 정말 기쁘다고 말했어. 봐.
나리: 정말 귀엽구나! 나는 그들의 이모지가 마음에 들어. 그 애들은 광선 막대기와 멋진 카메라를 가져올 거야.
지호: 그 말을 들으니 기쁘다. 우리는 정말 재미있을 거야!

A: 기분이 어떠니?
B: 나는 초조해. 수학 숙제 가져오는 걸 잊어버렸어. 너는 기분이 어떠니?
A: 나도 초조해. 내일 수학 시험이 있어. 같은 감정을 가진 사람을 찾아서 기뻐.
B: 나도 그래.

A: 기분이 어떠니?
B: 나는 기분이 좋아. 좋은 점수를 받았어. 너는 기분이 어떠니?
A: 나는 화가 나. 누군가가 내 안경을 망가뜨렸어.

Express Yourself A 1

G: _____ _____ you feeling today?

B: I'm really glad to _____ _____ _____ for my birthday.

G: What is the _____?

B: It's this drone, _____ our grandpa sent for my birthday.

G: Wow! I _____ _____ _____ it can fly.

B: _____ _____ _____ you.

G: Thanks.

Express Yourself A 2

G: _____ are you _____?

M: I'm really glad _____ _____ my _____ food.

G: I want to know _____ _____ _____.

M: It's *japchae*, _____ is _____ and _____.

G: I want _____ _____ some.

M: Okay. _____ _____ 30 minutes!

Check Yourself – Listen & Speak 1

G: Minsu, _____ _____ _____ _____?

B: I'm really _____, Miso. We _____ a new student _____ our class. His name is Kim Kihun.

G: So _____ are you _____?

B: He was a soccer player _____ his school _____. _____ _____ _____, my team _____ a player.

G: _____ _____ _____ _____ _____ that. I _____ he _____ your team.

B: Thanks a lot.

01 우리말에 맞도록 주어진 단어를 이용하여 5 단어로 쓰시오.

> 넌 오늘 기분이 어때? (how, feeling)

➡ _____

02 다음 대화의 빈칸에 들어갈 말로 알맞은 것은?

> W: Good morning, Mr. Lee. How are you feeling?
>
> M: I'm feeling very happy this morning. Some students are helping me clean the school.
>
> W: _____

① That's too bad.

② I'm sorry to hear that.

③ I don'k know how to help you.

④ You did a good job.

⑤ I'm glad to hear that.

03 다음 대화의 빈칸에 들어갈 말로 적절하지 <u>않은</u> 것은?

> B: You don't look happy. Are you all right?
>
> G: No, I'm really sad. _____
>
> B: That's too bad.

① I don't know whether Kirk likes me.

② I am having trouble with playing the guitar.

③ My dog is sick. He won't eat at all.

④ I'm glad to eat fried chicken!

⑤ My best friend Jihun is moving away.

04 다음 대화의 밑줄 친 우리말에 맞게 주어진 단어를 이용하여 문장의 빈칸을 채우시오.

> B: I'm excited to go to a whole new world, Yunju.
>
> G: I'm glad to hear that. <u>나는 너를 걱정했어</u>. (worry)

➡ I _____ you.

[01~02] 다음 대화를 읽고 물음에 답하시오.

G: Jihun, you're moving to another country next week. How are you ⓐfeeling?
B: I'm ⓑsad to go to a whole new world, Yunju.
G: I'm ⓒglad to hear that. I was ⓓworried about you.
B: Actually, I'm ⓔsad, too. I'll miss all of you a lot.
G: _____(A)_____
B: Okay. Let's have video chats often.

01 위 대화의 흐름상 밑줄 친 ⓐ~ⓔ 중 어휘의 쓰임이 어색한 것은?

① ⓐ   ② ⓑ   ③ ⓒ   ④ ⓓ   ⑤ ⓔ

02 위 대화의 빈칸 (A)에 들어갈 말로 알맞은 것은?

① I can visit you.
② We can write letters to each other.
③ My best friend is moving away, too.
④ Let's keep in touch online.
⑤ Why don't you buy a gift for me?

03 다음 대화의 밑줄 친 우리말에 맞게 주어진 단어를 이용하여 영어로 쓰시오.

A: How are you feeling today?
B: I'm feeling sad. My friend is sick.
A: 그 말을 들으니 안됐구나.

sorry / hear / that

➡ _____

[04~05] 다음 대화를 읽고 물음에 답하시오.

G: _____(A)_____
B: I'm really glad to get a present for my birthday.
G: What is the present?
B: It's this drone, which our grandpa sent for my birthday.
G: Wow! (B)그게 얼마나 높이 날 수 있는지 궁금하다.
B: Let me show you.
G: Thanks.

04 위 대화의 빈칸 (A)에 들어갈 말로 알맞은 것은?

① How are you feeling today?
② What's your favorite present for your birthday?
③ What do you think of this drone?
④ Do you like the present?
⑤ What do you want to get?

05 위 대화의 밑줄 친 (B)의 우리말에 맞게 주어진 단어를 이용하여 쓰시오.

wonder / high / it / can

➡ _____

06 다음 대화의 밑줄 친 부분의 의도로 알맞은 것은?

A: I have bad news.
B: What is it?
A: John fell down and broke his leg.
B: I'm sorry to hear that.

① 실망 표현하기   ② 상기시켜 주기
③ 격려에 답하기   ④ 기대 표현하기
⑤ 유감 표현하기

[07~08] 다음 대화를 읽고 물음에 답하시오.

Nari: Hi, Jiho. How are you feeling?

Jiho: I'm ⓐhappy than ever, Nari.

Nari: I know why. You did it, ⓑdidn't you?

Jiho: Yes. I finally ⓒbooked four tickets for the VTS concert!

Nari: Good job. Did you tell Minsu and Yujin about that?

Jiho: Sure. Oh, I just got messages from them. They said they are really happy. Look.

Nari: ⓓHow cute! I like their emojis. They will bring light sticks and a nice camera.

Jiho: I'm glad to hear that. We're going to have ⓔlots of fun!

 07 위 대화의 밑줄 친 ⓐ~ⓔ 중 어법상 어색한 것은?

① ⓐ   ② ⓑ   ③ ⓒ   ④ ⓓ   ⑤ ⓔ

 08 위 대화를 읽고 답할 수 없는 것은?

① How is Jiho feeling now?

② Why is Jiho so happy?

③ What did Minsu and Yujin send to Jiho?

④ How did Jiho book the tickets for the VTS concert?

⑤ What does Nari like?

서답형

09 다음 대화의 빈칸에 공통으로 들어갈 말에 대한 영어 풀이를 보고 주어진 철자로 시작하여 쓰시오.

> A: How are you feeling?
>
> B: I'm _____. I forgot to bring my math homework. How are you feeling?
>
> A: I'm _____, too. I have a math test tomorrow.

worried or frightened about something, and unable to relax

➡ n_____

10 주어진 문장에 이어질 대화의 순서로 알맞은 것은?

> G: How are you feeling?

> (A) I want to try some.
> (B) It's *japchae*, which is delicious and healthy.
> (C) I'm really glad to cook my favorite food.
> (D) I want to know what it is.

> M: Okay. Wait for 30 minutes!

① (B) – (A) – (C) – (D)

② (B) – (C) – (A) – (D)

③ (C) – (B) – (D) – (A)

④ (C) – (D) – (B) – (A)

⑤ (D) – (B) – (C) – (A)

중요

11 다음 두 사람의 대화가 어색한 것은?

① A: You don't look happy. Are you all right?

   B: No, I'm really sad.

② A: How are you feeling?

   B: I'm happier than ever.

③ A: My best friend is moving to another country next week.

   B: I'm glad to hear that.

④ A: Some students are helping me clean the school.

   B: I'm glad to hear that.

⑤ A: I'm feeling sad. My friend is sick.

   B: I'm sorry to hear that.

[01~02] 다음 대화를 읽고 물음에 답하시오.

> Nari: Hi, Jiho. How are you feeling?
>
> Jiho: (A)나는 어느 때보다 더 행복해, Nari.
>
> Nari: I know why. You did it, didn't you?
>
> Jiho: Yes. I finally booked four tickets for the VTS concert!
>
> Nari: Good job. Did you tell Minsu and Yujin about that?
>
> Jiho: Sure. Oh, I just got messages from them. They said they are really happy. Look.
>
> Nari: How cute! I like their emojis. They will bring light sticks and a nice camera.
>
> Jiho: I'm glad to hear that. We're going to have lots of fun!

01 위 대화를 읽고 다음 물음에 영어로 답하시오. (5 단어로 쓸 것)

Q: What does Nari think of the emojis?

➡ _____

02 위 대화의 밑줄 친 (A)의 우리말에 맞게 'happy'와 'ever'를 활용하여 영작하시오.

➡ _____

03 다음 대화의 빈칸에 들어갈 말로 자연스러운 것을 〈보기〉에 서 찾아 쓰시오.

> B: Yena, _____(A)_____
>
> G: I'm feeling very sad, Seho. My best friend Jihun is moving away.
>
> B: _____(B)_____ But don't be so sad. You two can have video chats online.
>
> G: You're right.
>
> B: _____(C)_____
>
> G: Great idea. I'm glad to give him something meaningful.

> ┤ 보기 ├
> • Why don't we make him a photo book as a goodbye gift?
> • how are you feeling?
> • Really? I'm sorry.

➡ (A) _____
　 (B) _____
　 (C) _____

04 다음 대화의 밑줄 친 질문에 대한 답을 주어진 단어를 활용 하여 〈조건〉에 맞게 영작하여 빈칸 (A)를 채우시오.

> ┤ 조건 ├
> • 관계대명사의 계속적 용법을 사용할 것.
> • this drone, our grandpa, send, for my birthday

> G: How are you feeling today?
>
> B: I'm really glad to get a present for my birthday.
>
> G: What is the present?
>
> B: _____(A)
>
> G: Wow! I wonder how high it can fly.
>
> B: Let me show you.
>
> G: Thanks.

➡ It's _____

_____ .

05 다음 대화의 빈칸에 들어갈 말을 주어진 단어를 알맞게 배 열하여 쓰시오.

> B: It'll be a good day today! Take a look at today's lunch menu.
>
> G: Wow! I'm glad to eat fried chicken!
>
> _____
>
> (for / break / I / can't / lunch / wait)

Grammar

교과서

1 간접의문문

• Everyone knows **what it means**. 모두가 그것이 무엇을 의미하는지 안다.

■ 형태: 의문사+주어+동사
의미: ~인지/일지

■ 다른 문장 뒤에 이어져서 간접의문문이 되며 '의문사+주어+동사'의 어순이 된다.
  • Do you know? + What time is it? (의문사+동사+주어)
  = Do you know **what time it is**? (의문사+주어+동사) 너는 몇 시인지 아니?

■ 의문사가 주어인 경우에는 의문사 뒤에 바로 동사가 이어진다.
  • Can you tell me? + Who visited our school today? (의문사(=주어)+동사)
  = Can you tell me **who visited our school today**? (의문사(=주어)+동사)
  오늘 누가 우리 학교를 방문했는지 내게 말해 줄 수 있니?

■ 'how often, how much, how many people, what kind of food'처럼 하나의 의미 단위로 쓰이는 의문사구는 하나의 의문사로 취급한다.
  • Tell me. + What kind of food does she enjoy? (의문사구+조동사+주어+동사원형)
  = Tell me **what kind of food she enjoys**. (○) 그녀가 어떤 종류의 음식을 좋아하는지 내게 말해 줘.
    Tell me what she enjoys kind of food. (✕)

■ 주절이 Do you think(believe, guess, suppose 등)일 때 간접의문문의 의문사는 맨 앞으로 보내진다.
  • Do you think? + When did Tom leave?
  = **When** do you think **Tom left**? 넌 Tom이 언제 떠났다고 생각하니?

■ 의문사가 없는 의문문은 의문사 대신 두 절을 연결하는 접속사로 whether 또는 if를 쓰고 '접속사+주어+동사'의 어순이 된다.
  • I wonder. + Is he satisfied with his job? (동사+주어)
  = I wonder **whether[if] he is satisfied with his job**. (접속사+주어+동사)
  그가 자기 직업에 만족하는지 궁금해.

핵심 Check

1. 다음 괄호 안에서 알맞은 것을 고르시오.
  (1) Do you know (who is he / who he is)?
  (2) Do you know (where does he come from / where he comes from)?
  (3) Tell me (how old he is / how he is old).

② 관계대명사의 계속적 용법

> • People also use ROFL, **which** means "Rolling On the Floor Laughing."
> 사람들은 또한 ROFL를 사용하는데, 그것은 '바닥을 구르면서 웃기'를 의미한다.

■ 형태: 쉼표(,) + 관계대명사
쓰임: 관계대명사절이 선행사에 대해 부연 설명할 때 사용함

■ 선행사가 사람이면 'who[whom]', 사람이 아니면 'which'를 사용한다. 그러나 'that'은 사용하지 않는다.

- Last Friday, I met my friend, Jack, **who** is a police officer.
  지난 금요일, 나는 내 친구 Jack을 만났는데, 그는 경찰관이다.
- This is my new laptop, **which** my mom bought for me.
  이것은 나의 새 노트북인데, 엄마가 나에게 사 주셨다.
- We visited the building, **which** was built by my company.
  우리는 그 건물을 방문했는데, 그것은 우리 회사에 의해서 지어졌다.

■ 관계대명사의 제한적 용법은 선행사를 꾸밀 때 사용하고 관계사절을 먼저 해석하지만, 관계대명사의 계속적 용법은 선행사를 부연 설명할 때 사용하므로 관계사절을 나중에 사용한다.

- Mrs. Irene has a daughter **who** is a lawyer. (Mrs. Irene은 변호사인 딸이 하나 있다. → 다른 직업을 가진 다른 딸이 있을 수 있음)
- Mrs. Irene has a daughter, **who** is a lawyer. (Mrs. Irene은 딸이 하나 있는데, 그녀는 변호사이다. → 딸이 한 명밖에 없고, 그 딸이 변호사임)

■ 선행사가 앞선 절의 일부이거나 전체인 경우, 'which'를 사용한 관계대명사의 계속적 용법으로 문장을 쓴다.

- He lost his new backpack, **which** made his mother angry. 〈선행사가 앞 문장 전체〉
  그는 그의 새 책가방을 잃어버렸는데, 그것이 그의 어머니를 화나게 만들었다.

핵심 Check

2. 다음 괄호 안에서 알맞은 것을 고르시오.

(1) This is Hannah, (who / that) is kind and smart.

(2) We wrote a letter to Jimin, (who / which) made him happy.

(3) My aunt, (who / that) is a teacher, lives in Incheon.

01 다음 우리말에 맞게 괄호 안에 주어진 어구를 바르게 배열하시오.

(1) 당신 학교의 이름이 무엇인지 제게 말해 주세요. (the name, tell, is, what, me, of your school)

➡ _____

(2) 저는 당신의 영어 선생님이 어디 출신인지 알고 싶습니다. (where, to know, like, your English teacher, I'd, comes from)

➡ _____

(3) 이 가방이 얼마인지 제게 말해 줄 수 있나요? (how much, tell, can, you, me, is, this bag)

➡ _____

(4) 저는 왜 당신이 슬픈지 알고 싶습니다. (why, to know, feeling, I'd like, sad, you, are)

➡ _____

02 다음 문장에서 어법상 <u>어색한</u> 부분을 바르게 고쳐 쓰시오.

(1) She has an office, where is located on Worchester Street.

_____ ➡ _____

(2) I have been to Wellington, that is the capital of New Zealand.

_____ ➡ _____

(3) Can you tell me where did Ann spend her vacation?

_____ ➡ _____

(4) I don't know why was he absent from school.

_____ ➡ _____

03 다음 우리말에 맞게 주어진 어휘를 바르게 배열하시오.

┌─ 보기 ├─

I asked Jane. + What did she eat for lunch yesterday?

→ I asked Jane what she ate for lunch yesterday.

└──────────

(1) Tell me. + When is your birthday?

➡ _____

(2) I didn't know. + What did she major in?

➡ _____

(3) Do you know? + What is the most famous online game these days?

➡ _____

01 다음 중 어법상 어색한 문장을 고르시오.

① Do you know who visited the museum?
② Can you tell me what it is time?
③ I wonder if we will have an exam.
④ What do you think he likes to eat for dinner?
⑤ I'm not sure how many people will come to my birthday party.

02 다음 두 문장을 한 문장으로 바르게 쓴 것을 고르시오.

> • Can you tell me?
> • How many hours do you sleep a day?

① Can you tell me how many hours do you sleep a day?
② Can you tell me how you sleep many hours a day?
③ How can you tell me many hours you sleep a day?
④ Can you tell me how many hours you sleep a day?
⑤ How many hours can you tell me sleep a day?

03 다음 빈칸에 들어갈 말로 적절한 것은?

> This is my friend, Minseung, _____ has a cute younger sister.

① that   ② who
③ whom   ④ whose
⑤ which

04 다음 빈칸에 들어갈 수 있는 말이 다른 하나는?

① She has a son, _____ is studying in Vancouver.
② My homeroom teacher, _____ teaches English, lives in Seoul.
③ Ted seems to like Jenny, _____ is very shocking to us.
④ I'm glad to meet Tom again, _____ I haven't heard from for a long time.
⑤ Look at that girl, _____ is smiling brightly.

05 빈칸에 들어갈 말을 순서대로 바르게 연결한 것은?

> • I wonder _____ he put his pencil case.
> • Can you guess _____ my brother got for his birthday?

① what – when
② where – how
③ how – who
④ how – when
⑤ where – what

06 다음 밑줄 친 who의 성격이 나머지 넷과 다른 것은?

① Can you guess <u>who</u> will be the next leader of our team?
② I haven't decided <u>who</u> to meet next Monday.
③ <u>Who</u> do you think is your best friend?
④ Please tell her <u>who</u> should be invited.
⑤ Meet my friend, Mingyu, <u>who</u> is the most popular boy.

서답형

07 다음 괄호 안에 주어진 단어들을 바르게 배열하여 문장을 완성하시오.

> The soccer ball is from Messi, (a big soccer game, whom, Amy, after, met).

➡ _____

08 다음 두 문장을 한 문장으로 바르게 옮긴 것은?

> • Do you know?
> • Does he have brothers or sisters?

① Do you know that he has brothers or sisters?
② Do you know whether does he have brothers or sisters?
③ Do you know whether he have brothers or sisters?
④ Do you know whether he has brothers or sisters?
⑤ Do you know he has brothers or sisters?

서답형

09 다음 문장에서 어법상 어색한 것을 바르게 고쳐 다시 쓰시오.

(1) I wonder how you need many books.

➡ _____

(2) Tell me why did he invent the machine.

➡ _____

서답형

10 다음 두 문장을 관계대명사의 계속적 용법을 사용하여 한 문장으로 바르게 바꿔 쓰시오.

> • I'm going to show you the photo.
> • My friend, Amy, sent it to me.

➡ _____
_____

 중요

11 다음 중 어법상 어색한 문장을 고르시오.

① She lives in Seoul, which is the biggest city in Korea.
② This is the microwave oven, which was invented by Dr. Spencer.
③ What do you think he will bring tomorrow?
④ I wonder that my teacher will ask me a question or not.
⑤ They welcomed me with a warm heart, which moved me.

서답형

12 다음 괄호 안에서 알맞은 말을 고르시오.

(1) I have grandparents, and (who / they) live in Busan.
(2) We sang a song, (who / which) sounded beautiful.
(3) She works at the bank, (which / where) is located on Downing Street.
(4) Mason won the gold medal, (which / who) made his family happy.
(5) I have a cat, (that / which) can jump high.

서답형

13 다음 괄호 안에 주어진 어구들을 바르게 배열하여 문장을 완성하시오.

> Can you tell me (for, many, we, class, to, pencils, how, need, bring, the next)?

➡ _____
_____

서답형

[14~15] 주어진 어휘를 이용하여 다음 우리말을 영어로 쓰시오.

14 너는 왜 과학자가 되고 싶은지 나에게 말해 줄 수 있니? (can, tell, why, become, scientist)

➡ _____

_____

15 나는 언니가 한 명 있는데, 그녀는 New York 에서 음악을 공부하는 중이야. (older, music, studying)

➡ _____

_____

16 다음 중 밑줄 친 부분의 쓰임이 <u>어색한</u> 것을 고르시오.

① This is Ms. Kim, <u>who</u> is my art teacher.

② My uncle has a son, <u>who</u> will go to high school next year.

③ I had dinner with Mike, <u>who</u> is one of my friends.

④ I bought a camera for June, <u>who</u> was very expensive.

⑤ I met an old friend, <u>who</u> didn't recognize me at first.

중요

17 빈칸에 들어갈 말을 순서대로 바르게 연결한 것은?

• This is Nancy, _____ took this photo.

• Do you know _____ your parents' favorite foods are.

① who – why　　② who – what

③ which – who　④ which – what

⑤ what – why

18 다음 문장에서 'who'가 들어갈 위치로 알맞은 것을 고르시오.

① Nancy, ② will throw ③ a birthday party tomorrow, ④ is ⑤ my classmate.

①　　②　　③　　④　　⑤

중요

19 다음 중 어법상 <u>어색한</u> 문장을 고르시오.

① I like Junho, who is gentle and kind.

② I met my friend at night, who was a secret.

③ I bought new pants, which were too tight.

④ I made friends with Chris, who speaks Korean fluently.

⑤ The books, which you gave me, were very helpful.

서답형

20 다음 문장을 두 문장으로 나누어 쓰시오.

(1) Do you know what the color red means?

➡ _____

(2) My best friends are Ken and Mary, who are nice and smart.

➡ _____

_____

(3) I wonder how often Mary meets Ken.

➡ _____

21 다음 빈칸에 들어갈 말이 순서대로 짝지어진 것은?

• I wonder _____ high the drone can fly.

• The present is this drone, _____ our grandpa sent to me for my birthday.

① why – what　　② how – who

③ how – which　④ when – which

⑤ why – which

01 다음 두 문장을 간접의문문을 이용하여 한 문장으로 연결하여 쓰시오.

(1) • Do you know?
• Why is Mira smiling?

➡ _____

(2) • Do you think?
• What is my dad cooking?

➡ _____

(3) • Do you guess?
• How did she find out the answer?

➡ _____

(4) • I want to know.
• What made him happy?

➡ _____

(5) • I wonder.
• How much time do they spend studying?

➡ _____

02 다음 우리말을 주어진 어휘를 이용하여 영어로 옮기시오.

(1) 나는 네가 그 인형을 어떻게 만들었는지 궁금해. (wonder, how, doll)

➡ _____

(2) 너는 그 영화가 언제 시작하는지 아니? (know, movie, start)

➡ _____

(3) 그녀에게 네가 뭐라고 말했는지 말해 줄 수 있니? (tell, what, said)

➡ _____

03 주어진 문장을 계속적 용법의 관계대명사를 사용하여 다시 쓰시오.

(1) Minsu got a drone from his grandpa, and he lives in Busan.

➡ _____

(2) He is cooking *japchae*, and he likes it the most.

➡ _____

04 잘못된 부분을 바르게 고쳐 문장을 다시 쓰시오.

(1) Do you know how he is old?

➡ _____

(2) The girl is Amy, that enjoys cooking.

➡ _____

(3) Look at this guitar, which I gave it to Amy for her birthday.

➡ _____

(4) The cute dog is Lucky, which like catching balls.

➡ _____

(5) Do you know when did he came to Korea?

➡ _____

05 다음 주어진 빈칸에 괄호 안의 문장을 알맞은 형태로 바꾸어 쓰시오.

> I want to learn _____.
> (What does he do in his free time?)

➡ _____

06 다음 괄호 안의 단어를 바르게 배열하여 대화를 완성하시오.

(1)

> A: Can you _____?
>   (live, tell, where, me, you)
> B: Sure, I live in Mokpo.

➡ _____

(2)

> A: Can you tell me _____?
>   (the, will, bus, when, come, next)
> B: Sure, it will come in 10 minutes.

➡ _____

07 다음 중 어법상 <u>어색한</u> 문장을 바르게 고치시오. (3개)

> a. Koreans use Hangeul, which was invented by King Sejong.
> b. Emma, who is very young, is good at chess.
> c. She wants to visit the Eiffel Tower, it is located in Paris.
> d. I climbed Mt. Halla with Mary, who is famous for its beauty.
> e. I hate those guys, who tells lies to me.

➡ _____ ➡ _____
_____ ➡ _____
_____ ➡ _____

08 다음 문장을 어법에 맞게 고쳐 쓰시오.

(1) She met my sister, who live in Hawaii.

➡ _____
_____

(2) He is dancing with Nancy, she is 20 years old.

➡ _____
_____

(3) He is happy to get a cat, Milky, that is white like milk.

➡ _____
_____

(4) Do you know why is the boy happy?

➡ _____
_____

(5) Do you guess what Mr. Lee is doing?

➡ _____
_____

09 두 문장을 간접의문문을 사용하여 한 문장으로 썼을 때, 빈칸에 해당하는 문장을 쓰시오.

(1) Do you know?
   + _____
   → Do you know when the game starts?

(2) I want to know.
   + Where did she go last night?
   → _____

(3) I wonder.
   + Who broke the glasses?
   → _____

(4) Can you tell me?
   + What color do you like?
   → _____

Reading

How Do You "Ha-Ha" in Your Texts?

Laughter is human. We laugh out loud when we hear a joke, see something funny, or feel happy. We laugh even in our writings, such as emails or texts, as we do in our conversations. How do we do that?

"Ha-ha" is a form of written laughter. Everyone knows what it means. Actually, it has been used since long ago. Even Shakespeare used "ha-ha" in his works.

DOGBERRY: Ha, ha, ha! Well, gentlemen, good night. And if anything important happens, find me and let me know.

(Shakespeare, *Much Ado About Nothing* Act 3, Scene 3, Page 4)

Another form of written laughter is LOL. It stands for "Laughing Out Loud." People also use ROFL quite often, which means "Rolling On the Floor Laughing." These expressions have become popular because they can be typed quite quickly.

A: Have a safe trip 2mrw. Make sure u don't miss me too much. LOL

B: OK. I'll try to make sure I don't miss u. LOL. Thanks for wishing me a safe trip.

XD also represents laughter in text. It shows a laughing face with a mouth open and eyes closed tightly. XD is not a word. It's an emoticon, which is a group of letters or symbols used to represent a facial expression. The emoticon XD expresses our happy feelings more visually than ha-ha and LOL do.

I can't wait to go to Disneyland. XD

text 글, 문서, 문자 메시지
conversation 대화
human 인간의, 인간적인
laugh out loud 큰 소리로 웃다
such as …와 같은
form 형식, 방식, 형태
written 글로 쓴, 글로 표현된
since …부터, … 이후
gentleman 신사
stand for …을 의미하다, …을 상징하다
type 치다, 입력하다
represent 나타내다, 대표하다
emoticon 이모티콘
　　　(emotion+icon)
a group of 한 무리의
symbol 상징
facial 얼굴의
visually 시각적으로

 확인문제

● 다음 문장이 본문의 내용과 일치하면 T, 일치하지 않으면 F를 쓰시오.

1 We laugh even in our writings. ☐

2 "Ha-ha" is a form of spoken laughter. ☐

3 Shakespeare didn't use "ha-ha" in his works. ☐

4 LOL stands for "Laughing Out Loud." ☐

5 XD is a word. ☐

These days, people use 😂 — a "face with tears of joy." This is a small picture called an "emoji." Lots of laughing emojis are available
앞에 나온 picture를 꾸며 주는 과거분사. 앞에 'which is'가 생략
to use online, so people can express their laughter in various ways.

그래서

A: I hit my head on the cupboard.

B: Oh, my! Are you okay?
아, 저런!

A: I hit my head on the cupboard. 😂

B: Uh-oh! Is the cupboard okay? 😂

Some emojis have grown bigger, and some even move or make
현재완료
laughing sounds.
웃음소리

A: So yesterday, I was in a restaurant, and I really needed to break
need to: ~할 필요가 있다
wind. 🐰

B: And ...

A: Well, the music was really loud, so I just did it.

B: And ...

A: And then I realized I was listening to music with my earphones.
I was 앞에 접속사 that이 생략

B: 🐰

Laughing marks can represent our facial expressions and deliver
represent와 병렬 관계
our voice tones. By using various laughing marks, we can show our
by –ing: ···함으로써
friends how much we care for them or how happy we are with them.
'show+간접목적어+직접목적어' (4형식 구문), 직접목적어에 간접의문문 두 개가 쓰였음
Laugh, even in written forms, and your friends will laugh with you.
명령문.+and ···: ~해라, 그러면 ···

A: Me when it's cold out

B: This was me yesterday

tear 눈물
joy 기쁨
emoji 이모지
available 구할 수 있는, 이용할 수 있는
various 다양한
cupboard 찬장
break wind 방귀를 뀌다
mark 기호, 표시
deliver 배달하다, 전달하다
tone 어조, 말투

📎 **확인문제**

● 다음 문장이 본문의 내용과 일치하면 T, 일치하지 않으면 F를 쓰시오.

1 😂 is known as a "face with tears of joy." ☐

2 Lots of laughing emojis are often used offline. ☐

3 Some emojis have grown bigger. ☐

4 Emojis can't move or make laughing sounds. ☐

5 Laughing marks can represent our facial expressions. ☐

6 Laughing marks can't deliver our voice tones. ☐

● 우리말을 참고하여 빈칸에 알맞은 말을 쓰시오.

1 _____ Do You "Ha-Ha" in Your _____?

2 Laughter is _____.

3 We _____ _____ _____ when we hear a joke, see something funny, or feel happy.

4 We _____ _____ _____ _____ _____, such as emails or texts, as we do in our conversations.

5 _____ do we do that?

6 "Ha-ha" is a form of _____ _____.

7 Everyone knows _____ _____ _____.

8 Actually, it _____ _____ _____ since long ago.

9 Even Shakespeare used "ha-ha" _____ _____ _____.

10 **DOGBERRY**: Ha, ha, ha! Well, _____, _____ night.

11 And if _____ _____ happens, find me and let me know.

12 (Shakespeare, *Much Ado About Nothing* _____ 3, _____ 3, Page 4)

13 Another form of _____ _____ is LOL.

14 It _____ _____ "Laughing Out Loud."

15 People also use ROFL quite often, which means "_____ _____ _____ _____ _____."

16 These expressions have become popular because they _____ _____ _____ quite quickly.

17 A: _____ _____ _____ _____ 2mrw.

18 _____ _____ u don't miss me too much. LOL

19 B: OK. I'll try to make sure I don't _____ _____. LOL

20 Thanks for _____ _____ _____ _____ _____.

21 XD also _____ laughter in text.

22 It shows a laughing face _____ a mouth _____ and eyes _____ _____.

23 XD is not _____ _____.

24 It's an emoticon, which is a group of letters or symbols _____ _____ _____ _____ _____ _____.

25 The emoticon XD expresses our happy feelings _____ _____ than ha-ha and LOL do.

26 I _____ _____ _____ go to Disneyland. XD

27 These days, people use 😂 — a "_____ _____ _____ _____ _____."

28 This is a small picture _____ an "emoji."

29 Lots of laughing emojis are _____ _____ _____ online, so people can express their laughter in _____ _____.

30 A: I _____ _____ _____ on the cupboard.

31 B: Oh, my! Are you _____?

32 A: I hit my head _____ _____ _____. 😂

33 B: Uh-oh! Is the cupboard _____? 😂

34 Some emojis _____ _____ bigger, and some even move or make _____ _____.

35 A: So yesterday, I was in a restaurant, and I really needed to _____ _____. 💨

36 B: And ...

37 A: Well, the music was really loud, so I _____ _____ _____.

38 B: And ...

39 A: And then I realized I was listening to music _____ _____ _____.

40 Laughing marks can represent our _____ _____ and deliver our _____ _____.

41 By using various laughing marks, we can show our friends how much we _____ _____ them or how happy we are _____ _____.

42 _____, even in written forms, _____ your friends will laugh with you.

43 Me when it's _____ _____

44 _____ _____ me yesterday

23 XD는 단어가 아니다.

24 그것은 이모티콘이고, 얼굴 표정을 나타내기 위해 사용되는 한 무리의 문자나 상징이다.

25 이모티콘 XD는 우리의 행복한 감정을 하하와 LOL보다 더 시각적으로 표현한다.

26 나는 디즈니랜드에 가는 게 몹시 기다려져. XD

27 요즘 사람들은 '기쁨의 눈물을 흘리는 얼굴'인 😂를 사용한다.

28 이것은 '이모지'라고 불리는 작은 그림이다.

29 많은 웃는 이모지가 온라인에서 사용될 수 있고, 그래서 사람들은 다양한 방식으로 자신들의 웃음을 표현할 수 있다.

30 A: 찬장에 머리를 부딪쳤어.

31 B: 오, 이런! 너 괜찮니?

32 A: 찬장에 머리를 부딪쳤어. 😂

33 B: 어 어! 찬장 괜찮니? 😂

34 어떤 이모지들은 크기가 커졌고, 또 어떤 것들은 심지어 움직이거나 웃음소리를 내기까지 한다.

35 A: 그래서 어제 나는 식당에 있었는데 정말 방귀를 뀌어야 했어.

36 B: 그리고 …

37 A: 음, 음악이 정말 시끄럽길래 나는 그냥 뀌어 버렸어.

38 B: 그리고 …

39 A: 그리고 그때 나는 내가 이어폰을 끼고 음악을 듣고 있다는 걸 깨달았지.

40 웃음 표시는 우리의 얼굴 표정을 나타내고 우리의 목소리 어조를 전달할 수 있다.

41 다양한 웃음 표시를 사용함으로써, 우리는 친구들을 얼마나 좋아하는지 또는 그들과 함께 있어서 얼마나 행복한지를 그들에게 보여 줄 수 있다.

42 웃어라, 문자로 된 형태로라도. 그러면 친구들도 여러분과 함께 웃을 것이다.

43 추울 때 내 모습이네.

44 이건 어제의 나야.

● 우리말을 참고하여 본문을 영작하시오.

1 글에서는 어떻게 "하하"라고 웃나요?
➡ _____

2 웃음은 인간 고유의 것이다.
➡ _____

3 우리는 농담을 듣거나 우스운 것을 보거나 행복감을 느끼면 소리 내어 웃는다.
➡ _____

4 우리는 이메일이나 문자 메시지 같은 글 속에서조차 대화에서 하듯이 웃는다.
➡ _____

5 어떻게 그렇게 하는가?
➡ _____

6 "하하"는 문자로 된 웃음의 한 형태이다.
➡ _____

7 모두가 그것이 무엇을 의미하는지 안다.
➡ _____

8 실제로 그것은 오래전부터 사용되어 왔다.
➡ _____

9 셰익스피어조차도 "하하"를 자신의 작품에 사용하였다.
➡ _____

10 DOGBERRY: 하하하! 자, 신사분들, 좋은 밤 보내시오.
➡ _____

11 그리고 만일 뭔가 중요한 일이 일어난다면 나를 찾아서 알려 주시오.
➡ _____

12 (셰익스피어. 헛소동. 3막 3장 4쪽)
➡ _____

13 또 다른 형태의 문자로 된 웃음은 LOL이다.
➡ _____

14 그것은 '크게 소리 내어 웃기'를 상징한다.
➡ _____

15 사람들은 또한 ROFL도 꽤 자주 사용하는데. 그것은 '바닥을 구르면서 웃기'를 의미한다.
➡ _____

16 이 표현들은 상당히 빠르게 타자를 칠 수 있어서 인기를 얻었다.
➡ _____

17 A: 내일 안전한 여행을 해.
➡ _____

18 나를 너무 많이 그리워하지 않도록 해. LOL
➡ _____

19 B: 좋아. 너를 그리워하지 않도록 할게. LOL.
➡ _____

20 안전한 여행을 기원해 줘서 고마워.
➡ _____

21 XD 또한 문자 메시지에서 웃음을 나타낸다.
➡ _____

22 그것은 입을 벌리고 눈을 질끈 감은 채 웃는 얼굴을 보여 준다.
➡ _____

23 XD는 단어가 아니다.
➡ _____

24 그것은 이모티콘이고, 얼굴 표정을 나타내기 위해 사용되는 한 무리의 문자나 상징이다.
➡ _____

25 이모티콘 XD는 우리의 행복한 감정을 하하와 LOL보다 더 시각적으로 표현한다.
➡ _____

26 나는 디즈니랜드에 가는 게 몹시 기다려져. XD
➡ _____

27 요즘 사람들은 '기쁨의 눈물을 흘리는 얼굴'인 😂 를 사용한다.
➡ _____

28 이것은 '이모지'라고 불리는 작은 그림이다.
➡ _____

29 많은 웃는 이모지가 온라인에서 사용될 수 있고, 그래서 사람들은 다양한 방식으로 자신들의 웃음을 표현할 수 있다.
➡ _____

30 A: 찬장에 머리를 부딪쳤어.
➡ _____

31 B: 오. 이런! 너 괜찮니?
➡ _____

32 A: 찬장에 머리를 부딪쳤어. 😂
➡ _____

33 B: 어 어! 찬장 괜찮니? 😂
➡ _____

34 어떤 이모지들은 크기가 커졌고, 또 어떤 것들은 심지어 움직이거나 웃음소리를 내기까지 한다.
➡ _____

35 A: 그래서 어제 나는 식당에 있었는데 정말 방귀를 뀌어야 했어. 💨
➡ _____

36 B: 그리고 …
➡ _____

37 A: 음, 음악이 정말 시끄럽길래 나는 그냥 뀌어 버렸어.
➡ _____

38 B: 그리고 …
➡ _____

39 A: 그리고 그때 나는 내가 이어폰을 끼고 음악을 듣고 있다는 걸 깨달았지.
➡ _____

40 웃음 표시는 우리의 얼굴 표정을 나타내고 우리의 목소리 어조를 전달할 수 있다.
➡ _____

41 다양한 웃음 표시를 사용함으로써, 우리는 친구들을 얼마나 좋아하는지 또는 그들과 함께 있어서 얼마나 행복한지를 그들에게 보여 줄 수 있다.
➡ _____

42 웃어라, 문자로 된 형태로라도. 그러면 친구들도 여러분과 함께 웃을 것이다.
➡ _____

43 추울 때 내 모습이네.
➡ _____

44 이건 어제의 나야.
➡ _____

[01~03] 다음 글을 읽고 물음에 답하시오.

XD also represents laughter in text. ⓐIt shows a laughing face with a mouth open and eyes closing tightly. XD is not a word. It's an emoticon, which is a group of letters or symbols used ⓑto represent a facial expression. The emoticon XD expresses our happy feelings more visually than ha-ha and LOL do.

서답형

01 위 글의 밑줄 친 ⓐ에서 어법상 틀린 부분을 찾아 고치시오.

_____ ➡ _____

02 아래 〈보기〉에서 위 글의 밑줄 친 ⓑto represent와 to부정사의 용법이 다른 것의 개수를 고르시오.

┌─── 보기 ───┐

① It is interesting to watch the show.
② You are nice to help the poor.
③ He has no house to live in.
④ My hobby is to play the piano.
⑤ He is a fool to say so.

① 1개 ② 2개 ③ 3개 ④ 4개 ⑤ 5개

03 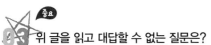 위 글을 읽고 대답할 수 없는 질문은?

① What does XD represent in text?
② What does XD show?
③ What is an emoticon?
④ What emoticon expresses our happy feelings most effectively?
⑤ Which expresses our happy feelings more visually, ha-ha or XD?

[04~06] 다음 글을 읽고 물음에 답하시오.

Laughter is human. We laugh out loud when we hear a joke, see something funny, or feel happy. We laugh even in our writings, such as emails or texts, ⓐas we do in our conversations. How do we do that?

"Ha-ha" is a form of written laughter. Everyone knows what it means. _____ⓑ_____, it has been used since long ago. Even Shakespeare used "ha-ha" in his works.

04 위 글의 밑줄 친 ⓐas와 같은 의미로 쓰인 것을 고르시오.

① As you were out, I left a message.
② He doesn't earn as much as me.
③ He sat watching her as she got ready.
④ He is famous as a statesman.
⑤ As you know, Mary is leaving soon.

05 위 글의 빈칸 ⓑ에 들어갈 알맞은 말을 고르시오.

① Therefore   ② However
③ Instead   ④ Actually
⑤ In other words

06 According to the passage, which is NOT true?

① Laughter is unique to humans.
② We laugh loudly when we hear a joke, see something funny, or feel happy.
③ It's impossible for us to laugh in our writings.
④ Everyone knows what "ha-ha" means.
⑤ "Ha-ha" was used even in Shakespeare's works.

[07~10] 다음 글을 읽고 물음에 답하시오.

These days, people use 😂 — a "face with tears of joy." ⓐThis is a small picture calling an "emoji." Lots of laughing emojis are available to use online, so people can express their laughter in various ways.

(1)
I hit my head on the cupboard.
Oh, my! Are you okay?

(2)
I hit my head on the cupboard.
Uh-oh! Is the cupboard okay?

서답형

07 다음 빈칸에 알맞은 단어를 넣어 😂에 대한 소개를 완성하시오.

It is a _____ _____ and is known as a "face with tears of joy."

08 다음 중 "emoji"에 해당하는 것을 고르시오.

① XD   ② ha-ha   ③ LOL
④ 👍   ⑤ ROFL

서답형

09 위 글의 밑줄 친 ⓐ에서 어법상 틀린 부분을 찾아 고치시오.

_____ ➡ _____

서답형

10 다음 빈칸 (A)와 (B)에 알맞은 단어를 넣어 위의 그림 (1)과 (2)의 차이점을 완성하시오.

The dialogue (2) which uses (A)_____ _____ can communicate laughter more visually than the dialogue (1) which

doesn't use an emoji. Besides, the woman in the second dialogue expresses the humorous mood more interestingly by replacing "Are you okay?" with "(B)_____ _____ _____ _____?"

[11~13] 다음 글을 읽고 물음에 답하시오.

Another form of written laughter is LOL. It stands for "Laughing Out Loud." People also use ROFL quite often, which means "Rolling On the Floor Laughing." These expressions have become popular because they can ⓐ_____ quite quickly.

서답형

11 위 글의 빈칸 ⓐ에 type를 알맞은 형태로 쓰시오.

➡ _____

중요

12 위 글의 앞에 올 내용으로 가장 알맞은 것을 고르시오.

① 대화에서 웃음을 터뜨리는 상황들 소개
② 문자로 된 웃음의 형태에 대한 소개
③ LOL이 생기게 된 배경 설명
④ ROFL을 주로 사용하는 상황들 소개
⑤ 이모티콘의 탄생 비화

서답형

13 Why have LOL and ROFL become popular? Fill in the blanks with suitable words.

Because people can type them _____ _____.

[14~16] 다음 글을 읽고 물음에 답하시오.

Laughter is human. We laugh out loud when we hear a joke, see something funny, or feel happy. We laugh even in our writings, such as emails or texts, as we do in our conversations. How do we do that?

"Ha-ha" is a form of written laughter. ⓐ모두가 그것이 무엇을 의미하는지 안다. Actually, ⓑit has been used since long ago. Even Shakespeare used "ha-ha" in his works.

서답형

14 위 글의 밑줄 친 ⓐ의 우리말에 맞게 주어진 어휘를 알맞게 배열하시오.

what / means / everyone / knows / it

➡ _____

서답형

15 위 글의 밑줄 친 ⓑit이 가리키는 것을 본문에서 찾아 쓰시오.

➡ _____

서답형

16 How can we laugh in our writings? Fill in the blanks below with suitable words. (two words)

We can use a form of _____ _____ like "ha-ha" in our writings.

[17~19] 다음 글을 읽고 물음에 답하시오.

Some emojis have grown bigger, and some even move or make laughing sounds.

A: So yesterday, I was in a restaurant, and I really needed to break wind.

B: And ...

A: Well, the music was really loud, so I just did it.

B: And ...

A: ⓐAnd then I realized I was listening to music with my earphones.

서답형

17 주어진 영영풀이에 해당하는 어구를 본문에서 찾아 쓰시오.

let gas out from the intestine

➡ _____

18 위 글의 밑줄 친 ⓐ에서 알 수 있는 'A'의 심경으로 가장 알맞은 것을 고르시오.

① disappointed   ② comfortable
③ refreshed   ④ pleased
⑤ embarrassed

서답형

19 Yesterday, could 'A' break wind undetected in a restaurant? Choose the right answer between (1) and (2) below. If you choose (2), write the reason by filling in the blanks ⓐ and ⓑ with suitable words. 〈*undetected: 아무에게도 들키지 않는〉

(1): Yes, he could.
(2): No, he couldn't. When he broke wind thinking the music was really ⓐ_____ in a restaurant, actually he was listening to music with ⓑ_____ _____.

➡ _____번,
ⓐ _____   ⓑ _____ _____

[20~23] 다음 글을 읽고 물음에 답하시오.

XD also represents laughter in text. It shows a laughing face (A)with a mouth open and eyes closed tightly. XD is not a word. It's an emoticon, which is a group of letters or symbols used to represent a facial expression. The emoticon XD expresses our happy feelings more ___ⓐ___ than ha-ha and LOL (B)do.

20 위 글의 빈칸 ⓐ에 들어갈 알맞은 말을 고르시오.

① musically   ② interestingly
③ indirectly   ④ visually
⑤ fantastically

21 위 글의 밑줄 친 (A)with와 문법적 쓰임이 같은 것을 모두 고르시오.

① She lives with her parents.
② Don't speak with your mouth full.
③ Look at the girl with red hair.
④ Cut it with a knife.
⑤ He stood there with his hands in his pockets.

서답형
22 위 글의 밑줄 친 (B)do가 가리키는 내용을 영어로 쓰시오.

➡ _____

23 본문의 그림 속에 밑줄 친 can't wait to go와 바꿔 쓸 수 없는 말을 고르시오.

① am looking forward to going
② am eager to go
③ am unwilling to go
④ am anxious to go
⑤ am dying to go

[24~26] 다음 글을 읽고 물음에 답하시오.

Laughter is human. We laugh out loud when we hear a joke, see something funny, or feel happy. We laugh even in our writings, ⓐsuch as emails or texts, as we do in our conversations. How do we do that?

"Ha-ha" is a form of written laughter. Everyone knows what it means. Actually, it has been used since long ago. Even Shakespeare used "ha-ha" in his works.

24 위 글의 밑줄 친 ⓐ를 한 단어로 바꿔 쓰시오.

➡ _____

25 위 글의 제목으로 알맞은 것을 고르시오.

① Various Kinds of Laughing Marks
② Can You Do "Ha-Ha" in Your Texts?
③ What Makes You Laugh?
④ How Can We Make Our Writings Fun?
⑤ Why Did Shakespeare Use "Ha-ha" in His Works?

서답형
26 본문의 내용과 일치하도록 다음 빈칸에 알맞은 단어를 쓰시오. (세 단어)

Jokes, funny sights, or happy feelings can make us _____ _____ _____ .

[01~03] 다음 글을 읽고 물음에 답하시오.

Laughter is human. We laugh out loud when we hear a joke, see something funny, or feel (A)[happy / happily]. We laugh even in our writings, such as emails or texts, as we (B) [are / do] in our conversations. How do we ⓐdo that?

"Ha-ha" is a form of written laughter. Everyone knows what it means. Actually, it has been used (C)[for / since] long ago. Even Shakespeare used "ha-ha" in his works.

01 위 글의 괄호 (A)~(C)에서 문맥이나 어법상 알맞은 낱말을 골라 쓰시오.

➡ (A) _____ (B) _____ (C) _____

02 다음 빈칸에 알맞은 단어를 넣어 위 글의 밑줄 친 ⓐdo that 이 가리키는 것을 완성하시오. (5 단어)

_____ _____ _____ _____

_____ as we do in our conversations

03 위 글의 내용을 다음과 같이 정리하고자 한다. 빈칸 (A)와 (B) 에 공통으로 들어갈 알맞은 단어를 본문에서 찾아 쓰시오.

Not only do we burst into (A)_____ when we experience something funny or happiness, but we can express laughing sound in our writings by using a form of written (B)_____, "ha-ha," as well.
*burst into: ~을 터뜨리다

➡ _____

[04~06] 다음 글을 읽고 물음에 답하시오.

Another form of written laughter is LOL. It stands for "Laughing Out Loud." People also use ROFL quite often, which means "Rolling On the Floor Laughing." These expressions have become popular because they can be typed quite quickly.

XD also represents laughter in text. ⓐ그것은 입을 벌리고 눈을 질끈 감은 채 웃는 얼굴을 보여 준다. XD is not a word. It's an emoticon, which is a group of letters or symbols used to represent a facial expression. The emoticon XD expresses our happy feelings more visually than ha-ha and LOL do.

04 What does ROFL stand for? Answer in English in a full sentence.

➡ _____

05 위 글의 밑줄 친 ⓐ의 우리말에 맞게 한 단어를 보충하여, 주어진 어휘를 알맞게 배열하시오.

a mouth / and / shows / closed tightly / it / open / a laughing face / eyes

➡ _____

_____

06 다음 문장에서 위 글의 내용과 <u>다른</u> 부분을 찾아서 고치시오.

LOL and ROFL are a group of letters or symbols used to represent a facial expression.

➡ _____ → _____ 또는

_____ → _____

[07~11] 다음 글을 읽고 물음에 답하시오.

Laughing marks can represent our facial expressions and deliver our voice tones. By using various laughing marks, we can show our friends how much we ⓐcare for them or how happy we are with ⓑthem. ⓒLaugh, even in written forms, and your friends will laugh with you.

07 위 글의 밑줄 친 ⓐcare for와 바꿔 쓸 수 있는 말을 한 단어로 쓰시오.

➡ _____

08 위 글의 밑줄 친 ⓑthem이 가리키는 것을 본문에서 찾아 쓰시오.

➡ _____

09 위 글의 밑줄 친 ⓒ를 It를 사용하여 고치시오.

➡ _____

_____

10 다음 빈칸 (A)와 (B)에 알맞은 단어를 넣어 laughing marks에 대한 설명을 완성하시오.

Using various laughing marks enables us to show our friends (A)_____ _____ we care for them or (B)_____ _____ we are with them.

11 What can laughing marks represent and deliver? Answer in English in a full sentence.

➡ _____

_____

[12~14] 다음 글을 읽고 물음에 답하시오.

Another form of written laughter is LOL. It ⓐstands for "Laughing Out Loud." People also use ROFL quite often, which means "Rolling On the Floor Laughing." These expressions have become popular because they can be typed quite quickly.

A: ⓑHave a safe trip 2mrw. Make sure u don't miss me too much. LOL
B: OK. I'll try to make sure I don't miss u. LOL. Thanks for wishing me a safe trip.

XD also represents laughter in text. It shows a laughing face with a mouth open and eyes closed tightly. XD is not a word. It's an emoticon, which is a group of letters or symbols used to represent a facial expression. The emoticon XD expresses our happy feelings more visually than ha-ha and LOL do.

12 위 글의 밑줄 친 ⓐstands for와 바꿔 쓸 수 있는 말을 본문에서 찾아 쓰시오.

➡ _____

13 위 글의 밑줄 친 ⓑ를 축약된 단어들의 본래 형태를 사용하여 문장을 다시 쓰시오.

➡ _____

_____

14 본문의 내용과 일치하도록 다음 빈칸 (A)와 (B)에 알맞은 단어를 쓰시오. (한 칸에 여러 단어를 쓸 수 있음.)

If you want to express your happy feelings more visually, it would be better for you to use (A)_____ than to use (B)_____ .

Self-study Guide

A: Can you tell me where you live?
tell의 직접목적어 자리에 사용된 간접의문문이다.

B: Sure. I live in Mokpo.
~에 살다

A: Could you tell me when the next bus will come?
정중한 부탁의 표현   tell의 직접목적어 자리에 사용된 간접의문문이다.

B: Sure. It will come in ten minutes.
in+시간: ~ 후에

Link to the World

Do you know what the color red means.
간접의문문: 의문사+주어+동사

• This is the uniform of the Reds, who cheer for the Korean soccer team. Red
관계대명사의 계속적 용법

  means "power" on this uniform.

• Red on a traffic light means "stop."

• Of all the meanings of red, "love" is my favorite. "Love never fails."
'all the+복수명사'의 어순

구문해설 • cheer for: ~을 응원하다   • of ~: ~ 중에서   • meaning: 의미

Express Yourself C

Yeji: Can you guess what my brother got for his birthday? He got a drone from
Can you guess?와 What did my brother get for his birthday?를 합친 간접의문문

  our grandpa, who lives in Busan.
= and he

구문해설 • guess: 추측하다   • drone: 드론   • grandpa: 할아버지(= grandfather)

해석

A: 당신이 어디에 사는지 제게 말해 줄 수 있나요?

B: 물론이죠. 저는 목포에 살아요.

A: 다음 버스가 언제 올지 제게 말씀해 주실 수 있으신가요?

B: 물론이죠. 그건 10분 후에 올겁니다.

빨간색이 무엇을 의미하는지 알고 있니?

• 이것은 붉은 악마들의 유니폼인데, 그들은 한국 축구팀을 응원한다. 이 유니폼에서 빨간색은 "힘"을 의미한다.

• 교통 신호등의 빨간색은 "멈추시오"라는 뜻이다.

• 빨간색의 모든 의미 중에서, '사랑'이 나는 가장 좋다. "사랑은 절대 실패하지 않는다."

예지: 내 남동생이 그의 생일 선물로 무엇을 받았는지 추측할 수 있니? 그는 우리 할아버지로부터 드론을 받았는데. 할아버지는 부산에 사셔.

01 다음 주어진 두 단어의 관계가 같도록 빈칸에 알맞은 단어를 쓰시오.

> popular – unpopular : _____ – partial

02 다음 글의 빈칸 (a)와 (b)에 들어갈 단어가 바르게 짝지어진 것은?

> • Laughing marks can represent our facial expression and (a) our voice tones.
> • Lots of laughing emojis are available to use online, so people can (b) their laughter in various ways.

① destroy – deliver ② make – buy
③ create – make   ④ deliver – express
⑤ deliver – form

[03~04] 다음 영영 풀이에 해당하는 것을 고르시오.

03
> involving writing rather than speaking

① typed   ② delivered
③ text   ④ represented
⑤ written

04
> a short set of keyboard symbols that represents the facial expression used in email, etc, to show feelings

① emoticon   ② sign
③ photograph   ④ symbol
⑤ signal

05 (A)와 (B)의 빈칸에 공통으로 들어갈 말을 쓰시오.

> (A) If you have been good, Santa will give you a nice _____ tomorrow!
> (B) Students in groups will _____ how they have reached their conclusions to certain questions.

➡ _____

06 다음 밑줄 친 부분의 뜻이 <u>잘못된</u> 것은?

① I'm glad to get a <u>book</u> from Junho. (예약하다)
② Can you <u>guess</u> who my mom met? (추측하다)
③ Shakespeare used "ha-ha" in his <u>works</u>. (작품들)
④ Another <u>form</u> of written laughter is LOL. (형태)
⑤ XD <u>represents</u> laughter in text. (나타내다)

07 다음 대화의 빈칸에 들어갈 말로 적절한 것은?

> G: _____ Are you all right?
> B: My mom won't let me play soccer after school.
> G: Why don't you ask her one more time?

① You look bored.
② You look upset.
③ You look tired.
④ You look refreshed.
⑤ You look pleased.

08 주어진 문장에 이어질 대화를 순서에 맞게 바르게 배열한 것은?

> Minsu, how are you feeling?

> (A) I'm glad to hear that. I hope he joins your team.
> (B) He was a soccer player on his school team. As you know, my team needs a player.
> (C) I'm really excited, Miso. We have a new student in our class. His name is Kim Kihun.
> (D) So why are you excited?

① (A) – (D) – (B) – (C)
② (B) – (A) – (C) – (D)
③ (B) – (D) – (C) – (A)
④ (C) – (A) – (D) – (B)
⑤ (C) – (D) – (B) – (A)

[09~10] 다음 대화를 읽고 물음에 답하시오.

A: How are you feeling?
B: I'm nervous. _____(A)_____ How are you feeling?
A: I'm nervous, too. I have a math test tomorrow. _____(B)_____
B: Me, too.

09 대화의 빈칸 (A)에 들어갈 말로 알맞은 것은?

① I got a good grade.
② I got a present for my birthday.
③ I forgot to bring my math homework.
④ I had a chance to travel to a new country.
⑤ It'll be a good day today!

10 대화의 빈칸 (B)에 들어갈 말을 주어진 단어를 알맞게 배열하여 쓰시오.

> (to / the / someone / I'm / feels / glad / find / who / same)

➡ _____
_____

[11~12] 다음 대화를 읽고 물음에 답하시오.

Nari: Hi, Jiho. How are you feeling?
Jiho: I'm happier than ever, Nari. (①)
Nari: I know why. You did it, didn't you?
Jiho: Yes. I finally booked four tickets for the VTS concert! (②)
Nari: Good job. Did you tell Minsu and Yujin about that? (③)
Jiho: Sure. Oh, I just got messages from them. They said they are really happy. Look. (④)
Nari: How cute! I like their emojis. (⑤)
Jiho: I'm glad to hear that. We're going to have lots of fun!

11 주어진 문장이 들어갈 위치로 알맞은 것은?

> They will bring light sticks and a nice camera.

①   ②   ③   ④   ⑤

12 위 대화의 내용과 일치하지 않는 것은?

① Jiho is happier than ever.
② Jiho booked four tickets for the VTS concert.
③ Minsu and Yujin sent messages with cute emojis.
④ Minsu and Yujin will not bring a camera.
⑤ Jiho told Minsu and Yujin about booking the tickets.

Grammar

13 다음 중 어법상 <u>어색한</u> 문장을 고르시오.

① Do you think who he liked?
② Can you tell me where she wants to go?
③ Who do you guess that man is?
④ What do you think is wrong with your computer?
⑤ I don't know if Jihoon likes inline skating.

14 다음 글에서 어법상 <u>어색한</u> 부분을 찾아 바르게 고치시오.

This is the uniform of the Reds, which cheer for the Korean soccer team. Red means "power" on this uniform.

_____ ➡ _____

15 주어진 〈조건〉에 맞추어, 괄호 안의 단어를 이용하여 영어로 쓰시오.

┌─── 조건 ├───
a. 우리말의 의미에 유의한다.
b. 필요하면 쉼표(,)를 적절히 사용한다.
c. 괄호 안에 주어진 영어 단어를 문법상 올바르게 변형한다.

(1) 그는 검은색인 고양이가 두 마리가 있다. (have, two cats, which)

➡ _____

(2) 그는 고양이가 두 마리 있는데, 그것들은 검은색이다. (have, two cats, which)

➡ _____

(3) 나는 노란 모자를 쓰고 있는 한 어린이를 보았다. (see, a child, who, wearing, a yellow cap)

➡ _____

(4) 나는 한 어린이를 보았는데, 그는 노란 모자를 쓰고 있었다. (see, a child, who, wearing, a yellow cap)

➡ _____

16 다음 두 문장을 한 문장으로 바르게 옮긴 것은?

Do you know? What does the color red mean?

① Do you know what the color red mean?
② Do you know what the color red means?
③ What do you know the color red means?
④ Do you know what the color red mean does?
⑤ Do you know what does the color red mean?

17 다음 중 어법상 <u>어색한</u> 문장의 개수로 알맞은 것은?

a. Do you think where they will go?
b. Do you know who invented the machine?
c. Did you ask me where did he go?
d. I met Jinhee, who was one of my classmates.
e. I borrowed a watch from Minji, who was broken.
f. I can't buy a car, which is very expensive.

① 1개 ② 2개 ③ 3개 ④ 4개 ⑤ 5개

18 다음 빈칸에 공통으로 알맞은 말을 쓰시오.

• I wonder _____ will win the contest.
• I read a book about a man, _____ sacrificed himself for others.

➡ _____

19 다음 우리말을 주어진 어휘를 이용하여 영어로 옮기시오.

(1) 너는 왜 선생님이 되고 싶은지 나에게 말해 줄 수 있니? (tell, me, want, be)

➡ _____

_____

(2) 너의 새로운 과학 선생님이 어떠신지 말해 줘. (Please, tell, what, science, like)

➡ _____

_____

Reading

[20~22] 다음 글을 읽고 물음에 답하시오.

Laughter is human. We laugh out loud when we hear a joke, see something funny, or feel happy. We laugh even in our ⓐ_____, such as emails or texts, as we do in our conversations. How do we do that?

"Ha-ha" is a form of written laughter. Everyone knows what it means. Actually, it ⓑhas been used since long ago. Even Shakespeare used "ha-ha" in his works.

20 위 글의 빈칸 ⓐ에 들어갈 알맞은 말을 고르시오.

① drawings ② writings ③ songs
④ pictures ⑤ poems

21 위 글의 밑줄 친 ⓑhas been used와 현재완료 용법이 같은 것을 모두 고르시오.

① How long has it been used in our writings?

② How many times has it been used in our writings?

③ It has already been used in our writings.

④ It has never been used in our writings.

⑤ It has been used for ten years in our writings.

22 위 글의 주제로 가장 알맞은 것을 고르시오.

① Laughter is human.

② We laugh out loud when we hear a joke.

③ We can laugh even in our writings.

④ "Ha-ha" is the most widely used written laughter.

⑤ We can find "ha-ha" even in Shakespeare's works.

[23~25] 다음 글을 읽고 물음에 답하시오.

Another form of written laughter is LOL. It stands for "Laughing Out Loud." People also use ROFL quite often, which means "Rolling On the Floor Laughing." These expressions have become popular ⓐ상당히 빠르게 타자를 칠 수 있어서.

XD also represents laughter in text. It shows a laughing face with a mouth open and eyes closed tightly. XD is not a word. ⓑIt's an emoticon, that is a group of letters or symbols used to represent a facial expression. The emoticon XD expresses our happy feelings more visually than ha-ha and LOL do.

23 위 글의 밑줄 친 ⓐ의 우리말에 맞게 주어진 어휘를 이용하여 7 단어로 영작하시오.

they, quite, typed

➡ _____

24 위 글의 밑줄 친 ⓑ에서 어법상 <u>틀린</u> 부분을 찾아 고치시오.

_____ ➡ _____

25 According to the passage, which is NOT true?

① LOL is a form of written laughter.

② ROFL is also used quite often.

③ XD represents alphabet X and D.

④ An emoticon is a group of letters or symbols used to represent a facial expression.

⑤ Ha-ha and LOL are less effective than XD in expressing our happy feelings visually.

[26~27] 다음 글을 읽고 물음에 답하시오.

Laughing marks can represent our facial expressions and deliver our voice tones. By using various laughing marks, we can show our friends how much we care for them or how happy we are with them. Laugh, even in written forms, and your friends will laugh with you.

26 위 글의 주제로 알맞은 것을 고르시오.

① pros and cons about laughing marks

② the role of laughing marks

③ the strong and weak points of laughing marks

④ the effective way of expressing laughter

⑤ various kinds of laughing marks

27 다음 중 위 글에 대한 이해가 올바르지 <u>못한</u> 사람을 고르시오.

① 수진: 웃음 표시는 우리의 얼굴 표정을 나타낼 수 있어..

② 미경: 웃음 표시로 우리의 목소리 어조를 전달하는 것은 힘들어.

③ 영미: 다양한 웃음 표시를 사용함으로써, 우리가 친구들을 얼마나 좋아하는지를 그들에게 보여줄 수 있어.

④ 진규: 다양한 웃음 표시를 사용함으로써, 우리는 또한 친구들과 함께 있어서 얼마나 행복한지도 그들에게 보여 줄 수 있어.

⑤ 희성: 문자로 된 형태라도 웃으면, 친구들도 우리와 함께 웃을 거야.

[28~29] 다음 글을 읽고 물음에 답하시오.

Minsu: _____ⓐ_____ She got a book from Junho, ⓑ<u>who every girl likes a lot.</u>

28 위 글의 빈칸 ⓐ에 Can you guess?와 Why is Mira smiling?을 한 문장으로 합쳐 쓰시오.

➡ _____

29 위 글의 밑줄 친 ⓑ를 다음과 같이 바꿔 쓸 때 빈칸에 들어갈 알맞은 말을 두 단어로 쓰시오.

➡ _____ every girl likes _____ a lot

🖊 출제율 90%

01 다음 짝지어진 단어의 관계가 같도록 빈칸에 알맞은 말을 쓰시오.

> chance : opportunity = diverse : _____

🖊 출제율 95%

02 다음 영영 풀이에 해당하는 단어는?

> a sign, shape, or object that is used to represent something else

① emoticon ② symbol
③ space ④ forest
⑤ emoji

🖊 출제율 90%

03 다음 대화를 읽고 Minsu의 상황에 맞는 Miso의 말을 빈칸 (A)에 영어 문장으로 완성하시오.

> G: Minsu, how are you feeling?
> B: I'm really excited, Miso. We have a new student in our class. His name is Kim Kihun.
> G: So why are you excited?
> B: He was a soccer player on his school team. As you know, my team needs a player.
> G: _____ (A) _____ I hope he joins your team.
> B: Thanks a lot.

➡ _____

[04~05] 다음 대화를 읽고 물음에 답하시오.

> B: Yena, how are you feeling?
> G: I'm feeling very sad, Seho. My best friend Jihun is moving away.
> B: Really? I'm sorry. But don't be so sad. You two can have video chats online.

> G: You're right.
> B: Why don't we make him a photo book as a goodbye gift?
> G: Great idea. 그에게 뭔가 의미 있는 것을 준다니 기뻐. (give / I'm / meaningful / to / something / him / glad)

🖊 출제율 100%

04 위 대화를 읽고 다음 빈칸에 알맞은 내용을 영어로 쓰시오. (to부정사로 시작하여 쓸 것.)

(1) Yena와 Jihun이 할 일: _____

_____

(2) Yena와 Seho가 할 일: _____

_____

🖊 출제율 90%

05 위 대화의 밑줄 친 우리말에 맞게 주어진 단어를 알맞게 배열하시오.

➡ _____

🖊 출제율 95%

06 다음 대화의 빈칸에 들어갈 말로 알맞은 것은?

> W: Good morning, Mr. Lee. How are you feeling?
> M: _____ Some students are helping me clean the school.
> W: I'm glad to hear that.

① I'm feeling very sad this morning.
② I'm nervous this morning.
③ I'm glad to hear that.
④ I'm feeling very happy this morning.
⑤ I'm very upset this morning.

G: Jihun, you ⓐare moving to another country next week. How are you feeling?

B: I'm ⓑexcited to go to a whole new world, Yunju.

G: I'm glad to hear that. I was ⓒworrying about you.

B: Actually, I'm sad, too. I'll miss all of you ⓓa lot.

G: Let's ⓔkeep in touch online.

B: Okay. Let's have video chats often.

07 위 글의 밑줄 친 ⓐ~ⓔ 중 어법상 어색한 것은?
출제율 95%

① ⓐ   ② ⓑ   ③ ⓒ   ④ ⓓ   ⑤ ⓔ

08 위 대화의 내용과 일치하지 않는 것은?
출제율 100%

① Jihun is going to move to another country next week.

② Yunju was concerned about Jihun.

③ Jihun was excited to move to a new country.

④ Jihun is sad as he will miss his friends.

⑤ Yunju is glad to hear that Jihun is moving to another country next week.

09 다음 대화의 빈칸 (A)와 (B)에 들어갈 표현으로 알맞은 것은?
출제율 90%

(1) B: You don't look happy. Are you all right?

  G: No, I'm really sad. My dog is sick. He won't eat at all.

  B: _____ (A)

(2) B: It'll be a good day today! Take a look at today's lunch menu.

  G: Wow! I'm glad to eat fried chicken! _____ (B)

① (A) That's too bad.
  (B) I'm not happy with today's lunch menu.

② (A) That's too bad.
  (B) I can't wait for lunch break.

③ (A) I'm glad to hear that.
  (B) I can't wait for lunch break.

④ (A) I'm happy to hear that.
  (B) I can wait for lunch break.

⑤ (A) I'm feeling very happy.
  (B) I'm happy with today's lunch menu.

10 다음 빈칸에 들어갈 말로 적절한 것을 모두 고르시오.
출제율 90%

That fire fighter is Fred, _____ saved a boy from the fire.

① which   ② he   ③ who
④ what   ⑤ and he

11 잘못된 부분을 바르게 고쳐 문장을 다시 쓰시오.
출제율 100%

(1) Do you know where did Tom work last year?

➡ _____

(2) She made chocolate cookies for me, which was very delicious.

➡ _____

_____

(3) I met Sue, who gives me a free ticket.

➡ _____

12 다음 밑줄 친 우리말을 괄호 안의 어구를 사용하여 영어로 옮기시오.

> (1) 빨간색이 무엇을 의미하는지 알고 있니? (color, mean) (8 words)
> (2) 이것은 붉은 악마들의 유니폼인데, 그들은 한국 축구팀을 응원한다. (uniform of the Reds, cheer) (14 words)

➡ (1) _____

(2) _____

_____

[13~15] 다음 글을 읽고 물음에 답하시오.

Laughter is human. We laugh out loud when we hear a joke, see something funny, or feel happy. We laugh even in our writings, such as emails or texts, as we do in our conversations. How do we do that?

"Ha-ha" is a form of ___ⓐ___ laughter. Everyone knows what it means. Actually, it has been used since long ago. Even Shakespeare used "ha-ha" in his ⓑworks.

13 위 글의 빈칸 ⓐ에 write를 알맞은 형태로 쓰시오.

➡ _____

14 위 글의 밑줄 친 ⓑworks와 같은 의미로 쓰인 것을 고르시오.

① She works for a bank.
② I have the complete works of J. K. Rowling.
③ He is the owner of the engineering works.
④ This machine works by electricity.
⑤ I'm interested in the works of a clock.

15 다음 중 위 글의 내용을 올바르게 이해하지 못한 사람을 고르시오.

① 수호: 웃음은 인간 고유의 것이야.
② 태경: 이메일을 보낼 때도 우리는 웃음을 표현할 수 있어.
③ 영미: 우리 모두 "하하"의 의미를 알지.
④ 철수: "하하"는 오래전부터 글 속에서 사용되어 왔어.
⑤ 희진: 셰익스피어가 글에서 "하하"를 사용한 첫 번째 작가야.

[16~18] 다음 글을 읽고 물음에 답하시오.

Another form of written laughter is LOL. It stands for "Laughing Out Loud." People also use ROFL quite often, (A)which means "Rolling On the Floor Laughing." These expressions have become popular because they can be typed quite quickly.

XD also represents laughter in text. It shows a laughing face with a mouth open and eyes closed tightly. XD is not a word. It's an emoticon, which is a group of letters or symbols used to represent a ___ⓐ___ expression. The emoticon XD expresses our happy feelings more visually than ha-ha and LOL do.

16 위 글의 한 단어를 변형하여 빈칸 ⓐ에 들어갈 알맞은 단어를 쓰시오.

➡ _____

17 위 글의 밑줄 친 (A)를 두 단어로 바꿔 쓰시오.

➡ _____

18 위 글의 제목으로 알맞은 것을 고르시오.

① Which Do You Prefer, LOL or ROFL?

② What Does XD Show?

③ How to Represent Laughter in Writings

④ What Is an Emoticon?

⑤ More Suitable Form for Expressing Happy Feelings Visually

[19~22] 다음 글을 읽고 물음에 답하시오.

These days, people use 😂 — a "face with tears of joy." This is a small picture called an "emoji." Lots of laughing emojis are available (A)to use online, so people can express their laughter in various ways.

A: I hit my head on the cupboard.
B: Oh, my! Are you okay?
A: I hit my head on the cupboard. 😂
B: Uh-oh! Is ___ⓐ___ okay? 😂

Some emojis have grown bigger, and some even move or make laughing sounds.

19 위 글의 대화가 더 유머러스한 분위기를 표현할 수 있도록, 본문의 단어를 사용하여 빈칸 ⓐ에 들어갈 알맞은 말을 쓰시오. (2 words)

➡ _____

20 위 글의 밑줄 친 (A)to use와 to부정사의 용법이 같은 것을 모두 고르시오.

① Can you tell me how to use it?

② I want a chance to use this coupon.

③ This tool is easy to use.

④ I would be happy to use this money.

⑤ He told me to use the locker.

21 According to the passage, which is NOT true?

① 😂 is known as a "face with tears of joy."

② We can find and use lots of laughing emojis online.

③ People can express their laughter in a few ways.

④ Some emojis even move.

⑤ Some emojis make laughing sounds.

22 What is an emoji? Answer in English in a full sentence.

➡ _____

_____

[23~24] 다음 글을 읽고 물음에 답하시오.

Laughing marks can represent our facial expressions and deliver our voice tones. By using various laughing marks, we can show our friends ⓐ친구들을 얼마나 좋아하는지 또는 그들과 함께 있어서 얼마나 행복한지를. Laugh, even in written forms, and your friends will laugh with you.

23 위 글의 밑줄 친 ⓐ의 우리말에 맞게 한 단어를 보충하여, 주어진 어휘를 알맞게 배열하시오.

them / we / how happy / care for / we are / or / them / how much

➡ _____

_____

24 위 글을 읽고 대답할 수 없는 것을 고르시오.

① What can laughing marks represent?

② What can laughing marks deliver?

③ What can you show by using various laughing marks?

④ What kind of laughing marks do people like most?

⑤ Can you make your friends laugh with you?

01 다음 대화의 우리말과 〈조건〉에 맞게 주어진 단어를 이용하여 영어로 쓰시오.

> (1) W: Good morning, Mr. Lee. How are you feeling?
>
> M: I'm feeling very happy this morning. (A)몇몇 학생들이 학교 청소하는 것을 돕고 있어요.
>
> W: I'm glad to hear that.
>
> (2) G: You look upset. Are you all right?
>
> B: (B)엄마가 방과 후에 축구하는 것을 허락하지 않으셔.
>
> G: Why don't you ask her one more time?

> ┤ 조건 ├
>
> (A) • 진행형을 사용할 것. / 목적보어 자리에 동사원형을 사용할 것.
>   • some / me / clean
>
> (B) • 미래 부정문의 축약형을 사용할 것.
>   • let / me / soccer / after school

➡ (A) _____

(B) _____

02 다음 대화의 흐름상 주어진 단어를 이용하여 빈칸 (A)에 들어갈 Miso의 질문을 완성하시오.

> G: Minsu, how are you feeling?
>
> B: I'm really excited, Miso. We have a new student in our class. His name is Kim Kihun.
>
> G: So _____(A)_____ (excited)
>
> B: He was a soccer player on his school team. As you know, my team needs a player.
>
> G: I'm glad to hear that. I hope he joins your team.

➡ _____

03 대화를 읽고 물음에 영어로 답하시오.

> Nari: Hi, Jiho. How are you feeling?
>
> Jiho: I'm happier than ever, Nari.
>
> Nari: I know why. You did it, didn't you?
>
> Jiho: Yes. I finally booked four tickets for the VTS concert!
>
> Nari: Good job. Did you tell Minsu and Yujin about that?
>
> Jiho: Sure. Oh, I just got messages from them. They said they are really happy. Look.
>
> Nari: How cute! I like their emojis. They will bring light sticks and a nice camera.
>
> Jiho: I'm glad to hear that. We're going to have lots of fun!

(1) Why is Jiho so happy?

➡ _____

(2) What did Minsu and Yujin send to Jiho?

➡ _____

04 〈보기〉에서 알맞은 문장을 골라 관계대명사의 계속적 용법으로 문장을 완성하시오.

> ┤ 보기 ├
>
> • The letter cheered him up.
> • She wrote a poem about love.

(1) My favorite poet is Alice. + _____

_____

→ My favorite poet is Alice, _____

_____ .

(2) Dennis got a letter. + _____

_____

→ Dennis got a letter, _____ .

05 다음 문장의 밑줄 친 부분을 '접속사+대명사'의 형태로 고치시오.

(1) The artist is Leonardo da Vinci, <u>who</u> painted the masterpiece, *The Last Supper*.

→ The artist is Leonardo da Vinci, _____ _____ painted the masterpiece, *The Last Supper*.

(2) I like my school bag, <u>which</u> was given to me by my mom for my birthday.

→ I like my school bag, _____ _____ was given to me by my mom for my birthday.

[06~08] 다음 글을 읽고 물음에 답하시오.

Laughter is human. We laugh out loud when we hear a joke, see something funny, or feel happy. We laugh even in our writings, such as emails or texts, as we (A)<u>do</u> in our conversations. How do we do that?

"Ha-ha" is a form of written laughter. Everyone knows what it means. Actually, it ⓐ_____ _____ _____ since long ago. Even Shakespeare used "ha-ha" in his works.

06 다음과 같은 뜻이 되도록 위 글의 빈칸 ⓐ에 들어갈 알맞은 말을 쓰시오. (세 단어)

Actually, it started to be used long ago and is still used now.

➡ _____

07 위 글의 밑줄 친 (A)<u>do</u>가 가리키는 것을 본문에서 찾아 쓰시오.

➡ _____

08 다음 빈칸 (A)와 (B)에 알맞은 단어를 넣어 "ha-ha"에 대한 소개를 완성하시오.

It is a form of written laughter which we use to laugh even in our (A)_____ as we do in our (B)_____.

[09~10] 다음 글을 읽고 물음에 답하시오.

Another form of written laughter is LOL. It stands for "Laughing Out Loud." People also use ROFL quite often, which means "Rolling On the Floor Laughing." These expressions have become popular because they can (A)[type / be typed] quite quickly.

XD also represents laughter in text. It shows a laughing face with a mouth (B)[open / opening] and eyes closed tightly. XD is not a word. It's an emoticon, which is a group of letters or symbols (C)[using / used] to represent a facial expression. The emoticon XD expresses our happy feelings more visually than ha-ha and LOL do.

09 위 글의 괄호 (A)~(C)에서 문맥이나 어법상 알맞은 낱말을 골라 쓰시오.

➡ (A) _____ (B) _____ (C) _____

10 본문의 내용과 일치하도록 다음 빈칸에 들어갈 알맞은 단어를 본문에서 찾아 쓰시오.

People can express laughter in their writings _____ _____ by using LOL instead of spelling the whole words "Laugh Out Loud."

창의사고력 서술형 문제

01 아래 표의 (A)는 감정 상태를, (B)는 그 이유를 나타낸다. 제시된 〈보기〉처럼 감정을 묻는 표현과 감정의 이유를 쓰시오.

(A)	(B)
• happy	• I got a good grade.
• nervous	• I forgot to bring my math homework.
• angry	• Someone broke my glasses.
• sad	• My brother is sick in bed.

보기

A: How are you feeling?

B: I'm nervous. I forgot to bring my math homework.

02 다음 〈보기〉와 같이, 관계대명사의 계속적 용법으로 부가 정보를 제공하는 문장을 쓰시오.

보기

I ate *Ceviche* in Peru, which is a traditional fish dish.

(1) My sister studied in Paris, _____.

(2) We learned Hula, _____.

(3) _____

(4) _____

03 다음 사진을 바탕으로 사진을 설명하는 글을 쓰시오.

A boy is holding a box with a white cat in it. The cat's name is Milky.

Yuna

Yuna: Can you guess (A)_____ the boy is happy? He is happy to get (B)_____, Milky, which is (C)_____ like milk.

단원별 모의고사

01 다음 단어에 대한 영어 설명이 <u>어색한</u> 것은?

① form: a type or variety of something
② since: from a time in the past until a later past time or until now
③ gentleman: a man who is polite, well educated and has excellent manners
④ deliver: to be accepted as meaning a certain thing
⑤ type: to write something using a computer or typewriter

02 다음 짝지어진 단어의 관계가 같도록 빈칸에 알맞은 말을 쓰시오.

> partial : whole = top : _____

03 다음 영영풀이에 해당하는 단어를 고르시오.

> in a way that is connected with seeing or sight

① variously
② visually
③ available
④ nervously
⑤ written

04 다음 대화의 빈칸에 알맞은 것은?

> G: You look upset. Are you all right?
> B: _____
> G: Why don't you ask her one more time?

① Someone broke my cell phone.
② My dad cooked my favorite pie.
③ My sister is sick in bed.
④ My mom won't let me play soccer after school.
⑤ My sister got a bad grade.

05 다음 대화의 빈칸에 들어갈 말로 알맞은 것을 고르시오.

> G: Jihun, you're moving to another country next week. How are you feeling?
> B: _____, Yunju.
> G: I'm glad to hear that. I was worried about you.
> B: Actually, I'm sad, too. I'll miss all of you a lot.
> G: Let's keep in touch online.
> B: Okay. Let's have video chats often.

① I'm really sad
② I'm so nervous to move to another country
③ I hope things will get better
④ That sounds like fun
⑤ I'm excited to go to a whole new world

06 다음 중 짝지어진 대화가 <u>어색한</u> 것은?

① A: How are you feeling?
   B: I'm happy. I got a good grade.
② A: How are you feeling today?
   B: I'm really glad to get a present for my birthday.
③ A: How are you feeling?
   B: I'm really bored to cook my favorite food.
④ A: How are you feeling?
   B: I'm really excited.
⑤ A: How are you feeling today?
   B: I'm feeling sad. My friend is sick.

[07~09] 다음 대화를 읽고 물음에 답하시오.

> (Nari and Jiho are at the bus stop.)
> Nari: Hi, Jiho. How are you feeling?
> Jiho: I'm happier than ever, Nari.
> Nari: I know why. (①) You did it, didn't you?
> Jiho: Yes. I finally booked four tickets for the VTS concert! (②)
> Nari: Good job. Did you tell Minsu and Yujin about that? (③)
> Jiho: Sure. Oh, I just got messages from them. (④) Look.
> Nari: How cute! I like their emojis. (⑤) They will bring light sticks and a nice camera.
> Jiho: I'm glad to hear that. We're going to have lots of fun!

07 위 대화의 ①~⑤ 중 주어진 문장이 들어갈 위치로 알맞은 것은?

> They said they are really happy.

①   ②   ③   ④   ⑤

08 What will Minsu and Yujin bring to the VTS concert? (9 단어로 답할 것)

➡ _____

09 다음은 위 대화를 요약한 문장이다. 빈칸에 알맞은 말을 찾아 쓰시오.

> Jiho is talking with Nari at the bus stop. He is _____ than ever because he _____ four tickets for the VTS concert. He told Minsu and Yujin about it, and they sent _____. Nari tells him that they will _____. Jiho is very glad to hear that.

10 다음 대화의 빈칸에 'how'를 이용하여 상대방의 감정에 대해 묻는 말을 완성하시오.

> A: _____ today?
> B: I'm feeling sad. My friend is sick.
> A: I'm sorry to hear that.

➡ _____

11 다음 주어진 문장에 이어질 대화의 순서로 알맞은 것은?

> G: Minsu, Jihun is moving to Abu Dhabi in the UAE next week. How are you feeling?

> (A) That's great! I'm glad to have a chance to travel to a new country.
> (B) I'm sad. I'm going to miss him a lot.
> (C) I'm sad, too, but I'm also happy. We can visit Abu Dhabi. He is going to invite us. He promised.

① (A) – (B) – (C)   ② (B) – (A) – (C)
③ (B) – (C) – (A)   ④ (C) – (A) – (B)
⑤ (C) – (B) – (A)

12 다음 대화의 빈칸에 들어갈 말로 알맞은 것은?

> B: Yena, how are you feeling?
> G: I'm feeling very sad, Seho. My best friend Jihun is moving away.
> B: Really? I'm sorry. But don't be so sad. You two can have video chats online.
> G: You're right.
> B: Why don't we make him a photo book as a goodbye gift?
> G: Great idea. _____

① We're going to have lots of fun!

② I'm sorry to hear that. But it was just a photo book.

③ I'm sorry to give him something simple.

④ I'm glad to give him something meaningful.

⑤ I'm glad to find someone who feels the same.

13 다음 중 어법상 올바른 문장을 고르시오.

① What do you think I should do?

② I wonder if what went wrong.

③ Do you know what do I mean?

④ I don't know whether can he do it.

⑤ Tell me who the window broke.

14 다음 우리말을 영어로 바르게 옮긴 것은?

너는 누가 다음 우승자가 될 것이라고 생각하니?

① Do you think who will become the next winner?

② Do you think who the next winner will become?

③ Do you think who will the next winner become?

④ Who do you think the next winner will become?

⑤ Who do you think will become the next winner?

15 주어진 문장을 활용하여 대화를 완성하시오.

A: The painting looks so special.
B: Right. It was painted by Basquiat, _____ . (Basquiat is one of the most famous artists of our time.)

16 다음 중 어법상 어색한 문장을 고르시오.

① Tell me why you didn't invite me.

② I want to know how the mountain is high.

③ I asked him how much money he earned a month.

④ I'm not sure who will be our new leader.

⑤ Do you know whom Daniel went out with?

17 우리말과 일치하도록 할 때, 빈칸에 알맞은 것은?

한 낯선 사람이 내게 내 휴대전화를 사용해도 되는지 물었다.
→ A stranger asked me _____ he could use my cell phone.

① whether　　② who　　③ that
④ how　　⑤ which

[18~19] 다음 글을 읽고 물음에 답하시오.

Laughter is human. (①) We laugh out loud when we hear a joke, see something funny, or feel happy. (②) We laugh even in our writings, such as emails or texts, as we do in our conversations. (③) How do we do that? (④) "Ha-ha" is a form of written laughter. (⑤) ⓐActually, it has been used since long ago. Even Shakespeare used "ha-ha" in his works.

18 위 글의 흐름으로 보아, 주어진 문장이 들어가기에 가장 적절한 곳은?

Everyone knows what it means.

①　　②　　③　　④　　⑤

19 위 글의 밑줄 친 ⓐActually와 바꿔 쓸 수 있는 말을 모두 고르시오.

① Probably   ② In fact
③ Exactly   ④ Especially
⑤ As a matter of fact

[20~22] 다음 글을 읽고 물음에 답하시오.

Another form of written laughter is LOL. It stands for "Laughing Out Loud." People also use ROFL quite often, which means "Rolling On the Floor Laughing." These expressions have become popular because ⓐthey can be typed quite quickly.

XD also represents laughter in text. It shows a laughing face with a mouth open and eyes closed tightly. XD is not a word. It's an emoticon, which is a group of letters or symbols ⓑused to represent a facial expression. The emoticon XD expresses our happy feelings more visually than ha-ha and LOL do.

20 위 글의 밑줄 친 ⓐthey가 가리키는 것을 본문에서 찾아 쓰시오.

➡ _____

21 위 글의 밑줄 친 ⓑ 앞에 생략된 말을 쓰시오.

➡ _____

22 위 글의 주제로 알맞은 것을 고르시오.

① What is the reason why we use LOL instead of "Laugh Out Loud"?
② Why have LOL and ROFL become popular?
③ We can represent laughter even in writings by using LOL, ROFL and XD.

④ There are many kinds of emoticons used to represent a facial expression.
⑤ Why is XD more effective than ha-ha to express our happy feelings visually?

[23~25] 다음 글을 읽고 물음에 답하시오.

Some emojis have ⓐgrown bigger, and some even move or make laughing sounds.

A: So yesterday, I was in a restaurant, and I really needed to break wind. 🐰

B: And ...

A: Well, the music was really loud, so I just ⓑ did it.

B: And ...

A: And then I realized I was listening to music with my earphones.

B: 😺

23 위 글의 밑줄 친 ⓐgrown과 바꿔 쓸 수 있는 말을 모두 고르시오.

① done   ② become
③ fallen   ④ gotten
⑤ given

24 요즈음 사용할 수 있는 이모지의 특성으로 언급되지 않은 것은? (2개)

① 크기가 커졌다.
② 움직이기도 한다.
③ 온라인에서만 사용할 수 있다.
④ 웃음소리를 내기까지 한다.
⑤ 색깔이 다양하다.

25 위 글의 밑줄 친 ⓑ가 가리키는 것을 영어로 쓰시오. (시제를 일치시킬 것.)

➡ _____

Lesson 2

Let's Make Our Town Better

🔍 **의사소통 기능**

- 주제 소개하기

  Let's talk about the class party.

- 감사하기

  Thank you for helping me.

🔍 **언어 형식**

- 과거완료

  I was glad my dad **had made** me wear gloves.

- 비교급 강조

  I had to admit the lot looked **much** better.

Words & Expressions

Key Words

- **activity** [æktívəti] 명 활동
- **admit** [ædmít] 동 인정하다, 시인하다
- **agree** [əgríː] 동 동의하다
- **among** [əmʌ́ŋ] 전 ~ 중에, ~ 사이에
- **assign** [əsáin] 동 배정하다, 배치하다, 맡기다
- **awful** [ɔ́ːfəl] 형 끔찍한, 지독한
- **bake** [beik] 동 굽다
- **bean** [biːn] 명 콩
- **board** [bɔːrd] 명 게시판
- **bring** [briŋ] 동 가져오다
- **bus stop** 버스 정류장
- **class leader** 반장
- **clean** [kliːn] 동 청소하다
- **complain** [kəmpléin] 동 불평하다, 투덜거리다
- **corner** [kɔ́ːrnər] 명 구석, 모서리
- **dirty** [dɔ́ːrti] 형 더러운
- **double** [dʌ́bl] 동 두 배가 되다
- **dust** [dʌst] 명 먼지
- **else** [els] 형 다른, 그 밖의
- **empty** [émpti] 형 텅 빈, 비어 있는
- **event** [ivént] 명 행사
- **far** [faːr] 부 (비교급 강조) 훨씬
- **fill** [fil] 동 채우다
- **fix** [fiks] 동 수리하다
- **guide** [gaid] 동 안내하다
- **hang** [hæŋ] 동 걸다, 매달다
- **heavy** [hévi] 형 무거운
- **helpful** [hélpfəl] 형 도움이 되는, 유용한
- **hit** [hit] 동 (생각이) ~에게 떠오르다
- **imagine** [imǽdʒin] 동 상상하다
- **kitchen** [kítʃən] 명 부엌
- **learn** [ləːrn] 동 알게 되다
- **lettuce** [létis] 명 상추
- **lot** [lɑt] 명 부지, 구획
- **mess** [mes] 명 쓰레기 더미, 지저분함, 엉망진창
- **neighborhood** [néibərhùd] 명 이웃, 인근 주민
- **newspaper** [njúːzpeipər] 명 신문(지)
- **noodle** [núːdl] 명 국수
- **nursing home** 양로원
- **plant** [plænt] 동 심다
- **pleasure** [pléʒər] 명 기쁨
- **popular** [pápjulər] 형 인기 있는
- **pot** [pɑt] 명 분, 항아리, 단지
- **put** [put] 동 두다
- **remember** [rimémbər] 동 기억하다
- **row** [rou] 명 열, 줄
- **sight** [sait] 명 광경
- **snake** [sneik] 명 뱀
- **sneeze** [sniːz] 동 재채기하다
- **string** [striŋ] 명 끈, 줄
- **suggest** [sədʒést] 동 제안하다
- **sweaty** [swéti] 형 땀투성이의, 땀에 젖은
- **the elderly** 노인들
- **tight** [tait] 부 단단히, 꽉
- **together** [təgéðər] 부 함께, 같이
- **tough** [tʌf] 형 힘든
- **trash** [træʃ] 명 쓰레기
- **trash bag** 쓰레기 봉투
- **ugly** [ʌ́gli] 형 추한, 보기 싫은
- **volunteer** [vàləntíər] 동 지원[자원]하다
- **volunteer work** 자원 봉사
- **water** [wɔ́ːtər] 동 물을 주다
- **wild plant** 야생식물
- **wonder** [wʌ́ndər] 동 궁금해 하다, ~할까 생각하다
- **wrap** [ræp] 명 포장지

Key Expressions

- **across from** ~ 맞은편에
- **be full of** ~로 가득 차다
- **be ready to-V** ~할 준비가 되다
- **divide A into B** A를 B로 나누다
- **fill A with B** A를 B로 채우다
- **How about+V-ing?** ~하는 게 어때?
- **I bet** 틀림없이 ~이다
- **in charge of** ~을 맡아, ~을 담당하여
- **let+목적어+동사원형** ~가 …하도록 허락하다
- **one of+복수명사** ~ 중 하나
- **pop up** 갑자기 나오다, 불쑥 나타나다
- **set up** 설치하다, 마련하다
- **Shall we+동사원형?** ~하는 게 어때?
- **take care of** ~을 돌보다
- **turn A into B** A를 B로 바꾸다
- **What do you think of ~?** ~을 어떻게 생각해?
- **Why don't you+동사원형?** ~하는 게 어때?
- **work on** ~에 공들이다[애쓰다]

Word Power

※ 서로 반대되는 뜻을 가진 어휘

- □ **popular**(인기 있는) ↔ **unpopular**(인기 없는)
- □ **fill** (채우다) ↔ **empty** (비우다)
- □ **remember** (기억하다) ↔ **forget** (잊다)

- □ **whole** (전체의) ↔ **partial** (일부분의)
- □ **awful** (끔찍한) ↔ **wonderful** (멋진)
- □ **empty** (비어 있는) ↔ **full** (가득 찬)

※ 서로 비슷한 뜻을 가진 어휘

- □ **awful** : **disgusting** (끔찍한, 역겨운)
- □ **empty** : **vacant** (비어 있는)
- □ **assign** : **allocate** (배치하다)
- □ **complain** : **moan** (불평하다)

- □ **plant** : **implant** (심다)
- □ **hang** : **suspend** (매달다)
- □ **fix** : **mend** (수리하다, 고치다)
- □ **string** : **cord** (끈)

English Dictionary

- □ **admit** 인정[시인]하다
  → to agree that something is true, especially unwillingly
  특히 내키지 않게 무언가가 사실이라는 것에 동의하다

- □ **assign** 배치하다, 맡기다
  → to give a particular job or piece of work to someone
  누군가에게 특정한 직업이나 일을 주다

- □ **awful** 끔찍한
  → extremely bad or unpleasant
  매우 나쁘거나 불쾌한

- □ **complain** 불평하다
  → to say that something is wrong or not satisfactory
  무언가 잘못되었거나 만족스럽지 않다고 말하다

- □ **double** 두 배가 되다
  → to make something twice as much or many
  어떤 것을 양이나 수가 두 배가 되게 하다

- □ **dust** 먼지
  → dry dirt in the form of powder that covers surfaces inside a building, or very small dry pieces of soil, sand, or other substances
  건물 내부의 표면을 덮는 분말 형태의 건조한 오물 또는 매우 작은 건조한 토양, 모래 또는 기타 물질 조각

- □ **empty** 텅 빈, 비어 있는
  → not containing any things or people
  어떤 물건이나 사람을 담고 있지 않은

- □ **fill** 채우다
  → to make or become full
  가득 채우거나 가득해지다

- □ **fix** 고치다
  → to repair something
  무언가를 수리하다

- □ **hang** 매달다
  → to put something in a position so that the top part is fixed or supported, and the bottom part is free to move and does not touch the ground
  상부가 고정 또는 지지되도록 어떤 위치에 놓이도록 하고, 바닥 부분은 자유롭게 이동할 수 있고, 지면에 닿지 않도록 하다

- □ **kitchen** 부엌
  → a room where food is kept, prepared, and cooked and where the dishes are washed
  음식이 보관, 준비, 조리되고, 설거지를 하는 방

- □ **lot** 부지, 구획
  → an area of land 땅의 한 구역

- □ **nursing home** 양로원
  → a place where very old people who are ill live and receive medical treatment and care
  병든 매우 나이 든 사람들이 살고 의학 치료와 돌봄을 받는 곳

- □ **row** 열, 줄
  → a line of things or people next to each other
  서로 옆에 있는 사물이나 사람의 줄

- □ **suggest** 제안하다
  → to tell someone your ideas about what they should do, where they should go, etc.
  자신이 무엇을 해야 하는지, 어디로 가야 하는지 등에 대한 당신의 생각을 누군가에게 말하다

- □ **sweaty** 땀에 젖은
  → covered in sweat or smelling of sweat
  땀 또는 땀 냄새로 뒤덮인

- □ **tough** 힘든
  → difficult to do or to deal with
  하거나 다루기에 어려운

- □ **volunteer** 자원하다
  → to offer to do something that you do not have to do
  할 필요가 없는 일을 하겠다고 제안하다

서답형

01 다음은 어떤 단어에 관한 영어 설명이다. 빈칸에 들어갈 알맞은 단어를 쓰시오.

> When you _____, air and often small drops of liquid suddenly come out of your nose and mouth in a way you cannot control.

중요

02 다음 빈칸에 들어갈 말로 가장 적절한 것은?

> The hotel was _____! To begin with, our room was too small.

① wonderful ② terrific
③ popular ④ awful
⑤ ugly

[03~04] 다음 영어 설명에 해당하는 단어를 고르시오.

03
> to say that something is wrong or not satisfactory

① blame ② appreciate
③ complain ④ praise
⑤ enable

중요

04
> a place where very old people who are ill live and receive medical treatment and care

① daycare center ② kindergarten
③ nursery ④ kitchen
⑤ nursing home

서답형

05 다음 우리말에 맞게 빈칸에 알맞은 단어를 쓰시오.

> 선생님은 학생들을 두 팀으로 나누었다.

➡ The teacher _____ the students _____ two teams.

06 빈칸에 공통으로 들어갈 말로 알맞은 것은? (대 · 소문자 무시)

> (A) _____ foods are fruits and vegetables that do not have a nice, visual appearance.
> (B) A goodwill basketball game between China and the United States turned _____.

① tough ② ugly
③ tasty ④ awesome
⑤ empty

중요

07 다음 짝지어진 단어의 관계가 같도록 알맞은 말을 쓰시오.

> string – cord : mend – _____

중요

08 다음 빈칸에 들어갈 말이 바르게 짝지어진 것은?

> • Recently, Hawking surprised the world by _____ a shocking idea.
> • Interestingly, a small colorful rainbow is _____ in the sky!

① suggesting – hanging
② suggesting – imagining
③ banning – hanging
④ banning – sneezing
⑤ suggesting – guiding

01 〈보기〉에서 알맞은 단어를 선택하여 문장의 빈칸을 완성하시오. (필요하면 변형하여 쓰시오.)

┌─ 보기 ─┐
hang   heavy   pot   corner   bring
└────────┘

(1) The woman placed the flower _____ next to the window.

(2) The _____ box doesn't move an inch.

(3) Jason is _____ a painting on the wall.

(4) Let's put this box in the _____.

02 다음 대화의 빈칸에 〈영영풀이〉에 해당하는 단어를 쓰시오.

┌─────────────────────────────┐
A: It smells good. What did you make?
B: I made a pizza. Let's eat it together.
A: Great. Then, let's _____ it into several pieces.
└─────────────────────────────┘

➡ _____

┌─────────────────────────────┐
〈영영풀이〉 to separate into parts or groups
└─────────────────────────────┘

03 다음 우리말에 맞게 주어진 문장의 빈칸에 알맞은 단어를 쓰시오.

┌─────────────────────────────┐
• 학급 반장들이 이 판에 몇 개의 포스터를 붙였습니다. 그 전에, 그들은 학교 정문 앞에 판을 세웠었습니다. 학급 반장들 덕분에, 이 장소는 이전보다 훨씬 더 인기 있습니다.

➡ The class _____ put up some posters on this board. Before that, they had _____ _____ the _____ in front of the school gate. Thanks to the class _____, this place is much more _____ than before.
└─────────────────────────────┘

04 영영풀이에 해당하는 단어를 〈보기〉에서 찾아 첫 번째 빈칸에 쓰고, 두 번째 빈칸에는 우리말 뜻을 쓰시오.

┌─ 보기 ─┐
dust   suggest   admit   kitchen
└────────┘

(1) _____: a room where food is kept, prepared, and cooked and where the dishes are washed: _____

(2) _____: dry dirt in the form of powder that covers surfaces inside a building, or very small dry pieces of soil, sand, or other substances: _____

(3) _____: to agree that something is true, especially unwillingly: _____

(4) _____: to tell someone your ideas about what they should do, where they should go, etc.: _____

05 다음 글의 빈칸에 주어진 철자로 시작하는 알맞은 단어를 쓰시오.

(1) My bedroom was a m_____, so my mom told me to clean it up.

(2) She hates summer because it is too hot and very s_____.

(3) Why didn't you cover your mouth when you s_____?

(4) My dad reads the n_____ every morning.

Conversation

- **Let's talk about the class party.** 학급 파티에 대해 이야기해 보자.

■ "Let's talk about ~."는 '~에 대해서 말해 보자.'라는 뜻으로 함께 대화하고자 하는 주제를 소개할 때 쓰는 표현이다. 또는 대화나 발표 도입부에서 특정 주제를 언급하고자 할 때 'I'd like to talk about ~.'을 쓸 수 있다. 상황에 따라 'talk about' 대신 'introduce', 'discuss', 'mention' 등도 사용할 수 있다. 또한 상대방과 친밀도가 높은 대화 상황에서는 'would like to' 대신 'want to'를 사용하는 것이 가능하다.

■ 이에 대한 응답으로 해당 주제에 관한 자신의 의견을 말할 수 있다.

주제를 소개하는 다른 표현들

- I'd like to say something about ~.
- I'd like to introduce ~.
- Let me tell you about ~.

- Why don't we talk about ~?
- I'd like to discuss ~.

자신의 의견을 말할 때

- I think ~. / How about ~? / In my opinion, ~.

- A: Let's talk about our trip. 우리의 여행에 대해 이야기해 보자.

  B: How about going to the national park? 국립공원으로 가는 게 어때?

- A: I'd like to talk about the movie we watched yesterday. 나는 어제 우리가 본 영화에 대해 얘기하고 싶어.

  B: Yes, what would you like to talk first? 그래. 어떤 부분을 먼저 말할래?

핵심 Check

1. 다음 대화의 빈칸에 들어갈 말로 알맞지 <u>않은</u> 것은?

   A: _____ a book I read recently.

   B: Please share your thoughts with us.

   ① Let's talk about
   ② It is likely that
   ③ Let me say something about
   ④ I'd like to say something about
   ⑤ Allow me to say something about

② 감사하기

> • **Thank you for helping me.** 도와줘서 고마워.

■ "Thank you for ~."는 '~에 대해서 고마워.'라는 뜻으로 감사를 나타낼 때 쓰는 표현이다. 이에 대한 응답으로 "You're welcome.", "(It's) My pleasure."와 같이 표현할 수 있다.

■ **감사하기 표현**

고마움과 감사의 표현으로 'Thank you'보다 더욱 공손하게 표현하고자 할 때는 'I appreciate ~.'를 사용할 수 있고 appreciate 뒤에는 목적어를 사용해야 한다.

  • A: I really appreciate your advice. 당신의 충고에 정말 감사드립니다.

  B: Not at all. I'm glad that I could help you. 천만에요. 당신을 도울 수 있어서 기쁩니다.

■ **감사하기 표현에 대한 응답 표현**

'Thank you.'나 'I appreciate ~.'에 대한 대답은 'You're welcome.', 'No problem.', 'Not at all.', 'Don't mention it.' 등을 사용한다.

  • A: Jihun, I heard you passed the math exam. 지훈아, 네가 수학 시험에 합격했다고 들었어.

  B: You helped me a lot. I really appreciate your help. 네가 많이 도와주었잖아. 너의 도움 정말 고마워.

  • A: I really appreciate your help. 도와줘서 정말 고마워.

  B: You're welcome. 천만에.

핵심 Check

2. 다음 우리말에 맞도록 빈칸에 들어갈 알맞은 말을 고르시오.

  • 그렇게 말해 주니 고마워.

  Thank you _____ that.

  ① of say   ② to say   ③ for saying

  ④ for to say   ⑤ with saying

Step Up – Real-life Scene

G1: ❶Let's talk about how we can make our town better.

B: ❷Let me tell you first. There's too much trash at the bus stop.

G2: I agree. ❸Why don't we clean the place together?

B: Good. We can put a bench there, too.

G1: Great idea. It'll be helpful for ❹the elderly.

G2: ❺How about putting some flower pots around the bench? They'll make the bus stop more beautiful.

G1: ❻Thank you for suggesting great ideas, everyone. Then, shall we start tomorrow?

G2, B: ❼No problem.

G1: 우리 마을을 어떻게 하면 더 좋게 만들 수 있을지를 이야기해 보자.

B: 내가 먼저 말할게. 버스 정류장에 쓰레기가 너무 많아.

G2: 동의해. 그 장소를 함께 치우는 게 어때?

B: 좋아. 우리가 거기에 벤치를 놓을 수도 있을 것 같아.

G1: 좋은 생각이야. 그것은 어르신들에게 도움이 될 거야.

G2: 벤치 주변에 화분도 좀 놓는 게 어때? 그것들은 버스 정류장을 더 아름답게 할 거야.

G1: 모두 좋은 의견을 내줘서 고마워. 그러면, 내일 시작하는 게 어때?

G2, B: 좋아.

❶ 'Let's talk about ~.'는 '~에 대해서 말해 보자'라는 뜻으로 함께 대화하고자 하는 주제를 소개할 때 쓰는 표현이다.
❷ 'Let+목적어+동사원형'은 '…가 ~하게 해주다'라는 의미이다.
❸ 'Why don't we+동사원형?'은 '~하는 게 어때?'라는 의미로 'Let's+동사원형'과 같이 주제를 소개할 때 쓰는 표현이다.
❹ 'the+형용사'는 복수명사로 '~한 사람들'의 의미로 '노인들'의 의미이다.
❺ 'How about+동명사?'는 '~는 어때?'라는 의미로 제안하는 표현이다.
❻ 'Thank you for+동명사'는 감사하는 표현으로 '~해 줘서 고마워'라는 의미이다.
❼ 감사하기 표현에 대한 응답 표현이다. 같은 표현으로 'You're welcome.' 'Not at all.' 'Don't mention it.' 등을 사용한다.

Check(√) True or False

(1) They are going to put a bench at the bus stop.   T ☐ F ☐

(2) Some flower pots will make the bench more beautiful.   T ☐ F ☐

Start Off – Listen & Talk B

G: Seho, we need something on the wall, too. Don't you think so?

B1: You're right. Let's talk about it together.

G: I think we need to put the club member list there. ❶It'll be helpful for us to learn the new members' names.

B2: That's a good idea. We also need our plan for this school year on the wall.

G: Right! That'll really ❷help us remember important school events.

B1: ❸Thank you for suggesting great ideas, everyone. We are a good team.

G: 세호야, 우리는 벽에도 뭔가 필요해. 그렇게 생각하지 않니?

B1: 네 말이 맞아. 그것에 대해서 함께 이야기해 보자.

G: 내 생각에는 거기에 동아리 회원 목록을 붙일 필요가 있는 것 같아. 그것은 우리가 신입 회원들의 이름을 알게 되는 데 도움이 될 거야.

B2: 좋은 생각이야. 이번 학년도의 우리 계획도 벽에 필요해.

G: 맞아! 그러면 우리가 중요한 학교 행사를 기억하는 데 정말 도움이 될 거야.

B1: 모두 좋은 의견을 내줘서 고마워. 우린 좋은 팀이야.

❶ It은 'to put the club member list there'를 가리키는 대명사이고, for us는 to부정사의 의미상 주어이다.
❷ 'help+목적어+목적보어(동사원형)' 형태로 '…가 ~하는 데 도움이 되다'라는 의미이다.
❸ 'Thank A for B' 구문은 'B 때문에 A에게 고마워하다'라는 의미로 전치사 for 뒤에는 동명사나 명사가 온다.

Check(√) True or False

(3) Seho doesn't think that they need something on the wall.   T ☐ F ☐

(4) Seho thanks G and B2 for suggesting great ideas.   T ☐ F ☐

Get Ready 2

(1) **B:** The flower pot ❶looks heavy. ❷Can I help you, Ms. Min?

W: You're so kind. Thank you very much.

(2) **G:** ❸Let me help you fix the bench.

M: Please hold this tight. ❹Thank you for helping me.

(3) **B:** Let's talk about ❺what we can do for our town.

G: ❻How about drawing pictures on the dirty walls?

B: Sounds good. ❼Anything else?

❶ 'look+형용사'는 '~하게 보이다'라는 의미이다.
❷ '도와 드릴까요?'라는 의미로 'May I help you?'를 대신 사용할 수 있다.
❸ 'let+목적어+동사원형'은 '…가 ~하게 하다'라는 의미이다.
❹ 감사를 표현하는 말로 전치사 for 뒤에는 동명사 helping이 온다.
❺ 전치사 about의 목적어 자리에 사용된 간접의문문으로 '의문사+주어+동사' 어순을 취한다.
❻ 'How about -ing?'는 '~하는 게 어때?'라는 의미로 'What about -ing?'를 사용할 수 있다.
❼ '-thing'으로 끝나는 부정대명사는 형용사가 뒤에서 수식한다.

 Start Off – Listen & Talk A

1. **B:** What do we need in our club room? ❶Let's talk about it.

G: Sure. Well, how about putting some flower pots by the windows? They'll ❷make our room prettier.

B: That's a good idea. Thank you, Jiu.

2. **B:** ❸How about hanging some pictures?

G: Good. ❹Why don't you bring one of your pictures? You're good at painting, Seho.

B: Thank you for saying that. I'll bring one of ❺mine.

3. **B:** Let's talk about the corner this time. Any ideas?

G: How about making a small library in the corner of the club room? I will bring some books tomorrow.

B: Great idea! Thank you for suggesting it, Minju.

❶ 'Let's talk about ~.'는 '~에 대해서 말해 보자'라는 뜻이다.
❷ 'make+목적어+목적보어(형용사)' 구문으로 '…을 ~하게 만들다'라는 뜻이다.
❸ 전치사 about 뒤에 동명사 hanging을 사용한다.
❹ 'Why don't you+동사원형?' 형태로 '(네가) ~하는 게 어때?'라는 제안의 표현이다.
❺ mine은 'my pictures'를 대신하는 소유대명사이다.

 Fun Time

A: Let's talk about the town party.

B: Okay. Why don't we cook *bibimbap*?

A: Wonderful. ❶Thank you for your idea.

❶ 감사의 표현으로 전치사 for 뒤에 명사가 온다.

Express Yourself A

1. **M1:** Thank you for coming, everyone. Let's talk about the Clean School Project.

W: I like the corner under the tree most. ❶ The Science Club cleaned around the corner and planted the tree.

M2: I like it, too. It is a very popular place among the students.

2. **M1:** Let's talk about the school gate this time. ❷What do you think of it?

W: The class leaders ❸set up the board and put up some posters. We can know ❹a lot more about school events.

M2: Right! They did a good job. Let's thank the class leaders.

❶ The Science Club cleaned ~ and planted ~ 형태로 동사 cleaned와 planted가 병렬 구조이다.
❷ 'What do you think of ~?'는 '~에 대해 어떻게 생각하니?'라는 뜻으로 의문사 'how'를 사용하지 않도록 주의한다.
❸ 동사 'set'과 'put'은 현재형과 과거형이 같은 형태의 동사로 여기서는 과거형으로 사용되었다.
❹ 'a lot'은 비교급 강조로 '훨씬'의 의미를 가진다. 'much, even, still, far' 등으로 바꾸어 사용할 수 있다.

● 다음 우리말과 일치하도록 빈칸에 알맞은 말을 쓰시오.

Get Ready 2

(1) B: The flower _____ looks _____. _____ _____ help you, Ms. Min?

 W: You're so kind. _____ _____ very much.

(2) G: _____ me _____ you _____ the bench.

 M: Please _____ this _____. Thank you _____ _____ me.

(3) B: _____ _____ _____ what we can do _____ our town.

 G: _____ _____ _____ pictures on the _____ walls?

 B: _____ good. _____ _____ _____?

Start Off – Listen & Talk A

1. B: What do we _____ in our club room? _____ talk about it.

 G: Sure. Well, _____ _____ _____ some _____ _____ _____ the windows? They'll _____ our room _____.

 B: That's a _____ _____. Thank you, Jiu.

2. B: How about _____ some pictures?

 G: Good. _____ _____ _____ _____ one of your pictures? You're good at _____, Seho.

 B: _____ you _____ _____ that. I'll _____ one of _____.

3. B: Let's talk _____ the _____ this time. _____ ideas?

 G: _____ _____ _____ a small library in the _____ of the club room? I will _____ some books tomorrow.

 B: Great idea! Thank you for _____ it, Minju.

Start Off – Listen & Talk B

 G: Seho, we need something on the wall, too. _____ you think so?

B1: You're right. _____ _____ about it _____.

 G: I think we need to _____ the club _____ list there. It'll be _____ _____ _____ _____ _____ _____ the new _____ names.

B2: That's a good idea. We also need our _____ for this _____ _____ on the wall.

 G: Right! That'll really _____ us _____ important school events.

B1: Thank you for _____ great ideas, everyone. We are a good team.

해석

(1) B: 화분이 무거워 보여요. 민 선생님, 도와드릴까요?
 W: 아주 친절하구나. 정말 고마워.

(2) G: 제가 의자 고치시는 걸 도와 드릴게요.
 M: 이걸 좀 꽉 잡아 다오. 도와줘서 고맙구나.

(3) B: 우리가 마을을 위해 무엇을 할 수 있는지 이야기해 보자.
 G: 지저분한 벽에 그림을 그리는 게 어떠니?
 B: 좋아. 또 다른 건?

1. B: 우리 동아리실에 무엇이 필요할까? 그것에 대해 이야기해 보자.
 G: 좋아. 음, 창가에 몇 개의 화분을 두는 게 어때? 그것들은 우리 동아리실을 더 예쁘게 할 거야.
 B: 좋은 생각이야. 지우야, 고마워.

2. B: 그림을 좀 거는 게 어때?
 G: 좋아. 네 그림 중의 하나를 가져오는 게 어때? 세호야, 넌 그림을 잘 그리잖아.
 B: 그렇게 말해 주니 고마워. 내가 내 그림 중에서 하나를 가져올게.

3. B: 이번에는 모퉁이에 대해 이야기해 보자. 의견 있니?
 G: 동아리실 모퉁이에 작은 도서관을 만드는 게 어때? 내가 내일 책 몇 권을 가져올게.
 B: 좋은 생각이야! 민주야, 제안해 줘서 고마워.

 G: 세호야, 우리는 벽에도 뭔가 필요해. 그렇게 생각하지 않니?
B1: 네 말이 맞아. 그것에 대해서 함께 이야기해 보자.
 G: 내 생각에는 거기에 동아리 회원 목록을 붙일 필요가 있는 것 같아. 그것은 우리가 신입 회원들의 이름을 알게 되는 데 도움이 될 거야.
B2: 좋은 생각이야. 이번 학년도의 우리 계획도 벽에 필요해.
 G: 맞아! 그러면 우리가 중요한 학교 행사를 기억하는 데 정말 도움이 될 거야.
B1: 모두 좋은 의견을 내줘서 고마워. 우린 좋은 팀이야.

Step Up – Real-life Scene

G1: Let's _____ _____ how we can make our town _____.

B: _____ me tell you first. There's too much _____ at the bus stop.

G2: I _____. _____ _____ _____ clean the place together?

B: Good. We can put a _____ there, too.

G1: Great idea. It'll be _____ for _____ _____.

G2: _____ _____ _____ some flower pots around the bench? They'll _____ the bus stop _____ _____.

G1: Thank you for _____ great ideas, everyone. Then, _____ _____ start tomorrow?

G2, B: No problem.

해석

G1: 우리 마을을 어떻게 하면 더 좋게 만들 수 있을지를 이야기해 보자.
B: 내가 먼저 말할게. 버스 정류장에 쓰레기가 너무 많아.
G2: 동의해. 그 장소를 함께 치우는 게 어때?
B: 좋아. 우리가 거기에 벤치를 놓을 수도 있을 것 같아.
G1: 좋은 생각이야. 그것은 어르신들에게 도움이 될 거야.
G2: 벤치 주변에 화분도 좀 놓는 게 어때? 그것들은 버스 정류장을 더 아름답게 할 거야.
G1: 모두 좋은 의견을 내줘서 고마워. 그러면, 내일 시작하는 게 어때?
G2, B: 좋아.

Fun Time

A: _____ _____ about the town party.

B: Okay. _____ _____ _____ cook *bibimbap*?

A: Wonderful. _____ you _____ your idea.

A: 마을 파티에 대해 이야기해 보자.
B: 좋아. 우리 비빔밥을 요리하는 게 어때?
A: 훌륭해. 의견을 내줘서 고마워.

Express Yourself A

1. **M1:** Thank you for _____, everyone. Let's _____ _____ the Clean School Project.

   W: I like the corner _____ the tree _____. The Science Club _____ around the corner and _____ the tree.

   M2: I like it, too. It is a very _____ place _____ the students.

2. **M1:** Let's talk about the _____ _____ this time. _____ _____ _____ _____ _____ it?

   W: The class _____ _____ _____ the board and _____ _____ some posters. We can know _____ _____ more about school _____.

   M2: Right! They did a good job. _____ _____ the class leaders.

1. **M1:** 모두 와 주셔서 감사합니다. '깨끗한 학교 프로젝트'에 대해 이야기해 봅시다.
   W: 저는 나무 아래의 모퉁이가 가장 마음에 듭니다. '과학 동아리'가 모퉁이 주변을 청소하고 나무를 심었어요.
   M2: 저도 마음에 듭니다. 그곳은 학생들 사이에 아주 인기 있습니다.

2. **M1:** 이번에는 학교 정문에 관해 이야기해 봅시다. 그것에 대해 어떻게 생각하나요?
   W: 학급 반장들이 판을 설치하고 몇 개의 포스터를 붙였어요. 우리가 학교 행사에 관해 훨씬 더 많이 알 수 있죠.
   M2: 맞아요! 정말 잘했어요. 학급 반장들에게 감사합시다.

01 다음 우리말에 맞도록 주어진 단어를 이용하여 5 단어로 쓰시오.

> 나를 도와줘서 고마워. (for, help)

➡ _____

02 다음 대화의 빈칸에 들어갈 말로 <u>어색한</u> 것은?

> B: Let's talk about what we can do for our town.
> G: _____
> B: Sounds good. Anything else?

① What about drawing pictures on the dirty walls?
② Shall we draw pictures on the dirty walls?
③ How about drawing pictures on the dirty walls?
④ Why didn't we draw pictures on the dirty walls?
⑤ Why don't we draw pictures on the dirty walls?

03 다음 대화의 빈칸에 들어갈 말로 적절한 것은?

> M1: Thank you for coming, everyone. Let's talk about the Clean School Project.
> W: I like the corner under the tree most. _____
> M2: I like it, too. It is a very popular place among the students.

① My friends played with the children under the tree.
② I took pictures of our town well.
③ Why don't we fly kites on the ground?
④ My classmates cooked for the elderly in the nursing home.
⑤ The Science Club cleaned around the corner and planted the tree.

04 다음 대화의 빈칸에 들어갈 말로 알맞은 것은?

> A: Let's talk about the class party. Who will make sandwiches?
> B: I will. I can do it well.
> A: Thank you for _____.

① making   ② volunteering   ③ playing
④ painting   ⑤ suggesting

[01~02] 다음 대화를 읽고 물음에 답하시오.

> B: ____(a)____ the corner this time. Any ideas?
> G: How about ___(A)___ (make) a small library in the corner of the club room? I will bring some books tomorrow.
> B: Great idea! Thank you for ___(B)___ (suggest) it, Minju.

01 위 대화의 빈칸 (a)에 들어갈 말로 알맞은 것은?

① Let us talk to
② Let's talk with
③ Let's talk to
④ Let's talk about
⑤ Let us to talk about

서답형

02 위 대화의 빈칸 (A)와 (B)에 주어진 단어를 알맞은 형태로 고치시오.

➡ (A) _____ (B) _____

서답형

03 다음 대화의 밑줄 친 우리말에 맞게 주어진 단어를 알맞은 순서로 배열하여 쓰시오.

> G: 제가 의자 고치시는 걸 도와 드릴게요. (fix / let / you / me / the bench / help)
> M: Please hold this tight. Thank you for helping me.

➡ _____

[04~05] 다음 대화를 읽고 물음에 답하시오.

> G: Seho, we need something on the wall, too. Don't you think so?
> B1: You're right. Let's talk about it together.

> G: I think we need to put the club member list there. It'll be ___(A)___ for us to learn the new members' names.
> B2: That's a good idea. We also need our plan for this school year on the wall.
> G: Right! That'll really help us remember important school events.
> B1: _____(B)_____, everyone. We are a good team.

서답형

04 위 대화의 빈칸 (A)에 들어갈 말에 대한 영어 풀이를 보고 주어진 철자로 시작하여 쓰시오.

> providing useful help in making a situation better or easier

➡ h_____

05 위 대화의 빈칸 (B)에 들어갈 말로 알맞은 것은?

① Thank you for informing me of the new members' names
② Thank you for teaching me how to make the wall
③ Thank you for suggesting great ideas
④ Thank you for volunteering
⑤ Thank you for helping me with remembering important school events

중요

06 다음 글의 밑줄 친 부분의 의도로 알맞은 것은?

> Let's talk about the school gate this time. What do you think of it?

① 실망 표현하기　　② 상기시켜 주기
③ 격려하기　　　　④ 기대 표현하기
⑤ 주제 소개하기

[07~08] 다음 대화를 읽고 물음에 답하시오.

> G1: Let's talk about _____ (A) _____ .
>
> B: Let me tell you first. There's too much trash at the bus stop.
>
> G2: I agree. Why don't we clean the place together?
>
> B: Good. We can put a bench there, too.
>
> G1: Great idea. It'll be helpful for the elderly.
>
> G2: How about putting some flower pots around the bench? They'll make the bus stop more beautiful.
>
> G1: Thank you for suggesting great ideas, everyone. Then, shall we start tomorrow?
>
> G2, B: No problem.

07 위 대화의 빈칸 (A)에 들어갈 말로 알맞은 것은?

① the class field trip

② how we can make our town better

③ how to make the town sports day more interesting

④ what we'll do to help the elderly

⑤ how we can make the trash can more beautiful

08 위 대화를 읽고 답할 수 <u>없는</u> 질문은?

① What is the problem in the town?

② What are they going to do after cleaning the bus stop?

③ Who is going to clean the bus stop?

④ What will they put on the bench?

⑤ When are they going to start working?

[09~10] 다음 대화를 읽고 물음에 답하시오.

> M1: Let's talk about the school gate this time. (A)그것에 대해 어떻게 생각하나요? (think of it)

> W: The class leaders set up the board and put up some posters. We can know a lot more about school events.
>
> M2: Right! They did a good job. Let's thank the class leaders.

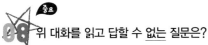
09 위 대화의 밑줄 친 우리말 (A)에 맞게 주어진 단어를 이용하여 영어로 쓰시오.

➡ _____

10 위 대화를 읽고 다음 질문에 영어로 답하시오.

Q: What did the class leaders do before they put up some posters on the board?

➡ They _____ .

[11~13] 다음 대화를 읽고 물음에 답하시오.

> B: How about hanging some pictures?
>
> G: Good. _____(A)_____ take one of your pictures? You're good at painting, Seho.
>
> B: Thank you for saying that. I'll bring one of (B)<u>mine</u>.

11 위 대화의 빈칸 (A)에 제안하는 표현을 세 단어로 쓰시오. (you를 이용할 것)

➡ _____

12 위 대화의 밑줄 친 (B)가 가리키는 것을 찾아 쓰시오.

➡ _____

13 위 대화에서 <u>어색하게 쓰인</u> 어휘를 하나 찾아서 바르게 고쳐 쓰시오.

_____ ➡ _____

[01~02] 다음 대화를 읽고 물음에 답하시오.

> **G1:** Let's talk about how we can make our town better.
>
> **B:** Let me tell you first. There's too much trash at the bus stop.
>
> **G2:** I agree. (A)<u>그 장소를 함께 치우는 게 어때?</u>
>
> **B:** Good. We can put a bench there, too.
>
> **G1:** Great idea. It'll be helpful for the elderly.
>
> **G2:** How about putting some flower pots around the bench? They'll make the bus stop more beautiful.
>
> **G1:** Thank you for suggesting great ideas, everyone. Then, shall we start tomorrow?
>
> **G2, B:** No problem.

01 위 대화를 읽고 다음 물음에 영어로 답하시오. (9 단어로 쓸 것)

> **Q:** What are they going to do to make the bus stop more beautiful?
>
> ⇒ _____

02 위 대화의 밑줄 친 (A)의 우리말에 맞게 'why'와 'we'를 활용하여 영작하시오.

> ⇒ _____

03 다음 대화의 빈칸에 들어갈 말로 자연스러운 것을 〈보기〉에서 찾아 쓰시오.

> **G:** Seho, we need something on the wall, too. Don't you think so?
>
> **B1:** You're right. _____(A)_____
>
> **G:** I think we need to put the club member list there. It'll be helpful for us to learn the new members' names.
>
> **B2:** That's a good idea. _____(B)_____

> **G:** Right! That'll really help us remember important school events.
>
> **B1:** _____(C)_____ We are a good team.

> ── 보기 ──
> • Thank you for suggesting great ideas, everyone.
> • Let's talk about it together.
> • Really? I'm sorry.
> • We also need our plan for this school year on the wall.

⇒ (A) _____
  (B) _____
  (C) _____

04 다음 대화의 밑줄 친 우리말을 주어진 〈조건〉에 맞게 영작하시오.

> **B:** Let's talk about the corner this time. Any ideas?
>
> **G:** <u>동아리실 모퉁이에 작은 도서관을 만드는 게 어때?</u> I will bring some books tomorrow.
>
> **B:** Great idea! Thank you for suggesting it, Minju.

> ── 조건 ──
> • 'How'를 사용할 것.
> • make, small, in the corner, the club room 등의 단어를 이용할 것.

⇒ _____
_____

Grammar

① 과거완료

> • I was glad my dad **had made** me wear gloves.
> 나는 아버지가 나를 장갑을 착용하게 하셔서 기뻤다.

■ 형태: had+과거분사(p.p.)
  의미: '~했었다'

■ 과거의 특정 시점보다 더 이전에 일어난 일이나 그때까지 지속된 상태

  • I looked at the photo that I **had taken** a week earlier.
  나는 일주일 전에 찍은 사진을 보았다. (사진을 본 것보다 사진을 찍은 것이 더 이전의 일)

  • When I arrived there, he **had been waiting** for me for 2 hours.
  내가 거기에 도착했을 때 그는 나를 2시간 동안 기다리고 있었다. (내가 거기에 도착한 과거의 특정 시점까지 그가 기다
  리는 행동이 그 이전부터 지속됨) (과거완료진행형)

■ 과거완료의 수동은 'had been+과거분사'로 쓰고, 과거완료의 진행은 'had been+현재분사'의 형태로
  쓴다.

  • My son spent all the money that **had been given** to him.
  나의 아들은 그에게 주어진 모든 돈을 다 써버렸다. (과거완료수동태)

  • When she visited my house, I **had been cleaning** the bathroom. (과거완료진행형)
  그녀가 나의 집을 방문했을 때 나는 욕실을 청소하고 있었다.

■ 역사적 사실은 과거완료를 쓰지 않고 항상 과거로 쓴다.

  • I knew that the North Korean army **had invaded** South Korea. (×)

  → I knew that the North Korean army **invaded** South Korea. (○)
  나는 북한군이 남한을 침략했다는 사실을 알고 있었다.

핵심 Check

1. 다음 괄호 안에서 알맞은 것을 고르시오.
  (1) I read the book that he (has / had) bought for me.
  (2) The old lady found out that she (left / had left) her key in the car.
  (3) When I (turned / had turned) on the radio, my favorite song had already been
     played.

② 비교급 강조

- **I had to admit the lot looked much better.**
  나는 그 지역이 훨씬 더 좋아 보이는 것을 인정해야만 했다.

- 형태: much/far/even/still/a lot + 비교급
  의미: 훨씬 더 ~한

- 'much/far/even/still/a lot'은 비교급 앞에서 '훨씬'의 뜻으로 비교급을 강조한다.
  - Your dog is **much** bigger than my dog. 너의 개가 나의 개보다 훨씬 더 크다.
  - The novel is **far** more interesting than the movie. 그 소설이 영화보다 훨씬 더 흥미롭다.

- 'very'는 원급을 강조할 때 쓰고, 비교급 강조에는 사용할 수 없다.
  - This computer is **very** cheap. (○)
    This computer is very cheaper than that phone. (×)
    → This computer is **much** cheaper than that phone. (○)
    이 컴퓨터는 저 전화기보다 훨씬 더 싸다.
  - My dad is **very** fat. (○)
    My dad is very fatter than my uncle. (×)
    → My dad is **even** fatter than my uncle. (○)
    나의 아빠는 삼촌보다 훨씬 더 뚱뚱하시다.

핵심 Check

2. 다음 괄호 안에서 알맞은 것을 고르시오.
   (1) The red shirt looks (many / much) more cheaper than the blue one.
   (2) I like summer (a lot / a lot of) more than winter.
   (3) We are (far / very) tired today.

Grammar 시험대비 기본평가

01 다음 우리말에 맞게 괄호 안에 주어진 단어를 이용하여 문장을 완성하시오.

(1) 수학 시험은 내가 예상한 것보다 훨씬 더 어려웠다. (much, difficult, expected)

➡ The math test _____.

(2) 그는 고양이보다 개를 훨씬 더 좋아한다. (much, cats)

➡ He likes _____.

(3) 너는 상자를 어디에 두었는지 기억했니? (where, put)

➡ Did you remember _____?

(4) 너는 그 집이 새로 칠해졌다는 것을 알아챘니? (newly, painted)

➡ Did you notice that _____?

02 다음 문장에서 어법상 <u>어색한</u> 부분을 바르게 고쳐 쓰시오.

(1) My teacher was looking at the pictures that her students had been drawn.

➡ _____

(2) When I arrived at the station, the train has just left.

➡ _____

(3) I jumped many higher than he did.

➡ _____

(4) He grew far tall than his father.

➡ _____

03 다음 〈보기〉의 문장을 참고하여 주어진 두 문장을 한 문장으로 바꾸어 쓰시오.

┌─ 보기 ├─────────────────────────
At 2, my mom left the house. + At 3, I arrived at the house.
→ When I arrived at the house, my mom had left the house.
└─────────────────────────────

(1) At 7, my friends prepared for my birthday party. + At 8, I entered the classroom.

➡ _____

(2) At 6 :30, my husband ate all the sandwiches. + At 7, I got up.

➡ _____

01 다음 빈칸에 들어갈 말로 적절하지 <u>않은</u> 것은?

> You helped me _____ more than anyone else.

① much ② still
③ far ④ really
⑤ even

 다음 중 어법상 <u>어색한</u> 문장을 고르시오.

① She was tired because she had run for hours.
② We hadn't met each other before we worked together.
③ The letter had already arrived at my office when I came in.
④ He said that he had heard about the rules before the contest.
⑤ The teacher said that the Civil War had been between the north and south part of America.

03 다음 빈칸에 들어갈 수 있는 말이 <u>다른</u> 하나는?

① You helped me _____. Thanks to you, I passed the test.
② She works out regularly these days. She looks _____ healthier than before.
③ As I'm working as a salesperson, I need to meet _____ people every day.
④ Learning Spanish is _____ more interesting than learning Japanese.
⑤ We hope you enjoy this show _____.

04 다음 두 문장을 '과거완료시제'를 사용하여 한 문장으로 바르게 바꾸면?

> • She was sick.
> • I found it later.

① I found that she was sick.
② I found that she had been sick.
③ I had found that she was sick.
④ She had been sick and I had found it.
⑤ She was sick and I had found it.

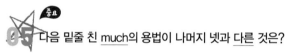 다음 밑줄 친 much의 용법이 나머지 넷과 <u>다른</u> 것은?

① We can't spend <u>much</u> time on this problem.
② The student has <u>much</u> interest in science.
③ The child wanted to have <u>much</u> more love.
④ Mike has never earned <u>much</u> money.
⑤ <u>Much</u> oil spilled out of the bottle.

빈칸에 들어갈 말을 순서대로 바르게 연결한 것은?

> Your brothers _____ the snowman that _____ by me.

① destroyed – made
② destroyed – had made
③ destroyed – had been made
④ had destroyed – had made
⑤ had destroyed – had been made

서답형

07 다음 괄호 안에 주어진 단어들을 바르게 배열하여 문장을 완성하시오.

> When I visited him, (fixed, he, already, bike, had, my).

➡ _____

중요

08 다음 중 어법상 <u>어색한</u> 문장을 고르시오.

① He said he had paid the phone bill.

② I remembered that I had once lived in Seoul.

③ Because she broke my earphones, I had yelled at my sister.

④ She was not the one who had broken the copy machine.

⑤ He had already packed his suitcase when I entered his room.

서답형

09 다음 문장에서 어법상 <u>어색한</u> 것을 바르게 고쳐 다시 쓰시오.

(1) When Jiyeon came back home, she found that her mother already set the table for her.

➡ _____

_____

(2) He is much more cool than you think. I'm sure you will like him.

➡ _____

_____

10 다음 빈칸에 들어갈 말로 <u>어색한</u> 것은?

> Ms. Miller was eating the chicken that her husband had _____.

① left   ② baked

③ cooked   ④ bought

⑤ took

11 다음 두 문장을 한 문장으로 바르게 옮긴 것은?

> • He moved to New York.
> • Before that, he lived in LA for 2 years.

① He lived in LA for 2 years before he had moved to New York.

② He had lived in LA for 2 years after he moved to New York.

③ He has lived in LA for 2 years before he moved to New York.

④ He had lived in LA for 2 years before he moved to New York.

⑤ After he lived in LA for 2 years, he had moved to New York.

서답형

12 다음 괄호 안에서 알맞은 말을 고르시오.

(1) I missed the bus because I (was / had) gotten up late.

(2) When they arrived at the party, their friends had already (leave / left) the party.

(3) She looks (so / even) younger than her age.

(4) Why don't you try much (hard / harder)?

(5) You need to be (a lot / lots of) nicer to the elderly.

중요

13 괄호 안의 단어가 들어갈 수 있는 적절한 위치를 고르시오.

> For me, ① science is ② more ③ difficult ④ than math ⑤. (a lot)

①   ②   ③   ④   ⑤

서답형

14 다음 괄호 안에 주어진 단어 중 필요한 단어만 골라 바르게 배열하여 문장을 완성하시오.

> 그녀는 자기 딸보다 훨씬 어려 보인다.
> She (many, than, looks, young, even, her daughter, younger, more).

➡ She _____.

서답형

15 주어진 어휘를 활용하여 다음 우리말을 영어로 쓰시오.

> 그녀는 내가 예상한 것보다 훨씬 더 친절하게 행동했다. (behave, kindly, expect)

➡ _____

_____

서답형

16 〈보기〉에서 적절한 단어를 골라 빈칸을 알맞은 형태로 완성하시오.

┌─── 보기 ───┐
cook   fix   wash
└──────────┘

When Mr. Han came back home,
(1) he found somebody _____ rice for him.
(2) he was surprised that somebody _____ his T-shirt.
(3) he was happy that somebody _____ his chair.

17 빈칸에 공통으로 들어갈 말을 고르시오.

> • Today is _____ colder than yesterday.
> • I have _____ interest in films.

① very   ② so   ③ much
④ a lot   ⑤ even

서답형

18 주어진 어휘를 이용하여 다음 우리말을 영어로 쓰시오.

> 그는 문을 잠그지 않아서 놀랐다. (surprise, that, had, lock)

➡ _____

_____

19 다음 중 어법상 어색한 문장을 고르시오.

① Can you run much faster than your dog?
② The bag looks even heavier than the book.
③ My grandfather always gets up much more early than me.
④ Alex works a lot harder than anyone else in his company.
⑤ I can eat even more than my friends.

중요

20 다음 중 밑줄 친 부분의 쓰임이 어색한 것을 고르시오.

① Her hair is much longer than mine.
② This shirt is far cheaper than that one.
③ My bed is a lot more comfortable than yours.
④ This cake tastes even better than that one.
⑤ Dogs are very smarter than birds.

21 다음 중 어법상 어색한 문장의 개수로 알맞은 것은?

> a. Your car is much more expensive than me.
> b. I feel much lonelier than usual.
> c. You look even more lovely than before.
> d. He was very more handsome than I thought.
> e. Is an ostrich a lot faster than a cheetah?

① 1개   ② 2개   ③ 3개   ④ 4개   ⑤ 5개

01 과거완료시제를 이용하여 두 문장을 하나로 연결하시오.

(1) • Where did you put the book?
   • Did you remember it?

   ➡ _____

   _____

(2) • Somebody broke in.
   • When I came back home, I found it.

   ➡ _____

   _____

(3) • The house was newly painted.
   • Did you notice it?

   ➡ _____

   _____

(4) • I lost my bag.
   • Mom bought it for me.

   ➡ _____

   _____

(5) • My teacher already left the classroom.
   • When I entered the classroom, I found it.

   ➡ _____

   _____

02 우리말과 같은 뜻이 되도록 빈칸에 알맞은 말을 쓰시오.

그녀는 어제보다 훨씬 더 아름답게 춤을 추었다.
→ She danced _____ than yesterday.

➡ _____

03 다음 그림을 보고 괄호 안의 단어를 바르게 배열하여 문장을 완성하시오.

(1)

A: Look at these shoes. Which one do you like?
B: I like the sneakers. They _____. (comfortable, than, others, the, more, look, much)

➡ _____

(2)

A: Which one will you buy?
B: I'll buy the backpack. It is _____. (cheaper, the, than, hand bag, much)

➡ _____

04 주어진 문장의 밑줄 친 부분을 괄호 안의 단어로 바꾸어 문장을 다시 쓰시오.

(1) Eric played the violin very <u>well</u>. (better)

   ➡ _____

(2) You should work very <u>hard</u>. (harder)

   ➡ _____

05 다음 우리말을 주어진 어휘를 이용하여 영어로 옮기시오.

(1) 어제보다 훨씬 더 비가 심하게 오는 중이다.
(raining, lot, harder)

➡ _____

_____

(2) 너의 책은 다른 어떤 것보다 읽기에 훨씬 쉽다.
(even, to read, anything)

➡ _____

_____

(3) 이 책은 저것보다 훨씬 더 어려워 보인다.
(much, difficult, one)

➡ _____

_____

06 다음 빈칸에 괄호 안의 단어를 알맞은 형태로 바꾸어 쓰시오.

> She _____ New York until she became
> 20 years old. (never, visit)

➡ _____

07 〈보기〉를 참고하여 주어진 두 문장을 한 문장으로 바르게 바꾸시오.

> ┤ 보기 ├
> Mina wrote a letter to Jenny.
> + Jenny read the letter.
> → Jenny read the letter that Mina had written to her.

(1) Jack sent a gift to Tony.
 + Tony threw away the gift by mistake.

➡ _____

_____

(2) Yuna showed me the notebook.
 + She wrote down a poem on the notebook.

➡ _____

_____

08 잘못된 부분을 바르게 고쳐 문장을 다시 쓰시오.

(1) Jack lost the umbrella that his friend has lent to him.

➡ _____

_____

(2) When I called her, she has already gone to sleep.

➡ _____

_____

(3) Before I get to the theater, the movie had already finished.

➡ _____

_____

(4) When I arrived at the airport, the plane was already left.

➡ _____

_____

(5) Did you eat the pie that Dad has baked?

➡ _____

_____

09 괄호 안의 단어를 빈칸에 알맞은 형태로 쓰시오.

(1) When Mr. Han came back home, he found somebody _____ his house. (clean)

(2) I think sandwiches are much _____ than *gimbap*. (healthy)

(3) When he _____, I had already eaten lunch. (call)

(4) He couldn't open the door because he _____ his key. (lose)

(5) He got up late because he _____ to bed late. (go)

Reading

Green Thumbs

I complained the whole day. My parents were making me work on the neighborhood project, but I had far better things to do. I didn't understand why we were working on this place. It was just the ugly, old, empty lot across from Johnny's Shop. It was full of wild plants, fast food wraps, old newspapers, broken glass, and every other kind of dirty trash you can imagine. As I looked at it that first morning, I thought, "I bet there are snakes in there, too."

There were twenty of us — all ages and sizes — ready to work that day. I didn't think that we could clean up this awful mess and turn it into a garden. We were all wondering where to begin. Then Mr. Hernandez said, "The only way to do it is just to start." Then, he divided the lot into four parts with string and assigned five people to each part.

By lunchtime, I was hot, sweaty, and glad my dad had made me wear gloves. We filled fifty trash bags with waste and were ready to pull wild plants. As we pulled and pulled, dust filled the air and made us sneeze. At the end of the day, I had to admit the lot looked much better.

green thumb 원예의 재능(식물을 잘 키우는 사람)
neighborhood 이웃
wrap 포장지; 포장하다
ugly 불쾌한, 볼품없는
empty 텅 빈
lot 지역, 부지
be full of …으로 가득 차다
newspaper 신문
bet …이 틀림없다, 확신하다
snake 뱀
awful 끔찍한, 지독한
mess 쓰레기 더미, 혼잡
divide … into ~ …를 ~로 나누다
string 끈, 줄
assign 맡기다, 배정하다
sweaty 땀에 젖은, 땀이 나는
fill …을 채우다
trash bag 쓰레기 봉투
be ready to …할 준비가 되어 있다
dust 먼지
sneeze 재채기하다
admit 인정하다

 확인문제

● 다음 문장이 본문의 내용과 일치하면 T, 일치하지 않으면 F를 쓰시오.

1 The writer complained the whole day. ☐

2 The neighborhood project was working on the town garden across from Johnny's Shop. ☐

3 The place was full of wild plants, fast food wraps, old newspapers, broken glass, etc. ☐

4 Mr. Hernandez divided the lot into four parts with chalk. ☐

5 By lunchtime, the writer was hot and sweaty. ☐

6 The writer filled fifty trash bags with wild plants. ☐

That first day was the toughest. On the weekends that followed, we
최상급

made rows, planted flower and vegetable seeds, and watered them.
V1   V2   V3

After about two weeks, I stopped complaining when I found the plants
stop ~ing: ~하는 것을 그만두다. to complain(×)

had started popping up! First, the lettuce and then the beans and the
= to pop. start는 목적어로 동명사와 to부정사를 쓸 수 있다.

tomatoes. They grew so fast. I couldn't believe it! The bean plants
the lettuce. the beans and the tomatoes

grew an inch, and the tomatoes doubled in size in just a few days.
단지 며칠 만에

Now, two months later, I like to go there every day to see what new
to부정사의 부사적 용법(목적)

flowers are ready to pop up. Lots of people in the neighborhood meet
to부정사의 부사적 용법(형용사 수식)

there to enjoy the sights and to talk together.
to부정사의 부사적 용법(목적)   to부정사의 부사적 용법(목적)

Tonight, it suddenly hit me — what a good thing we did! I'm proud I
= occurred to = struck: ~에게 생각이 떠올랐다

have been a part of it. I'm in charge of picking flowers for the nursing
be in charge of: ~을 담당하다, ~을 책임지고 있다

home on Fourth Street. The vegetables will go to every kitchen in our

town. But even better, an ugly and dirty lot that people didn't like has
비교급 강조(훨씬)   = which(관계대명사 목적격)

become a pretty garden for everyone.

---

tough 힘든, 질긴
row 열, 줄
pop up 갑자기 나오다
lettuce 상추
bean 콩
complain 불평하다
suddenly 갑자기
double 두 배가 되다
hit (생각 등이 불현듯) 떠오르다
in charge of ···을 맡아서, 담당해서
nursing home 양로원
kitchen 부엌, 주방

확인문제

● 다음 문장이 본문의 내용과 일치하면 T, 일치하지 않으면 F를 쓰시오.

1 That first day was the toughest. ☐

2 After about two weeks, the writer kept complaining. ☐

3 The lettuce, the beans and the tomatoes grew so fast. ☐

4 The bean plants doubled in size in just a few days. ☐

5 The writer is in charge of picking flowers for the nursing home on Fourth Street. ☐

6 The vegetables will go to the participants in the project. ☐

● 우리말을 참고하여 빈칸에 알맞은 말을 쓰시오.

1 Green _____

2 I _____ the whole day.

3 My parents were making me _____ on the neighborhood project, but I had _____ _____ things to do.

4 I didn't understand _____ _____ _____ _____ on this place.

5 It was just the ugly, old, empty lot _____ _____ Johnny's Shop.

6 It _____ _____ _____ wild plants, fast food wraps, old newspapers, broken glass, and every other kind of dirty trash _____ _____ _____.

7 As I looked at it that first morning, I thought, "_____ _____ there are snakes in there, too."

8 There were twenty of us — _____ _____ _____ — ready to work that day.

9 I didn't think that we could clean up _____ _____ _____ and turn it into a garden.

10 We were all wondering _____ _____ _____.

11 Then Mr. Hernandez said, "The only way to do it is _____ _____ _____."

12 Then, he _____ the lot _____ four parts with string and _____ five people _____ each part.

13 _____ _____, I was hot, sweaty, and glad my dad had made me _____ gloves.

14 We _____ fifty trash bags _____ waste and _____ _____ _____ pull wild plants.

15 As we pulled and pulled, dust filled the air and _____ _____ _____.

---

1 식물을 잘 키우는 사람들

2 나는 온종일 불평했다.

3 우리 부모님은 나를 이웃 프로젝트에서 일하게 하셨지만, 나에게는 훨씬 더 나은 할 일들이 있었다.

4 나는 우리가 왜 이곳에서 일하고 있어야 하는지 이해하지 못했다.

5 그곳은 그저 Johnny's Shop 건너편에 있는 볼품없고, 오래되고, 텅 빈 지역이었다.

6 그곳은 잡초와 패스트푸드 포장지와 낡은 신문, 깨진 유리, 그리고 상상할 수 있는 모든 다른 종류의 더러운 쓰레기로 가득 차 있었다.

7 그 첫날 아침에 그곳을 보았을 때, 나는 "틀림없이 저 안에는 뱀들도 있을 거야."라고 생각했다.

8 그날 일할 준비가 된 —모든 연령대와 몸집을 가진 — 우리 20명이 있었다.

9 나는 이 끔찍하게 더러운 곳을 청소하여 정원으로 바꿀 수 있다고 생각하지 않았다.

10 우리는 모두 어디서부터 시작해야 할지 궁금해 하고 있었다.

11 그때 Hernandez 씨가 "그것을 할 유일한 방법은 그냥 시작하는 것입니다."라고 말했다.

12 그러고 나서, 그는 그 지역을 끈으로 네 구역으로 나누고, 5명을 각 구역에 배치했다.

13 점심 무렵, 나는 덥고, 땀이 났으며, 아버지가 나에게 장갑을 끼도록 한 것이 기뻤다.

14 우리는 쓰레기 봉투 50개를 쓰레기로 채웠고, 잡초를 뽑을 준비가 되어 있었다.

15 우리가 뽑으면 뽑을수록, 먼지가 공기를 가득 메워서 재채기가 나왔다.

16 _____ _____ _____ _____ the day, I had to admit the lot looked much better.

17 That first day was _____ _____ .

18 On the weekends that followed, we _____ _____ , planted flower and vegetable seeds, and watered them.

19 After about two weeks, I _____ _____ when I found the plants had started popping up!

20 _____ , _____ _____ and then the beans and the tomatoes.

21 They grew _____ _____ .

22 I _____ _____ it!

23 The bean plants grew an inch, and the tomatoes doubled _____ _____ _____ _____ _____ _____ .

24 Now, two months later, I like to go there every day to see _____ _____ _____ _____ to pop up.

25 Lots of people in the neighborhood meet there to _____ _____ _____ and to talk together.

26 Tonight, it suddenly _____ _____ — what a good thing we did!

27 I'm proud I _____ _____ _____ _____ of it.

28 _____ _____ _____ _____ picking flowers for the nursing home on Fourth Street.

29 The vegetables _____ _____ _____ every kitchen in our town.

30 But _____ _____ , an ugly and dirty lot _____ people didn't like has become a pretty garden for everyone.

16 그날이 끝날 무렵, 나는 그 지역이 훨씬 더 나아 보인다는 것을 인정해야 했다.

17 그 첫날이 가장 힘들었다.

18 그다음 주말에 우리는 열을 만들고, 꽃과 채소 씨앗을 심고, 물을 주었다.

19 약 2주 뒤, 나는 식물들이 자라나기 시작한 것을 발견했을 때 불평하는 것을 멈추었다!

20 처음에는 상추, 그러고 나서, 콩과 토마토.

21 그것들은 아주 빨리 자랐다.

22 나는 믿을 수가 없었다!

23 콩 식물은 1인치 자라났고, 토마토는 며칠 만에 크기가 두 배가 되었다.

24 두 달이 지난 지금, 나는 매일 어떤 새로운 꽃들이 피어날 준비가 되었는지 보러 그곳에 가는 것을 좋아한다.

25 이웃의 많은 사람이 그곳에서 만나 풍경을 즐기고 함께 이야기를 나눈다.

26 오늘 밤, 갑자기 생각났다 — 우리가 얼마나 좋은 일을 했는가!

27 나는 내가 그 일의 일부였다는 것이 자랑스럽다.

28 나는 'Fourth Street'에 있는 양로원을 위해 꽃을 따는 일을 맡았다.

29 채소들은 우리 마을의 모든 부엌으로 갈 것이다.

30 하지만 훨씬 더 좋은 것은, 사람들이 좋아하지 않았던 볼품없고 더러운 지역이 모두를 위한 예쁜 정원이 되었다는 것이다.

• 우리말을 참고하여 본문을 영작하시오.

1 식물을 잘 키우는 사람들

➡ _____

2 나는 온종일 불평했다.

➡ _____

3 우리 부모님은 나를 이웃 프로젝트에서 일하게 하셨지만, 나에게는 훨씬 더 나은 할 일들이 있었다.

➡ _____

4 나는 우리가 왜 이곳에서 일하고 있어야 하는지 이해하지 못했다.

➡ _____

5 그곳은 그저 Johnny's Shop 건너편에 있는 볼품없고, 오래되고, 텅 빈 지역이었다.

➡ _____

6 그곳은 잡초와 패스트푸드 포장지와 낡은 신문, 깨진 유리, 그리고 상상할 수 있는 모든 다른 종류의 더러운 쓰레기로 가득 차 있었다.

➡ _____

_____

7 그 첫날 아침에 그곳을 보았을 때, 나는 "틀림없이 저 안에는 뱀들도 있을 거야."라고 생각했다.

➡ _____

8 그날 일할 준비가 된 ―모든 연령대와 몸집을 가진 ― 우리 20명이 있었다.

➡ _____

9 나는 이 끔찍하게 더러운 곳을 청소하여 정원으로 바꿀 수 있다고 생각하지 않았다.

➡ _____

10 우리는 모두 어디서부터 시작해야 할지 궁금해 하고 있었다.

➡ _____

11 그때 Hernandez 씨가 "그것을 할 유일한 방법은 그냥 시작하는 것입니다."라고 말했다.

➡ _____

12 그러고 나서, 그는 그 지역을 끈으로 네 구역으로 나누고, 5명을 각 구역에 배치했다.

➡ _____

13 점심 무렵, 나는 덥고, 땀이 났으며, 아버지가 나에게 장갑을 끼도록 한 것이 기뻤다.

➡ _____

14 우리는 쓰레기 봉투 50개를 쓰레기로 채웠고, 잡초를 뽑을 준비가 되어 있었다.

➡ _____

15 우리가 뽑으면 뽑을수록, 먼지가 공기를 가득 메워서 재채기가 나왔다.

➡ _____

16 그날이 끝날 무렵, 나는 그 지역이 훨씬 더 나아 보인다는 것을 인정해야 했다.

➡ _____

17 그 첫날이 가장 힘들었다.

➡ _____

18 그다음 주말에 우리는 열을 만들고, 꽃과 채소 씨앗을 심고, 물을 주었다.

➡ _____

19 약 2주 뒤, 나는 식물들이 자라나기 시작한 것을 발견했을 때 불평하는 것을 멈추었다!

➡ _____

20 처음에는 상추, 그러고 나서, 콩과 토마토.

➡ _____

21 그것들은 아주 빨리 자랐다.

➡ _____

22 나는 믿을 수가 없었다!

➡ _____

23 콩 식물은 1인치 자라났고, 토마토는 며칠 만에 크기가 두 배가 되었다.

➡ _____

24 두 달이 지난 지금, 나는 매일 어떤 새로운 꽃들이 피어날 준비가 되었는지 보러 그곳에 가는 것을 좋아한다.

➡ _____

25 이웃의 많은 사람이 그곳에서 만나 풍경을 즐기고 함께 이야기를 나눈다.

➡ _____

26 오늘 밤, 갑자기 생각났다 — 우리가 얼마나 좋은 일을 했는가!

➡ _____

27 나는 내가 그 일의 일부였다는 것이 자랑스럽다.

➡ _____

28 나는 'Fourth Street'에 있는 양로원을 위해 꽃을 따는 일을 맡았다.

➡ _____

29 채소들은 우리 마을의 모든 부엌으로 갈 것이다.

➡ _____

30 하지만 훨씬 더 좋은 것은, 사람들이 좋아하지 않았던 볼품없고 더러운 지역이 모두를 위한 예쁜 정원이 되었다는 것이다.

➡ _____

[01~03] 다음 글을 읽고 물음에 답하시오.

I (A)[complained / complained about] the whole day. My parents were making me work on the neighborhood project, but I had far better things to do. I didn't understand why we were working on ①this place. ②It was just the ugly, old, empty lot across from ③ Johnny's Shop. ⓐIt was full of wild plants, fast food wraps, old newspapers, (B)[breaking / broken] glass, and every other (C)[kind / kinds] of dirty trash you can imagine. As I looked at ④it that first morning, I thought, "I bet there are snakes in ⑤there, too."

서답형

01 위 글의 괄호 (A)~(C)에서 어법상 알맞은 낱말을 골라 쓰시오.

➡ (A) _____ (B) _____ (C) _____

중요

02 밑줄 친 ①~⑤ 중에서 가리키는 대상이 나머지 넷과 다른 것은?

①   ②   ③   ④   ⑤

서답형

03 위 글의 밑줄 친 ⓐ를 다음과 같이 바꿔 쓸 때 빈칸에 들어갈 알맞은 말을 두 단어로 쓰시오.

➡ It was _____ wild plants

[04~07] 다음 글을 읽고 물음에 답하시오.

There were twenty of us — all ages and sizes — ready to work that day. (A)I didn't think that we could clean up this terrific mess and turn it into a garden. We were all wondering where to begin. Then Mr.

Hernandez said, "(B)The only way to do it is just to start." Then, he divided the lot into four parts with string and assigned ___ ⓐ ___ people to each part.

서답형

04 위 글의 빈칸 ⓐ에 들어갈 알맞은 단어를 쓰시오.

➡ _____

서답형

05 위 글의 밑줄 친 (A)에서 흐름상 어색한 부분을 찾아 고치시오.

_____ ➡ _____

중요

06 위 글의 밑줄 친 (B)에 어울리는 속담으로 가장 알맞은 것을 고르시오.

① Look before you leap.
② Well begun is half done.
③ Too many cooks spoil the broth.
④ Make hay while the sun shines.
⑤ It never rains but it pours.

07 본문의 내용과 일치하도록 다음 빈칸 (A)~(C)에 알맞은 단어를 쓰시오.

When the twenty people were (A)_____ where they should begin, Mr. Hernandez (B)_____ the lot into four parts with string and (C)_____ five people to each part.

[08~11] 다음 글을 읽고 물음에 답하시오.

That first day was the toughest. (①) On the weekends ⓐthat followed, we made rows, planted flower and vegetable seeds, and watered them. (②) After about two weeks, I stopped complaining when I found the plants had started popping up! (③) First, the lettuce and then the beans and the tomatoes. (④) They grew so fast. (⑤) The bean plants grew an inch, and the tomatoes ⓑ며칠 만에 크기가 두 배가 되었다.

서답형

08 위 글의 흐름으로 보아, 주어진 문장이 들어가기에 가장 적절한 곳은?

I couldn't believe it!

①   ②   ③   ④   ⑤

위 글의 제목으로 알맞은 것을 고르시오.

① The Toughest Day in a Week
② Unbelievable! I have a Green Thumb!
③ The Difficulty of Growing Vegetables
④ How to Plant Flower Seeds
⑤ A Shortcut to Grow Vegetables!

10 아래 <보기>에서 위 글의 밑줄 친 ⓐthat과 문법적 쓰임이 같은 것의 개수를 고르시오.

┌─── 보기 ├──
① It's the best novel that I've ever read.
② The watch that you gave me keeps perfect time.
③ I am glad that I found you.
④ I'm so tired that I cannot do my homework.
⑤ Where's the letter that came yesterday?
└──────────────

① 1개   ② 2개   ③ 3개   ④ 4개   ⑤ 5개

서답형

11 위 글의 밑줄 친 ⓑ의 우리말에 맞게 주어진 어휘를 이용하여 8 단어로 영작하시오.

doubled, just a few

➡ _____

[12~13] 다음 글을 읽고 물음에 답하시오.

Tonight, it suddenly hit me — what a good thing we did! I'm proud I have been a part of it. I'm in ⓐcharge of picking flowers for the nursing home on Fourth Street. The vegetables will go to every kitchen in our town. But even better, an ugly and dirty lot that people didn't like has become a pretty garden for everyone.

12 위 글의 밑줄 친 ⓐcharge와 같은 의미로 쓰인 것을 고르시오.

① He took charge of the farm then.
② Delivery is free of charge.
③ What did they charge for the repairs?
④ She rejected the charge that the story was untrue.
⑤ They began to charge the enemy.

13 According to the passage, which is NOT true?

① Tonight, it suddenly occurred to the writer that they did a very good thing.
② The writer was proud of having been a part of it.
③ The writer was in charge of picking flowers for the nursing home.
④ The writer brought the vegetables to every kitchen in his or her town.
⑤ People didn't like the ugly and dirty lot before it became a pretty garden for everyone.

[14~16] 다음 글을 읽고 물음에 답하시오.

I complained the whole day. My parents were making me work on the neighborhood project, but ⓐI had far good things to do. I didn't understand why we were working on this place. It was just the ugly, old, empty lot across from Johnny's Shop. It was full of wild plants, fast food wraps, old newspapers, broken glass, and every other kind of dirty trash you can imagine. ⓑAs I looked at it that first morning, I thought, "I bet there are snakes in there, too."

서답형

14 위 글의 밑줄 친 ⓐ에서 어법상 틀린 부분을 찾아 고치시오.

_____ ➡ _____

중요

15 위 글의 마지막 부분 ⓑ에서 알 수 있는 'I'의 심경으로 가장 알맞은 것을 고르시오.

① ashamed   ② excited

③ reluctant   ④ willing

⑤ calm

16 According to the passage, which is NOT true?

① The writer was full of complaints the whole day.

② The writer's parents had the writer work on the neighborhood project.

③ The writer didn't figure out why they were working on the neighborhood project.

④ The place was just the ordinary empty lot across from Johnny's Shop.

⑤ The place was full of wild plants, fast food wraps, old newspapers, etc.

[17~19] 다음 글을 읽고 물음에 답하시오.

That first day was the toughest. On the weekends that followed, we made ⓐrows, planted flower and vegetable seeds, and watered them. After about two weeks, I stopped complaining ⓑwhen I found the plants had started popping up! First, the lettuce and then the beans and the tomatoes. They grew so fast. I couldn't believe it! The bean plants grew an inch, and the tomatoes doubled in size in just a few days.

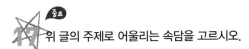

17 위 글의 주제로 어울리는 속담을 고르시오.

① The more the better.

② Prevention is better than cure.

③ Haste makes waste.

④ Sweet after bitter.

⑤ It never rains but it pours.

18 위 글의 밑줄 친 ⓐrows와 같은 의미로 쓰인 것을 모두 고르시오.

① He rows around the island.

② She rows against the flood.

③ The vegetables were planted in neat rows.

④ There were endless rows of identical houses.

⑤ The fisherman rows them back to the shore.

서답형

19 위 글의 밑줄 친 ⓑ를 다음과 같이 바꿔 쓸 때 빈칸에 들어갈 알맞은 말을 두 단어로 쓰시오.

➡ when I found the plants had started _____ _____ up

[20~22] 다음 글을 읽고 물음에 답하시오.

(A)There were twenty of us — all ages and sizes — ready to work that day. I didn't think that we could clean up this awful mess and turn it ___ⓐ___ a garden. We were all wondering where to begin. Then Mr. Hernandez said, "The only way to do it is just (B)to start." Then, he divided the lot into four parts with string and assigned five people ___ⓑ___ each part.

20 위 글의 빈칸 ⓐ와 ⓑ에 들어갈 전치사가 바르게 짝지어진 것은?

	ⓐ	ⓑ			ⓐ	ⓑ
①	for – to			②	into – on	
③	to – from			④	for – on	
⑤	into – to					

서답형

21 위 글의 밑줄 친 (A)를 다음과 같이 바꿔 쓸 때 빈칸에 들어갈 알맞은 단어를 철자 d로 시작하여 쓰시오.

➡ There were twenty of us who were ready to work that day, and our ages and our sizes were all _____.

중요

22 위 글의 밑줄 친 (B)to start와 to부정사의 용법이 다른 것을 모두 고르시오.

① Give me something hot to drink.
② To get up early is good for your health.
③ I'm pleased to meet you again.
④ I took a subway to get there on time.
⑤ We decided to go to the museum.

[23~25] 다음 글을 읽고 물음에 답하시오.

Tonight, ⓐit suddenly hit me — what a good thing we did! I'm proud I have been a part of it. I'm in charge of picking flowers for the nursing home on Fourth Street. The vegetables will go to every kitchen in our town. But ⓑeven better, ⓒ사람들이 좋아하지 않았던 볼품없고 더러운 지역이 모두를 위한 예쁜 정원이 되었다.

23 위 글의 밑줄 친 ⓐ와 바꿔 쓸 수 없는 말을 고르시오.

① I suddenly hit on it
② it suddenly occurred to me
③ a light suddenly went on in my room
④ it suddenly struck me
⑤ I suddenly came up with it

중요

24 위 글의 밑줄 친 ⓑeven과 같은 의미로 쓰인 것을 고르시오.

① Even a child can understand it.
② Our scores are now even.
③ 4, 6, 8, 10 are all even numbers.
④ You need an even surface to work on.
⑤ You know even less about it than I do.

서답형

25 위 글의 밑줄 친 ⓒ의 우리말에 맞게 주어진 어휘를 알맞게 배열하시오.

has become / that / a pretty garden / for everyone / didn't like / an ugly and dirty lot / people

➡ _____

_____

[01~03] 다음 글을 읽고 물음에 답하시오.

I complained the whole day. My parents were making me work on the neighborhood project, but ⓐ나에게는 훨씬 더 나은 할 일들이 있었다. I didn't understand why we were working on this place. It was just the ugly, old, empty lot across from Johnny's Shop. It was full of wild plants, fast food wraps, old newspapers, broken glass, and every other kind of dirty trash you can imagine. As I looked at it that first morning, I thought, "ⓑI bet there are snakes in there, too."

01 위 글의 밑줄 친 ⓐ의 우리말에 맞게 주어진 어휘를 이용하여 7 단어로 영작하시오.

far

➡ _____

02 위 글의 밑줄 친 ⓑ를 다음과 같이 바꿔 쓸 때 빈칸에 들어갈 알맞은 단어를 쓰시오.

➡ There _____ be snakes in there, too.
= I'm _____ that there are snakes in there, too.

03 다음 문장에서 위 글의 내용과 <u>다른</u> 부분을 찾아서 고치시오.

The writer was willing to work on the neighborhood project.

_____ ➡ _____

[04~06] 다음 글을 읽고 물음에 답하시오.

There were twenty of us — all ages and sizes — ready to work that day. I didn't think that we could clean up this awful (A)[mass / mess] and turn it into a garden. We were

all (B)[wandering / wondering] ⓐwhere to begin. Then Mr. Hernandez said, "The only way to do it is just to start." Then, he (C)[decided / divided] the lot into four parts with string and assigned five people to each part.

04 위 글의 괄호 (A)~(C)에서 문맥상 알맞은 낱말을 골라 쓰시오.

➡ (A) _____ (B) _____ (C) _____

05 위 글의 밑줄 친 ⓐ를 다음과 같이 바꿔 쓸 때 빈칸에 들어갈 알맞은 말을 두 단어로 쓰시오.

➡ where _____ _____ begin.

06 주어진 영영풀이에 해당하는 단어를 본문에서 찾아 쓰시오.

gave someone some work to do

➡ _____

[07~09] 다음 글을 읽고 물음에 답하시오.

By lunchtime, I was hot, sweaty, and glad my dad ___ⓐ___ me wear gloves. We filled fifty trash bags with waste and were ready to pull wild plants. As we pulled and pulled, ⓑdust filled the air and made us sneeze. At the end of the day, I had to admit the lot looked much better.

07 위 글의 빈칸 ⓐ에 make를 알맞은 형태로 쓰시오.

➡ _____

08 위 글의 밑줄 친 ⓑ를 다음과 같이 바꿔 쓸 때 빈칸에 들어갈 알맞은 말을 of를 포함하여 두 단어로 쓰시오.

➡ we sneezed _____ _____ the dust which filled the air

09 본문의 내용과 일치하도록 다음 빈칸 (A)와 (B)에 공통으로 들어갈 알맞은 단어를 쓰시오.

> After the people filled fifty trash bags with waste, they pulled and pulled wild plants. At the end of the day, the writer had to admit the (A)_____ looked a (B)_____ better.

[10~12] 다음 글을 읽고 물음에 답하시오.

> That first day was the toughest. On the weekends that followed, we ___ⓐ___ rows, ___ⓑ___ flower and vegetable seeds, and ___ⓒ___ them. After about two weeks, I stopped complaining when I found the plants had started popping up! First, the lettuce and then the beans and the tomatoes. ⓓThey grew so fast. I couldn't believe it! The bean plants grew an inch, and the tomatoes doubled in size in just a few days.

10 위 글의 빈칸 ⓐ~ⓒ에 make, plant, water를 각각 알맞은 형태로 쓰시오.

➡ ⓐ _____ ⓑ _____ ⓒ _____

11 위 글의 밑줄 친 ⓓThey가 가리키는 것을 본문에서 찾아 쓰시오.

➡ _____

12 What made the writer stop complaining after about two weeks? Fill in the blank with a suitable word.

> The sight of the _____ that had popped up made the writer stop complaining.

[13~16] 다음 글을 읽고 물음에 답하시오.

> Tonight, it suddenly hit me — what ⓐa good thing we did! ⓑI'm proud I have been a part of it. ⓒI'm in charge of picking flowers for the nursing home on Fourth Street. The vegetables will go to every kitchen in our town. ⓓBut even better, an ugly and dirty lot that people didn't like has become a pretty garden for everyone.

13 위 글의 밑줄 친 ⓐ의 구체적인 내용을 본문에서 찾아 쓰시오.

➡ _____
_____

14 위 글의 밑줄 친 ⓑ를 동명사를 사용하여 고치시오.

➡ _____

15 위 글의 밑줄 친 ⓒ를 다음과 같이 바꿔 쓸 때 빈칸에 들어갈 알맞은 말을 두 단어로 쓰시오.

➡ I'm _____ _____ picking flowers for the nursing home on Fourth Street.

16 위 글의 밑줄 친 ⓓ에서 생략할 수 있는 말을 생략하고 문장을 다시 쓰시오.

➡ _____
_____

After You Read A

해석

June 17

I visited the town garden after school. Some people were talking while they
visited to(×)   방과 후에   ~하는 동안
were looking at the beautiful garden. I picked some flowers and took them to
= some flowers
the nursing home. I'm proud that we made a pretty garden for everyone.
접속사: [원인·이유] …이므로, …이기 때문에

구문해설 · visit: 방문하다 · pick: 꺾다 · nursing home: 양로원

6월 17일

나는 방과 후에 마을 정원을 방문했다. 몇몇 사람들이 아름다운 정원을 보면서 이야기하고 있었다. 나는 꽃을 몇 송이 꺾어서 양로원에 가지고 갔다. 우리가 모두를 위한 예쁜 정원을 만든 것이 자랑스럽다.

Do It Yourself

Our Town Symbol

This is Oksig, which I drew as a symbol of my town. I designed this after I
관계대명사의 계속적 용법   ~으로(전치사)   과거
had taken pictures of many different kinds of corn. Oksig is much cuter than
과거완료 (두 동사 간의 시간의 순서를 알려준다.)   비교급 강조 (= still/far/even/a lot)
real corn. I hope everybody likes it.
Oksig

구문해설 · symbol: 상징 · design: 디자인하다 · take pictures of : ~를 사진 찍다

우리 동네 상징

이것은 Oksig이고, 내가 나의 동네 상징으로 그렸습니다. 나는 많은 다양한 종류의 옥수수 사진을 찍은 후에 이것을 디자인했습니다. Oksig은 진짜 옥수수보다 훨씬 더 귀엽습니다. 나는 모든 사람들이 이것을 좋아하길 바랍니다.

Link to the World

· Kampong Ayer is the largest "water village" in the world. It is made up of
the+최상급+단수명사+in+단수 명사(범위/장소)   ~로 구성되다(= consists of
                                                    = is composed of)
about 40 small villages.

· All the houses are built over the water.
수동태: 지어지다
· There are schools, police stations, gas stations, and post offices.
There are+복수명사: ~가 있다
· It is much more beautiful than you think. It is called the Venice of Asia.
비교급 강조: 훨씬(= even. still. far. a lot)   수동태: ~라 불리다

구문해설 · village 마을 · be made up of ~로 이루어져 있다 · gas station 주유소
· Venice 베니스

· 캄퐁 아에르는 세상에서 가장 큰 '수상 마을'이다. 그것은 40개의 작은 마을들로 이루어져 있다.

· 모든 집은 물 위에 지어져 있다.

· 학교, 경찰서, 주유소, 우체국이 있다.

· 그곳은 여러분이 생각하는 것보다 훨씬 더 아름답다. 그곳은 아시아의 베니스라고 불린다.

01 다음 주어진 두 단어의 관계가 같도록 빈칸에 알맞은 단어를 쓰시오.

> fill – empty : wonderful – a_____

02 다음 문장의 빈칸 (a)와 (b)에 들어갈 단어가 바르게 짝지어진 것은?

> • John wasn't invited to the party, so we were surprised when he (a)_____.
> • The (b)_____ of the mountains was so beautiful that she cried.

① didn't come – sight
② didn't come – top
③ was delivered – hillside
④ popped up – seed
⑤ popped up – sight

[03~04] 다음 영영풀이에 해당하는 것을 고르시오.

03
> to offer to do something that you do not have to do

① fill   ② volunteer
③ hang   ④ represent
⑤ suggest

04
> a line of things or people next to each other

① row   ② law
③ low   ④ raw
⑤ lot

05 다음 대화의 빈칸에 들어갈 말을 〈영영풀이〉에 맞게 두 단어로 쓰시오.

> A: Hi, Molly. Are you good with plants?
> B: Not really.
> A: Do you know someone?
> B: Ask Susan. She has a _____.
> A: Thanks.

> 〈영영풀이〉 considerable talent or ability to grow plants

➡ _____

06 다음 밑줄 친 부분의 뜻이 잘못된 것은?

① I don't use plastic wrap. (포장지)
② She cut the lettuce and made a salad. (상추)
③ My mother often makes rice mixed with beans. (콩)
④ Do not complain about small things. (배정하다)
⑤ Kevin is always late, so I bet that he will be late today. (확신하다)

07 다음 대화의 빈칸에 들어갈 말로 문법상 적절하지 않은 것은?

> B: Let's talk about what we can do for our town.
> G: _____ on the dirty walls?
> B: Sounds good. Anything else?

① How about drawing pictures
② What about drawing pictures
③ What do you say to draw pictures
④ Why don't we draw pictures
⑤ Shall we draw pictures

08 다음 대화의 순서를 바르게 배열한 것은?

> (A) I like it, too. It is a very popular place among the students.
>
> (B) I like the corner under the tree most. The Science Club cleaned around the corner and planted the tree.
>
> (C) Thank you for coming, everyone. Let's talk about the Clean School Project.

① (A) – (B) – (C)
② (B) – (A) – (C)
③ (C) – (A) – (B)
④ (C) – (B) – (A)
⑤ (A) – (C) – (B)

09 다음 짝지어진 대화 중 <u>어색한</u> 것은?

① A: Who will make posters for school flea market?
　B: I will. I can do it well.
② A: Thank you for taking care of my dog.
　B: My pleasure.
③ A: Thank you for teaching me how to ride a bike.
　B: No problem.
④ A: How about hanging some pictures?
　B: Good.
⑤ A: Let's talk about our club room this time. Any ideas?
　B: Great idea!

[10~11] 다음 대화를 읽고 물음에 답하시오.

G1: Let's talk about how we can make our town better.

B: ①<u>Let me tell</u> you first. There's too much trash at the bus stop.

G2: I agree. ②<u>Why don't we cleaning</u> the place together?

B: Good. We can put a bench there, too.

G1: Great idea. It'll be helpful for ③<u>the elderly</u>.

G2: ④<u>How about putting</u> some flower pots around the bench? They'll make the bus stop more beautiful.

G1: Thank you ⑤<u>for suggesting</u> great ideas, everyone. Then, shall we start tomorrow?

G2, B: No problem.

10 위 대화의 제목으로 가장 적절한 것은?

① Making the Bus Stop More Beautiful
② How to Choose Flower Pots
③ Meeting for Making Our Town Better.
④ How to Suggest a Great Idea
⑤ The Influence of Trash at the Bus Stop on the Town

11 위 대화의 밑줄 친 ①~⑤ 중 어법상 <u>어색한</u> 것은?

①　　②　　③　　④　　⑤

12 다음 대화의 밑줄 친 우리말 해석에 맞게 주어진 단어를 알맞게 배열하여 쓰시오.

> G: Seho, we need something on the wall, too. Don't you think so?
> B1: You're right. Let's talk about it together.
> G: I think we need to put the club member list there. <u>그것은 우리가 신입 회원들의 이름을 알게 되는 데 도움이 될 거야.</u>
> B2: That's a good idea.

(learn / new / helpful / us / to / the / members' / for / be / names)

➡ It'll _____

_____.

Grammar

13 다음 중 어법상 어색한 문장을 모두 고르시오.

① Skiing is much more difficult than it looks.
② Driving a car is far more easy than I think.
③ Today is more worse than yesterday.
④ The giraffe is much taller than the deer.
⑤ A whale is still bigger than a dolphin.

14 다음 글에서 어법상 어색한 부분을 찾아 바르게 고치시오.

> **Our Town Symbol**
> This is Oksig, which I drew as a symbol of my town. I designed this after I had taken pictures of many different kinds of corn. Oksig is very cuter than real corn. I hope everybody likes it.

➡ _____

15 다음 두 문장을 한 문장으로 바르게 옮긴 것은?

> • I missed the bus.
> • So, I was late for school.

① Because I was late for school, I had missed the bus.
② Because I had been late for school, I missed the bus.
③ Because I missed the bus, I had been late for school.
④ Because I had missed the bus, I had been late for school.
⑤ Because I had missed the bus, I was late for school.

16 괄호 안의 단어를 알맞은 형태로 쓰시오.

> A: The class leaders set up the board and put some posters. We can know (1)(a lot, much) about school events than before.
> B: Right! They did a good job. Let's thank the class leaders.
>
> A: The Green Club cleaned the pond and put some fish into it.
> B: Right! Thanks to the Green Club, this place looks (2)(much, good) than before.
>
> A: The Art Club drew flowers and wings on this wall.
> B: Right! Thanks to the Art Club, this place is (3)(much, popular) than before.

➡ (1) _____ (2) _____
(3) _____

17 다음 빈칸에 공통으로 알맞은 말을 쓰시오.

> • Unfortunately, we do not have _____ information on this accident.
> • You look _____ better than before.

➡ _____

18 다음 우리말을 주어진 어휘를 이용하여 영어로 옮기시오.

(1) Bill Gates는 나보다 훨씬 더 부자이다. (much, rich)

➡ _____

(2) 이 책이 저 책보다 훨씬 인기 있다. (even, popular)

➡ _____

(3) 너는 나보다 훨씬 더 우아하게 춤을 춘다. (far, gracefully)

➡ _____

Reading

[19~20] 다음 글을 읽고 물음에 답하시오.

I complained the whole day. ⓐMy parents were making me to work on the neighborhood project, but I had far better things to do. I didn't understand why we were working on this place. It was just the ugly, old, empty ⓑ lot across from Johnny's Shop. It was full of wild plants, fast food wraps, old newspapers, broken glass, and every other kind of dirty trash you can imagine. As I looked at it that first morning, I thought, "I bet there are snakes in there, too."

19 위 글의 밑줄 친 ⓐ에서 어법상 틀린 부분을 찾아 고치시오.

_____ ➡ _____

20 위 글의 밑줄 친 ⓑlot과 같은 의미로 쓰인 것을 고르시오.

① A lot of people are coming to the meeting.
② She felt dissatisfied with her lot.
③ I like him quite a lot.
④ You have to find a parking lot there.
⑤ They choose a person by lot.

[21~23] 다음 글을 읽고 물음에 답하시오.

By lunchtime, I was hot, sweaty, and glad my dad had made me wear gloves. We filled fifty trash bags with (A)waste and were ready to pull wild plants. As we pulled and pulled, dust filled the air and made us sneeze. At the end of the day, I had to admit the lot looked ⓐ better.

21 위 글의 빈칸 ⓐ에 들어갈 수 없는 말을 고르시오.

① even   ② still
③ very   ④ much
⑤ far

22 위 글의 밑줄 친 (A)waste와 같은 의미로 쓰인 것을 고르시오.

① It's a waste of money to do such a thing.
② Don't waste a good opportunity.
③ Use your waste talents.
④ I have no time to waste.
⑤ Don't throw industrial waste into the river.

23 본문의 내용과 일치하도록 다음 빈칸에 들어갈 두 단어를 쓰시오.

> Before the people pulled wild plants, they _____ _____ fifty trash bags with waste.

[24~26] 다음 글을 읽고 물음에 답하시오.

> ### Let's Change the Dirty Lot ⓐ_____ a Pretty Garden!
>
> • When: Apr. 17
> • Where: at the empty lot across from Johnny's Shop
> • What to do: to pull wild plants and clean the lot
> • What to bring: gloves, trash bags
> • How: We'll divide the lot ⓑ_____ four parts. Five people will clean each part.
>
> *If you have any questions, call Mr. Hernandez.*

24 위 글의 빈칸 ⓐ와 ⓑ에 공통으로 들어갈 알맞은 전치사를 고르시오.

① for   ② from
③ into   ④ in
⑤ to

25 위 글의 종류로 알맞은 것을 고르시오.

① article   ② notice
③ catalog   ④ review
⑤ advertisement

---

26 위 글을 읽고 알 수 <u>없는</u> 것을 고르시오.

① 모임 시기   ② 모임 장소
③ 모임 활동 내용   ④ 준비물
⑤ 참가 가능 연령

[27~28] 다음 글을 읽고 물음에 답하시오.

> June 17
> I visited the town garden after school. Some people were talking while they were looking at the beautiful garden. I picked some flowers and took ⓐ<u>them</u> to the nursing home. I'm proud that we made a pretty garden for everyone.

27 위 글의 밑줄 친 ⓐ가 가리키는 것을 본문에서 찾아 쓰시오.

➡ _____

28 What is the writer proud of? Fill in the blanks with suitable words.

> The writer is proud of having made a _____ _____ for everyone.

01 다음 짝지어진 단어의 관계가 같도록 빈칸에 알맞은 말을 쓰시오.

> remember – forget : partial – _____

02 다음 영영풀이에 해당하는 단어는?

> to make something twice as much or many

① hang   ② double   ③ second

④ mess   ⑤ two

03 다음 대화를 읽고 B의 말에 대한 A의 대답을 〈조건〉에 맞게 쓰시오.

┌─ 보기 ─┐
- 감사의 표현을 사용할 것.
- 본문에 나오는 한 단어를 활용할 것.

A: Let's talk about the volunteer work for our town. Who will play with the children?
B: I will. I can do it well.
A: _____

➡ _____

[04~05] 다음 대화를 읽고 물음에 답하시오.

G: Seho, we need something on the wall, too. Don't you think so? (①)
B1: You're right. Let's talk about it together.
G: (②) I think we need to put the club member list there. (③) It'll be helpful for us to learn the new members' names.
B2: That's a good idea. (④)
G: Right! That'll really help us remember important school events. (⑤)
B1: Thank you for suggesting great ideas, everyone. We are a good team.

04 위 대화의 (①)~(⑤) 중 주어진 문장이 들어갈 위치로 알맞은 것은?

> We also need our plan for this school year on the wall.

①   ②   ③   ④   ⑤

05 위 대화를 읽고 Seho와 그의 친구들이 할 일 두 가지 내용을 영어로 쓰시오. (to부정사로 시작하여 쓸 것)

➡ _____ and their plan _____ on the wall

06 다음 대화의 빈칸에 들어갈 말로 어색한 것은?

> A: Thank you for taking care of my dog.
> B: _____

① My pleasure.
② No problem.
③ Don't worry about it.
④ Don't mention it.
⑤ Not at all.

07 다음 대화의 빈칸 (A)에 들어갈 문장을 주어진 어휘를 배열하여 완성하시오.

> B: How about hanging some pictures?
> G: Good. Why don't you bring one of your pictures? You're good at painting, Seho.
> B: _____ (A) _____
> (you / saying / thank / that / for). I'll bring one of mine.

➡ _____

08 다음 대화의 빈칸 (A)와 (B)에 들어갈 표현으로 알맞은 것은?

> B: Let's talk about what we can do for our town.
> G: _____(A)_____
> B: Sounds good. Anything else?
> G: Let me help you fix the bench.
> M: Please hold this tight. _____(B)_____

① (A) Why don't we do a funny dance?
　(B) Thank you for your idea.

② (A) How about drawing pictures on the dirty walls?
　(B) Thank you for helping me.

③ (A) Let's talk about the town party.
　(B) Wonderful.

④ (A) Who will make posters for school flea market?
　(B) My pleasure.

⑤ (A) I can do it well.
　(B) Thank you for volunteering.

[09~10] 다음 대화를 읽고 물음에 답하시오.

> G1: Let's talk about how we can make our town better.
> B: Let me tell you first. There's too much trash at the bus stop.
> (A) Great idea. It'll be helpful for the elderly.
> (B) Good. We can put a bench there, too.
> (C) How about putting some flower pots around the bench? They'll make the bus stop more beautiful.
> (D) I agree. Why don't we clean the place together?
> G1: Thank you for suggesting great ideas, everyone. Then, shall we start tomorrow?
> G2, B: No problem.

09 위 대화의 (A)~(D)를 알맞은 순서로 배열하시오.

➡ _____

10 위 대화의 내용과 일치하지 <u>않는</u> 것은?

① There is too much trash at the bus stop.
② All of them will clean the place together.
③ They will put a bench there for the elderly.
④ They will put some flower pots around the bench.
⑤ They will start working right now.

11 다음 문장에서 어법상 <u>어색한</u> 부분을 찾아 바르게 고치시오.

> When my brother came back home, I have already done the dishes.

_____ ➡ _____

12 다음 글에서 밑줄 친 우리말을 괄호 안에 주어진 단어를 사용하여 영어로 옮기시오.

> **Our Town Symbol**
> 　This is Oksig, which I drew as a symbol of my town. I designed this (1) 많은 다양한 종류의 옥수수 사진을 찍은 후에 (had, different). (2)Oksig은 진짜 옥수수보다 훨씬 더 귀엽습니다.(cuter, real) I hope everybody likes it.

➡ (1) _____
　(2) _____

13 잘못된 부분을 바르게 고쳐 문장을 다시 쓰시오.

(1) When we visited her, she said she studied music for 5 years in Paris.

➡ _____

_____

(2) It was strange that he didn't remember the movie that we have watched the other day.

➡ _____

_____

(3) Walking is much helpful for your health than running.

➡ _____

_____

(4) The building is very larger than I expected.

➡ _____

_____

[14~15] 다음 글을 읽고 물음에 답하시오.

I _____ⓐ_____ the whole day. My parents were making me work on the neighborhood project, but I had far better things to do. I didn't understand why we were working on ⓑthis place. It was just the ugly, old, empty lot across from Johnny's Shop. It was full of wild plants, fast food wraps, old newspapers, broken glass, and every other kind of dirty trash you can imagine. As I looked at it that first morning, I thought, "I bet there are snakes in there, too."

14 위 글의 빈칸 ⓐ에 들어갈 알맞은 말을 고르시오.

① apologized
② complimented
③ complained
④ rewarded
⑤ offered

15 다음 빈칸 (A)와 (B)에 서로 상반되는 의미의 단어를 넣어 ⓑthis place에 대한 소개를 완성하시오.

It was just the (A)_____ lot which was (B)_____ of wild plants, fast food wraps, old newspapers, broken glass, and every other sort of dirty trash imaginable.

[16~17] 다음 글을 읽고 물음에 답하시오.

That first day was the toughest. On the weekends that followed, we made rows, planted flower and vegetable seeds, and watered them. After about two weeks, I stopped complaining when I found the plants ⓐhad started popping up! First, the lettuce and then the beans and the tomatoes. They grew so fast. I couldn't believe it! The bean plants grew an inch, and the tomatoes doubled in size in just a few days.

16 위 글의 밑줄 친 ⓐhad started와 과거완료의 용법이 같은 것을 고르시오.

① I did not tell her at first, for I had never seen her before.
② I lost the pen that I had bought a few days before.
③ When I met her, she had been ill for two weeks.
④ He said he had been to New York twice.
⑤ He had lived there for ten years when his father died.

17 According to the passage, which is NOT true?

① That first day was the hardest day for the writer.
② After about two weeks, the writer stopped complaining.
③ The tomatoes popped up first.

④ The lettuce, the beans and the tomatoes grew so fast.

⑤ The tomatoes doubled in size in just a few days.

[18~19] 다음 글을 읽고 물음에 답하시오.

Now, two months later, I like ①to go there every day ②to see what new flowers are ready ③to pop up. ⓐLots of people in the neighborhood meet there ④to enjoy the sights and ⑤to talk together.

18 밑줄 친 ①~⑤ 중에서 to부정사의 용법이 나머지 넷과 다른 것은?

①   ②   ③   ④   ⑤

19 위 글의 밑줄 친 ⓐLots of와 바꿔 쓸 수 있는 말을 두 개 쓰시오.

➡ _____, _____

[20~21] 다음 글을 읽고 물음에 답하시오.

Tonight, ⓐit suddenly hit me — what a good thing we did! I'm proud I have been a part of it. I'm in charge of picking flowers for the nursing home on Fourth Street. The vegetables will go to every kitchen in our town. But even better, an ugly and dirty lot that people didn't like has become a pretty garden for everyone.

20 위 글의 밑줄 친 ⓐit이 가리키는 것을 본문에서 찾아 쓰시오.

➡ _____

21 다음 빈칸 (A)와 (B)에 알맞은 단어를 넣어 글쓴이의 감상문을 완성하시오.

At first, people didn't like the ugly and dirty lot, but it became (A)_____ _____ _____ for everyone, and the writer is proud of himself because he has been (B)_____ _____ of such a good thing.

[22~23] 다음 글을 읽고 물음에 답하시오.

The Art Club drew wings on this wall. Before that, they ____ⓐ____ flowers. Thanks to the Art Club, this place is much more popular than before.

- the Green Club
Apr. 1: clean it
Apr. 5: put some fish into it

- the Art Club
Mar. 15: draw flowers
Mar. 17: draw wings

The Green Club put some fish into this pond. Before that, they ____ⓑ____ the pond. Thanks to the Green Club, this place is much more popular than before.

22 위 글의 빈칸 ⓐ와 ⓑ에 draw와 clean을 각각 알맞은 형태로 쓰시오.

➡ ⓐ _____ ⓑ _____

23 본문의 내용과 일치하도록 다음 빈칸 (A)와 (B)에 알맞은 단어를 쓰시오.

Thanks to the (A)_____ _____ and the (B)_____ _____, the environment of the town has changed for the better.

01 다음 대화의 빈칸 (A)와 (B)에 주어진 〈조건〉의 어구와 우리말을 이용하여 알맞은 말을 쓰시오.

> B: What do we need in our club room? Let's talk about it.
> G: Sure. Well, _____(A)_____? They'll make our room prettier.
> B: That's a good idea. Thank you, Jiu.
>
> B: Let's talk about the corner this time. Any ideas?
> G: How about making a small library in the corner of the club room? I will bring some books tomorrow.
> B: Great idea! _____(B)_____, Minju.

┌─ 조건 ─┐
(A) • how about / the windows / put / flower pots / by / some
(B) • 감사 표현 / for / suggest / it
└────────┘

➡ (A) _____
　 (B) _____

02 다음 대화의 빈칸에 들어갈 문장을 〈조건〉에 맞게 쓰시오.

> A: _____
> 　 Who will cook for the elderly?
> B: I will. I can do it well.
> A: Thank you for volunteering.

┌─ 조건 ─┐
• 주제는 '마을(our town)을 위한 자원봉사'에 관한 것으로 Let's를 이용하여 대화의 주제를 소개하는 문장을 쓰시오.
└────────┘

➡ _____

03 다음 대화를 읽고 물음에 영어로 답하시오.

> G1: Let's talk about how we can make our town better.
> B: Let me tell you first. There's too much trash at the bus stop.
> G2: I agree. Why don't we clean the place together?
> B: Good. We can put a bench there, too.
> G1: Great idea. It'll be helpful for the elderly.
> G2: How about putting some flower pots around the bench? They'll make the bus stop more beautiful.
> G1: Thank you for suggesting great ideas, everyone. Then, shall we start tomorrow?
> G2, B: No problem.

(1) What is the problem in the town?
　 ➡ _____
(2) What are they going to do after cleaning the bus stop?
　 ➡ _____

04 다음 글에서 어법상 틀린 곳의 기호를 쓰고 바르게 고치시오.

> **Our Town Symbol**
> 　This is Oksig, ⓐthat I drew as a symbol of my town. I designed this after I ⓑhave taken pictures of many different ⓒkinds of corn. Oksig is ⓓmuch cuter than real corn. I hope everybody likes ⓔthem.

➡ (1) _____　(2) _____
　 (3) _____

05 〈보기〉에 주어진 단어 중 의미상 적절한 것을 골라 다음 문장의 빈칸 하나에 한 단어씩 알맞은 형태로 써 넣으시오.

┌─── 보기 ───┐
live   see   tell   have   go
└──────────────┘

(1) We _____ _____ a good time before Mom came home.

(2) Yesterday I found out that my friend _____ _____ a lie to me.

(3) Mark _____ _____ with his family before he got married to Irene.

[06~08] 다음 글을 읽고 물음에 답하시오.

I complained the whole day. My parents were making me work on the neighborhood project, but I had far better things to do. I didn't understand (A)우리가 왜 이곳에서 일하고 있어야 하는지. It was just the ugly, old, empty lot across from Johnny's Shop. It was full of wild plants, fast food wraps, old newspapers, broken glass, and (B)every other kind of dirty trash you can imagine. As I looked at it that first morning, I thought, "_____ ⓐ _____ there are snakes in there, too."

06 다음과 같은 뜻이 되도록 위 글의 빈칸 ⓐ에 들어갈 알맞은 말을 쓰시오. (2 단어)

┌──────────────────────┐
It is certain that
└──────────────────────┘

➡ _____

---

07 위 글의 밑줄 친 (A)의 우리말에 맞게 주어진 어휘를 알맞게 배열하시오.

┌──────────────────────┐
working / place / were / this / we / why / on
└──────────────────────┘

➡ _____

08 위 글의 밑줄 친 (B)에 생략된 한 단어를 넣어 다시 쓰시오.

➡ _____

_____

[09~10] 다음 글을 읽고 물음에 답하시오.

That first day was the toughest. On the weekends that followed, we made rows, planted flower and vegetable seeds, and watered them. ⓐAfter about two weeks, I stopped to complain when I found the plants had started popping up! First, the lettuce and then the beans and the tomatoes. ⓑThey grew so fast. I couldn't believe it! The bean plants grew an inch, and the tomatoes doubled in size in just a few days.

09 위 글의 밑줄 친 ⓐ에서 어법상 틀린 부분을 찾아 고치시오.

_____ ➡ _____

10 위 글의 밑줄 친 ⓑ의 예를 본문에서 찾아 우리말로 쓰시오.

➡ 콩 식물은 _____

_____ .

01 아래 표의 (A)와 (B)는 학교 행사 준비에 필요한 일들을 적어둔 것이다. 제시된 〈보기〉의 문장처럼 주제 소개와 감사의 표현을 쓰시오.

(A)	(B)
• class party	• make sandwiches
• class field trip	• take pictures of our activities
• club festival	• make posters
• sports day	• run a 100 meter race

보기

A: Let's talk about the class party. Who will make sandwiches?
B: I will. I can do it well.
A: Thank you for volunteering.

02 과거완료시제를 이용하여 주어진 문장의 원인을 자유롭게 쓰시오.

(1) I didn't do well on the test this morning because _____.

(2) He lost some weight because _____.

(3) Jen needed to buy new shoes because _____.

(4) Sera felt bored during the movie because _____.

03 다음 내용을 바탕으로 교내 환경의 변화된 모습을 알리는 홍보문을 쓰시오.

• the Art Club	• the Green Club
Mar. 15: draw flowers	Apr. 1: clean it
Mar. 17: draw wings	Apr. 5: put some fish into it

The Art Club (A)_____ on this wall. Before that, they (B)_____.
Thanks to the Art Club, this place is much more popular than before.
The Green Club (C)_____ into this pond. Before that, they (D)_____
the pond. Thanks to the Green Club, this place is much more popular than before.

단원별 모의고사

01 다음 단어에 대한 영어 설명이 <u>어색한</u> 것은?

① suggest: to give a particular job or piece of work to someone

② empty: not containing any things or people

③ tough: difficult to do or to deal with

④ hang: to put something in a position so that the top part is fixed or supported, and the bottom part is free to move and does not touch the ground

⑤ sweaty: covered in sweat or smelling of sweat

02 다음 짝지어진 단어의 관계가 같도록 빈칸에 알맞은 말을 쓰시오.

complain – moan : disgusting – a_____

03 다음 영영풀이에 해당하는 단어를 고르시오.

to mention an idea, possible plan, or action for other people to consider

① volunteer   ② admit
③ suggest   ④ fill
⑤ sneeze

04 다음 중 짝지어진 대화가 <u>어색한</u> 것은?

① A: Let's talk about the corner. What do you think of it?
   B: I like it very much.

② A: Shall we start working tomorrow?
   B: No problem.

③ A: Bread is very popular.
   B: I think *gimbap* is much more popular than bread.

④ A: Let's talk about the town party.
   B: Okay. Why don't we play the ukulele?

⑤ A: Let's talk about the volunteer work for our town. Who will guide visitors?
   B: How about going to the national park?

[05~06] 다음 대화의 빈칸에 들어갈 말로 알맞은 것을 고르시오.

05

B: How about hanging some pictures?
G: Good. _____
   You're good at painting, Seho.
B: Thank you for saying that. I'll bring one of mine.

① How about making a small library in the corner of the club room?

② Thank you for teaching me how to ride a bike.

③ Who will take pictures of our activities?

④ Why don't you bring one of your pictures?

⑤ How about drawing pictures on the dirty walls?

06

A: _____ Who will paint the dirty wall?
B: I will. I can do it well.
A: Thank you for volunteering.

① Let's talk about the class field trip.

② Let's talk about the volunteer work for our town.

③ Let's talk about the club festival.

④ Let's talk about the town sports day.

⑤ Let's talk about the pond.

[07~08] 다음 대화를 읽고 물음에 답하시오.

G: Seho, we need something on the wall, too. ①Don't you think so?

B1: You're right. ②Let's talk about it together.

G: I think we need to put the club member list there. (A)It'll be helpful ③for us to learn the new members' names.

B2: That's a good idea. We also need our plan for this school year on the wall.

G: Right! That'll really help us ④remember important school events.

B1: Thank you for ⑤suggest great ideas, everyone. We are a good team.

07 위 대화의 밑줄 친 ①~⑤ 중 어법상 어색한 것은?

① ② ③ ④ ⑤

08 위 대화의 밑줄 친 (A)의 'It'이 가리키는 말을 찾아 영어로 쓰시오. (9 단어로 답할 것)

➡ _____

[09~10] 다음 대화를 읽고 물음에 답하시오.

G1: ①Let's talk about how we can make our town better.

B: ②Let me tell you first. There's too much trash at the bus stop.

G2: I agree. ③Why don't we clean the place together?

B: Good. We can put a bench there, too.

G1: Great idea. (A)그것은 어르신들에게 도움이 될 거야.

G2: ④How about putting some flower pots around the bench? They'll make the bus stop more beautiful.

G1: Thank you for suggesting great ideas, everyone. Then, ⑤shall we start tomorrow?

G2, B: No problem.

09 위 대화의 밑줄 (A)의 우리말에 맞게 주어진 단어를 활용하여 영작하시오.

(it / be / help / for / elderly)

➡ _____

10 위 대화의 밑줄 친 ①~⑤ 중 의도가 다른 것은?

① ② ③ ④ ⑤

11 다음 중 어법상 올바른 문장을 고르시오.

① Their baby was crying much loudly than usual.

② My health is far more important than my wealth.

③ Your car looks much more cheap than mine.

④ Russia is very bigger than my country.

⑤ We need to spend our allowance much wiser.

12 다음 두 문장을 한 문장으로 바르게 옮긴 것은?

• Mom remembered his name.
• Mom saw him before.

① Mom had remembered his name because she saw him before.

② Mom remembered his name because she saw him before.

③ Mom remembered his name because she had seen him before.

④ Mom remembered his name because she has seen him before.

⑤ Mom had remembered his name because she had seen him before.

13 다음 우리말을 영어로 바르게 옮긴 것은?

> 그녀는 나보다 훨씬 더 부지런하게 일한다.

① She works more diligent than me.
② She works much more diligent than me.
③ She works more diligently than me.
④ She works much diligently than me.
⑤ She works much more diligently than me.

14 〈보기〉에서 내용의 흐름상 적절한 문장을 골라 알맞은 형태로 대화를 완성하시오.

┌─ 보기 ┤
• They draw flowers.
• They clean the pond.
• They set up the board.
└──────

A: The class leaders put some posters. Before that, (1)_____.
We can know a lot more about school events.
B: Right! They did a good job. Let's thank the class leaders.
A: The Green Club put some fish into the pond. Before that, (2)_____ _____.
B: Right! Thanks to the Green Club, this place looks much better than before.
A: The Art Club drew wings on this wall. Before that, (3)_____ _____.
B: Right! Thanks to the Art Club, this place is much more popular than before.

15 두 문장의 의미가 같도록 주어진 동사를 활용하여 빈칸에 알맞은 말을 쓰시오.

> Jihoo visited the zoo for the first time last month.
> = Jihoo _____ _____ _____ the zoo before last month.

[16~17] 다음 글을 읽고 물음에 답하시오.

I complained the whole day. My parents were making me work on the neighborhood project, but I had far better things @to do. I didn't understand why we were working on this place. It was just the ugly, old, empty lot across from Johnny's Shop. It was full of wild plants, fast food wraps, old newspapers, broken glass, and every other kind of dirty trash ⓑyou can imagine. As I looked at it that first morning, I thought, "I bet there are snakes in there, too."

16 아래 〈보기〉에서 위 글의 밑줄 친 @to do와 to부정사의 용법이 같은 것의 개수를 고르시오.

┌─ 보기 ┤
① I think it wrong to do such a thing.
② He was the last man to do it.
③ It is time for me to do the dishes.
④ It was impossible for him to do the work.
⑤ She must be mad to do such a thing.
└──────

① 1개   ② 2개   ③ 3개   ④ 4개   ⑤ 5개

17 위 글의 밑줄 친 ⓑ를 한 단어의 형용사로 고치시오.

➡ _____

[18~19] 다음 글을 읽고 물음에 답하시오.

There were twenty of us — all ages and sizes — ready to work that day. ⓐ나는 우리가 이 끔찍하게 더러운 곳을 청소하여 정원으로 바꿀 수 있다고 생각하지 않았다. We were all wondering where to begin. Then Mr. Hernandez said, "The only way to do it is just to start." Then, he divided the lot into four parts with string and assigned five people to each part.

18 위 글의 밑줄 친 ⓐ의 우리말에 맞게 주어진 어휘를 알맞게 배열하시오.

this / mess / a garden / could / awful / clean up / we / and / into / didn't think / turn / that / I / it / .

➡ _____

_____

19 According to the passage, which is NOT true?

① Twenty people gathered at the place.
② The ages and sizes of the people were all different.
③ The people didn't know where to begin.
④ Mr. Hernandez divided the lot into five parts with string.
⑤ Mr. Hernandez assigned five people to each part.

[20~21] 다음 글을 읽고 물음에 답하시오.

That first day was the toughest. On the weekends that followed, we made rows, planted flower and vegetable seeds, and watered ⓐthem. After ⓑabout two weeks, I stopped complaining when I found the plants had started popping up! First, the lettuce and then the beans and the tomatoes. They grew so fast. I couldn't believe it! The bean plants grew an inch, and the tomatoes doubled in size in just a few days.

20 위 글의 밑줄 친 ⓐ가 가리키는 것을 본문에서 찾아 쓰시오.

➡ _____

21 위 글의 밑줄 친 ⓑabout과 같은 의미로 쓰인 것을 고르시오.

① What's she so angry about?
② They are about to cross the street.
③ She is about my age.
④ He walked about the room.
⑤ She wore a shawl about her shoulders.

[22~23] 다음 글을 읽고 물음에 답하시오.

Tonight, it suddenly hit me — what a good thing we did! I'm ___ⓐ___ I have been a part of it. I'm in charge of picking flowers for the nursing home on Fourth Street. The vegetables will go to every kitchen in our town. ⓑBut even worse, an ugly and dirty lot that people didn't like has become a pretty garden for everyone.

22 위 글의 빈칸 ⓐ에 들어갈 알맞은 말을 고르시오.

① ashamed   ② disappointed
③ nervous   ④ proud
⑤ upset

23 위 글의 밑줄 친 ⓑ에서 흐름상 어색한 부분을 찾아 고치시오.

_____ ➡ _____

Lesson 3

Laugh First and Then Think

 의사소통 기능

- 기대 표현하기
  I'm looking forward to seeing you at the race.

- 기원하기
  I'll keep my fingers crossed!

 언어 형식

- enough to
  Is this research project good **enough to** win a Nobel Prize?

- not only ~ but also ...
  Not only the winners' fun studies **but also** the ceremony makes people laugh.

Words & Expressions

Key Words

- **accept**[æksépt] 동 받아들이다
- **actually**[ǽktʃuəli] 부 실제로, 사실은
- **afraid**[əfréid] 형 두려운
- **award**[əwɔ́ːrd] 동 수여하다 명 상
- **backward**[bǽkwərd] 부 뒤로 형 뒤의
- **bomb**[bɑm] 명 폭탄
- **brave**[breiv] 형 용감한
- **ceremony**[sérəmòuni] 명 의식, 식
- **cheer**[tʃiər] 동 응원하다
- **cross**[krɔːs] 동 교차하다 명 십자가
- **discovery**[diskʌ́vəri] 명 발견
- **eager**[íːgər] 형 열렬한, 간절히 바라는
- **economics** 명 경제학
- **feeder**[fíːdər] 명 모이통
- **field trip** 명 현장 학습, 수학여행
- **float**[flout] 동 뜨다
- **guess**[ges] 동 추측하다
- **honor**[ɑ́nər] 동 존중하다 명 명예
- **imaginative**[imǽdʒənətiv] 형 창의적인, 상상력이 풍부한
- **interest**[íntərəst] 명 관심
- **invent**[invént] 동 발명하다
- **invention**[invénʃən] 명 발명, 발명품
- **join**[dʒɔin] 동 참가하다
- **laughable**[lǽfəbl] 형 웃기는
- **live**[laiv] 형 살아 있는
- **lovely**[lʌ́vli] 형 귀여운
- **magnet**[mǽgnit] 명 자석

- **maybe**[méibiː] 부 아마도
- **mistake**[mistéik] 명 실수
- **navy**[néivi] 명 해군
- **nervous**[nə́ːrvəs] 형 긴장한, 초조한
- **opening**[óupəniŋ] 명 개막
- **peace**[piːs] 명 평화
- **perform**[pərfɔ́ːrm] 동 공연하다
- **practice**[prǽktis] 동 연습하다 명 연습
- **present**[prizént] 동 수여하다
- **prize**[praiz] 명 상
- **project**[prɑ́dʒekt] 명 과제
- **race**[reis] 명 경주, 달리기
- **receive**[risíːv] 동 받다
- **repeatedly**[ripíːtidli] 부 반복적으로
- **research**[risə́ːrtʃ] 명 연구, 조사 동 조사하다
- **sailor**[séilər] 명 선원
- **solve**[sɑlv] 동 풀다, 해결하다
- **store**[stɔːr] 동 저장하다
- **study**[stʌ́di] 명 연구
- **tradition**[trədíʃən] 명 전통
- **trillion**[tríljən] 명 1조
- **university**[jùːnəvə́ːrsəti] 명 대학, 대학교
- **unusual**[ənjúːʒuəl] 형 드문, 특이한
- **useful**[júːsfəl] 형 유용한
- **while**[hwail] 접 ~하는 동안, ~인 반면에
- **winner**[wínər] 명 수상자
- **worth**[wəːrθ] 명 가치 형 ~의 가치가 있는

Key Expressions

- **a number of** 얼마간의, 다수의
- **be eager to** ~을 (열렬히) 하고 싶어 하다
- **be filled with** ~로 가득 차다
- **can't wait for** ~를 몹시 기다리다
- **closing speech** 폐막 연설
- **get bored** 지루해지다
- **get out of** ~에서 떠나다, 나가다
- **How about ~?** ~하는 것이 어때?
- **instead of** ~ 대신에
- **keep A from -ing** A가 ~하지 못하게 하다

- **keep -ing** 계속 ~하다
- **keep one's fingers crossed** 행운을 빌다
- **laugh out loud** 큰 소리로 웃다
- **less than** ~ 이하, ~보다 적은
- **look forward to** ~을 기대하다
- **run away** 달아나다
- **sense of humor** 유머 감각
- **succeed in** ~에 성공하다
- **take part in** ~에 참여하다
- **talent show** 장기 자랑

Word Power

※ 서로 비슷한 뜻을 가진 어휘

- accept 받다 : obtain 얻다
- cheer 응원하다 : encourage 장려하다
- actually 실제로 : really 사실은
- imaginative 상상력이 풍부한 : original 독창적인

※ 서로 반대의 뜻을 가진 어휘

- accept 받다 ↔ reject 거절하다
- backward 뒤로 ↔ forward 앞으로
- opening 개막 ↔ closing 폐막
- usual 일상적인 ↔ unusual 드문, 특이한
- float 뜨다 ↔ sink 가라앉다
- nervous 불안한 ↔ calm 차분한
- present 수여하다 ↔ receive 받다
- useful 유용한 ↔ useless 쓸모없는

※ 형용사 – 명사

- dark 어두운 – darkness 어두움
- happy 행복한 – happiness 행복
- sad 슬픈 – sadness 슬픔
- eager 열렬한 – eagerness 열망
- kind 친절한 – kindness 친절
- soft 부드러운 – softness 부드러움

English Dictionary

- accept 받아들이다
  → to take something offered 제안된 어떤 것을 취하다
- award 수여하다
  → to give a prize 상을 주다
- backward 뒤의
  → looking or facing in the direction that is behind you
  뒤쪽 방향을 보거나 향하고 있는
- discovery 발견
  → the act of finding something for the first time
  처음으로 어떤 것을 발견하는 행위
- eager 열렬한, 간절히 바라는
  → wanting very much to do or have something
  어떤 것을 하거나 갖기를 매우 원하는
- float 뜨다, 띄우다
  → to be on a liquid and not sink
  액체의 위에 있고 가라앉지 않다
- honor (명) 명예
  → something you are proud to do
  하기를 자랑스러워하는 어떤 것
  (동) 존경하다
  → to show great respect for someone, esp. in public
  특히 공공연히 누군가에 대한 대단한 존경을 보여주다
- imaginative 창의적인, 상상력이 풍부한
  → having or showing new and exciting ideas
  새롭고 흥미로운 생각을 갖거나 보여주는
- invent 발명하다
  → to make, design, or think of a new type of thing
  새로운 것을 만들거나 디자인하거나 생각해 내다
- live 살아 있는
  → not dead 죽지 않은
- magnet 자석
  → a piece of metal that attracts other iron
  다른 철을 끌어당기는 금속 조각
- navy 해군
  → a military force made up of boats and ships
  배와 함선으로 이루어진 군대
- research 연구, 조사
  → the study of something to discover new facts
  새로운 사실들을 발견하기 위한 어떤 것의 연구
- sailor 선원
  → someone who works on a ship 배에서 일하는 사람
- trillion 1조
  → the number 1,000,000,000,000
  1,000,000,000,000이라는 수
- university 대학
  → an educational institution at the highest level, where you study for a degree
  학위를 받기 위해서 공부하는 가장 높은 수준의 교육 기관

서답형

01 다음 글의 빈칸에 〈영어 설명〉에 알맞은 단어를 쓰시오.

> Finding the new land was an amazing
> _____.
> 〈영어 설명〉 the act of finding something
> for the first time

중요

02 다음 빈칸에 공통으로 들어갈 말로 가장 적절한 것은?

> • The friendship between the cat and the
>   dog is quite _____.
> • Some people keep _____ pets such
>   as pigs, iguanas, and even snakes.

① ugly   ② unusual
③ popular   ④ useful
⑤ wonderful

[03~04] 다음 영어 설명에 해당하는 단어를 고르시오.

03
> an educational institution at the highest
> level, where you study for a degree

① navy   ② honor
③ bomb   ④ university
⑤ research

04
> someone who works on a boat or ship

① sail   ② peace
③ nurse   ④ navy
⑤ sailor

서답형

05 다음 우리말에 맞게 주어진 단어를 이용하여 쓰시오.

> 아이들은 어서 수업을 마치고 놀기 시작하고 싶
> 어 했다. (eager / finish)

➡ The children _____
   class and start playing.

06 다음 빈칸에 공통으로 들어갈 말로 알맞은 것은?

> (A) On July 16, the Korean _____
>   contest was held in California, U.S.
> (B) The boy gave a _____ in front of
>   the class.

① research   ② science
③ speech   ④ trillion
⑤ ceremony

서답형

07 다음 짝지어진 단어의 관계가 같도록 알맞은 말을 쓰시오.

> sad – sadness : dark – _____

중요

08 다음 빈칸에 들어갈 말이 바르게 짝지어진 것은?

> (A) The gate _____ people from
>   entering the park.
> (B) The paintings of Leonardo da Vinci
>   are _____ a lot of money.

① keeps – worth
② keeps – eager
③ receives – worth
④ gets – unusual
⑤ gets – eager

01 〈보기〉에서 알맞은 단어를 선택하여 문장의 빈칸을 완성하시오. (필요하면 변형하여 쓰시오.)

┌─ 보기 ─────────────────┐
    receive   repeated   bore   number
└──────────────────────┘

(1) Bring games on an airplane not to get _____.

(2) The kids sang their favorite song _____.

(3) _____ of students failed the test.

(4) He _____ a special card from his grandfather last Christmas.

02 대화의 빈칸에 〈영영 풀이〉에 해당하는 단어를 쓰시오.

B: Minji, you're a happy girl. I think you'll get the Ms. Cheerful _____. I'll keep my fingers crossed!

G: Oh, thank you, Jiho.

┌────────────────────────┐
〈영영 풀이〉 a prize or other marks of recognition given in honor of an achievement
└────────────────────────┘

➡ _____

03 영영 풀이에 해당하는 단어를 〈보기〉에서 찾아 첫 번째 빈칸에 쓰고, 두 번째 빈칸에는 우리말 뜻을 쓰시오.

┌─ 보기 ─────────────────┐
    ceremony   magnet   invent   navy
└──────────────────────┘

(1) _____: a military force made up of boats and ships: _____

(2) _____: a piece of metal that attracts other iron: _____

(3) _____: to make, design, or think of a new type of thing: _____

(4) _____: a formal public event with special traditions: _____

04 다음 우리말에 맞게 주어진 글의 빈칸에 알맞은 단어를 쓰시오.

┌────────────────────────┐
이것은 '커피 애호가를 위한 우산'입니다. 당신은 그것을 우산뿐만 아니라 컵 걸이로도 사용할 수 있습니다. 이 발명품은 당신의 삶을 훨씬 더 편안하게 할 정도로 충분히 유용합니다.
└────────────────────────┘

➡ This is the Umbrella for Coffee Lovers. You can use it _____ as an umbrella _____ as a cup holder. This _____ is _____ to make your life much easier.

05 다음 글의 빈칸에 주어진 철자로 시작하는 알맞은 단어를 쓰시오.

(1) The workers at this company didn't a_____ any gifts from customers.

(2) I think I have a good sense of h_____.

(3) I will study e_____ at university to become a banker.

(4) The large box is f_____ with warm clothes for the poor.

(5) The writer of the children's story is very i_____.

Conversation

1 기대 표현하기

> • **I'm looking forward to seeing you at the race.** 나는 경기에서 너를 보기를 기대해.

- 앞으로 일어날 일이나 하고 싶은 일에 대한 기대를 표현할 때 '~을 기대한다'의 의미로 'I'm looking forward to ~.'나 'I look forward to ~.'의 표현을 사용한다. '빨리 ~하고 싶다, ~을 너무 하고 싶다.'의 뜻으로 'I can't wait for ~.', 'I am dying to ~.', 'I'm expecting to ~.'라고 하기도 한다.

- '~을 기대하다'라는 의미의 'look forward to'에서 to가 전치사이기 때문에 그 뒤에 명사나 동명사가 온다. 'I can't wait for ~.'는 원하던 일이 다가오고 있어 빨리하고 싶은 기대감을 나타내는 표현이며, 직역의 의미는 '~하는 것을 기다릴 수 없다.'이고, 보통 '당장 ~하고 싶다, 빨리 ~했으면 좋겠다.'로 해석한다. to 뒤에는 동사원형의 형태가 오는데, 뒤에 명사구가 올 경우에는 'I can't wait for+명사[명사구]'의 형태로 쓰기도 한다.

- '기대하다'라는 의미의 expect를 써서 'I'm expecting to 동사원형 ~.'이라고 하거나 '열망하다'라는 의미의 동사 long을 써서 'I'm longing to+동사원형', 'I'm longing for+명사'라고 하거나, 형용사 eager(열망하는)를 써서 'I'm eager to+동사원형', 'I'm eager for+명사'의 형태로 나타내기도 한다.

기대 표현하기

- I'm looking forward to+명사(구) (~을 기대한다.)
- I can't wait for+명사/to+동사원형 (빨리 ~했으면 좋겠다.)
- I am expecting to+동사원형 (~하기를 기대한다.)
- I am longing for+명사/to+동사원형 (~하기를 열망한다.)
- I am eager for+명사/to+동사원형 (~하기를 기대한다.)

핵심 Check

1. 다음 우리말과 일치하도록 주어진 단어를 포함하여 적절한 형태로 빈칸에 알맞은 말을 쓰시오.

   A: We're going on a field trip next Tuesday. What are you going to do in the talent show, Jimin?

   B: I'm going to talk like our teachers do in class and tell some jokes.

   A: Wow! _____. (나는 정말로 그것이 기대가 돼.) (be, really, forward, it)

   B: Will everyone like my show? I'm not sure.

   ➡ _____

② 기원하기

> • I'll keep my fingers crossed. 행운을 빌어.

■ 상대가 하는 일이 잘 되기를 기원하면서 '행운을 빌어!'라고 할 때 'I'll keep my finger's crossed (for you)!'라고 한다. 'keep one's fingers crossed'란 집게손가락 위에 가운데 손가락을 교차시켜서 소원이 이루어지도록(= hope for something) 행운을 비는 동작을 묘사한 말로 '기도하다, 좋은 결과나 행운을 빌어준다'라는 의미이다.

■ 흔히 상대에게 행운을 비는 말은 'Good luck!'이고, 'Have a nice ~!'도 상대에게 행운을 기원하는 말이다. 기원이나 기대를 나타내는 wish, expect, hope, pray를 사용하여 행운을 기원하기도 한다. 'Break a leg!(행운을 빌어!)'라는 표현은 주로 공연이나 행사, 경기 등을 앞두고 있는 사람에게 '행운을 빌어!'라고 격려할 때 자주 쓰인다.

■ 긴장한 상대에게 긴장을 풀어주는 표현 'Don't worry.', 'Don't be worried.', 'Just relax.', 'Take it easy.', 'Loosen up.', 'Don't be too nervous.'(긴장 풀어. 너무 긴장하지 마.)에 이어서 행운을 빌어주는 표현을 쓰는 경우가 많다. '기원하다'라는 의미의 'wish'는 'wish+명사, wish+주어+동사'의 형태이다.

기대 표현하기

- I'll keep my fingers crossed (for you)! (행운을 빌게!)
- Let's keep our fingers crossed for you. (행운을 빌어.)
- Good luck! / Good luck to you! (행운을 빌어!)
- I wish you luck! (행운이 함께 하기를 빌어!)
- I wish/hope/pray ~. (나는 ~하길 바란다.)
- I hope everything goes well with you. / Everything will be okay. (다 잘 될 거야.)
- Break a leg! (행운을 빌어!)
- I wish you all the best. (행운이 있기를 빌어.)

핵심 Check

2. 다음 주어진 말에 이어지는 대화의 순서를 바르게 배열하시오.

W: Soyun, are you going to take part in any races on the sports day?

(A) Just do your best. I'll keep my fingers crossed!

(B) Wow, I'm looking forward to seeing you at the race.

(C) But, Mom, I'm not sure I'll win the race.

(D) Sure. I'm going to run a 100 meter race at the end of the day.

➡ _____

Step Up – Real-life Scene

Miso: We're going on a field trip next Tuesday. ❶What are you going to do in the talent show, Jimin?

Jimin: I'm going to talk like our teachers ❷do in class and tell some jokes.

Miso: Wow! I'm really ❸looking forward to it.

Jimin: Will everyone like my show? I'm not sure.

Miso: Don't worry. I'm sure you'll do great. I'll ❹keep my fingers crossed!

Jimin: Thank you, Miso. ❺Let me show you one part of my act. Guess who? "Goood Jooob!"

Miso: Ha-ha, you sound like our English teacher.

Jimin: Do I? I'm going to show you more at the show.

Miso: Great! You always ❻make us laugh out loud.

미소: 다음 주 화요일에 수학여행을 갈 거야. 지민아, 너는 장기 자랑에서 뭘 할 거니?

지민: 나는 수업 시간에 선생님들이 말하는 것을 흉내 내고 농담도 할 거야.

미소: 와! 정말 기대되는데.

지민: 모든 사람이 나의 쇼를 좋아할까? 잘 모르겠어.

미소: 걱정하지 마. 나는 네가 잘할 거라고 확신해. 행운을 빌어 줄게!

지민: 고마워, 미소야. 내가 나의 연기의 한 부분을 보여 줄게. 누군지 맞힐 수 있겠니? "잘~ 했어~요!"

미소: 하하. 우리 영어 선생님처럼 들리는데.

지민: 그래? 장기 자랑에서 더 많이 보여 줄게.

미소: 멋지다! 너는 항상 우리를 웃게 만들어.

❶ 미래의 계획을 물을 때 사용하는 표현으로 "무엇을 할 예정이니?"의 의미이다.
❷ 앞 문장의 'talk'을 대신하는 대동사이다.
❸ 앞으로 일어날 일이나 하고 싶은 일에 대한 기대를 표현하는 말로, 'look forward to+명사/동명사' 형태이다.
❹ 행운을 빌어줄 때 사용하는 표현으로 '동사(keep)+목적어(my fingers)+목적보어(crossed: 과거분사)'의 5형식 구문이다.
❺ 'let+목적어+동사원형'은 '…가 ~하게 하다'라는 의미이다.
❻ 'make(사역동사)+목적어+목적보어(동사원형)' 구문으로 '…가 ~하게 하다'라는 의미이다.

Check(√) True or False

(1) Miso is looking forward to Jimin's show.   T ☐ F ☐

(2) Miso is not sure whether Jimin will do great.   T ☐ F ☐

Start Off – Listen & Talk A 1

G: Mom, ❶I can't wait for the sports day.

W: What are you going to do on that day, Minji?

G: I'm going to play basketball for my class. ❷We've practiced hard for a few weeks.

W: Oh, I'm looking forward to your game.

G: Actually, ❸I'm a little worried. I'm afraid I'll make a mistake.

W: Don't worry. You'll do a good job. I'll keep my fingers crossed!

G: 엄마, 체육 대회가 정말 기다려져요.

W: 민지야, 너는 그날 무엇을 할 거니?

G: 저는 학급을 대표해서 농구를 할 거예요. 우리는 몇 주간 열심히 연습해 왔어요.

W: 오, 너의 경기가 기대되는구나.

G: 사실은, 전 조금 걱정이 돼요. 제가 실수를 할까봐 겁나요.

W: 걱정하지 마. 넌 잘할 거야. 행운을 빌어 줄게!

❶ '~이 정말 기다려져'의 뜻으로 기대를 표현할 때 사용한다.
❷ 현재완료(have practiced)는 기간을 나타내는 for a few weeks와 함께 사용되어 과거부터 현재까지의 계속적인 일을 나타낸다.
❸ '걱정하다'라는 표현으로 'be worried'를 사용한다. a little은 '약간, 조금'의 의미로 과거분사 worried를 수식한다.

Check(√) True or False

(3) Minji is looking forward to the sports day.   T ☐ F ☐

(4) Minji's mother is afraid Minji will make a mistake.   T ☐ F ☐

Start Off – Listen & Talk B

G: Mom, ❶are you coming to the sports day?

W: Sure. I'm going to play the game Kick a Shoe. This will be the first time ❷for me to try it.

G: Don't worry. I'm sure you'll ❸do great. I'll keep my fingers crossed for you!

W: Thank you. I'm also going to perform a funny dance with some other mothers.

G: ❹That sounds fun. I'm looking forward to watching you on the stage.

G: 엄마, 체육 대회에 오실 거예요?

W: 물론이지. 나는 'Kick a Shoe' 게임에 참가할 거야. 이번에 처음 해 보는 거야.

G: 걱정하지 마세요. 엄마는 잘하실 거예요. 행운을 빌어 드릴게요!

W: 고맙다. 나는 다른 엄마들과 코믹 댄스도 할 거야.

G: 재밌겠네요. 무대에 선 엄마 모습을 보는 것이 기대돼요.

❶ 'are coming(현재진행형)'은 미래 시점과 사용이 될 때 미래의 일을 나타낼 수 있다.

❷ 'for me(for+목적격)'는 to부정사의 의미상의 주어로 '내가'로 해석한다. to부정사 'to try it'은 'the first time'을 수식하는 형용사 용법이다. it = the game Kick a Shoe

❸ do great: 잘하다

❹ 'sound+형용사'로 '~처럼 들리다'라는 뜻이다.

Check(√) True or False

(5) The girl's mom have played the game Kick a Shoe before.　T ☐ F ☐

(6) The girl is looking forward to watching her mom on the stage.　T ☐ F ☐

Fun Time

A: I'm going to travel to Jejudo next week.

B: Wow! That sounds great.

A: Yeah, I'm really looking forward to it.

A: I'm going to ❶enter the dance contest next week, but ❷I'm worried about it.

B: Don't worry. You'll do great. I'll keep my fingers crossed.

A: Thank you.

A: 나는 다음 주에 제주도를 여행할 거야.

B: 와! 멋지다.

A: 응, 난 그것이 정말 기대돼.

A: 난 다음 주에 춤 대회에 나갈 건데, 걱정이 된다.

B: 걱정하지 마. 넌 잘할 거야. 행운을 빌어 줄게.

A: 고마워.

❶ enter는 타동사이므로 전치사 없이 목적어를 취한다.

❷ 'be worried about ~'은 '~에 관해 걱정하다'라는 뜻이다.

Check(√) True or False

(7) A will travel to Jejudo next week.　T ☐ F ☐

(8) B hopes A will do great at the dance contest next week.　T ☐ F ☐

Get Ready 2

(1) G: You solved ❶a lot of problems in class. I'm sure you'll win the Class Brain award.

B: Do you really think so?

G: Of course. I'll keep my fingers crossed for you, Sangjun!

(2) B: The winner of the Oh So Sweet award will get some candies.

G: Oh, I ❷want to get the prize.

B: ❸I'm sure you'll get the prize this time. Good luck, Jiu!

(3) B: ❹I'm looking forward to the Best Joker award this time.

G: Ha-ha. You always ❺make us laugh out loud. So you'll get the prize, Yunki. Good luck.

B: Thank you.

(4) B: Minji, you're a happy girl. I think you'll get the Ms. Cheerful award. I'll keep my fingers crossed!

G: Oh, thank you, Jiho.

❶ 여기서 'a lot of'는 'many'의 의미로 'lots of, plenty of'로 바꾸어 쓸 수 있다.

❷ 'want'는 목적어로 'to-V'를 취한다.

❸ '～을 확신하다'라는 표현으로 'I'm sure (that)+주어+동사 ～'를 사용한다.

❹ 앞으로 일어날 일에 대한 기대를 표현하는 말로 'to'는 전치사로 뒤에 명사나 동명사가 온다.

❺ 'make(사역동사)+목적어+목적보어(동사원형)' 구문으로 '…가 ～하게 하다'라는 의미이다.

 Start Off – Listen & Talk A 2

W: Soyun, ❶are you going to take part in any races on the sports day?

G: Sure. ❷I'm going to run a 100 meter race at the end of the day.

W: Wow, ❸I'm looking forward to seeing you at the race.

G: But, Mom, I'm not sure I'll win the race.

W: Just do your best. I'll keep my fingers crossed!

❶ 'take part in ～'은 '～에 참가하다'라는 의미이고, 의문문에서는 '어떤'의 의미로 'any'를 사용한다.

❷ 'be going to+동사원형'은 '～할 예정이다'라는 미래의 일을 나타낼 때 사용한다.

❸ 'look forward to+동명사(seeing)'는 '～을 기대하다'라는 뜻이다.

 Start Off – Speak Up

A: I'm looking forward to the model airplane contest tomorrow. Are you ready?

B: Well, ❶I think so, but I'm nervous.

A: You will do well. ❷I'll keep my fingers crossed!

❶ I think so = I think (that) I'm ready

❷ 상대가 하는 일이 잘 되기를 기원하면서 "행운을 빌어!"라고 할 때 사용하는 표현이다.

Express Yourself A

1. G: Can you tell me something about your invention?

B: They are ❶a pair of special shoes. You can also clean the floor with them.

G: Great! I'm sure you'll win a prize. I'll keep my fingers crossed!

2. B: This ❷looks interesting. Is this a cutting board or a bird feeder?

G: It is ❸not only a cutting board but also a bird feeder. You can do two things ❹at the same time.

B: That's a great idea!

G: Do you really think so?

B: Yes. ❺I'm really looking forward to using it.

❶ '신발 한 켤레'를 나타낼 때는 'a pair of shoes'를 쓴다.

❷ 'look+형용사'로 '～처럼 보이다'라는 의미이다.

❸ 'not only A but also B'는 'A뿐만 아니라 B도'의 의미이다.

❹ at the same time: 동시에

❺ 'look forward to+동명사(using)'는 '～을 기대하다'라는 뜻이다.

Conversation 교과서 확인학습

● 다음 우리말과 일치하도록 빈칸에 알맞은 말을 쓰시오.

Get Ready 2

(1) **G:** You _____ _____ _____ _____ problems in class.
_____ _____ you'll win the Class Brain _____.
B: Do you really _____ _____?
G: Of course. I'll _____ my fingers _____ for you, Sangjun!

(2) **B:** The _____ of the Oh So Sweet _____ will get some candies.
G: Oh, I want _____ _____ the _____.
B: _____ _____ you'll get the prize this time. _____
_____, Jiu!

(3) **B:** I'm _____ _____ _____ the Best Joker award this time.
G: Ha-ha. You always _____ us _____ out loud. So you'll
_____ _____ _____, Yunki. Good luck.
B: Thank you.

(4) **B:** Minji, you're a happy girl. I think you'll get the Ms. Cheerful
award. I'll _____ _____ _____ _____!
G: Oh, thank you, Jiho.

Start Off – Listen & Talk A

1. **G:** Mom, I _____ _____ _____ the sports day.
W: _____ are you _____ _____ _____ on that day, Minji?
G: I'm going to play basketball for my class. We've _____ hard
_____ a few weeks.
W: Oh, I'm _____ _____ _____ your game.
G: _____, I'm _____ _____ _____. I'm _____ I'll
_____ a _____.
W: _____ _____. You'll _____ a good _____. I'll keep
_____ _____ _____ _____!

2. **W:** Soyun, are you going to _____ _____ _____ any races
on the sports day?
G: Sure. I'_____ _____ _____ run a 100 meter race at the
_____ of the day.
W: Wow, I'm looking _____ to _____ you at the race.
G: But, Mom, I'm not _____ I'll _____ the race.
W: Just _____ _____ _____. I'll _____ _____
_____ _____!

해석

(1) **G:** 너는 수업 중 많은 문제를 해결했잖아. 나는 네가 'Class Brain'상을 탈 거라고 확신해.
B: 정말 그렇게 생각하니?
G: 물론이야. 행운을 빌게, 상준아!

(2) **B:** 'Oh So Sweet'상 수상자는 사탕을 받을 거야.
G: 오, 그 상을 받고 싶다.
B: 네가 이번에는 그 상을 탈 거라고 확신해. 행운을 빌어, 지우야!

(3) **B:** 난 이번에 'Best Joker'상을 받기를 기대해.
G: 하하. 너는 항상 우리를 웃게 하잖아. 그러니 네가 그 상을 탈 거야, 윤기야. 행운을 빌어.
B: 고마워.

(4) **B:** 민지야, 너는 쾌활한 아이야. 나는 네가 'Ms. Cheerful'상을 탈 거라고 생각해. 행운을 빌게!
G: 오, 고마워, 지호야.

1. **G:** 엄마, 체육 대회가 정말 기다려져요.
W: 민지야, 너는 그날 무엇을 할 거니?
G: 저는 학급을 대표해서 농구를 할 거예요. 우리는 몇 주간 열심히 연습해 왔어요.
W: 오, 너의 경기가 기대되는구나.
G: 사실은, 전 조금 걱정이 돼요. 제가 실수를 할까봐 겁나요.
W: 걱정하지 마. 넌 잘할 거야. 행운을 빌어줄게!

2. **W:** 소윤아, 넌 체육 대회에서 경주에 참가하니?
G: 물론이죠. 전 그날 마지막에 있는 100 미터 달리기를 뛸 거예요.
W: 와, 네가 경주에서 달리는 모습을 보는 것이 기대되는구나.
G: 하지만 엄마, 전 경주에서 이길지 잘 모르겠어요.
W: 그냥 최선을 다하렴. 행운을 빌어줄게!

Start Off – Listen & Talk B

G: Mom, _____ _____ _____ to the sports day?

W: Sure. I'm _____ to play the game Kick a Shoe. This will be the first time _____ _____ _____ _____ it.

G: Don't worry. I'm _____ you'll _____ _____. I'll _____ my fingers _____ for you!

W: Thank you. I'm also going to _____ a funny dance with some _____ mothers.

G: That _____ _____. I'm _____ _____ to _____ you on the _____.

G: 엄마, 체육 대회에 오실 거예요?
W: 물론이지. 나는 'Kick a Shoe' 게임에 참가할 거야. 이번에 처음 해 보는 거야.
G: 걱정하지 마세요. 엄마는 잘하실 거예요. 행운을 빌어 드릴게요!
W: 고맙다. 나는 다른 엄마들과 코믹 댄스도 할 거야.
G: 재밌겠네요. 무대에 선 엄마 모습을 보는 것이 기대돼요.

Start Off – Speak Up

A: I'm _____ _____ _____ the _____ airplane contest tomorrow. Are you _____?

B: Well, I think _____, but I'm _____.

A: You will _____ _____. I'll _____ my fingers _____!

B: 나는 내일 모형 비행기 대회가 기대돼. 너는 준비됐니?
G: 음, 그런 것 같아, 하지만 긴장돼.
B: 너는 잘할 거야. 내가 행운을 빌어 줄게!

Step Up – Real-life Scene

Miso: We're going on a _____ _____ next Tuesday. What are you going to do in the _____ _____, Jimin?

Jimin: I'm going to talk _____ our teachers _____ in class and tell some _____.

Miso: Wow! I'm really _____ _____ _____ _____.

Jimin: Will everyone like my _____? I'm not _____.

Miso: Don't _____. I'm sure you'll _____ _____. I'll _____ _____ _____ _____!

Jimin: Thank you, Miso. _____ me _____ you one part of my act. _____ who? "Goood Jooob!"

Miso: Ha-ha, you _____ _____ our English teacher.

Jimin: Do I? I'm going to _____ you more at the show.

Miso: Great! You always _____ us _____ _____ _____.

미소: 다음 주 화요일에 수학여행을 갈 거야. 지민아, 너는 장기 자랑에서 뭘 할 거니?
지민: 나는 수업 시간에 선생님들이 말하는 것을 흉내 내고 농담도 할 거야.
미소: 와! 정말 기대되는데.
지민: 모든 사람이 나의 쇼를 좋아할까? 잘 모르겠어.
미소: 걱정하지 마. 나는 네가 잘할 거라고 확신해. 행운을 빌어 줄게!
지민: 고마워, 미소야. 내가 나의 연기의 한 부분을 보여 줄게. 누군지 맞힐 수 있겠니? "잘~ 했어~요!"
미소: 하하. 우리 영어 선생님처럼 들리는데.
지민: 그래? 장기 자랑에서 더 많이 보여 줄게.
미소: 멋지다! 너는 항상 우리를 웃게 만들어.

Fun Time

A: I'_____ _____ _____ travel to Jejudo next week.

B: Wow! That _____ _____.

A: Yeah, I'_____ _____ _____ _____ _____ it.

A: I'm going to _____ the dance contest next week, but I'_____ _____ _____ it.

B: Don't worry. You'll do great. I'll _____ _____ _____ _____.

A: Thank you.

해석

A: 나는 다음 주에 제주도를 여행할 거야.
B: 와! 멋지다.
A: 응, 난 그것이 정말 기대돼.

A: 난 다음 주에 춤 대회에 나갈 건데, 걱정이 된다.
B: 걱정하지 마. 넌 잘할 거야. 행운을 빌어 줄게.
A: 고마워.

Express Yourself A

1. **G:** _____ _____ _____ _____ something about your _____?

   B: They are _____ _____ _____ _____ shoes. You can also _____ the _____ with them.

   G: Great! I'm sure you'll _____ _____ _____. I'll _____ my fingers crossed!

2. **B:** This looks _____. Is this a _____ _____ or a bird _____?

   G: It is _____ _____ a cutting _____ _____ _____ a bird _____. You can do two things _____ _____ _____ _____.

   B: That's a great _____!

   G: Do you really think so?

   B: Yes. I'm really _____ _____ to _____ it.

1. **G:** 너의 발명품에 관해 이야기를 좀 해 줄래?
   B: 그것은 특별한 신발이야. 너는 그것으로 바닥을 청소할 수도 있어.
   G: 멋지다! 네가 상을 탈 거라고 확신해. 행운을 빌게!

2. **B:** 이것은 흥미로워 보여. 도마니, 아니면 새 모이통이니?
   G: 그것은 도마일 뿐만 아니라 새 모이통이기도 해. 너는 동시에 두 가지를 할 수 있어.
   B: 멋진 아이디어야!
   G: 정말 그렇게 생각하니?
   B: 응. 난 그것을 사용해 보는 게 정말 기대가 되는 걸.

01 다음 우리말에 맞도록 주어진 단어를 활용하여 4단어로 쓰시오.

> 행운을 빌어. (keep, fingers, cross)

➡ I'll _____ .

02 다음 대화의 빈칸에 들어갈 말로 알맞은 것은?

> B: I'm looking forward to the Best Joker award this time.
> G: Ha-ha. _____ So you'll get the prize, Yunki. Good luck.
> B: Thank you.

① We've practiced hard for a few weeks.
② I'm looking forward to seeing your photos.
③ You always make us laugh out loud.
④ That sounds great.
⑤ Joker is my favorite movie of all.

03 다음 대화의 빈칸에 들어갈 말로 적절한 것은?

> B: The winner of the Oh So Sweet award will get some candies.
> G: Oh, I want to get the prize.
> B: _____ Good luck, Jiu!

① Eating too many candies isn't good for your teeth.
② I'm sure you'll like the candies.
③ Why don't you bring some sweets to your classmates?
④ I don't think so.
⑤ I'm sure you'll get the prize this time.

04 다음 대화의 빈칸에 들어갈 말로 알맞은 것은?

> A: I'm looking forward to the model airplane contest tomorrow. Are you ready?
> B: Well, I think so, but I'm _____ .
> A: You will do well.

① proud   ② nervous   ③ funny
④ cheerful   ⑤ useful

[01~02] 다음 대화를 읽고 물음에 답하시오.

W: Soyun, are you going to take part in any races on the sports day?

G: Sure. I'm going to run a 100 meter race at the end of the day.

W: Wow, I'm looking forward to ___(A)___ (see) you at the race.

G: But, Mom, I'm not sure I'll win the race.

W: Just do your best. I'll keep my fingers ___(B)___ (cross)!

서답형

01 위 대화의 빈칸 (A)와 (B)에 주어진 단어를 알맞은 형태로 고치시오.

➡ (A) _____ (B) _____

중요

02 위 대화의 내용과 일치하지 <u>않는</u> 것은?

① They are talking about the sports day.

② Soyun is going to run a 100 meter race.

③ Soyun's mom wants to run the race.

④ Soyun is not sure she'll win the race.

⑤ Soyun's mom hopes that Soyun will do her best.

[03~05] 다음 대화를 읽고 물음에 답하시오.

G: Mom, are you coming to the sports day?

W: Sure. I'm going @to play the game Kick a Shoe. This will be the first time ⓑfor me to try it.

G: Don't worry. I'm sure you'll ⓒdo great. (A) I'll keep my fingers crossed for you!

W: Thank you. I'm also going to perform a funny dance with some ⓓother mothers.

G: That sounds fun. I'm looking forward ⓔto watch you on the stage.

중요

03 위 대화의 밑줄 친 @~ⓔ 중 어법상 <u>어색한</u> 것은?

① @ ② ⓑ ③ ⓒ ④ ⓓ ⑤ ⓔ

04 위 대화의 밑줄 친 (A)와 바꾸어 사용할 수 <u>없는</u> 표현은?

① Let's keep our fingers crossed for you.

② Good luck to you!

③ I wish you all the best.

④ Don't be worried. Just relax.

⑤ Break a leg!

서답형

05 위 대화를 읽고 다음 질문에 영어로 답하시오.

Q: What is Mom going to take part in?

➡ She is going to take part in _____

_____

_____ .

[06~07] 다음 대화를 읽고 물음에 답하시오.

B: This looks interesting. Is this a cutting board or a bird feeder?

G: _____(A)_____ You can do two things at the same time.

B: That's a great idea!

G: Do you really think so?

B: Yes. (B)난 그것을 사용해 보는 게 정말 기대가 되는 걸.

06 위 대화의 빈칸 (A)에 들어갈 말로 알맞은 것은?

① It is either a cutting board or a bird feeder.

② You can use it only as a bird feeder.

③ It is neither a cutting board nor a bird feeder.

④ It is only a cutting board.

⑤ It is not only a cutting board but also a bird feeder.

서답형

07 위 대화의 밑줄 친 (B)의 우리말에 맞게 주어진 단어를 활용하여 영어로 쓰시오.

> be, really, forward, use, it

➡ _____

[08~09] 다음 대화를 읽고 물음에 답하시오.

Miso: We're going on a field trip next Tuesday. What are you going to do in the talent show, Jimin? (①)

Jimin: I'm going to talk like our teachers do in class and tell some jokes. (②)

Miso: Wow! I'm really looking forward to it.

Jimin: Will everyone like my show? I'm not sure.

Miso: Don't worry. (③) I'm sure you'll do great. I'll keep my fingers crossed!

Jimin: Thank you, Miso. (④) Guess who? "Goood Jooob!" (⑤)

Miso: Ha-ha, you sound like our English teacher.

Jimin: Do I? I'm going to show you more at the show.

Miso: Great! You always make us laugh out loud.

08 위 대화의 (①)~(⑤) 중 주어진 문장이 들어갈 위치로 알맞은 것은?

> Let me show you one part of my act.

①   ②   ③   ④   ⑤

09 위 대화를 읽고 답할 수 없는 질문은?

① What are Jimin and Miso talking about?

② When is the field trip?

③ What is Jimin going to do in the talent show?

④ Why is Miso looking forward to Jimin's show?

⑤ How many times has Jimin ever taken part in a talent show?

[10~11] 다음 대화를 읽고 물음에 답하시오.

G: Mom, _____ (A) _____

W: What are you going to do on that day, Minji?

G: I'm going to play basketball for my class. We've practiced hard for a few weeks.

W: Oh, (B)너의 경기가 기대되는구나.

G: Actually, I'm a little worried. I'm afraid I'll make a mistake.

W: Don't worry. You'll do a good job. I'll keep my fingers crossed!

중요

10 위 대화의 빈칸 (A)에 들어갈 말로 알맞은 것은?

① are you going to take part in any races on the sports day?

② are you coming on the sports day?

③ I think I'll get the Ms. Cheerful award.

④ I can't wait for the sports day.

⑤ are you ready?

서답형

11 위 대화의 밑줄 친 (B)의 우리말에 맞게 주어진 단어를 활용하여 영작하시오.

(be / look / to / your game)

➡ _____

[01~02] 다음 대화를 읽고 물음에 답하시오.

Miso: We're going on a field trip next Tuesday. What are you going to do in the talent show, Jimin?

Jimin: I'm going to talk like our teachers do in class and tell some jokes.

Miso: Wow! _____ (A)

Jimin: Will everyone like my show? I'm not sure.

Miso: Don't worry. I'm sure you'll do great.
_____ (B)

Jimin: Thank you, Miso. Let me show you one part of my act. Guess who? "Goood Jooob!"

Miso: Ha-ha, you sound like our English teacher.

Jimin: Do I? I'm going to show you more at the show.

Miso: Great! You always make us laugh out loud.

01 위 대화의 빈칸 (A)와 (B)에 들어갈 말을 〈조건〉에 맞게 영어로 쓰시오.

┌─ 조건 ┐
(A) • 기대를 표현하는 말을 쓸 것.
• 현재진행형과 대명사 'it'을 사용할 것.
(B) • 기원을 표현하는 말을 쓸 것.
• 'keep'과 'cross'를 활용할 것.
└─────┘

➡ (A) _____
(B) _____

02 위 대화를 읽고 다음 물음에 영어로 답하시오.

Who did Jimin talk like in the dialog?

➡ _____

03 다음 대화의 밑줄 친 부분과 같은 의미가 되도록 주어진 단어를 써서 문장을 다시 쓰시오.

B: This looks interesting. Is this a cutting board or a bird feeder?

G: It is a bird feeder as well as a cutting board.(only, also) You can do two things at the same time.

B: That's a great idea!

G: Do you really think so?

B: Yes. I'm really looking forward to using it.

➡ _____

[04~05] 다음 대화를 읽고 물음에 답하시오.

G: Mom, (a)체육 대회가 정말 기다려져요.

W: What are you going to do on that day, Minji?

G: I'm going to play basketball for my class. We've practiced hard for a few weeks.

W: Oh, I'm looking forward to your game.

G: Actually, I'm a little worried.
_____ (A)

W: Don't worry. You'll do a good job.

04 위 대화의 흐름상 빈칸 (A)에 들어갈 말을 주어진 단어를 이용하여 영작하시오.

(afraid, a mistake)

➡ _____

05 위 대화의 밑줄 친 (a)의 우리말을 주어진 〈조건〉을 이용하여 영작하시오.

┌─ 조건 ┐
• 'wait'을 이용할 것.
• the sports day
└─────┘

➡ _____

Grammar

1 enough to

- Is this research project good **enough to** win a Nobel Prize?
  이 연구 과제는 노벨상을 받을 정도로 훌륭할까?

■ 형태: 형용사/부사+enough to+동사원형

  의미: '~할 만큼 충분히 ~한/하게'

■ 'enough'는 형용사/부사 뒤에 위치한다.

- My bag is big **enough to** hold as many as 5 books.
  나의 가방은 책을 5권이나 담을 수 있을 만큼 충분히 크다.

■ to부정사의 의미상 주어가 문장의 주어와 다를 경우 to부정사 앞에 'for+목적격'을 쓴다.

- The weather was warm **enough for the kids to play** outside.
  날씨가 아이들이 밖에 나가서 놀 수 있을 만큼 충분히 따뜻했다.

■ 'so+형용사/부사+that+주절의 주어(또는 의미상 주어)+can+동사원형(+목적어)'으로 바꾸어 쓸 수 있다.

- She is **smart enough to understand** the difficult question.

  = She is **so smart that she can understand** the difficult question.
  그녀는 그 어려운 문제를 이해할 만큼 충분히 똑똑하다.

- This soup tastes **good enough <u>for me</u> to enjoy**.

  = This soup tastes **so good that <u>I</u> can enjoy <u>it</u>**.
  이 수프는 내가 즐기기에 충분히 맛이 좋다.

핵심 Check

1. 다음 괄호 안에서 알맞은 것을 고르시오.

   (1) I'm (enough strong / strong enough) to carry the big box.

   (2) Did you work hard enough (winning / to win) the contest?

   (3) This textbook is easy enough (for young students / of young students) to read.

2 not only ~ but also ...

> • **Not only** the winners' fun studies **but also** the ceremony makes people laugh.
> 수상자들의 재밌는 연구들뿐만 아니라 시상식도 또한 사람들을 웃게 만든다.

■ 형태: not only ~ but also …
　 의미: ~뿐만 아니라 …도

■ 두 단어가 짝을 이루어 하나의 접속사 역할을 하는 상관접속사로, 상관접속사로 연결되는 두 어구의 형태를 일치시킨다.

　• Jack is **not only** kind **but also** smart. (형용사)
　　Jack은 친절할 뿐만 아니라 똑똑하기도 하다.

　• We can **not only** meet the singer **but also** take a picture with him. (동사원형)
　　우리는 그 가수를 만날 수 있을 뿐만 아니라 그와 사진을 찍을 수도 있다.

■ '… as well as ~'로 바꾸어 쓸 수 있다.

　• This coffee **not only** tastes fresh **but also** has rich aromas.

　　= This coffee has rich aromas **as well as** tastes fresh.
　　이 커피는 맛이 신선할 뿐만 아니라 풍부한 향을 가지고 있다.

■ 'Not only ~ but also …'가 주어로 쓰일 경우 수의 일치는 'but also'와 쓰인 주어에 맞춘다.

　• **Not only** Jenny **but also** her parents were born in New Zealand.
　　Jenny뿐만 아니라 그녀의 부모님들도 뉴질랜드에서 태어났다.

핵심 Check

2. 다음 괄호 안에서 알맞은 것을 고르시오.

(1) The dancers performed not only beautifully but also (intense / intensely).

(2) This vegetable is not only nutritious (and / but) also delicious.

(3) Not only (they are / are they) dangerous but also they can harm the environment.

Grammar 시험대비 기본평가

01 다음 우리말에 맞게 괄호 안에 주어진 단어를 이용하여 문장을 완성하시오.

(1) 그 밴드는 상을 수상할 정도로 충분히 인기 있다. (popular, win, award)

➡ The band is _____.

(2) 우리의 노래들은 부르기에 충분히 쉽다. (easy, sing)

➡ Our songs _____.

(3) 그는 용감할 뿐만 아니라 매우 친절하다. (brave, nice)

➡ He is not only _____.

(4) Ann은 사랑스러울 뿐만 아니라 똑똑하다. (lovely, smart)

➡ Ann _____.

02 다음 문장에서 어법상 어색한 부분을 바르게 고쳐 쓰시오.

(1) Their music is enough great to make their fans excited.

➡ _____

(2) Their fans are excited enough crying out.

➡ _____

(3) Pinocchio is not only popular but also very nicely.

➡ _____

(4) I know not only the meaning of "eager" but also "eagerness".

➡ _____

03 다음 〈보기〉의 문장을 참고하여 주어진 두 문장을 한 문장으로 바꾸어 쓰시오.

┤ 보기 ├

My mom is brave. She can climb the high mountain.

→ My mom is brave enough to climb the high mountain.

(1) The singer is tall. She can reach the shelf.

➡ _____

(2) The flower is big. It can cover the woman's face.

➡ _____

01 다음 빈칸에 'enough'가 들어갈 수 없는 하나를 고르시오.

① She is rich _____ to have a fancy car.
② Ann is brave _____ to catch the bug.
③ I have _____ time to meet you.
④ Do we have _____ paint for the wall?
⑤ Leslie is _____ shy to raise her hand.

02 다음 두 문장을 한 문장으로 바르게 바꾸면?

> • I teach German to the students.
> • Oliver teaches German to the students, too.

① Either I or Oliver teaches German to the students.
② Not only I but also Oliver teach German to the students.
③ Oliver as well as I teaches German to the students.
④ Neither I nor Oliver teaches German to the students.
⑤ Both I and Oliver teaches German to the students.

03 다음 빈칸에 들어갈 말로 적절한 것은?

> It was warm _____ for children to play soccer outside.

① so   ② very   ③ too
④ enough   ⑤ as

04 다음 중 어법상 어색한 문장을 고르시오.

① He is not only kind but also intelligent.
② I like to play soccer as well as basketball.
③ Not only Tom but also Susie will take part in the contest.
④ You as well as he have a sister.
⑤ He enjoys not only cooking but also to eat.

05 다음 문장의 뜻이 나머지 넷과 다른 것은?

① Because it was so cold, we stayed in the classroom.
② It was so cold that we stayed in the classroom.
③ It was very cold, so we stayed in the classroom.
④ It was cold enough for us to stay in the classroom.
⑤ It was too cold for us to stay in the classroom.

06 빈칸에 들어갈 말을 순서대로 바르게 연결한 것은?

> • The movie was _____ touching that I almost cried.
> • She was _____ sad to go to the party.

① so   – so
② so   – enough
③ so   – too
④ enough   – too
⑤ enough   – so

서답형

07 다음 괄호 안에 주어진 어구를 바르게 배열하여 문장을 다시 쓰시오.

> The room is (enough, up to 100 people, to accommodate, big).

➡ _____

_____

08 다음 문장과 같은 뜻을 가진 것은?

> She is so tall that she can reach the ceiling.

① She is tall enough that she can reach the ceiling.
② She is too tall to reach the ceiling.
③ She is enough tall to reach the ceiling.
④ She is tall enough to reach the ceiling.
⑤ She is so tall to reach the ceiling.

서답형

09 다음 문장에서 어법상 어색한 것을 바르게 고쳐 다시 쓰시오.

(1) He was so diligent that he can finish the work.

➡ _____

_____

(2) Tom as well as his parents are eating chicken.

➡ _____

_____

서답형

10 다음 두 문장을 'enough to'를 사용하여 한 문장으로 바꿔 쓰시오.

> • The puzzle was so easy.
> • I could solve it.

➡ _____

중요

11 다음 중 어법상 어색한 문장을 고르시오.

① Not only my dad but also my uncle are going to quit smoking.
② Harry as well as you is very famous now.
③ Not only children but also adults like the movie *Frozen*.
④ Not only you but also he was interested in the game.
⑤ Not only the teacher but also her students try their best.

서답형

12 다음 괄호 안에서 알맞은 말을 고르시오.

(1) The girl was (enough nice / nice enough) to help the poor.
(2) The box is (too / enough) big to put in the car.
(3) The princess was brave enough (to fight / fighting) the monster.
(4) This coat is so warm that I (wear / wear it) in winter.
(5) The computer is so fast that (to run / it can run) the program.

13 다음 밑줄 친 우리말을 영어로 바르게 옮긴 것은? (2개)

> <u>Mary뿐만 아니라 John도</u> joined the drama club.

① Not only Mary but also John
② Not John but Mary
③ Neither Mary nor John
④ John as well as Mary
⑤ Either John or Mary

서답형

14 다음 괄호 안에 주어진 어구를 바르게 배열하여 문장을 다시 쓰시오.

> This building (to survive / is / strong / a heavy storm / enough).

➡ _____

_____

서답형

15 주어진 어휘를 이용하여 다음 우리말을 영어로 쓰시오.

> 그 책은 여러 번 읽을 만큼 충분히 흥미롭다. (interesting, several times)

➡ _____

_____

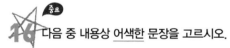

다음 중 내용상 어색한 문장을 고르시오.

① He was so young that he couldn't go to school.
② It was so hot that we went to the pool.
③ She was brave enough to stand up for the truth.
④ He was too strong to carry all the books.
⑤ The box is light enough for a young child to lift up.

17 빈칸에 들어갈 말을 순서대로 바르게 연결한 것은?

> • Both Tom and Ann _____ late.
> • I'm hungry _____ to eat all the food.

① were – too
② was – enough
③ were – so
④ was – too
⑤ were – enough

서답형

18 주어진 어휘를 이용하여 다음 우리말을 영어로 쓰시오.

> 그 강은 거대한 배가 항해할 수 있을 만큼 충분히 깊다. (a huge ship, enough, sail on, deep)

➡ _____

_____

19 다음 두 문장을 한 문장으로 바르게 옮긴 것은?

> • He is very smart.
> • He can put a 500-piece puzzle together.

① He is too smart to put a 500-piece puzzle together.
② He is so smart to put a 500-piece puzzle together.
③ He is smart enough to put a 500-piece puzzle together.
④ He is smart so that he can put a 500-piece puzzle together.
⑤ He is smart so that he can't put a 500-piece puzzle together.

서답형

20 대화의 빈칸에 적절한 말을 주어진 단어를 알맞은 형태로 바꾸어 써 넣으시오.

(1) A: I think Winnie the Pooh is very heavy. What do you think?
   B: He is not only heavy but also very _____. (love)

(2) A: I think Hong Gildong is very fast. What do you think?
   B: He is not only fast but also very _____. (strength)

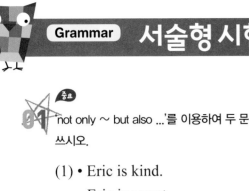

01 'not only ~ but also ...'를 이용하여 두 문장을 한 문장으로 쓰시오.

(1) • Eric is kind.
   • Eric is smart.
   ➡ _____

(2) • Jake is a student.
   • You are a student.
   ➡ _____

(3) • She was hardworking.
   • She was honest.
   ➡ _____

(4) • You run fast.
   • He runs fast.
   ➡ _____

(5) • You are going to join our club.
   • He is going to join our club.
   ➡ _____

02 다음 우리말을 주어진 어휘를 이용하여 영어로 옮기시오.

(1) 이 발명품은 너의 삶을 훨씬 쉽게 만들어 줄 만큼 충분히 유용하다. (invention, useful, enough, make, much easier)
   ➡ _____
   _____

(2) 너의 미소는 교실을 밝혀줄 만큼 충분히 환하다. (smile, bright, enough, light up)
   ➡ _____
   _____

(3) 너는 우리를 행복하게 만들 뿐만 아니라 우리가 잘 지내도록 도와준다. (not only, make, help, get along well)
   ➡ _____
   _____

03 다음 문장을 괄호 안의 어구를 써서 문장을 다시 쓰시오.

(1) You can use it not only as a door but also as a table for playing table tennis. (as well as)
   ➡ _____
   _____

(2) She was so kind that she showed me how to use chopsticks. (enough to)
   ➡ _____
   _____

04 잘못된 부분을 바르게 고쳐 문장을 다시 쓰시오.

(1) Mark visited not only his mother also his friends.
   ➡ _____
   _____

(2) This building is strong enough surviving a heavy storm.
   ➡ _____
   _____

(3) He is enough tall to touch the ceiling.
   ➡ _____
   _____

(4) They sell not only eggs but also to milk.
   ➡ _____
   _____

(5) The box is too heavy for the girl to move it.
   ➡ _____
   _____

05 다음 두 문장을 'enough to부정사'를 이용하여 한 문장으로 바르게 바꿔 쓰시오.

> • The water is very clean.
> • We can drink it.

➡ _____

06 다음 그림을 보고 괄호 안의 단어를 활용하여 문장을 완성하시오.

(1)
Umbrella for Coffee Lovers

> This is the Umbrella for Coffee Lovers.
> You can use it not only as an umbrella
> _____. (but also, cup holder)

(2)
Magic Stairs

> These are Magic Stairs. You can use
> them not only for going up and down
> _____. (but also, store,
> things)

(3)
LED Shoes

> These are LED Shoes. You can use them
> not only as shoes _____.
> (but also, lights)

07 다음 (A), (B) 문장을 괄호 안의 지시대로 바꿔 쓰시오.

> (A) He is not only a teacher but also a
>   painter. (as well as를 써서)
> (B) She looks wise as well as friendly.
>   (not only ~ but also를 써서)

➡ (A) _____
　 (B) _____

08 다음 문장을 어법에 맞게 고쳐 쓰시오.

(1) He is tall very to be a basketball player.
　➡ _____
　 _____

(2) Sumin ran enough fast to get there on time.
　➡ _____
　 _____

(3) The girl was brave too to speak in front of many people.
　➡ _____
　 _____

(4) It is warm enough plays outside.
　➡ _____
　 _____

(5) He's cheerful enough making us feel happy.
　➡ _____
　 _____

The Ig Nobel Prize

"What happens when you walk backward while you are carrying a cup of coffee?" Han Jiwon, a Korean high school student, did research on this topic in 2015. Is this research project good enough to win a
to부정사의 부사적 용법(부사 수식 용법). ~ enough to = so ~ that … can
Nobel Prize? Maybe not. But how about an Ig Nobel Prize? He won
Maybe not. = Maybe this research project is not good enough to win a Nobel Prize.
one in 2017 for this fun research.

The Ig Nobel Prizes are awarded for discoveries that "first make one
= which makes(×)
laugh and then think." They were started in 1991 by *AIR* magazine
The Ig Nobel Prizes
to increase people's interest in science by honoring the unusual and
to부정사의 부사적 용법(목적) = unusual people
the imaginative.
= imaginative people: the+형용사 = 복수 보통명사
The prizes are presented by real Nobel winners in Sanders Theater
= awarded
at Harvard University. The room is usually filled with people who are
eager to cheer for the brave scientists with their "laughable" research.
be eager(anxious/dying) to 동사원형: ~하고 싶은 생각이 간절하다
The U.K. Navy won the Ig Nobel Prize for Peace in 2000. To save
money, the Navy made its sailors shout, "Bang!" instead of using real
사역동사(made)+목적어+목적격보어(동사원형)
bombs. Is that funny enough for you to laugh out loud?

Andre Geim also won an award that year. He succeeded in floating
succeed in ~ing: ~하는 데 성공하다
a live frog in the air by using magnets. "In my experience, if people
= Unless people have
don't have a sense of humor, they are usually not very good scientists,"
he said when he accepted his award.

magnet 자석
float 뜨다, 띄우다
research 연구, 조사
award 상; 수여하다
discovery 발견
increase 증가시키다, 늘리다
honor 명예; 존경하다
unusual 특이한, 색다른
imaginative 창의적인, 상상력이 풍부한
university 대학교
be filled with …로 가득 차다
eager 열렬한, 간절히 바라는
be eager to …을 (열렬히) 하고 싶어 하다
peace 평화
sailor 선원
instead of … 대신에
bomb 폭탄
navy 해군
succeed 성공하다
sense 감각
humor 유머, 익살
accept 받아들이다

 확인문제

● 다음 문장이 본문의 내용과 일치하면 T, 일치하지 <u>않으면</u> F를 쓰시오.

1 Han Jiwon won an Ig Nobel Prize in 2017 for this fun research. ☐

2 The Ig Nobel Prizes are awarded for discoveries that "first make one think and then laugh." ☐

3 *AIR* magazine started the Ig Nobel Prizes in 1991. ☐

4 The Ig Nobel Prizes are presented by former Ig Nobel winners. ☐

5 The U.K. Navy won the Ig Nobel Prize for Peace in 2000. ☐

If that still does not bring a smile to your face, how about this?
In 2005, Gauri Nanda won the Ig Nobel Prize in Economics for inventing an alarm clock. It keeps running away until the sleeper finally gets out of bed.

Not only the winners' fun studies but also the ceremony for the Ig Nobel Prizes makes people laugh. There are a number of interesting things that keep people from getting bored. The opening and closing speeches are just two words each: "Welcome. Welcome." and "Goodbye. Goodbye." If someone talks for too long, an eight-year-old girl called Miss Sweetie Poo shouts repeatedly, "Please stop! I'm bored." Each winner receives ten trillion Zimbabwean dollars, which is worth less than one U.S. dollar. Throwing paper planes is another fun tradition.

The Ig Nobel Prize ceremony ends with the words, "If you didn't win a prize — and if you did — better luck next year!" The winners do not receive lots of money. And the awards are not great honors like the Nobel Prizes. But the Ig Nobel Prizes make science a lot more fun!

economics 경제학
get out of …에서 떠나다, 나가다
ceremony 의식, 식
a number of 얼마간의, 다수의
keep … from …가 ~하지 못하게 하다
get bored 지루해지다
speech 연설, 담화
repeatedly 반복적으로
receive 받다
trillion 1조
worth …의 가치가 있는

확인문제

● 다음 문장이 본문의 내용과 일치하면 T, 일치하지 않으면 F를 쓰시오.

1 In 2005, Gauri Nanda won the Ig Nobel Prize in Economics for inventing an alarm clock. ☐

2 The alarm clock keeps running after the sleeper until the sleeper finally gets out of bed. ☐

3 The ceremony for the Ig Nobel Prizes as well as the winners' fun studies makes people laugh. ☐

4 There are a number of things that keep people bored. ☐

5 The opening and closing speeches are just two words each. ☐

6 Ten trillion Zimbabwean dollars is worth more than one U.S. dollar. ☐

● 우리말을 참고하여 빈칸에 알맞은 말을 쓰시오.

1 The _____ _____ Prize

2 "What _____ when you walk _____ while you are carrying a cup of coffee?"

3 Han Jiwon, a Korean high school student, _____ _____ on this topic in 2015.

4 Is this research project good _____ _____ win a Nobel Prize?

5 _____ not.

6 But _____ _____ an Ig Nobel Prize?

7 He won _____ in 2017 for this fun research.

8 The Ig Nobel Prizes _____ _____ _____ discoveries that "first make one _____ and then _____."

9 They were started in 1991 by *AIR* magazine to increase people's interest in science _____ _____ _____ _____ and _____ _____.

10 The prizes _____ _____ _____ real Nobel winners in Sanders Theater at Harvard University.

11 The room _____ usually _____ _____ people who are eager to cheer for the brave scientists with their "_____" research.

12 The U.K. Navy won the Ig Nobel Prize _____ Peace in 2000.

13 _____ _____ money, the Navy made its sailors shout, "Bang!" _____ _____ using real bombs.

14 Is that funny enough for you to _____ _____ _____?

15 Andre Geim also _____ _____ _____ that year.

16 He _____ _____ _____ a live frog in the air by using magnets.

---

1 이그노벨상

2 "당신이 커피 한 잔을 들고 가면서 뒤로 걸을 때 무슨 일이 일어날까?"

3 한국의 한 고등학생인 한지원은 2015년에 이 주제에 관해 연구했다.

4 이 연구 과제는 노벨상을 받을 정도로 훌륭할까?

5 아마도 아닐 것이다.

6 하지만 이그노벨상은 어떤가?

7 그는 이 재미있는 연구로 2017년에 상을 탔다.

8 이그노벨상은 '먼저 웃기고 나서 다음에 생각하게 하는' 발견에 수여된다.

9 그것은 특이하고 창의적인 사람들을 높이 평가함으로써 과학에 대한 사람들의 흥미를 늘리기 위해 AIR 잡지에 의해 1991년에 시작되었다.

10 그 상들은 하버드 대학의 Sanders 극장에서 진짜 노벨상 수상자들에 의해 수여된다.

11 그 방은 대개 '웃기는' 연구를 한 용감한 과학자들을 열렬히 격려하고자 하는 사람들로 가득 찬다.

12 영국 해군은 2000년에 이그노벨 평화상을 탔다.

13 돈을 아끼기 위해, 해군에서는 선원들에게 진짜 폭탄을 사용하는 대신에 "쾅!"이라고 소리치게 했다.

14 그것이 당신이 큰 소리로 웃을 정도로 우스운가?

15 Andre Geim도 그해에 상을 탔다.

16 그는 자석을 이용해서 살아 있는 개구리를 공중에 띄우는 데 성공했다.

17 "In my experience, if people don't have _____ _____ _____ _____, they are usually not very good scientists," he said when he accepted his award.

18 If that still does not _____ a smile _____ your face, how about this?

19 In 2005, Gauri Nanda won the Ig Nobel Prize _____ Economics _____ inventing an alarm clock.

20 It _____ _____ _____ until the sleeper finally gets out of bed.

21 _____ _____ the winners' fun studies _____ _____ the ceremony for the Ig Nobel Prizes _____ people laugh.

22 There are _____ _____ _____ interesting things that _____ people _____ _____ _____.

23 The opening and closing speeches are just _____ _____ _____: "Welcome. Welcome." and "Goodbye. Goodbye."

24 If someone talks for too long, _____ _____ _____ _____ Miss Sweetie Poo shouts repeatedly, "Please stop! I'm bored."

25 Each winner receives ten trillion Zimbabwean dollars, which is _____ _____ _____ one U.S. dollar.

26 _____ paper planes _____ another fun tradition.

27 The Ig Nobel Prize ceremony _____ _____ the words, "If you didn't win a prize — and if you _____ — better luck next year!"

28 The winners _____ _____ _____ lots of money.

29 And the awards are not _____ _____ _____ the Nobel Prizes.

30 But the Ig Nobel Prizes make science _____ _____ _____ _____!

● 우리말을 참고하여 본문을 영작하시오.

1 이그노벨상
➡ _____

2 "당신이 커피 한 잔을 들고 가면서 뒤로 걸을 때 무슨 일이 일어날까?"
➡ _____

3 한국의 한 고등학생인 한지원은 2015년에 이 주제에 관해 연구했다.
➡ _____

4 이 연구 과제는 노벨상을 받을 정도로 훌륭할까?
➡ _____

5 아마도 아닐 것이다.
➡ _____

6 하지만 이그노벨상은 어떤가?
➡ _____

7 그는 이 재미있는 연구로 2017년에 상을 탔다.
➡ _____

8 이그노벨상은 '먼저 웃기고 나서 다음에 생각하게 하는' 발견에 수여된다.
➡ _____

9 그것은 특이하고 창의적인 사람들을 높이 평가함으로써 과학에 대한 사람들의 흥미를 늘리기
위해 AIR 잡지에 의해 1991년에 시작되었다.
➡ _____
_____

10 그 상들은 하버드 대학의 Sanders 극장에서 진짜 노벨상 수상자들에 의해 수여된다.
➡ _____

11 그 방은 대개 '웃기는' 연구를 한 용감한 과학자들을 열렬히 격려하고자 하는 사람들로 가득 찬다.
➡ _____
_____

12 영국 해군은 2000년에 이그노벨 평화상을 탔다.
➡ _____

13 돈을 아끼기 위해, 해군에서는 선원들에게 진짜 폭탄을 사용하는 대신에 "쾅!"이라고 소리치게 했다.
➡ _____

14 그것이 당신이 큰 소리로 웃을 정도로 우스운가?
➡ _____

15 Andre Geim도 그해에 상을 탔다.
➡ _____

16 그는 자석을 이용해서 살아 있는 개구리를 공중에 띄우는 데 성공했다.

➡ _____

17 그는 상을 받을 때, "내 경험상, 사람들이 유머 감각이 없다면, 그들은 대개 별로 훌륭한 과학자가 아니다."라고 말했다.

➡ _____

_____

18 그것이 아직도 당신의 얼굴에 미소를 띠게 하지 않는다면, 이것은 어떤가?

➡ _____

19 2005년에 Gauri Nanda는 자명종을 발명해서 이그노벨 경제학상을 받았다.

➡ _____

20 그것은 잠자는 사람이 결국 침대 밖으로 나올 때까지 계속 도망을 다닌다.

➡ _____

21 수상자들의 재미있는 연구뿐만 아니라 이그노벨상 시상식도 또한 사람들을 웃게 만든다.

➡ _____

22 사람들이 지루해하지 않도록 하는 재미있는 것들이 많이 있다.

➡ _____

23 개회사와 폐회사는 단지 두 마디이다: "환영합니다. 환영합니다."와 "안녕. 안녕."

➡ _____

24 만일 누군가가 너무 오랫동안 말을 하면, Miss Sweetie Poo라고 하는 여덟 살짜리 여자아이가 "제발 멈춰요! 지루해요."라고 계속 외친다.

➡ _____

_____

25 각 수상자는 10조의 짐바브웨 달러를 받는데, 그것은 미국의 1달러보다 가치가 낮다.

➡ _____

26 종이비행기를 날리는 것은 또 다른 재미있는 전통이다.

➡ _____

27 이그노벨상 시상식은 "만일 당신이 상을 타지 못했다면 – 그리고 만일 탔다면 – 내년에는 좀 더 많은 행운이 있기를!"이라는 말로 끝이 난다.

➡ _____

_____

28 수상자들은 많은 상금을 받지 않는다.

➡ _____

29 그리고 그 상은 노벨상같이 훌륭한 영광은 아니다.

➡ _____

30 하지만 이그노벨상은 과학을 훨씬 더 재미있게 만든다!

➡ _____

[01~03] 다음 글을 읽고 물음에 답하시오.

"What happens when you walk backward while you are carrying a cup of coffee?" (①) Han Jiwon, a Korean high school student, did research ___ⓐ___ this topic in 2015. (②) Is this research project good enough to win a Nobel Prize? (③) But how about an Ig Nobel Prize? (④) He won one in 2017 ___ⓑ___ this fun research. (⑤)

The Ig Nobel Prizes are awarded for discoveries that "first make one laugh and then think." They were started in 1991 by *AIR* magazine to increase people's interest in science by honoring the unusual and the imaginative.

01 위 글의 빈칸 ⓐ와 ⓑ에 들어갈 전치사가 바르게 짝지어진 것은?

	ⓐ	ⓑ		ⓐ	ⓑ
①	on	in	②	about	of
③	about	in	④	at	for
⑤	on	for			

02 위 글의 흐름으로 보아, 주어진 문장이 들어가기에 가장 적절한 곳은?

> Maybe not.

①   ②   ③   ④   ⑤

03 According to the passage, which is NOT true?

① Han Jiwon was a Korean high school student.
② Han Jiwon studied about the topic "What happens when you walk backward while you are carrying a cup of coffee?"

③ Han Jiwon won an Ig Nobel Prize in 2017.
④ The Ig Nobel Prizes are awarded for discoveries that "first make one think and then laugh."
⑤ The Ig Nobel Prizes were started in 1991 by *AIR* magazine.

[04~06] 다음 글을 읽고 물음에 답하시오.

The prizes are presented by real Nobel winners in Sanders Theater at Harvard University. The room is usually filled with people who (A)are eager to cheer for the brave scientists with their "laughable" research.

The U.K. Navy won the Ig Nobel Prize for Peace in 2000. (B)To save money, the Navy made its sailors shouting, "Bang!" instead of using ___ⓐ___. Is that funny enough for you to laugh out loud?

04 위 글의 빈칸 ⓐ에 들어갈 알맞은 말을 고르시오.

① real knives   ② fake blows
③ fake bombs   ④ artificial knives
⑤ real bombs

05 위 글의 밑줄 친 (A)와 바꿔 쓸 수 없는 말을 고르시오.

① are anxious to cheer
② long to cheer
③ are anxious about cheering
④ long for cheering
⑤ are dying to cheer

서답형

06 위 글의 밑줄 친 (B)에서 어법상 **틀린** 부분을 찾아 고치시오.

_____ ➡ _____

[07~09] 다음 글을 읽고 물음에 답하시오.

The U.K. Navy won the Ig Nobel Prize for Peace in 2000. To save money, the Navy made its sailors shout, "Bang!" instead of using real bombs. ⓐIs that _____ out loud?

Andre Geim also won an award that year. He succeeded in floating a ⓑlive frog in the air by using magnets. "In my experience, if people don't have a sense of humor, they are usually not very good scientists," he said when he accepted his award.

서답형

07 위 글의 문장 ⓐ의 빈칸에 알맞은 단어를 넣어 다음 문장과 같은 뜻이 되도록 하시오. (여섯 단어)

Is that so funny that you can laugh out loud?

➡ _____

서답형

08 When did Andre Geim win the Ig Nobel Prize? Answer in English in a full sentence. (5 words)

➡ _____

09 위 글의 밑줄 친 ⓑlive와 같은 의미로 쓰인 것을 고르시오.

① The doctors said he only had six months to live.
② The show is going out live.
③ We saw a real live rattlesnake!
④ The club has live music most nights.
⑤ Their names live in our memory.

[10~12] 다음 글을 읽고 물음에 답하시오.

Not only the winners' fun studies but also the ceremony for the Ig Nobel Prizes makes people laugh. There are a number of interesting things that keep people from getting bored. The opening and closing speeches are just two words each: "Welcome. Welcome." and "Goodbye. Goodbye." If someone talks for too long, an eight-year-old girl called Miss Sweetie Poo shouts ⓐrepeatedly, "Please stop! I'm bored." ⓑEach winner receives ten trillion Zimbabwean dollars, which are worth less than one U.S. dollar. Throwing paper planes is another fun tradition.

10 위 글의 밑줄 친 ⓐrepeatedly와 바꿔 쓸 수 **없는** 말을 **모두** 고르시오.

① again and again
② over and over
③ all of a sudden
④ all at once
⑤ over and over again

서답형

11 위 글의 밑줄 친 ⓑ에서 어법상 **틀린** 부분을 찾아서 고치시오.

_____ ➡ _____

중요

12 다음 중 이그노벨상 시상식의 재미있는 전통에 해당하지 <u>않</u>는 것은?

① The opening speech is "Welcome. Welcome."
② The closing speech is "Goodbye. Goodbye."
③ The winners must give a long speech.
④ Miss Sweetie Poo is an eight-year-old girl.
⑤ The prize money is ten trillion Zimbabwean dollars.

[13~15] 다음 글을 읽고 물음에 답하시오.

The Ig Nobel Prize ceremony ends with the words, "If you didn't win a prize — and if you (A)did — better luck next year!" The winners do not receive lots of money. And the awards are not great honors (B)like the Nobel Prizes. But the Ig Nobel Prizes make science ____ⓐ____ more fun!

13 위 글의 빈칸 ⓐ에 들어갈 수 <u>없는</u> 말을 고르시오.

① much ② very ③ even
④ a lot ⑤ still

14 위 글의 밑줄 친 (A)did와 바꿔 쓸 수 있는 말을 쓰시오. (세 단어)

➡ _____

15 위 글의 밑줄 친 (B)like와 같은 의미로 쓰인 것을 고르시오.

① How did you <u>like</u> the movie?
② She responded in <u>like</u> manner.
③ I don't <u>like</u> the way he's looking at me.
④ He ran <u>like</u> the wind.
⑤ <u>Like</u> I said, you're always welcome to stay.

[16~18] 다음 글을 읽고 물음에 답하시오.

The prizes are (A)presented by real Nobel winners in Sanders Theater at Harvard University. The room is usually filled with people who are eager to cheer for the brave scientists with their "laughable" research.

The U.K. Navy won the Ig Nobel Prize for Peace in 2000. To save money, the Navy made its sailors shout, "Bang!" ____ⓐ____ using real bombs. Is that funny enough for you to laugh out loud?

16 위 글의 빈칸 ⓐ에 들어갈 알맞은 말을 고르시오.

① besides ② instead of
③ along with ④ in spite of
⑤ in addition to

17 위 글의 밑줄 친 (A)presented와 바꿔 쓸 수 있는 단어를 철자 a로 시작하여 쓰시오.

➡ _____

18 위 글을 읽고 'the Ig Nobel Prize'에 대해 알 수 <u>없는</u> 것을 고르시오.

① 상의 수여자 ② 시상식 장소
③ 시상식 참여자 ④ 시상식 시기
⑤ 2000년 수상자

[19~21] 다음 글을 읽고 물음에 답하시오.

Andre Geim also won an award that year. He succeeded in floating a live frog in the air by using magnets. "In my experience, if people don't have a sense of humor, they are usually not very good scientists," he said when he accepted his award.

If that still does not bring ____ⓐ____ to your face, how about this? In 2005, Gauri Nanda won the Ig Nobel Prize in Economics for inventing an alarm clock. It keeps ____ⓑ____ away until the sleeper finally gets out of bed.

19 위 글의 빈칸 ⓐ에 들어갈 가장 알맞은 말을 고르시오.

① some comfort ② your regret
③ some respect ④ inner peace
⑤ a smile

서답형

20 위 글의 빈칸 ⓑ에 run을 알맞은 형태로 쓰시오.

➡ _____

서답형

21 How did Andre Geim succeed in floating a live frog in the air? Fill in the blanks with suitable words.

He accomplished it by _____ _____.

[22~24] 다음 글을 읽고 물음에 답하시오.

The Ig Nobel Prize ceremony ends (A)[up / with] the words, "(A)If you didn't win a prize — and if you (B)[did / were] — better luck next year!" The winners do not receive lots of money. And the awards are not great honors (C)[alike / like] the Nobel Prizes. But the Ig Nobel Prizes make science a lot more fun!

서답형

22 위 글의 괄호 (A)~(C)에서 문맥이나 어법상 알맞은 낱말을 골라 쓰시오.

➡ (A) _____ (B) _____ (C) _____

서답형

23 위 글의 밑줄 친 (A)를 Unless를 사용하여 고치시오.

➡ _____

서답형

24 본문의 내용과 일치하도록 다음 빈칸 (A)~(C)에 알맞은 단어를 쓰시오. (한 칸에 두 단어도 가능)

Though the prize money of the (A)_____ Prize is not big and the winners don't gain great honors like the (B)_____ Prize winners, the (C)_____ Prizes make science much more fun.

[25~27] 다음 글을 읽고 물음에 답하시오.

"What happens when you walk backward while you are carrying a cup of coffee?" Han Jiwon, a Korean high school student, did research on this topic in 2015. Is this research project good enough ⓐto win a Nobel Prize? Maybe not. But how about an Ig Nobel Prize? He won one in 2017 for this fun research.

The Ig Nobel Prizes are awarded for discoveries that "first make one laugh and then think." ⓑThey were started in 1991 by *AIR* magazine to increase people's interest in science by honoring ⓒthe unusual and ⓓthe imaginative.

25 위 글의 밑줄 친 ⓐto win과 to부정사의 용법이 같은 것을 고르시오.

① He cannot be a gentleman to do such a thing.

② She is studying English to get a good job.

③ He worked too slowly to finish it in time.

④ He left his native country never to return.

⑤ She smiled to see the monkey.

서답형

26 위 글의 밑줄 친 ⓑThey가 가리키는 것을 본문에서 찾아 쓰시오.

➡ _____

서답형

27 위 글의 밑줄 친 ⓒthe unusual, ⓓthe imaginative와 바꿔쓸 수 있는 말을 각각 두 단어로 쓰시오.

➡ ⓐ _____ ⓓ _____

[01~03] 다음 글을 읽고 물음에 답하시오.

"What happens when you walk backward while you are carrying a cup of coffee?" Han Jiwon, a Korean high school student, did research on this topic in 2015. ⓐ이 연구 과제는 노벨상을 받을 정도로 훌륭할까? Maybe not. But how about an Ig Nobel Prize? He won one in 2017 for this fun research.

The Ig Nobel Prizes are (A)[awarded / rewarded] for discoveries that "first make one laugh and then think." They were started in 1991 by *AIR* magazine to increase people's interest in science by (B)[honoring / ignoring] the unusual and the imaginative.

01 위 글의 괄호 (A)~(B)에서 문맥상 알맞은 낱말을 골라 쓰시오.

➡ (A) _____ (B) _____

02 위 글의 밑줄 친 ⓐ의 우리말에 맞게 주어진 어휘를 알맞게 배열하시오.

> a Nobel Prize / enough / research project / good / this / to win / is / ?

➡ _____

_____

03 다음 빈칸 (A)와 (B)에 알맞은 단어를 넣어 Han Jiwon에 대한 소개를 완성하시오.

> He was a Korean high school student and won an (A)_____ _____ _____ in 2017 because of the (B)_____ research that he had done in 2015.

[04~06] 다음 글을 읽고 물음에 답하시오.

ⓐThe prizes are presented by real Nobel winners in Sanders Theater at Harvard University. The room is usually filled with people who are eager to cheer for the brave scientists with their "laughable" research.

The U.K. Navy won the Ig Nobel Prize for Peace in 2000. To save money, the Navy made its sailors shout, "Bang!" instead of using real bombs. Is ⓑthat funny enough for you to laugh out loud?

04 위 글의 밑줄 친 ⓐ를 능동태로 고치시오.

➡ _____

_____

05 Why did the U.K. Navy make its sailors shout, "Bang!" instead of using real bombs? Fill in the blanks with suitable words.

> Because it wanted to _____ _____.

06 위 글의 밑줄 친 ⓑthat이 가리키는 것을 본문에서 찾아 쓰시오.

➡ _____

_____

[07~08] 다음 글을 읽고 물음에 답하시오.

Andre Geim also won an Ig Nobel Prize that year. He succeeded in floating a live frog in the air by using magnets. "In my experience, ⓐif people don't have a sense of humor, they are usually not very good scientists," he said when he accepted his award.

07 위 글의 밑줄 친 ⓐ를 unless를 사용하여 고치시오.

➡ _____

08 다음 빈칸 (A)와 (B)에 알맞은 단어를 넣어 Andre Geim에 대한 소개를 완성하시오.

> Andre Geim was successful in (A)_____ a live frog in the air by using magnets, and won an Ig Nobel Prize. In his acceptance speech, he referred to (B)_____ _____ _____ _____ as an essential qualification of a good scientist.

[09~10] 다음 글을 읽고 물음에 답하시오.

> ⓐNot only the winners' fun studies but also the ceremony for the Ig Nobel Prizes makes people laugh. There are ⓑa number of interesting things that keep people from getting bored. The opening and closing speeches are just two words each: "Welcome. Welcome." and "Goodbye. Goodbye." If someone talks for too long, an eight-year-old girl called Miss Sweetie Poo shouts repeatedly, "Please stop! I'm bored." Each winner receives ten trillion Zimbabwean dollars, which is worth less than one U.S. dollar. Throwing paper planes is another fun tradition.

09 위 글의 밑줄 친 ⓐ를 as well as을 사용하여 고치시오.

➡ _____
_____

10 위 글의 밑줄 친 ⓑ에 해당하는 것을 우리말로 쓰시오. (네 가지)

➡ _____
_____
_____
_____
_____

[11~12] 다음 글을 읽고 물음에 답하시오.

> "What happens when you walk backward while you are carrying a cup of coffee?" Han Jiwon, a Korean high school student, did research on this topic in 2015. Is this research project good enough to win a Nobel Prize? ⓐ Maybe not. But how about an Ig Nobel Prize? He won one in 2017 for this fun research.
>
> The Ig Nobel Prizes are awarded for discoveries that "first make one laugh and then think." They were started in 1991 by *AIR* magazine to increase people's interest in science by honoring the unusual and the imaginative.

11 위 글의 밑줄 친 ⓐ에 생략된 부분을 넣어 완전한 문장으로 쓰시오.

➡ _____
_____

12 Why did *AIR* magazine start the Ig Nobel Prizes? Fill in the blanks with suitable words.

> *AIR* magazine started them to increase people's _____ _____ _____ by honoring the unusual and the imaginative.

구석구석

Self-study Guide

- New words again!

- He showed great eagerness to learn new things.
  명사를 수식하는 형용사 용법

- Oh, I get the meaning of "-ness."
  = understand

- Now I know not only the meaning of "eager" but also the meaning of "eagerness."

구문해설 • eagerness: 열정 • meaning: 의미 • not only A but also B: A뿐만 아니라 B도
  • eager: 열렬한, 간절히 바라는

• 또 새 단어네!

• 그는 새로운 것들을 배우고자 하는 열정을 보여주었다.

• 오, 나는 '-ness'의 의미를 알았어.

• 이제 나는 'eager'의 뜻뿐만 아니라 'eagerness'의 뜻도 알아.

Express Yourself C

Magic Stairs

These are Magic Stairs. You can use them not only for going up and down
　　　　　　　　　　　　　　not only A but also B = B as well as A: A뿐만 아니라 B도　　　동명사
but also for storing things. This invention is useful enough to make your life
　　　　　　동명사　　　　　　　　　　　　　　　~ enough to = so ~ that … can
much easier.
비교급 강조(훨씬)

구문해설 • stair: 계단 • store: 저장[보관]하다 • invention: 발명

마법의 계단

이것은 '마법의 계단'입니다. 당신은 그것을 올라가고 내려가기 위해서 뿐만 아니라 물건을 보관하기 위해서도 사용할 수 있습니다. 이 발명품은 당신의 삶을 훨씬 더 편안하게 할 정도로 충분히 유용합니다.

Link to the World

The Nobel Prize

The Nobel Prize was named after Alfred Nobel, a Swedish scientist. It is
　　　　　　　be named after: ~의 이름을 따서 짓다　　　ㄴ　동격
awarded to people who have done great work for the world.
수동태　　　　주격 관계대명사
Of all the winners, Malala Yousafzai is the youngest. She won the Nobel Prize
~ 중에서
at the age of 17 because she had fought for women's and children's rights.
~의 나이에　　　　　　　　　과거완료
The Curie family received the Nobel Prize three times. Not only Marie Curie

but also her daughter was awarded the Nobel Prize.
= Her daughter as well as Marie Curie

구문해설 • be named after: ~의 이름을 따서 짓다 • Swedish: 스웨덴의 • award: 수여하다
  • right: 권리

노벨상

노벨상은 스웨덴 과학자인 Alfred Nobel의 이름을 따서 지었다. 그 상은 세계를 위해 위대한 일을 행한 사람들에게 수여된다.

모든 수상자들 중에서, Malala Yousafzai가 최연소이다. 그녀는 여성과 어린이의 권리를 위해서 싸웠기 때문에 17세의 나이에 노벨상을 수상했다.

Curie 가족은 노벨상을 3번 수상했다. Marie Curie뿐만 아니라 그녀의 딸도 노벨상을 수상했다.

01 다음 주어진 두 단어의 관계가 같도록 빈칸에 알맞은 단어를 쓰시오.

> useful – useless : usual – _____

02 다음 문장의 빈칸 (a)와 (b)에 들어갈 단어가 바르게 짝지어진 것은?

> • We had to ____(a)____ the swimming pool as it rained.
> • The nation's president hoped to end the war and bring ____(b)____ .

① wait for – peace
② get into – discovery
③ get out of – peace
④ get out of – discovery
⑤ wait for – honor

03 다음 대화의 빈칸에 들어갈 말을 〈영영 풀이〉를 참고하여 대화에 나오는 한 단어를 이용하여 쓰시오.

> A: I'm going to enter the dance contest next week, but I'm _____ about it.
> B: Don't worry. You'll do great. I'll keep my fingers crossed.
> A: Thank you.

> <영영 풀이> unhappy because you are thinking about problems or unpleasant things that might happen

➡ _____

[04~05] 다음 영영 풀이에 해당하는 것을 고르시오.

04
> to be on a liquid and not sink

① fill
② volunteer
③ hang
④ represent
⑤ float

05
> something you are proud to do

① honor
② humor
③ sense
④ trillion
⑤ sailor

06 다음 중 밑줄 친 부분의 뜻이 잘못된 것은?

① Everyone went underground before the bomb went off. (폭탄)
② He wanted to join the navy instead of the army. (해군)
③ The student did research on the Internet to learn about King Sejong. (조사)
④ The writer of the children's story is very imaginative. (가상의)
⑤ The store increased the price of toys. (증가시키다, 늘리다)

07 다음 대화에서 어법상 어색한 부분을 찾아 바르게 고치시오.

> B: I'm looking forward to the Best Joker award this time.
> G: Ha-ha. You always make us laughing out loud. So you'll get the prize, Yunki. Good luck.
> B: Thank you.

_____ ➡ _____

08 다음 짝지어진 대화 중 어색한 것은?

① A: What kind of prize did Han Jiwon win in 2017?

B: He won an Ig Nobel Prize.

② A: I'm going to travel to Jejudo next week.

B: Wow! That sounds great.

③ A: I'm going to enter the speech contest tomorrow.

B: Me, too. I'm looking forward to it.

④ A: I'm going to join the dance contest next Friday.

B: Are you? I'm looking forward to watching you dance.

⑤ A: I'm looking forward to the funny dance contest tomorrow. Are you ready?

B: Well, I think so, but I'm confident.

[09~11] 다음 대화를 읽고 물음에 답하시오.

Miso: We're going on a field trip next Tuesday. What are you going to do in the talent show, Jimin?

Jimin: I'm going to talk like our teachers do in class and tell some jokes.

Miso: Wow! I'm really ⓐlooking forward to it.

Jimin: Will everyone like my show? I'm not sure.

Miso: Don't worry. I'm sure you'll do great. I'll ⓑkeep my fingers crossed!

Jimin: Thank you, Miso. ⓒLet me to show you one part of my act. Guess who? "Goood Jooob!"

Miso: Ha-ha, you ⓓsound like our English teacher.

Jimin: Do I? I'm going to show you more at the show.

Miso: Great! You always make us ⓔlaugh out loud.

09 위 대화의 밑줄 친 부분 중 어법상 틀린 것은?

① ⓐ   ② ⓑ   ③ ⓒ   ④ ⓓ   ⑤ ⓔ

10 위 대화의 제목으로 가장 적절한 것은?

① Difficulty of Imitating Teachers' Voice

② Doing the Show Which Everyone likes

③ Choosing the Place of a Field Trip

④ Looking Forward to the Talent Show

⑤ Making Others Laugh out Loud

11 위 대화의 내용과 일치하지 않는 것을 고르시오.

① They are talking about the talent show.

② The field trip is next Tuesday.

③ Miso is going to talk like the teachers do in class and tell some jokes.

④ Jimin always makes Miso laugh out loud.

⑤ Jimin talked like his English teacher.

Grammar

12 주어진 문장의 밑줄 친 that과 용법이 같은 것은?

The dinner at that famous restaurant was so nice that I couldn't forget it.

① I hope that I can see your face.

② The report shows that we need to have healthier food.

③ The money that you saved will be used to buy a bike.

④ That is the jacket that my aunt made for me.

⑤ The old lady is so wise that we always get advice from her.

13 다음 글에서 어법상 어색한 부분을 찾아 바르게 고치시오.

> The Curie family received the Nobel Prize three times. Not only Marie Curie but also her daughter were awarded the Nobel Prize.

➡ _____

_____

14 다음 주어진 우리말과 의미가 다른 하나를 고르시오.

> 방이 너무 어두워서 나는 책을 읽을 수 없었다.

① It was so dark in the room that I couldn't read books.
② Because it was so dark in the room, I couldn't read books.
③ It was dark enough in the room for me to read books.
④ It was too dark in the room for me to read books.
⑤ It was very dark in the room, so I wasn't able to read books.

15 다음 중 어법상 어색한 문장의 개수로 알맞은 것은?

> a. Kate not only runs fast but also jump high.
> b. Mike drinks a lot as well as eats a lot.
> c. She is such smart that she can make those decisions.
> d. This is not only an umbrella but also a coffee holder.
> e. It is useful enough making my life much easier.
> f. He was clever enough to understand the question.

① 1개 ② 2개 ③ 3개 ④ 4개 ⑤ 5개

16 주어진 문장과 같은 뜻이 되도록 'as well as'를 써서 바꿔 쓸 때 빈칸에 알맞은 말을 쓰시오.

> We communicate not only on the phone but also by email.
> = We communicate _____.

➡ _____

17 다음 우리말을 주어진 어휘를 이용하여 영어로 옮기시오.

(1) Ted는 나의 가방을 들어줄 만큼 충분히 친절했다. (kind, enough, carry)
➡ _____

(2) Vivian은 많은 돈을 저축할 만큼 충분히 열심히 일했다. (hard, to save, lots)
➡ _____

(3) 그 마당은 매우 커서 우리 모두 자전거를 탈 수 있다. (yard, so big, bikes, in)
➡ _____

18 다음 우리말을 영어로 바르게 옮긴 것은?

> Mary는 불을 끌 수 있을 정도로 키가 크다.

① Mary is tall enough to turn on the light.
② Mary is tall enough to turn off the light.
③ Mary is so tall that she can't turn off the light.
④ Mary is so tall that she can turn on the light.
⑤ Mary is too tall not to turn off the light.

Reading

[19~20] 다음 글을 읽고 물음에 답하시오.

Not only the winners' fun studies but also the ceremony for the Ig Nobel Prizes makes people laugh. There are a number of interesting things that keep people from getting bored. The opening and closing speeches are just two words each: "Welcome. Welcome." and "Goodbye. Goodbye." If someone talks for too long, an eight-year-old girl ⓐcalled Miss Sweetie Poo shouts repeatedly, "Please stop! I'm bored." Each winner receives ten trillion Zimbabwean dollars, which is worth less than one U.S. dollar. ⓑThrowing paper planes is another fun tradition.

19 위 글의 밑줄 친 ⓐcalled 앞에 생략된 말을 쓰시오.

➡ _____

20 아래 〈보기〉에서 위 글의 밑줄 친 ⓑThrowing과 문법적 쓰임이 같은 것의 개수를 고르시오.

┌─ 보기 ├─
① We stopped throwing paper planes.
② They are throwing paper planes.
③ Do you know the boys throwing paper planes?
④ They are fond of throwing paper planes.
⑤ I saw them throwing paper planes.
└──────────

① 1개　② 2개　③ 3개　④ 4개　⑤ 5개

[21~23] 다음 글을 읽고 물음에 답하시오.

"What happens when you walk backward while you are carrying a cup of coffee?" Han Jiwon, a Korean high school student, did research on this topic in 2015. (A)Is this research project good enough to win a Nobel Prize? Maybe not. But how about an Ig Nobel Prize? He won (B)one in 2017 for this fun research.

The Ig Nobel Prizes are awarded for discoveries that "first make (C)one laugh and then think." They were started in 1991 ⓐ_____ AIR magazine to increase people's interest in science ⓑ_____ honoring the unusual and the imaginative.

21 위 글의 빈칸 ⓐ와 ⓑ에 공통으로 들어갈 알맞은 전치사를 쓰시오.

➡ _____

22 다음 빈칸에 알맞은 단어를 넣어 위 글의 밑줄 친 (A)를 복문으로 고치시오.

➡ Is this research project _____ good _____ it _____ win a Nobel Prize?

23 아래 〈보기〉에서 위 글의 밑줄 친 (B)one, (C)one과 같은 의미로 쓰인 것을 각각 고르시오.

┌─ 보기 ├─
① One must obey one's parents.
② I'd like an ice cream. Are you having one, too?
③ One can be glad and sorry at the same time.
④ I don't have a pen. Can you lend me one?
⑤ Do you have a watch? — Yes, I have one.
└──────────

➡ (B) one: _____　(C) one: _____

[24~25] 다음 글을 읽고 물음에 답하시오.

Andre Geim also won an award that year. He succeeded in floating a live frog in the air by using magnets. "In my experience, if people don't have a sense of humor, they are usually not very good scientists," he said when he accepted his award.

If that still does not bring a smile to your face, how about this? In 2005, Gauri Nanda won the Ig Nobel Prize in Economics for inventing an alarm clock. It keeps running away until the sleeper ⓐfinally gets out of bed.

24 위 글의 밑줄 친 ⓐfinally와 바꿔 쓸 수 없는 말을 모두 고르시오.

① at last   ② in the end
③ above all   ④ at least
⑤ in the long run

25 다음 중 위 글에 대한 설명을 바르게 하지 못한 사람을 고르시오.

① 형규: Andre Geim은 자석을 사용해서 살아 있는 개구리를 공중에 띄울 수 있었어.

② 수희: Andre Geim에 따르면, 대체로 아주 훌륭한 과학자가 되려면 유머 감각이 필요하다고 해.

③ 민수: 2005년에 Gauri Nanda가 이그노벨상을 탔어.

④ 세진: 응, 자명종을 발명해서 이그노벨 경제학상을 받은 거야.

⑤ 나리: 그 자명종은 잠자는 사람이 깨어날 때까지 쫓아다닌대.

[26~28] 다음 글을 읽고 물음에 답하시오.

Umbrella for Coffee Lovers

This is the Umbrella for Coffee Lovers. You can use it not only ⓐas an umbrella but also as a cup holder. ⓑThis invention is useful enough to make your life much easier.

Magic Stairs

These are Magic Stairs. ⓒYou can use them not only for going up and down but also for storing things. This invention is useful enough to make your life much easier.

26 위 글의 밑줄 친 ⓐas와 같은 의미로 쓰인 것을 고르시오.

① As he is honest, he is trusted by everyone.
② This box will serve as a table.
③ Susan is not as pretty as Jane.
④ As I entered the room, they cried.
⑤ Her anger grew as she talked.

27 위 글의 밑줄 친 ⓑ를 복문으로 고치시오.

➡ _____

_____

28 다음 중 위 글의 밑줄 친 문장 ⓒ와 의미가 같지 않은 문장을 고르시오.

① You can use them not just for going up and down but also for storing things.
② You can use them not simply for going up and down but also for storing things.
③ You can use them for storing things as well as for going up and down.
④ You can use them not for going up and down but for storing things.
⑤ You can use them not only for going up and down but for storing things as well.

01 출제율 90%

다음 짝지어진 단어의 관계가 같도록 빈칸에 알맞은 말을 쓰시오.

> backward – forward : sink – _____

02 출제율 95%

다음 영영 풀이에 해당하는 단어는?

> a weapon made of material that will explode

① magnet   ② navy   ③ bomb
④ army   ⑤ science

03 출제율 100%

다음 대화를 읽고 B의 빈칸에 들어갈 말을 〈조건〉에 맞게 쓰시오.

> ┤ 보기 ├
> • 행운을 빌어주는 표현을 쓸 것.
> • 'leg'를 사용할 것.

> A: I'm going to enter the dance contest next week, but I'm worried about it.
> B: Don't worry. You'll do great. _____!
> A: Thank you.

➡ _____

[04~05] 다음 대화를 읽고 물음에 답하시오.

> Miso: We're going on a field trip next Tuesday. What are you going to do in the talent show, Jimin?
> Jimin: I'm going to talk like our teachers do in class and tell some jokes.
>
> (A) Will everyone like my show? I'm not sure.
> (B) Thank you, Miso. Let me show you one part of my act. Guess who? "Goood Jooob!"
> (C) Ha-ha, you sound like our English teacher.
> (D) Don't worry. I'm sure you'll do great. I'll keep my fingers crossed!
> (E) Wow! I'm really looking forward to it.
>
> Jimin: Do I? I'm going to show you more at the show.
> Miso: Great! You always make us laugh out loud.

04 출제율 100%

위 대화의 (A)~(E) 중 흐름상 네 번째 위치할 대화는?

① (A)   ② (B)   ③ (C)   ④ (D)   ⑤ (E)

05 출제율 90%

위 대화를 읽고 다음 질문에 영어로 답하시오.

> Q: What is Jimin going to do in the talent show?

➡ _____
_____

06 출제율 95%

다음 대화의 빈칸에 들어갈 말로 어색한 것은?

> A: I'm looking forward to the model airplane contest tomorrow. Are you ready?
> B: Well, I think so, but I'm nervous.
> A: You will do well. _____

① I'll keep my fingers crossed!
② Good luck!
③ Don't give up!
④ I wish you all the best.
⑤ Don't be worried.

07 대화에서 단어의 쓰임이 <u>어색한</u> 곳을 찾아 바르게 고치시오. (2개)

> B: This looks interesting. Is this a cutting board and a bird feeder?
> G: It is not only a cutting board but also a bird feeder. You can do one thing at the same time.
> B: That's a great idea!
> G: Do you really think so?
> B: Yes. I'm really looking forward to using it.

_____ ➡ _____ , _____ ➡ _____

[08~09] 다음 대화를 읽고 물음에 답하시오.

> G: Mom, I can't wait for the sports day.
> W: What are you going to do on that day, Minji?
> G: I'm going to play basketball for my class. We've practiced hard for a few weeks.
> W: Oh, I'm looking forward to your game.
> G: Actually, I'm a little worried. I'm afraid I'll make a mistake.
> W: Don't worry. You'll do a good job. _____ (A) _____!

08 위 대화의 빈칸 (A)에 들어갈 알맞은 말을 주어진 단어를 이용하여 쓰시오.

> (keep, fingers, crossed)

➡ _____

09 위 대화의 내용과 일치하지 <u>않는</u> 것은?

① They are talking about the sports day.
② Minji will play basketball for her class.
③ Minji is looking forward to the sports days.
④ Minji's mom is expecting to play basketball.
⑤ Minji is afraid she'll make a mistake.

10 다음 대화의 빈칸에 들어갈 말로 <u>어색한</u> 것은?

> (A) B: The winner of the Oh So Sweet award will get some candies.
> G: Oh, I want to get the prize.
> B: I'm sure you'll get the prize this time. _____, Jiu!
> (B) B: I'm looking forward to the Best Joker award this time.
> G: Ha-ha. You always make us laugh out loud. So you'll get the prize, Yunki. _____.
> B: Thank you.

① Good luck
② I knock on wood for you
③ I hope everything goes well with you
④ I'll keep my fingers crossed for you
⑤ I can't wait to get the prize

11 다음 문장에서 어법상 <u>어색한</u> 부분을 찾아 바르게 고치시오.

> You can use it not only putting on your back but also for controlling the TV.

_____ ➡ _____

12 다음 빈칸에 들어갈 말로 적절하지 <u>않은</u> 것을 고르시오.

> He gave me not _____ clothes but also money.

① only   ② just   ③ rather
④ simply   ⑤ merely

13 우리말과 같은 뜻이 되도록 괄호 안에 주어진 말과 'not only ~ but also ...'를 사용하여 한 문장으로 쓰시오. *출제율 90%*

(1) Tommy는 힘이 셀뿐만 아니라 현명하기도 해.
(strong, wise)

➡ _____

(2) 그녀는 지식뿐만 아니라 용기도 가지고 있다.
(knowledge, courage)

➡ _____

(3) 나는 춤추는 것뿐만 아니라 노래도 잘한다.
(good at, dancing, singing)

➡ _____

(4) 너뿐만 아니라 그도 그 영화를 보고 싶어 한다.
(want, see the movie)

➡ _____

[14~16] 다음 글을 읽고 물음에 답하시오.

"What happens when you walk backward while you are carrying a cup of coffee?" Han Jiwon, a Korean high school student, did research on ⓐthis topic in 2015. Is this research project good enough to win a Nobel Prize? Maybe not. But how about an Ig Nobel Prize? He won one in 2017 for this fun research.

The Ig Nobel Prizes are awarded for discoveries ⓑthat "first make one laugh and then think." ⓒThey were started in 1991 by _AIR_ magazine to increase people's interest in science by honoring the unusual and the imaginative.

14 위 글의 밑줄 친 ⓐthis topic이 가리키는 것을 본문에서 찾아 쓰시오. *출제율 90%*

➡ _____

_____

15 위 글의 밑줄 친 ⓑthat과 문법적 쓰임이 같은 것을 모두 고르시오. *출제율 95%*

① Look at that man over there.
② Who was the first man that came here?
③ The trouble is that we are short of money.
④ This is my sister and that is my cousin.
⑤ Is this the farm that they spoke of?

16 위 글의 밑줄 친 ⓒ를 능동태로 고치시오. *출제율 90%*

➡ _____

[17~18] 다음 글을 읽고 물음에 답하시오.

Andre Geim also won an award that year. He (A)succeeded in floating a live frog in the air by using magnets. "In my experience, if people don't have a sense of humor, they are usually not very good scientists," he said when he accepted his award.

If that still does not bring a smile to your face, how about this? In 2005, Gauri Nanda won the Ig Nobel Prize ⓐ_____ Economics ⓑ_____ inventing an alarm clock. It keeps running away until the sleeper finally gets out of bed.

17 위 글의 빈칸 ⓐ와 ⓑ에 들어갈 전치사가 바르게 짝지어진 것은? *출제율 95%*

	ⓐ	ⓑ		ⓐ	ⓑ
①	for	at	②	in	at
③	in	for	④	to	by
⑤	to	for			

18 위 글의 밑줄 친 (A)를 다음과 같이 바꿔 쓸 때, 빈칸에 들어갈 알맞은 단어를 쓰시오. *출제율 90%*

➡ was _____ in floating

[19~21] 다음 글을 읽고 물음에 답하시오.

	Since 1991
The 27th	First make one
Ig Nobel	laugh and
Prize Ceremony	then think

Thursday, September 14, 2017 6:00 PM
in Sanders Theater at Harvard University
Join us for the awarding of 10 new Ig Nobel Prizes
Winners of 2017:
Han Jiwon, Korea
"How to Carry Your Coffee"

출제율 100%

19 위 글의 종류로 알맞은 것을 고르시오.

① diary　　② summary　　③ article
④ invitation　　⑤ advertisement

출제율 90%

20 To win an Ig Nobel Prize, which is more important, making one laugh or making one think? Fill in the blanks (A) and (B) with suitable words.

> To win an Ig Nobel Prize, making one (A)_____ is more important than making one (B)_____.

출제율 95%

21 위 글을 읽고 답할 수 없는 질문을 고르시오.

① When was the Ig Nobel Prize started?
② What is the condition of winning the prize?
③ When will the ceremony be held?
④ Where will the ceremony be held?
⑤ Who will present the prizes?

[22~24] 다음 글을 읽고 물음에 답하시오.

Not only the winners' fun studies but also the ceremony for the Ig Nobel Prizes makes people laugh. There are a number of interesting things that ⓐkeep people from getting bored. The opening and closing speeches are just two words each: "Welcome. Welcome." and "Goodbye. Goodbye." If someone talks for too long, an eight-year-old girl called Miss Sweetie Poo shouts repeatedly, "Please stop! I'm bored." Each winner receives ten trillion Zimbabwean dollars, which is worth less than one U.S. dollar. ⓑThrowing paper planes is another fun tradition.

출제율 90%

22 위 글의 밑줄 친 ⓐkeep과 바꿔 쓸 수 있는 말을 모두 고르시오.

① stop　　② prevent　　③ prohibit
④ allow　　⑤ encourage

출제율 95%

23 밑줄 친 ⓑ를 다음과 같이 바꿔 쓸 때 빈칸에 들어갈 알맞은 말을 두 단어로 쓰시오.

➡ It is another fun tradition _____ _____ paper planes.

출제율 100%

24 According to the passage, which is NOT true?

① The winners' fun studies make people laugh.
② The ceremony for the Ig Nobel Prizes also makes people laugh.
③ There are many interesting things that keep people interested.
④ The opening speeches are just four words: "Welcome. Welcome." and "Goodbye. Goodbye."
⑤ Miss Sweetie Poo is eight years old.

01 다음 대화의 우리말에 맞게 주어진 단어를 활용하여 영어로 쓰시오.

> G: Mom, are you coming to the sports day?
>
> W: Sure. I'm going to play the game Kick a Shoe. This will be the first time for me to try it.
>
> G: Don't worry. I'm sure you'll do great. I'll keep my fingers crossed for you!
>
> W: Thank you. I'm also going to perform a funny dance with some other mothers.
>
> G: That sounds fun. <u>무대에 선 엄마 모습을 보는 것이 기대돼요.</u> (I'm / look / watch / on the stage)

➡ _____

02 다음 대화를 읽고 요약문을 완성하시오.

> A: We're going on a field trip next Tuesday. What are you going to do in the talent show, Jimin?
>
> B: I'm going to talk like our teachers do in class and tell some jokes.
>
> A: Wow! I'm really looking forward to it.
>
> B: Will everyone like my show? I'm not sure.
>
> A: Don't worry. I'm sure you'll do great. I'll keep my fingers crossed!
>
> B: Thank you, Miso. Let me show you one part of my act. Guess who? "Goood Jooob!"
>
> A: Ha-ha, you sound like our English teacher.
>
> B: Do I? I'm going to show you more at the show.
>
> A: Great! You always make us laugh out loud.

> Jimin and Miso are talking about the _____. Jimin is going to _____ their teachers do in class and _____. Miso is _____ his show.

03 대화의 흐름상 빈칸에 들어갈 문장을 〈조건〉에 맞게 쓰시오.

> W: Soyun, are you going to take part in any races on the sports day?
>
> G: Sure. I'm going to run a 100 meter race at the end of the day.
>
> W: Wow, _____
>
> G: But, Mom, I'm not sure I'll win the race.
>
> W: Just do your best. I'll keep my fingers crossed!

┤ 조건 ├
- 진행형을 이용하여 '기대를 표현하는 말'을 쓸 것.
- look / see / you / at the race를 사용할 것.

➡ _____

04 다음 글에서 어법상 틀린 곳의 기호를 쓰고 바르게 고쳐 쓰시오. (3개)

> **The Nobel Prize**
>
> The Nobel Prize (a)<u>named</u> after Alfred Nobel, a Swedish scientist. It (b)<u>is awarded</u> to people who (c)<u>has</u> done great work for the world.
>
> The Curie family (d)<u>received</u> the Nobel Prize three times. Not only Marie Curie but also her daughter (e)<u>were awarded</u> the Nobel Prize.

➡ _____

"What happens when you walk backward while you are carrying a cup of coffee?" Han Jiwon, a Korean high school student, did research on this topic in 2015. Is this research project good enough to win a Nobel Prize? Maybe not. ⓐBut how about an Ig Nobel Prize? He won one in 2017 for this fun research.

The Ig Nobel Prizes are awarded for discoveries that "first make one laugh and then think." They were started in 1991 by *AIR* magazine to increase people's interest in science by honoring ⓑ특이하고 창의적인 사람들.

05 위 글의 밑줄 친 ⓐ를 다음과 같이 바꿔 쓸 때 빈칸에 들어갈 알맞은 말을 두 단어로 쓰시오.

➡ But is this research project _____ _____ to win an Ig Nobel Prize?

06 위 글의 밑줄 친 ⓑ의 우리말에 맞게 주어진 단어를 사용하여 5 단어로 영작하시오. (unusual, imaginative)

➡ _____

07 다음 빈칸 (A)와 (B)에 알맞은 단어를 넣어 the Ig Nobel Prizes에 대한 소개를 완성하시오.

> *AIR* magazine started them in 1991 for the purpose of increasing people's interest in science. If a discovery first makes one (A)_____ and then (B)_____, it can award the prize.

Not only the winners' fun studies but also the ceremony for the Ig Nobel Prizes (A)[make / makes] people laugh. ⓐ사람들이 지루하지 않도록 하는 재미있는 것들이 많이 있다. The opening and closing speeches are just two words each: "Welcome. Welcome." and "Goodbye. Goodbye." If someone talks for too long, an eight-year-old girl called Miss Sweetie Poo shouts repeatedly, "Please stop! I'm bored." Each winner receives ten trillion Zimbabwean dollars, which (B)[is / are] worth less than one U.S. dollar. Throwing paper planes (C)[is / are] another fun tradition.

08 위 글의 괄호 (A)~(C)에서 어법상 알맞은 낱말을 골라 쓰시오.

➡ (A) _____ (B) _____ (C) _____

09 위 글의 밑줄 친 ⓐ의 우리말에 맞게 주어진 어휘를 이용하여 13 단어로 영작하시오.

> a number of, keep, bored

➡ _____
_____

10 What is the closing speech of the Ig Nobel Prizes? Answer in English in a full sentence. (4 words)

➡ _____

01 〈보기〉의 (A)는 기대를 표현하는 대화이고, (B)는 기원을 표현하는 대화이다. 〈보기〉를 보고 (A), (B)의 표현을 써서 대화를 완성하시오.

(A)	(B)
• travel to Jejudo	• have a basketball game
• go camping with my parents	• enter the dance contest
• club festival	• join the invention contest
• see a musical	• have an important meeting

┤ 보기 ├

(A) A: I'm going to travel to Jejudo next week.

   B: Wow! That sounds great.

   A: Yeah, I'm really looking forward to it.

(B) A: I'm going to enter the dance contest next week, but I'm worried about it.

   B: Don't worry. You'll do great. I'll keep my fingers crossed.

   A: Thank you.

02 〈보기〉에 주어진 표현을 사용하여 'not only ~ but also ...' 또는 'enough to부정사'의 문장을 쓰시오.

┤ 보기 ├

understand the novel	buy the building	speak English	speak Chinese
interested in basketball	interested in volleyball	watch the drama	play the game

rich   clever   young   old   careful   foolish   cheap   expensive

(1) _____

(2) _____

(3) _____

(4) _____

단원별 모의고사

01 다음 단어에 대한 영어 설명이 어색한 것은?

① backward: looking or facing in the direction that is behind you

② imaginative: having or showing new and exciting ideas

③ live: not dead

④ million: the number 1,000,000,000,000

⑤ university: an educational institution of learning of the highest level

02 다음 짝지어진 단어의 관계가 같도록 빈칸에 알맞은 말을 쓰시오.

> happy – happiness : eager – _____

03 다음 영영풀이에 해당하는 단어를 고르시오.

> to achieve something that you planned to do

① reach ② accept ③ succeed
④ fill ⑤ throw

[04~05] 다음 대화의 빈칸에 들어갈 말로 알맞은 것을 고르시오.

04

> A: I'm going to enter the dance contest next week, but I'm worried about it.
> B: _____ I'll keep my fingers crossed.
> A: Thank you.

① Why don't you practice dancing hard?
② Don't worry. You'll do great.
③ Who will take part in the dance contest?
④ I'm looking forward to it.
⑤ Wow! That sounds great.

05

> B: _____ award this time.
> G: Ha-ha. You always make us laugh out loud. So you'll get the prize, Yunki. Good luck.
> B: Thank you.

① I'm looking forward to the Best Joker
② I'm looking forward to the Class Brain
③ I'm looking forward to Oh So Sweet
④ I'm looking forward to the Ms. Cheerful
⑤ I'm looking forward to the Best Note Keeper

06 다음 중 짝지어진 대화가 어색한 것은?

① A: These are special shoes. I hope to win a prize with this invention.
B: I'm sure you will.

② A: I'm looking forward to the funny dance contest tomorrow. Are you ready?
B: Well, I think so, but I'm nervous.

③ A: I'm going to enter the photo contest tomorrow.
B: Are you? I'll keep my fingers crossed!

④ A: I'm going to go camping with my parents next week.
B: Wow! That sounds great.

⑤ A: Minho always makes us laugh out loud.
B: Don't worry. You'll do great. I'll keep my fingers crossed.

07 대화의 흐름상 밑줄 친 ①~⑤ 중 어휘의 쓰임이 어색한 것은?

G: Mom, I ①can't wait for the sports day.

W: What are you going to do on that day, Minji?

G: I'm going to play basketball for my class. We've ②practiced hard for a few weeks.

W: Oh, ③I'm looking forward to your game.

G: Actually, ④I'm little worried. I'm afraid I'll make a mistake.

W: Don't worry. You'll do a good job. I'll ⑤keep my fingers crossed!

①   ②   ③   ④   ⑤

[08~09] 다음 대화를 읽고 물음에 답하시오.

G: Mom, are you coming to the sports day?

W: Sure. I'm going to play the game Kick a Shoe. (①) This will be the first time for me to try it. (②)

G: Don't worry. I'm sure you'll do great. I'll keep my fingers ___(A)___ (cross) for you! (③)

W: Thank you. (④)

G: That sounds fun. (⑤) I'm looking forward to ___(B)___ (watch) you on the stage.

08 위 대화의 (①)~(⑤) 중 주어진 문장이 들어갈 위치로 알맞은 곳은?

I'm also going to perform a funny dance with some other mothers.

①   ②   ③   ④   ⑤

09 위 대화의 (A)와 (B)에 주어진 단어를 알맞은 형태로 쓰시오.

➡ (A) _____ (B) _____

[10~12] 다음 대화를 읽고 물음에 답하시오.

Miso: We're going on a field trip next Tuesday. What are you going to do in the talent show, Jimin?

Jimin: I'm going to talk like our teachers (A)do in class and tell some jokes.

Miso: Wow! I'm really looking forward to it.

Jimin: Will everyone like my show? I'm not sure.

Miso: Don't worry. I'm sure you'll do great. I'll keep my fingers crossed!

Jimin: Thank you, Miso. Let me show you one part of my act. Guess who? "Goood Jooob!"

Miso: Ha-ha, you sound like our English teacher.

Jimin: (B)Do I? I'm going to show you more at the show.

Miso: Great! You always make us laugh out loud.

10 위 대화의 내용과 일치하도록 Jimin의 장기 자랑 계획을 영어로 쓰시오. (to부정사로 문장을 시작하시오.)

➡ Jimin's Plan for the Talent Show

(1) _____

(2) _____

11 위 대화의 밑줄 친 (A)의 'do'가 의미하는 바로 알맞은 것은?

① teach   ② like   ③ talk
④ make   ⑤ go

12 위 대화의 밑줄 친 (B)의 'Do I?'를 완전한 문장으로 쓰시오.

➡ _____

[13~15] 괄호 안에 주어진 표현을 사용하여 우리말을 영어로 완성하시오.

13 (as well as, nice)

A: I think Pinocchio is popular. What do you think?
B: 그는 친절할 뿐만 아니라 인기 있어.

➡ _____

14 (both ~ and ..., lovely)

A: I think Rapunzel is very beautiful. What do you think?
B: 그녀는 예쁘고 사랑스러워.

➡ _____

15 (neither ~ nor ···, creative)

A: I think Ms. Marple is very smart. What do you think?
B: 그녀는 똑똑하지도 창의적이지도 않아.

➡ _____

16 다음 중 어법상 어색한 문장을 고르시오.

① This hall is big enough to hold 1,000 people.
② Mr. Kim is old enough to drive a car.
③ Jimin was smart enough to solve the difficult problem.
④ Sue sings not only beautifully but also happy.
⑤ He teaches not just English but science.

17 다음 두 문장을 한 문장으로 바르게 옮긴 것을 모두 고르시오.

- The lake is deep.
- You can't swim in the lake.

① The lake is so deep that you can't swim in the lake.
② The lake is so deep for you to swim in the lake.
③ The lake is too deep for you to swim in the lake.
④ The lake is too deep for you to swim in.
⑤ The lake is so deep that you can't swim in.

18 다음 중 어법상 <u>어색한</u> 문장의 개수로 알맞은 것은?

> a. You can use it not only for holding paper but also to put your phone on it.
> b. She not only sang well but also dance perfectly.
> c. The cat was not only tired but also hungry.
> d. This water is so clean that we could drink it.
> e. Her voice was loud enough to wake the boy up.

① 1개 ② 2개 ③ 3개 ④ 4개 ⑤ 5개

[19~22] 두 문장이 같은 뜻이 되도록 괄호 안의 어구를 사용하여 문장을 쓰시오.

19 We were so brave that we faced the strong enemy. (enough to)

➡ _____

_____

20 Ted is old enough to talk about the topic. (so ... that ~ can)

➡ _____

_____

21 He has experience as well as knowledge. (not only ~ but also ...)

➡ _____

_____

22 I must not only feed the animals but also look after the children. (as well as)

➡ _____

_____

23 다음 문장에서 밑줄 친 우리말을 영어로 옮기시오.

> You can use it not only for (1)피자를 자르기 (2)피자 한 조각을 집기 위해서도.

➡ (1) _____
(2) _____

24 주어진 〈보기〉를 참고하여 두 문장을 하나의 문장으로 쓰시오.

> ┤ 보기 ├
> You like the movie.
> + Eric likes the movie, too.
> → Not only you but also Eric likes the movie.

(1) She has to leave here.
+ You have to leave here, too.

➡ _____

_____

(2) I like to play with dogs.
+ My brothers like to play with dogs, too.

➡ _____

_____

(3) I am from Busan.
+ My best friend is from Busan, too.

➡ _____

_____

[25~26] 다음 글을 읽고 물음에 답하시오.

"What happens when you walk backward while you are carrying a cup of coffee?" Han Jiwon, a Korean high school student, did research on this topic in 2015. Is this research project good enough to win a Nobel Prize? Maybe not. But how about an Ig Nobel Prize? He won ⓐone in 2017 for ⓑthis fun research. ⓒThe Ig Nobel Prizes are awarded for discoveries that "first makes one laugh and then think." They were started in 1991 by *AIR* magazine to increase people's interest in science by honoring the unusual and the imaginative.

25 위 글의 밑줄 친 ⓐone이 가리키는 것을 본문에서 찾아 쓰고, ⓑthis fun research의 조사 내용을 우리말로 쓰시오.

➡ ⓐ _____

　ⓑ _____

26 위 글의 밑줄 친 ⓒ에서 어법상 틀린 부분을 찾아 고치시오.

_____ ➡ _____

[27~28] 다음 글을 읽고 물음에 답하시오.

The prizes are presented by real Nobel winners in Sanders Theater at Harvard University. The room is usually filled with people who are eager ⓐto cheer for the brave scientists with their "laughable" research.

The U.K. Navy won the Ig Nobel Prize for Peace in 2000. To save money, the Navy made its sailors shout, "Bang!" instead of using real bombs. Is that funny enough for you to laugh out loud?

27 아래 <보기>에서 위 글의 밑줄 친 ⓐto cheer와 to부정사의 용법이 같은 것의 개수를 고르시오.

　　┤ 보기 ├
① To hear him talk, you would take him for a fool.
② My plan is to go to the movies tonight.
③ The mother was pleased to see her son well.
④ He didn't live to see the work finished.
⑤ What a fool she is to believe such a thing!

① 1개　② 2개　③ 3개　④ 4개　⑤ 5개

28 According to the passage, which is NOT true?

① The prizes are presented by real Ig Nobel winners.
② The prizes are presented in Sanders Theater at Harvard University.
③ People who are eager to cheer for the brave scientists with their "laughable" research usually fill the room.
④ The U.K. Navy won the Ig Nobel Prize for Peace in 2000.
⑤ To save money, the Navy made its sailors shout, "Bang!" instead of using real bombs.

[29~30] 다음 글을 읽고 물음에 답하시오.

Andre Geim also won an award that year. He succeeded in floating a live frog in the air by using magnets. "In my experience, if people don't have a sense of humor, they are usually not very good scientists," he said when he accepted his award.

If that still does not bring a smile to your face, how about this? In 2005, Gauri Nanda won the Ig Nobel Prize in Economics for inventing an alarm clock. It keeps running away until the sleeper finally gets out of bed.

29 본문의 내용과 일치하도록 다음 빈칸에 알맞은 단어들을 쓰시오.

> According to Andre Geim, _____ _____ _____ _____ is usually a necessary condition to be a very good scientist.

30 다음 빈칸 (A)와 (B)에 알맞은 단어를 넣어 Gauri Nanda에 대한 소개를 완성하시오.

> Gauri Nanda won the Ig Nobel Prize in Economics in 2005 because she invented (A)_____ _____ _____ which the sleeper can stop only after he or she finally (B)_____ _____ _____ _____.

[31~32] 다음 글을 읽고 물음에 답하시오.

Not only the winners' fun studies but also the ceremony for the Ig Nobel Prizes makes people laugh. ⓐThere are the number of interesting things that keeps people from getting bored. The opening and closing speeches are just two words each: "Welcome. Welcome." and "Goodbye. Goodbye." If someone talks for too long, an eight-year-old girl called Miss Sweetie Poo shouts repeatedly, "Please stop! I'm bored." Each winner receives ten trillion Zimbabwean dollars, ⓑ그것은 미국의 1달러보다 가치가 낮다. Throwing paper planes is another fun tradition.

31 위 글의 밑줄 친 ⓐ에서 어법상 틀린 부분을 찾아 고치시오. (두 군데)

_____ ➡ _____

_____ ➡ _____

32 위 글의 밑줄 친 ⓑ의 우리말에 맞게 주어진 어휘를 알맞게 배열하시오.

> one U.S. dollar / worth / than / which / less / is

➡ _____

Dreaming of My Future

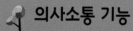 **의사소통 기능**

- 슬픔, 불만족, 실망의 원인에 대해 묻기
  Why are you disappointed?

- 충고 구하기
  Do you think I should keep trying?

 언어 형식

- 분사구문
  Hearing this, I felt really sorry for her.

- 관계대명사 'what'
  That's **what** I need to learn from her.

Words & Expressions

Key Words

- **a white school** 백인학교
- **ability** [əbíləti] 명 능력
- **accept** [æksépt] 동 받아들이다
- **African-American** 명 아프리카계 미국인
- **against** [əgénst] 전 ~에 반대하여, ~에 맞서
- **allow** [əláu] 동 허락하다
- **as** [æz] 전 ~처럼
- **audition** [ɔ:díʃən] 명 오디션
- **baker** [béikər] 명 제빵사
- **career** [kəríər] 명 직업, 직장 생활
- **case** [keis] 명 소송 사건
- **character** [kǽriktər] 명 등장인물
- **colored** [kʌ́lərd] 형 색깔이 있는, 유색 인종의
- **competition** [kàmpətíʃən] 명 대회, 시합
- **control** [kəntróul] 동 조종하다
- **cook** [kuk] 명 요리사
- **courage** [kə́:ridʒ] 명 용기
- **decorate** [dékərèit] 동 장식하다
- **disappointed** [dìsəpɔ́intid] 형 실망한
- **engineer** [èndʒiníər] 명 기술자, 엔지니어
- **expert** [ékspə:rt] 명 전문가
- **face** [feis] 동 (상황에) 직면하다
- **figure** [fígjər] 명 (중요한) 인물, 거물, 숫자, 피규어(모형 장난감)
- **grade** [greid] 명 성적
- **hanger** [hǽŋər] 명 옷걸이
- **hidden** [hídn] 형 숨겨진, 비밀의

- **impress** [imprés] 동 감명을 주다, 깊은 인상을 주다
- **install** [instɔ́:l] 동 설치하다
- **job festival** 진로 박람회, 직업 설명회
- **judge** [dʒʌdʒ] 명 판사
- **later** [léitər] 부 나중에, 후에
- **laughter** [lǽftər] 명 웃음(소리)
- **line** [lain] 명 (연극, 영화 등의) 대사
- **lose** [lu:z] 동 지다, 패배하다
- **magic trick** 마술 묘기
- **magician** [mədʒíʃən] 명 마술사
- **manager** [mǽnidʒər] 명 관리자, 경영자
- **match** [mætʃ] 명 시합, 경기
- **matter** [mǽtər] 동 중요하다, 문제가 되다
- **offer** [ɔ́:fər] 명 제의, 제안
- **permission** [pərmíʃən] 명 허락
- **presentation** [prèzəntéiʃən] 명 발표
- **programmer** [próugræmər] 명 프로그래머
- **recognize** [rékəgnàiz] 동 알아보다, 인정하다
- **record** [rékɔ:rd] 명 기록
- **reporter** [ripɔ́:rtər] 명 기자
- **rocket** [rákit] 명 로켓
- **space** [speis] 명 우주
- **speech** [spi:tʃ] 명 연설, 말
- **tip** [tip] 명 조언
- **useful** [júːsfəl] 형 유용한
- **Your Honor** 판사님, 재판장님

Key Expressions

- **a little** 약간, 조금
- **be afraid of** ~을 두려워하다
- **be against** ~에 반대하다
- **break down** ~을 부수다
- **get over** ~을 극복하다
- **get upset** 기분이 상하다
- **give permission** 허가하다
- **give up** 포기하다
- **have no choice but to** ~할 수밖에 없다
- **How about -ing?** ~하는 것이 어때?
- **keep ~ in mind** ~을 명심하다

- **keep -ing** 계속 ~하다
- **laugh at** ~을 비웃다
- **look down** 우울해 보이다
- **make a suggestion** 제안하다
- **prepare for** ~을 준비하다
- **set a goal** 목표를 정하다
- **stand up for** ~을 옹호하다, 지지하다
- **take a class** 수업을 받다
- **Take it easy.** 걱정하지 마., 진정해.
- **thanks to** ~ 덕분에
- **Why don't you ~?** ~하는 게 어때?

Word Power

※ 서로 비슷한 뜻을 가진 어휘

- □ **ability** 능력 : **capability** 능력
- □ **competition** 대회, 시합 : **match** 시합
- □ **hidden** 숨겨진, 비밀의 : **veiled** 숨겨진
- □ **recognize** 알아보다 : **perceive** 인식하다

- □ **allow** 허락하다 : **permit** 허락하다
- □ **courage** 용기 : **bravery** 용기
- □ **matter** 중요하다 : **count** 중요하다
- □ **reporter** 기자 : **journalist** 기자

※ 서로 반대의 뜻을 가진 어휘

- □ **accept** 받아들이다 ↔ **reject** 거절하다
- □ **colored** 유색 인종의 ↔ **white** 백인의
- □ **expert** 전문가 ↔ **novice** 초보자
- □ **lose** 지다, 패배하다 ↔ **win** 이기다
- □ **useful** 유용한 ↔ **useless** 쓸모없는

- □ **allow** 허락하다 ↔ **forbid** 금지하다
- □ **courage** 용기 ↔ **cowardice** 비겁함
- □ **install** 설치하다 ↔ **remove** 제거하다
- □ **permission** 허락 ↔ **prohibition** 금지

※ 동사 – 명사

- □ **accept** 받아들이다 – **acceptance** 수용
- □ **compete** 경쟁하다 – **competition** 대회, 시합
- □ **impress** 깊은 인상을 주다 – **impression** 인상
- □ **prepare** 준비하다 – **preparation** 준비

- □ **allow** 허락하다 – **allowance** 허용
- □ **decorate** 장식하다 – **decoration** 장식
- □ **permit** 허가하다 – **permission** 허락
- □ **recognize** 인정하다 – **recognition** 인식

English Dictionary

- □ **allow** 허락하다
  → to let someone do something
  어떤 사람이 무엇을 하도록 내버려 두다

- □ **career** 직업, 직장 생활
  → the series of jobs that you do during your working life 직장 생활 동안 하는 일련의 직업

- □ **colored** 유색 인종의
  → of a race other than white 백인종을 제외한 인종의

- □ **courage** 용기
  → the ability to control your fear in a dangerous or difficult situation
  위험하거나 어려운 상황에서 두려움을 조절하는 능력

- □ **engineer** 기술자, 엔지니어
  → a person who designs, builds, or maintains machines
  기계를 설계하고, 만들고 또는 유지하는 사람

- □ **expert** 전문가
  → a person with a high level of knowledge or skill in a particular area
  어떤 특정한 분야에서 높은 수준의 지식 또는 기술을 가진 사람

- □ **face** (상황에) 직면하다
  → to deal with a difficult situation 어려운 상황을 처리하다

- □ **figure** (중요한) 인물, 거물
  → a well-known person 잘 알려진 사람

- □ **hidden** 숨겨진, 비밀의
  → not easy to find 찾기가 쉽지 않은

- □ **judge** 판사
  → the person in a court who decides how criminals should be punished
  법정에서 범죄자들이 어떻게 처벌 받아야 하는지를 결정하는 사람

- □ **laughter** 웃음(소리)
  → the act or sound of laughing 웃는 행동 또는 소리

- □ **manager** 관리자, 경영자
  → a person who is responsible for controlling an organization 조직을 통제할 책임이 있는 사람

- □ **permission** 허락
  → the action of allowing someone to do something
  누군가에게 무엇을 하도록 허용해 주는 행위

- □ **space** 우주
  → the region beyond the Earth's atmosphere or beyond the solar system
  지구의 대기 또는 태양계 너머의 지역

서답형

01 다음 글의 빈칸에 〈영어 설명〉에 맞게 두 단어로 쓰시오.

> They _____ me when I made a mistake.
> <영어 설명> to show that you think someone or something is stupid

중요

02 다음 빈칸에 공통으로 들어갈 말로 가장 적절한 것은?

> • The _____ sentenced him to three years in prison.
> • It's very wrong to _____ people by their skin color.

① cook   ② judge
③ report   ④ grade
⑤ expert

[03~04] 다음 설명에 해당하는 단어를 고르시오.

03

> the region beyond the Earth's atmosphere or beyond the solar system

① permission   ② rocket
③ engineer   ④ university
⑤ space

중요

04

> the ability to control your fear in a dangerous or difficult situation

① programmer   ② peace
③ courage   ④ permission
⑤ laughter

서답형

05 다음 우리말에 맞게 주어진 단어를 이용하여 쓰시오.

> 그는 실패를 두려워하지 않을 만큼 충분히 대담했다. (afraid)

➡ He was bold enough not to _____ failure.

06 다음 빈칸에 들어갈 말이 바르게 짝지어진 것은?

> (A) Did you _____ the new program on your computer?
> (B) The dancer _____ her teacher with her excellent dance skills.

① offer – faced
② offer – recognized
③ install – impressed
④ break down – allowed
⑤ install – offered

서답형

07 다음 짝지어진 단어의 관계가 같도록 알맞은 말을 쓰시오.

> accept – acceptance : allow – _____

중요

08 다음 빈칸에 공통으로 들어갈 말로 알맞은 것은?

> (A) Walt Disney is an important cultural _____ in history.
> (B) The _____ is lower than the OECD average of $6,741.

① figure   ② match
③ programmer   ④ laughter
⑤ suggestion

01 〈보기〉에서 알맞은 단어를 선택하여 문장의 빈칸을 완성하시오. (필요하면 변형하고 단어를 추가하여 쓰시오.)

┌─ 보기 ─┐
later   thank   laugh   engineer
└──────┘

(1) _____ his brother's advice, Minho could become a doctor.
(2) How many _____ designed this bridge?
(3) _____, the poor boy became the President.
(4) I believe that _____ is the best medicine.

02 대화의 빈칸에 〈영영풀이〉에 해당하는 단어를 주어진 철자로 쓰시오.

┌─────────────────────────┐
A: Why are you d_____?
B: I lost the tennis game. Do you think I should practice harder?
A: Yes, I think so.
└─────────────────────────┘

┌─────────────────────────┐
<영영풀이> sad because something is not as good as you expected, or because something did not happen
└─────────────────────────┘

➡ _____

03 다음 우리말과 같도록 문장의 빈칸에 주어진 철자로 시작하는 한 단어를 쓰시오.

(1) 그런 상황에서, 어떻게 미래 직업을 준비할 수 있는가?
➡ In such conditions, how should one prepare for his or her future c_____?

(2) 어쨌든 우주에는 숨겨진 보석이 있었다.
➡ There was a h_____ gem in the universe after all.

(3) 세계는 한글이 매우 독창적이고 과학적이라고 인정합니다.
➡ The world r_____ that Hangul is very unique and scientific.

04 영영풀이에 해당하는 단어를 〈보기〉에서 찾아 첫 번째 빈칸에 쓰고, 두 번째 빈칸에는 우리말 뜻을 쓰시오.

┌─ 보기 ─┐
permission   expert   manager   face
└──────┘

(1) _____ : to deal with a difficult situation: _____
(2) _____ : a person with a high level of knowledge or skill in a particular area: _____
(3) _____ : the action of allowing someone to do something: _____
(4) _____ : a person who is responsible for controlling an organization: _____

05 빈칸에 주어진 철자로 시작하는 알맞은 단어를 쓰시오.

(1) Do you have your own way to g_____ over the cold?
(2) One eighth of the whole population in the U.S. was c_____ slaves.
(3) A spelling bee is a spelling c_____ in the U.S.

Conversation

1 슬픔, 불만족, 실망의 원인에 대해 묻기

• **Why are you disappointed?** 너는 왜 실망하고 있니?

■ 'Why are you disappointed?(너는 왜 실망하고 있니?)'는 실망하고 있는 상대방에게 그 이유를 묻는 표현이다. 상대방이 뭔가에 불만족하거나 실망하고 있는 것을 보고 사용하는 표현으로, 그 원인을 물을 때 'What's the matter (with you)?(무슨 일 있니?)'라고 물을 수 있다.

■ 'Why are you disappointed?'처럼 상대방의 걱정, 슬픔이나 불만족, 실망의 원인에 대해 물을 때 사용되는 일반적인 표현으로 'What's the matter (with ~)?'가 쓰이며 '무슨 일 있니?'라는 뜻으로 다음 표현으로 바꿔 쓸 수 있다. (What's wrong? = What's the problem? = Is there anything wrong? = What happened? = Why the long face?)

■ 걱정이나 두려움을 나타내는 표현으로는 'be anxious about ~(~에 대해 걱정하다)', 'be worried about ~', 'be concerned about ~(~에 대해 걱정이다)' 등이 있고, 상대방의 걱정, 염려, 슬픔, 불만족, 실망에 대해, Don't worry. / I'm sorry to hear that. / That's too bad. / Cheer up! 등과 같은 위로하는 표현을 쓸 수 있다.

슬픔, 불만족, 실망의 원인에 대해 묻는 표현

• Why are you disappointed? 너는 왜 실망하고 있니?

• What's the matter? 무슨 문제가 있니?

• What's wrong? 뭐가 잘못되었니?

• What's the problem? 무슨 문제 있니?

• Why the long face? 왜 그렇게 우울한 얼굴이니?

• What makes you sad/depressed/disappointed? 무엇 때문에 슬프니/우울하니/실망했니?

• Is there anything wrong? 잘못된 일 있니?

핵심 Check

1. 다음 밑줄 친 (A) 대신 쓰기에 적절하지 <u>않은</u> 것은?

G: You look down today. (A) <u>What's the matter?</u>

B: I want to take dance classes, but my father doesn't like that idea. He thinks that boys should play sports.

G: I'm sorry to hear that.

① Why are you disappointed? ② What matters the most?
③ What's wrong? ④ What's the problem?
⑤ Why the long face?

② 충고 구하기

• **Do you think I should keep trying?** 너는 내가 계속 노력해야 한다고 생각하니?

■ 'Do you think I should ~?(너는 내가 ~해야 한다고 생각하니?)'는 상대방으로부터 충고를 구하는 표현이다. 이 질문에 대해 'Yes.'나 'No.'로 대답한 후, '(I think) You should[had better] ~(내 생각에는 ~해야 해.)', 'Why don't you ~?(~하는 것이 어떠니?)', 'How[What] about -ing?(~하는 것이 어떨까?)' 등과 같이 부연해서 조언해 줄 수 있다.

충고를 구하는 표현

• Do you think I'd better ~? 너는 내가 ~해야 한다고 생각하니?

• If you were me, would you ~? 네가 나라면 너는 ~할 거니?

• What would you do if you were in my shoes? 네가 내 입장이라면 너는 무엇을 할래?

• What should I do? 내가 무엇을 해야 할까?

• What do you think I should do? 너는 내가 무엇을 해야 한다고 생각하니?

• What would you advise me to do? 너는 나에게 무엇을 하라고 충고할 거니?

■ 실망하거나 낙담한 상대방에게 처음부터 조언이나 충고를 하는 것보다는 위로나 위안의 말을 먼저 건네는 것이 더 자연스러운 대화가 될 수 있다.

위로 · 위안의 표현

• Come on. 힘 내.

• Take it easy. 진정해.

• I'm sorry to hear that. 그 말을 들으니 유감이다.

• Everything will be fine. 다 잘 될 거야.

핵심 Check

2. 다음 대화의 내용으로 보아, 빈칸에 들어가기에 적절한 것은?

G: Why are you disappointed?

B: I'm preparing for the ski competition, but my record is not good. _____

G: I think you should keep practicing more. I'm sure you'll get better and better.

① What's the matter?　　　　② I'm sorry to hear that.

③ What would you do?　　　　④ Will you do me a favor?

⑤ What should I do?

Step Up – Real-life Scene

Jisu: ❶Why are you so disappointed, Ryan?

Ryan: My parents won't ❷let me enter Superstar 101, a singing competition.

Jisu: ❸I'm sorry to hear that. Why are they against it?

Ryan: ❹They want me to study hard and be a doctor. ❺They're always worried about my grades.

Jisu: Did you tell your parents you really want to be a singer?

Ryan: Not yet. ❻Do you think I should talk with them about it?

Jisu: Yes. Just show them ❼how much you love singing. ❽Why don't you sing the songs you made in front of them?

Ryan: Okay. I'll try. Thank you for your advice, Jisu.

지수: 너는 왜 그렇게 실망하고 있니, Ryan?

Ryan: 부모님은 내가 노래 경연 대회인 슈퍼스타 101에 참가하는 걸 허락하지 않으실 거야.

지수: 그 말을 들으니 유감이구나. 왜 부모님은 그것에 반대하시니?

Ryan: 부모님은 내가 열심히 공부해서 의사가 되기를 원하셔. 항상 내 성적을 걱정하시지.

지수: 부모님께 네가 정말로 가수가 되고 싶다고 말씀드렸니?

Ryan: 아니 아직. 너는 내가 부모님께 그것에 대해 말씀드려야 한다고 생각하니?

지수: 응. 그냥 부모님께 네가 얼마나 노래 부르는 것을 좋아하는지 보여 드려. 부모님 앞에서 네가 만든 노래를 부르는 건 어때?

Ryan: 알았어. 시도해 볼게. 조언해 줘서 고마워, 지수야.

❶ 'disappoint'는 '실망시키다'라는 뜻의 동사로 사람이 실망한 것은 과거분사 'disappointed'를 사용한다.
❷ '사역동사+목적어+동사원형'의 형태로 '…이 ~하도록 허락하다'라는 뜻이다.
❸ 상대방의 좋지 않은 일에 대해 유감을 표현하는 말이다.
❹ '동사(want)+목적어(me)+목적보어(to부정사)'의 5형식 구문으로 '…가 ~하기를 원하다'로 해석한다.
❺ 'be worried about'은 '~에 관해 걱정하다'라는 뜻이다.
❻ 'Do you think I should ~?(너는 내가 ~해야 한다고 생각하니?)'는 상대방으로부터 충고를 구하는 표현이다.
❼ 동사 'show'의 직접목적어로 '의문사(how much)+주어(you)+동사(love)' 어순의 '간접의문문'이다.
❽ 'Why don't you+동사원형?'은 '~하는 게 어떠니?'라는 뜻으로 제안할 때 사용한다.

Check(√) True or False

(1) Ryan is disappointed because he failed a singing competition. T ☐ F ☐

(2) Jisu wants Ryan to tell his parents about his dream. T ☐ F ☐

Start Off A – Listen & Talk 1

B: You don't ❶look happy. Why are you disappointed?

G: We lost the basketball game ❷because of my mistake.

B: Come on. ❸Everyone makes mistakes.

G: Do you think I should practice more?

B: Well, yes. You know, practice makes perfect.

B: 너는 기분이 좋아 보이지 않는구나. 왜 실망하고 있니?
G: 내 실수 때문에 우리가 농구 시합에서 졌어.
B: 괜찮아. 모든 사람은 실수하기 마련이야.
G: 내가 더 연습해야 한다고 생각하니?
B: 음, 그래. 너도 알다시피, 연습이 완벽을 만들잖아.

❶ 'look+형용사'로 '~처럼 보이다'라는 의미이다.
❷ '~ 때문에'라는 의미로 'because of+명사(구)' 또는 'because+주어+동사'를 사용할 수 있다. 즉, because of my mistake는 because I made a mistake.로 바꾸어 쓸 수 있다.
❸ 'Everyone'은 '모든 사람들'의 의미로 단수 취급한다.

Check(√) True or False

(3) Because everyone makes mistakes, the girl isn't disappointed. T ☐ F ☐

(4) The boy advises the girl to practice more. T ☐ F ☐

Get Ready 2

(1) G: You look down today. ❶What's the matter?
   B: I want to take dance classes, but my father doesn't like that idea. He thinks ❷ that boys should play sports.
   G: I'm sorry to hear that.

(2) G: Why are you disappointed?
   B: I'm preparing for the ski jumping competition, but my record is not good. What should I do?
   G: ❸I think you should keep practicing more. I'm sure ❹you'll get better and better.

(3) B: I want to be a cook, but everybody laughs at me. Do you think I should give up my dream?
   G: No, never give up. I think you're really good at cooking. You'll be a great cook!
   B: Thank you.

❶ 실망이나 불만족하는 원인을 물을 때 사용하는 표현이다.
❷ 'that'은 동사 'think'의 목적어를 이끄는 접속사이다.
❸ 'I think' 뒤에는 목적어를 이끄는 접속사 'that'이 생략되어 있다. 'keep -ing(동명사)'는 '계속 ~하다'라는 의미이다.
❹ 'get+비교급 and 비교급'은 '점점 더 ~해지다'라는 의미이다.

Start Off – Listen & Talk A 2

G: Why are you disappointed?
B: I didn't give a good presentation.
G: ❶Take it easy. Your speech was a little fast, but I liked your presentation.
B: Do you think I should speak more slowly?
G: Yes. It will ❷help your classmates understand you better.

❶ 위로·위안의 표현으로 '괜찮아.', '진정해.' 등의 의미로 해석할 수 있다.
❷ 'help+목적어+동사원형'으로 '…가 ~하는 데 도움이 되다'로 해석한다.

Start Off – Listen & Talk B

G: Junsu, you look down today. ❶Why are you disappointed?
B: I lost the cooking competition.
G: I'm sorry to hear that. I know you tried hard.
B: Yeah, but maybe that wasn't enough. ❷Do you think I should learn more cooking tips?
G: Yes. I think they will help. ❸How about getting useful tips from cooking shows online?
B: Okay. I'll try. Thank you for your advice, Mina.
G: You're welcome. Just remember I'm a fan of your dishes.

❶ 'What makes you disappointed?'로 바꾸어 쓸 수 있다.
❷ 'Do you think I should ~?(너는 내가 ~해야 한다고 생각하니?)'는 상대방으로부터 충고를 구하는 표현이다.
❸ 'How about+동명사 ~?'는 '~하는 게 어때?'라는 뜻으로 제안할 때 사용한다.

Start Off – Speak Up

B: ❶Why are you disappointed?
G: I failed the audition for the Mapo Youth Band. Do you think I should keep trying?
B: Sure. Don't give up. You'll do better next time.
G: Thank you.

❶ 슬픔, 불만족, 실망의 원인에 대해 묻는 표현으로 'What's the matter?', 'What's the problem?' 등으로 바꾸어 쓸 수 있다.

Express Yourself A

1. W: You don't look happy. Why are you disappointed?
   B: I ❶want to be a wonderful magician like you, but I failed the magic competition. Do you think I should give up?
   W: No. Practice hard every day and you'll get better and better. ❷It's important to keep trying.
   B: Okay, I'll try. Thank you for your advice.

2. W: Please come in. ❸Are you interested in designing things?
   B: Yes, I want to be a product designer. Do you think I should go to design school?
   W: I think that will help, but ❹it's more important to practice drawing every day. ❺Reading design magazines will also help you.
   B: Thank you. I'll keep that in mind.

❶ 'want'는 to부정사를 목적어로 취하는 동사이다.
❷ 가주어(It) ~ 진주어(to keep trying) 구문으로 가주어는 '그것'으로 해석하지 않는다.
❸ 'be interested in'은 '~에 관심이 있다'라는 의미로 전치사 뒤에 동명사(designing)가 온다.
❹ 가주어(it) ~ 진주어(to practice) 구문이다. 'practice'는 동명사를 목적어로 취하는 동사이다.
❺ 동명사(Reading) 주어로 '읽는 것은'으로 해석한다.

Learning Diary – Listen & Speak 1

B: You look down today, Minji. Why are you disappointed?
G: We lost the soccer game ❶because I made a mistake.
B: Don't be so sad. It can happen to anyone.
G: Do you think I should practice more?
B: Well, yes. I can help you if you want. You know, I'm a good soccer player.
G: Really? Thank you, Seho.

❶ because는 접속사로 '주어+동사'가 나온다.

● 다음 우리말과 일치하도록 빈칸에 알맞은 말을 쓰시오.

Get Ready 2

(1) G: You _____ _____ today. What's _____ _____?
　　B: I want _____ _____ dance classes, but my father doesn't like _____ _____. He thinks _____ boys _____ play sports.
　　G: I'm _____ _____ _____ _____.

(2) G: Why are you _____?
　　B: I'm _____ for the ski jumping _____, but my _____ is not good. _____ should I do?
　　G: I think you should _____ _____ more. I'm _____ you'll _____ _____ _____ _____.

(3) B: I want _____ _____ a _____, but everybody _____ _____ me. Do you think I should _____ _____ my dream?
　　G: No, _____ _____ _____. I think you're really _____ _____ _____. You'll be a great _____!
　　B: Thank you.

Start Off – Listen & Talk A

1. B: You don't _____ happy. _____ are you _____?
　　G: We _____ the basketball game _____ _____ my _____.
　　B: Come on. Everyone _____ _____.
　　G: Do you think I should _____ more?
　　B: Well, yes. You know, _____ _____ _____.

2. G: Why _____ _____ _____?
　　B: I didn't _____ a good _____.
　　G: _____ it _____. Your _____ was _____ _____ fast, but I liked your _____.
　　B: Do you think I should speak _____ _____?
　　G: Yes. It will _____ your classmates _____ you better.

Start Off – Listen & Talk B

G: Junsu, you _____ _____ today. Why are you _____?
B: I _____ the cooking _____.
G: I'm _____ _____ _____ _____. I know you tried _____.
B: Yeah, but _____ that wasn't _____. Do you think I should learn more _____ _____?
G: Yes. I think they will help. _____ _____ _____ _____ tips from cooking shows online?
B: Okay. I'll _____. Thank you _____ your _____, Mina.
G: You're welcome. Just _____ I'm a fan of your _____.

해석

(1) G: 너는 오늘 우울해 보이는구나. 무슨 일이니?
　　B: 나는 춤 수업을 듣고 싶은데, 아버지는 그 생각을 마음에 들어하지 않으셔. 아버지는 남자아이들은 운동을 해야 한다고 생각하셔.
　　G: 그것 참 안됐구나.
(2) G: 너는 왜 실망하고 있니?
　　B: 스키 점프 대회를 준비하고 있는데, 내 기록이 좋지 않아. 내가 무엇을 해야 할까?
　　G: 네가 계속 더 많이 연습해야 한다고 생각해. 난 네가 점점 더 나아질 거라고 확신해.
(3) B: 나는 요리사가 되고 싶은데, 모두 나를 비웃어. 너는 내가 꿈을 포기해야 한다고 생각하니?
　　G: 아니, 절대 포기하지 마. 나는 네가 정말 요리를 잘한다고 생각해. 너는 훌륭한 요리사가 될 거야!
　　B: 고마워.

1. B: 너는 기분이 좋아 보이지 않는구나. 왜 실망하고 있니?
　　G: 내 실수 때문에 우리가 농구 시합에서 졌어.
　　B: 괜찮아. 모든 사람은 실수하기 마련이야.
　　G: 내가 더 연습해야 한다고 생각하니?
　　B: 음, 그래. 너도 알다시피, 연습이 완벽을 만들잖아.
2. G: 너는 왜 실망하고 있니?
　　B: 나는 발표를 잘하지 못했어.
　　G: 괜찮아. 너의 발표는 약간 빨랐지만, 나는 너의 발표가 마음에 들었어.
　　B: 너는 내가 더 천천히 말해야 한다고 생각하니?
　　G: 응. 그러면 너의 학급 친구들이 네 말을 더 잘 이해하게 될 거야.

G: 준수야, 너 오늘 우울해 보이는구나. 왜 실망하고 있니?
B: 요리 대회에서 떨어졌어.
G: 그것 참 안됐구나. 네가 열심히 노력했다는 걸 알아.
B: 응, 하지만 아마 그게 충분하지는 않았나 봐. 너는 내가 더 많은 요리 요령들을 배워야 한다고 생각하니?
G: 응. 나는 그것이 도움이 될 거라고 생각해. 온라인 요리 영상에서 유용한 조언들을 얻는 게 어때?
B: 알았어. 시도해 볼게. 조언해 줘서 고마워, 미나야.
G: 천만에. 내가 네 요리의 팬이라는 것만 기억해.

Start Off – Speak Up

B: _____ are you _____?
G: I _____ the _____ for the Mapo Youth Band. Do you think I should _____ _____?
B: Sure. _____ _____ _____. You'll do _____ next time.
G: Thank you.

Start Up – Real-life Scene

Jisu: Why are you so _____, Ryan?
Ryan: My parents _____ _____ me _____ Superstar 101, a singing competition.
Jisu: I'm _____ _____ that. Why are they _____ it?
Ryan: They want me _____ _____ hard and be a doctor. They're always _____ _____ my grades.
Jisu: Did you tell your _____ you really want _____ a singer?
Ryan: _____ _____. Do you think I should _____ _____ them about it?
Jisu: Yes. Just show them _____ _____ you love singing. _____ _____ _____ _____ the songs you made _____ _____ _____ them?
Ryan: Okay. I'll try. _____ _____ _____ your advice, Jisu.

Express Yourself A

1. W: You don't look happy. Why are you _____?
   B: I want to be a wonderful _____ _____ you, but I _____ the magic _____. Do you think I should _____ _____?
   W: No. _____ every day and you'll _____ _____ and _____. It's important _____ _____ _____.
   B: Okay, I'll try. Thank you for _____ _____.
2. W: Please _____ _____. _____ you _____ _____ _____ things?
   B: Yes, I want to be a _____ _____. Do you think I should go to _____ school?
   W: I think that will help, but _____ more important _____ _____ _____ every day. _____ design _____ will also help you.
   B: Thank you. I'll _____ _____ _____ _____.

Learning Diary– Listen & Speak 1

B: You _____ _____ today, Minji. _____ _____ _____?
G: We _____ the soccer game _____ I made a mistake.
B: _____ _____ so sad. It can _____ to _____.
G: Do you think I should _____ _____?
B: Well, yes. I can help you _____ you want. _____ _____, I'm a good soccer player.
G: Really? Thank you, Seho.

해석

B: 너는 왜 실망하고 있니?
G: 나는 마포 청소년 밴드 오디션에서 떨어졌어. 너는 내가 계속 노력해야 한다고 생각하니?
B: 물론이지. 포기하지 마. 너는 다음번에 더 잘할 거야.
G: 고마워.

지수: 너는 왜 그렇게 실망하고 있니, Ryan?
Ryan: 부모님은 내가 노래 경연 대회인 슈퍼스타 101에 참가하는 걸 허락하지 않으실 거야.
지수: 그 말을 들으니 유감이구나. 왜 부모님은 그것에 반대하시니?
Ryan: 부모님은 내가 열심히 공부해서 의사가 되기를 원하셔. 항상 내 성적을 걱정하시지.
지수: 부모님께 네가 정말로 가수가 되고 싶다고 말씀드렸니?
Ryan: 아니 아직. 너는 내가 부모님께 그것에 대해 말씀드려야 한다고 생각하니?
지수: 응. 그냥 부모님께 네가 얼마나 노래 부르는 것을 좋아하는지 보여 드려. 부모님 앞에서 네가 만든 노래를 부르는 건 어때?
Ryan: 알았어. 시도해 볼게. 조언해 줘서 고마워, 지수야.

1. W: 기분이 안 좋아 보이네요. 왜 실망하고 있나요?
   B: 저는 당신처럼 멋진 마술사가 되고 싶은데, 마술 대회에서 떨어졌어요. 제가 포기해야 한다고 생각하나요?
   W: 아뇨. 매일 열심히 연습하면 점점 더 나아질 거예요. 계속 노력하는 것이 중요해요.
   B: 네, 노력해 볼게요. 조언해 주셔서 감사합니다.
2. W: 어서 들어오세요. 물건을 디자인하는 것에 관심이 있나요?
   B: 네, 저는 상품 디자이너가 되고 싶어요. 제가 디자인 학교에 가야 한다고 생각하나요?
   W: 그것이 도움이 될 거라고 생각해요. 하지만 매일 그림을 연습하는 것이 더 중요해요. 디자인 잡지를 읽는 것도 도움이 될 거예요.
   B: 감사합니다. 그 점을 명심할게요.

B: 오늘 우울해 보이는구나, 민지야. 왜 실망하고 있니?
G: 내가 실수를 해서 우리가 축구 시합에서 졌거든.
B: 너무 슬퍼하지 마. 그런 일은 누구에게나 일어날 수 있어.
G: 넌 내가 더 연습해야 한다고 생각하니?
B: 음, 그래. 네가 원한다면 내가 너를 도와줄 수 있어. 너도 알다시피, 내가 축구를 잘하잖아.
G: 정말이니? 고마워, 세호야.

Conversation 시험대비 기본평가

01 다음 우리말에 맞도록 주어진 단어를 활용하여 빈칸을 채우시오.

> 너는 왜 실망하고 있니? (disappoint)

➡ Why _____ you _____?

02 다음 대화의 빈칸에 들어갈 말로 어색한 것은?

> G: You look down today. _____
>
> B: I want to take dance classes, but my father doesn't like that idea. He thinks that boys should play sports.
>
> G: I'm sorry to hear that.

① What's wrong?　　　　② Is there anything wrong?

③ What's the matter?　　④ Why the long face?

⑤ Do you think I should keep trying?

03 다음 대화의 빈칸에 들어갈 말로 적절한 것은?

> B: I want to be a cook, but everybody laughs at me. _____
>
> G: No, never give up. I think you're really good at cooking. You'll be a great cook!
>
> B: Thank you.

① Does anybody want to share your ideas?

② Do you think I should keep trying?

③ Do you think I should give up my dream?

④ Everything will be fine.

⑤ Do you think I should learn more cooking tips?

04 다음 대화의 밑줄 친 말의 의도로 알맞은 것은?

> A: Do you think I should have a role model for my future?
>
> B: Yes. I think that will help.

① 관심 표현하기　　　　② 충고 구하기

③ 의견 표현하기　　　　④ 위로 표현하기

⑤ 실망의 원인에 대해 묻기

Conversation 시험대비 실력평가

[01~02] 다음 대화를 읽고 물음에 답하시오.

B: You look down today, Minji. Why are you (a)disappointed?

G: We lost the soccer game (b)because of I made a mistake.

B: (c)Don't be so sad. It can (d)happen to anyone.

G: _____ (A) _____

B: Well, yes. I can help you (e)if you want. You know, I'm a good soccer player.

G: Really? Thank you, Seho.

01 위 대화의 빈칸 (A)에 들어갈 말로 알맞은 것은?

① Do you think I should go to design school?
② Do you think I should give up?
③ Are you happy with your team?
④ Do you think I should practice more?
⑤ Should I want to be a soccer player?

서답형
02 위 대화의 (a)~(e) 중 어법상 틀린 것을 찾아 바르게 고치시오. (1개)

➡ 틀린 것: _____

➡ 고치기: _____ ➡ _____

[03~04] 다음 대화를 읽고 물음에 답하시오.

W: Please come in. Are you interested in designing things?

B: Yes, I want to be a product designer. _____ (A) _____ go to design school?

W: I think that will help, but it's more important to practice drawing every day. Reading design magazines will also help you.

B: Thank you. _____ (B) _____

03 위 대화의 빈칸 (A)에 들어갈 말로 알맞은 것은?

① Do you have to
② Do you want to
③ Do you think I should
④ Why do I have to
⑤ Do I think you should

중요

04 위 대화의 흐름상 (B)에 들어갈 알맞은 표현은?

① Let's keep our fingers crossed for you.
② I'll keep that in mind.
③ I wish you all the best.
④ You can be what you act.
⑤ Break a leg!

[05~06] 다음 대화를 읽고 물음에 답하시오.

G: Junsu, you look (a)down today. Why are you disappointed?

B: I lost the cooking competition.

G: I'm (b)pleased to hear that. I know you tried hard.

B: Yeah, but maybe that wasn't (c)enough. Do you think I should learn more cooking tips?

G: Yes. I think they will help. How about getting useful tips from cooking shows online?

B: Okay. I'll try. Thank you for your (d)advice, Mina.

G: You're welcome. Just (e)remember I'm a fan of your dishes.

05 위 대화의 (a)~(e) 중 흐름상 어휘의 쓰임이 어색한 것은?

① (a)   ② (b)   ③ (c)   ④ (d)   ⑤ (e)

06 위 대화에서 요리 대회에 떨어진 Junsu에게 해줄 수 있는 조언으로 알맞은 것은?

① Killing two birds with one stone.
② Birds of a feather flock together.
③ Curiosity killed the cat.
④ Every failure is a step closer to success.
⑤ Actions speak louder than words.

07 다음 대화의 빈칸에 들어갈 단어를 주어진 영영풀이를 보고 쓰시오.

> B: Why are you disappointed?
> G: I failed the _____ for the Mapo Youth Band.

> <영영풀이> a short performance that someone gives to try to get a job as an actor, musician, dancer, etc.

➡ _____

[08~09] 다음 대화를 읽고 물음에 답하시오.

Jisu: Why are you so disappointed, Ryan?
Ryan: My parents won't let me (a)enter Superstar 101, a singing competition.
Jisu: I'm sorry (b)to hear that. Why are they against it?
Ryan: They want me (c)to study hard and be a doctor. They're always worried about my grades.
Jisu: Did you tell your parents you really want to be a singer?
Ryan: Not yet. Do you think I should talk with them about it?
Jisu: Yes. Just show them (d)how many you love singing. (e)Why don't you sing the songs you made in front of them?
Ryan: Okay. I'll try. Thank you for your advice, Jisu.

08 위 대화를 읽고 답할 수 없는 질문은?

① Why is Ryan disappointed?
② What is Superstar 101?
③ Why are Ryan's parents against his entering Superstar 101?
④ What does Ryan want to be?
⑤ How many songs did Ryan make?

09 위 대화의 (a)~(e) 중 어법상 어색한 것은?

① (a) ② (b) ③ (c) ④ (d) ⑤ (e)

[10~11] 다음 대화를 읽고 물음에 답하시오.

B: You don't look happy. Why are you disappointed?
G: We lost the basketball game because of my mistake.
B: Come on. _____(A)_____
G: Do you think I should practice more?
B: Well, yes. You know, _____(B)_____.

10 위 대화의 빈칸 (A)에 들어갈 말로 알맞은 것은?

① Everyone makes mistakes.
② Faith without deeds is useless.
③ We give advice, but we cannot give conduct.
④ Habit is second nature.
⑤ When you are in trouble, you find out who your real friends are.

서답형
11 위 대화의 흐름상 빈칸 (B)에 들어갈 말을 주어진 단어를 이용하여 영어로 쓰시오.

> practice / perfect

➡ _____

[01~02] 다음 대화를 읽고 물음에 답하시오.

Jisu: _____(A)_____, Ryan?

Ryan: My parents won't let me enter Superstar 101, a singing competition.

Jisu: I'm sorry to hear that. Why are they against it?

Ryan: They want me to study hard and be a doctor. They're always worried about my grades.

Jisu: Did you tell your parents you really want to be a singer?

Ryan: Not yet. _____(B)_____ talk with them about it?

Jisu: Yes. Just show them how much you love singing. Why don't you sing the songs you made in front of them?

Ryan: Okay. I'll try. Thank you for your advice, Jisu.

01 위 대화를 읽고 다음 물음에 영어로 답하시오. (Because를 사용할 것)

Q: Why are Ryan's parents against his entering Superstar 101?

➡ _____

02 위 대화의 빈칸 (A)와 (B)에 들어갈 말을 〈조건〉에 맞게 영어로 쓰시오.

┌─ 조건 ─┐
(A) • 실망하고 있는 상대방에게 그 이유를 묻는 표현을 쓸 것.
• 'disappoint'와 'so'를 이용할 것.
(B) • '너는 내가 ~해야 한다고 생각하니?'의 의미가 되도록 상대방으로부터 충고를 구하는 표현을 쓸 것.

➡ (A) _____
   (B) _____

03 다음 대화의 빈칸 (A)에 들어갈 표현을 주어진 〈조건〉에 맞게 쓰시오.

G: Junsu, you look down today. Why are you disappointed?

B: I lost the cooking competition.

G: _____(A)_____ I know you tried hard.

B: Yeah, but maybe that wasn't enough. Do you think I should learn more cooking tips?

G: Yes. I think they will help.

┌─ 조건 ─┐
• 'sorry'와 'that'을 이용하여 유감이나 동정을 나타내는 표현을 쓸 것.

➡ _____

[04~05] 다음 대화를 읽고 물음에 답하시오.

W: Please come in. (A)물건을 디자인하는 것에 관심이 있나요?

B: Yes, I want to be a product designer. Do you think I should go to design school?

W: I think that will help, but (B)매일 그림을 연습하는 것이 더 중요해요. Reading design magazines will also help you.

B: Thank you. I'll keep that in mind.

04 위 대화에서 (A)의 우리말을 'interest'와 'design things'를 활용하여 영작하시오.

➡ _____

05 위 대화의 (B)의 우리말에 맞게 주어진 어구를 알맞은 순서로 배열하시오.

┌─────────────────────────────┐
more / to / it / practice / is / drawing / important / every day
└─────────────────────────────┘

➡ _____

Grammar

1 분사구문

> • **Hearing** this, I felt really sorry for her. 이 말을 듣고서, 나는 그녀가 정말로 안됐다고 느꼈다.

- 형태: '접속사+주어+동사'를 현재분사(동사원형+-ing)를 써서 간략하게 나타낸 것
  의미: 때, 이유, 동시동작, 연속상황, 조건 등의 뜻을 나타내는 일종의 부사구

- 분사구문 만드는 법
  (1) 접속사를 생략
  (2) 접속사절의 반복 주어를 생략
  (3) 접속사절의 동사를 현재분사(Ving)로 바꿈
  (4) 주절은 그대로 둠

  • As I felt sick, I went to bed early. → **Feeling** sick, I went to bed early. (이유)
  아파서, 나는 일찍 잠자리에 들었다.

- 분사구문에서 Being이나 Having been은 보통 생략한다.

  • As my friend was embarrassed by his mistake, he couldn't say anything.
  → (Being) **Embarrassed** by his mistake, my friend couldn't say anything. (이유)
  자신의 실수에 당혹스러워서, 내 친구는 아무 말도 하지 못했다.

- 부사절과 주절의 주어가 다를 때는 부사절의 주어를 생략하지 않고 사용한다.

  • If it rains tomorrow, we will play futsal indoors.
  → **It raining** tomorrow, we will play futsal indoors. (조건)
  내일 비가 오면, 우리는 실내에서 풋살을 할 거야.

- 분사구문으로 바꿀 부사절이 부정문이면 'not+현재분사'의 형태로 쓴다.

  • As I don't know what to say, I will keep silent.
  → **Not knowing** what to say, I will keep silent.
  무슨 말을 해야 할지 모르기 때문에, 나는 계속 조용히 있을 거야.

핵심 Check

1. 다음 두 문장이 같은 뜻이 되도록 분사구문을 사용하여 빈칸에 알맞은 말을 쓰시오.
   (1) As my daughter had her leg broken, she couldn't walk.
   = _____ her leg broken, my daughter couldn't walk.
   (2) If you turn left, you can see my house next to the post office.
   = _____ left, you can see my house next to the post office.

② 관계대명사 'what'

> - That's **what** I need to learn from her. 그것이 내가 그녀에게서 배울 필요가 있는 점이다.
> - The judge was impressed by **what** she said and finally gave her permission.
>   판사는 그녀가 말한 것에 감명을 받고 마침내 그녀에게 허락해 주었다.

■ 형태: what = the thing(s) that[which]
　의미: (…하는) 것

■ 선행사 the thing(s)을 포함한 관계대명사로 명사절의 역할(주어, 목적어, 보어)을 한다.

- **What you broke** is my mom's favorite dish. (주어)
  네가 깨트린 것은 우리 엄마가 가장 좋아하는 접시야.

- I understand **what you said**. (목적어)
  나는 네가 말한 것을 이해한다.

- This is what **I recommended to you**. (보어)
  이것이 내가 너에게 추천했던 것이다.

■ 선행사를 포함하는 관계대명사이므로 앞에 명사(선행사)가 나오면 안 된다.

- You should get ready for the thing what lies ahead of you. （×）

  → You should get ready for ~~the thing~~ what lies ahead of you. （○）
  너는 네 앞에 놓여 있는 것에 대비해야 한다.

핵심 Check

2. 다음 괄호 안에서 알맞은 것을 고르시오.

(1) I agree with the thing (what / that) you said.

(2) This is (what / that) I'd like to buy.

(3) (What/ That) he said was true.

01 다음 우리말에 맞게 괄호 안에 주어진 단어를 이용하여 문장을 완성하시오.

(1) 돈이 없어서, 그들은 먹을 것을 살 수 없다. (having, money)

➡ _____, they can't buy anything to eat.

(2) 거리를 걸으면서, 그는 지도를 보았다. (walking, street)

➡ _____, he looked at the map.

(3) 네가 원하는 것을 나에게 말해 줘. (what, want)

➡ Tell me _____.

(4) 우리에게 필요한 것은 약간의 공간이다. (what, need)

➡ _____ is a little space.

02 다음 문장에서 어법상 <u>어색한</u> 부분을 바르게 고쳐 다시 쓰시오.

(1) Feel tired, he sat on a bench.

➡ _____

(2) Watched the news, she called her mom.

➡ _____

(3) Let me tell you that I heard yesterday.

➡ _____

(4) Show me the things what you have in your pocket.

➡ _____

03 다음 〈보기〉의 문장을 참고하여 빈칸을 완성하시오.

┌─ 보기 ├─────────────────────────────
  When I heard the news, I ran to my teacher.
  = Hearing the news, I ran to my teacher.
└──────────────────────────────────────

(1) As he was surprised at his test result, he dropped the cup.

= _____, he dropped the cup.

(2) If you feel happy with what you are doing, don't let anything stop you from doing it.

= _____, don't let anything stop you from doing it.

01 다음 빈칸에 들어갈 말이 나머지와 다른 하나를 고르시오.

① The detective believed _____ Tim told her.

② I can't remember _____ time we should meet in front of this building.

③ I think _____ impressed me most in this book is his courage.

④ It is believed _____ hundreds of wild animals still survive in the forest.

⑤ Have you decided _____ to buy for her?

02 중요 다음 밑줄 친 부분을 바꾸어 쓸 때 가장 적절한 것은?

Being on a diet, he doesn't eat any bread.

① Though he is on a diet, he doesn't eat any bread.

② As he is on a diet, he doesn't eat any bread.

③ Before he was on a diet, he doesn't eat any bread.

④ Because he was on a diet, he doesn't eat any bread.

⑤ If he is on a diet, he doesn't eat any bread.

03 다음 빈칸에 들어갈 말로 적절한 것을 모두 고르시오.

Climbing the mountain, he ran into a grizzly bear.
= _____ he was climbing the mountain, he ran into a grizzly bear.

① As   ② Though   ③ If
④ While   ⑤ Until

04 중요 다음 중 어법상 어색한 문장을 고르시오.

① What I want is the smartphone.

② What you should do is to check all the e-mails.

③ I think what she said is not true.

④ Leaving this crowded city is all what I want.

⑤ I remember what you did to me last night.

05 다음 중 어법상 어색한 것은?

① When she arrived at home, she found out that she had left her bag at the party.

② Arriving at home, she found out that she had left her bag at the party.

③ As she arrived at home, she found out that she had left her bag at the party.

④ When arrived at home, she found out that she had left her bag at the party.

⑤ When arriving at home, she found out that she had left her bag at the party.

06 서답형 다음 괄호 안에 주어진 단어들을 바르게 배열하여 문장을 완성하시오.

I'm sorry, but this (we, not, ordered, what, is).

➡ _____

07 빈칸에 들어갈 말을 순서대로 바르게 연결한 것은?

> • This is _____ I want to read.
> • I couldn't believe the things _____ I saw yesterday.

① what   –   what
② what   –   that
③ which   –   what
④ that   –   what
⑤ that   –   which

08 다음 문장과 같은 의미의 문장으로 바꿔 쓴 것으로 어법상 어색한 것은?

> This book is what I bought yesterday.

① This book is the thing I bought yesterday.
② This book is the thing that I bought yesterday.
③ This book is the thing which I bought yesterday.
④ This is the book that I bought yesterday.
⑤ This is the book what I bought yesterday.

09 다음 중 어법상 어색한 문장을 고르시오.

① Not knowing the password, I couldn't go into the house.
② I did my homework, listening to the radio.
③ Being angry at him, the woman shouted.
④ Stayed in New York, he had a chance to eat the famous burger.
⑤ Tired after the long walk, my grandma decided to take a rest on the bench.

서답형

10 다음 문장에서 어법상 어색한 것을 바르게 고쳐 다시 쓰시오. (선행사를 사용하지 말 것)

(1) That he said is true.
➡ _____

(2) I know which you did yesterday.
➡ _____

서답형

11 다음 두 문장을 관계대명사 'what'을 사용하여 한 문장으로 쓰시오.

> • This bag is the thing.
> • I want to buy it.

➡ _____

서답형

12 다음 괄호 안에서 알맞은 말을 고르시오.

(1) I watched a TV show, (eat / eating) fried chicken.
(2) (Cooked / Cooking) dinner, he sang a song.
(3) He listened to music, (did / doing) his homework.
(4) (Say / Saying) good-bye, he left the classroom.
(5) (Get / Getting) up early, and you will be on time.

서답형

13 다음 괄호 안에 주어진 단어들을 바르게 배열하여 문장을 완성하시오.

> The boy (sad, loudly, cried, feeling).

➡ _____

14 다음 우리말을 영어로 바르게 옮긴 것은?

> 내 남동생은 원하는 것을 받았다.

① My brother got that he wanted.
② My brother got the thing he wanted it.
③ My brother got what he wanted.
④ My brother got the thing what he wanted.
⑤ My brother got what he wanted it.

서답형

15 다음 우리말을 주어진 어휘를 이용하여 빈칸을 채우시오.

> 오늘 할 수 있는 것을 내일로 미루지 마라. (do / what / today)

➡ Don't put off _____.

16 다음 중 어법상 어색한 문장을 고르시오.

① Reaching the top of the mountain, I took a picture of myself there.
② Feeling not well, I went to see a doctor.
③ It being nice, we had a nice family trip.
④ Knowing how to fix it, he helped me with my copying machine.
⑤ Talking on the phone, Dad kept smoking.

서답형

17 두 대화에 공통으로 들어갈 말을 두 대화 중에 쓰인 단어들을 이용하여 쓰시오.

(1) A: Is this bed what you want?
   B: No. That's not _____. This is what I need.
(2) A: Do you like this ball?
   B: Yes. That's exactly _____.

18 대화의 빈칸에 들어갈 말을 순서대로 바르게 연결한 것은?

> A: Is this book _____ you are looking for?
> B: Yes, that is the book _____ I am looking for.

① what – which
② what – what
③ that – what
④ that – that
⑤ which – what

서답형

19 주어진 어휘를 이용하여 다음 우리말을 영어로 쓰시오.

> 그들은 음악에 맞춰 춤을 추면서, 길을 건넜다. (to, crossed, dancing, the street, they, the music)

➡ _____

_____

20 다음 두 문장을 한 문장으로 바르게 옮긴 것은?

> • I opened the box.
> • I found a gift in it.

① When I open the box, I found a gift in it.
② Open the box, I found a gift in it.
③ Opened the box, I found a gift in it.
④ Opening the box, I found a gift in it.
⑤ I opened the box, I found a gift in it.

21 다음 중 어법상 어색한 문장의 개수로 알맞은 것은?

> a. This book is what I needed.
> b. I couldn't understand what he said.
> c. What you did were very brave.
> d. Writing in Chinese, the letter was difficult to read.
> e. Hearing the news, he was surprised.

① 1개 ② 2개 ③ 3개 ④ 4개 ⑤ 5개

01 'what'을 이용하여 두 문장을 한 문장으로 쓰시오.

(1) • Don't always believe the things.
　• You see them.

➡ _____

(2) • Never put off the things.
　• You can do them today.

➡ _____

(3) • The thing is your health.
　• It is the most important.

➡ _____

(4) • I'm not interested in the things.
　• He showed them to me.

➡ _____

(5) • The thing was eating spicy food.
　• I get used to it in Korea

➡ _____

02 다음 우리말을 괄호 안에 주어진 어휘를 이용하여 분사구문으로 시작하는 영어 문장으로 쓰시오.

(1) TV를 보다가, 그는 잠이 들었다. (watch, fall, asleep)

➡ _____

(2) 노래를 부르면서, 그녀는 행복하게 춤을 추었다. (a song, happily)

➡ _____

(3) 파일럿으로 일하기 때문에, 그는 여행을 많이 한다. (work, a pilot, travel, a lot)

➡ _____

03 주어진 문장을 의미가 같도록 분사구문을 이용하여 다시 쓰시오.

(1) She left the room, as she was singing a song.

➡ _____

_____

(2) As there were no tickets left, we couldn't go to the concert.

➡ _____

_____

04 잘못된 부분을 바르게 고쳐 문장을 다시 쓰시오.

(1) She walked in the park, she ate bread.

➡ _____

또는 _____

(2) Is this cap that you wanted?

➡ _____

(3) This key is what I was looking for it.

➡ _____

(4) Had no money, I can't help you.

➡ _____

(5) I humming a song, I vacuumed the floor.

➡ _____

(6) I hope he remembers that I did for him.

➡ _____

05 다음 두 문장을 분사구문을 이용하여 하나의 문장으로 쓰시오.

• I didn't know what to say.
• I just stood around like a fool.

➡ _____

06 우리말과 같은 뜻이 되도록 괄호 안의 단어들을 바르게 배열하시오.

사과를 먹으면서, Amy는 그녀의 개를 산책시켰다.
(an, Amy, walked, apple, dog, her, eating)

➡ _____

07 다음 그림을 보고 괄호 안의 단어를 활용하여 빈칸에 알맞은 분사구문을 쓰시오.

(1)

_____, Katherine solved a very difficult math problem. (write, board)

(2)

_____, Charlie walked with Snoopy. (hold, flower)

(3)

_____, the dog enjoyed the summer. (swim, pool)

08 주어진 〈보기〉를 참고하여 같은 뜻의 문장을 쓰시오.

보기
When I visited Busan, I met my cousin.
→ Visiting Busan, I met my cousin.

(1) While I was climbing a mountain, I fell down.
➡ _____

(2) As he dislikes watching TV, he only listens to music.
➡ _____

(3) Although I don't have time to see the movie "Frozen", I know who the Olaf is.
➡ _____

(4) Dad took me to the kitchen, and showed me what he had cooked.
➡ _____

The Hidden Figures of NASA

I watched the movie *Hidden Figures* last weekend. It was a movie about three African-American women who worked at NASA. They began their career in the 1960s as "human computers." However, they dreamed of becoming space experts at NASA and tried hard to get over difficulties.

Katherine Johnson was one of the three "hidden figures" in this movie. She worked hard and showed a talent in math, and her manager Al Harrison recognized her ability. One day, he got upset when Katherine was missing from her desk for too long. Al asked where Katherine had been, and she answered.

Katherine: The bathroom. There are no COLORED bathrooms in this building. I have to run half a mile away just to use the bathroom.

Hearing this, I felt really sorry for her. However, I was glad that she had courage to talk to the manager about the problem. This made Al Harrison break down the "Colored Ladies Room" sign.

Mary Jackson was the character I liked the most of the three. She wanted to learn more about rocket science, but she wasn't allowed to go to a white school. So, she asked a judge to give her permission.

---

hidden 숨겨진, 비밀의

figure (중요한) 인물, 거물, 숫자, 피규어 (모형 장난감)

career 직업, 직장 생활

space 우주

expert 전문가

get over ~을 극복하다

manager 관리자, 경영자

recognize 알아보다, 인정하다

ability 능력

colored 색깔이 있는, 유색 인종의

courage 용기

break down ~을 부수다

rocket 로켓

allow 허락하다

judge 판사

permission 허락

 확인문제

● 다음 문장이 본문의 내용과 일치하면 T, 일치하지 <u>않으면</u> F를 쓰시오.

1 *Hidden Figures* was a movie about three African-American women who worked at NASA. ☐

2 The three African-American women began their career in the 1960s as computer programmers. ☐

3 Katherine Johnson worked hard and showed a talent in math. ☐

4 Katherine Johnson had to run half a mile away just to use the bathroom. ☐

5 Mary Jackson wanted to learn more about rocket science, and she was allowed to go to a white school. ☐

Mary: I can't change the color of my skin. So ... I have no choice but
to be the first. Your Honor, of all the cases you'll hear today, which one
will matter in a hundred years? Which one will make you the "first?"

The judge was impressed by what she said and finally gave her
permission. Mary stood up for herself and for other African-Americans.
That was what impressed me most in the movie. Finally, she became
the first African-American woman engineer at NASA.

Dorothy Vaughan was the last "hidden figure." When IBM
computers were installed at NASA in 1961, she was worried the "human
computers" would lose their jobs. She studied a new programming
language, FORTRAN. She also taught it to her team members. Later,
when she was asked to be the leader of a new IBM team, she made a
suggestion.

Dorothy: I'm not accepting the offer if I can't bring my ladies with me.
We need a lot of people to program that machine. I can't do it alone.
My girls are ready.

Thanks to Dorothy, her team members could become programmers.
She wasn't afraid of change and used it as a chance. That's what I need
to learn from her.

Watching this movie, I could learn how to face challenges in life.
I won't forget the tears and laughter of Katherine, Mary, and Dorothy.

have no choice but to ~할 수밖에 없다

impress 감명을 주다, 깊은 인상을 주다

stand up for ~을 옹호하다, 지지하다

engineer 기술자, 엔지니어

install 설치하다

later 나중에, 후에

offer 제의, 제안

thanks to ~ 덕분에

programmer 프로그래머

be afraid of ~을 두려워하다

face (상황에) 직면하다

laughter 웃음(소리)

확인문제

● 다음 문장이 본문의 내용과 일치하면 T, 일치하지 않으면 F를 쓰시오.

1 Mary had no choice but to be the first. ☐

2 Mary stood up for herself and for other American women. ☐

3 Mary became the first African-American woman engineer at NASA. ☐

4 When IBM computers were installed at NASA in 1961, Dorothy Vaughan lost her
job. ☐

5 Dorothy Vaughan studied a new programming language, FORTRAN. ☐

6 Thanks to Dorothy, her team members could become human computers. ☐

● 우리말을 참고하여 빈칸에 알맞은 말을 쓰시오.

1 The _____ _____ of NASA

2 I watched the movie *Hidden Figures* _____ _____.

3 It was a movie about three _____ women who worked at NASA.

4 They began their career _____ _____ _____ _____ "human computers."

5 However, they dreamed of becoming _____ _____ at NASA and tried hard _____ _____ _____ _____.

6 **Katherine Johnson** was one of the _____ "_____ _____" in this movie.

7 She worked hard and _____ _____ _____ _____ math, and her manager Al Harrison recognized her ability.

8 One day, he _____ _____ when Katherine was missing from her desk for too long.

9 Al asked _____ _____ _____ _____, and she answered.

10 Katherine: The _____.

11 There are no _____ _____ in this building.

12 I have to run half a mile away _____ _____ _____ the bathroom.

13 _____ _____, I felt really sorry for her.

14 However, I was glad that she _____ _____ _____ to the manager about the problem.

15 This made Al Harrison _____ _____ the "Colored Ladies Room" sign.

16 **Mary Jackson** was the _____ I liked the most of the three.

17 She wanted to learn more about rocket science, but she _____ _____ _____ go to a white school.

18 So, she asked a judge _____ _____ _____ _____.

19 Mary: I _____ _____ the color of my skin.

1 NASA의 숨겨진 인물들

2 나는 지난 주말에 〈히든 피겨스〉라는 영화를 보았다.

3 그것은 NASA에서 일했던 세 명의 아프리카계 미국인 여성들에 대한 영화였다.

4 그들은 1960년대에 '인간 컴퓨터(계산원)'로 일을 시작했다.

5 하지만 그들은 NASA에서 우주 전문가가 되기를 꿈꾸었고 어려움을 극복하기 위해 열심히 노력했다.

6 Katherine Johnson은 이 영화에서 세 명의 '숨겨진 인물들' 중 한 명이었다.

7 그녀는 열심히 일했고 수학에서 재능을 보였으며, 그녀의 상사인 Al Harrison은 그녀의 능력을 알아차렸다.

8 어느 날, 그는 Katherine이 너무 오래 자리를 비웠을 때 화가 났다.

9 Al은 Katherine에게 어디에 갔었는지 물었고 그녀는 대답했다.

10 Katherine: 화장실요.

11 이 건물에는 유색 인종 전용 화장실이 없어요.

12 저는 단지 화장실을 사용하기 위해 반 마일을 달려가야 해요.

13 이 말을 듣고서, 나는 그녀가 정말로 안됐다고 느꼈다.

14 그러나 나는 그 문제에 대해 상사에게 말한 그녀의 용기를 보고 기뻤다.

15 이것은 Al Harrison으로 하여금 '유색 여성 화장실' 표지판을 부수게 만들었다.

16 Mary Jackson은 셋 중에 가장 나의 마음에 드는 인물이었다.

17 그녀는 로켓 공학에 대해 더 많이 배우고 싶었지만 백인 학교에 다니는 것이 허락되지 않았다.

18 그래서 그녀는 판사에게 허락해 달라고 요청했다.

19 Mary: 저는 제 피부색을 바꿀 수 없어요.

20 So ... I _____ _____ _____ _____ be the first.

21 Your Honor, of all the cases you'll hear today, which one will matter _____ _____ _____ _____?

22 _____ _____ will make you the "first?"

23 The judge was _____ by _____ she said and finally gave her permission.

24 Mary _____ _____ _____ herself and for other African-Americans.

25 That was _____ _____ _____ _____ in the movie.

26 Finally, she became the _____ _____ _____ _____ at NASA.

27 **Dorothy Vaughan** was _____ _____ "hidden figure."

28 When IBM computers _____ _____ at NASA in 1961, she was worried the "human computers" _____ _____ their jobs.

29 She studied a _____ _____ _____, FORTRAN.

30 She also _____ _____ to her team members.

31 Later, when she _____ _____ _____ be the leader of a new IBM team, she made a suggestion.

32 Dorothy: _____ _____ _____ the offer if I can't bring my ladies with me.

33 We need a lot of people _____ _____ that machine.

34 I can't do it _____.

35 My girls _____ _____.

36 _____ _____ Dorothy, her team members could become programmers.

37 She _____ _____ _____ change and used it _____ _____ _____.

38 That's _____ _____ _____ _____ _____ from her.

39 Watching this movie, I could learn _____ _____ _____ _____ in life.

40 I won't forget the _____ _____ _____ of Katherine, Mary, and Dorothy.

---

20 그래서⋯ 저는 '최초'가 되는 것 이외에는 선택이 없어요.

21 판사님, 당신이 오늘 들을 모든 사건 중에서, 백 년 뒤에 어느 것이 중요할까요?

22 어느 것이 판사님을 '최초'로 만들까요?

23 판사는 그녀가 말한 것에 감명을 받고 마침내 그녀에게 허락해 주었다.

24 Mary는 그녀 자신과 다른 아프리카계 미국인들의 편에 섰다.

25 그것은 영화에서 나를 가장 감동하게 한 점이었다.

26 마침내 그녀는 NASA에서 최초의 아프리카계 미국인 여성 공학자가 되었다.

27 Dorothy Vaughan은 마지막 '히든 피겨(숨은 인물)'였다.

28 1961년 NASA에 IBM 컴퓨터가 설치되었을 때, 그녀는 '인간 컴퓨터(계산원)'들이 직업을 잃을까봐 걱정했다.

29 그녀는 새로운 프로그래밍 언어인 포트란을 공부했다.

30 그녀는 또한 그것을 그녀의 팀원들에게 가르쳤다.

31 나중에 그녀가 새 IBM 팀의 리더가 되도록 요청받았을 때, 그녀는 제안했다.

32 Dorothy: 저는 저의 여성 팀원들을 데려올 수 없다면 그 제안을 받아들이지 않겠습니다.

33 그 기계의 프로그램을 짜기 위해서는 많은 사람이 필요합니다.

34 저는 그것을 혼자 할 수 없습니다.

35 제 여성 팀원들은 준비가 되어 있습니다.

36 Dorothy 덕분에, 그녀의 팀원들은 프로그래머가 될 수 있었다.

37 그녀는 변화를 두려워하지 않고 그것을 기회로 이용했다.

38 그것이 내가 그녀에게서 배울 필요가 있는 점이다.

39 이 영화를 보면서, 나는 삶에서 어떻게 도전에 직면해야 하는지 배울 수 있었다.

40 나는 Katherine, Mary, 그리고 Dorothy의 눈물과 웃음을 잊지 않을 것이다.

● 우리말을 참고하여 본문을 영작하시오.

1 NASA의 숨겨진 인물들

➡ _____

2 나는 지난 주말에 〈히든 피겨스〉라는 영화를 보았다.

➡ _____

3 그것은 NASA에서 일했던 세 명의 아프리카계 미국인 여성들에 대한 영화였다.

➡ _____

4 그들은 1960년대에 '인간 컴퓨터(계산원)'로 일을 시작했다.

➡ _____

5 하지만 그들은 NASA에서 우주 전문가가 되기를 꿈꾸었고 어려움을 극복하기 위해 열심히 노력했다.

➡ _____

6 Katherine Johnson은 이 영화에서 세 명의 '숨겨진 인물들' 중 한 명이었다.

➡ _____

7 그녀는 열심히 일했고 수학에서 재능을 보였으며, 그녀의 상사인 Al Harrison은 그녀의 능력을 알아차렸다.

➡ _____

8 어느 날, 그는 Katherine이 너무 오래 자리를 비웠을 때 화가 났다.

➡ _____

9 Al은 Katherine에게 어디에 갔었는지 물었고 그녀는 대답했다.

➡ _____

10 Katherine: 화장실요.

➡ _____

11 이 건물에는 유색 인종 전용 화장실이 없어요.

➡ _____

12 저는 단지 화장실을 사용하기 위해 반 마일을 달려가야 해요.

➡ _____

13 이 말을 듣고서, 나는 그녀가 정말로 안됐다고 느꼈다.

➡ _____

14 그러나 나는 그 문제에 대해 상사에게 말한 그녀의 용기를 보고 기뻤다.

➡ _____

15 이것은 Al Harrison으로 하여금 '유색 여성 화장실' 표지판을 부수게 만들었다.

➡ _____

16 Mary Jackson은 셋 중에 가장 나의 마음에 드는 인물이었다.

➡ _____

17 그녀는 로켓 공학에 대해 더 많이 배우고 싶었지만 백인 학교에 다니는 것이 허락되지 않았다.

➡ _____

18 그래서 그녀는 판사에게 허락해 달라고 요청했다.

➡ _____

19 Mary: 저는 제 피부색을 바꿀 수 없어요.

➡ _____

20 그래서… 저는 '최초'가 되는 것 이외에는 선택이 없어요.
➡ _____

21 판사님, 당신이 오늘 들을 모든 사건 중에서, 백 년 뒤에 어느 것이 중요할까요?
➡ _____

22 어느 것이 판사님을 '최초'로 만들까요?
➡ _____

23 판사는 그녀가 말한 것에 감명을 받고 마침내 그녀에게 허락해 주었다.
➡ _____

24 Mary는 그녀 자신과 다른 아프리카계 미국인들의 편에 섰다.
➡ _____

25 그것은 영화에서 나를 가장 감동하게 한 점이었다.
➡ _____

26 마침내 그녀는 NASA에서 최초의 아프리카계 미국인 여성 공학자가 되었다.
➡ _____

27 Dorothy Vaughan은 마지막 '히든 피겨(숨은 인물)'였다.
➡ _____

28 1961년 NASA에 IBM 컴퓨터가 설치되었을 때, 그녀는 '인간 컴퓨터(계산원)'들이 직업을 잃을까 봐 걱정했다.
➡ _____
_____

29 그녀는 새로운 프로그래밍 언어인 포트란을 공부했다.
➡ _____

30 그녀는 또한 그것을 그녀의 팀원들에게 가르쳤다.
➡ _____

31 나중에 그녀가 새 IBM 팀의 리더가 되도록 요청받았을 때, 그녀는 제안했다.
➡ _____

32 Dorothy: 저는 저의 여성 팀원들을 데려올 수 없다면 그 제안을 받아들이지 않겠습니다.
➡ _____

33 그 기계의 프로그램을 짜기 위해서는 많은 사람이 필요합니다.
➡ _____

34 저는 그것을 혼자 할 수 없습니다.
➡ _____

35 제 여성 팀원들은 준비가 되어 있습니다.
➡ _____

36 Dorothy 덕분에, 그녀의 팀원들은 프로그래머가 될 수 있었다.
➡ _____

37 그녀는 변화를 두려워하지 않고 그것을 기회로 이용했다.
➡ _____

38 그것이 내가 그녀에게서 배울 필요가 있는 점이다.
➡ _____

39 이 영화를 보면서, 나는 삶에서 어떻게 도전에 직면해야 하는지 배울 수 있었다.
➡ _____

40 나는 Katherine, Mary, 그리고 Dorothy의 눈물과 웃음을 잊지 않을 것이다.
➡ _____

[01~03] 다음 글을 읽고 물음에 답하시오.

I watched the movie *Hidden* (A)*Figures* last weekend. It was a movie about three African-American women who worked at NASA. They began their career in the 1960s as "human computers." _____ⓐ_____, they dreamed of becoming space experts at NASA and tried hard to get over difficulties.

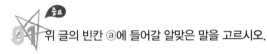

01 위 글의 빈칸 ⓐ에 들어갈 알맞은 말을 고르시오.

① For example ② However
③ Therefore ④ That is
⑤ In addition

02 위 글의 밑줄 친 (A)*Figures*와 같은 의미로 쓰인 것을 고르시오.

① She figures if she takes the night train, she can be in Scotland by morning.
② Tell me the latest sales figures.
③ Inflation is in double figures.
④ He figures the attendance at 1,500.
⑤ I met many leading figures in the music industry.

03 According to the passage, which is NOT true?

① The writer watched the movie *Hidden Figures* last weekend.
② *Hidden Figures* was a movie about three African-American women who worked at NASA.
③ The three women began their career in the 1960s as "human computers."

④ The three women dreamed of becoming space astronauts at NASA.
⑤ The three women tried hard to get over difficulties.

[04~06] 다음 글을 읽고 물음에 답하시오.

Katherine Johnson was one of the three "hidden figures" in this movie. She worked hard and showed a talent _____ⓐ_____ math, and her manager Al Harrison recognized her ability. One day, he got upset when Katherine was missing from her desk for too long. Al asked where Katherine had been, and she answered.
Katherine: The bathroom. There are no COLORED bathrooms in this building. I have to run half a mile away just to use the bathroom.

Hearing (A)this, I felt really sorry _____ⓑ_____ her. However, I was glad that she had courage to talk to the manager about the problem. This made Al Harrison break down the "Colored Ladies Room" sign.

04 위 글의 빈칸 ⓐ와 ⓑ에 들어갈 전치사가 바르게 짝지어진 것은?

	ⓐ	ⓑ		ⓐ	ⓑ
①	of	for	②	in	for
③	in	of	④	for	on
⑤	of	on			

서답형
05 위 글의 밑줄 친 (A)this가 가리키는 내용을 우리말로 쓰시오.

➡ _____

_____

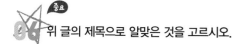

06 위 글의 제목으로 알맞은 것을 고르시오.

① The Three "Hidden Figures" at NASA
② Katherine's Wonderful Ability
③ Al Harrison Got Upset
④ No More "Colored Ladies Room"
⑤ Al Harrison, a Strict Manager

[07~09] 다음 글을 읽고 물음에 답하시오.

Mary Jackson was the character I liked the most of the three. She wanted to learn more about rocket science, but she wasn't allowed to go to a white school. So, she asked a judge to give her ⓐ_____.

Mary: I can't change the color of my skin. So … I have no choice but to be the first. Your Honor, of all the cases you'll hear today, which one will matter in a hundred years? Which one will make you ⓑthe "first?"

The judge was impressed by what she said and ⓒfinally gave her permission. Mary stood up for herself and for other African-Americans. That was what impressed me most in the movie. Finally, she became the first African-American woman engineer at NASA.

서답형

07 위 글의 빈칸 ⓐ에 permit을 알맞은 형태로 쓰시오.

➡ _____

서답형

08 다음 빈칸 (A)와 (B)에 알맞은 단어를 넣어, 밑줄 친 ⓑthe first가 무엇을 의미하는지 완성하시오.

It means the first judge who allowed a (A)_____ student to take classes with (B)_____ students.

09 위 글의 밑줄 친 ⓒfinally와 바꿔 쓸 수 없는 말을 고르시오.

① eventually   ② after all
③ in the end   ④ at least
⑤ in the long run

[10~12] 다음 글을 읽고 물음에 답하시오.

I watched the movie *Hidden Figures* (A)[last / latest] weekend. It was a movie about ⓐ세 명의 아프리카계 미국인 여성들 who worked at NASA. They began their career in the 1960s as "human computers." However, they dreamed of becoming space (B)[experts / exports] at NASA and tried (C)[hard / hardly] ⓑto get over difficulties.

서답형

10 위 글의 괄호 (A)~(C)에서 문맥상 알맞은 낱말을 골라 쓰시오.

➡ (A)_____ (B)_____ (C)_____

서답형

11 위 글의 밑줄 친 ⓐ의 우리말에 맞게 3 단어로 영작하시오.

➡ _____

12 위 글의 밑줄 친 ⓑto get over와 to부정사의 용법이 다른 것을 모두 고르시오.

① I want to know how to get over difficulties.
② He was too weak to get over difficulties.
③ It is the fastest way to get over difficulties.
④ I tried to get over difficulties.
⑤ She was relieved to get over difficulties.

[13~14] 다음 글을 읽고 물음에 답하시오.

ⓐWatching this movie, ⓑI could learn how to face challenges in life. I won't forget the tears and laughter of Katherine, Mary, and Dorothy.

13 위 글의 밑줄 친 ⓐWatching과 문법적 쓰임이 같은 것을 고르시오.

① He was fond of watching movies.
② Do you know the man watching a movie there?
③ My brother was watching a movie.
④ Who enjoys watching the movie?
⑤ His hobby is watching movies.

서답형
14 위 글의 밑줄 친 ⓑ를 다음과 같이 바꿔 쓸 때 빈칸에 들어갈 알맞은 말을 두 단어로 쓰시오.

➡ I could learn how _____ face challenges in life.

[15~17] 다음 글을 읽고 물음에 답하시오.

(ⓐ) **Dorothy Vaughan** was the last "hidden figure." (ⓑ) When IBM computers were installed at NASA in 1961, she was worried ①the "human computers" would lose ②their jobs. (ⓒ) She also taught it to ③her team members. (ⓓ) Later, when she was asked to be the leader of a new IBM team, she made a suggestion. (ⓔ)

Dorothy: I'm not accepting the offer if I can't bring ④my ladies with me. ⑤We need a lot of people to program that machine. I can't do it alone. My girls are ready.

Thanks to Dorothy, her team members could become programmers. She wasn't afraid of change and used it as a chance. That's what I need to learn from her.

15 위 글의 흐름으로 보아, 주어진 문장이 들어가기에 가장 적절한 곳은?

> She studied a new programming language, FORTRAN.

① ⓐ ② ⓑ ③ ⓒ ④ ⓓ ⑤ ⓔ

16 위 글의 밑줄 친 ①~⑤ 중에서 가리키는 대상이 나머지 넷과 다른 것은?

① ② ③ ④ ⑤

17 According to the passage, which is NOT true?

① When IBM computers were installed at NASA in 1961, Dorothy Vaughan was worried the "human computers" would lose their jobs.
② Dorothy Vaughan studied a new programming language, FORTRAN.
③ Dorothy Vaughan taught FORTRAN to her team members.
④ Thanks to Dorothy, her team members could become programmers.
⑤ Dorothy Vaughan was afraid of using the change as a chance.

[18~21] 다음 글을 읽고 물음에 답하시오.

Katherine Johnson was one of the three "hidden figures" in this movie. She worked hard and showed a talent in math, and her manager Al Harrison recognized her ability. One day, he got ___ⓐ___ when Katherine was missing from her desk for too long. Al asked where Katherine had been, and she answered.

Katherine: The bathroom. (①) There are no COLORED bathrooms in this building. (②) I have to run half a mile away just to use the bathroom. (③)

Hearing this, I felt really sorry for her. (④) This made Al Harrison break down the "Colored Ladies Room" sign. (⑤)

18 위 글의 빈칸 ⓐ에 들어갈 알맞은 말을 고르시오.

① ashamed ② satisfied ③ upset
④ relieved ⑤ embarrassed

19 위 글의 흐름으로 보아, 주어진 문장이 들어가기에 가장 적절한 곳은?

> However, I was glad that she had courage to talk to the manager about the problem.

① ② ③ ④ ⑤

20 위 글을 읽고 알 수 없는 것을 고르시오.

① Who are the three "hidden figures" in the movie?
② In what did Katherine Johnson show a talent?
③ Who was Al Harrison?
④ Why did Al Harrison get upset?
⑤ Why was Katherine missing from her desk for too long?

서답형
21 다음 빈칸에 알맞은 단어를 넣어 Katherine Johnson에 대한 소개를 완성하시오.

> Katherine Johnson was a _____ _____ who made Al Harrison break down the "Colored Ladies Room" sign.

[22~24] 다음 글을 읽고 물음에 답하시오.

Mary Jackson was the character I liked the most of the three. She wanted to learn more about rocket science, but she wasn't allowed to go to a white school. So, she asked a judge to give her permission.

Mary: I can't change the color of my skin. So ... I have no choice but to be the first. Your Honor, of all the cases you'll hear today, which one will ⓐmatter in a hundred years? Which one will make you the "first?"

The judge was impressed by what she said and finally gave her ⓑpermission. Mary stood up for herself and for other African-Americans. That was what impressed me most in the movie. Finally, she became the first African-American woman engineer at NASA.

22 위 글의 밑줄 친 ⓐmatter와 같은 의미로 쓰인 것을 고르시오.

① They had an important matter to discuss.
② He wants to study the properties of matter.
③ It doesn't matter whether you are rich or not.
④ She didn't approve of their choice of reading matter.
⑤ Is anything the matter?

서답형
23 위 글의 밑줄 친 ⓑpermission 뒤에 생략된 말을 본문에서 찾아 쓰시오.

➡ _____

24 위 글의 종류로 알맞은 것을 고르시오.

① essay ② anecdote ③ review
④ article ⑤ book report

[01~03] 다음 글을 읽고 물음에 답하시오.

I watched the movie *Hidden Figures* last weekend. ⓐIt was a movie about three African-American women who worked at NASA. They began their career in the ⓑ1960s as "human computers." However, they dreamed of becoming space experts at NASA and tried hard to ⓒget over difficulties.

01 위 글의 밑줄 친 ⓐIt이 가리키는 것을 본문에서 찾아 쓰시오.

➡ _____

02 위 글의 밑줄 친 ⓑ1960s를 영어로 읽으시오.

➡ _____

03 위 글의 밑줄 친 ⓒget over와 바꿔 쓸 수 있는 단어를 쓰시오.

➡ _____

[04~07] 다음 글을 읽고 물음에 답하시오.

Katherine Johnson was one of the three "hidden figures" in this movie. She worked hard and showed a talent in math, and her manager Al Harrison recognized her ability. One day, he got upset when Katherine was missing from her desk for too long. Al asked where Katherine had been, and she answered.

Katherine: The bathroom. There are no COLORED bathrooms in this building. I have to run half a mile away just to use the bathroom.

ⓐHearing this, I felt really sorry for her. However, I was glad that she had courage to talk to the manager about the problem. ⓑThis made Al Harrison to break down the "Colored Ladies Room" sign.

04 Why did Katherine have to run half a mile away just to use the bathroom? Answer in English beginning with "Because". (9 words)

➡ _____
_____

05 위 글의 밑줄 친 ⓐHearing this를 부사절로 고치시오.

➡ _____

06 위 글의 밑줄 친 ⓑ에서 어법상 틀린 부분을 찾아 고치시오.

_____ ➡ _____

07 다음 빈칸에 알맞은 단어를 넣어 위 글을 읽고 추론할 수 있는 내용을 완성하시오.

In the past, the colored people faced the racial discrimination. For example, even such a smart woman as Katherine could not use the _____ bathrooms with whites and was forced to use separate bathrooms.

*racial discrimination: 인종차별

[08~10] 다음 글을 읽고 물음에 답하시오.

Mary Jackson was the character I liked the most of the three. She wanted to learn more about rocket science, but she wasn't allowed to go to a white school. So, she asked a judge to give her permission.

Mary: I can't change the color of my skin. So ...
ⓐI have no choice but to be the first. Your Honor, of all the cases you'll hear today,

which one will matter in a hundred years? Which one will make you the "first?"

The judge was impressed by what she said and finally gave her permission. Mary stood up for herself and for other African-Americans. ⓑ그것이 영화에서 나를 가장 감동하게 한 것이었다. Finally, she became the first African-American woman engineer at NASA.

08 위 글의 밑줄 친 ⓐ를 다음과 같이 바꿔 쓸 때 빈칸에 들어갈 알맞은 단어를 쓰시오.

➡ I cannot help _____ the first. = I cannot but _____ the first.

09 위 글의 밑줄 친 ⓑ의 우리말에 맞게 주어진 어휘를 이용하여 9 단어로 영작하시오.

> That, impressed, most

➡ _____

10 다음 빈칸 (A)와 (B)에 알맞은 단어를 넣어 Mary Jackson에 대한 소개를 완성하시오.

> Mary Jackson learned more about (A)_____ _____ at a white school, and became the first African-American woman (B)_____ at NASA.

[11~13] 다음 글을 읽고 물음에 답하시오.

Dorothy Vaughan was the last "hidden figure." When IBM computers were installed at NASA in 1961, she was worried the "human computers" would lose their jobs.

She studied a new programming language, FORTRAN. She also taught it to her team members. Later, when she was asked to be the leader of a new IBM team, she made a suggestion.

Dorothy: I'm not accepting the offer ⓐif I can't bring my ladies with me. We need a lot of people to program that machine. I can't do it alone. My girls are ready.

Thanks to Dorothy, her team members could become programmers. She wasn't afraid of change and used it as a chance. ⓑThat's what I need to learn from her.

Watching this movie, I could learn how to face challenges in life. I won't forget the tears and laughter of Katherine, Mary, and Dorothy.

11 위 글의 밑줄 친 ⓐ를 unless를 사용하여 고치시오.

➡ _____

12 위 글의 밑줄 친 ⓑThat이 가리키는 것을 본문에서 찾아 쓰시오.

➡ _____
_____

13 다음 빈칸 (A)와 (B)에 알맞은 단어를 넣어 Dorothy Vaughan에 대한 소개를 완성하시오.

> Dorothy Vaughan was a hidden figure who studied a (A)_____ _____ _____, FORTRAN, and helped her team members become (B)_____ by teaching them FORTRAN.

Express Yourself C

1. I had a good time with the baker. He told me about his job, decorating some
   분사구문으로 '~하면서'로 해석한다.
   cupcakes. I will not forget what he said, "Make what your family love."
   관계대명사   Make의 목적어로 사용된 관계대명사절

2. I had a good time with the actor. He told me about his job, saying his
   동시동작의 분사구문
   famous lines. I will not forget what he said, "You can be what you act."
   forget의 목적어로 사용된 관계대명사절   be동사의 보어로 사용된 관계대명사절

구문해설 · **baker**: 제빵사 · **decorate**: 장식하다 · **forget**: 잊다 · **actor**: 배우 · **line**: 대사

After You Read A

Katherine Johnson: I made my manager break down the "Colored Ladies
                                              to break(×)
Room" sign.

Mary Jackson: I asked the judge to allow me to study at a white school.
                         ask+목적어+to부정사   allow+목적어+to부정사

Dorothy Vaughan: I studied a new programming language to prepare for
                                                                to부정사의 부사적 용법(목적)
change.

구문해설 · **manager**: 관리자, 경영자 · **break down**: ~을 부수다 · **colored**: 색깔이 있는, 유색 인종의
· **judge**: 판사 · **allow**: 허락하다 · **prepare for**: ~을 준비하다

Link to the World

Q1 What do you do at this restaurant?

A1 I make various Italian dishes and desserts.

Q2 What is difficult about your job?

A2 I have so many things to do other than cooking. I have to buy fresh meat
                         형용사적 용법: ~해야 할
and vegetables every day. I also wash the dishes and keep my kitchen clean.
                                                        keep   목적어   목적보어(형용사)

Q3 Are you happy with your job?

A3 Yes, I am. It's a tough job, but I love what I do. I feel proud, seeing people
                                          선행사를 포함한 관계대명사: ~하는 것   분사구문: ~하면서
enjoy my dishes.

구문해설 · **various**: 다양한 · **dessert**: 후식 · **other than**: ~ 이외에도 · **tough**: 힘든

해석

1. 저는 제빵사와 즐거운 시간을 보냈습니다. 그는 컵케이크에 장식하며 그의 직업에 대해 말해 주었습니다. 저는 그가 말한 것을 잊지 않을 것입니다. "가족이 좋아하게 될 것을 만드세요."

2. 저는 그 배우와 즐거운 시간을 보냈습니다. 그는 자신의 유명한 대사를 말하면서 그의 직업에 대해 말해 주었습니다. 저는 그가 말한 것을 잊지 않을 것입니다. "당신은 자신이 연기하는 것이 될 수 있습니다."

Katherine Johnson: 나는 나의 상사로 하여금 '유색 여성 화장실' 표지판을 부수게 만들었다.

Mary Jackson: 나는 판사에게 백인 학교에서 공부하도록 허락해 달라고 요청했다.

Dorothy Vaughan: 나는 변화에 대비해 준비하기 위하여 새로운 프로그래밍 언어를 공부했다.

Q1. 당신은 이 식당에서 무엇을 합니까?
A1. 저는 다양한 이탈리아 요리와 후식을 만듭니다.
Q2. 당신 직업의 어려운 점은 무엇입니까?
A2. 저는 요리 외에도 할 일이 많습니다. 저는 매일 신선한 고기와 채소를 사야 합니다. 또한 설거지하고 주방을 깨끗이 유지합니다.
Q3. 당신은 당신의 직업에 만족합니까?
A3. 네, 그렇습니다. 힘든 직업이지만, 저는 제가 하는 일을 좋아합니다. 저는 사람들이 제 요리를 즐기는 것을 보면서 자부심을 느낍니다.

01 다음 주어진 두 단어의 관계가 같도록 빈칸에 알맞은 단어를 쓰시오.

> courage – cowardice : novice – _____

02 다음 문장의 빈칸 (a)와 (b)에 들어갈 말이 바르게 짝지어진 것은?

> • Anger can be a good thing because it helps you ___(a)___ yourself when you are treated unfairly.
> • Teachers, journalists, and public civil servants cannot ___(b)___ expensive gifts.

① break down – accept
② get over – allow
③ stand up for – accept
④ stand up for – remove
⑤ get over – compete

[03~04] 다음 영영풀이에 해당하는 것을 고르시오.

03

> the person in a court who decides how criminals should be punished

① magician   ② volunteer   ③ manager
④ reporter   ⑤ judge

04

> a large cylinder-shaped object that moves very fast and is used for space travel

① rocket   ② permission   ③ ability
④ figure   ⑤ plane

05 빈칸에 들어갈 전치사를 〈영영풀이〉를 참고하여 쓰시오.

> A: Why are you disappointed?
> B: My parents won't let me join the dance club.
> A: I'm sorry to hear that. Why are they _____ it?
> B: They want me to study hard to be a lawyer. They're always worried about my grades.

> 〈영영풀이〉 disagreeing with a plan or activity

➡ _____

06 다음 밑줄 친 부분의 뜻이 잘못된 것은?

① I'm concerned about my low grades. (성적)
② The actors went to the audition for the movie. (관객)
③ Bibimbap is one of the most popular Korean dishes. (요리)
④ I'm worried about my presentation tomorrow. (발표)
⑤ They laughed at me when I made a mistake. (비웃었다)

07 다음 대화에서 단어의 쓰임이 어색한 부분을 찾아 바르게 고치시오.

> B: I want to be a cooker, but everybody laughs at me. Do you think I should give up my dream?
> G: No, never give up. I think you're really good at cooking.

_____ ➡ _____

08 주어진 문장에 이어질 대화를 순서에 맞게 바르게 배열한 것은?

> G: Why are you disappointed?
> (A) Yes. It will help your classmates understand you better.
> (B) I didn't give a good presentation.
> (C) Do you think I should speak more slowly?
> (D) Take it easy. Your speech was a little fast, but I liked your presentation.

① (B) – (A) – (C) – (D)
② (B) – (D) – (C) – (A)
③ (C) – (B) – (D) – (A)
④ (D) – (A) – (C) – (B)
⑤ (D) – (B) – (A) – (C)

09 다음 짝지어진 대화 중 어색한 것은?

① A: Why are you disappointed?
　 B: I didn't give a good presentation.
② A: Why are you disappointed?
　 B: I failed the math exam.
③ A: Do you think I should learn more cooking tips?
　 B: Yes. I think they will help.
④ A: Do you think I should study harder for my future?
　 B: Yes. I think you should read many books.
⑤ A: Do you think I should have a role model for my future?
　 B: Yes. Making a model plane is not easy.

[10~12] 다음 대화를 읽고 물음에 답하시오.

> Jisu: Why are you so disappointed, Ryan?
> Ryan: My parents (a)won't let me enter Superstar 101, a singing competition.

Jisu: I'm sorry to hear that. Why are they (b)for it?
Ryan: They want me to study hard and be a doctor. They're always (c)worried about my grades.
Jisu: Did you tell your parents you really want to be a singer?
Ryan: (d)Not yet. Do you think I should talk with them about it?
Jisu: Yes. Just show them how much you (e)love singing. Why don't you sing the songs you made in front of them?
Ryan: Okay. I'll try. Thank you for your advice, Jisu.

10 위 대화의 밑줄 친 (a)~(e) 중 어휘의 쓰임이 어색한 것은?

① (a)　　② (b)　　③ (c)　　④ (d)　　⑤ (e)

11 위 대화의 제목으로 가장 적절한 것은?

① How to Enter a Singing Competition
② Disagreement Between Parents and Their Child
③ Difficulty in Making Songs
④ I Want to Be a Singer
⑤ Saying and Doing are Two Different Things

12 위 대화의 내용과 일치하지 않는 것을 고르시오.

① Ryan is disappointed because his parents won't let him enter Superstar 101.
② Ryan's parents aren't worried about his grade but they want him to be a doctor.
③ Jisu advises him to tell his parents about his dream.
④ Ryan wants to enter a singing competition.
⑤ Ryan thanks Jisu for her advice.

Grammar

13 주어진 문장의 밑줄 친 what과 쓰임이 같은 것은?

> Q3 Are you happy with your job?
>
> A3 Yes, I am. It's a tough job, but I love what I do. I feel proud, seeing people enjoy my dishes.

① Not knowing what to do, I asked him for help.
② Judging from what he's wearing, he's probably a soldier.
③ Can you tell me what the main ingredients are in this dish?
④ I want to know what reason you are crying for.
⑤ I don't remember what color she likes.

14 다음 문장에서 어법상 어색한 부분을 찾아 바르게 고치시오.

> Leaving alone in the room, the baby began to cry.

➡ _____

15 다음 우리말을 바르게 영작한 것은?

> 비가 와서, 우리는 밖에서 축구를 하지 않았다.

① Raining, we didn't play soccer outside.
② It raining, we didn't play soccer outside.
③ As rained, we didn't play soccer outside.
④ As was raining, we didn't play soccer outside.
⑤ Raining it, we didn't play soccer outside.

16 다음 중 어법상 어색한 문장의 개수로 알맞은 것은?

> a. Walk along the street, I saw a big cat.
> b. Lives in America, he speaks English very well.
> c. When he saw me, he ran away.
> d. They sat on the beach, looked at the rising sun.
> e. While I was walking the dog, I saw a UFO over the roof.
> f. As he was running down the stairs, he fell down.

① 1개 ② 2개 ③ 3개 ④ 4개 ⑤ 5개

17 다음 중 밑줄 친 부분의 쓰임이 나머지 넷과 다른 하나는?

① I can't believe what I saw.
② Baseball is what I like most.
③ I'm sorry, but this isn't what we ordered.
④ I don't know what your name is.
⑤ What I need is a new computer.

18 밑줄 친 부분에 유의하여, 바르게 해석하시오.

(1) David remembers what she said.
  ➡ _____
(2) That's what you should learn.
  ➡ _____
(3) What matters is that you tried your best.
  ➡ _____

19 다음 빈칸에 들어갈 말로 적절하지 않은 것을 고르시오.

> Tell me _____ you did yesterday.

① the things ② what
③ that ④ anything
⑤ the things that

Reading

[20~21] 다음 글을 읽고 물음에 답하시오.

Katherine Johnson was one of the three "hidden figures" in this movie. She worked hard and showed a talent in math, and her manager Al Harrison recognized her ability. One day, he got upset when Katherine was missing from her desk for too long. ⓐAl은 Katherine에게 어디에 갔었는지 물었고, and she answered.

Katherine: The bathroom. There are no COLORED bathrooms in this building. I have to run half a mile away just to use the bathroom.

Hearing this, I felt really sorry for her. However, I was glad that she had courage to talk to the manager about the problem. This made Al Harrison break down the "Colored Ladies Room" sign.

20 위 글의 밑줄 친 ⓐ의 우리말에 맞게 주어진 어휘를 알맞게 배열하시오.

Katherine / asked / had / Al / been / where

➡ _____

21 According to the passage, which is NOT true?

① There were two more "hidden figures" except Katherine Johnson in the movie.
② Katherine Johnson worked hard and showed a talent in math.
③ Al Harrison was Katherine's manager and envied her ability.
④ There were no COLORED bathrooms in the building.
⑤ Al Harrison was a considerate man.

[22~24] 다음 글을 읽고 물음에 답하시오.

Mary Jackson was the character I liked the most of the three. She wanted to learn more about rocket science, but she wasn't allowed to go to a white school. So, she asked a judge to give her permission.

Mary: I can't change the color of my skin. So ... I have no choice but to be the first. Your Honor, of all the ⓐcases you'll hear today, which one will matter in a hundred years? Which one will make you the "first?"

The judge was impressed by what she said and finally gave her permission. Mary stood up for herself and for other African-Americans. That was what impressed me most in the movie. Finally, she became the first African-American woman engineer at NASA.

22 위 글의 밑줄 친 ⓐcases와 같은 의미로 쓰인 것을 고르시오.

① In some cases people have had to wait several weeks for an appointment.
② She has won many court cases until now.
③ The most serious cases were treated at the scene of the accident.
④ The museum was full of stuffed animals in glass cases.
⑤ In some cases, you can't really tell people the truth.

23 위 글의 제목으로 알맞은 것을 고르시오.

① My Favorite Character of the Three
② How to Learn More about Rocket Science
③ I Can't Change the Color of My Skin
④ A Woman Who Had No Choice but to Be the First
⑤ Which One Will Make You the "First?"

24 위 글의 내용과 일치하도록 다음 빈칸 (A)와 (B)에 알맞은 단어를 쓰시오.

> Mary Jackson was given (A)_____ _____ to go to a white school, where she learned more about rocket science, and she (B)_____ _____ for herself and for other African-Americans.

[25~27] 다음 글을 읽고 물음에 답하시오.

Dorothy: I'm not accepting the offer if I can't bring my ladies with me. We need a lot of people to program that machine. (A)I can't do it alone. My girls are ready.

____ⓐ____ Dorothy, her team members could become programmers. She wasn't afraid of change and used (B)it as a chance. That's what I need to learn from her.

Watching this movie, I could learn how to face challenges in life. I won't forget the tears and laughter of Katherine, Mary, and Dorothy.

25 위 글의 빈칸 ⓐ에 들어갈 알맞은 말을 고르시오.

① In spite of   ② Thanks to
③ Rather than   ④ In terms of
⑤ Instead of

26 위 글의 밑줄 친 (A)를 다음과 같이 바꿔 쓸 때 빈칸에 들어갈 알맞은 말을 두 단어로 쓰시오.

➡ I can't do it _____.

27 위 글의 밑줄 친 (B)it이 가리키는 것을 본문에서 찾아 쓰시오.

➡ _____

[28~29] 다음 글을 읽고 물음에 답하시오.

I had a good time with the baker. He told me about his job, ⓐdecorating some cupcakes. I will not forget ⓑwhat he said, "Make what your family will love."

28 위 글의 밑줄 친 ⓐdecorating some cupcakes를 부사절로 고치시오.

➡ _____

29 위 글의 밑줄 친 ⓑwhat과 문법적 쓰임이 같은 것을 모두 고르시오.

① What kind of music do you like?
② What you need is a good meal.
③ What is your name?
④ What a beautiful house!
⑤ She pointed to what looked like a bird.

출제율 90%

01 다음 짝지어진 단어의 관계가 같도록 빈칸에 알맞은 말을 쓰시오.

> accept – acceptance : compete – _____

출제율 95%

02 다음 영영풀이에 해당하는 단어는?

> the series of jobs that you do during your working life

① figure   ② expert   ③ career
④ engineer   ⑤ courage

출제율 90%

03 다음 대화를 읽고 빈칸에 들어갈 말을 〈조건〉에 맞게 쓰시오.

> ─── 조건 ───
> • 슬픔, 불만족, 실망의 원인에 대해 물을 것.
> • 'face'를 사용하여 4 단어로 쓸 것.

> B: _____
> G: I failed the audition for the Mapo Youth Band. Do you think I should keep trying?
> B: Sure. Don't give up. You'll do better next time.
> G: Thank you.

➡ _____

[04~05] 다음 대화를 읽고 물음에 답하시오.

> (A) Please come in. Are you interested in designing things?
> (B) I think that will help, but it's more important to practice drawing every day. Reading design magazines will also help you.
> (C) Yes, I want to be a product designer. Do you think I should go to design school?
> Boy: Thank you. I'll keep that in mind.

출제율 100%

04 위 대화의 (A)~(C)를 순서대로 배열하시오.

➡ _____

출제율 95%

05 위 대화를 읽고 다음 질문에 영어로 답하시오.

> Q: What should the boy do to be a product designer?

➡ _____
    _____

출제율 100%

06 다음 대화의 빈칸에 들어갈 말로 알맞은 것은?

> W: You don't look happy. Why are you disappointed?
> B: I want to be a wonderful magician like you, but I failed the magic competition.
> _____
> W: No. Practice hard every day and you'll get better and better. It's important to keep trying.
> B: Okay, I'll try. Thank you for your advice.

① Do you like this trick?
② Do you think I should keep trying?
③ Do you think I should give up?
④ Do you think I should study harder?
⑤ Do you think I should practice harder?

07 아래 대화에서 다음 문장이 들어갈 위치로 알맞은 것은?

> How about getting useful tips from cooking shows online?

> G: Junsu, you look down today. Why are you disappointed? (①)
> B: I lost the cooking competition.
> G: I'm sorry to hear that. I know you tried hard. (②)
> B: Yeah, but maybe that wasn't enough. (③) Do you think I should learn more cooking tips? (④)
> G: Yes. I think they will help. (⑤)
> B: Okay. I'll try. Thank you for your advice, Mina.
> G: You're welcome. Just remember I'm a fan of your dishes.

①   ②   ③   ④   ⑤

08 다음 대화의 빈칸 (A)에 들어갈 말로 적절하지 않은 것은?

> B: You look down today, Minji.
>   (A)
> G: We lost the soccer game because I made a mistake.
> B: Don't be so sad. It can happen to anyone.
> G: Do you think I should practice more?
> B: Well, yes. I can help you if you want. You know, I'm a good soccer player.
> G: Really? Thank you, Seho.

① Why are you disappointed?
② What's wrong?
③ Is there anything wrong?
④ Why don't you play soccer with us?
⑤ Why the long face?

09 빈칸에 들어갈 말로 알맞은 것은?

> B: You don't look happy. Why are you disappointed?
> G: We lost the basketball game because of my mistake.
> B: Come on. Everyone makes mistakes.
> G: _____
> B: Well, yes. You know, practice makes perfect.

① Why don't you practice dancing hard?
② Do you think I should practice more?
③ Why don't you perform in front of them?
④ Do you think I should give up?
⑤ Do you think I should go to design school?

10 밑줄 친 부분에 유의하여, 바르게 해석하시오.

> (1) Having a cold, he went to bed early.
> (2) Arriving at the airport, she called her parents.
> (3) Drinking a lot of water, you will be healthier.

➡ (1) _____
(2) _____
(3) _____

11 밑줄 친 부분과 바꾸어 쓸 수 없는 것은? (2개)

> While I was walking down the street, I saw my cat cross the street.

① While walking   ② Walking
③ While I walking   ④ While walked
⑤ As I was walking

12 잘못된 부분을 바르게 고쳐 문장을 다시 쓰시오.

(1) Make the things what your family will love.

➡ _____

(2) Design that you dream of.

➡ _____

(3) I will not forget what he said it.

➡ _____

(4) She told me about her job, and drawing some product designs.

➡ _____

_____

(5) You can be which you act.

➡ _____

13 괄호 안에 주어진 표현을 사용하여 우리말로 된 대화를 영어로 완성하시오.

(1) (That, what, want)

A: Do you like this book?

B: Yes. 그것이 내가 읽기를 원하는 것이야.

➡ _____

(2) (That, what, looking)

A: Here is your cap.

B: Thanks. 그것이 내가 찾고 있었던 것이야.

➡ _____

(3) (That, what, have, mind)

A: Is this doll what you want?

B: No. 그것은 내가 생각하는 것이 아니야.

➡ _____

[14~15] 다음 글을 읽고 물음에 답하시오.

I watched the movie *Hidden Figures* last weekend. It was a movie about three African-American women who worked at NASA. They began their ____ⓐ____ in the 1960s ⓑas "human computers." However, they dreamed of becoming space experts at NASA and tried hard to get over difficulties.

14 주어진 영영풀이를 참고하여 빈칸 ⓐ에 철자 c로 시작하는 단어를 쓰시오.

> the job or profession that someone does for a long period of their life

➡ _____

15 위 글의 밑줄 친 ⓑas와 같은 의미로 쓰인 것을 고르시오.

① They did as I had asked.

② He runs as fast as you run.

③ I respect him as a doctor.

④ As you were out, I left a message.

⑤ Such flowers as the rose require special care.

[16~18] 다음 글을 읽고 물음에 답하시오.

Katherine Johnson was one of the three "hidden figures" in this movie. She worked hard and showed a talent in math, and her manager Al Harrison recognized her ability. ⓐOne day, he got upset when Katherine was missed from her desk for too long. Al asked where Katherine had been, and she answered.

Katherine: The bathroom. There are no COLORED bathrooms in this building. I have to run half a mile away just to use the bathroom.

Hearing this, I felt really sorry for her. However, I was glad that she had courage ⓑ to talk to the manager about the problem. This made Al Harrison break down the "Colored Ladies Room" sign.

🖊 출제율 95%

16 위 글의 밑줄 친 ⓐ에서 어법상 틀린 부분을 찾아 고치시오

_____ ➡ _____

🖊 출제율 90%

17 아래 〈보기〉에서 위 글의 밑줄 친 ⓑto talk와 to부정사의 용법이 같은 것의 개수를 고르시오.

┌─── 보기 ───┐

① He grew up to be a movie director.
② She had the kindness to show me the way.
③ It is a lot of fun to play tennis.
④ He was the first man to land on the moon.
⑤ His dream is to start a business.

① 1개   ② 2개   ③ 3개   ④ 4개   ⑤ 5개

🖊 출제율 95%

18 What made Al Harrison break down the "Colored Ladies Room" sign? Fill in the blank with a suitable word.

Katherine's _____ to his question got him to break down the "Colored Ladies Room" sign.

[19~21] 다음 글을 읽고 물음에 답하시오.

Mary Jackson was the character I liked the most of the three. She wanted to learn more about rocket science, but she wasn't allowed to go to a white school. So, she asked a judge to give her permission.

Mary: I can't change the color of my skin. So ... I have no choice but to be the first. Your Honor, of all the cases you'll hear today, which one will matter in a hundred years? Which one will make you the "first?"

(A)판사는 그녀가 말한 것에 감명을 받고 마침내 그녀에게 허락해 주었다. Mary stood up for herself and for other African-Americans. That was _____ⓐ impressed me most in the movie. Finally, she became the first African-American woman engineer at NASA.

🖊 출제율 95%

19 위 글의 빈칸 ⓐ에 들어갈 알맞은 말을 고르시오.

① which   ② why   ③ how
④ that   ⑤ what

🖊 출제율 90%

20 위 글의 밑줄 친 (A)의 우리말에 맞게 주어진 어휘를 알맞게 배열하시오.

she / permission / finally / said / the judge / impressed / gave / what / and / by / her / was

➡ _____
_____

🖊 출제율 100%

21 According to the passage, which is NOT true?

① The writer liked Mary Jackson the most of the three.
② Mary Jackson asked a judge to give her permission to go to a white school.
③ Mary Jackson couldn't be the first.
④ Mary Jackson supported herself and other African-Americans.
⑤ There was no other African-American woman engineer at NASA before Mary Jackson.

01 다음 대화의 우리말에 맞게 주어진 단어를 알맞은 순서로 배열하시오.

> B: You don't look happy. Why are you disappointed?
> G: We lost the basketball game because of my mistake.
> B: Come on. Everyone makes mistakes.
> G: 내가 더 연습해야 한다고 생각하니? (do / I / practice / you / should / more / think / ?)
> B: Well, yes. You know, practice makes perfect.

➡ _____

02 다음 대화를 읽고 요약문을 완성하시오.

> Jisu: Why are you so disappointed, Ryan?
> Ryan: My parents won't let me enter Superstar 101, a singing competition.
> Jisu: I'm sorry to hear that. Why are they against it?
> Ryan: They want me to study hard and be a doctor. They're always worried about my grades.
> Jisu: Did you tell your parents you really want to be a singer?
> Ryan: Not yet. Do you think I should talk with them about it?
> Jisu: Yes. Just show them how much you love singing. Why don't you sing the songs you made in front of them?
> Ryan: Okay. I'll try. Thank you for your advice, Jisu.

> Ryan's _____ is to be a singer, so he wants to _____ a singing competition. But his parents are _____ it because they want him to be a _____. Ryan

> is very _____. Jisu _____ him to tell his parents about his dream and to _____ them _____ _____ he loves singing. Ryan _____ Jisu for her _____.

03 다음 글에서 어법상 틀린 곳의 기호를 쓰고 바르게 고치시오.

> Q2 What is difficult about your job?
> A2 I have so many things ㉠doing other than cooking. I have to buy fresh meat and vegetables every day. I also wash the dishes and keep my kitchen ㉡clean.
> Q3 Are you happy ㉢with your job?
> A3 Yes, I am. It's a tough job, but I love ㉣which I do. I feel proud, ㉤see people enjoy my dishes.

(1) ____ → _____   (2) ____ → _____
(3) ____ → _____

04 〈보기〉의 문장을 참고하여 그림에 나타난 사람들을 설명하는 문장을 괄호 안에 주어진 단어를 사용하여 완성하시오

┤ 보기 ├
> Listening to music, Amy jumped rope.

(1) (sing, song), Jack danced wonderfully.
➡ _____
(2) (drink, milk), Sam walked his dog.
➡ _____
(3) Eating some cookies, (read, book).
➡ _____
(4) Holding some balloons, (kick, ball).
➡ _____

Mary Jackson was the character I liked the most of the three. She wanted to learn more about rocket science, but she wasn't allowed ⓐ to a white school. So, she asked a judge to give her permission.

Mary: I can't change the color of my skin. So ... I have no choice but to be the first. Your Honor, of all the cases you'll hear today, which one will matter in a hundred years? Which one will make you the "first?"

The judge was impressed by what she said and finally gave her permission. Mary stood up for herself and for other African-Americans. That was what impressed me most in the movie. Finally, she became the first African-American woman engineer at NASA.

05 위 글의 빈칸 ⓐ에 go를 알맞은 형태로 쓰시오.

➡ _____

06 다음 문장에서 위 글의 내용과 다른 부분을 찾아서 고치시오.

> Mary Jackson became the first woman engineer at NASA.

_____ ➡ _____

07 본문의 내용과 일치하도록 다음 빈칸 (A)와 (B)에 알맞은 단어를 쓰시오.

> Mary Jackson was a hidden figure who made the judge become the (A)_____ who permitted a black student to take classes with white students. She also (B)_____ African-Americans as well as herself.

Dorothy Vaughan was the last "hidden figure." ⓐWhen IBM computers installed at NASA in 1961, she was worried the "human computers" would lose their jobs. She studied a new programming language, FORTRAN. She also taught it to her team members. Later, when she was asked to be the leader of a new IBM team, she made a suggestion.

Dorothy: I'm not accepting the offer if I can't bring my ladies with me. We need a lot of people to program that machine. I can't do it alone. My girls are ready.

Thanks to Dorothy, her team members could become programmers. ⓑ그녀는 변화를 두려워하지 않고 그것을 기회로 이용했다. That's what I need to learn from her.

ⓒWatching this movie, I could learn how to face challenges in life. I won't forget the tears and laughter of Katherine, Mary, and Dorothy.

08 위 글의 밑줄 친 ⓐ에서 어법상 틀린 부분을 찾아 고치시오.

_____ ➡ _____

09 위 글의 밑줄 친 ⓑ의 우리말에 맞게 주어진 어휘를 알맞게 배열하시오.

> afraid / a chance / used / of / change / wasn't / and / it / as / she

➡ _____

10 위 글의 밑줄 친 ⓒWatching this movie를 부사절로 고치시오.

➡ _____

01 아래 표의 (A)의 고민과 어울리는 충고의 말을 (B)에서 골라 〈보기〉와 같이 대화를 완성하시오.

(A)	(B)
• lost the dance competition	• study harder
• got a bad grade	• practice harder
• fought with my friend	• talk to my friend about it

— 보기 —

A: Why are you disappointed?

B: I got a bad grade. Do you think I should study harder?

A: Yes, I think so.

02 다음 내용을 바탕으로 빈칸을 채워 직업에 대한 부스 체험 소감문을 완성하시오.

1. W: Please come in. Are you interested in designing things?

   B: Yes, I want to be a product designer. Do you think I should go to design school?

   W: I think that will help, but it's more important to design what you dream of. Reading design magazines will also help you.

   B: Thank you. I'll keep that in mind.

2. W: You don't look happy. Why are you disappointed?

   B: I want to be a wonderful magician like you, but I failed the magic competition. Do you think I should give up?

   W: No. Practice hard every day and you'll get better and better. It's important not to believe what you see.

   B: Okay, I'll try. Thank you for your advice.

1. I had a good time with the (A)_____. She told me about her job, drawing some product designs. I will not forget what she said, "Design (B)_____."

2. I had a good time with the (C)_____. She told me about her job, doing some magic tricks. I will not forget what she said, "Don't believe (D)_____."

단원별 모의고사

01 다음 단어에 대한 영어 설명이 <u>어색한</u> 것은?

① hidden: not easy to find
② figure: a well-known person
③ recognize: to know someone or something because you have experienced it before
④ courage: the skill or qualities that you need to do something
⑤ impress: to cause someone to feel admiration or respect

02 다음 짝지어진 단어의 관계가 같도록 빈칸에 알맞은 말을 쓰시오.

> courage – bravery : veiled – _____

03 다음 영영풀이에 해당하는 단어를 고르시오.

> to put a machine or a piece of equipment into position and to make it ready to use

① reach   ② accept   ③ install
④ fill   ⑤ throw

04 다음 중 짝지어진 대화가 <u>어색한</u> 것은?

① A: Do you like this book?
   B: Yes. That's what I want to read.
② A: Do you like this camera?
   B: Yes. That's what I want.
③ A: Here is your notebook.
   B: Thanks. That's what I was looking for.
④ A: Is this doll what you want?
   B: No. That's not what I have in mind.
⑤ A: Do you think I should take magic lessons?
   B: I want to be a magician like you.

05 대화의 흐름상 빈칸에 들어갈 문장을 〈조건〉에 맞게 쓰시오.

> G: Junsu, you look down today. Why are you disappointed?
> B: I lost the cooking competition.
> G: I'm sorry to hear that. I know you tried hard.
> B: Yeah, but maybe that wasn't enough. Do you think I should learn more cooking tips?
> G: Yes. I think they will help. _____ from cooking shows online?
> B: Okay. I'll try. Thank you for your advice, Mina.
> G: You're welcome. Just remember I'm a fan of your dishes.

> ┤ 조건 ├
> • How about을 이용하여 '~하는 게 어때?'라는 제안의 표현을 쓸 것.
> • 'get useful tips'를 이용할 것.

➡ _____

06 다음 빈칸에 들어갈 말로 <u>어색한</u> 것은?

> G: You look down today. _____
> B: I want to take dance classes, but my father doesn't like that idea. He thinks that boys should play sports.
> G: I'm sorry to hear that.

① What's the matter?
② Why are you disappointed?
③ What happened?
④ What makes you so sad?
⑤ What are you looking forward to?

07 대화의 흐름상 밑줄 친 ①~⑤ 중 어색한 것은?

W: You don't ①look sad. Why are you disappointed?

B: I want to ②be a wonderful magician like you, but I ③failed the magic competition. Do you think I should give up?

W: No. Practice hard every day and you'll ④get better and better. It's important to keep trying.

B: Okay, I'll try. ⑤Thank you for your advice.

①   ②   ③   ④   ⑤

08 다음 대화의 빈칸에 들어갈 말로 알맞은 것은?

G: Why are you disappointed?

B: I didn't give a good presentation.

G: Take it easy. Your speech was a little fast, but I liked your presentation.

B: _____

G: Yes. It will help your classmates understand you better.

① Do you think I should talk with them about it?

② Do you think I should speak more slowly?

③ Do you think I should keep trying?

④ Do you think I should give up my dream?

⑤ Do you think I should practice more?

09 다음 주어진 문장에 이어질 대화 순서를 알맞게 배열하시오.

A: Why are you disappointed?

(A) I'm sorry to hear that.

(B) Sure. You'll do better next time.

(C) I failed the audition for the band.

(D) Do you think I should keep trying?

➡ _____

[10~11] 다음 대화를 읽고 물음에 답하시오.

W: Please come in. Are you interested in designing things? (①)

B: Yes, I want to be a product designer. (②) Do you think I should go to design school? (③)

W: I think that will help, but it's more important to practice drawing every day. (④)

B: Thank you. (⑤) I'll ___(A)___ that in mind.

10 위 대화의 (①)~(⑤) 중 주어진 문장이 들어갈 위치로 알맞은 곳은?

Reading design magazines will also help you.

①   ②   ③   ④   ⑤

11 위 대화의 빈칸 (A)에 들어갈 단어를 쓰시오.

➡ _____

[12~14] 다음 대화를 읽고 물음에 답하시오.

Jisu: Why are you so disappointed, Ryan?

Ryan: My parents won't let me enter Superstar 101, a singing competition.

Jisu: I'm sorry to hear that. Why are they (a) against it?

Ryan: _____(A)_____ They're always worried about my grades.

Jisu: Did you tell your parents you really want to be a singer?

Ryan: Not yet. Do you think I should talk with them about it?

Jisu: Yes. Just show them how much you love singing. Why don't you sing the songs you made in front of them?

Ryan: Okay. I'll try. Thank you for your advice, Jisu.

12 위 대화의 빈칸 (A)에 들어갈 말로 알맞은 것은?

① They want me to pursue my dream.

② They really want me to sing a song at Superstar 101.

③ They want me to be a singer.

④ They don't want to talk with me.

⑤ They want me to study hard and be a doctor.

13 위 대화를 읽고 다음 질문에 영어로 답하시오.

Q: Why is Ryan disappointed?

➡ _____

14 위 대화의 밑줄 친 (a)의 'against'와 같은 의미로 사용된 것은?

① I was standing, leaning against Mahatma Gandhi's statue.

② They took precautions against fire.

③ In 1959, Tibetan people rose up in a movement against the Chinese rule.

④ His red clothes stood out clearly against the snow.

⑤ You must weigh the benefits against the cost.

15 다음 중 어법상 어색한 문장을 모두 고르시오.

① This is the thing that she likes it.

② He gave me what I wanted.

③ He read a newspaper, drank coffee.

④ Feeling sick, I had to take the test.

⑤ He had breakfast, going to work.

16 다음 주어진 문장과 뜻이 가장 가까운 문장은?

Doing a lot of exercise, I'm still gaining weight.

① If I do a lot of exercise, I'm still gaining weight.

② As I do a lot of exercise, I'm still gaining weight.

③ Because I do a lot of exercise, I'm still gaining weight.

④ Though I do a lot of exercise, I'm still gaining weight.

⑤ After I do a lot of exercise, I'm still gaining weight.

17 다음 우리말을 영어로 바르게 옮긴 것은?

> 그는 손을 흔들며 작별인사를 했다.

① Saying good-bye, waving his hand.
② He said good-bye, waving his hand.
③ He saying good-bye, waved his hand.
④ As he said good-bye, waving his hand.
⑤ He said good-bye, waved his hand.

18 다음은 직업 체험에 대한 소감의 일부이다. 〈보기〉에 주어진 표현을 골라 분사구문을 사용하여 글을 완성하시오.

> ┌── 보기 ├──
> • decorate some cupcakes
> • control robots
> • do some magic tricks
> • say one's famous lines
> • show ... one's news reports

(1) I had a good time with the baker, _____.

(2) I had a good time with the actor. He told me about his job, _____ _____.

(3) I had a good time with the magician. She told me about her job, _____ _____.

(4) I had a good time with the TV reporter. He told me about his job, _____.

(5) I had a good time with the robot scientist. She told me about her job, _____.

19 다음 주어진 우리말을 관계대명사 'what'을 사용하여 영어로 옮기시오.

> (1) 당신이 보는 것을 믿지 마세요.
> (2) 사실인 것을 보도하세요.
> (3) 로봇은 당신이 할 수 없는 것을 할 수 있습니다.

(1) Don't believe _____.
(2) Report _____.
(3) Robots can do _____.

[20~22] 다음 글을 읽고 물음에 답하시오.

Dorothy Vaughan was the last "hidden figure." When IBM computers were installed at NASA in 1961, she was worried the "human computers" would lose their jobs. She studied a new programming language, FORTRAN. She also taught it to her team members. Later, when she was asked to be the leader of a new IBM team, she made a suggestion.

Dorothy: I'm not accepting @the offer if I can't bring my ladies with me. We need a lot of people to program that machine. I can't do it alone. My girls are ready.

Thanks to Dorothy, her team members could become programmers. She wasn't afraid of change and used it as a chance. That's what I need to learn from her.

Watching this movie, I could learn how to ⓑ face challenges in life. I won't forget the tears and laughter of Katherine, Mary, and Dorothy.

20 위 글의 밑줄 친 @the offer가 가리키는 내용을 우리말로 쓰시오.

➡ _____

21 위 글의 밑줄 친 ⓑface와 바꿔 쓸 수 없는 말을 고르시오.

① confront
② cope with
③ tackle
④ overlook
⑤ deal with

22 What was FORTRAN? Answer in English in a full sentence. (6 words)

➡ _____

[23~25] 다음 글을 읽고 물음에 답하시오.

Katherine Johnson was one of the three "hidden figures" in this movie. She worked hard and showed a talent in math, and her manager Al Harrison recognized her ability. One day, he got upset when Katherine was missing from her desk for too long. Al asked where Katherine had been, and she answered.

Katherine: The bathroom. There are no COLORED bathrooms in this building. I have to run half a mile away just to use the bathroom.

Hearing this, I felt really sorry for her. _____ⓐ_____ , I was glad that ⓑshe had courage to talk to the manager about the problem. This made Al Harrison break down the "Colored Ladies Room" sign.

23 위 글의 빈칸 ⓐ에 들어갈 알맞은 말을 고르시오.

① Moreover
② Thus
③ Similarly
④ As a result
⑤ However

24 위 글의 밑줄 친 ⓑ를 다음과 같이 바꿔 쓸 때 빈칸에 공통으로 들어갈 알맞은 단어를 쓰시오.

➡ she was _____ enough to talk to the manager about the problem
= she was so _____ as to talk to the manager about the problem

25 위 글에서 알 수 있는 Al Harrison의 심경 변화로 가장 알맞은 것을 고르시오.

① upset → disappointed
② nervous → satisfied
③ unpleasant → sympathetic
④ bored → upset
⑤ satisfied → disappointed

[26~28] 다음 글을 읽고 물음에 답하시오.

Mary Jackson was the (A)character I liked the most of the three. (①) So, she asked a judge to give her permission. (②)

Mary: I can't change the color of my skin. (③) So ... I have no choice but to be the first. (④) Your Honor, of all the cases you'll hear today, which one will matter _____ⓐ_____ a hundred years? (⑤) Which one will make you the "first?"

The judge was impressed by what she said and finally gave her permission. Mary stood up _____ⓑ_____ herself and _____ⓑ_____ other African-Americans. That was what impressed me most in the movie. Finally, she became the first African-American woman engineer at NASA.

26 위 글의 빈칸 ⓐ와 ⓑ에 들어갈 전치사가 바르게 짝지어진 것은?

	ⓐ	ⓑ		ⓐ	ⓑ
①	for	to	②	in	for
③	in	to	④	for	by
⑤	at	for			

27 위 글의 흐름으로 보아, 주어진 문장이 들어가기에 가장 적절한 곳은?

> She wanted to learn more about rocket science, but she wasn't allowed to go to a white school.

①   ②   ③   ④   ⑤

28 위 글의 밑줄 친 (A)character와 같은 의미로 쓰인 것을 고르시오.

① She has a strong character.
② The modern hotels here have no real character.
③ Please write in a large character.
④ Who is the leading character in this drama?
⑤ He was a man of good character.

[29~30] 다음 글을 읽고 물음에 답하시오.

Dorothy Vaughan was the last "hidden figure." When IBM computers were installed at NASA in 1961, she was worried the "human computers" would lose their jobs. She studied a new programming language, FORTRAN. She also taught it to her team members. Later, when she was asked to be the leader of a new IBM team, she made a suggestion.

Dorothy: I'm not accepting the offer if I can't bring my ladies with me. We need a lot of people to program that machine. I can't do it alone. My girls are ready.

Thanks to Dorothy, her team members could become programmers. She wasn't afraid of change and used it as a chance. That's what I need to learn from her.

Watching this movie, I could learn how to face challenges in life. I won't forget the tears and laughter of Katherine, Mary, and Dorothy.

29 위 글의 제목으로 가장 알맞은 것을 고르시오.

① Who Was the Last Hidden Figure?
② What If the "Human Computers" Would Lose Their Jobs?
③ Don't Be Afraid of Change
④ Are You Afraid of Change?
⑤ What Do You Need to Learn from Her?

30 Which question CANNOT be answered after reading the passage?

① When were IBM computers installed at NASA?
② What was Dorothy worried about?
③ Did Dorothy lose her job when IBM computers were installed at NASA?
④ What did Dorothy suggest before accepting the offer?
⑤ How many team members could become programmers thanks to Dorothy?

The Frog Prince Continued

교과서
Words & Expressions

Key Words

- **anything**[éniθiŋ] 대 (부정문·의문문·조건문) 아무것도, 어떤 일도
- **believe**[bilíːv] 동 믿다
- **bright**[brait] 형 밝은, 눈부신
- **cart**[kɑːrt] 명 수레
- **chance**[tʃæns] 명 기회
- **clothes**[klouz] 명 옷, 의복
- **delicious**[dilíʃəs] 형 맛있는
- **enough**[ináf] 부 충분히
- **even**[íːvən] 부 ~조차도; 훨씬
- **ever**[évər] 부 언제나, 항상, (부정문, 의문문에 쓰여) 한 번도
- **fairy**[fέəri] 명 요정
- **fat**[fæt] 형 통통한, 살찐
- **find**[faind] 동 찾다
- **fool**[fuːl] 명 바보, 멍청이
- **frog**[frɔːg] 명 개구리
- **funny**[fáni] 형 웃긴
- **hit**[hit] 동 치다, 때리다
- **inside**[ìnsáid] 부 안에, 안으로
- **instead**[instéd] 부 대신에
- **invite**[inváit] 동 초대하다
- **kill**[kil] 동 죽이다
- **lesson**[lésn] 명 교훈, 단원
- **matter**[mǽtər] 동 중요하다, 문제가 되다
- **mess**[mes] 명 엉망진창
- **monster**[mánstər] 명 괴물
- **oops**[ups] 감 아이쿠, 이런
- **people**[píːpl] 명 백성, 국민, 사람들
- **pond**[pɑnd] 명 연못
- **princess**[prínsis] 명 공주
- **problem**[prάbləm] 명 문제
- **rest**[rest] 명 (the ~) 나머지
- **save**[seiv] 동 구하다
- **serve**[səːrv] 동 대접하다
- **shout**[ʃaut] 동 외치다
- **still**[stil] 부 여전히, 아직도
- **stuck**[stʌk] 형 꼼짝 못 하는, 움직일 수 없는
- **unhappily**[ənhǽpəli] 부 불행하게
- **water**[wɔ́ːtər] 동 침이 고이다, 침을 흘리다
- **wave**[weiv] 동 (손을) 흔들다
- **wheel**[hwiːl] 명 바퀴
- **witch**[witʃ] 명 마녀
- **worry**[wə́ːri] 동 걱정하다

Key Expressions

- **be better off** 더 잘 살다
- **by the name of** ~라는 이름의
- **feel like -ing** ~하고 싶다
- **from now on** 지금부터 죽
- **give it a try** 한번 해 보다, 시도하다
- **hand in hand** 손에 손을 잡고
- **hundreds of** 수백 개의 ~
- **jump around** 뛰어다니다
- **keep one's fingers crossed** 행운을 빌다
- **let+목적어+동사원형** …가 ~하도록 허락하다
- **look forward to+명사[동명사]** ~을 고대하다
- **look like** ~처럼 보이다
- **not ~ anymore** 더 이상 ~ 않다
- **on one's way to** ~에 가는 길[도중]에
- **pick up** 줍다, 집어들다
- **run away** 도망가다, 달아나다
- **so (that)+주어+can** ~ 하기 위해
- **thank A for B** B에 대해 A에게 감사하다
- **these days** 요즘에
- **to oneself** 혼자
- **turn … into** ~ …을 ~로 바꾸다
- **What's wrong with you?** 무슨 문제가 있니?
- **wait a minute** 잠깐

Word Power

※ 서로 비슷한 뜻을 가진 어휘

- □ **save** : **rescue** (구하다)
- □ **matter** : **count** (중요하다)
- □ **delicious** : **tasty** (맛있는)
- □ **chance** : **opportunity** (기회)

- □ **hit** : **strike** (때리다)
- □ **mess** : **untidiness** (엉망진창)
- □ **shout** : **yell** (외치다)
- □ **stuck** : **fixed** (움직이지 않는)

※ 서로 반대의 뜻을 가진 어휘

- □ **funny** (웃긴) ↔ **serious** (진지한)
- □ **believe** (믿다) ↔ **disbelieve** (믿지 않다)
- □ **bright** (밝은) ↔ **dark** (어두운)
- □ **find** (찾다) ↔ **lose** (잃어버리다)

- □ **inside** (안에) ↔ **outside** (밖에)
- □ **thin** (마른) ↔ **fat** (퉁퉁한, 살찐)
- □ **wrong** (잘못된) ↔ **right** (옳은)
- □ **happily** (행복하게) ↔ **unhappily** (불행하게)

English Dictionary

□ **cart** 수레
→ a vehicle with wheels that is pulled by an animal
동물이 끄는 바퀴가 달린 탈것

□ **delicious** 맛있는
→ very good to eat or drink
먹거나 마시기에 매우 좋은

□ **fairy** 요정
→ an imaginary creature like a small person with wings who has magic powers
마법의 힘을 가진 날개가 있는 작은 사람 같은 상상 속의 생명체

□ **frog** 개구리
→ a small, green animal with long back legs for jumping, that lives in or near water
물속이나 물가에 사는, 점프하기 위한 긴 뒷다리를 가진 작은 녹색의 동물

□ **hit** 치다, 때리다
→ to touch something or someone quickly and with force, usually hurting or damaging something
대개 무언가를 다치게 하거나 손상시키기 위해 물건이나 사람을 힘을 가해 빠르게 손을 대다

□ **invite** 초대하다
→ to ask someone to come to your house, to a party, etc.
누군가에게 당신의 집이나 파티에 오라고 청하다

□ **monster** 괴물
→ an imaginary creature that is large, ugly, and frightening
크고, 추하고, 무서운 상상 속의 생명체

□ **princess** 공주
→ the daughter of a king or queen, or one of their close female relatives
왕이나 왕비의 딸, 또는 그들의 가까운 여성 친척 중 한 명

□ **rest** 나머지
→ the part of something that remains
어떤 것의 남아 있는 일부

□ **shout** 외치다
→ to say something very loudly
무언가를 매우 크게 말하다

□ **stuck** 꼼짝 못하는
→ not able to move anywhere
아무데도 움직일 수 없는

□ **wave** (손을) 흔들다
→ to put your hand up and move it from side to side in order to attract someone's attention or to say goodbye
누군가의 관심을 끌거나 작별 인사를 하기 위해 손을 위로 올리고 좌우로 움직이다

□ **wheel** 바퀴
→ a circular object fixed under a vehicle so that it moves smoothly over the ground
지면 위로 차량이 부드럽게 움직이도록 차량 아래에 고정되어 있는 원형 물체

□ **witch** 마녀
→ in stories, a woman who has magical powers
이야기에서 마법의 힘을 가진 여자

The Frog Prince Continued

Characters: Frog Prince, Princess, Witch 1, Witch 2, Fairy

Scene 1: In a room

(Prince comes in, jumping around.)
'뛰면서'의 뜻으로 동시동작을 나타내는 분사구문

Princess: Stop jumping around, honey.
stop+동명사: ~하기를 멈추다, stop+to부정사: ~하기 위해 멈추다

Prince: Well, I just can't stop.

Princess: You're not a frog anymore.

Prince: What's wrong with you? You don't go down to the pond these days.

Princess: I don't like it when you jump around in the room. Go out to
'when' 이하의 내용을 받는 것
kill monsters and save our people.

Prince: I don't want to go out and kill anything. I just feel like running away. *(Picking up a book)* Listen! "They lived happily ever after. The end." I'm living my life as the book says, but we're not happy.
~하는 대로, ~하는 바와 같이'(접속사)
What's the problem?

Princess: What's the problem? There are hundreds of problems! Sometimes I think we were better off when you were still a frog.
'I think' 뒤에 접속사 'that'이 생략된 구문   '더 잘 살다, 더 부유하다'(be well off'의 비교급)

Prince: Still a frog .... Yes! That's it! *(Goes out)*

Scene 2: On the mountain

Prince: *(To himself)* I need to find the witch, who will turn me back into
재귀대명사   계속적 용법의 관계대명사
a frog.

　(Shouting) Ms. Witch, Ms. Witch. Where are you? Please help me!

Witch 1: *(Coming out of the house)* Hi, Prince. How are you feeling?

Prince: I'm glad to meet you. I'm the Frog Prince. I hope you can turn me back into a frog so I can live happily ever after.

Witch 1: Frog Prince, you say? That's funny. You don't look like a frog. Well, it doesn't matter. If you're a prince, you're a prince. And I won't let you save Snow White. Here, eat the rest of this apple.
let+목적어+목적격보어(동사원형): 목적어가 ~하도록 내버려 두다

Prince: No, thank you. That's not what I want! *(Runs away)*
선행사를 포함한 관계대명사: ~하는 것

---

witch 마녀

fairy 요정

princess 공주

not ~ anymore 더 이상 ~ 않다

pond 연못

these days 요즘에

monster 괴물

save 구하다

feel like -ing ~하고 싶다

pick up 줍다, 집어들다

ever 언제나, 항상; (부정문, 의문문에 쓰여) 한 번도

problem 문제

hundreds of 수백 개의 ~

be better off 더 잘 살다

still 여전히, 아직도

to oneself 혼잣말로

turn … into ~ …을 ~로 바꾸다

look like ~처럼 보이다

matter 중요하다; 문제가 되다

rest 나머지

run away 도망가다, 달아나다

(Prince and Witch 2 come in.)

Prince: Ms. Witch, Ms. Witch. Where are you? Please help me! I'm the Frog ....

Witch 2: If you're a frog, I'm the King of France.

Prince: No, I'm not a frog. I'm the Frog Prince. But I need a witch to turn me back into a frog so I can live happily ever after. Can you do it?

Witch 2: Let's talk about it inside. I will serve you a delicious lunch. Come in.

Prince: Thank you for inviting me. Oh, this house is made of cookies and candies. Wait a minute. Do you know any children by the name of Hansel and Gretel?

Witch 2: Yes, Prince, I do. *(With her mouth watering)* They are not fat enough yet, but you are ....

(Prince runs away and finds a fairy.)

Prince: I'm glad to meet you, Ms. Fairy. I am the Frog Prince. Could you turn me back into a frog so I can live happily ever after?

Fairy: Well, I'm on my way to see Cinderella, but I'll give it a try. It's my first time, you know. *(Fairy turns Prince into a wheel.)*

Fairy: Oops! Sorry, but don't worry. Everything will be okay.

Prince: *(To himself)* Oh, what a fool I've been! I want to be sitting at home with the Princess, living happily ever after. But instead, I'm stuck here under this cart and I'll live unhappily ever after.

(The clock hits twelve, and the wheel turns into Prince.)

Prince: I can't believe this. Thank you for giving me a second chance. Now I know how I should live my life. *(Goes out)*

Fairy: *(Waving her hand)* You learned a good lesson. I'll keep my fingers crossed.

Scene 3: In the Frog Prince's house

(Prince runs in, smiling.)

Princess: Where have you been? I've been worried. Your clothes are a mess.

Prince: *(Looking at Princess)* You believed me when no one else in the world did. You loved me even when I was a frog. From now on, I will make you happier.

Princess: I'm glad to hear that. I'll make you even happier.

Prince: Great! I'm looking forward to our bright future. Ha-ha ....

(They run to the pond together, jumping hand in hand.)

---

inside 안에, 안으로

serve 대접하다

delicious 맛있는

wait a minute 잠깐

by the name of ~라는 이름의

water 침이 고이다, 침을 흘리다

fat 통통한, 살찐

on one's way to ~에 가는 길[도중]에

give it a try 한번 해 보다, 시도하다

fool 바보, 멍청이

instead 대신에

stuck 꼼짝 못 하는, 움직일 수 없는

cart 수레

wave (손을) 흔들다

lesson 교훈; 단원

keep one's fingers crossed 행운을 빌다

clothes 의복, 옷

mess 엉망진창

even ~조차도; 훨씬

from now on 지금부터 죽

hand in hand 손에 손을 잡고

● 우리말을 참고하여 빈칸에 알맞은 말을 쓰시오.

1 The _____ _____ Continued

2 _____ : Frog Prince, Princess, Witch 1, Witch 2, Fairy

3 _____ 1: In a room

4 *(Prince comes in, _____ around.)*

5 Princess: _____ _____ around, honey.

6 Prince: Well, I just _____ _____ .

7 Princess: You're not a frog _____ .

8 Prince: _____ _____ _____ you? You don't go down to the pond these days.

9 Princess: _____ _____ _____ _____ _____ you jump around in the room. Go out to kill monsters and save our people.

10 Prince: I don't want to go out and kill anything. I just _____ _____ _____ away. *(Picking up a book)* Listen! "They lived happily ever after. The end." I'm living my life _____ the book says, but we're not happy. What's the problem?

11 Princess: What's the problem? There are _____ _____ problems! Sometimes I think we _____ _____ _____ when you were still a frog.

12 Prince: Still a frog .... Yes! _____ _____ ! *(Goes out)*

13 _____ 2: On the mountain

14 Prince: *(_____ _____)* I need to find the witch, who will turn me back _____ a frog. *(Shouting)* Ms. Witch, Ms. Witch. Where are you? Please help me!

15 Witch 1: *(Coming out of the house)* Hi, Prince. _____ are you feeling?

16 Prince: I'm glad to meet you. I'm the Frog Prince. I hope you can _____ _____ _____ _____ a frog so I can live happily _____ _____.

17 Witch 1: Frog Prince, you say? That's funny. You don't _____ _____ a frog. Well, it doesn't matter. If you're a prince, you're a prince. And I won't _____ _____ _____ Snow White. Here, eat the rest of this apple.

18 Prince: No, thank you. That's not what I _____! *(Runs away)*

19 *(Prince and Witch 2 _____ _____.)*

20 Prince: Ms. Witch, Ms. Witch. _____ are you? Please help me! I'm the Frog ....

21 Witch 2: _____ you're a frog, I'm the King of France.

22 Prince: No, I'm not a frog. I'm the Frog Prince. But I need a witch to _____ _____ _____ _____ a frog so I can _____ _____ ever after. Can you do it?

23 Witch 2: Let's talk about it inside. I will _____ you a delicious lunch. Come in.

24 Prince: Thank you for inviting me. Oh, this house _____ _____ _____ _____ and candies. Wait a minute. Do you know any children _____ _____ _____ _____ Hansel and Gretel?

25 Witch 2: Yes, Prince, _____ _____. *(With her mouth watering)* They are not fat enough yet, but you are ....

26 *(Prince _____ _____ and finds a fairy.)*

27 Prince: I'm glad to meet you, Ms. Fairy. I am the Frog Prince. _____ _____ turn me back into a frog _____ I can live happily ever after?

16 왕자: 당신을 만나서 기뻐요. 저는 개구리 왕자예요. 저는 당신이 저를 다시 개구리로 바꿔줘서 제가 앞으로 행복하게 살 수 있게 되기를 원해요.

17 마녀 1: 개구리 왕자라고 했어요? 그거 웃기는군요. 당신은 개구리처럼 보이지 않아요. 음, 그건 중요하지 않아요. 당신이 왕자라면 왕자인 거죠. 그리고 나는 당신이 백설공주를 구하도록 놔두지 않을 거예요. 여기, 이 사과의 나머지를 먹어요.

18 왕자: 고맙지만 됐어요. 그건 제가 원하는 게 아니에요! (도망간다)

19 (왕자와 마녀 2가 등장한다.)

20 왕자: 마녀님, 마녀님. 어디 계세요? 저 좀 도와주세요! 저는 개구리 ….

21 마녀 2: 당신이 개구리라면 나는 프랑스의 왕이에요.

22 왕자: 아니요, 저는 개구리가 아니에요. 저는 개구리 왕자예요. 하지만 저를 다시 개구리로 바꿔 줘서 제가 앞으로 행복하게 살 수 있게 해 줄 마녀가 필요해요. 그렇게 해 주실 수 있나요?

23 마녀 2: 안에서 그것에 관해 이야기해 봅시다. 내가 당신에게 맛있는 점심을 대접할게요. 들어와요.

24 왕자: 저를 초대해 주셔서 감사합니다. 오, 이 집은 과자와 사탕으로 만들어져 있네요. 잠깐만요. 당신은 헨젤과 그레텔이라는 이름의 아이들을 혹시 알아요?

25 마녀 2: 그래요, 왕자님. 알고 있어요. (그녀가 군침을 흘리면서) 그 애들은 아직 충분히 살이 찌지 않았지만, 당신은 ….

26 (왕자는 도망치다가 요정을 발견한다.)

27 왕자: 만나게 되어 기쁩니다, 요정님. 저는 개구리 왕자예요. 저를 다시 개구리로 바꿔 앞으로 행복하게 살 수 있게 해 주실 수 있나요?

28 **Fairy:** Well, I'm _____ _____ _____ to see Cinderella, but I'll _____ _____ _____ _____. It's my first time, you know. *(Fairy turns Prince into a wheel.)*

29 **Fairy:** Oops! Sorry, but don't worry. Everything _____ _____ _____.

30 **Prince:** *(To himself)* Oh, _____ _____ _____ I've been! I want to be sitting at home with the Princess, living happily ever after. But instead, I'm _____ here under this cart and I'll live _____ ever after.

31 *(The clock hits twelve, and the wheel _____ _____ Prince.)*

32 **Prince:** I can't believe this. Thank you for _____ _____ _____ _____ _____. Now I know _____ _____ _____ my life. *(Goes out)*

33 **Fairy:** *(Waving her hand)* You learned a good lesson. I'll _____ _____ _____ _____.

34 **Scene 3:** In the Frog Prince's house

35 *(Prince runs in, _____.)*

36 **Princess:** Where _____ _____ _____? I've been worried. Your clothes are a mess.

37 **Prince:** *(Looking at Princess)* You believed me when no one _____ in the world _____. You loved me even when I was a frog. From now on, I will make you happier.

38 **Princess:** I'm glad to hear that. I'll make you _____ happier.

39 **Prince:** Great! I'm _____ _____ _____ our bright future. Ha-ha ....

40 *(They run to the pond together, jumping _____ _____ _____.)*

28 요정: 음, 저는 신데렐라를 만나러 가는 길이지만, 한번 해 볼게요. 아시다시피 이건 제가 처음으로 해 보는 거예요. (요정이 왕자를 바퀴로 바꾼다.)

29 요정: 이런! 미안하지만 걱정하지 마세요. 모든 게 잘될 거예요.

30 왕자: (혼잣말로) 오, 내가 얼마나 바보였던가! 앞으로 행복하게 살면서 집에서 공주와 함께 앉아 있고 싶구나. 하지만 대신에 여기 이 수레 아래에 붙박여 있고 앞으로 불행하게 살게 되겠구나.

31 (시계가 12시를 치자 바퀴가 왕자로 바뀐다.)

32 왕자: 믿을 수가 없네. 두 번째 기회를 주셔서 감사합니다. 이제 나는 내 인생을 어떻게 살아야 할지 알겠어요. (퇴장한다)

33 요정: (손을 흔들며) 좋은 교훈을 배웠군요. 행운을 빌어요.

34 장면 3: 개구리 왕자의 집 안에서

35 (왕자가 미소를 지으며 뛰어 들어온다.)

36 공주: 어디 있었어요? 걱정했잖아요. 옷이 엉망진창이네요.

37 왕자: (공주를 바라보며) 당신은 세상 어느 누구도 나를 믿지 않을 때 나를 믿어 주었어요. 당신은 내가 개구리일 때조차도 나를 사랑해 주었죠. 이제부터는 내가 당신을 더 행복하게 해 주겠어요.

38 공주: 그 말을 들으니 기뻐요. 제가 당신을 훨씬 더 행복하게 해 줄게요.

39 왕자: 좋아요! 난 우리의 밝은 미래를 기대할게요. 하하 ….

40 (그들은 서로 손을 잡고 함께 연못으로 뛰어간다.)

● 우리말을 참고하여 본문을 영작하시오.

1 계속된 개구리 왕자
➡ _____

2 등장인물: 개구리 왕자, 공주, 마녀 1, 마녀 2, 요정
➡ _____

3 장면 1: 방 안에서
➡ _____

4 (왕자가 이리저리 뛰어다니며 등장한다.)
➡ _____

5 공주: 여보, 이리저리 뛰어다니지 마세요.
➡ _____

6 왕자: 저, 나는 단지 멈출 수 없을 뿐이에요.
➡ _____

7 공주: 당신은 이제 개구리가 아니에요.
➡ _____

8 왕자: 당신한테 무슨 문제가 있어요? 요즘 당신은 연못으로 내려가지도 않잖아요.
➡ _____

9 공주: 나는 당신이 방 안에서 이리저리 뛰어다니는 게 마음에 안 들어요. 나가서 괴물들을 죽이고 우리 백성을 구하세요.
➡ _____
_____

10 왕자: 나는 밖에 나가서 아무것도 죽이고 싶지 않아요. 나는 단지 멀리 뛰어다니고 싶을 뿐이오. (책을 집어 들고) 들어 봐요! "그들은 그 후로 행복하게 살았다. 끝." 나는 책에서 말한 것처럼 내 인생을 살고 있지만, 우리는 행복하지 않아요. 뭐가 문제일까요?
➡ _____
_____
_____

11 공주: 뭐가 문제냐고요? 수백 가지 문제가 있어요! 가끔 나는 당신이 아직 개구리일 때 더 잘 살지 않았나 생각해요.
➡ _____
_____

12 왕자: 아직 개구리라 …. 그래! 바로 그거요! (퇴장한다.)
➡ _____

13 장면 2: 산속에서
➡ _____

14 왕자: (혼잣말로) 나는 마녀를 찾아야 해. 그녀가 나를 다시 개구리로 바꿔 줄 거야.
(소리치며) 마녀님, 마녀님. 어디 계세요? 저 좀 도와주세요!

➡ _____

_____

15 마녀 1: (집 밖으로 나오며) 안녕, 왕자님. 기분이 어때요?

➡ _____

16 왕자: 당신을 만나서 기뻐요. 저는 개구리 왕자예요. 저는 당신이 저를 다시 개구리로 바꿔줘서
제가 앞으로 행복하게 살 수 있게 되기를 원해요.

➡ _____

_____

17 마녀 1: 개구리 왕자라고 했어요? 그거 웃기는군요. 당신은 개구리처럼 보이지 않아요. 음, 그건
중요하지 않아요. 당신이 왕자라면 왕자인 거죠. 그리고 나는 당신이 백설공주를 구하도록 놔두지
않을 거예요. 여기, 이 사과의 나머지를 먹어요.

➡ _____

_____

_____

18 왕자: 고맙지만 됐어요. 그건 제가 원하는 게 아니에요! (도망간다)

➡ _____

19 (왕자와 마녀 2가 등장한다.)

➡ _____

20 왕자: 마녀님, 마녀님. 어디 계세요? 저 좀 도와주세요! 저는 개구리 ….

➡ _____

21 마녀 2: 당신이 개구리라면 나는 프랑스의 왕이에요.

➡ _____

22 왕자: 아니요, 저는 개구리가 아니에요. 저는 개구리 왕자예요. 하지만 저를 다시 개구리로 바꿔
줘서 제가 앞으로 행복하게 살 수 있게 해 줄 마녀가 필요해요. 그렇게 해 주실 수 있나요?

➡ _____

_____

23 마녀 2: 안에서 그것에 관해 이야기해 봅시다. 내가 당신에게 맛있는 점심을 대접할게요. 들어와요.

➡ _____

24 왕자: 저를 초대해 주셔서 감사합니다. 오, 이 집은 과자와 사탕으로 만들어져 있네요. 잠깐만요.
당신은 헨젤과 그레텔이라는 이름의 아이들을 혹시 알아요?

➡ _____

_____

25 마녀 2: 그래요, 왕자님, 알고 있어요. (그녀가 군침을 흘리면서) 그 애들은 아직 충분히 살이
찌지 않았지만, 당신은 ….

➡ _____

26 (왕자는 도망치다가 요정을 발견한다.)

➡ _____

27 왕자: 만나게 되어 기쁩니다, 요정님. 저는 개구리 왕자예요. 저를 다시 개구리로 바꿔 앞으로 행복하게 살 수 있게 해 주실 수 있나요?

➡ _____

➡ _____

28 요정: 음, 저는 신데렐라를 만나러 가는 길이지만, 한번 해 볼게요. 아시다시피 이건 제가 처음으로 해 보는 거예요. (요정이 왕자를 바퀴로 바꾼다.)

➡ _____

➡ _____

29 요정: 이런! 미안하지만 걱정하지 마세요. 모든 게 잘될 거예요

➡ _____

30 왕자: (혼잣말로) 오, 내가 얼마나 바보였던가! 앞으로 행복하게 살면서 집에서 공주와 함께 앉아 있고 싶구나. 하지만 대신에 여기 이 수레 아래에 붙박여 있고 앞으로 불행하게 살게 되겠구나.

➡ _____

➡ _____

31 (시계가 12시를 치자 바퀴가 왕자로 바뀐다.)

➡ _____

32 왕자: 믿을 수가 없네. 두 번째 기회를 주셔서 감사합니다. 이제 나는 내 인생을 어떻게 살아야 할지 알겠어요. (퇴장한다)

➡ _____

➡ _____

33 요정: (손을 흔들며) 좋은 교훈을 배웠군요. 행운을 빌어요.

➡ _____

34 장면 3: 개구리 왕자의 집 안에서

➡ _____

35 (왕자가 미소를 지으며 뛰어 들어온다.)

➡ _____

36 공주: 어디 있었어요? 걱정했잖아요. 옷이 엉망진창이네요.

➡ _____

37 왕자: (공주를 바라보며) 당신은 세상 어느 누구도 나를 믿지 않을 때 나를 믿어 주었어요. 당신은 내가 개구리일 때조차도 나를 사랑해 주었죠. 이제부터는 내가 당신을 더 행복하게 해 주겠어요.

➡ _____

➡ _____

38 공주: 그 말을 들으니 기뻐요. 제가 당신을 훨씬 더 행복하게 해 줄게요.

➡ _____

39 왕자: 좋아요! 난 우리의 밝은 미래를 기대할게요. 하하….

➡ _____

40 (그들은 서로 손을 잡고 함께 연못으로 뛰어간다.)

➡ _____

01 다음 문장에 공통으로 들어갈 말을 쓰시오.

> (1) On hot summer days, you often _____ eating ice cream.
> (2) It is so cold that I _____ we are in the North Pole!

02 영영풀이에 해당하는 단어를 〈보기〉에서 찾아 첫 번째 빈칸에 쓰고, 두 번째 빈칸에는 우리말 뜻을 쓰시오.

> ┤ 보기 ├
> wheel　fairy　princess　frog

(1) _____ : a circular object fixed under a vehicle so that it moves smoothly over the ground: _____

(2) _____ : a small, green animal with long back legs for jumping, that lives in or near water : _____

(3) _____ : the daughter of a king or queen, or one of their close female relatives: _____

(4) _____ : an imaginary creature like a small person with wings who has magic powers : _____

03 다음 우리말에 맞게 빈칸에 알맞은 말을 쓰시오.

(1) 고르디아스 왕은 황소 수레를 갖고 있었다.
➡ King Gordias had an ox c_____.

(2) 가장 가까운 쉼터에서, 우리는 점심 시간 동안 음식을 대접했어.
➡ At the closest shelter, we s_____ food during lunch time.

(3) 대신에, 그녀는 그녀의 방에서 대략 하루 동안 혼자 기도했습니다.
➡ I_____, she prayed alone for about a day in her room.

04 다음 우리말을 주어진 어휘를 이용하여 영어로 옮기시오.

(1) 음악을 들으면서, 그녀는 창문을 닦았다. (listening, wiped)
➡ _____

(2) 그 소식을 들었을 때, 그녀는 울기 시작했다. (hearing, news, began)
➡ _____

(3) 지금 떠나면, 너는 지각하지 않을 거야. (leaving, won't, late)
➡ _____

05 다음 문장에서 어법상 <u>어색한</u> 부분을 찾아 바르게 고치시오.

> I couldn't understand which the teacher said.

_____ ➡ _____

[06~08] 다음 글을 읽고 물음에 답하시오.

Scene 1: In a room
(Prince comes in, jumping around.)
Princess: (A)Stop to jump around, honey.
Prince: Well, I just can't stop.
Princess: You're not a frog anymore.
Prince: What's wrong with you? You don't go down to the pond these days.
Princess: I don't like it when you jump around in the room. Go out to kill monsters and save our people.

Prince: I don't want to go out and kill anything. I just feel like ___ⓐ___ away. *(Picking up a book)* Listen! "They lived happily ever after. The end." I'm living my life as the book says, but we're not happy. What's the problem?

Princess: What's the problem? There are hundreds of problems! Sometimes I think we were better off when you were still a frog.

Prince: Still a frog .... Yes! That's it! *(Goes out)*

06 위 글의 빈칸 ⓐ에 run을 알맞은 형태로 쓰시오.

➡ _____

07 위 글의 밑줄 친 (A)에서 어법상 틀린 부분을 찾아 고치시오.

_____ ➡ _____

08 본문의 내용과 일치하도록 다음 빈칸 (A)와 (B)에 알맞은 단어를 쓰시오.

Princess doesn't like it when Prince (A)_____ _____ in the room, and tells Prince to go out to kill monsters and save the people, but Prince (B)_____ _____ to go out and kill anything.

[09~11] 다음 글을 읽고 물음에 답하시오.

Scene 2: On the mountain

Prince: *(To (A)[him / himself)]* I need to find the witch, who will turn me back into a frog.
(Shouting) Ms. Witch, Ms. Witch. Where are you? Please help me!

Witch 1: *(Coming out of the house)* Hi, Prince. (B)[How / What] are you feeling?

Prince: I'm glad to meet you. I'm the Frog Prince. I hope you can turn me back into a frog so I can live happily ever after.

Witch 1: Frog Prince, you say? That's funny. You don't (C)[look / look like] a frog. Well, it doesn't matter. If you're a prince, you're a prince. ⓐAnd I won't let you save Snow White. Here, eat the rest of this apple.

Prince: No, thank you. That's not what I want! *(Runs away)*

09 위 글의 괄호 (A)~(C)에서 문맥이나 어법상 알맞은 낱말을 골라 쓰시오.

➡ (A) _____ (B) _____ (C) _____

10 위 글의 밑줄 친 ⓐ를 다음과 같이 바꿔 쓸 때 빈칸에 들어갈 알맞은 말을 두 단어로 쓰시오.

➡ And I won't allow you _____ _____ Snow White.

11 Why does Prince want Witch 1 to turn him back into a frog? Answer in English beginning with "Because".

➡ _____
_____

출제율 90%

01 다음 단어에 대한 영어 설명이 어색한 것은?

① stuck: not able to move anywhere
② dinosaur: an imaginary creature that is large, ugly, and frightening
③ witch: in stories, a woman who has magical powers
④ delicious: very good to eat or drink
⑤ wave: to put your hand up and move it from side to side in order to attract someone's attention or to say goodbye

출제율 95%

02 다음 짝지어진 단어의 관계가 같도록 빈칸에 알맞은 말을 쓰시오.

save : rescue – yell : _____

출제율 90%

03 다음 영영풀이에 해당하는 단어를 고르시오.

to touch something or someone quickly and with force, usually hurting or damaging something

① hit　　　　② wound
③ rest　　　　④ save
⑤ worry

출제율 95%

04 다음 문장에 공통으로 들어갈 단어를 쓰시오.

• The smells from the kitchen made our mouths _____.
• Rain is the result of the circulation of _____ in nature.　　*circulation 순환

출제율 95%

05 다음 문장의 밑줄 친 어구와 의미가 같은 말을 5 단어로 쓰시오.

I am longing to watch this movie.

➡ _____

출제율 100%

06 다음 빈칸에 들어갈 말이 알맞게 짝지어진 것은?

• They run to the pond together, jumping hand _____ hand.
• Could you turn me back _____ a frog so I can live happily ever after?
• Do you know any children _____ the name of Hansel and Gretel?

① on – with – down
② into – of – up
③ by – of – up
④ in – into – by
⑤ by – of – down

출제율 95%

07 다음 중 짝지어진 단어의 관계가 다른 것은?

① funny : serious　　② bright : dark
③ win : lose　　　　④ shout : yell
⑤ wrong : right

출제율 95%

08 다음 문장의 빈칸에 공통으로 들어갈 말을 쓰시오.

• Taking a _____ helps you be more energetic and active.
• For the _____ of the break, we're going to Disneyland!

09 다음 빈칸에 들어갈 말을 〈보기〉에서 찾아 쓰시오. (필요하면 변형하여 쓰시오.)

┤ 보기 ├

run away   from now on   good off

(1) He is far _____ than he was three years ago.

(2) If a strange adult comes to you or call you, _____.

(3) _____, we will not sell any Japanese products.

10 〈보기〉의 밑줄 친 As[as]와 의미가 같은 것은?

┤ 보기 ├

<u>As</u> I told you before, I want some time to think by myself.

① <u>As</u> times goes by, you will understand everything.

② We were busy <u>as</u> we had a lot of guests.

③ The boys laughed <u>as</u> she passed by.

④ <u>As</u> I took a shower, someone knocked the door.

⑤ Please be prepared <u>as</u> you promised me.

11 다음 중 밑줄 친 단어의 쓰임이 <u>다른</u> 하나를 고르시오.

① It's too hot here. I feel like <u>drinking</u> iced coffee.

② I'm sorry about <u>breaking</u> your favorite plates.

③ Jenny's job is <u>writing</u> lyrics for pop music.

④ He got lost, <u>being</u> a stranger there.

⑤ I'm looking forward to <u>seeing</u> your family sometime.

12 주어진 〈보기〉를 참고하여 같은 의미의 문장을 쓰시오.

┤ 보기 ├

He sent me a birthday present, and it made me happy.

→ He sent me a birthday present, which made me happy.

(1) We went to the hospital, but it was closed because it was Sunday.

➡ We went to the hospital, _____ _____.

(2) Jake works for a bank, and it is located near my school.

➡ Jake works for a bank, _____ _____.

(3) Cathy likes a Chinese actor, and he is good at kung fu.

➡ Cathy likes a Chinese actor, _____ _____.

13 다음 주어진 문장과 의미가 같은 문장을 고르시오.

You did a really foolish thing.

① How foolish a thing is!

② How foolish thing you did!

③ What a foolish you did a thing!

④ What really foolish thing you did!

⑤ What a foolish thing you did!

14 다음 주어진 우리말에 맞게 괄호 안에서 필요한 단어만 골라 영어로 쓰시오.

아버지는 내가 밤을 새우는 것을 허락하지 않으실 거야.

(my, not, let, allow, dad, me, up, down, every, will, night, all, stay)

➡ _____

15 다음 빈칸에 들어갈 말이 순서대로 짝지어진 것은?

> • I have a stomachache. I should stop _____.
>
> • A boy was looking for his toy, so I stopped _____ him.

① eat – help

② eating – helping

③ eating – to help

④ to eat – to help

⑤ to eat – helping

16 다음 중 어법상 어색한 문장을 고르시오.

① Ms. Lee, who lives in New York, wants to be a musical actress.

② I have a friend, who was born in France.

③ Jen is holding a poodle which has curly brown hair.

④ I want to see the robot that was made by Dr. Kim.

⑤ Can you be friends with Thomas, that you have never met before?

17 다음 중 어법상 어색한 문장을 고르시오.

① My shoes were covered with mud.

② Cheese is made from milk.

③ BTS is known to people from all over the world.

④ The library is filled with old books.

⑤ The house is made by candies and cookies.

18 밑줄 친 부분이 〈보기〉와 쓰임이 같은 것을 고르시오.

> ┤ 보기 ├
> He asked me to tell the truth and I did.

① I did the dishes at least once a week for my family.

② You should say what you did yesterday.

③ The wind moved slowly, so did the clouds.

④ When I was younger, I did my homework right after school.

⑤ All of the athletes did their best to win gold medals.

[19~21] 다음 글을 읽고 물음에 답하시오.

> Scene 2: On the mountain
>
> Prince: (To ①himself) I need to find the witch, who will turn me back into a frog.
> (Shouting) Ms. Witch, Ms. Witch. Where are ②you? Please help me!
>
> Witch 1: (Coming out of the house) Hi, Prince. How are ③you feeling?
>
> Prince: I'm glad to meet you. I'm the Frog Prince. I hope you can turn me back into a frog so ④I can live happily ever after.
>
> Witch 1: Frog Prince, ⑤you say? That's funny. You don't look like a frog. Well, it doesn't matter. If you're a prince, you're a prince. And I won't let you save Snow White. Here, eat the rest of this apple.
>
> Prince: No, thank you. That's not _____ⓐ_____ I want! (Runs away)

19 위 글의 빈칸 ⓐ에 들어갈 알맞은 말을 고르시오.

① that   ② whom

③ how   ④ which

⑤ what

20 밑줄 친 ①~⑤ 중에서 가리키는 대상이 나머지 넷과 <u>다른</u> 것은?

①   ②   ③   ④   ⑤

21 Which question CANNOT be answered after reading the passage?

① Where is the setting of Scene 2?

② Whom does Prince want to meet?

③ What does Prince want Witch 1 to do?

④ What will Prince give Witch 1 as the price for turning him back into a frog?

⑤ Why does Witch 1 tell Prince "That's funny?"

[22~24] 다음 글을 읽고 물음에 답하시오.

Scene 1: In a room

(Prince comes in, jumping around.)

Princess: Stop jumping around, honey.

Prince: Well, I just can't stop.

Princess: You're not a frog anymore.

Prince: What's wrong with you? You don't go down to the pond these days.

Princess: I don't like it when you jump around in the room. Go out to kill monsters and save our people.

Prince: I don't want to go out and kill anything. I just feel like running away. *(Picking up a book)* Listen! "They lived happily ever after. The end." I'm living my life ⓐas the book says, but we're not happy. What's the problem?

Princess: What's the problem? There are hundreds of problems! Sometimes I think we were better off when you were still a frog.

Prince: Still a frog .... Yes! That's it! *(Goes out)*

22 위 글의 밑줄 친 ⓐas와 같은 의미로 쓰인 것을 고르시오.

① <u>As</u> you were out, I left a message.

② Treat me <u>as</u> a friend.

③ Susan is not <u>as</u> pretty as Jane.

④ <u>As</u> the poet says, a little learning is a dangerous thing.

⑤ He sat watching her <u>as</u> she got ready.

23 위 글의 종류로 알맞은 것을 고르시오.

① article   ② play

③ biography   ④ essay

⑤ review

24 According to the passage, which is NOT true?

① Princess tells Prince to stop jumping around.

② Prince just can't stop.

③ Prince doesn't go down to the pond these days.

④ Prince doesn't want to go out and kill anything.

⑤ Prince just feels inclined to run away.

[25~27] 다음 글을 읽고 물음에 답하시오.

(Prince and Witch 2 come in.)

Prince: Ms. Witch, Ms. Witch. Where are you? Please help me! I'm the Frog ....

Witch 2: (A)If you're a frog, I'm the King of France.

Prince: No, I'm not a frog. I'm the Frog Prince. But I need a witch to turn me back ⓐ a frog so I can live happily ever after. Can you do it?

Witch 2: Let's talk about it inside. I will serve you a delicious lunch. Come in.

Prince: Thank you for inviting me. Oh, this house is made ___ⓑ___ cookies and candies. Wait a minute. (B)당신은 헨젤과 그레텔이라는 이름의 아이들을 알아요?

Witch 2: Yes, Prince, I do. *(With her mouth watering)* They are not fat enough yet, but you are ....

출제율 95%

25 위 글의 빈칸 ⓐ와 ⓑ에 들어갈 전치사가 바르게 짝지어진 것은?

ⓐ	ⓑ	ⓐ	ⓑ

① into – from ② for – of
③ in – from ④ in – to
⑤ into – of

출제율 95%

26 위 글의 밑줄 친 (A)에서 알 수 있는 'Witch 2'의 심경으로 가장 알맞은 것을 고르시오.

① excited ② doubtful
③ bored ④ depressed
⑤ satisfied

출제율 90%

27 위 글의 밑줄 친 (B)의 우리말에 맞게 주어진 어휘를 이용하여 12 단어로 영작하시오.

> any children, Hansel and Gretel

➡ _____

_____

[28~30] 다음 글을 읽고 물음에 답하시오.

Prince: *(To himself)* Oh, (A)what a fool I've been! I want to be sitting at home with the Princess, living happily ever after. But instead, I'm stuck here under this cart and I'll live unhappily ever after.

(The clock hits twelve, and the wheel turns into Prince.)

Prince: I can't believe this. Thank you for giving me ___ⓐ___. Now I know how I should live my life. *(Goes out)*

Fairy: *(Waving her hand)* You learned a good lesson. I'll keep my fingers crossed.

출제율 95%

28 위 글의 빈칸 ⓐ에 들어갈 알맞은 말을 고르시오.

① all the challenges
② a handsome appearance
③ the popular identity
④ a second chance
⑤ an attractive personality

출제율 90%

29 위 글의 밑줄 친 (A)를 how를 사용하여 고치시오.

➡ _____

출제율 100%

30 According to the passage, which is NOT true?

① Prince wants to stay at home with the Princess.
② Prince wants to live happily with the Princess.
③ Fairy made Prince turn into a frog.
④ Fairy gave a good lesson to Prince.
⑤ When the clock hits twelve, the wheel turns into Prince.

MEMO

MEMO

Middle School 3-1
학교시험 완벽 대비

1학기 전과정
plus⁺
적중100
영어 기출문제집

영어 중 3

천재 | 정사열

Best Collection

내용문의 중등영어발전소 적중100 편집부 TEL 070-7707-0457

INSIGHT
on the textbook

교과서 파헤치기

영어 기출 문제집
적중 100 plus
1학기 전과정

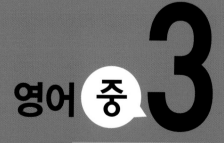

영어 중 3

천재 | 정사열

INSIGHT
on the textbook

교과서 파헤치기

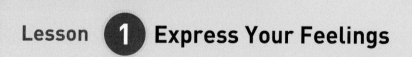

※ 다음 영어를 우리말로 쓰시오.

01 healthy	22 facial	
02 joke	23 lunch break	
03 book	24 since	
04 deliver	25 wonder	
05 miss	26 finally	
06 available	27 promise	
07 nervous	28 laughter	
08 expression	29 represent	
09 written	30 even	
10 gentleman	31 letter	
11 actually	32 meaningful	
12 guess	33 tear	
13 present	34 move	
14 human	35 keep in touch	
15 various	36 such as	
16 tone	37 care for	
17 break wind	38 stand for	
18 visually	39 laugh out loud	
19 popular	40 grow+비교급	
20 whole	41 the same ~ as	
21 chance	42 can't wait for	
	43 with+명사+형용사~	

※ 다음 우리말을 영어로 쓰시오.

01	농담	
02	실제로	
03	막대기, 나뭇가지	
04	의미 있는	
05	전달하다	
06	표현	
07	웃음	
08	신사	
09	드디어, 마지막으로	
10	구할 수 있는, 이용할 수 있는	
11	예매하다, 예약하다	
12	건강에 좋은	
13	완전한, 전체의	
14	인간적인, 인간의	
15	약속하다; 약속	
16	어조, 말투	
17	그리워하다	
18	얼굴의	
19	글로 쓴, 글로 표현된	
20	시각적으로	
21	초조한	

22	인기 있는	
23	선물	
24	꽤	
25	나타내다, 대표하다	
26	이사하다	
27	추측하다, 짐작하다	
28	궁금해 하다	
29	기회, 가능성	
30	눈물	
31	다양한	
32	문자	
33	찬장	
34	기름에 튀긴	
35	큰 소리로 웃다	
36	~을 몹시 기다리다	
37	~을 의미하다, 상징하다	
38	~와 같은 …	
39	~을 좋아하다	
40	계속해서 연락하다	
41	어느 때보다 행복한	
42	~을 보다	
43	~에 대해 걱정하다	

※ 다음 영영풀이에 알맞은 단어를 <보기>에서 골라 쓴 후, 우리말 뜻을 쓰시오.

1 _____ : having many different features: _____

2 _____ : a type or variety of something: _____

3 _____ : involving writing rather than speaking: _____

4 _____ : able to be bought or used: _____

5 _____ : in a way that is connected with seeing or sight: _____

6 _____ : from a time in the past until a later past time or until now: _____

7 _____ : to write something using a computer or typewrite: _____

8 _____ : to bring goods, letter, etc. to the proper person: _____

9 _____ : a man who is polite, well educated and has excellent manners: _____

10 _____ : to be accepted as meaning a certain thing: _____

11 _____ : an informal talk involving a small group of people or only two: _____

12 _____ : a sign, shape, or object that is used to represent something else: _____

13 _____ : to arrange to have a seat, room, performer, etc. at a particular time in the future: _____

14 _____ : a short set of keyboard symbols that represents the facial expression used in email, etc. to show feelings: _____

15 _____ : being, relating to, or belonging to a person or to people as opposed to animals: _____

16 _____ : to give an answer to a particular question when you do not have all the facts and so cannot be certain if you are correct: _____

보기			
book	since	form	conversation
available	gentleman	various	deliver
human	symbol	written	visually
guess	represent	emoticon	type

※ 다음 우리말과 일치하도록 빈칸에 알맞은 말을 쓰시오.

Get Ready 2

(1) **B:** You don't _____ _____ . Are you all _____ ?

    G: No, I'm _____ _____ . My dog is _____ . He won't eat _____ _____ .

    B: _____ _____ _____ _____ .

(2) **B:** It'll _____ a _____ _____ today! _____ _____ _____ at today's lunch menu.

    G: Wow! I'm _____ _____ _____ _____ fried chicken! I _____ _____ _____ _____ _____ _____ .

(3) **W:** Good morning, Mr. Lee. _____ are you _____ ?

    M: I'm _____ very happy this morning. Some students are _____ me _____ the school.

    W: I'm_____ _____ _____ _____ .

(4) **G:** You look _____ . Are you _____ _____ ?

    B: My mom won't _____ me _____ soccer _____ _____ .

    G: _____ _____ _____ ask her one more time?

Start Off – Listen & Talk A

1. **G:** Jihun, you're _____ to _____ _____ next week. _____ are you _____ ?

    B: I'm _____ _____ go to a _____ new world, Yunju.

    G: I'm glad _____ _____ that. I _____ _____ you.

    B: _____ , I'm sad, too. I'll _____ all of you _____ _____ .

    G: Let's _____ _____ _____ online.

    B: Okay. _____ _____ video chats often.

2. **G:** Minsu, Jihun _____ _____ to Abu Dhabi in the UAE next week. _____ are you _____ ?

    B: I'm sad. I'm _____ _____ _____ him a lot.

    G: I'm sad, too, but I'm also happy. We can visit Abu Dhabi. He _____ _____ to _____ us. He _____ .

    B: That's great! I'm _____ _____ _____ a _____ to _____ to a new country.

B: Yena, _____ _____ _____ _____?

G: I'm _____ very _____, Seho. My best friend Jihun is _____
_____.

B: Really? I'm _____. But _____ _____ so sad. You two can
have _____ _____ online.

G: You're right.

B: _____ _____ _____ make him a photo book _____ a
_____ _____?

G: Great idea. I'm glad to give him _____ _____.

Start Off – Speak Up – Mission

A: _____ _____ _____ feeling today?

B: I'm _____ happy. Today's lunch is great.

A: I'm _____ _____ _____ _____.

Step Up – Real-life Scene

I Like Their Emojis

Nari: Hi, Jiho. _____ are you _____?

Jiho: I'm _____ than _____, Nari.

Nari: I know _____. You did it, _____ _____?

Jiho: Yes. I finally _____ four tickets for the VTS concert!

Nari: Good job. Did you tell Minsu and Yujin _____ that?

Jiho: Sure. Oh, I just _____ _____ from them. They said they are
really happy. Look.

Nari: _____ _____! I like their _____. They will _____
_____ _____ and a nice camera.

Jiho: _____ _____ _____ _____ _____. We're going to
have _____ _____ _____!

Fun Time

A: _____ are you _____?

B: I'm _____. I _____ _____ _____ my math homework.
_____ _____ you feeling?

A: I'm _____, _____. I have a math test tomorrow. I'm _____
_____ someone _____ _____ the same.

B: Me, _____.

A: _____ are you feeling?

B: I'm _____. I _____ a good _____. How are you feeling?

A: I'm _____. Someone _____ my glasses.

B: 예나야, 기분이 어떠니?

G: 아주 슬퍼, 세호야. 내 가장 친한 친구인 지훈이가 이사 간대.

B: 정말? 유감이구나. 하지만 너무 슬퍼하지 마. 너희 둘은 온라인으로 화상 채팅을 할 수 있잖아.

G: 네 말이 맞아.

B: 우리 이별 선물로 그에게 사진책을 만들어 주는 게 어때?

G: 좋은 생각이야. 그에게 뭔가 의미 있는 것을 준다니 기뻐.

A: 오늘 기분이 어떠니?

B: 기분이 좋아. 오늘 점심이 훌륭해.

A: 그 말을 들으니 기쁘구나.

나는 그들의 이모지가 마음에 들어

나리: 안녕, 지호. 기분이 어떠니?

지호: 어떤 때보다 행복해, 나리야.

나리: 왜 그런지 알겠다. 너 해냈구나, 그렇지?

지호: 그래. 내가 마침내 VTS 콘서트 표를 4장 예매했어!

나리: 잘했어. 민수와 유진이에게도 그것에 대해 말했니?

지호: 물론이지. 오, 그들에게서 방금 메시지를 받았어. 그 애들도 정말 기쁘다고 말했어. 봐.

나리: 정말 귀엽구나! 나는 그들의 이모지가 마음에 들어. 그 애들은 광선 막대기와 멋진 카메라를 가져올 거야.

지호: 그 말을 들으니 기쁘다. 우리는 정말 재미있을 거야!

A: 기분이 어떠니?

B: 나는 초조해. 수학 숙제 가져오는 걸 잊어버렸어. 너는 기분이 어떠니?

A: 나도 초조해. 내일 수학 시험이 있어. 같은 감정을 가진 사람을 찾아서 기뻐.

B: 나도 그래.

A: 기분이 어떠니?

B: 나는 기분이 좋아. 좋은 점수를 받았어. 너는 기분이 어떠니?

A: 나는 화가 나. 누군가가 내 안경을 망가뜨렸어.

Express Yourself A 1

G: _____ _____ you feeling today?

B: I'm really _____ _____ _____ _____ _____ for my birthday.

G: What is the _____?

B: It's this drone, _____ our grandpa _____ _____ my birthday.

G: Wow! I _____ _____ _____ it _____ _____.

B: _____ _____ _____ you.

G: Thanks.

G: 넌 오늘 기분이 어때?
B: 생일 선물을 받아서 정말 기뻐.
G: 선물이 뭔데?
B: 이 드론인데, 우리 할아버지가 내 생일에 보내 주셨어.
G: 와! 그게 얼마나 높이 날 수 있는지 궁금하다.
B: 내가 보여 줄게.
G: 고마워.

Express Yourself A 2

G: _____ are you _____?

M: I'm really glad _____ _____ my _____ food.

G: I want _____ _____ _____ _____ _____.

M: It's *japchae*, _____ is _____ and _____.

G: I want _____ _____ some.

M: Okay. _____ _____ 30 _____!

G: 기분이 어떠세요?
M: 내가 가장 좋아하는 음식을 요리해서 정말 기뻐.
G: 그게 뭔지 알고 싶은데요.
M: 그건 잡채인데, 맛있고 건강에도 좋아.
G: 저도 좀 먹어 보고 싶어요.
M: 좋아. 30분만 기다려!

Check Yourself – Listen & Speak 1

G: Minsu, _____ _____ _____ _____ _____?

B: I'm really _____, Miso. We _____ a new student _____ _____ _____. His name is Kim Kihun.

G: So _____ are you _____?

B: He was a soccer player _____ his school _____. _____ _____ _____, my team _____ a player.

G: _____ _____ _____ _____ _____ that. I _____ he _____ your team.

B: Thanks a lot.

G: 민수야, 기분이 어떠니?
B: 나 정말 신나, 미소야. 우리 반에 새 학생이 한 명 왔어. 이름은 김기훈이야.
G: 그래서 네가 왜 신나는데?
B: 그는 학교 팀 축구 선수였대. 너도 알다시피, 우리 팀은 선수가 한 명 필요하잖아.
G: 그 말을 들으니 기뻐. 그가 너희 팀에 합류하길 바랄게.
B: 고마워.

※ 다음 우리말에 맞도록 대화를 영어로 쓰시오.

Get Ready 2

(1) B: _____

G: _____

B: _____

(2) B: _____

G: _____

(3) W: _____

M: _____

W: _____

(4) G: _____

B: _____

G: _____

(1) B: 기분이 좋아 보이지 않는구나. 너 괜찮니?

G: 아니, 나 정말 슬퍼. 내 개가 아파. 그는 아무것도 안 먹으려고 해.

B: 정말 안됐구나.

(2) B: 오늘은 좋은 날이 될 거야! 오늘 점심 메뉴 좀 봐.

G: 와! 닭튀김을 먹게 되어 기뻐! 점심시간이 무척 기다려져.

(3) W: 안녕하세요, 이 선생님. 기분이 어떠세요?

M: 오늘 아침에는 기분이 아주 좋습니다. 몇몇 학생들이 학교 청소하는 것을 돕고 있어요.

W: 그 말을 들으니 기쁘군요.

(4) G: 기분이 언짢아 보인다. 너 괜찮니?

B: 엄마가 방과 후에 축구하는 것을 허락하지 않으셔.

G: 한 번 더 말씀드려 보지 그러니?

Start Off – Listen & Talk A

1. G: _____

B: _____

G: _____

B: _____

G: _____

B: _____

2. G: _____

_____

B: _____

G: _____

_____

B: _____

1. G: 지훈아, 너 다음 주에 다른 나라로 이사가지. 기분이 어때?

B: 완전히 새로운 나라에 가게 되어 흥분돼, 윤주야.

G: 그 말을 들으니 기쁘구나. 나는 너를 걱정했어.

B: 사실, 슬프기도 해. 너희 모두를 많이 그리워할 거야.

G: 온라인으로 계속 연락하자.

B: 좋아. 자주 화상 채팅하자.

2. G: 민수야, 지훈이가 다음 주에 아랍에미리트의 아부다비로 이사 간대. 기분이 어떠니?

B: 슬퍼. 그 애가 많이 보고 싶을 거야.

G: 나도 슬퍼, 하지만 기쁘기도 해. 우리는 아부다비를 방문할 수 있잖아. 그가 우리를 초대할 거야. 약속했어.

B: 그거 굉장하다! 새로운 나라로 여행할 기회를 얻게 되어 기뻐.

Start Off – Listen & Talk B

B: _____

G: _____

B: _____

G: _____

B: _____

G: _____

Start Off – Speak Up – Mission

A: _____

B: _____

A: _____

Step Up – Real-life Scene

I Like Their Emojis

Nari: _____

Jiho: _____

Nari: _____

Jiho: _____

Nari: _____

Jiho: _____

_____

Nari: _____

Jiho: _____

Fun Time

A: _____

B: _____

A: _____

_____

B: _____

A: _____

B: _____

A: _____

B: 예나야, 기분이 어떠니?

G: 아주 슬퍼, 세호야. 내 가장 친한 친구인 지훈이가 이사 간대.

B: 정말? 유감이구나. 하지만 너무 슬퍼하지 마. 너희 둘은 온라인으로 화상 채팅을 할 수 있잖아.

G: 네 말이 맞아.

B: 우리 이별 선물로 그에게 사진책을 만들어 주는 게 어때?

G: 좋은 생각이야. 그에게 뭔가 의미 있는 것을 준다니 기뻐.

A: 오늘 기분이 어떠니?

B: 기분이 좋아. 오늘 점심이 훌륭해.

A: 그 말을 들으니 기쁘구나.

나는 그들의 이모지가 마음에 들어

나리: 안녕, 지호. 기분이 어떠니?

지호: 어떤 때보다 행복해, 나리야.

나리: 왜 그런지 알겠다. 너 해냈구나, 그렇지?

지호: 그래. 내가 마침내 VTS 콘서트 표를 4장 예매했어!

나리: 잘했어. 민수와 유진이에게도 그것에 대해 말했니?

지호: 물론이지. 오, 그들에게서 방금 메시지를 받았어. 그 애들도 정말 기쁘다고 말했어. 봐.

나리: 정말 귀엽구나! 나는 그들의 이모지가 마음에 들어. 그 애들은 광선 막대기와 멋진 카메라를 가져올 거야.

지호: 그 말을 들으니 기쁘다. 우리는 정말 재미있을 거야!

A: 기분이 어떠니?

B: 나는 초조해. 수학 숙제 가져오는 걸 잊어버렸어. 너는 기분이 어떠니?

A: 나도 초조해. 내일 수학 시험이 있어. 같은 감정을 가진 사람을 찾아서 기뻐.

B: 나도 그래.

A: 기분이 어떠니?

B: 나는 기분이 좋아. 좋은 점수를 받았어. 너는 기분이 어떠니?

A: 나는 화가 나. 누군가가 내 안경을 망가뜨렸어.

Express Yourself A 1

G: _____

B: _____

G: _____

B: _____

G: _____

B: _____

G: _____

G: 넌 오늘 기분이 어때?
B: 생일 선물을 받아서 정말 기뻐.
G: 선물이 뭔데?
B: 이 드론인데, 우리 할아버지가 내 생일에 보내 주셨어.
G: 와! 그게 얼마나 높이 날 수 있는지 궁금하다.
B: 내가 보여 줄게.
G: 고마워.

Express Yourself A 2

G: _____

M: _____

G: _____

M: _____

G: _____

M: _____

G: 기분이 어떠세요?
M: 내가 가장 좋아하는 음식을 요리해서 정말 기뻐.
G: 그게 뭔지 알고 싶은데요.
M: 그건 잡채인데, 맛있고 건강에도 좋아.
G: 저도 좀 먹어 보고 싶어요.
M: 좋아. 30분만 기다려!

Check Yourself – Listen & Speak 1

G: _____

B: _____

_____

G: _____

B: _____

G: _____

B: _____

G: 민수야, 기분이 어떠니?
B: 나 정말 신나, 미소야. 우리 반에 새 학생이 한 명 왔어. 이름은 김기훈이야.
G: 그래서 네가 왜 신나는데?
B: 그는 학교 팀 축구 선수였대. 너도 알다시피, 우리 팀은 선수가 한 명 필요하잖아.
G: 그 말을 들으니 기뻐. 그가 너희 팀에 합류하길 바랄게.
B: 고마워.

※ 다음 우리말과 일치하도록 빈칸에 알맞은 것을 골라 쓰시오.

1 _____ Do You "Ha-Ha" _____ Your _____?
A. Texts   B. How   C. in

2 _____ is _____.
A. human   B. laughter

3 We _____ _____ _____ when we hear a _____, see something funny, or feel happy.
A. out   B. joke   C. loud   D. laugh

4 We laugh _____ in our _____, such _____ emails or texts, as we do in our _____.
A. writings   B. even   C. as   D. conversations

5 _____ do _____ do _____?
A. that   B. we   C. how

6 "Ha-ha" is a _____ of _____ _____.
A. written   B. form   C. laughter

7 Everyone knows _____ _____ _____.
A. it   B. what   C. means

8 Actually, it _____ _____ _____ _____ long ago.
A. been   B. since   C. has   D. used

9 _____ Shakespeare used "ha-ha" _____ his _____.
A. works   B. even   C. in

10 **DOGBERRY**: Ha, ha, ha! Well, _____, _____ _____.
A. good   B. gentlemen   C. night

11 And if _____ _____ _____, find me and _____ me know.
A. important   B. let   C. happens   D. anything

12 (Shakespeare, _____ *Ado About Nothing* _____ 3, _____ 3, Page 4)
A. Act   B. Much   C. Scene

13 _____ form of _____ _____ is LOL.
A. written   B. another   C. laughter

14 It _____ _____ "Laughing _____ _____."
A. for   B. Loud   C. stands   D. Out

15 People also use ROFL _____ often, which means " _____ the Floor _____."
A. on   B. Laughing   C. quite   D. Rolling

---

1 글에서는 어떻게 "하하"라고 웃나요?

2 웃음은 인간 고유의 것이다.

3 우리는 농담을 듣거나 우스운 것을 보거나 행복감을 느끼면 소리 내어 웃는다.

4 우리는 이메일이나 문자 메시지 같은 글 속에서조차 대화에서 하듯이 웃는다.

5 어떻게 그렇게 하는가?

6 "하하"는 문자로 된 웃음의 한 형태이다.

7 모두가 그것이 무엇을 의미하는지 안다.

8 실제로 그것은 오래전부터 사용되어 왔다.

9 셰익스피어조차도 "하하"를 자신의 작품에 사용하였다.

10 DOGBERRY: 하하하! 자, 신사분들, 좋은 밤 보내시오.

11 그리고 만일 뭔가 중요한 일이 일어난다면 나를 찾아서 알려주시오.

12 (셰익스피어. 헛소동. 3막 3장 4쪽)

13 또 다른 형태의 문자로 된 웃음은 LOL이다.

14 그것은 '크게 소리 내어 웃기'를 상징한다.

15 사람들은 또한 ROFL도 꽤 자주 사용하는데. 그것은 '바닥을 구르면서 웃기'를 의미한다.

16 These _____ have become _____ because they can _____ _____ quite quickly.

A. popular   B. expressions   C. typed   D. be

17 A: _____ a _____ _____ 2mrw.

A. trip   B. safe   C. have

18 _____ _____ u _____ _____ me too much. LOL

A. miss   B. sure   C. don't   D. make

19 B: OK. I'll _____ to make _____ I don't _____ u. LOL

A. miss   B. sure   C. try

20 Thanks _____ _____ me a _____ _____ .

A. wishing   B. for   C. trip   D. safe

21 XD also _____ _____ in _____ .

A. text   B. represents   C. laughter

22 It shows a laughing face _____ a mouth _____ and eyes _____ _____ .

A. open   B. with   C. tightly   D. closed

23 XD is _____ _____ _____ .

A. not   B. word   C. a

24 It's an emoticon, which is a group of letters or symbols _____ to _____ a _____ _____ .

A. represent   B. expression   C. used   D. facial

25 The _____ XD _____ our happy _____ more _____ than ha-ha and LOL do.

A. visually   B. emoticon   C. feelings   D. expresses

26 I _____ _____ _____ go to Disneyland. XD

A. to   B. can't   C. wait

27 These days, people use 😂 — a "face _____ _____ _____ _____ ."

A. tears   B. joy   C. of   D. with

28 This is a _____ picture _____ an "_____ ."

A. emoji   B. small   C. called

29 Lots of _____ emojis are _____ to use online, so people can express their _____ in _____ ways.

A. available   B. various   C. laughter   D. laughing

30 A: I _____ my _____ on the _____ .

A. cupboard   B. hit   C. head

31 B: Oh, my! _____ you _____ ?

A. okay   B. are

16 이 표현들은 상당히 빠르게 타자를 칠 수 있어서 인기를 얻었다.

17 A: 내일 안전한 여행을 해.

18 나를 너무 많이 그리워하지 않도록 해. LOL

19 B: 좋아. 너를 그리워하지 않도록 할게. LOL

20 안전한 여행을 기원해 줘서 고마워.

21 XD 또한 문자 메시지에서 웃음을 나타낸다.

22 그것은 입을 벌리고 눈을 질끈 감은 채 웃는 얼굴을 보여 준다.

23 XD는 단어가 아니다.

24 그것은 이모티콘이고, 얼굴 표정을 나타내기 위해 사용되는 한 무리의 문자나 상징이다.

25 이모티콘 XD는 우리의 행복한 감정을 하하와 LOL보다 더 시각적으로 표현한다.

26 나는 디즈니랜드에 가는 게 몹시 기다려져. XD

27 요즘 사람들은 '기쁨의 눈물을 흘리는 얼굴'인 😂를 사용한다.

28 이것은 '이모지'라고 불리는 작은 그림이다.

29 많은 웃는 이모지가 온라인에서 사용될 수 있고, 그래서 사람들은 다양한 방식으로 자신들의 웃음을 표현할 수 있다.

30 A: 찬장에 머리를 부딪쳤어.

31 B: 오. 이런! 너 괜찮니?

32 A: I _____ my _____ on the _____. 😂
　A. head　　　　B. cupboard　　C. hit

33 B: Uh-oh! _____ the _____ _____? 😂
　A. okay　　　　B. cupboard　　C. is

34 Some emojis _____ _____ bigger, and some even move or make _____ _____.
　A. grown　　　B. sounds　　C. have　　D. laughing

35 A: So yesterday, I was in a restaurant, and I really _____ _____ _____ _____. 🦋
　A. break　　　B. wind　　C. to　　D. needed

36 B: And ...

37 A: Well, the music was really _____, _____ I _____ _____ it.
　A. so　　　　B. loud　　C. did　　D. just

38 B: And ...

39 A: And then I _____ I was _____ to music _____ my _____.
　A. with　　　B. realized　　C. listening　　D. earphones

40 Laughing marks can represent our _____ _____ and deliver our _____ _____.
　A. tones　　　B. expressions　　C. voice　　D. facial

41 _____ using various laughing marks, we can show our friends how much we _____ _____ them or how happy we are _____ them.
　A. care　　　B. for　　C. by　　D. with

42 _____, even in _____ _____, _____ your friends will laugh with you.
　A. written　　B. and　　C. laugh　　D. forms

43 Me _____ it's _____ _____
　A. out　　　　B. when　　C. cold

44 This _____ _____ _____ _____
　A. yesterday　　B. was　　C. me

32 A: 찬장에 머리를 부딪쳤어. 😂

33 B: 어 어! 찬장 괜찮니? 😂

34 어떤 이모지들은 크기가 커졌고, 또 어떤 것들은 심지어 움직이거나 웃음소리를 내기까지 한다.

35 A: 그래서 어제 나는 식당에 있었는데 정말 방귀를 뀌어야 했어.

36 B: 그리고 …

37 A: 음, 음악이 정말 시끄럽길래 나는 그냥 뀌어 버렸어.

38 B: 그리고 …

39 A: 그리고 그때 나는 내가 이어폰을 끼고 음악을 듣고 있다는 걸 깨달았지.

40 웃음 표시는 우리의 얼굴 표정을 나타내고 우리의 목소리 어조를 전달할 수 있다.

41 다양한 웃음 표시를 사용함으로써, 우리는 친구들을 얼마나 좋아하는지 또는 그들과 함께 있어서 얼마나 행복한지를 그들에게 보여 줄 수 있다.

42 웃어라, 문자로 된 형태로라도. 그러면 친구들도 여러분과 함께 웃을 것이다.

43 추울 때 내 모습이네.

44 이건 어제의 나야.

※ 다음 우리말과 일치하도록 빈칸에 알맞은 것을 골라 쓰시오.

1 _____ Do You "Ha-Ha" in Your _____?

2 _____ is _____.

3 We _____ _____ _____ when we hear a joke, see _____ _____, or feel happy.

4 We _____ _____ _____ _____ _____, such as emails or texts, _____ we do in our conversations.

5 _____ do we do _____?

6 "Ha-ha" is a _____ of _____ _____.

7 Everyone knows _____ _____ _____.

8 Actually, it _____ _____ _____ _____ long ago.

9 Even Shakespeare used "ha-ha" _____ _____ _____.

10 **DOGBERRY**: Ha, ha, ha! Well, _____, _____ night.

11 And if _____ _____ happens, find me and let me know.

12 (Shakespeare, *Much Ado About Nothing* _____ 3, _____ 3, Page 4)

13 _____ form of _____ _____ is LOL.

14 It _____ _____ "_____ Out _____."

15 People also use ROFL quite often, which means "_____ _____ _____ _____ _____."

16 These _____ have become popular _____ they _____ _____ _____ quite quickly.

17 A: _____ _____ _____ _____ 2mrw.

18 _____ _____ u don't _____ me too much. LOL

19 B: OK. I'll try to make sure I don't _____ _____. LOL

20 Thanks for _____ _____ _____ _____ _____.

21 XD also _____ _____ in text.

22 It shows a _____ _____ _____ a mouth _____ and eyes _____ _____.

1 글에서는 어떻게 "하하"라고 웃나요?

2 웃음은 인간 고유의 것이다.

3 우리는 농담을 듣거나 우스운 것을 보거나 행복감을 느끼면 소리 내어 웃는다.

4 우리는 이메일이나 문자 메시지 같은 글 속에서조차 대화에서 하듯이 웃는다.

5 어떻게 그렇게 하는가?

6 "하하"는 문자로 된 웃음의 한 형태이다.

7 모두가 그것이 무엇을 의미하는지 안다.

8 실제로 그것은 오래전부터 사용되어 왔다.

9 셰익스피어조차도 "하하"를 자신의 작품에 사용하였다.

10 DOGBERRY: 하하하! 자, 신사분들, 좋은 밤 보내시오.

11 그리고 만일 뭐가 중요한 일이 일어난다면 나를 찾아서 알려 주시오.

12 (셰익스피어. 헛소동. 3막 3장 4쪽)

13 또 다른 형태의 문자로 된 웃음은 LOL이다.

14 그것은 '크게 소리 내어 웃기'를 상징한다.

15 사람들은 또한 ROFL도 꽤 자주 사용하는데, 그것은 '바닥을 구르면서 웃기'를 의미한다.

16 이 표현들은 상당히 빠르게 타자를 칠 수 있어서 인기를 얻었다.

17 A: 내일 안전한 여행을 해.

18 나를 너무 많이 그리워하지 않도록 해. LOL

19 B: 좋아. 너를 그리워하지 않도록 할게. LOL.

20 안전한 여행을 기원해 줘서 고마워.

21 XD 또한 문자 메시지에서 웃음을 나타낸다.

22 그것은 입을 벌리고 눈을 질끈 감은 채 웃는 얼굴을 보여 준다.

23 XD is not _____ _____.

24 It's an emoticon, _____ is a group of letters or symbols _____ _____ _____ _____ _____ _____.

25 The emoticon XD _____ our happy feelings _____ _____ than ha-ha and LOL do.

26 I _____ _____ _____ go to Disneyland. XD

27 _____ _____, people use 😂 — a "_____ _____ _____ _____ _____."

28 This is a small picture _____ an "emoji."

29 Lots of laughing emojis are _____ _____ _____ online, so people can express their laughter in _____ _____.

30 A: I _____ _____ _____ on the cupboard.

31 B: Oh, my! Are you _____?

32 A: I _____ my head _____ _____ _____ _____. 😆

33 B: Uh-oh! Is the cupboard _____? 😆

34 Some emojis _____ _____ _____, and some _____ _____ or make _____ _____.

35 A: So yesterday, I was in a restaurant, and I really _____ _____ _____. 🐰

36 B: And ...

37 A: Well, the music was really _____, _____ I _____ _____ _____.

38 B: And ...

39 A: And then I _____ I was _____ _____ music _____ _____.

40 Laughing marks can _____ our _____ and _____ our _____ _____.

41 _____ _____ various laughing marks, we can show our friends how much we _____ _____ them or how happy we are _____ _____.

42 _____, even in _____ _____, _____ your friends will _____ with you.

43 Me when it's _____ _____

44 _____ _____ me yesterday

---

23 XD는 단어가 아니다.

24 그것은 이모티콘이고, 얼굴 표정을 나타내기 위해 사용되는 한 무리의 문자나 상징이다.

25 이모티콘 XD는 우리의 행복한 감정을 하하와 LOL보다 더 시각적으로 표현한다.

26 나는 디즈니랜드에 가는 게 몹시 기다려져. XD

27 요즘 사람들은 '기쁨의 눈물을 흘리는 얼굴'인 😂를 사용한다.

28 이것은 '이모지'라고 불리는 작은 그림이다.

29 많은 웃는 이모지가 온라인에서 사용될 수 있고, 그래서 사람들은 다양한 방식으로 자신들의 웃음을 표현할 수 있다.

30 A: 찬장에 머리를 부딪쳤어.

31 B: 오. 이런! 너 괜찮니?

32 A: 찬장에 머리를 부딪쳤어. 😆

33 B: 어 어! 찬장 괜찮니? 😆

34 어떤 이모지들은 크기가 커졌고, 또 어떤 것들은 심지어 움직이거나 웃음소리를 내기까지 한다.

35 A: 그래서 어제 나는 식당에 있었는데 정말 방귀를 뀌어야 했어.

36 B: 그리고 …

37 A: 음, 음악이 정말 시끄럽길래 나는 그냥 뀌어 버렸어.

38 B: 그리고 …

39 A: 그리고 그때 나는 내가 이어폰을 끼고 음악을 듣고 있다는 걸 깨달았지.

40 웃음 표시는 우리의 얼굴 표정을 나타내고 우리의 목소리 어조를 전달할 수 있다.

41 다양한 웃음 표시를 사용함으로써, 우리는 친구들을 얼마나 좋아하는지 또는 그들과 함께 있어서 얼마나 행복한지를 그들에게 보여 줄 수 있다.

42 웃어라, 문자로 된 형태로라도. 그러면 친구들도 여러분과 함께 웃을 것이다.

43 추울 때 내 모습이네.

44 이건 어제의 나야.

※ 다음 문장을 우리말로 쓰시오.

1 How Do You "Ha-Ha" in Your Texts?

➡ _____

2 Laughter is human.

➡ _____

3 We laugh out loud when we hear a joke, see something funny, or feel happy.

➡ _____

4 We laugh even in our writings, such as emails or texts, as we do in our conversations.

➡ _____

5 How do we do that?

➡ _____

6 "Ha-ha" is a form of written laughter.

➡ _____

7 Everyone knows what it means.

➡ _____

8 Actually, it has been used since long ago.

➡ _____

9 Even Shakespeare used "ha-ha" in his works.

➡ _____

10 DOGBERRY: Ha, ha, ha! Well, gentlemen, good night.

➡ _____

11 And if anything important happens, find me and let me know.

➡ _____

12 (Shakespeare, Much Ado About Nothing Act 3, Scene 3, Page 4)

➡ _____

13 Another form of written laughter is LOL.

➡ _____

14 It stands for "Laughing Out Loud."

➡ _____

15 People also use ROFL quite often, which means "Rolling on the Floor Laughing."

➡ _____

16 These expressions have become popular because they can be typed quite quickly.

➡ _____

17 A: Have a safe trip 2mrw.

➡ _____

18 Make sure u don't miss me too much. LOL

➡ _____

19 B: OK. I'll try to make sure I don't miss u. LOL.

➡ _____

20 Thanks for wishing me a safe trip.

➡ _____

21 XD also represents laughter in text.

➡ _____

22 It shows a laughing face with a mouth open and eyes closed tightly.

➡ _____

23 XD is not a word.

➡ _____

24 It's an emoticon, which is a group of letters or symbols used to represent a facial expression.

➡ _____

25 The emoticon XD expresses our happy feelings more visually than ha-ha and LOL do.

➡ _____

26 I can't wait to go to Disneyland. XD

➡ _____

27 These days, people use 😂 — a "face with tears of joy."

➡ _____

28 This is a small picture called an "emoji."

➡ _____

29 Lots of laughing emojis are available to use online, so people can express their laughter in various ways.

➡ _____

30 A: I hit my head on the cupboard.

➡ _____

31 B: Oh, my! Are you okay?

➡ _____

32 A: I hit my head on the cupboard. 😂

➡ _____

33 B: Uh-oh! Is the cupboard okay? 😂

➡ _____

34 Some emojis have grown bigger, and some even move or make laughing sounds.

➡ _____

35 A: So yesterday, I was in a restaurant, and I really needed to break wind. 🐰

➡ _____

36 B: And ...

➡ _____

37 A: Well, the music was really loud, so I just did it.

➡ _____

38 B: And ...

➡ _____

39 A: And then I realized I was listening to music with my earphones.

➡ _____

40 Laughing marks can represent our facial expressions and deliver our voice tones.

➡ _____

41 By using various laughing marks, we can show our friends how much we care for them or how happy we are with them.

➡ _____

_____

42 Laugh, even in written forms, and your friends will laugh with you.

➡ _____

43 Me when it's cold out

➡ _____

44 This was me yesterday

➡ _____

※ 다음 괄호 안의 단어들을 우리말에 맞도록 바르게 배열하시오.

1 (Do / How / "Ha-Ha" / You / in / Texts? / Your)
➡ _____

2 (is / Laughter / human.)
➡ _____

3 (laugh / we / loud / out / we / when / hear / joke, / a / see / funny, / something / or / happy. / feel)
➡ _____
_____

4 (laugh / we / in / even / writings, / our / as / such / or / emails / texts, / we / as / do / our / in / conversations.)
➡ _____
_____

5 (do / how / do / we / that?)
➡ _____

6 (is / "ha-ha" / form / a / written / of / laughter.)
➡ _____

7 (knows / everyone / it / what / means.)
➡ _____

8 (it / actually, / has / used / been / long / since / ago.)
➡ _____

9 (Shakespeare / even / "ha-ha" / used / in / works. / his)
➡ _____

10 (DOGBERRY: / ha, / ha! / ha, / gentlemen, / well, / night. / good)
➡ _____

11 (if / and / anything / happens, / important / me / find / and / me / let / know.)
➡ _____

12 ((Much / Shakespeare, / Ado / Nothing / About / 3, / Act / Scene / 4 / 3, / Page)
➡ _____

13 (form / another / written / of / is / laughter / LOL.)
➡ _____

14 (stands / it / for / Out / "Laughing / Loud.")
➡ _____

15 (also / people / FOFL / use / often, / quite / means / which / on / "Rolling / the / Laughing." / Floor)
➡ _____
_____

1 글에서는 어떻게 "하하"라고 웃나요?

2 웃음은 인간 고유의 것이다.

3 우리는 농담을 듣거나 우스운 것을 보거나 행복감을 느끼면 소리 내어 웃는다.

4 우리는 이메일이나 문자 메시지 같은 글 속에서조차 대화에서 하듯이 웃는다.

5 어떻게 그렇게 하는가?

6 "하하"는 문자로 된 웃음의 한 형태이다.

7 모두가 그것이 무엇을 의미하는지 안다.

8 실제로 그것은 오래전부터 사용되어 왔다.

9 셰익스피어조차도 "하하"를 자신의 작품에 사용하였다.

10 DOGBERRY: 하하하! 자, 신사분들, 좋은 밤 보내시오.

11 그리고 만일 뭔가 중요한 일이 일어난다면 나를 찾아서 알려 주시오.

12 (셰익스피어. 헛소동. 3막 3장 4쪽)

13 또 다른 형태의 문자로 된 웃음은 LOL이다.

14 그것은 '크게 소리 내어 웃기'를 상징한다.

15 사람들은 또한 ROFL도 꽤 자주 사용하는데, 그것은 '바닥을 구르면서 웃기'를 의미한다.

16 (expressions / these / become / have / because / popular / can / they / typed / be / quickly. / quite)

➡ _____

_____

17 (A: / a / have / safe / 2mrw. / trip)

➡ _____

18 (sure / make / don't / u / me / miss / much. / too / LOL)

➡ _____

19 (B: / OK. // try / I'll / make / to / I / sure / miss / don't / u. / LOL.)

➡ _____

20 (for / thanks / me / wishing / safe / a / trip.)

➡ _____

21 (also / XD / laughter / represents / text. / in)

➡ _____

22 (shows / it / laughing / a / with / face / mouth / a / open / eyes / and / tightly. / closed)

➡ _____

23 (is / XD / a / not / word.)

➡ _____

24 (an / it's / emoticon, / is / which / group / a / letters / of / or / uesed / symbols / represent / to / facial / a / expression.)

➡ _____

_____

25 (emoticon / the / expresses / XD / happy / our / more / feelings / than / visually / ha-ha / LOL / and / do.)

➡ _____

_____

26 (can't / I / to / wait / to / go / XD / Disneyland.)

➡ _____

27 (days, / these / use / people / 😂 / – / "face / a / tears / with / joy." / of)

➡ _____

28 (is / small / this / picture / a / called / "emoji." / an)

➡ _____

29 (of / lots / emojis / laughing / available / are / use / to / online, / people / so / express / can / laughter / their / various / in / ways.)

➡ _____

_____

30 (A: / hit / I / head / my / on / cupboard. / the)

➡ _____

31 (B: / my! / oh, // you / are / okay?)

➡ _____

16 이 표현들은 상당히 빠르게 타자를 칠 수 있어서 인기를 얻었다.

17 A: 내일 안전한 여행을 해.

18 나를 너무 많이 그리워하지 않도록 해. LOL

19 B: 좋아. 너를 그리워하지 않도록 할게. LOL

20 안전한 여행을 기원해 줘서 고마워.

21 XD 또한 문자 메시지에서 웃음을 나타낸다.

22 그것은 입을 벌리고 눈을 질끈 감은 채 웃는 얼굴을 보여 준다.

23 XD는 단어가 아니다.

24 그것은 이모티콘이고, 얼굴 표정을 나타내기 위해 사용되는 한 무리의 문자나 상징이다.

25 이모티콘 XD는 우리의 행복한 감정을 하하와 LOL보다 더 시각적으로 표현한다.

26 나는 디즈니랜드에 가는 게 몹시 기다려져. XD

27 요즘 사람들은 '기쁨의 눈물을 흘리는 얼굴'인 😂를 사용한다.

28 이것은 '이모지'라고 불리는 작은 그림이다.

29 많은 웃는 이모지가 온라인에서 사용될 수 있고, 그래서 사람들은 다양한 방식으로 자신들의 웃음을 표현할 수 있다.

30 A: 찬장에 머리를 부딪쳤어.

31 B: 오. 이런! 너 괜찮니?

32 (A: / hit / I / head / my / the / on / cupboard. / 😆)

➡ _____

33 (B: /uh-oh! / the / is / okay? / cupboa😆/)

➡ _____

34 (emojis / some / grown / have / bigger, / some / and / move / even / make / or / sounds. / laughing)

➡ _____

_____

35 (A: yesterday, / so / was / I / in / restaurant, / a / and / really / I / to / needed / wind. / break / 🐿)

➡ _____

_____

36 (B: / ... / and)

➡ _____

37 (A: / the / well, / music / really / was / so / loud, / just / I / it. / did)

➡ _____

38 (B: / ... / and)

➡ _____

39 (A: / then / and / I / realized / I / listening / was / music / to / my / with / earphones.)

➡ _____

_____

40 (marks / laughing / represent / can / facial / our / expressions / and / our / deliver / tones. / voice)

➡ _____

_____

41 (using / by / laughing / various / marks, / can / we / our / show / friends / much / how / care / we / for / or / them / happy / how / are / we / them. / with)

➡ _____

_____

42 (even / laugh, / written / in / forms, / your / and / will / friends / with / laugh / you.)

➡ _____

_____

43 (when / me / cold / it's / out)

➡ _____

44 (was / this / yesterday / me)

➡ _____

32 A: 찬장에 머리를 부딪쳤어. 😆

33 B: 어 어! 찬장 괜찮니? 😆

34 어떤 이모지들은 크기가 커졌고, 또 어떤 것들은 심지어 움직이거나 웃음소리를 내기까지 한다.

35 A: 그래서 어제 나는 식당에 있었는데 정말 방귀를 뀌어야 했어.

36 B: 그리고 …

37 A: 음, 음악이 정말 시끄럽길래 나는 그냥 뀌어 버렸어.

38 B: 그리고 …

39 A: 그리고 그때 나는 내가 이어폰을 끼고 음악을 듣고 있다는 걸 깨달았지.

40 웃음 표시는 우리의 얼굴 표정을 나타내고 우리의 목소리 어조를 전달할 수 있다.

41 다양한 웃음 표시를 사용함으로써, 우리는 친구들을 얼마나 좋아하는지 또는 그들과 함께 있어서 얼마나 행복한지를 그들에게 보여 줄 수 있다.

42 웃어라, 문자로 된 형태로라도. 그러면 친구들도 여러분과 함께 웃을 것이다.

43 추울 때 내 모습이네.

44 이건 어제의 나야.

※ 다음 우리말을 영어로 쓰시오.

1 글에서는 어떻게 "하하"라고 웃나요?
➡ _____

2 웃음은 인간 고유의 것이다.
➡ _____

3 우리는 농담을 듣거나 우스운 것을 보거나 행복감을 느끼면 소리 내어 웃는다.
➡ _____

4 우리는 이메일이나 문자 메시지 같은 글 속에서조차 대화에서 하듯이 웃는다.
➡ _____

5 어떻게 그렇게 하는가?
➡ _____

6 "하하"는 문자로 된 웃음의 한 형태이다.
➡ _____

7 모두가 그것이 무엇을 의미하는지 안다.
➡ _____

8 실제로 그것은 오래전부터 사용되어 왔다.
➡ _____

9 셰익스피어조차도 "하하"를 자신의 작품에 사용하였다.
➡ _____

10 DOGBERRY: 하하하! 자, 신사분들, 좋은 밤 보내시오.
➡ _____

11 그리고 만일 뭔가 중요한 일이 일어난다면 나를 찾아서 알려 주시오.
➡ _____

12 (셰익스피어. 헛소동. 3막 3장 4쪽)
➡ _____

13 또 다른 형태의 문자로 된 웃음은 LOL이다.
➡ _____

14 그것은 '크게 소리 내어 웃기'를 상징한다.
➡ _____

15 사람들은 또한 ROFL도 꽤 자주 사용하는데. 그것은 '바닥을 구르면서 웃기'를 의미한다.
➡ _____

16 이 표현들은 상당히 빠르게 타자를 칠 수 있어서 인기를 얻었다.
➡ _____

17 A: 내일 안전한 여행을 해.
➡ _____

18 나를 너무 많이 그리워하지 않도록 해. LOL
➡ _____

19 B: 좋아. 너를 그리워하지 않도록 할게. LOL
➡ _____

20 안전한 여행을 기원해 줘서 고마워.
➡ _____

21 XD 또한 문자 메시지에서 웃음을 나타낸다.
➡ _____

22 그것은 입을 벌리고 눈을 질끈 감은 채 웃는 얼굴을 보여 준다.
➡ _____

23 XD는 단어가 아니다.
➡ _____

24 그것은 이모티콘이고, 얼굴 표정을 나타내기 위해 사용되는 한 무리의 문자나 상징이다.
➡ _____

25 이모티콘 XD는 우리의 행복한 감정을 하하와 LOL보다 더 시각적으로 표현한다.
➡ _____

26 나는 디즈니랜드에 가는 게 몹시 기다려져. XD
➡ _____

27 요즘 사람들은 '기쁨의 눈물을 흘리는 얼굴'인 😂를 사용한다.
➡ _____

28 이것은 '이모지'라고 불리는 작은 그림이다.
➡ _____

29 많은 웃는 이모지가 온라인에서 사용될 수 있고, 그래서 사람들은 다양한 방식으로 자신들의 웃음을 표현할 수 있다.
➡ _____

30 A: 찬장에 머리를 부딪쳤어.
➡ _____

31 B: 오. 이런! 너 괜찮니?
➡ _____

32 A: 찬장에 머리를 부딪쳤어. 😂
➡ _____

33 B: 어 어! 찬장 괜찮니? 😂
➡ _____

34 어떤 이모지들은 크기가 커졌고, 또 어떤 것들은 심지어 움직이거나 웃음소리를 내기까지 한다.
➡ _____

35 A: 그래서 어제 나는 식당에 있었는데 정말 방귀를 뀌어야 했어.
➡ _____

36 B: 그리고 …
➡ _____

37 A: 음, 음악이 정말 시끄럽길래 나는 그냥 뀌어 버렸어.
➡ _____

38 B: 그리고 …
➡ _____

39 A: 그리고 그때 나는 내가 이어폰을 끼고 음악을 듣고 있다는 걸 깨달았지.
➡ _____

40 웃음 표시는 우리의 얼굴 표정을 나타내고 우리의 목소리 어조를 전달할 수 있다.
➡ _____

41 다양한 웃음 표시를 사용함으로써, 우리는 친구들을 얼마나 좋아하는지 또는 그들과 함께 있어서 얼마나 행복한지를 그들에게 보여 줄 수 있다.
➡ _____

42 웃어라, 문자로 된 형태로라도. 그러면 친구들도 여러분과 함께 웃을 것이다.
➡ _____

43 추울 때 내 모습이네.
➡ _____

44 이건 어제의 나야.
➡ _____

※ 다음 우리말과 일치하도록 빈칸에 알맞은 말을 쓰시오.

Self-study Guide

1. A: Can you tell me _____ _____ _____?

2. B: Sure. I _____ _____ Mokpo.

3. A: _____ _____ tell me _____ _____ _____ _____
_____ _____?

4. B: Sure. It will come _____ _____ _____.

1. A: 당신이 어디에 사는지 제게 말해 줄
   수 있나요?
2. B: 물론이죠. 저는 목포에 살아요.
3. A: 다음 버스가 언제 올지 제게 말씀
   해 주실 수 있으신가요?
4. B: 물론이죠. 그건 10분 후에 올 겁니다.

Link to the World

1. Do you know _____ _____ _____ _____ _____.

2. • This is the uniform of the Reds, _____ _____ _____ the
Korean soccer team. Red _____ "power" on this uniform.

3. • Red on a _____ _____ means "stop."

4. • _____ _____ _____ _____ of red, "love" is my favorite.
"Love _____ _____."

1. 빨간색이 무엇을 의미하는지 알고 있니?
2. • 이것은 붉은 악마들의 유니폼인데,
   그들은 한국 축구팀을 응원한다. 이 유
   니폼에서 빨간색은 "힘"을 의미한다.
3. • 교통 신호등의 빨간색은 "멈추시
   오"라는 뜻이다.
4. • 빨간색의 여러 의미 중에서, '사랑'
   이 나는 가장 좋다. "사랑은 절대 실패
   하지 않는다."

Express Yourself C

1. Yeji: Can you _____ _____ _____ _____ for
his birthday?

2. He _____ a drone _____ our grandpa, _____ _____
_____ Busan.

1. 예지: 내 남동생이 그의 생일 선물로
   무엇을 받았는지 추측할 수 있니?
2. 그는 우리 할아버지로부터 드론을 받
   았는데, 할아버지는 부산에 사셔.

※ 다음 우리말을 영어로 쓰시오.

Self-study Guide

1. A: 당신이 어디에 사는지 제게 말해 줄 수 있나요?

➡ _____

2. B: 물론이죠. 저는 목포에 살아요.

➡ _____

3. A: 다음 버스가 언제 올지 제게 말씀해 주실 수 있으신가요?

➡ _____

4. B: 물론이죠. 그건 10분 후에 올 겁니다.

➡ _____

Link to the World

1. 빨간색이 무엇을 의미하는지 알고 있니?

➡ _____

2. • 이것은 붉은 악마들의 유니폼인데, 그들은 한국 축구팀을 응원한다. 이 유니폼에서 빨간색은 "힘"을 의미한다.

➡ _____

_____

3. • 교통 신호등의 빨간색은 "멈추시오"라는 뜻이다.

➡ _____

4. • 빨간색의 여러 의미 중에서, '사랑'이 나는 가장 좋다. "사랑은 절대 실패하지 않는다."

➡ _____

Express Yourself C

1. 예지: 내 남동생이 그의 생일 선물로 무엇을 받았는지 추측할 수 있니?

➡ _____

2. 그는 우리 할아버지로부터 드론을 받았는데. 할아버지는 부산에 사셔.

➡ _____

Step1

※ 다음 영어를 우리말로 쓰시오.

01	awful	
02	sweaty	
03	class leader	
04	dirty	
05	double	
06	activity	
07	else	
08	empty	
09	suggest	
10	sneeze	
11	pleasure	
12	trash bag	
13	hang	
14	string	
15	tough	
16	fill	
17	complain	
18	fix	
19	admit	
20	dust	
21	lettuce	

22	neighborhood	
23	among	
24	trash	
25	wrap	
26	imagine	
27	bean	
28	helpful	
29	wonder	
30	mess	
31	assign	
32	sight	
33	tight	
34	popular	
35	work on	
36	in charge of	
37	set up	
38	take care of	
39	fill A with B	
40	divide A into B	
41	turn A into B	
42	be ready to-V	
43	pop up	

※ 다음 우리말을 영어로 쓰시오.

01 끔찍한, 지독한

02 더러운

03 제안하다

04 두 배가 되다

05 채우다

06 불평하다, 투덜거리다

07 수리하다

08 쓰레기 봉투

09 먼지

10 도움이 되는, 유용한

11 (생각이) ~에게 떠오르다

12 끈, 줄

13 배정하다, 배치하다, 맡기다

14 상상하다

15 단단히, 꽉

16 텅 빈, 비어 있는

17 기쁨

18 인정하다, 시인하다

19 ~ 중에, ~ 사이에

20 포장지

21 땀투성이의, 땀에 젖은

22 콩

23 재채기하다

24 걸다. 매달다

25 힘든

26 인기 있는

27 열, 줄

28 광경

29 쓰레기

30 상추

31 쓰레기 더미, 지저분함

32 이웃, 인근 주민

33 양로원

34 무거운

35 ~로 가득 차다

36 ~을 돌보다

37 설치하다, 마련하다

38 A를 B로 바꾸다

39 ~에 공들이다[애쓰다]

40 ~할 준비가 되다

41 A를 B로 나누다

42 ~ 맞은편에

43 ~을 맡아, ~을 담당하여

※ 다음 영영풀이에 알맞은 단어를 <보기>에서 골라 쓴 후, 우리말 뜻을 쓰시오.

1 _____ : an area of land: _____

2 _____ : to repair something: _____

3 _____ : to make or become full: _____

4 _____ : extremely bad or unpleasant: _____

5 _____ : difficult to do or to deal with: _____

6 _____ : covered in sweat or smelling of sweat: _____

7 _____ : not containing any things or people: _____

8 _____ : to offer to do something that you do not have to do: _____

9 _____ : to say that something is wrong or not satisfactory: _____

10 _____ : to make something twice as much or many: _____

11 _____ : to agree that something is true, especially unwillingly: _____

12 _____ : to give a particular job or piece of work to someone: _____

13 _____ : to tell someone your ideas about what they should do, where they should go etc.: _____

14 _____ : dry dirt in the form of powder that covers surfaces inside a building, or very small dry pieces of soil, sand, or other substances: _____

15 _____ : a place where very old people who are ill live and receive medical treatment and care: _____

16 _____ : to put something in a position so that the top part is fixed or supported, and the bottom part is free to move and does not touch the ground: _____

dust	admit	empty	volunteer
hang	tough	lot	awful
suggest	assign	nursing home	double
fill	complain	fix	sweaty

※ 다음 우리말과 일치하도록 빈칸에 알맞은 말을 쓰시오.

Get Ready 2

(1) B: The _____ _____ looks _____. _____ _____ help you, Ms. Min?

   W: You're so _____. _____ _____ very much.

(2) G: _____ _____ _____ you _____ the bench.

   M: Please _____ this _____. Thank you _____ _____ me.

(3) B: _____ _____ _____ what we can do _____ our town.

   G: _____ _____ _____ pictures on the _____ walls?

   B: _____ good. _____ _____?

Start Off – Listen & Talk A

1. B: What do we _____ in our club room? _____ talk about it.

   G: Sure. Well, _____ _____ _____ _____ some _____ _____ _____ the windows? They'll _____ our room _____.

   B: That's a _____ _____. Thank you, Jiu.

2. B: _____ _____ _____ some pictures?

   G: Good. _____ _____ _____ _____ one of your pictures? You're _____ _____ _____, Seho.

   B: _____ you _____ _____ that. I'll _____ one of _____.

3. B: Let's talk _____ the _____ this time. _____ ideas?

   G: _____ _____ _____ a small library in the _____ of the club room? I will _____ some books tomorrow.

   B: Great idea! Thank you _____ _____ it, Minju.

Start Off – Listen & Talk B

G: Seho, we need something on the wall, too. _____ you think so?

B1: You're _____. _____ _____ about it _____.

G: I think we _____ _____ _____ the club _____ list there. It'll be _____ _____ _____ _____ _____ _____ the new _____ names.

B2: That's a good idea. We _____ _____ _____ our _____ for this _____ _____ on the wall.

G: Right! That'll really _____ us _____ important school events.

B1: Thank you for _____ great ideas, everyone. We are a good team.

Step Up – Real-life Scene

G1: Let's _____ _____ how we can make our town _____.

B: _____ _____ _____ you first. There's too much _____ at the _____ _____.

G2: I _____. _____ _____ _____ clean the place together?

B: Good. We _____ _____ a _____ there, _____.

G1: Great idea. It'll be _____ for _____ _____.

G2: _____ _____ _____ some flower pots _____ the bench? They'll _____ the bus stop _____ _____.

G1: Thank you _____ _____ great ideas, everyone. Then, _____ _____ start tomorrow?

G2, B: No _____.

Fun Time

A: _____ _____ about the _____ _____.

B: Okay. _____ _____ _____ _____ *bibimbap*?

A: Wonderful. _____ you _____ your idea.

Express Yourself A

1. **M1:** Thank you _____ _____, everyone. Let's _____ _____ the Clean School Project.

   W: I like the corner _____ the tree _____. The Science Club _____ _____ the corner and _____ the tree.

   M2: I like it, too. It is a very _____ _____ _____ the students.

2. **M1:** _____ _____ about the _____ _____ this time. _____ _____ _____ _____ _____ it?

   W: The class _____ _____ the board and _____ _____ some posters. We can know _____ _____ about school _____.

   M2: Right! They did a good job. _____ _____ the _____ _____.

G1: 우리 마을을 어떻게 하면 더 좋게 만들 수 있을지를 이야기해 보자.

B: 내가 먼저 말할게. 버스 정류장에 쓰레기가 너무 많아.

G2: 동의해. 그 장소를 함께 치우는 게 어때?

B: 좋아. 우리가 거기에 벤치를 놓을 수도 있을 것 같아.

G1: 좋은 생각이야. 그것은 어르신들에게 도움이될 거야.

G2: 벤치 주변에 화분도 좀 놓는 게 어때? 그것들은 버스 정류장을 더 아름답게 할 거야.

G1: 모두 좋은 의견을 내줘서 고마워. 그러면, 내일 시작하는 게 어때?

G2, B: 좋아.

A: 마을 파티에 대해 이야기해 보자.

B: 좋아. 우리 비빔밥을 요리하는 게 어때?

A: 훌륭해. 의견을 내줘서 고마워.

1. M1: 모두 와 주셔서 감사합니다. '깨끗한 학교 프로젝트'에 대해 이야기해 봅시다.

   W: 저는 나무 아래의 모퉁이가 가장 마음에 듭니다. '과학 동아리'가 모퉁이 주변을 청소하고 나무를 심었어요.

   M2: 저도 마음에 듭니다. 그곳은 학생들 사이에 아주 인기 있습니다.

2. M1: 이번에는 학교 정문에 관해 이야기해 봅시다. 그것에 대해 어떻게 생각하나요?

   W: 학급 반장들이 판을 설치하고 몇 개의 포스터를 붙였어요. 우리가 학교 행사에 관해 훨씬 더 많이 알 수 있죠.

   M2: 맞아요! 정말 잘했어요. 학급 반장들에게 감사합시다.

※ 다음 우리말에 맞도록 대화를 영어로 쓰시오.

Get Ready 2

(1) B: _____

　　 W: _____

(2) G: _____

　　 M: _____

(3) B: _____

　　 G: _____

　　 B: _____

Start Off – Listen & Talk A

1. B: _____

　 G: _____

　　 _____

　 B: _____

2. B: _____

　 G: _____

　　 _____

　 B: _____

3. B: _____

　 G: _____

　　 _____

　 B: _____

Start Off – Listen & Talk B

G: _____

B1: _____

G: _____

　 _____

B2: _____

G: _____

B1: _____

해석

(1) B: 화분이 무거워 보여요. 민 선생님, 도와드릴까요?
　 W: 아주 친절하구나. 정말 고마워.

(2) G: 제가 의자 고치시는 걸 도와 드릴 게요.
　 M: 이걸 좀 꽉 잡아 다오. 도와줘서 고맙구나.

(3) B: 우리가 마을을 위해 무엇을 할 수 있는지 이야기해 보자.
　 G: 지저분한 벽에 그림을 그리는 게 어떠니?
　 B: 좋아. 또 다른 건?

1. B: 우리 동아리실에 무엇이 필요할까? 그것에 대해 이야기해 보자.
　 G: 좋아. 음, 창가에 몇 개의 화분을 두는 게 어때? 그것들은 우리 동아리실을 더 예쁘게 할 거야.
　 B: 좋은 생각이야. 지우야, 고마워.

2. B: 그림을 좀 거는 게 어때?
　 G: 좋아. 네 그림 중의 하나를 가져오는 게 어때? 세호야, 넌 그림을 잘 그리잖아.
　 B: 그렇게 말해 주니 고마워. 내가 내 그림 중에서 하나를 가져올게.

3. B: 이번에는 모퉁이에 대해 이야기해 보자. 의견 있니?
　 G: 동아리실 모퉁이에 작은 도서관을 만드는 게 어때? 내가 내일 책 몇 권을 가져올게.
　 B: 좋은 생각이야! 민주야, 제안해 줘서 고마워.

G: 세호야, 우리는 벽에도 뭔가 필요해. 그렇게 생각하지 않니?
B1: 네 말이 맞아. 그것에 대해서 함께 이야기해 보자.
G: 내 생각에는 거기에 동아리 회원 목록을 붙일 필요가 있는 것 같아. 그것은 우리가 신입 회원들의 이름을 알게 되는 데 도움이 될 거야.
B2: 좋은 생각이야. 이번 학년도의 우리 계획도 벽에 필요해.
G: 맞아! 그러면 우리가 중요한 학교 행사를 기억하는 데 정말 도움이 될 거야.
B1: 모두 좋은 의견을 내줘서 고마워. 우린 좋은 팀이야.

Step Up – Real-life Scene

G1: _____

B: _____

G2: _____

B: _____

G1: _____

G2: _____

_____

G1: _____

G2, B: _____

G1: 우리 마을을 어떻게 하면 더 좋게 만들 수 있을지를 이야기해 보자.

B: 내가 먼저 말할게. 버스 정류장에 쓰레기가 너무 많아.

G2: 동의해. 그 장소를 함께 치우는 게 어때?

B: 좋아. 우리가 거기에 벤치를 놓을 수도 있을 것 같아.

G1: 좋은 생각이야. 그것은 어르신들에게 도움이될 거야.

G2: 벤치 주변에 화분도 좀 놓는 게 어때? 그것들은 버스 정류장을 더 아름답게 할 거야.

G1: 모두 좋은 의견을 내줘서 고마워. 그러면, 내일 시작하는 게 어때?

G2, B: 좋아.

Fun Time

A: _____

B: _____

A: _____

A: 마을 파티에 대해 이야기해 보자.

B: 좋아. 우리 비빔밥을 요리하는 게 어때?

A: 훌륭해. 의견을 내줘서 고마워.

Express Yourself A

1. M1: _____

W: _____

_____

M2: _____

2. M1: _____

W: _____

_____

M2: _____

1. M1: 모두 와 주셔서 감사합니다. '깨끗한 학교 프로젝트'에 대해 이야기해 봅시다.

W: 저는 나무 아래의 모퉁이가 가장 마음에 듭니다. '과학 동아리'가 모퉁이 주변을 청소하고 나무를 심었어요.

M2: 저도 마음에 듭니다. 그곳은 학생들 사이에 아주 인기 있습니다.

2. M1: 이번에는 학교 정문에 관해 이야기해 봅시다. 그것에 대해 어떻게 생각하나요?

W: 학급 반장들이 판을 설치하고 몇 개의 포스터를 붙였어요. 우리가 학교 행사에 관해 훨씬 더 많이 알 수 있죠.

M2: 맞아요! 정말 잘했어요. 학급 반장들에게 감사합시다.

※ 다음 우리말과 일치하도록 빈칸에 알맞은 것을 골라 쓰시오.

1
_____ _____
A. Thumbs   B. Green

2 I _____ the _____ _____ .
A. whole   B. complained   C. day

3 My parents were making me _____ on the _____ project, but I had _____ _____ things to do.
A. far   B. neighborhood C. better   D. work

4 I didn't understand _____ _____ _____ _____ on this place.
A. were   B. why   C. working   D. we

5 It was just the _____ ugly, old, _____ lot _____ _____ Johnny's Shop.
A. across   B. ugly   C. from   D. empty

6 It was _____ of wild plants, fast food _____ , old newspapers, broken glass, and every _____ kind of dirty trash you can _____ .
A. imagine   B. full   C. wraps   D. other

7 As I looked _____ it that first morning, I thought, "I _____ _____ are snakes in there, _____ ."
A. bet   B. at   C. too   D. there

8 There were twenty of us — all _____ and _____ — to _____ that day.
A. ages   B. ready   C. sizes   D. work

9 I didn't think that we could clean _____ this _____ and turn it _____ a garden.
A. mess   B. up   C. awful   D. into

10 We were all wondering _____ _____ _____ .
A. begin   B. to   C. where

11 Then Mr. Hernandez said, "The _____ to do it is _____ to _____ ."
A. way   B. start   C. only   D. just

12 Then, he _____ the lot _____ four parts with string and _____ five people _____ each part.
A. assigned   B. into   C. divided   D. to

13 _____ _____ , I was hot, _____ , and glad my dad had made me _____ gloves.
A. sweaty   B. lunchtime   C. wear   D. by

14 We _____ fifty trash bags _____ waste and were _____ to _____ wild plants.
A. with   B. ready   C. filled   D. pull

15 As we pulled and pulled, dust _____ the air and _____ _____ .
A. sneeze   B. filled   C. us   D. made

---

1 식물을 잘 키우는 사람들

2 나는 온종일 불평했다.

3 우리 부모님은 나를 이웃 프로젝트에서 일하게 하셨지만, 나에게는 훨씬 더 나은 할 일들이 있었다.

4 나는 우리가 왜 이곳에서 일하고 있어야 하는지 이해하지 못했다.

5 그곳은 그저 Johnny's Shop 건너편에 있는 볼품없고, 오래되고, 텅 빈 지역이었다.

6 그곳은 잡초와 패스트푸드 포장지와 낡은 신문, 깨진 유리, 그리고 상상할 수 있는 모든 다른 종류의 더러운 쓰레기로 가득 차 있었다.

7 그 첫날 아침에 그곳을 보았을 때, 나는 "틀림없이 저 안에는 뱀들도 있을 거야."라고 생각했다.

8 그날 일할 준비가 된 — 모든 연령대와 몸집을 가진 — 우리 20명이 있었다.

9 나는 이 끔찍하게 더러운 곳을 청소하여 정원으로 바꿀 수 있다고 생각하지 않았다.

10 우리는 모두 어디서부터 시작해야 할지 궁금해 하고 있었다.

11 그때 Hernandez 씨가 "그것을 할 유일한 방법은 그냥 시작하는 것입니다."라고 말했다.

12 그러고 나서, 그는 그 지역을 끈으로 네 구역으로 나누고, 5명을 각 구역에 배치했다.

13 점심 무렵, 나는 덥고, 땀이 났으며, 아버지가 나에게 장갑을 끼도록 한 것이 기뻤다.

14 우리는 쓰레기 봉투 50개를 쓰레기로 채웠고, 잡초를 뽑을 준비가 되어 있었다.

15 우리가 뽑으면 뽑을수록, 먼지가 공기를 가득 메워서 재채기가 나왔다.

16 At the _____ of the day, I had to _____ the lot looked _____ _____.

A. much　　　　B. admit　　　　C. better　　　　D. end

17 That _____ day was _____ _____.

A. toughest　　　B. the　　　　C. first

18 On the weekends that _____, we made _____, planted flower and vegetable _____, and _____ them.

A. watered　　　B. rows　　　　C. seeds　　　　D. followed

19 After _____ two weeks, I _____ _____ when I found the plants had started popping _____!

A. complaining　　B. up　　　　C. stopped　　　D. about

20 _____, the _____ and _____ the _____ and the tomatoes.

A. beans　　　　B. lettuce　　　C. then　　　　D. first

21 They _____ _____ _____.

A. fast　　　　B. so　　　　C. grew

22 I _____ _____ it!

A. believe　　　B. couldn't

23 The bean plants grew an inch, and the tomatoes _____ in _____ in just a _____ days.

A. few　　　　B. doubled　　　C. grew　　　　D. size

24 Now, two months _____, I like to go there _____ day to see _____ new flowers are _____ to pop up.

A. what　　　　B. later　　　C. ready　　　　D. every

25 _____ of people in the neighborhood meet _____ to _____ the _____ and to talk together.

A. sights　　　B. lots　　　C. enjoy　　　　D. there

26 Tonight, it _____ _____ me — _____ a good _____ we did!

A. hit　　　　B. suddenly　　C. thing　　　　D. what

27 I'm _____ I _____ a _____ of it.

A. part　　　　B. been　　　C. proud　　　　D. have

28 I'm in _____ of _____ flowers for the _____ on Fourth Street.

A. nursing　　　B. picking　　C. charge　　　D. home

29 The vegetables _____ _____ _____ every kitchen _____ our town.

A. to　　　　B. will　　　C. in　　　　D. go

30 But _____ _____, an ugly and dirty lot _____ people didn't like has _____ a pretty garden for everyone.

A. better　　　B. that　　　C. even　　　　D. become

16 그날이 끝날 무렵, 나는 그 지역이 훨씬 더 나아 보인다는 것을 인정해야 했다.

17 그 첫날이 가장 힘들었다.

18 그다음 주말에 우리는 열을 만들고, 꽃과 채소 씨앗을 심고, 물을 주었다.

19 약 2주 뒤, 나는 식물들이 자라나기 시작한 것을 발견했을 때 불평하는 것을 멈추었다!

20 처음에는 상추, 그러고 나서, 콩과 토마토.

21 그것들은 아주 빨리 자랐다.

22 나는 믿을 수가 없었다!

23 콩 식물은 1인치 자라났고, 토마토는 며칠 만에 크기가 두 배가 되었다.

24 두 달이 지난 지금, 나는 매일 어떤 새로운 꽃들이 피어날 준비가 되었는지 보러 그곳에 가는 것을 좋아한다.

25 이웃의 많은 사람이 그곳에서 만나 풍경을 즐기고 함께 이야기를 나눈다.

26 오늘 밤, 갑자기 생각났다 — 우리가 얼마나 좋은 일을 했는가!

27 나는 내가 그 일의 일부였다는 것이 자랑스럽다.

28 나는 'Fourth Street'에 있는 양로원을 위해 꽃을 따는 일을 맡았다.

29 채소들은 우리 마을의 모든 부엌으로 갈 것이다.

30 하지만 훨씬 더 좋은 것은, 사람들이 좋아하지 않았던 볼품없고 더러운 지역이 모두를 위한 예쁜 정원이 되었다는 것이다.

※ 다음 우리말과 일치하도록 빈칸에 알맞은 말을 쓰시오.

1 Green _____

2 I _____ the _____ _____.

3 My parents were _____ me _____ on the neighborhood project, but I had _____ _____ things _____ _____.

4 I didn't understand _____ _____ _____ _____ on this place.

5 It was just the _____, old, _____ lot _____ _____ Johnny's Shop.

6 It _____ _____ _____ wild plants, fast food _____, old newspapers, _____ glass, and _____ _____ _____ of dirty trash _____ _____ _____.

7 As I looked at it that first morning, I thought, "_____ _____ _____ _____ snakes in there, _____."

8 There were twenty of us — _____ _____ _____ _____ — _____ _____ _____ that day.

9 I didn't think that we could _____ _____ _____ and _____ it _____ a garden.

10 We were all wondering _____ _____ _____.

11 Then Mr. Hernandez said, "The _____ _____ it is _____ _____ _____."

12 Then, he _____ the lot _____ four parts _____ _____ and _____ five people _____ each part.

13 _____ _____, I was hot, _____, and glad my dad had made me _____ _____.

14 We _____ fifty trash bags _____ _____ and _____ _____ _____ _____ wild plants.

15 _____ we pulled and pulled, _____ _____ the air and _____ _____ _____.

1 식물을 잘 키우는 사람들

2 나는 온종일 불평했다.

3 우리 부모님은 나를 이웃 프로젝트에서 일하게 하셨지만, 나에게는 훨씬 더 나은 할 일들이 있었다.

4 나는 우리가 왜 이곳에서 일하고 있어야 하는지 이해하지 못했다.

5 그곳은 그저 Johnny's Shop 건너편에 있는 볼품없고, 오래되고, 텅 빈 지역이었다.

6 그곳은 잡초와 패스트푸드 포장지와 낡은 신문, 깨진 유리, 그리고 상상할 수 있는 모든 다른 종류의 더러운 쓰레기로 가득 차 있었다.

7 그 첫날 아침에 그곳을 보았을 때, 나는 "틀림없이 저 안에는 뱀들도 있을 거야."라고 생각했다.

8 그날 일할 준비가 된 — 모든 연령대와 몸집을 가진 — 우리 20명이 있었다.

9 나는 이 끔찍하게 더러운 곳을 청소하여 정원으로 바꿀 수 있다고 생각하지 않았다.

10 우리는 모두 어디서부터 시작해야 할지 궁금해 하고 있었다.

11 그때 Hernandez 씨가 "그것을 할 유일한 방법은 그냥 시작하는 것입니다."라고 말했다.

12 그러고 나서, 그는 그 지역을 끈으로 네 구역으로 나누고, 5명을 각 구역에 배치했다.

13 점심 무렵, 나는 덥고, 땀이 났으며, 아버지가 나에게 장갑을 끼도록 한 것이 기뻤다.

14 우리는 쓰레기 봉투 50개를 쓰레기로 채웠고, 잡초를 뽑을 준비가 되어 있었다.

15 우리가 뽑으면 뽑을수록, 먼지가 공기를 가득 메워서 재채기가 나왔다.

16 _____ _____ _____ the day, I _____ _____ _____ the lot looked _____ _____.

17 That first day was _____ _____.

18 On the weekends that followed, we _____ _____, planted flower and vegetable seeds, and _____ them.

19 After about two weeks, I _____ _____ when I found the plants had started _____ _____!

20 _____, _____ _____ and then the beans and the tomatoes.

21 They _____ _____ _____.

22 I _____ _____ it!

23 The bean plants grew an inch, and the tomatoes doubled _____ _____ _____ _____ _____ _____ _____.

24 Now, two months _____, I like to go there every day to see _____ _____ _____ _____ _____ _____ to pop up.

25 _____ _____ people in the neighborhood meet there _____ _____ _____ and to talk together.

26 Tonight, it _____ _____ _____ — what a good thing we did!

27 I'm _____ I _____ _____ _____ _____ _____ of it.

28 _____ _____ _____ _____ _____ _____ flowers for the _____ _____ on Fourth Street.

29 The vegetables _____ _____ _____ every kitchen in our town.

30 But _____ _____, an ugly and dirty lot _____ people didn't like _____ _____ a pretty garden for everyone.

---

16 그날이 끝날 무렵, 나는 그 지역이 훨씬 더 나아 보인다는 것을 인정해야 했다.

17 그 첫날이 가장 힘들었다.

18 그다음 주말에 우리는 열을 만들고, 꽃과 채소 씨앗을 심고, 물을 주었다.

19 약 2주 뒤, 나는 식물들이 자라나기 시작한 것을 발견했을 때 불평하는 것을 멈추었다!

20 처음에는 상추, 그러고 나서, 콩과 토마토.

21 그것들은 아주 빨리 자랐다.

22 나는 믿을 수가 없었다!

23 콩 식물은 1인치 자라났고, 토마토는 며칠 만에 크기가 두 배가 되었다.

24 두 달이 지난 지금, 나는 매일 어떤 새로운 꽃들이 피어날 준비가 되었는지 보러 그곳에 가는 것을 좋아한다.

25 이웃의 많은 사람이 그곳에서 만나 풍경을 즐기고 함께 이야기를 나눈다.

26 오늘 밤, 갑자기 생각났다 — 우리가 얼마나 좋은 일을 했는가!

27 나는 내가 그 일의 일부였다는 것이 자랑스럽다.

28 나는 'Fourth Street'에 있는 양로원을 위해 꽃을 따는 일을 맡았다.

29 채소들은 우리 마을의 모든 부엌으로 갈 것이다.

30 하지만 훨씬 더 좋은 것은, 사람들이 좋아하지 않았던 볼품없고 더러운 지역이 모두를 위한 예쁜 정원이 되었다는 것이다.

※ 다음 문장을 우리말로 쓰시오.

1 Green Thumbs

➡ _____

2 I complained the whole day.

➡ _____

3 My parents were making me work on the neighborhood project, but I had far better things to do.

➡ _____

4 I didn't understand why we were working on this place.

➡ _____

5 It was just the ugly, old, empty lot across from Johnny's Shop.

➡ _____

6 It was full of wild plants, fast food wraps, old newspapers, broken glass, and every other kind of dirty trash you can imagine.

➡ _____

_____

7 As I looked at it that first morning, I thought, "I bet there are snakes in there, too."

➡ _____

8 There were twenty of us — all ages and sizes — ready to work that day.

➡ _____

9 I didn't think that we could clean up this awful mess and turn it into a garden.

➡ _____

10 We were all wondering where to begin.

➡ _____

11 Then Mr. Hernandez said, "The only way to do it is just to start."

➡ _____

12 Then, he divided the lot into four parts with string and assigned five people to each part.

➡ _____

13 By lunchtime, I was hot, sweaty, and glad my dad had made me wear gloves.

➡ _____

14 We filled fifty trash bags with waste and were ready to pull wild plants.

➡ _____

15 As we pulled and pulled, dust filled the air and made us sneeze.

➡ _____

16 At the end of the day, I had to admit the lot looked much better.

➡ _____

17 That first day was the toughest.

➡ _____

18 On the weekends that followed, we made rows, planted flower and vegetable seeds, and watered them.

➡ _____

19 After about two weeks, I stopped complaining when I found the plants had started popping up!

➡ _____

20 First, the lettuce and then the beans and the tomatoes.

➡ _____

21 They grew so fast.

➡ _____

22 I couldn't believe it!

➡ _____

23 The bean plants grew an inch, and the tomatoes doubled in size in just a few days.

➡ _____

24 Now, two months later, I like to go there every day to see what new flowers are ready to pop up.

➡ _____

25 Lots of people in the neighborhood meet there to enjoy the sights and to talk together.

➡ _____

26 Tonight, it suddenly hit me — what a good thing we did!

➡ _____

27 I'm proud I have been a part of it.

➡ _____

28 I'm in charge of picking flowers for the nursing home on Fourth Street.

➡ _____

29 The vegetables will go to every kitchen in our town.

➡ _____

30 But even better, an ugly and dirty lot that people didn't like has become a pretty garden for everyone.

➡ _____

※ 다음 괄호 안의 단어들을 우리말에 맞도록 바르게 배열하시오.

1   (Thumbs / Green)
➡ _____

2   (complained / I / whole / the / day.)
➡ _____

3   (parents / my / making / were / work / me / on / neighborhood / the / project, / but / had / I / better / far / to / do. / things)
➡ _____

4   (didn't / I / why / understand / we / working / were / this / on / place.)
➡ _____

5   (was / it / just / ugly, / the / old, / lot / empty / from / across / Shop. / Johnny's)
➡ _____

6   (was / it / full / wild / of / plants, / food / fast / wraps, / newspapers, / old / glass, / broken / and / other / every / kind / dirty / of / you / trash / imagine. / can)
➡ _____

7   (I / as / looked / at / that / it / morning, / first / thought, / I / "I / there / bet / are / in / snakes / there, / too.")
➡ _____

8   (were / there / of / us / twenty / — / ages / all / sizes / and / — / to / ready / work / day. / that)
➡ _____

9   (didn't / I / that / think / could / we / clean / this / up / mess / awful / and / it / turn / into / garden. / a)
➡ _____

10   (were / we / wondering / all / to / where / begin.)
➡ _____

11   (Mr. / then / Hernandes / said, / "the / way / only / do / to / is / it / to / just / start.")
➡ _____

12   (he / then, / divided / lot / the / four / into / with / parts / string / assinged / and / people / five / each / to / part.)
➡ _____

13   (lunchtime, / by / was / I / hot, / and / sweaty, / glad / dad / my / made / had / wear / me / gloves.)
➡ _____

14   (filled / we / trash / fifty / with / bags / waste / and / ready / were / pull / to / plants. / wild)
➡ _____

15   (we / as / pulled / and / dust / pulled / filled / air / the / and / us / made / sneeze.)
➡ _____

---

1 식물을 잘 키우는 사람들

2 나는 온종일 불평했다.

3 우리 부모님은 나를 이웃 프로젝트에서 일하게 하셨지만, 나에게는 훨씬 더 나은 할 일들이 있었다.

4 나는 우리가 왜 이곳에서 일하고 있어야 하는지 이해하지 못했다.

5 그곳은 그저 Johnny's Shop 건너편에 있는 볼품없고, 오래되고, 텅 빈 지역이었다.

6 그곳은 잡초와 패스트푸드 포장지와 낡은 신문, 깨진 유리, 그리고 상상할 수 있는 모든 다른 종류의 더러운 쓰레기로 가득 차 있었다.

7 그 첫날 아침에 그곳을 보았을 때, 나는 "틀림없이 저 안에는 뱀들도 있을 거야."라고 생각했다.

8 그날 일할 준비가 된 — 모든 연령대와 몸집을 가진 — 우리 20명이 있었다.

9 나는 이 끔찍하게 더러운 곳을 청소하여 정원으로 바꿀 수 있다고 생각하지 않았다.

10 우리는 모두 어디서부터 시작해야 할지 궁금해 하고 있었다.

11 그때 Hernandez 씨가 "그것을 할 유일한 방법은 그냥 시작하는 것입니다."라고 말했다.

12 그리고 나서, 그는 그 지역을 끈으로 네 구역으로 나누고, 5명을 각 구역에 배치했다.

13 점심 무렵, 나는 덥고, 땀이 났으며, 아버지가 나에게 장갑을 끼도록 한 것이 기뻤다.

14 우리는 쓰레기 봉투 50개를 쓰레기로 채웠고, 잡초를 뽑을 준비가 되어 있었다.

15 우리가 뽑으면 뽑을수록, 먼지가 공기를 가득 메워서 재채기가 나왔다.

16 (the / at / of / end / day, / the / had / I / admit / to / lot / the / looked / better. / much)
➡ _____

17 (first / that / was / day / toughest. / the)
➡ _____

18 (the / on / weekends / followed, / that / made / we / rows, / flower / planted / and / seeds, / vegetable / watered / and / them.)
➡ _____
_____

19 (about / after / weeks, / two / stopped / I / when / complaining / I / the / found / plants / started / had / up! / popping)
➡ _____
_____

20 (the / first, / and / lettuce / then / beans / the / and / tomatoes. / the)
➡ _____

21 (grew / they / fast. / so)
➡ _____

22 (couldn't / I / it! / believe)
➡ _____

23 (bean / the / grew / plants / inch, / an / and / tomatoes / the / in / doubled / size / just / in / few / a / days.)
➡ _____
_____

24 (two / now, / later, / months / like / I / go / to / every / there / day / see / to / new / what / flowers / ready / are / pop / to / up.)
➡ _____
_____

25 (of / lots / people / the / in / neighborhood / there / meet / enjoy / to / sights / the / to / and / together. / talk)
➡ _____
_____

26 (it / tonight, / suddenly / me / hit / — / a / what / thing / good / did! / we)
➡ _____

27 (proud / I'm / have / I / been / part / a / it. / of)
➡ _____

28 (in / I'm / of / charge / flowers / picking / the / for / home / nursing / on / Street. / Fourth)
➡ _____
_____

29 (vegetables / the / go / will / every / to / in / kitchen / our / town.)
➡ _____

30 (even / but / better, / ugly / an / and / lot / dirty / that / didn't / people / like / become / has / pretty / a / for / garden / everyone.)
➡ _____
_____

16 그날이 끝날 무렵, 나는 그 지역이 훨씬 더 나아 보인다는 것을 인정해야 했다.

17 그 첫날이 가장 힘들었다.

18 그다음 주말에 우리는 열을 만들고, 꽃과 채소 씨앗을 심고, 물을 주었다.

19 약 2주 뒤, 나는 식물들이 자라나기 시작한 것을 발견했을 때 불평하는 것을 멈추었다!

20 처음에는 상추, 그러고 나서, 콩과 토마토.

21 그것들은 아주 빨리 자랐다.

22 나는 믿을 수가 없었다!

23 콩 식물은 1인치 자라났고, 토마토는 며칠 만에 크기가 두 배가 되었다.

24 두 달이 지난 지금, 나는 매일 어떤 새로운 꽃들이 피어날 준비가 되었는지 보러 그곳에 가는 것을 좋아한다.

25 이웃의 많은 사람이 그곳에서 만나 풍경을 즐기고 함께 이야기를 나눈다.

26 오늘 밤, 갑자기 생각났다 — 우리가 얼마나 좋은 일을 했는가!

27 나는 내가 그 일의 일부였다는 것이 자랑스럽다.

28 나는 'Fourth Street'에 있는 양로원을 위해 꽃을 따는 일을 맡았다.

29 채소들은 우리 마을의 모든 부엌으로 갈 것이다.

30 하지만 훨씬 더 좋은 것은, 사람들이 좋아하지 않았던 볼품없고 더러운 지역이 모두를 위한 예쁜 정원이 되었다는 것이다.

※ **다음 우리말을 영어로 쓰시오.**

1 식물을 잘 키우는 사람들

➡ _____

2 나는 온종일 불평했다.

➡ _____

3 우리 부모님은 나를 이웃 프로젝트에서 일하게 하셨지만, 나에게는 훨씬 더 나은 할 일들이 있었다.

➡ _____

4 나는 우리가 왜 이곳에서 일하고 있어야 하는지 이해하지 못했다.

➡ _____

5 그곳은 그저 Johnny's Shop 건너편에 있는 볼품없고, 오래되고, 텅 빈 지역이었다.

➡ _____

6 그곳은 잡초와 패스트푸드 포장지와 낡은 신문, 깨진 유리, 그리고 상상할 수 있는 모든 다른 종류의 더러운 쓰레기로 가득 차 있었다.

➡ _____

_____

7 그 첫날 아침에 그곳을 보았을 때, 나는 "틀림없이 저 안에는 뱀들도 있을 거야."라고 생각했다.

➡ _____

8 그날 일할 준비가 된 — 모든 연령대와 몸집을 가진 — 우리 20명이 있었다.

➡ _____

9 나는 이 끔찍하게 더러운 곳을 청소하여 정원으로 바꿀 수 있다고 생각하지 않았다.

➡ _____

10 우리는 모두 어디서부터 시작해야 할지 궁금해 하고 있었다.

➡ _____

11 그때 Hernandez 씨가 "그것을 할 유일한 방법은 그냥 시작하는 것입니다."라고 말했다.

➡ _____

12 그러고 나서, 그는 그 지역을 끈으로 네 구역으로 나누고, 5명을 각 구역에 배치했다.

➡ _____

13 점심 무렵, 나는 덥고, 땀이 났으며, 아버지가 나에게 장갑을 끼도록 한 것이 기뻤다.

➡ _____

14 우리는 쓰레기 봉투 50개를 쓰레기로 채웠고, 잡초를 뽑을 준비가 되어 있었다.

➡ _____

15 우리가 뽑으면 뽑을수록, 먼지가 공기를 가득 메워서 재채기가 나왔다.

➡ _____

16 그날이 끝날 무렵, 나는 그 지역이 훨씬 더 나아 보인다는 것을 인정해야 했다.

➡ _____

17 그 첫날이 가장 힘들었다.

➡ _____

18 그다음 주말에 우리는 열을 만들고, 꽃과 채소 씨앗을 심고, 물을 주었다.

➡ _____

19 약 2주 뒤, 나는 식물들이 자라나기 시작한 것을 발견했을 때 불평하는 것을 멈추었다!

➡ _____

20 처음에는 상추, 그러고 나서, 콩과 토마토.

➡ _____

21 그것들은 아주 빨리 자랐다.

➡ _____

22 나는 믿을 수가 없었다!

➡ _____

23 콩 식물은 1인치 자라났고, 토마토는 며칠 만에 크기가 두 배가 되었다.

➡ _____

24 두 달이 지난 지금, 나는 매일 어떤 새로운 꽃들이 피어날 준비가 되었는지 보러 그곳에 가는 것을 좋아한다.

➡ _____

25 이웃의 많은 사람이 그곳에서 만나 풍경을 즐기고 함께 이야기를 나눈다.

➡ _____

26 오늘 밤, 갑자기 생각났다 — 우리가 얼마나 좋은 일을 했는가!

➡ _____

27 나는 내가 그 일의 일부였다는 것이 자랑스럽다.

➡ _____

28 나는 'Fourth Street'에 있는 양로원을 위해 꽃을 따는 일을 맡았다.

➡ _____

29 채소들은 우리 마을의 모든 부엌으로 갈 것이다.

➡ _____

30 하지만 훨씬 더 좋은 것은, 사람들이 좋아하지 않았던 볼품없고 더러운 지역이 모두를 위한 예쁜 정원이 되었다는 것이다.

➡ _____

※ 다음 우리말과 일치하도록 빈칸에 알맞은 말을 쓰시오.

After You Read A

June 17

1. I _____ the town garden _____ _____.

2. Some people were talking _____ they _____ _____ at the beautiful garden.

3. I _____ some _____ and _____ them _____ the _____ _____.

4. I'm _____ _____ we _____ a pretty garden _____ _____.

6월 17일
1. 나는 방과 후에 마을 정원을 방문했다.
2. 몇몇 사람들이 아름다운 정원을 보면서 이야기하고 있었다.
3. 나는 꽃을 몇 송이 꺾어서 양로원에 가지고 갔다.
4. 우리가 모두를 위한 예쁜 정원을 만든 것이 자랑스럽다.

Do It Yourself

1. _____ Town _____

2. This is Oksig, _____ I _____ _____ a symbol of _____ _____.

3. I _____ this after I _____ _____ pictures of _____ _____ _____ _____ _____.

4. Oksig is _____ _____ _____ real corn.

5. I hope _____ _____ _____ _____.

1. 우리 동네 상징
2. 이것은 Oksig이고, 내가 나의 동네 상징으로 그렸습니다.
3. 나는 많은 다양한 종류의 옥수수 사진을 찍은 후에 이것을 디자인했습니다.
4. Oksig은 진짜 옥수수보다 훨씬 더 귀엽습니다.
5. 나는 모든 사람들이 이것을 좋아하길 바랍니다.

Link to the World

1. • Kampong Ayer is _____ _____ "water village" _____ _____ _____.

2. It _____ _____ _____ about 40 small villages.

3. • All the houses _____ _____ _____ the water.

4. • _____ _____ schools, _____ _____, gas stations, and _____ _____.

5. • It is _____ _____ beautiful _____ you think.

6. It _____ _____ the Venice of Asia.

1. • 캄퐁 아에르는 세상에서 가장 큰 '수상 마을'이다.
2. 그것은 40개의 작은 마을들로 이루어져 있다.
3. • 모든 집은 물 위에 지어져 있다.
4. • 학교, 경찰서, 주유소, 우체국이 있다.
5. • 그곳은 여러분이 생각하는 것보다 훨씬 더 아름답다.
6. 그곳은 아시아의 베니스라고 불린다.

※ 다음 우리말을 영어로 쓰시오.

After You Read A

1. 나는 방과 후에 마을 정원을 방문했다.

　➡ _____

2. 몇몇 사람들이 아름다운 정원을 보면서 이야기하고 있었다.

　➡ _____

3. 나는 꽃을 몇 송이 꺾어서 양로원에 가지고 갔다.

　➡ _____

4. 우리가 모두를 위한 예쁜 정원을 만든 것이 자랑스럽다.

　➡ _____

Do It Yourself

1. 우리 동네 상징

　➡ _____

2. 이것은 Oksig이고, 내가 나의 동네 상징으로 그렸습니다.

　➡ _____

3. 나는 많은 다양한 종류의 옥수수 사진을 찍은 후에 이것을 디자인했습니다.

　➡ _____

4. Oksig은 진짜 옥수수보다 훨씬 더 귀엽습니다.

　➡ _____

5. 나는 모든 사람들이 이것을 좋아하길 바랍니다.

　➡ _____

Link To The World

1. • 캄퐁 아에르는 세상에서 가장 큰 '수상 마을'이다.

　➡ _____

2. 그것은 40개의 작은 마을들로 이루어져 있다.

　➡ _____

3. • 모든 집은 물 위에 지어져 있다.

　➡ _____

4. • 학교, 경찰서, 주유소, 우체국이 있다.

　➡ _____

5. • 그곳은 여러분이 생각하는 것보다 훨씬 더 아름답다.

　➡ _____

6. 그곳은 아시아의 베니스라고 불린다.

　➡ _____

※ 다음 영어를 우리말로 쓰시오.

01 brave _____

02 discovery _____

03 university _____

04 backward _____

05 bomb _____

06 float _____

07 mistake _____

08 honor _____

09 imaginative _____

10 maybe _____

11 award _____

12 opening _____

13 invention _____

14 laughable _____

15 ceremony _____

16 store _____

17 worth _____

18 accept _____

19 magnet _____

20 eager _____

21 repeatedly _____

22 cheer _____

23 tradition _____

24 perform _____

25 actually _____

26 economics _____

27 navy _____

28 present _____

29 interest _____

30 research _____

31 sailor _____

32 useful _____

33 trillion _____

34 unusual _____

35 instead of _____

36 keep -ing _____

37 succeed in _____

38 laugh out loud _____

39 take part in _____

40 keep A from -ing _____

41 be eager to _____

42 get out of _____

43 keep one's fingers crossed _____

※ 다음 우리말을 영어로 쓰시오.

01	받아들이다	
02	개막	
03	뒤로	
04	발견	
05	열렬한, 간절히 바라는	
06	반복적으로	
07	공연하다	
08	경제학	
09	뜨다	
10	평화	
11	존중하다; 명예	
12	폭탄	
13	용감한	
14	수여하다; 상	
15	의식, 식	
16	발명, 발명품	
17	~하는 동안, ~인 반면에	
18	웃기는	
19	실제로, 사실은	
20	드문, 특이한	
21	해군	

22	자석	
23	아마도	
24	실수	
25	선원	
26	전통	
27	연구, 조사; 조사하다	
28	1조	
29	유용한	
30	가치; ~의 가치가 있는	
31	창의적인, 상상력이 풍부한	
32	관심	
33	대학, 대학교	
34	받다	
35	~ 이하, ~보다 적은	
36	~ 대신에	
37	~에 성공하다	
38	~에 참여하다	
39	큰 소리로 웃다	
40	계속 ~하다	
41	~에서 떠나다, 나가다	
42	~을 (열렬히) 하고 싶어 하다	
43	A가 ~하지 못하게 하다	

※ 다음 영영풀이에 알맞은 단어를 <보기>에서 골라 쓴 후, 우리말 뜻을 쓰시오.

1 _____ : not dead: _____

2 _____ : to give a prize: _____

3 _____ : someone who works on a ship: _____

4 _____ : the number 1,000,000,000,000: _____

5 _____ : to take something offered: _____

6 _____ : a piece of metal that attracts other iron: _____

7 _____ : a military force made up of boats and ships: _____

8 _____ : looking or facing in the direction that is behind you: _____

9 _____ : the act of finding something for the first time: _____

10 _____ : to be on a liquid and not sink: _____

11 _____ : the study of something to discover new facts: _____

12 _____ : to make, design, or think of a new type of thing: _____

13 _____ : wanting very much to do or have something: _____

14 _____ : • something you are proud to do: _____

　　　　　　　　 • to show great respect for someone, esp. in public: _____

15 _____ : having or showing new and exciting ideas: _____

16 _____ : an educational institution at the highest level, where you study for a
　　　　　　　　degree: _____

 보기

honor	float	live	sailor
backward	invent	accept	navy
university	award	imaginative	trillion
eager	research	magnet	discovery

※ 다음 우리말과 일치하도록 빈칸에 알맞은 말을 쓰시오.

Get Ready 2

(1) **G:** You _____ _____ _____ _____ problems in class. _____ _____ you'll _____ the Class Brain _____.

B: Do you really _____ _____?

G: Of course. I'll _____ my fingers _____ for you, Sangjun!

(2) **B:** The _____ of the Oh So Sweet _____ will get some candies.

G: Oh, I want _____ _____ the _____.

B: _____ _____ you'll _____ the _____ this time. _____ _____, Jiu!

(3) **B:** I'm _____ _____ _____ the Best Joker award this time.

G: Ha-ha. You always _____ us _____ _____ _____. So you'll _____ _____ _____, Yunki. Good luck.

B: Thank you.

(4) **B:** Minji, you're a happy girl. I think you'll _____ the Ms. Cheerful _____. I'll _____ _____ _____ _____!

G: Oh, thank you, Jiho.

Start Off – Listen & Talk A

1. **G:** Mom, I _____ _____ _____ the sports day.

W: _____ are you _____ _____ _____ on that day, Minji?

G: I'm going to play basketball for my class. We've _____ hard _____ _____ _____ _____ _____.

W: Oh, I'm _____ _____ _____ your game.

G: _____, I'm _____ _____ _____. I'm _____ I'll _____ a _____.

W: _____ _____. You'll _____ a good _____. I'll keep _____ _____ _____!

2. **W:** Soyun, are you going to _____ _____ _____ any races on the sports day?

G: Sure. I'_____ _____ _____ _____ a 100 meter race at the _____ of the day.

W: Wow, I'm _____ _____ to _____ you at the race.

G: But, Mom, I'm not _____ I'll _____ the race.

W: Just _____ _____ _____. I'll _____ _____ _____ _____!

해석

(1) **G:** 너는 수업 중 많은 문제를 해결했 잖아. 나는 네가 'Class Brain'상 을 탈 거라고 확신해.

B: 정말 그렇게 생각하니?

G: 물론이야. 행운을 빌게, 상준아!

(2) **B:** 'Oh So Sweet'상 수상자는 사탕 을 받을 거야.

G: 오, 그 상을 받고 싶다.

B: 네가 이번에는 그 상을 탈 거라고 확신해. 행운을 빌어, 지우야!

(3) **B:** 난 이번에 'Best Joker'상을 받기 를 기대해.

G: 하하. 너는 항상 우리를 웃게 하잖 아. 그러니 네가 그 상을 탈 거야, 윤기야. 행운을 빌어.

B: 고마워.

(4) **B:** 민지야, 너는 쾌활한 아이야. 나는 네가 'Ms. Cheerful'상을 탈 거라 고 생각해. 행운을 빌게!

G: 오, 고마워, 지호야.

1. **G:** 엄마, 체육 대회가 정말 기다려져 요.

W: 민지야, 너는 그날 무엇을 할 거 니?

G: 저는 학급을 대표해서 농구를 할 거예요. 우리는 몇 주간 열심히 연 습해 왔어요.

W: 오, 너의 경기가 기대되는구나.

G: 사실은, 전 조금 걱정이 돼요. 제 가 실수를 할까봐 겁나요.

W: 걱정하지 마. 넌 잘할 거야. 행운 을 빌어줄게!

2. **W:** 소윤아, 넌 체육 대회에서 경주에 참가하니?

G: 물론이죠. 전 그날 마지막에 있는 100 미터 달리기를 뛸 거예요.

W: 와, 네가 경주에서 달리는 모습을 보는 것이 기대되는구나.

G: 하지만 엄마, 전 경주에서 이길지 잘 모르겠어요.

W: 그냥 최선을 다하렴. 행운을 빌어 줄게!

Start Off – Listen & Talk B

G: Mom, _____ _____ _____ to the sports day?

W: Sure. I'm _____ _____ _____ the game Kick a Shoe. This will be the first time _____ _____ _____ _____ it.

G: Don't worry. I'm _____ you'll _____ _____. I'll _____ my _____ _____ for you!

W: Thank you. I'm also _____ _____ _____ a funny dance with some _____ _____.

G: That _____ _____. I'm _____ _____ to _____ you on the _____.

Start Off – Speak Up

A: I'm _____ _____ _____ the _____ airplane contest tomorrow. Are you _____?

B: Well, I think _____, but I'm _____.

A: You will _____ _____. I'll _____ _____ _____ _____ _____!

Step Up – Real-life Scene

Miso: We're going on a _____ _____ next Tuesday. What are you going to do in the _____ _____, Jimin?

Jimin: I'm _____ _____ talk _____ our teachers _____ _____ _____ and tell some _____.

Miso: Wow! I'm really _____ _____ _____ _____ _____.

Jimin: Will everyone like my _____? I'm not _____.

Miso: Don't _____. I'm sure you'll _____ _____. I'll _____ _____ _____ _____!

Jimin: Thank you, Miso. _____ _____ _____ you one part of my _____. _____ who? "Goood Jooob!"

Miso: Ha-ha, you _____ _____ our English teacher.

Jimin: Do I? I'm _____ _____ _____ you more at the show.

Miso: Great! You always _____ us _____ _____ _____.

G: 엄마, 체육 대회에 오실 거예요?
W: 물론이지. 나는 'Kick a Shoe' 게임에 참가할 거야. 이번에 처음 해 보는 거야.
G: 걱정하지 마세요. 엄마는 잘하실 거예요. 행운을 빌어 드릴게요!
W: 고맙다. 나는 다른 엄마들과 코믹 댄스도 할 거야.
G: 재밌겠네요. 무대에 선 엄마 모습을 보는 것이 기대돼요.

B: 나는 내일 모형 비행기 대회가 기대돼. 너는 준비됐니?
G: 음, 그런 것 같아, 하지만 긴장돼.
B: 너는 잘할 거야. 내가 행운을 빌어 줄게!

미소: 다음 주 화요일에 수학여행을 갈 거야. 지민아, 너는 장기 자랑에서 뭘 할 거니?
지민: 나는 수업 시간에 선생님들이 말하는 것을 흉내 내고 농담도 할 거야.
미소: 와! 정말 기대되는데..
지민: 모든 사람이 나의 쇼를 좋아할까? 잘 모르겠어.
미소: 걱정하지 마. 나는 네가 잘할 거라고 확신해. 행운을 빌어 줄게!
지민: 고마워, 미소야. 내가 나의 연기의 한 부분을 보여 줄게. 누군지 맞힐 수 있겠니? "잘~ 했어~요!"
미소: 하하. 우리 영어 선생님처럼 들리는데.
지민: 그래? 장기 자랑에서 더 많이 보여 줄게.
미소: 멋지다! 너는 항상 우리를 웃게 만들어.

Fun Time

A: I'_____ _____ _____ _____ to Jejudo next week.

B: Wow! That _____ _____.

A: Yeah, I'_____ _____ _____ _____ _____ it.

A: I'm _____ _____ _____ the dance contest next week, but I'_____ _____ _____ it.

B: _____ _____. You'll do great. I'll _____ _____ _____ _____.

A: Thank you.

A: 나는 다음 주에 제주도를 여행할 거야.

B: 와! 멋지다.

A: 응, 난 그것이 정말 기대돼.

A: 난 다음 주에 춤 대회에 나갈 건데, 걱정이 된다.

B: 걱정하지 마. 넌 잘할 거야. 행운을 빌어 줄게.

A: 고마워.

Express Yourself A

1. **G:** _____ _____ _____ _____ something about your _____?

   B: They are _____ _____ _____ _____ shoes. You can also _____ the _____ with them.

   G: Great! I'm sure you'll _____ _____ _____. I'll _____ my fingers _____!

2. **B:** This _____ _____. Is this a _____ _____ or a bird _____?

   G: It is _____ _____ a cutting _____ _____ _____ a bird _____. You can do two things _____ _____ _____ _____.

   B: That's a great _____!

   G: Do you _____ _____ _____?

   B: Yes. I'm really _____ _____ to _____ it.

1. G: 너의 발명품에 관해 이야기를 좀 해 줄래?

   B: 그것은 특별한 신발이야. 너는 그것으로 바닥을 청소할 수도 있어.

   G: 멋지다! 네가 상을 탈 거라고 확신해. 행운을 빌게!

2. B: 이것은 흥미로워 보여. 도마니, 아니면 새 모이통이니?

   G: 그것은 도마일 뿐만 아니라 새 모이통이기도 해. 너는 동시에 두 가지를 할 수 있어.

   B: 멋진 아이디어야!

   G: 정말 그렇게 생각하니?

   B: 응. 난 그것을 사용해 보는 게 정말 기대가 되는 걸.

※ 다음 우리말에 맞도록 대화를 영어로 쓰시오.

Get Ready 2

(1) G: _____

    _____

    B: _____

    G: _____

(2) B: _____

    G: _____

    B: _____

(3) B: _____

    G: _____

    _____

    B: _____

(4) B: _____

    G: _____

Start Off – Listen & Talk A

1. G: _____

    W: _____

    G: _____

    W: _____

    G: _____

    W: _____

2. W: _____

    G: _____

    W: _____

    G: _____

    W: _____

해석

(1) G: 너는 수업 중 많은 문제를 해결했잖아. 나는 네가 'Class Brain'상을 탈 거라고 확신해.
B: 정말 그렇게 생각하니?
G: 물론이야. 행운을 빌게, 상준아!

(2) B: 'Oh So Sweet'상 수상자는 사탕을 받을 거야.
G: 오, 그 상을 받고 싶다.
B: 네가 이번에는 그 상을 탈 거라고 확신해. 행운을 빌어, 지우야!

(3) B: 난 이번에 'Best Joker'상을 받기를 기대해.
G: 하하. 너는 항상 우리를 웃게 하잖아. 그러니 네가 그 상을 탈 거야, 윤기야. 행운을 빌어.
B: 고마워.

(4) B: 민지야, 너는 쾌활한 아이야. 나는 네가 'Ms. Cheerful'상을 탈 거라고 생각해. 행운을 빌게!
G: 오, 고마워, 지호야.

1. G: 엄마, 체육 대회가 정말 기다려져요.
W: 민지야, 너는 그날 무엇을 할 거니?
G: 저는 학급을 대표해서 농구를 할 거예요. 우리는 몇 주간 열심히 연습해 왔어요.
W: 오, 너의 경기가 기대되는구나.
G: 사실은, 전 조금 걱정이 돼요. 제가 실수를 할까봐 겁나요.
W: 걱정하지 마. 넌 잘할 거야. 행운을 빌어줄게!

2. W: 소윤아, 넌 체육 대회에서 경주에 참가하니?
G: 물론이죠. 전 그날 마지막에 있는 100 미터 달리기를 뛸 거예요.
W: 와, 네가 경주에서 달리는 모습을 보는 것이 기대되는구나.
G: 하지만 엄마, 전 경주에서 이길지 잘 모르겠어요.
W: 그냥 최선을 다하렴. 행운을 빌어줄게!

Start Off – Listen & Talk B

G: _____

W: _____

_____

G: _____

W: _____

G: _____

Start Off – Speak Up

A: _____

B: _____

A: _____

Step Up – Real-life Scene

Miso: _____

_____

Jimin: _____

Miso: _____

Jimin: _____

Miso: _____

Jimin: _____

_____

Miso: _____

Jimin: _____

Miso: _____

G: 엄마, 체육 대회에 오실 거예요?

W: 물론이지. 나는 'Kick a Shoe' 게임에 참가할 거야. 이번에 처음 해 보는 거야.

G: 걱정하지 마세요. 엄마는 잘하실 거예요. 행운을 빌어 드릴게요!

W: 고맙다. 나는 다른 엄마들과 코믹 댄스도 할 거야.

G: 재밌겠네요. 무대에 선 엄마 모습을 보는 것이 기대돼요.

B: 나는 내일 모형 비행기 대회가 기대돼. 너는 준비됐니?

G: 음, 그런 것 같아, 하지만 긴장돼.

B: 너는 잘할 거야. 내가 행운을 빌어 줄게!

미소: 다음 주 화요일에 수학여행을 갈 거야. 지민아, 너는 장기 자랑에서 뭘 할 거니?

지민: 나는 수업 시간에 선생님들이 말하는 것을 흉내 내고 농담도 할 거야.

미소: 와! 정말 기대되는데.

지민: 모든 사람이 나의 쇼를 좋아할까? 잘 모르겠어.

미소: 걱정하지 마. 나는 네가 잘할 거라고 확신해. 행운을 빌어 줄게!

지민: 고마워, 미소야. 내가 나의 연기의 한 부분을 보여 줄게. 누군지 맞힐 수 있겠니? "잘~ 했어~요!"

미소: 하하. 우리 영어 선생님처럼 들리는데.

지민: 그래? 장기 자랑에서 더 많이 보여 줄게.

미소: 멋지다! 너는 항상 우리를 웃게 만들어.

Fun Time

A: _____

B: _____

A: _____

A: _____

B: _____

A: _____

A: 나는 다음 주에 제주도를 여행할 거야.
B: 와! 멋지다.
A: 응, 난 그것이 정말 기대돼.

A: 난 다음 주에 춤 대회에 나갈 건데, 걱정이 된다.
B: 걱정하지 마. 넌 잘할 거야. 행운을 빌어 줄게.
A: 고마워.

Express Yourself A

1. G: _____

   B: _____

   G: _____

2. B: _____

   G: _____

   _____

   B: _____

   G: _____

   B: _____

1. G: 너의 발명품에 관해 이야기를 좀 해 줄래?
   B: 그것은 특별한 신발이야. 너는 그 것으로 바닥을 청소할 수도 있어.
   G: 멋지다! 네가 상을 탈 거라고 확신해. 행운을 빌게!

2. B: 이것은 흥미로워 보여. 도마니, 아니면 새 모이통이니?
   G: 그것은 도마일 뿐만 아니라 새 모이통이기도 해. 너는 동시에 두 가지를 할 수 있어.
   B: 멋진 아이디어야!
   G: 정말 그렇게 생각하니?
   B: 응. 난 그것을 사용해 보는 게 정말 기대가 되는 걸.

※ 다음 우리말과 일치하도록 빈칸에 알맞은 것을 골라 쓰시오.

1 The _____ _____ _____
A. Prize   B. Nobel   C. Ig

1 이그노벨상

2 "What _____ when you walk _____ _____ you are _____ a cup of coffee?"
A. backward   B. happens   C. carrying   D. while

2 "당신이 커피 한 잔을 들고 가면서 뒤로 걸을 때 무슨 일이 일어날까?"

3 Han Jiwon, a Korean high school student, _____ _____ _____ this _____ in 2015.
A. research   B. on   C. did   D. topic

3 한국의 한 고등학생인 한지원은 2015년에 이 주제에 관해 연구했다.

4 Is this _____ project good _____ _____ _____ a Nobel Prize?
A. win   B. research   C. enough   D. to

4 이 연구 과제는 노벨상을 받을 정도로 훌륭할까?

5 _____ _____.
A. not   B. maybe

5 아마도 아닐 것이다.

6 But _____ _____ an Ig Nobel Prize?
A. about   B. how

6 하지만 이그노벨상은 어떤가?

7 He _____ one in 2017 for this _____ _____.
A. fun   B. won   C. research

7 그는 이 재미있는 연구로 2017년에 상을 탔다.

8 The Ig Nobel Prizes are _____ _____ discoveries that "first make one _____ and then _____."
A. awarded   B. laugh   C. for   D. think

8 이그노벨상은 '먼저 웃기고 나서 다음에 생각하게 하는' 발견에 수여된다.

9 They were started in 1991 by *AIR* magazine to increase people's _____ in science by _____ the _____ and the _____.
A. interest   B. imaginative   C. honoring   D. unusual

9 그것은 특이하고 창의적인 사람들을 높이 평가함으로써 과학에 대한 사람들의 흥미를 늘리기 위해 AIR 잡지에 의해 1991년에 시작되었다.

10 The prizes _____ _____ _____ real Nobel _____ in Sanders Theater at Harvard University.
A. winners   B. are   C. by   D. presented

10 그 상들은 하버드 대학의 Sanders 극장에서 진짜 노벨상 수상자들에 의해 수여된다.

11 The room is usually _____ _____ people who are eager to _____ for the brave scientists with their "_____" research.

A. cheer   B. with   C. laughable   D. filled

12 The U.K. Navy _____ the Ig Nobel Prize _____ Peace _____ 2000.

A. for   B. won   C. in

13 _____ _____ money, the Navy made its sailors shout, "Bang!" _____ _____ using real bombs.

A. of   B. save   C. to   D. instead

14 Is that funny _____ for you to _____ _____ _____?

A. laugh   B. loud   C. enough   D. out

15 Andre Geim _____ _____ an _____ that year.

A. award   B. also   C. won

16 He _____ _____ _____ a live frog in the air by _____ magnets.

A. using   B. succeeded   C. floating   D. in

17 "In my experience, if people don't have a _____ of _____, they are usually not very good scientists," he said when he _____ his _____.

A. humor   B. accepted   C. sense   D. award

18 If that still does not _____ a smile _____ your _____, _____ about this?

A. to   B. bring   C. how   D. face

19 In 2005, Gauri Nanda won the Ig Nobel Prize _____ Economics _____ an _____ clock.

A. for   B. alarm   C. inventing   D. in

20 It _____ _____ _____ until the sleeper finally gets _____ of bed.

A. away   B. out   C. running   D. keeps

---

11 그 방은 대개 '웃기는' 연구를 한 용감한 과학자들을 열렬히 격려하고자 하는 사람들로 가득 찬다.

12 영국 해군은 2000년에 이그노벨 평화상을 탔다.

13 돈을 아끼기 위해, 해군에서는 선원들에게 진짜 폭탄을 사용하는 대신에 "쾅!"이라고 소리치게 했다.

14 그것이 당신이 큰 소리로 웃을 정도로 우스운가?

15 Andre Geim도 그해에 상을 탔다.

16 그는 자석을 이용해서 살아 있는 개구리를 공중에 띄우는 데 성공했다.

17 그는 상을 받을 때, "내 경험상, 사람들이 유머 감각이 없다면, 그들은 대개 별로 훌륭한 과학자가 아니다."라고 말했다.

18 그것이 아직도 당신의 얼굴에 미소를 띠게 하지 않는다면, 이것은 어떤가?

19 2005년에 Gauri Nanda는 자명종을 발명해서 이그노벨 경제학상을 받았다.

20 그것은 잠자는 사람이 결국 침대 밖으로 나올 때까지 계속 도망을 다닌다.

21 _____ _____ the winners' fun studies _____ also the ceremony for the Ig Nobel Prizes _____ people laugh.

    A. but   B. only   C. makes   D. not

22 There are a _____ of interesting things that _____ people _____ getting _____.

    A. from   B. number   C. bored   D. keep

23 The _____ and _____ speeches are just two _____ _____: "Welcome. Welcome." and "Goodbye. Goodbye."

    A. each   B. closing   C. words   D. opening

24 If someone talks for too long, an eight-year-old girl _____ Miss Sweetie Poo _____ _____, "Please stop! I'm _____."

    A. called   B. bored   C. repeatedly   D. shouts

25 Each winner receives ten _____ Zimbabwean dollars, _____ is _____ _____ than one U.S. dollar.

    A. less   B. trillion   C. worth   D. which

26 _____ paper planes _____ _____ fun _____.

    A. is   B. throwing   C. tradition   D. another

27 The Ig Nobel Prize ceremony _____ _____ the words, "If you didn't _____ a prize — and if you _____ — better luck next year!"

    A. with   B. did   C. win   D. ends

28 The _____ do not _____ _____ _____ money.

    A. receive   B. lots   C. winners   D. of

29 And the _____ are not _____ _____ _____ the Nobel Prizes.

    A. honors   B. awards   C. like   D. great

30 But the Ig Nobel Prizes make science _____ _____ _____!

    A. fun   B. a   C. more   D. lot

21 수상자들의 재미있는 연구뿐만 아니라 이그노벨상 시상식도 또한 사람들을 웃게 만든다.

22 사람들이 지루해하지 않도록 하는 재미있는 것들이 많이 있다.

23 개회사와 폐회사는 단지 두 마디이다: "환영합니다. 환영합니다."와 "안녕. 안녕."

24 만일 누군가가 너무 오랫동안 말을 하면, Miss Sweetie Poo 라고 하는 여덟 살짜리 여자아이가 "제발 멈춰요! 지루해요." 라고 계속 외친다.

25 각 수상자는 10조의 짐바브웨 달러를 받는데, 그것은 미국의 1 달러보다 가치가 낮다.

26 종이비행기를 날리는 것은 또 다른 재미있는 전통이다.

27 이그노벨상 시상식은 "만일 당신이 상을 타지 못했다면 – 그리고 만일 탔다면 – 내년에는 좀 더 많은 행운이 있기를!"이라는 말로 끝이 난다.

28 수상자들은 많은 상금을 받지 않는다.

29 그리고 그 상은 노벨상같이 훌륭한 영광은 아니다.

30 하지만 이그노벨상은 과학을 훨씬 더 재미있게 만든다!

※ 다음 우리말과 일치하도록 빈칸에 알맞은 말을 쓰시오.

1　The _____ _____ _____

2　"What _____ when you walk _____ _____ you are _____ a cup of coffee?"

3　Han Jiwon, a Korean high school student, _____ _____ on this _____ in 2015.

4　Is this research project _____ _____ _____ _____ a Nobel Prize?

5　_____ not.

6　But _____ _____ an Ig Nobel Prize?

7　He _____ _____ in 2017 for this _____ _____.

8　The Ig Nobel Prizes _____ _____ _____ _____ that "first make one _____ and then _____."

9　They were started in 1991 by *AIR* magazine _____ _____ people's _____ in science _____ _____ _____ and _____ _____.

10　The prizes _____ _____ _____ _____ _____ _____ in Sanders Theater at Harvard University.

1　이그노벨상

2　"당신이 커피 한 잔을 들고 가면서 뒤로 걸을 때 무슨 일이 일어날까?"

3　한국의 한 고등학생인 한지원은 2015년에 이 주제에 관해 연구했다.

4　이 연구 과제는 노벨상을 받을 정도로 훌륭할까?

5　아마도 아닐 것이다.

6　하지만 이그노벨상은 어떤가?

7　그는 이 재미있는 연구로 2017년에 상을 탔다.

8　이그노벨상은 '먼저 웃기고 나서 다음에 생각하게 하는' 발견에 수여된다.

9　그것은 특이하고 창의적인 사람들을 높이 평가함으로써 과학에 대한 사람들의 흥미를 늘리기 위해 AIR 잡지에 의해 1991년에 시작되었다.

10　그 상들은 하버드 대학의 Sanders 극장에서 진짜 노벨상 수상자들에 의해 수여된다.

11 The room _____ usually _____ _____ people who are _____ _____ _____ for the brave scientists with their "_____" research.

12 The U.K. Navy _____ the Ig Nobel Prize _____ Peace in 2000.

13 _____ _____ money, the Navy _____ its sailors _____, "Bang!" _____ _____ _____ real bombs.

14 Is that _____ _____ for you to _____ _____ _____?

15 Andre Geim also _____ _____ _____ that year.

16 He _____ _____ _____ a live frog in the air _____ _____ _____.

17 "In my experience, if people don't have _____ _____ _____ _____, they are usually not very good scientists," he said _____ he _____ his _____.

18 If that still does not _____ a smile _____ your face, _____ _____ this?

19 In 2005, Gauri Nanda won the Ig Nobel Prize _____ Economics _____ _____ an alarm clock.

20 It _____ _____ _____ until the sleeper finally _____ _____ _____ bed.

11 그 방은 대개 '웃기는' 연구를 한 용감한 과학자들을 열렬히 격려하고자 하는 사람들로 가득 찬다.

12 영국 해군은 2000년에 이그노벨 평화상을 탔다.

13 돈을 아끼기 위해, 해군에서는 선원들에게 진짜 폭탄을 사용하는 대신에 "쾅!"이라고 소리치게 했다.

14 그것이 당신이 큰 소리로 웃을 정도로 우스운가?

15 Andre Geim도 그해에 상을 탔다.

16 그는 자석을 이용해서 살아 있는 개구리를 공중에 띄우는 데 성공했다.

17 그는 상을 받을 때, "내 경험상, 사람들이 유머 감각이 없다면, 그들은 대개 별로 훌륭한 과학자가 아니다."라고 말했다.

18 그것이 아직도 당신의 얼굴에 미소를 띠게 하지 않는다면, 이것은 어떤가?

19 2005년에 Gauri Nanda는 자명종을 발명해서 이그노벨 경제학상을 받았다.

20 그것은 잠자는 사람이 결국 침대 밖으로 나올 때까지 계속 도망을 다닌다.

21 _____ _____ the winners' fun studies _____ _____ the ceremony for the Ig Nobel Prizes _____ people _____.

22 There are _____ _____ _____ interesting things that _____ people _____ _____ _____.

23 The _____ and _____ _____ are just _____ _____ _____: "Welcome. Welcome." and "Goodbye. Goodbye."

24 If someone talks for too long, _____ _____ _____ _____ Miss Sweetie Poo shouts _____, "Please stop! I'm bored."

25 Each winner receives _____ _____ Zimbabwean dollars, _____ is _____ _____ _____ one U.S. dollar.

26 _____ paper planes _____ another fun _____.

27 The Ig Nobel Prize ceremony _____ _____ the words, "If you didn't _____ a _____ — and if you _____ — better luck next year!"

28 The winners _____ _____ _____ lots of money.

29 And the awards are not _____ _____ _____ the Nobel Prizes.

30 But the Ig Nobel Prizes make science _____ _____ _____!

21 수상자들의 재미있는 연구뿐만 아니라 이그노벨상 시상식도 또한 사람들을 웃게 만든다.

22 사람들이 지루해하지 않도록 하는 재미있는 것들이 많이 있다.

23 개회사와 폐회사는 단지 두 마디이다: "환영합니다. 환영합니다."와 "안녕. 안녕."

24 만일 누군가가 너무 오랫동안 말을 하면, Miss Sweetie Poo 라고 하는 여덟 살짜리 여자아이가 "제발 멈춰요! 지루해요." 라고 계속 외친다.

25 각 수상자는 10조의 짐바브웨 달러를 받는데, 그것은 미국의 1 달러보다 가치가 낮다.

26 종이비행기를 날리는 것은 또 다른 재미있는 전통이다.

27 이그노벨상 시상식은 "만일 당신이 상을 타지 못했다면 - 그리고 만일 탔다면 - 내년에는 좀 더 많은 행운이 있기를!"이라는 말로 끝이 난다.

28 수상자들은 많은 상금을 받지 않는다.

29 그리고 그 상은 노벨상같이 훌륭한 영광은 아니다.

30 하지만 이그노벨상은 과학을 훨씬 더 재미있게 만든다!

※ 다음 문장을 우리말로 쓰시오.

1 The Ig Nobel Prize

➡ _____

2 "What happens when you walk backward while you are carrying a cup of coffee?"

➡ _____

3 Han Jiwon, a Korean high school student, did research on this topic in 2015.

➡ _____

4 Is this research project good enough to win a Nobel Prize?

➡ _____

5 Maybe not.

➡ _____

6 But how about an Ig Nobel Prize?

➡ _____

7 He won one in 2017 for this fun research.

➡ _____

8 The Ig Nobel Prizes are awarded for discoveries that "first make one laugh and then think."

➡ _____

9 They were started in 1991 by AIR magazine to increase people's interest in science by honoring the unusual and the imaginative.

➡ _____

_____

10 The prizes are presented by real Nobel winners in Sanders Theater at Harvard University.

➡ _____

11 The room is usually filled with people who are eager to cheer for the brave scientists with their "laughable" research.

➡ _____

12 The U.K. Navy won the Ig Nobel Prize for Peace in 2000.

➡ _____

13 To save money, the Navy made its sailors shout, "Bang!" instead of using real bombs.

➡ _____

14 Is that funny enough for you to laugh out loud?

➡ _____

15 Andre Geim also won an award that year.

➡ _____

16 He succeeded in floating a live frog in the air by using magnets.

➡ _____

17 "In my experience, if people don't have a sense of humor, they are usually not very good scientists," he said when he accepted his award.

➡ _____

18 If that still does not bring a smile to your face, how about this?

➡ _____

19 In 2005, Gauri Nanda won the Ig Nobel Prize in Economics for inventing an alarm clock.

➡ _____

20 It keeps running away until the sleeper finally gets out of bed.

➡ _____

21 Not only the winners' fun studies but also the ceremony for the Ig Nobel Prizes makes people laugh.

➡ _____

22 There are a number of interesting things that keep people from getting bored.

➡ _____

23 The opening and closing speeches are just two words each: "Welcome. Welcome." and "Goodbye. Goodbye."

➡ _____

24 If someone talks for too long, an eight-year-old girl called Miss Sweetie Poo shouts repeatedly, "Please stop! I'm bored."

➡ _____

_____

25 Each winner receives ten trillion Zimbabwean dollars, which is worth less than one U.S. dollar.

➡ _____

26 Throwing paper planes is another fun tradition.

➡ _____

27 The Ig Nobel Prize ceremony ends with the words, "If you didn't win a prize — and if you did — better luck next year!"

➡ _____

_____

28 The winners do not receive lots of money.

➡ _____

29 And the awards are not great honors like the Nobel Prizes.

➡ _____

30 But the Ig Nobel Prizes make science a lot more fun!

➡ _____

※ 다음 괄호 안의 단어들을 우리말에 맞도록 바르게 배열하시오.

1 (Ig / The / Prize / Nobel)
➡ _____

2 (happens / "what / you / when / backward / walk / you / while / carrying / are / cup / a / of / coffee?")
➡ _____

3 (Jiwon, / Han / Korean / a / school / high / student, / research / did / this / on / topic / 2015. / in)
➡ _____

4 (this / is / project / research / enough / good / win / to / a / Prize? / Nobel)
➡ _____

5 (not. / maybe)
➡ _____

6 (how / but / an / about / Nobel / Ig / Prize?)
➡ _____

7 (won / he / in / one / 2017 / this / for / research. / fun)
➡ _____

8 (Ig / The / Prizes / Nobel / awarded / are / discoveries / for / "first / that / one / make / laugh / then / and / think.")
➡ _____

9 (were / they / in / started / 1991 / *AIR* / by / to / magazine / interest / people's / increase / in / by / science / the / honoring / unusual / and / imaginative. / the)
➡ _____

10 (prizes / the / presented / are / real / by / winners / Nobel / Sanders / in / Theater / Harvard / at / University.)
➡ _____

1 이그노벨상

2 "당신이 커피 한 잔을 들고 가면서 뒤로 걸을 때 무슨 일이 일어날까?"

3 한국의 한 고등학생인 한지원은 2015년에 이 주제에 관해 연구했다.

4 이 연구 과제는 노벨상을 받을 정도로 훌륭할까?

5 아마도 아닐 것이다.

6 하지만 이그노벨상은 어떤가?

7 그는 이 재미있는 연구로 2017년에 상을 탔다.

8 이그노벨상은 '먼저 웃기고 나서 다음에 생각하게 하는' 발견에 수여된다.

9 그것은 특이하고 창의적인 사람들을 높이 평가함으로써 과학에 대한 사람들의 흥미를 늘리기 위해 AIR 잡지에 의해 1991년에 시작되었다.

10 그 상들은 하버드 대학의 Sanders 극장에서 진짜 노벨상 수상자들에 의해 수여된다.

11 (room / the / usually / is / with / filled / who / people / eager / are / to / for / cheer / the / scientists / brave / their / with / research. / "laughable")

➡ _____

_____

12 (U.K. / the / won / Navy / Ig / the / Prize / Nobel / Peace / in / 2000. / for)

➡ _____

13 (save / to / money, / Navy / the / its / made / sailors / "Bang!" / shout, / of / instead / using / of / bombs. / real)

➡ _____

_____

14 (that / is / enough / funny / you / for / laugh / to / loud? / out)

➡ _____

15 (Geim / Andre / won / also / award / an / year. / that)

➡ _____

16 (succeeded / he / floating / in / live / a / in / frog / the / by / air / magnets. / using)

➡ _____

17 (my / "in / experience, / people / if / have / don't / sense / a / of / they / humor, / are / not / usually / very / scientists," / good / said / he / he / when / his / award. / accepted)

➡ _____

_____

18 (that / if / does / still / bring / not / smile / a / your / to / face, / about / this? / how)

➡ _____

19 (2005, / in / Nanda / Gauri / the / won / Nobel / Ig / in / Prize / for / Economics / inventing / alarm / an / clock.)

➡ _____

20 (keeps / it / away / running / the / until / finally / sleeper / out / gets / of / bed. / of)

➡ _____

11 그 방은 대개 '웃기는' 연구를 한 용감한 과학자들을 열렬히 격려하고자 하는 사람들로 가득 찬다.

12 영국 해군은 2000년에 이그노벨 평화상을 탔다.

13 돈을 아끼기 위해, 해군에서는 선원들에게 진짜 폭탄을 사용하는 대신에 "쾅!"이라고 소리치게 했다.

14 그것이 당신이 큰 소리로 웃을 정도로 우스운가?

15 Andre Geim도 그해에 상을 탔다.

16 그는 자석을 이용해서 살아 있는 개구리를 공중에 띄우는 데 성공했다.

17 그는 상을 받을 때, "내 경험상, 사람들이 유머 감각이 없다면, 그들은 대개 별로 훌륭한 과학자가 아니다."라고 말했다.

18 그것이 아직도 당신의 얼굴에 미소를 띠게 하지 않는다면, 이것은 어떤가?

19 2005년에 Gauri Nanda는 자명종을 발명해서 이그노벨 경제학상을 받았다.

20 그것은 잠자는 사람이 결국 침대 밖으로 나올 때까지 계속 도망을 다닌다.

21 (only / not / winners' / the / studies / fun / also / but / ceremony / the / the / for / Ig / Prizes / Nobel / people / laugh. / makes)

➡ _____

_____

22 (are / there / number / a / interesting / of / that / things / people / keep / from / bored. / getting)

➡ _____

_____

23 (opening / the / and / speeches / closing / just / are / words / two / each: / "welcome. / goodbye." / welcome." / and / "goodbye.)

➡ _____

_____

24 (someone / if / for / talks / long, / too / eight-year-old / an / called / girl / Sweetie / Miss / shouts / Poo / repeatedly, / stop! / "please / bored." / I'm)

➡ _____

_____

25 (winner / each / ten / receives / trillion / dollars, / Zimbabwean / is / which / less / worth / one / than / dollar. / U.S.)

➡ _____

_____

26 (paper / throwing / planes / another / is / tradition. / fun)

➡ _____

27 (Ig / The / Prize / ceremony / with / ends / words, / the / you / "if / win / didn't / prize / a / – / if / and / did / you / – / luck / year!" / better / next)

➡ _____

_____

28 (winners / the / not / do / lots / receive / money. / of)

➡ _____

29 (the / and / are / awards / great / not / like / honors / the / Prizes. / Nobel)

➡ _____

30 (the / but / Nobel / Ig / make / Prizes / a / science / more / lot / fun!)

➡ _____

21 수상자들의 재미있는 연구뿐만 아니라 이그노벨상 시상식도 또한 사람들을 웃게 만든다.

22 사람들이 지루해하지 않도록 하는 재미있는 것들이 많이 있다.

23 개회사와 폐회사는 단지 두 마디이다: "환영합니다. 환영합니다."와 "안녕. 안녕."

24 만일 누군가가 너무 오랫동안 말을 하면, Miss Sweetie Poo 라고 하는 여덟 살짜리 여자아이가 "제발 멈춰요! 지루해요." 라고 계속 외친다.

25 각 수상자는 10조의 짐바브웨 달러를 받는데, 그것은 미국의 1 달러보다 가치가 낮다.

26 종이비행기를 날리는 것은 또 다른 재미있는 전통이다.

27 이그노벨상 시상식은 "만일 당신이 상을 타지 못했다면 – 그리고 만일 탔다면 – 내년에는 좀 더 많은 행운이 있기를!"이라는 말로 끝이 난다.

28 수상자들은 많은 상금을 받지 않는다.

29 그리고 그 상은 노벨상같이 훌륭한 영광은 아니다.

30 하지만 이그노벨상은 과학을 훨씬 더 재미있게 만든다!

※ 다음 우리말을 영어로 쓰시오.

1 이그노벨상

➡ _____

2 "당신이 커피 한 잔을 들고 가면서 뒤로 걸을 때 무슨 일이 일어날까?"

➡ _____

3 한국의 한 고등학생인 한지원은 2015년에 이 주제에 관해 연구했다.

➡ _____

4 이 연구 과제는 노벨상을 받을 정도로 훌륭할까?

➡ _____

5 아마도 아닐 것이다.

➡ _____

6 하지만 이그노벨상은 어떤가?

➡ _____

7 그는 이 재미있는 연구로 2017년에 상을 탔다.

➡ _____

8 이그노벨상은 '먼저 웃기고 나서 다음에 생각하게 하는' 발견에 수여된다.

➡ _____

9 그것은 특이하고 창의적인 사람들을 높이 평가함으로써 과학에 대한 사람들의 흥미를 늘리기 위해 AIR 잡지에 의해 1991년에 시작되었다.

➡ _____

_____

10 그 상들은 하버드 대학의 Sanders 극장에서 진짜 노벨상 수상자들에 의해 수여된다.

➡ _____

11 그 방은 대개 '웃기는' 연구를 한 용감한 과학자들을 열렬히 격려하고자 하는 사람들로 가득 찬다.

➡ _____

_____

12 영국 해군은 2000년에 이그노벨 평화상을 탔다.

➡ _____

13 돈을 아끼기 위해, 해군에서는 선원들에게 진짜 폭탄을 사용하는 대신에 "쾅!"이라고 소리치게 했다.

➡ _____

14 그것이 당신이 큰 소리로 웃을 정도로 우스운가?

➡ _____

15 Andre Geim도 그해에 상을 탔다.

➡ _____

16 그는 자석을 이용해서 살아 있는 개구리를 공중에 띄우는 데 성공했다.

➡ _____

17 그는 상을 받을 때, "내 경험상, 사람들이 유머 감각이 없다면, 그들은 대개 별로 훌륭한 과학자가 아니다."라고 말했다.

➡ _____

_____

18 그것이 아직도 당신의 얼굴에 미소를 띠게 하지 않는다면, 이것은 어떤가?

➡ _____

19 2005년에 Gauri Nanda는 자명종을 발명해서 이그노벨 경제학상을 받았다.

➡ _____

20 그것은 잠자는 사람이 결국 침대 밖으로 나올 때까지 계속 도망을 다닌다.

➡ _____

21 수상자들의 재미있는 연구뿐만 아니라 이그노벨상 시상식도 또한 사람들을 웃게 만든다.

➡ _____

22 사람들이 지루해하지 않도록 하는 재미있는 것들이 많이 있다.

➡ _____

23 개회사와 폐회사는 단지 두 마디이다: "환영합니다. 환영합니다."와 "안녕. 안녕."

➡ _____

24 만일 누군가가 너무 오랫동안 말을 하면, Miss Sweetie Poo라고 하는 여덟 살짜리 여자아이가 "제발 멈춰요! 지루해요."라고 계속 외친다.

➡ _____

_____

25 각 수상자는 10조의 짐바브웨 달러를 받는데, 그것은 미국의 1달러보다 가치가 낮다.

➡ _____

26 종이비행기를 날리는 것은 또 다른 재미있는 전통이다.

➡ _____

27 이그노벨상 시상식은 "만일 당신이 상을 타지 못했다면 – 그리고 만일 탔다면 – 내년에는 좀 더 많은 행운이 있기를!"이라는 말로 끝이 난다.

➡ _____

_____

28 수상자들은 많은 상금을 받지 않는다.

➡ _____

29 그리고 그 상은 노벨상같이 훌륭한 영광은 아니다.

➡ _____

30 하지만 이그노벨상은 과학을 훨씬 더 재미있게 만든다!

➡ _____

※ 다음 우리말과 일치하도록 빈칸에 알맞은 말을 쓰시오.

Self-study Guide

1. New _____ again!

2. He _____ great _____ _____ _____ new things.

3. Oh, I _____ the _____ of "-ness."

4. Now I know _____ _____ the meaning of "eager" _____
_____ the meaning of "eagerness."

1. 또 새 단어네!
2. 그는 새로운 것들을 배우고자 하는 열정을 보여주었다.
3. 오, 나는 '-ness'의 의미를 알았어.
4. 이제 나는 'eager'의 뜻뿐만 아니라 'eagerness'의 뜻도 알아.

Express Yourself C

1. Magic _____

2. _____ are _____ Stairs.

3. You can use them _____ _____ for _____ up and down
_____ _____ for _____ things.

4. This invention is _____ _____ _____ _____ your life
_____ _____ .

1. 마법의 계단
2. 이것은 '마법의 계단'입니다.
3. 당신은 그것을 올라가고 내려가기 위해서 뿐만 아니라 물건을 보관하기 위해서도 사용할 수 있습니다.
4. 이 발명품은 당신의 삶을 훨씬 더 편안하게 할 정도로 충분히 유용합니다.

Link to the World

1. The _____ _____

2. The Nobel Prize was _____ _____ Alfred Nobel, a _____
_____ .

3. It _____ _____ _____ people _____ have done _____
_____ for the world.

4. Of _____ _____ _____ , Malala Yousafzai is _____ _____ .

5. She won the Nobel Prize _____ _____ _____ _____ 17
because she _____ _____ for women's and _____ _____ .

6. The Curie family _____ the Nobel Prize _____ _____ .

7. _____ _____ Marie Curie _____ _____ her daughter
_____ the Nobel Prize.

1. 노벨상
2. 노벨상은 스웨덴 과학자인, Alfred Nobel의 이름을 따서 지었다.
3. 그 상은 세계를 위해 위대한 일을 행한 사람들에게 수여된다.
4. 모든 수상자들 중에서, Malala Yousafzai가 최연소이다.
5. 그녀는 여성과 어린이의 권리를 위해서 싸웠기 때문에 17세의 나이에 노벨상을 수상했다.
6. Curie 가족은 노벨상을 3번 수상했다.
7. Marie Curie뿐만 아니라 그녀의 딸도 노벨상을 수상했다.

※ 다음 우리말을 영어로 쓰시오.

Self-study Guide

1. 또 새 단어네!

➡ _____

2. 그는 새로운 것들을 배우고자 하는 열정을 보여주었다.

➡ _____

3. 오, 나는 '-ness'의 의미를 알았어.

➡ _____

4. 이제 나는 'eager'의 뜻뿐만 아니라 'eagerness'의 뜻도 알아.

➡ _____

Express Yourself C

1. 마법의 계단

➡ _____

2. 이것은 '마법의 계단'입니다.

➡ _____

3. 당신은 그것을 올라가고 내려가기 위해서 뿐만 아니라 물건을 보관하기 위해서도 사용할 수 있습니다.

➡ _____

4. 이 발명품은 당신의 삶을 훨씬 더 편안하게 할 정도로 충분히 유용합니다.

➡ _____

Link to the World

1. 노벨상

➡ _____

2. 노벨상은 스웨덴 과학자인, Alfred Nobel의 이름을 따서 지었다.

➡ _____

3. 그 상은 세계를 위해 위대한 일을 행한 사람들에게 수여된다.

➡ _____

4. 모든 수상자들 중에서, Malala Yousafzai가 최연소이다.

➡ _____

5. 그녀는 여성과 어린이의 권리를 위해서 싸웠기 때문에 17세의 나이에 노벨상을 수상했다.

➡ _____

6. Curie 가족은 노벨상을 3번 수상했다.

➡ _____

7. Marie Curie뿐만 아니라 그녀의 딸도 노벨상을 수상했다.

➡ _____

※ 다음 영어를 우리말로 쓰시오.

01	recognize	
02	career	
03	competition	
04	hidden	
05	ability	
06	impress	
07	case	
08	face	
09	judge	
10	magician	
11	expert	
12	permission	
13	control	
14	figure	
15	laughter	
16	match	
17	line	
18	presentation	
19	useful	
20	accept	
21	matter	

22	courage	
23	record	
24	colored	
25	manager	
26	offer	
27	decorate	
28	character	
29	hanger	
30	disappointed	
31	install	
32	against	
33	allow	
34	later	
35	get upset	
36	stand up for	
37	give up	
38	break down	
39	get over	
40	thanks to	
41	prepare for	
42	laugh at	
43	have no choice but to	

※ 다음 우리말을 영어로 쓰시오.

01 능력 _____

02 숨겨진, 비밀의 _____

03 감명을 주다,
   깊은 인상을 주다 _____

04 용기 _____

05 받아들이다 _____

06 장식하다 _____

07 색깔이 있는, 유색 인종의 _____

08 직업, 직장 생활 _____

09 ~에 반대하여, ~에 맞서 _____

10 등장인물 _____

11 실망한 _____

12 발표 _____

13 소송 사건 _____

14 기록 _____

15 마술사 _____

16 (중요한) 인물, 거물, 숫자 _____

17 허락 _____

18 알아보다, 인정하다 _____

19 조종하다 _____

20 설치하다 _____

21 판사 _____

22 나중에, 후에 _____

23 중요하다, 문제가 되다 _____

24 제의, 제안 _____

25 지다, 패배하다 _____

26 전문가 _____

27 (상황에) 직면하다 _____

28 시합, 경기 _____

29 (연극, 영화 등의) 대사 _____

30 대회, 시합 _____

31 유용한 _____

32 연설, 말 _____

33 관리자, 경영자 _____

34 웃음(소리) _____

35 포기하다 _____

36 ~ 덕분에 _____

37 ~을 옹호하다, 지지하다 _____

38 우울해 보이다 _____

39 ~을 명심하다 _____

40 ~을 극복하다 _____

41 계속 ~하다 _____

42 ~을 비웃다 _____

43 ~을 부수다 _____

※ 다음 영영풀이에 알맞은 단어를 <보기>에서 골라 쓴 후, 우리말 뜻을 쓰시오.

1 _____ : of a race other than white: _____

2 _____ : not easy to find: _____

3 _____ : a well-known person: _____

4 _____ : someone who bakes bread, cakes, etc.: _____

5 _____ : to deal with a difficult situation: _____

6 _____ : to let someone do something: _____

7 _____ : the act or sound of laughing: _____

8 _____ : the series of jobs that you do during your working life: _____

9 _____ : a person who designs, builds, or maintains machines: _____

10 _____ : the ability to control your fear in a dangerous or difficult situation: _____

11 _____ : the action of allowing someone to do something: _____

12 _____ : a person with a high level of knowledge or skill in a particular area: _____

13 _____ : the person in a court who decides how criminals should be punished: _____

14 _____ : a person who is responsible for controlling an organization: _____

15 _____ : the region beyond the Earth's atmosphere or beyond the solar system: _____

16 _____ : a written account of something that is kept so that it can be looked at and used in the future: _____

보기			
figure	judge	allow	laughter
space	permission	hidden	colored
engineer	manager	career	face
courage	expert	record	baker

※ 다음 우리말과 일치하도록 빈칸에 알맞은 말을 쓰시오.

해석

Get Ready 2

(1) G: You _____ _____ today. What's _____ _____?
   B: I want _____ _____ _____ _____, but my father doesn't like _____ _____. He thinks _____ boys _____ play sports.
   G: I'm _____ _____ _____ _____.

(2) G: Why are you _____?
   B: I'm _____ _____ the ski jumping _____, but my _____ is not good. _____ should I do?
   G: I think you should _____ _____ more. I'm _____ you'll _____ _____ _____ _____.

(3) B: I want _____ _____ a _____, but everybody _____ _____ me. Do you think I should _____ _____ my dream?
   G: No, _____ _____ _____. I think you're really _____ _____ _____. You'll be a great _____!
   B: Thank you.

Start Off – Listen & Talk A

1. B: You don't _____ happy. _____ are you _____?
   G: We _____ the basketball game _____ _____ my _____.
   B: Come on. Everyone _____ _____.
   G: Do you think I _____ _____ _____?
   B: Well, yes. You know, _____ _____ _____.
2. G: Why_____ _____ _____?
   B: I didn't _____ a good _____.
   G: _____ it _____. Your _____ was _____ _____ fast, but I liked your _____.
   B: Do you think I should speak _____ _____?
   G: Yes. It will _____ your classmates _____ you _____.

Start Off – Listen & Talk B

G: Junsu, you _____ _____ today. Why are you _____?
B: I _____ the _____ _____.
G: I'm _____ _____ _____ _____. I know you _____ _____.
B: Yeah, but _____ that wasn't _____. Do you think I should _____ _____ _____ _____?
G: Yes. I think they will help. _____ _____ _____ _____ tips _____ cooking shows _____?
B: Okay. I'll _____. Thank you _____ your _____, Mina.
G: You're _____. Just _____ I'm a fan of your _____.

(1) G: 너는 오늘 우울해 보이는구나. 무슨 일이니?
   B: 나는 춤 수업을 듣고 싶은데, 아버지는 그 생각을 마음에 들어하지 않으셔. 아버지는 남자아이들은 운동을 해야 한다고 생각하셔.
   G: 그것 참 안됐구나.
(2) G: 너는 왜 실망하고 있니?
   B: 스키 점프 대회를 준비하고 있는데, 내 기록이 좋지 않아. 내가 무엇을 해야 할까?
   G: 네가 계속 더 많이 연습해야 한다고 생각해. 난 네가 점점 더 나아질 거라고 확신해.
(3) B: 나는 요리사가 되고 싶은데, 모두 나를 비웃어. 너는 내가 꿈을 포기해야 한다고 생각하니?
   G: 아니, 절대 포기하지 마. 나는 네가 정말 요리를 잘한다고 생각해. 너는 훌륭한 요리사가 될 거야!
   B: 고마워.

1. B: 너는 기분이 좋아 보이지 않는구나. 왜 실망하고 있니?
   G: 내 실수 때문에 우리가 농구 시합에서 졌어.
   B: 괜찮아. 모든 사람은 실수하기 마련이야.
   G: 내가 더 연습해야 한다고 생각하니?
   B: 음, 그래. 너도 알다시피, 연습이 완벽을 만들잖아.
2. G: 너는 왜 실망하고 있니?
   B: 나는 발표를 잘하지 못했어.
   G: 괜찮아. 너의 발표는 약간 빨랐지만, 나는 너의 발표가 마음에 들었어.
   B: 너는 내가 더 천천히 말해야 한다고 생각하니?
   G: 응. 그러면 너의 학급 친구들이 네 말을 더 잘 이해하게 될 거야.

G: 준수야, 너 오늘 우울해 보이는구나. 왜 실망하고 있니?
B: 요리 대회에서 떨어졌어.
G: 그것 참 안됐구나. 네가 열심히 노력했다는 걸 알아.
B: 응, 하지만 아마 그게 충분하지는 않았나 봐. 너는 내가 더 많은 요리 요령들을 배워야 한다고 생각하니?
G: 응. 나는 그것이 도움이 될 거라고 생각해. 온라인 요리 영상에서 유용한 조언들을 얻는 게 어때?
B: 알았어. 시도해 볼게. 조언해 줘서 고마워, 미나야.
G: 천만에. 내가 네 요리의 팬이라는 것만 기억해.

Start Off – Speak Up

B: _____ are you _____?
G: I _____ the _____ for the Mapo Youth Band. Do you think I should _____ _____?
B: Sure. _____ _____ _____. You'll do _____ next time.
G: Thank you.

Start Up – Real-life Scene

Jisu: Why are you so _____, Ryan?
Ryan: My parents _____ _____ me _____ Superstar 101, a _____ _____.
Jisu: I'm _____ _____ _____ that. Why are they _____ it?
Ryan: They want me _____ _____ _____ and be a doctor. They're always _____ _____ _____ _____.
Jisu: Did you tell your _____ you really want _____ _____ a singer?
Ryan: _____ _____. Do you think I should _____ them about it?
Jisu: Yes. Just show them _____ _____ you love singing. _____ _____ _____ _____ _____ the songs you made _____ _____ _____ them?
Ryan: Okay. I'll try. _____ _____ _____ your advice, Jisu.

Express Yourself A

1. W: You don't _____ _____. Why are you _____?
   B: I want to be a wonderful _____ _____ you, but I _____ the magic _____. Do you think I should _____ _____?
   W: No. _____ _____ every day and you'll _____ _____ and _____. _____ important _____ _____ _____.
   B: Okay, I'll try. Thank you for _____ _____.
2. W: Please _____ _____. _____ you _____ _____ _____ _____?
   B: Yes, I want to be a _____ _____. Do you think I should go to _____ school?
   W: I think that will help, but _____ more important _____ _____ _____ _____ every day. _____ design _____ _____ _____ you.
   B: Thank you. I'll _____ _____ _____ _____ _____.

Learning Diary– Listen & Speak 1

B: You _____ _____ today, Minji. _____ _____ _____?
G: We _____ the soccer game _____ I _____ a _____.
B: _____ _____ so sad. It can _____ to _____.
G: Do you think I should _____ _____?
B: Well, yes. I can help you _____ you want. _____, I'm a good soccer player.
G: Really? Thank you, Seho.

B: 너는 왜 실망하고 있니?
G: 나는 마포 청소년 밴드 오디션에서 떨어졌어. 너는 내가 계속 노력해야 한다고 생각하니?
B: 물론이지. 포기하지 마. 너는 다음번에 더 잘할 거야.
G: 고마워.

지수: 너는 왜 그렇게 실망하고 있니, Ryan?
Ryan: 부모님은 내가 노래 경연 대회인 슈퍼스타 101에 참가하는 걸 허락하지 않으실 거야.
지수: 그 말을 들으니 유감이구나. 왜 부모님은 그것에 반대하시니?
Ryan: 부모님은 내가 열심히 공부해서 의사가 되기를 원하셔. 항상 내 성적을 걱정하시지.
지수: 부모님께 네가 정말로 가수가 되고 싶다고 말씀드렸니?
Ryan: 아니 아직. 너는 내가 부모님께 그것에 대해 말씀드려야 한다고 생각하니?
지수: 응. 그냥 부모님께 네가 얼마나 노래 부르는 것을 좋아하는지 보여 드려. 부모님 앞에서 네가 만든 노래를 부르는 건 어때?
Ryan: 알았어. 시도해 볼게. 조언해 줘서 고마워, 지수야.

1. W: 기분이 안 좋아 보이네요. 왜 실망하고 있나요?
   B: 저는 당신처럼 멋진 마술사가 되고 싶은데, 마술 대회에서 떨어졌어요. 제가 포기해야 한다고 생각하나요?
   W: 아뇨. 매일 열심히 연습하면 점점 더 나아질 거예요. 계속 노력하는 것이 중요해요.
   B: 네, 노력해 볼게요. 조언해 주셔서 감사합니다.
2. W: 어서 들어오세요. 물건을 디자인하는 것에 관심이 있나요?
   B: 네, 저는 상품 디자이너가 되고 싶어요. 제가 디자인 학교에 가야 한다고 생각하나요?
   W: 그것이 도움이 될 거라고 생각해요. 하지만 매일 그림을 연습하는 것이 더 중요해요. 디자인 잡지를 읽는 것도 도움이될 거예요.
   B: 감사합니다. 그 점을 명심할게요.

B: 오늘 우울해 보이는구나, 민지야. 왜 실망하고 있니?
G: 내가 실수를 해서 우리가 축구 시합에서 졌거든.
B: 너무 슬퍼하지 마. 그런 일은 누구에게나 일어날 수 있어.
G: 넌 내가 더 연습해야 한다고 생각하니?
B: 음, 그래. 네가 원한다면 내가 너를 도와줄 수 있어. 너도 알다시피, 내가 축구를 잘하잖아.
G: 정말이니? 고마워, 세호야.

※ 다음 우리말에 맞도록 대화를 영어로 쓰시오.

Get Ready 2

(1) G: _____
   B: _____
   _____
   G: _____

(2) G: _____
   B: _____
   _____
   G: _____

(3) B: _____
   _____
   G: _____
   _____
   B: _____

Start Off – Listen & Talk A

1. B: _____
   G: _____
   B: _____
   G: _____
   B: _____

2. G: _____
   B: _____
   G: _____
   B: _____
   G: _____

Start Off – Listen & Talk B

G: _____
B: _____
G: _____
B: _____

G: _____

B: _____
G: _____

해석

(1) G: 너는 오늘 우울해 보이는구나. 무슨 일이니?
   B: 나는 춤 수업을 듣고 싶은데, 아버지는 그 생각을 마음에 들어하지 않으셔. 아버지는 남자아이들은 운동을 해야 한다고 생각하셔.
   G: 그것 참 안됐구나.

(2) G: 너는 왜 실망하고 있니?
   B: 스키 점프 대회를 준비하고 있는데, 내 기록이 좋지 않아. 내가 무엇을 해야 할까?
   G: 네가 계속 더 많이 연습해야 한다고 생각해. 난 네가 점점 더 나아질 거라고 확신해.

(3) B: 나는 요리사가 되고 싶은데, 모두 나를 비웃어. 너는 내가 꿈을 포기해야 한다고 생각하니?
   G: 아니, 절대 포기하지 마. 나는 네가 정말 요리를 잘한다고 생각해. 너는 훌륭한 요리사가 될 거야!
   B: 고마워.

1. B: 너는 기분이 좋아 보이지 않는구나. 왜 실망하고 있니?
   G: 내 실수 때문에 우리가 농구 시합에서 졌어.
   B: 괜찮아. 모든 사람은 실수하기 마련이야.
   G: 내가 더 연습해야 한다고 생각하니?
   B: 음, 그래. 너도 알다시피, 연습이 완벽을 만들잖아.

2. G: 너는 왜 실망하고 있니?
   B: 나는 발표를 잘하지 못했어.
   G: 괜찮아. 너의 발표는 약간 빨랐지만, 나는 너의 발표가 마음에 들었어.
   B: 너는 내가 더 천천히 말해야 한다고 생각하니?
   G: 응. 그러면 너의 학급 친구들이 네 말을 더 잘 이해하게 될 거야.

G: 준수야, 너 오늘 우울해 보이는구나. 왜 실망하고 있니?
B: 요리 대회에서 떨어졌어.
G: 그것 참 안됐구나. 네가 열심히 노력했다는 걸 알아.
B: 응, 하지만 아마 그게 충분하지는 않았나 봐. 너는 내가 더 많은 요리 요령들을 배워야 한다고 생각하니?
G: 응. 나는 그것이 도움이 될 거라고 생각해. 온라인 요리 영상에서 유용한 조언들을 얻는 게 어때?
B: 알았어. 시도해 볼게. 조언해 줘서 고마워, 미나야.
G: 천만에. 내가 네 요리의 팬이라는 것만 기억해.

Start Off – Speak Up

B: _____

G: _____

_____

B: _____

G: _____

Start Up – Real-life Scene

Jisu: _____

Ryan: _____

Jisu: _____

Ryan: _____

_____

Jisu: _____

Ryan: _____

Jisu: _____

_____

Ryan: _____

Express Yourself A

1. W: _____

B: _____

_____

W: _____

_____

B: _____

2. W: _____

B: _____

_____

W: _____

_____

B: _____

Learning Diary– Listen & Speak 1

B: _____

G: _____

B: _____

G: _____

B: _____

G: _____

B: 너는 왜 실망하고 있니?

G: 나는 마포 청소년 밴드 오디션에서 떨어졌어. 너는 내가 계속 노력해야 한다고 생각하니?

B: 물론이지. 포기하지 마. 너는 다음번에 더 잘할 거야.

G: 고마워.

지수: 너는 왜 그렇게 실망하고 있니, Ryan?

Ryan: 부모님은 내가 노래 경연 대회인 슈퍼스타 101에 참가하는 걸 허락하지 않으실 거야.

지수: 그 말을 들으니 유감이구나. 왜 부모님은 그것에 반대하시니?

Ryan: 부모님은 내가 열심히 공부해서 의사가 되기를 원하셔. 항상 내 성적을 걱정하시지.

지수: 부모님께 네가 정말로 가수가 되고 싶다고 말씀드렸니?

Ryan: 아니 아직. 너는 내가 부모님께 그것에 대해 말씀드려야 한다고 생각하니?

지수: 응. 그냥 부모님께 네가 얼마나 노래 부르는 것을 좋아하는지 보여 드려. 부모님 앞에서 네가 만든 노래를 부르는 건 어때?

Ryan: 알았어. 시도해 볼게. 조언해 줘서 고마워, 지수야.

1. W: 기분이 안 좋아 보이네요. 왜 실망하고 있나요?

B: 저는 당신처럼 멋진 마술사가 되고 싶은데, 마술 대회에서 떨어졌어요. 제가 포기해야 한다고 생각하나요?

W: 아뇨. 매일 열심히 연습하면 점점 더 나아질 거예요. 계속 노력하는 것이 중요해요.

B: 네, 노력해 볼게요. 조언해 주셔서 감사합니다.

2. W: 어서 들어오세요. 물건을 디자인하는 것에 관심이 있나요?

B: 네, 저는 상품 디자이너가 되고 싶어요. 제가 디자인 학교에 가야 한다고 생각하나요?

W: 그것이 도움이 될 거라고 생각해요. 하지만 매일 그림을 연습하는 것이 더 중요해요. 디자인 잡지를 읽는 것도 도움이될 거예요.

B: 감사합니다. 그 점을 명심할게요.

B: 오늘 우울해 보이는구나, 민지야. 왜 실망하고 있니?

G: 내가 실수를 해서 우리가 축구 시합에서 졌거든.

B: 너무 슬퍼하지 마. 그런 일은 누구에게나 일어날 수 있어.

G: 넌 내가 더 연습해야 한다고 생각하니?

B: 음, 그래. 네가 원한다면 내가 너를 도와줄 수 있어. 너도 알다시피, 내가 축구를 잘하잖아.

G: 정말이니? 고마워, 세호야.

※ 다음 우리말과 일치하도록 빈칸에 알맞은 것을 골라 쓰시오.

1 The _____ _____ of _____
A. Figures   B. Hidden   C. NASA

2 I _____ the _____ *Hidden Figures* _____ _____.
A. last   B. movie   C. watched   D. weekend

3 It was a movie about three _____ _____ _____ _____ at NASA.
A. worked   B. women   C. African-American   D. who

4 They began their _____ _____ the 1960s _____ " _____ computers."
A. human   B. career   C. as   D. in

5 However, they dreamed of becoming space _____ at NASA and tried hard to _____ _____ _____.
A. over   B. experts   C. get   D. difficulties

6 **Katherine Johnson** was _____ of the three " _____ _____ " in this _____.
A. one   B. hidden   C. figures   D. movie

7 She worked _____ and showed a _____ in math, and her manager Al Harrison _____ her _____.
A. ability   B. talent   C. hard   D. recognized

8 One day, he _____ _____ when Katherine was _____ from her desk _____ too long.
A. missing   B. upset   C. got   D. for

9 Al asked _____ _____ _____ _____, and she answered.
A. been   B. where   C. had   D. Katherine

10 **Katherine:** _____ _____.
A. bathroom   B. the

11 _____ _____ no _____ _____ in this building.
A. are   B. bathrooms   C. COLORED   D. there

12 I _____ to run _____ a mile _____ just to _____ the bathroom.
A. use   B. half   C. away   D. have

13 _____ this, I _____ really _____ for her.
A. sorry   B. felt   C. hearing

1 NASA의 숨겨진 인물들

2 나는 지난 주말에 〈히든 피겨스〉라는 영화를 보았다.

3 그것은 NASA에서 일했던 세 명의 아프리카계 미국인 여성들에 대한 영화였다.

4 그들은 1960년대에 '인간 컴퓨터(계산원)'로 일을 시작했다.

5 하지만 그들은 NASA에서 우주 전문가가 되기를 꿈꾸었고 어려움을 극복하기 위해 열심히 노력했다.

6 Katherine Johnson은 이 영화에서 세 명의 '숨겨진 인물들' 중 한 명이었다.

7 그녀는 열심히 일했고 수학에서 재능을 보였으며, 그녀의 상사인 Al Harrison은 그녀의 능력을 알아차렸다.

8 어느 날, 그는 Katherine이 너무 오래 자리를 비웠을 때 화가 났다.

9 Al은 Katherine에게 어디에 갔었는지 물었고 그녀는 대답했다.

10 Katherine: 화장실요.

11 이 건물에는 유색 인종 전용 화장실이 없어요.

12 저는 단지 화장실을 사용하기 위해 반 마일을 달려가야 해요.

13 이 말을 듣고서, 나는 그녀가 정말로 안됐다고 느꼈다.

14 However, I was glad that she _____ _____ _____ _____ to the manager about the problem.

A. to   B. had   C. talk   D. courage

15 This _____ Al Harrison _____ _____ the "Colored Ladies Room" _____.

A. sign   B. break   C. down   D. made

16 **Mary Jackson** was the _____ I liked the _____ of the _____.

A. most   B. character   C. three

17 She wanted to _____ more about rocket science, but she _____ _____ _____ go to a white school.

A. allowed   B. learn   C. to   D. wasn't

18 So, she asked a _____ to _____ _____ _____.

A. permission   B. judge   C. her   D. give

19 **Mary:** I _____ _____ the _____ of my _____.

A. color   B. can't   C. skin   D. change

20 So ... I have _____ _____ _____ be the first.

A. but   B. no   C. to   D. choice

21 Your Honor, of all the _____ you'll hear today, _____ one will _____ in a hundred _____?

A. matter   B. cases   C. years   D. which

22 _____ _____ will _____ you the "first?"

A. one   B. which   C. make

23 The judge was _____ by _____ she said and _____ gave her _____.

A. what   B. permission   C. impressed   D. finally

24 Mary _____ _____ for _____ and for _____ African-Americans.

A. other   B. stood   C. herself   D. up

25 That was _____ _____ _____ _____ in the movie.

A. most   B. what   C. me   D. impressed

26 Finally, she became the _____ _____ _____ at NASA.

A. engineer   B. first   C. woman   D. African-American

---

14 그러나 나는 그 문제에 대해 상사에게 말한 그녀의 용기를 보고 기뻤다.

15 이것은 Al Harrison으로 하여금 '유색 여성 화장실' 표지판을 부수게 만들었다.

16 Mary Jackson은 셋 중에 가장 나의 마음에 드는 인물이었다.

17 그녀는 로켓 공학에 대해 더 많이 배우고 싶었지만 백인 학교에 다니는 것이 허락되지 않았다.

18 그래서 그녀는 판사에게 허락해 달라고 요청했다.

19 Mary: 저는 제 피부색을 바꿀 수 없어요.

20 그래서… 저는 '최초'가 되는 것 이외에는 선택이 없어요.

21 판사님, 당신이 오늘 들을 모든 사건 중에서, 백 년 뒤에 어느 것이 중요할까요?

22 어느 것이 판사님을 '최초'로 만들까요?

23 판사는 그녀가 말한 것에 감명을 받고 마침내 그녀에게 허락해 주었다.

24 Mary는 그녀 자신과 다른 아프리카계 미국인들의 편에 섰다.

25 그것은 영화에서 나를 가장 감동하게 한 점이었다.

26 마침내 그녀는 NASA에서 최초의 아프리카계 미국인 여성 공학자가 되었다.

27 **Dorothy Vaughan** was _____ _____ "_____ _____."

    A. last   B. the   C. figure   D. hidden

28 When IBM computers were _____ at NASA in 1961, she was _____ the "human computers" _____ _____ their jobs.

    A. installed   B. lose   C. would   D. worried

29 She studied a _____ _____ _____, FORTRAN.

    A. programming   B. new   C. language

30 She also _____ _____ to her team _____.

    A. members   B. taught   C. it

31 Later, when she was _____ _____ be the leader of a new IBM team, she _____ a _____.

    A. suggestion   B. asked   C. made   D. to

32 Dorothy: I'm not _____ the _____ if I can't _____ my ladies _____ me.

    A. bring   B. accepting   C. offer   D. with

33 We _____ a _____ of people _____ _____ that machine.

    A. lot   B. program   C. need   D. to

34 I _____ _____ it _____.

    A. do   B. can't   C. alone

35 My girls _____ _____.

    A. ready   B. are

36 _____ _____ Dorothy, her team members could _____ _____.

    A. to   B. become   C. thanks   D. programmers

37 She wasn't _____ _____ change and used it _____ a _____.

    A. chance   B. afraid   C. as   D. of

38 That's _____ I _____ _____ from her.

    A. need   B. what   C. learn   D. to

39 Watching this movie, I could learn _____ _____ _____ in life.

    A. to   B. challenges   C. face   D. how

40 I _____ _____ the _____ and _____ of Katherine, Mary, and Dorothy.

    A. tears   B. won't   C. laughter   D. forget

27 Dorothy Vaughan은 마지막 '히든 피겨(숨은 인물)'였다.

28 1961년 NASA에 IBM 컴퓨터가 설치되었을 때, 그녀는 '인간 컴퓨터(계산원)'들이 직업을 잃을까봐 걱정했다.

29 그녀는 새로운 프로그래밍 언어인 포트란을 공부했다.

30 그녀는 또한 그것을 그녀의 팀원들에게 가르쳤다.

31 나중에 그녀가 새 IBM 팀의 리더가 되도록 요청받았을 때, 그녀는 제안했다.

32 Dorothy: 저는 저의 여성 팀원들을 데려올 수 없다면 그 제안을 받아들이지 않겠습니다.

33 그 기계의 프로그램을 짜기 위해서는 많은 사람이 필요합니다.

34 저는 그것을 혼자 할 수 없습니다.

35 제 여성 팀원들은 준비가 되어 있습니다.

36 Dorothy 덕분에, 그녀의 팀원들은 프로그래머가 될 수 있었다.

37 그녀는 변화를 두려워하지 않고 그것을 기회로 이용했다.

38 그것이 내가 그녀에게서 배울 필요가 있는 점이다.

39 이 영화를 보면서, 나는 삶에서 어떻게 도전에 직면해야 하는지 배울 수 있었다.

40 나는 Katherine, Mary, 그리고 Dorothy의 눈물과 웃음을 잊지 않을 것이다.

※ 다음 우리말과 일치하도록 빈칸에 알맞은 말을 쓰시오.

1 The _____ _____ of NASA

2 I _____ the movie *Hidden Figures* _____ _____.

3 It was a movie about three _____ _____ who _____ _____ NASA.

4 They began their career _____ _____ _____ "human computers."

5 However, they dreamed _____ _____ _____ _____ _____ at NASA and tried hard _____ _____ _____ _____.

6 **Katherine Johnson** was one of the _____ " _____ _____ " in this movie.

7 She worked hard and _____ _____ _____ _____ _____ math, and her manager Al Harrison _____ _____ _____.

8 One day, he _____ _____ when Katherine _____ _____ from her desk for too long.

9 Al asked _____ _____ _____ _____, and she answered.

10 **Katherine:** The _____.

11 _____ are no _____ _____ in this building.

12 I have to run _____ _____ _____ away _____ _____ _____ the bathroom.

13 _____ _____, I _____ really _____ for her.

14 _____, I was glad that she _____ _____ _____ _____ to the manager about the problem.

15 This made Al Harrison _____ _____ the "Colored Ladies Room" sign.

16 **Mary Jackson** was the _____ I liked the most of the three.

17 She wanted to learn more about rocket science, but she _____ _____ _____ go to a _____ _____.

18 So, she asked a judge _____ _____ _____ _____.

19 **Mary:** I _____ _____ the color of my _____.

1 NASA의 숨겨진 인물들

2 나는 지난 주말에 〈히든 피겨스〉라는 영화를 보았다.

3 그것은 NASA에서 일했던 세 명의 아프리카계 미국인 여성들에 대한 영화였다.

4 그들은 1960년대에 '인간 컴퓨터(계산원)'로 일을 시작했다.

5 하지만 그들은 NASA에서 우주 전문가가 되기를 꿈꾸었고 어려움을 극복하기 위해 열심히 노력했다.

6 Katherine Johnson은 이 영화에서 세 명의 '숨겨진 인물들' 중 한 명이었다.

7 그녀는 열심히 일했고 수학에서 재능을 보였으며, 그녀의 상사인 Al Harrison은 그녀의 능력을 알아차렸다.

8 어느 날, 그는 Katherine이 너무 오래 자리를 비웠을 때 화가 났다.

9 Al은 Katherine에게 어디에 갔었는지 물었고 그녀는 대답했다.

10 Katherine: 화장실요.

11 이 건물에는 유색 인종 전용 화장실이 없어요.

12 저는 단지 화장실을 사용하기 위해 반 마일을 달려가야 해요.

13 이 말을 듣고서, 나는 그녀가 정말로 안됐다고 느꼈다.

14 그러나 나는 그 문제에 대해 상사에게 말한 그녀의 용기를 보고 기뻤다.

15 이것은 Al Harrison으로 하여금 '유색 여성 화장실' 표지판을 부수게 만들었다.

16 Mary Jackson은 셋 중에 가장 나의 마음에 드는 인물이었다.

17 그녀는 로켓 공학에 대해 더 많이 배우고 싶었지만 백인 학교에 다니는 것이 허락되지 않았다.

18 그래서 그녀는 판사에게 허락해 달라고 요청했다.

19 Mary: 저는 제 피부색을 바꿀 수 없어요.

20 So ... I _____ _____ _____ _____ _____ be the first.

21 Your Honor, of all the _____ you'll hear today, which one will matter _____ _____ _____ _____?

22 _____ _____ will make you the "first?"

23 The judge was _____ by _____ she said and _____ _____ her _____.

24 Mary _____ _____ _____ _____ and for _____ African-Americans.

25 That was _____ _____ _____ _____ in the movie.

26 Finally, she became the _____ _____ _____ _____ at NASA.

27 **Dorothy Vaughan** was _____ _____ "hidden figure."

28 When IBM computers _____ _____ at NASA in 1961, she was worried the "human computers" _____ _____ their jobs.

29 She studied a _____ _____ _____, FORTRAN.

30 She also _____ _____ to her team members.

31 Later, when she _____ _____ _____ be the leader of a new IBM team, she _____ a _____.

32 Dorothy: _____ _____ _____ the _____ if I can't bring my ladies with me.

33 We need a _____ of people _____ _____ that machine.

34 I can't do it _____.

35 My girls _____ _____.

36 _____ _____ Dorothy, her team members could become programmers.

37 She _____ _____ _____ change and used it _____ _____ _____.

38 That's _____ _____ _____ _____ _____ from her.

39 _____ this movie, I could learn _____ _____ _____ _____ in life.

40 I won't forget the _____ _____ _____ of Katherine, Mary, and Dorothy.

20 그래서… 저는 '최초'가 되는 것 이외에는 선택이 없어요.

21 판사님, 당신이 오늘 들을 모든 사건 중에서, 백 년 뒤에 어느 것이 중요할까요?

22 어느 것이 판사님을 '최초'로 만들까요?

23 판사는 그녀가 말한 것에 감명을 받고 마침내 그녀에게 허락해 주었다.

24 Mary는 그녀 자신과 다른 아프리카계 미국인들의 편에 섰다.

25 그것은 영화에서 나를 가장 감동하게 한 점이었다.

26 마침내 그녀는 NASA에서 최초의 아프리카계 미국인 여성 공학자가 되었다.

27 Dorothy Vaughan은 마지막 '히든 피겨(숨은 인물)'였다.

28 1961년 NASA에 IBM 컴퓨터가 설치되었을 때, 그녀는 '인간 컴퓨터(계산원)'들이 직업을 잃을까봐 걱정했다.

29 그녀는 새로운 프로그래밍 언어인 포트란을 공부했다.

30 그녀는 또한 그것을 그녀의 팀원들에게 가르쳤다.

31 나중에 그녀가 새 IBM 팀의 리더가 되도록 요청받았을 때, 그녀는 제안했다.

32 Dorothy: 저는 저의 여성 팀원들을 데려올 수 없다면 그 제안을 받아들이지 않겠습니다.

33 그 기계의 프로그램을 짜기 위해서는 많은 사람이 필요합니다.

34 저는 그것을 혼자 할 수 없습니다.

35 제 여성 팀원들은 준비가 되어 있습니다.

36 Dorothy 덕분에, 그녀의 팀원들은 프로그래머가 될 수 있었다.

37 그녀는 변화를 두려워하지 않고 그것을 기회로 이용했다.

38 그것이 내가 그녀에게서 배울 필요가 있는 점이다.

39 이 영화를 보면서, 나는 삶에서 어떻게 도전에 직면해야 하는지 배울 수 있었다.

40 나는 Katherine, Mary, 그리고 Dorothy의 눈물과 웃음을 잊지 않을 것이다.

※ 다음 문장을 우리말로 쓰시오.

1 The Hidden Figures of NASA
➡ _____

2 I watched the movie *Hidden Figures* last weekend.
➡ _____

3 It was a movie about three African-American women who worked at NASA.
➡ _____

4 They began their career in the 1960s as "human computers."
➡ _____

5 However, they dreamed of becoming space experts at NASA and tried hard to get over difficulties.
➡ _____

6 Katherine Johnson was one of the three "hidden figures" in this movie.
➡ _____

7 She worked hard and showed a talent in math, and her manager Al Harrison recognized her ability.
➡ _____

8 One day, he got upset when Katherine was missing from her desk for too long.
➡ _____

9 Al asked where Katherine had been, and she answered.
➡ _____

10 Katherine: The bathroom.
➡ _____

11 There are no COLORED bathrooms in this building.
➡ _____

12 I have to run half a mile away just to use the bathroom.
➡ _____

13 Hearing this, I felt really sorry for her.
➡ _____

14 However, I was glad that she had courage to talk to the manager about the problem.
➡ _____

15 This made Al Harrison break down the "Colored Ladies Room" sign.
➡ _____

16 Mary Jackson was the character I liked the most of the three.
➡ _____

17 She wanted to learn more about rocket science, but she wasn't allowed to go to a white school.
➡ _____

18 So, she asked a judge to give her permission.
➡ _____

19 Mary: I can't change the color of my skin.
➡ _____

20 So ... I have no choice but to be the first.
➡ _____

21 Your Honor, of all the cases you'll hear today, which one will matter in a hundred years?
➡ _____

22 Which one will make you the "first?"
➡ _____

23 The judge was impressed by what she said and finally gave her permission.
➡ _____

24 Mary stood up for herself and for other African-Americans.
➡ _____

25 That was what impressed me most in the movie.
➡ _____

26 Finally, she became the first African-American woman engineer at NASA.
➡ _____

27 Dorothy Vaughan was the last "hidden figure."
➡ _____

28 When IBM computers were installed at NASA in 1961, she was worried the "human computers" would lose their jobs.
➡ _____

29 She studied a new programming language, FORTRAN.
➡ _____

30 She also taught it to her team members.
➡ _____

31 Later, when she was asked to be the leader of a new IBM team, she made a suggestion.
➡ _____

32 Dorothy: I'm not accepting the offer if I can't bring my ladies with me.
➡ _____

33 We need a lot of people to program that machine.
➡ _____

34 I can't do it alone.
➡ _____

35 My girls are ready.
➡ _____

36 Thanks to Dorothy, her team members could become programmers.
➡ _____

37 She wasn't afraid of change and used it as a chance.
➡ _____

38 That's what I need to learn from her.
➡ _____

39 Watching this movie, I could learn how to face challenges in life.
➡ _____

40 I won't forget the tears and laughter of Katherine, Mary, and Dorothy.
➡ _____

Step4

※ 다음 괄호 안의 단어들을 우리말에 맞도록 바르게 배열하시오.

1 (Hidden / The / Figures / NASA / of)
➡ _____

2 (watched / I / movie / the / *Figures* / *Hidden* / weekend. / last)
➡ _____

3 (was / it / movie / a / three / about / women / African-American / worked / who / NASA. / at)
➡ _____

4 (began / they / career / their / the / in / 1960s / computers." / as / "human)
➡ _____

5 (they / however, / dreamed / becoming / of / experts / space / NASA / at / tried / and / to / hard / get / difficulties. / over)
➡ _____
_____

6 (Johnson / Katherine / one / was / of / three / the / figures" / "hidden / this / in / movie.)
➡ _____

7 (worked / she / hard / showed / and / talent / a / math, / in / her / and / AI / manager / recognized / Harrison / ability. / her)
➡ _____
_____

8 (day, / one / got / he / when / upset / Katherine / missing / was / her / from / desk / too / for / long.)
➡ _____
_____

9 (asked / AI / Katherine / where / been, / had / she / and / answered.)
➡ _____

10 (Katherine: / bathroom. / the)
➡ _____

11 (are / there / COLORED / no / bathrooms / this / in / building.)
➡ _____

12 (have / I / run / to / a / half / away / mile / to / just / the / use / bathroom.)
➡ _____

13 (this, / hearing / felt / I / sorry / really / her. / for)
➡ _____

1 NASA의 숨겨진 인물들

2 나는 지난 주말에 〈히든 피겨스〉라는 영화를 보았다.

3 그것은 NASA에서 일했던 세 명의 아프리카계 미국인 여성들에 대한 영화였다.

4 그들은 1960년대에 '인간 컴퓨터(계산원)'로 일을 시작했다.

5 하지만 그들은 NASA에서 우주 전문가가 되기를 꿈꾸었고 어려움을 극복하기 위해 열심히 노력했다.

6 Katherine Johnson은 이 영화에서 세 명의 '숨겨진 인물들' 중 한 명이었다.

7 그녀는 열심히 일했고 수학에서 재능을 보였으며, 그녀의 상사인 AI Harrison은 그녀의 능력을 알아차렸다.

8 어느 날, 그는 Katherine이 너무 오래 자리를 비웠을 때 화가 났다.

9 AI은 Katherine에게 어디에 갔었는지 물었고 그녀는 대답했다.

10 Katherine: 화장실요.

11 이 건물에는 유색 인종 전용 화장실이 없어요.

12 저는 단지 화장실을 사용하기 위해 반 마일을 달려가야 해요.

13 이 말을 듣고서, 나는 그녀가 정말로 안됐다고 느꼈다.

14 (I / however, / was / that / glad / had / she / to / courage / talk / to / the / about / manager / problem. / the)

➡ _____

_____

15 (made / this / Harrison / AI / down / break / the / Ladies / "Colored / sign. / Room")

➡ _____

16 (Jackson / Mary / the / was / character / liked / I / most / the / of / three. / the)

➡ _____

17 (wanted / she / learn / to / about / more / science, / rocket / she / but / allowed / wasn't / go / to / a / to / school. / white)

➡ _____

_____

18 (she / so, / a / asked / to / judge / give / permission. / her)

➡ _____

19 (Mary: / can't / I / the / change / color / my / of / skin.)

➡ _____

20 (I / … / so / no / have / but / choice / be / to / first. / the)

➡ _____

21 (Honor, / Your / all / of / cases / the / hear / you'll / today, / one / which / matter / will / a / in / years? / hundred)

➡ _____

_____

22 (one / which / make / will / the / you / "first?")

➡ _____

23 (judge / the / impressed / was / what / by / said / she / and / gave / finally / permission. / her)

➡ _____

24 (stood / Mary / for / up / and / herself / other / for / African-Americans.)

➡ _____

25 (was / that / impressed / what / most / me / the / in / movie.)

➡ _____

26 (she / finally, / the / became / first / woman / African-American / at / engineer / NASA.)

➡ _____

---

14 그러나 나는 그 문제에 대해 상사에게 말한 그녀의 용기를 보고 기뻤다.

15 이것은 AI Harrison으로 하여금 '유색 여성 화장실' 표지판을 부수게 만들었다.

16 Mary Jackson은 셋 중에 가장 나의 마음에 드는 인물이었다.

17 그녀는 로켓 공학에 대해 더 많이 배우고 싶었지만 백인 학교에 다니는 것이 허락되지 않았다.

18 그래서 그녀는 판사에게 허락해 달라고 요청했다.

19 Mary: 저는 제 피부색을 바꿀 수 없어요.

20 그래서… 저는 '최초'가 되는 것 이외에는 선택이 없어요.

21 판사님, 당신이 오늘 들을 모든 사건 중에서, 백 년 뒤에 어느 것이 중요할까요?

22 어느 것이 판사님을 '최초'로 만들까요?

23 판사는 그녀가 말한 것에 감명을 받고 마침내 그녀에게 허락해 주었다.

24 Mary는 그녀 자신과 다른 아프리카계 미국인들의 편에 섰다.

25 그것은 영화에서 나를 가장 감동하게 한 점이었다.

26 마침내 그녀는 NASA에서 최초의 아프리카계 미국인 여성 공학자가 되었다.

27 (Vaughan / Dorothy / the / was / last / figure." / "hidden)

➡ _____

28 (IBM / when / were / computers / at / installed / NASA / 1961, / in / was / she / the / worried / computers" / "human / lose / would / jobs. / their)

➡ _____

_____

29 (studied / she / a / new / language, / programming / FORTRAN.)

➡ _____

30 (also / she / it / taught / her / to / members. / team)

➡ _____

31 (when / later, / was / she / to / asked / be / leader / the / a / of / IBM / new / team, / made / she / suggestion. / a)

➡ _____

_____

32 (Dorothy: / not / I'm / accepting / offer / the / I / if / bring / can't / ladies / my / me. / with)

➡ _____

33 (need / we / lot / a / of / to / people / program / machine. / that)

➡ _____

34 (can't / I / it / do / alone.)

➡ _____

35 (girls / my / ready. / are)

➡ _____

36 (to / thanks / Dorothy, / team / her / could / members / programmers. / become)

➡ _____

37 (wasn't / she / of / afraid / and / change / used / as / it / chance. / a)

➡ _____

38 (what / that's / need / I / learn / to / her. / from)

➡ _____

39 (this / watchinig / movie, / could / I / how / learn / to / challenges / in / face / life.)

➡ _____

40 (won't / I / the / forget / tears / and / of / laughter / Katherine, / and / Mary, / Dorothy.)

➡ _____

27 Dorothy Vaughan은 마지막 '히든 피겨(숨은 인물)'였다.

28 1961년 NASA에 IBM 컴퓨터가 설치되었을 때, 그녀는 '인간 컴퓨터(계산원)'들이 직업을 잃을까봐 걱정했다.

29 그녀는 새로운 프로그래밍 언어인 포트란을 공부했다.

30 그녀는 또한 그것을 그녀의 팀원들에게 가르쳤다.

31 나중에 그녀가 새 IBM 팀의 리더가 되도록 요청받았을 때, 그녀는 제안했다.

32 Dorothy: 저는 저의 여성 팀원들을 데려올 수 없다면 그 제안을 받아들이지 않겠습니다.

33 그 기계의 프로그램을 짜기 위해서는 많은 사람이 필요합니다.

34 저는 그것을 혼자 할 수 없습니다.

35 제 여성 팀원들은 준비가 되어 있습니다.

36 Dorothy 덕분에, 그녀의 팀원들은 프로그래머가 될 수 있었다.

37 그녀는 변화를 두려워하지 않고 그것을 기회로 이용했다.

38 그것이 내가 그녀에게서 배울 필요가 있는 점이다.

39 이 영화를 보면서, 나는 삶에서 어떻게 도전에 직면해야 하는지 배울 수 있었다.

40 나는 Katherine, Mary, 그리고 Dorothy의 눈물과 웃음을 잊지 않을 것이다.

※ 다음 우리말을 영어로 쓰시오.

1 NASA의 숨겨진 인물들
➡ _____

2 나는 지난 주말에 〈히든 피겨스〉라는 영화를 보았다.
➡ _____

3 그것은 NASA에서 일했던 세 명의 아프리카계 미국인 여성들에 대한 영화였다.
➡ _____

4 그들은 1960년대에 '인간 컴퓨터(계산원)'로 일을 시작했다.
➡ _____

5 하지만 그들은 NASA에서 우주 전문가가 되기를 꿈꾸었고 어려움을 극복하기 위해 열심히 노력했다.
➡ _____

6 Katherine Johnson은 이 영화에서 세 명의 '숨겨진 인물들' 중 한 명이었다.
➡ _____

7 그녀는 열심히 일했고 수학에서 재능을 보였으며, 그녀의 상사인 Al Harrison은 그녀의 능력을 알아차렸다.
➡ _____

8 어느 날, 그는 Katherine이 너무 오래 자리를 비웠을 때 화가 났다.
➡ _____

9 Al은 Katherine에게 어디에 갔었는지 물었고 그녀는 대답했다.
➡ _____

10 Katherine: 화장실요.
➡ _____

11 이 건물에는 유색 인종 전용 화장실이 없어요.
➡ _____

12 저는 단지 화장실을 사용하기 위해 반 마일을 달려가야 해요.
➡ _____

13 이 말을 듣고서, 나는 그녀가 정말로 안됐다고 느꼈다.
➡ _____

14 그러나 나는 그 문제에 대해 상사에게 말한 그녀의 용기를 보고 기뻤다.
➡ _____

15 이것은 Al Harrison으로 하여금 '유색 여성 화장실' 표지판을 부수게 만들었다.
➡ _____

16 Mary Jackson은 셋 중에 가장 나의 마음에 드는 인물이었다.
➡ _____

17 그녀는 로켓 공학에 대해 더 많이 배우고 싶었지만 백인 학교에 다니는 것이 허락되지 않았다.
➡ _____

18 그래서 그녀는 판사에게 허락해 달라고 요청했다.
➡ _____

19 Mary: 저는 제 피부색을 바꿀 수 없어요.
➡ _____

20 그래서… 저는 '최초'가 되는 것 이외에는 선택이 없어요.
➡ _____

21 판사님, 당신이 오늘 들을 모든 사건 중에서, 백 년 뒤에 어느 것이 중요할까요?
➡ _____

22 어느 것이 판사님을 '최초'로 만들까요?
➡ _____

23 판사는 그녀가 말한 것에 감명을 받고 마침내 그녀에게 허락해 주었다.
➡ _____

24 Mary는 그녀 자신과 다른 아프리카계 미국인들의 편에 섰다.
➡ _____

25 그것은 영화에서 나를 가장 감동하게 한 점이었다.
➡ _____

26 마침내 그녀는 NASA에서 최초의 아프리카계 미국인 여성 공학자가 되었다.
➡ _____

27 Dorothy Vaughan은 마지막 '히든 피겨(숨은 인물)'였다.
➡ _____

28 1961년 NASA에 IBM 컴퓨터가 설치되었을 때, 그녀는 '인간 컴퓨터(계산원)'들이 직업을 잃을까 봐 걱정했다.
➡ _____

29 그녀는 새로운 프로그래밍 언어인 포트란을 공부했다.
➡ _____

30 그녀는 또한 그것을 그녀의 팀원들에게 가르쳤다.
➡ _____

31 나중에 그녀가 새 IBM 팀의 리더가 되도록 요청받았을 때, 그녀는 제안했다.
➡ _____

32 Dorothy: 저는 저의 여성 팀원들을 데려올 수 없다면 그 제안을 받아들이지 않겠습니다.
➡ _____

33 그 기계의 프로그램을 짜기 위해서는 많은 사람이 필요합니다.
➡ _____

34 저는 그것을 혼자 할 수 없습니다.
➡ _____

35 제 여성 팀원들은 준비가 되어 있습니다.
➡ _____

36 Dorothy 덕분에, 그녀의 팀원들은 프로그래머가 될 수 있었다.
➡ _____

37 그녀는 변화를 두려워하지 않고 그것을 기회로 이용했다.
➡ _____

38 그것이 내가 그녀에게서 배울 필요가 있는 점이다.
➡ _____

39 이 영화를 보면서, 나는 삶에서 어떻게 도전에 직면해야 하는지 배울 수 있었다.
➡ _____

40 나는 Katherine, Mary, 그리고 Dorothy의 눈물과 웃음을 잊지 않을 것이다.
➡ _____

※ 다음 우리말과 일치하도록 빈칸에 알맞은 말을 쓰시오.

Express Yourself C

1. 1. I _____ _____ _____ _____ _____ the baker.

2. He _____ _____ about his job, _____ some cupcakes.

3. I will not forget _____ _____ _____, "Make _____ _____ _____ _____."

4. 2. I _____ _____ _____ _____ _____ the actor.

5. He _____ _____ _____ his job, _____ _____ _____ _____.

6. I will not forget _____ _____ _____, "You can be _____ _____ _____."

After You Read A

1. **Katherine Johnson:** I _____ _____ _____ _____ the "Colored Ladies Room" _____.

2. **Mary Jackson:** I _____ _____ _____ _____ me _____ _____ at a white school.

3. **Dorothy Vaughan:** I studied a new programming language _____ _____ _____ _____.

Link to the World

1. Q1 _____ do you do _____ _____ _____?

2. A1 I _____ _____ _____ _____ and desserts.

3. Q2 What _____ _____ about _____ _____?

4. A2 I have so _____ _____ _____ _____ _____ than cooking.

5. I _____ _____ _____ _____ _____ and vegetables _____ _____.

6. I also _____ _____ _____ and _____ _____ _____ _____.

7. Q3 _____ you _____ _____ your job?

8. A3 Yes, I am. It's a _____ _____, but I love _____ _____ _____.

9. I _____ _____, _____ _____ _____ _____ my dishes.

---

1. 1. 저는 제빵사와 즐거운 시간을 보냈습니다.
2. 그는 컵케이크에 장식하며 그의 직업에 대해 말해 주었습니다.
3. 저는 그가 말한 것을 잊지 않을 것입니다. "가족이 좋아하게 될 것을 만드세요."
4. 2. 저는 배우와 즐거운 시간을 보냈습니다.
5. 그는 자신의 유명한 대사를 말하면서 그의 직업에 대해 말해 주었습니다.
6. 저는 그가 말한 것을 잊지 않을 것입니다. "당신은 자신이 연기하는 것이 될 수 있습니다."

1. Katherine Johnson: 나는 나의 상사로 하여금 '유색 여성 화장실' 표지판을 부수게 만들었다.
2. Mary Jackson: 나는 판사에게 백인 학교에서 공부하도록 허락해 달라고 요청했다.
3. Dorothy Vaughan: 나는 변화에 대비해 준비하기 위하여 새로운 프로그래밍 언어를 공부했다.

1. Q1. 당신은 이 식당에서 무엇을 합니까?
2. A1. 저는 다양한 이탈리아 요리와 후식을 만듭니다.
3. Q2. 당신 직업의 어려운 점은 무엇입니까?
4. A2. 저는 요리 외에도 할 일이 많습니다.
5. 저는 매일 신선한 고기와 채소를 사야 합니다.
6. 또한 설거지하고 주방을 깨끗이 유지합니다.
7. Q3. 당신은 당신의 직업에 만족합니까?
8. A3. 네, 그렇습니다. 힘든 직업이지만, 저는 제가 하는 일을 좋아합니다.
9. 저는 사람들이 제 요리를 즐기는 것을 보면서 자부심을 느낍니다.

※ 다음 우리말을 영어로 쓰시오.

Express Yourself C

1. 1. 저는 제빵사와 즐거운 시간을 보냈습니다.
➡ _____

2. 그는 컵케이크에 장식하며 그의 직업에 대해 말해 주었습니다.
➡ _____

3. 저는 그가 말한 것을 잊지 않을 것입니다. "가족이 좋아하게 될 것을 만드세요."
➡ _____

4. 2. 저는 배우와 즐거운 시간을 보냈습니다.
➡ _____

5. 그는 자신의 유명한 대사를 말하면서 그의 직업에 대해 말해 주었습니다.
➡ _____

6. 저는 그가 말한 것을 잊지 않을 것입니다. "당신은 자신이 연기하는 것이 될 수 있습니다."
➡ _____

After You Read A

1. Katherine Johnson: 나는 나의 상사로 하여금 '유색 여성 화장실' 표지판을 부수게 만들었다.
➡ _____

2. Mary Jackson: 나는 판사에게 백인 학교에서 공부하도록 허락해 달라고 요청했다.
➡ _____

3. Dorothy Vaughan: 나는 변화에 대비해 준비하기 위하여 새로운 프로그래밍 언어를 공부했다.
➡ _____

Link to the World

1. Q1. 당신은 이 식당에서 무엇을 합니까?
➡ _____

2. A1. 저는 다양한 이탈리아 요리와 후식을 만듭니다.
➡ _____

3. Q2. 당신 직업의 어려운 점은 무엇입니까?
➡ _____

4. A2. 저는 요리 외에도 할 일이 많습니다.
➡ _____

5. 저는 매일 신선한 고기와 채소를 사야 합니다.
➡ _____

6. 또한 설거지하고 주방을 깨끗이 유지합니다.
➡ _____

7. Q3. 당신은 당신의 직업에 만족합니까?
➡ _____

8. A3. 네, 그렇습니다. 힘든 직업이지만, 저는 제가 하는 일을 좋아합니다.
➡ _____

9. 저는 사람들이 제 요리를 즐기는 것을 보면서 자부심을 느낍니다.
➡ _____

※ 다음 영어를 우리말로 쓰시오.

01 anything	_____	22 lesson	_____
02 believe	_____	23 matter	_____
03 cart	_____	24 wheel	_____
04 wave	_____	25 serve	_____
05 delicious	_____	26 witch	_____
06 enough	_____	27 mess	_____
07 fairy	_____	28 princess	_____
08 fat	_____	29 frog	_____
09 people	_____	30 rest	_____
10 bright	_____	31 shout	_____
11 find	_____	32 stuck	_____
12 fool	_____	33 unhappily	_____
13 chance	_____	34 worry	_____
14 monster	_____	35 from now on	_____
15 water	_____	36 hand in hand	_____
16 clothes	_____	37 to oneself	_____
17 hit	_____	38 pick up	_____
18 inside	_____	39 run away	_____
19 instead	_____	40 on one's way to	_____
20 save	_____	41 be better off	_____
21 kill	_____	42 by the name of	_____
		43 give it a try	_____

※ 다음 우리말을 영어로 쓰시오.

01	수레	22	(손을) 흔들다
02	괴물	23	중요하다, 문제되다
03	맛있는	24	기회
04	충분히	25	~조차도; 훨씬
05	믿다	26	나머지
06	요정	27	외치다
07	통통한, 살찐	28	연못
08	마녀	29	불행하게
09	엉망진창	30	침이 고이다, 침을 흘리다
10	구하다	31	교훈, 단원
11	꼼짝 못 하는, 움직일 수 없는	32	공주
12	밝은, 눈부신	33	걱정하다
13	바보, 멍청이	34	웃긴
14	백성, 국민	35	손에 손을 잡고
15	대접하다	36	더 이상 ~ 않다
16	치다, 때리다	37	~에 가는 길(도중)에
17	안에, 안으로	38	더 잘 살다
18	여전히, 아직도	39	수백 개의 ~
19	대신에	40	지금부터 죽
20	옷, 의복	41	도망가다, 달아나다
21	죽이다	42	뛰어다니다
		43	혼자

※ 다음 영영풀이에 알맞은 단어를 <보기>에서 골라 쓴 후, 우리말 뜻을 쓰시오.

1 _____ : the part of something that remains: _____

2 _____ : to say something very loudly: _____

3 _____ : very good to eat or drink: _____

4 _____ : not able to move anywhere: _____

5 _____ : learned through experience: _____

6 _____ : in stories, a woman who has magical powers: _____

7 _____ : a vehicle with wheels that is pulled by an animal: _____

8 _____ : to ask someone to come to your house, to a party, etc.: _____

9 _____ : an imaginary creature that is large, ugly, and frightening: _____

10 _____ : an area of water that is surrounded by land and that is smaller than a lake: _____

11 _____ : the daughter of a king or queen, or one of their close female relatives: _____

12 _____ : a small, green animal with long back legs for jumping, that lives in or near water: _____

13 _____ : a circular object fixed under a vehicle so that it moves smoothly over the ground: _____

14 _____ : an imaginary creature like a small person with wings who has magic powers: _____

15 _____ : to put your hand up and move it from side to side in order to attract someone's attention or to say goodbye: _____

16 _____ : to touch something or someone quickly and with force, usually hurting or damaging something: _____

보기			
frog	wheel	cart	rest
hit	fairy	delicious	monster
princess	pond	invite	stuck
wave	lesson	shout	witch

※ 다음 우리말과 일치하도록 빈칸에 알맞은 것을 골라 쓰시오.

1   **The** _____ _____ _____
    A. Frog   B. Continued   C. Prince

2   _____ : Frog Prince, _____ , Witch 1, Witch 2, _____
    A. Fairy   B. Princess   C. Characters

3   _____ **1:** _____ a _____
    A. in   B. Scene   C. room

4   *(Prince comes _____ , _____ _____ .)*
    A. in   B. around   C. jumping

5   **Princess:** _____ _____ _____ , honey.
    A. jumping   B. stop   C. around

6   **Prince:** Well, I _____ _____ _____ .
    A. can't   B. just   C. stop

7   **Princess:** You're not _____ _____ _____ .
    A. anymore   B. frog   C. a

8   **Prince:** What's _____ with you? You don't go _____ to the _____ _____ days.
    A. wrong   B. these   C. down   D. pond

9   **Princess:** I don't like it when you jump _____ in the room. Go out to _____ _____ and _____ our people.
    A. save   B. around   C. monsters   D. kill

10   **Prince:** I don't want to go out and kill anything. I just _____ like running _____ . *(Picking up a book)* Listen! "They lived happily ever _____ . The end." I'm living my life _____ the book says, but we're not happy. What's the problem?
    A. away   B. as   C. after   D. feel

11   **Princess:** What's the problem? There are _____ _____ problems! Sometimes I think we were _____ _____ when you were still a frog.
    A. better   B. hundreds   C. off   D. of

12   **Prince:** _____ a frog .... Yes! That's _____ ! *(Goes _____)*
    A. out   B. still   C. it

13   _____ **2:** _____ the _____
    A. mountain   B. Scene   C. on

14   **Prince:** *(To _____)* I need to find the _____ , who will _____ me _____ into a frog. *(Shouting)* Ms. Witch, Ms. Witch. Where are you? Please help me!
    A. back   B. himself   C. turn   D. witch

15   **Witch 1:** *(Coming _____ _____ the house)* Hi, Prince. _____ are you _____ ?
    A. of   B. how   C. out   D. feeling

---

1   계속된 개구리 왕자

2   등장인물: 개구리 왕자, 공주, 마녀 1, 마녀 2, 요정

3   장면 1: 방 안에서

4   (왕자가 이리저리 뛰어다니며 등장한다.)

5   공주: 여보, 이리저리 뛰어다니지 마세요.

6   왕자: 저, 나는 단지 멈출 수 없을 뿐이에요.

7   공주: 당신은 이제 개구리가 아니에요.

8   왕자: 당신한테 무슨 문제가 있어요? 요즘 당신은 연못으로 내려가지도 않잖아요.

9   공주: 나는 당신이 방 안에서 이리저리 뛰어다니는 게 마음에 안 들어요. 나가서 괴물들을 죽이고 우리 백성을 구하세요.

10   왕자: 나는 밖에 나가서 아무것도 죽이고 싶지 않아요. 나는 단지 멀리 뛰어다니고 싶을 뿐이오. (책을 집어 들고) 들어 봐요! "그들은 그 후로 행복하게 살았다. 끝." 나는 책에서 말한 것처럼 내 인생을 살고 있지만, 우리는 행복하지 않아요. 뭐가 문제일까요?

11   공주: 뭐가 문제냐고요? 수백 가지 문제가 있어요! 가끔 나는 당신이 아직 개구리일 때 더 잘 살지 않았나 생각해요.

12   왕자: 아직 개구리라 ⋯. 그래! 바로 그거요! (퇴장한다.)

13   장면 2: 산속에서

14   왕자: (혼잣말로) 나는 마녀를 찾아야 해. 그녀가 나를 다시 개구리로 바꿔 줄 거야. (소리치며) 마녀님, 마녀님. 어디 계세요? 저 좀 도와주세요!

15   마녀 1: (집 밖으로 나오며) 안녕, 왕자님. 기분이 어때요?

16 Prince: I'm glad to _____ you. I'm the Frog Prince. I hope you can turn me back _____ a frog so I can live happily _____ _____.

    A. ever   B. into   C. meet   D. after

17 Witch 1: Frog Prince, you say? That's funny. You don't look _____ a frog. Well, it doesn't _____. If you're a prince, you're a prince. And I won't _____ you _____ Snow White. Here, eat the rest of this apple.

    A. matter   B. like   C. save   D. let

18 Prince: No, thank you. That's not _____ I _____! *(Runs _____)*

    A. away   B. what   C. want

19 *(Prince and Witch 2 _____ _____.)*

    A. in   B. come

20 Prince: Ms. Witch, Ms. Witch. _____ are you? _____ _____ me! I'm the Frog ....

    A. help   B. where   C. please

21 Witch 2: _____ you're a _____, I'm the King of _____.

    A. frog   B. if   C. France

22 Prince: No, I'm not a frog. I'm the Frog Prince. But I need a witch to _____ me _____ into a frog so I can _____ _____ ever after. Can you do it?

    A. happily   B. turn   C. live   D. back

23 Witch 2: _____ talk about it _____. I will _____ you a _____ lunch. Come in.

    A. serve   B. inside   C. delicious   D. let's

24 Prince: Thank you for inviting me. Oh, this house is _____ _____ cookies and candies. Wait a minute. Do you know any children _____ the _____ of Hansel and Gretel?

    A. by   B. made   C. of   D. name

25 Witch 2: Yes, Prince, I do. *(_____ her mouth _____)* They are not _____ _____ yet, but you are ....

    A. enough   B. watering   C. with   D. fat

26 *(Prince _____ _____ and _____ a fairy.)*

    A. finds   B. runs   C. away

27 Prince: I'm glad to meet you, Ms. Fairy. I am the Frog Prince. _____ you _____ me back into a frog _____ I can live happily ever _____?

    A. so   B. could   C. after   D. turn

---

16 왕자: 당신을 만나서 기뻐요. 저는 개구리 왕자예요. 저는 당신이 저를 다시 개구리로 바꿔줘서 제가 앞으로 행복하게 살 수 있게 되기를 원해요.

17 마녀 1: 개구리 왕자라고 했어요? 그거 웃기는군요. 당신은 개구리처럼 보이지 않아요. 음, 그건 중요하지 않아요. 당신이 왕자라면 왕자인 거죠. 그리고 나는 당신이 백설공주를 구하도록 놔두지 않을 거예요. 여기, 이 사과의 나머지를 먹어요.

18 왕자: 고맙지만 됐어요. 그건 제가 원하는 게 아니에요! (도망간다)

19 (왕자와 마녀 2가 등장한다.)

20 왕자: 마녀님, 마녀님. 어디 계세요? 저 좀 도와주세요! 저는 개구리 ….

21 마녀 2: 당신이 개구리라면 나는 프랑스의 왕이에요.

22 왕자: 아니요. 저는 개구리가 아니에요. 저는 개구리 왕자예요. 하지만 저를 다시 개구리로 바꿔 줘서 제가 앞으로 행복하게 살 수 있게 해 줄 마녀가 필요해요. 그렇게 해 주실 수 있나요?

23 마녀 2: 안에서 그것에 관해 이야기해 봅시다. 내가 당신에게 맛있는 점심을 대접할게요. 들어와요.

24 왕자: 저를 초대해 주셔서 감사합니다. 오, 이 집은 과자와 사탕으로 만들어져 있네요. 잠깐만요. 당신은 헨젤과 그레텔이라는 이름의 아이들을 혹시 알아요?

25 마녀 2: 그래요, 왕자님, 알고 있어요. (그녀가 군침을 흘리면서) 그 애들은 아직 충분히 살이 찌지 않았지만, 당신은 ….

26 (왕자는 도망치다가 요정을 발견한다.)

27 왕자: 만나게 되어 기쁩니다, 요정님. 저는 개구리 왕자예요. 저를 다시 개구리로 바꿔 앞으로 행복하게 살 수 있게 해 주실 수 있나요?

28 Fairy: Well, I'm _____ my _____ to see Cinderella, but I'll give it a _____. It's my first time, you know. *(Fairy turns Prince _____ a wheel.)*

A. try   B. into   C. way   D. on

29 Fairy: Oops! Sorry, but don't _____. Everything _____ _____ _____.

A. worry   B. okay   C. be   D. will

30 Prince: *(To himself)* Oh, _____ a _____ I've been! I want to be sitting at home with the Princess, living happily ever after. But instead, I'm _____ here under this cart and I'll live _____ ever after.

A. stuck   B. unhappily   C. fool   D. what

31 *(The clock _____ twelve, and the wheel _____ _____ Prince.)*

A. into   B. turns   C. hits

32 Prince: I can't believe this. Thank you for giving me a second _____. Now I know _____ I _____ _____ my life. *(Goes out)*

A. chance   B. should   C. how   D. live

33 Fairy: *(_____ her hand)* You learned a good _____. I'll _____ my fingers _____.

A. lesson   B. crossed   C. keep   D. waving

34 **Scene 3:** _____ the Frog _____ _____

A. in   B. house   C. Prince's

35 *(Prince _____ _____, _____.)*

A. in   B. runs   C. smiling

36 Princess: Where have you _____? I've been _____. Your _____ are a _____.

A. been   B. mess   C. worried   D. clothes

37 Prince: *(Looking at Princess)* You _____ me when no one _____ in the world _____. You loved me even when I was a frog. From now _____, I will make you happier.

A. else   B. on   C. believed   D. did

38 Princess: I'm _____ to _____ that. I'll _____ you _____ happier.

A. hear   B. even   C. make   D. glad

39 Prince: Great! I'm _____ _____ to our _____ _____. Ha-ha ....

A. bright   B. looking   C. future   D. forward

40 *(They run _____ the pond together, _____ hand _____.)*

A. hand   B. to   C. in   D. jumping

28 요정: 음, 저는 신데렐라를 만나러 가는 길이지만, 한번 해 볼게요. 아시다시피 이건 제가 처음으로 해 보는 거예요. (요정이 왕자를 바퀴로 바꾼다.)

29 요정: 이런! 미안하지만 걱정하지 마세요. 모든 게 잘될 거예요.

30 왕자: (혼잣말로) 오, 내가 얼마나 바보였던가! 앞으로 행복하게 살면서 집에서 공주와 함께 앉아 있고 싶구나. 하지만 대신에 여기 이 수레 아래에 붙박여 있고 앞으로 불행하게 살게 되겠구나.

31 (시계가 12시를 치자 바퀴가 왕자로 바뀐다.)

32 왕자: 믿을 수가 없네. 두 번째 기회를 주셔서 감사합니다. 이제 나는 내 인생을 어떻게 살아야 할지 알겠어요. (퇴장한다)

33 요정: (손을 흔들며) 좋은 교훈을 배웠군요. 행운을 빌어요.

34 장면 3: 개구리 왕자의 집 안에서

35 (왕자가 미소를 지으며 뛰어 들어온다.)

36 공주: 어디 있었어요? 걱정했잖아요. 옷이 엉망진창이네요.

37 왕자: (공주를 바라보며) 당신은 세상 어느 누구도 나를 믿지 않을 때 나를 믿어 주었어요. 당신은 내가 개구리일 때조차도 나를 사랑해 주었죠. 이제부터는 내가 당신을 더 행복하게 해 주겠어요.

38 공주: 그 말을 들으니 기뻐요. 제가 당신을 훨씬 더 행복하게 해 줄게요.

39 왕자: 좋아요! 난 우리의 밝은 미래를 기대할게요. 하하 ….

40 (그들은 서로 손을 잡고 함께 연못으로 뛰어간다.)

※ 다음 우리말과 일치하도록 빈칸에 알맞은 것을 골라 쓰시오.

1 The _____ _____ _____

2 _____ : Frog Prince, _____ , Witch 1, Witch 2, _____

3 _____ **1:** _____ a room

4 *(Prince comes in, _____ _____ .)*

5 Princess: _____ _____ around, honey.

6 Prince: Well, I just _____ _____ .

7 Princess: You're not a frog _____ .

8 Prince: _____ _____ _____ you? You don't go down to the pond _____ _____ .

9 Princess: _____ _____ _____ _____ _____ you jump around in the room. Go out to _____ _____ and _____ our people.

10 Prince: I don't want to go out and kill anything. I just _____ _____ _____ _____ . (_____ _____ a book) Listen! "They lived happily ever after. The end." I'm living my life _____ the book says, but we're not happy. What's the problem?

11 Princess: What's the problem? There are _____ _____ problems! Sometimes I think we _____ _____ _____ _____ you _____ _____ a frog.

12 Prince: Still a frog .... Yes! _____ _____ ! *(Goes out)*

13 _____ **2:** _____ the mountain

14 Prince: *(_____ _____)* I need to find the witch, who will _____ me back _____ a frog. *(Shouting)* Ms. Witch, Ms. Witch. Where are you? Please help me!

15 Witch 1: *(Coming _____ _____ the house)* Hi, Prince. _____ are you feeling?

---

1 계속된 개구리 왕자

2 등장인물: 개구리 왕자, 공주, 마녀 1, 마녀 2, 요정

3 장면 1: 방 안에서

4 (왕자가 이리저리 뛰어다니며 등장한다.)

5 공주: 여보, 이리저리 뛰어다니지 마세요.

6 왕자: 저, 나는 단지 멈출 수 없을 뿐이에요.

7 공주: 당신은 이제 개구리가 아니에요.

8 왕자: 당신한테 무슨 문제가 있어요? 요즘 당신은 연못으로 내려가지도 않잖아요.

9 공주: 나는 당신이 방 안에서 이리저리 뛰어다니는 게 마음에 안 들어요. 나가서 괴물들을 죽이고 우리 백성을 구하세요.

10 왕자: 나는 밖에 나가서 아무것도 죽이고 싶지 않아요. 나는 단지 멀리 뛰어다니고 싶을 뿐이오. (책을 집어 들고) 들어 봐요! "그들은 그 후로 행복하게 살았다. 끝." 나는 책에서 말한 것처럼 내 인생을 살고 있지만, 우리는 행복하지 않아요. 뭐가 문제일까요?

11 공주: 뭐가 문제냐고요? 수백 가지 문제가 있어요! 가끔 나는 당신이 아직 개구리일 때 더 잘 살지 않았나 생각해요.

12 왕자: 아직 개구리라 …. 그래! 바로 그거요! (퇴장한다.)

13 장면 2: 산속에서

14 왕자: (혼잣말로) 나는 마녀를 찾아야 해. 그녀가 나를 다시 개구리로 바꿔 줄 거야. (소리치며) 마녀님. 마녀님. 어디 계세요? 저 좀 도와주세요!

15 마녀 1: (집 밖으로 나오며) 안녕, 왕자님. 기분이 어때요?

16 Prince: I'm glad to meet you. I'm the Frog Prince. I hope you can _____ _____ _____ _____ a frog _____ I can _____ _____ _____ _____.

17 Witch 1: Frog Prince, you say? That's funny. You don't _____ _____ a frog. Well, it _____ _____. If you're a prince, you're a prince. And I won't _____ _____ _____ Snow White. Here, eat the _____ of this apple.

18 Prince: No, thank you. That's not what I _____! *(Runs away)*

19 *(Prince and Witch 2 _____ _____.)*

20 Prince: Ms. Witch, Ms. Witch. _____ are you? Please help me! I'm the Frog ....

21 Witch 2: _____ you're a frog, I'm the King of France.

22 Prince: No, I'm not a frog. I'm the Frog Prince. But I need a witch to _____ _____ _____ _____ a frog so I can _____ _____ ever after. Can you do it?

23 Witch 2: _____ talk about it inside. I will _____ you a _____ lunch. Come in.

24 Prince: Thank you _____ _____ me. Oh, this house _____ _____ _____ _____ and candies. Wait a minute. Do you know any children _____ _____ _____ _____ Hansel and Gretel?

25 Witch 2: Yes, Prince, _____ _____. *(With her mouth watering)* They are not _____ _____ yet, but you are ....

26 *(Prince _____ _____ and finds a fairy.)*

27 Prince: I'm glad to meet you, Ms. Fairy. I am the Frog Prince. _____ _____ turn me back into a frog _____ I can live happily ever after?

---

16 왕자: 당신을 만나서 기뻐요. 저는 개구리 왕자예요. 저는 당신이 저를 다시 개구리로 바꿔줘서 제가 앞으로 행복하게 살 수 있게 되기를 원해요.

17 마녀 1: 개구리 왕자라고 했어요? 그거 웃기는군요. 당신은 개구리처럼 보이지 않아요. 음, 그건 중요하지 않아요. 당신이 왕자라면 왕자인 거죠. 그리고 나는 당신이 백설공주를 구하도록 놔두지 않을 거예요. 여기, 이 사과의 나머지를 먹어요.

18 왕자: 고맙지만 됐어요. 그건 제가 원하는 게 아니에요! (도망간다)

19 (왕자와 마녀 2가 등장한다.)

20 왕자: 마녀님, 마녀님. 어디 계세요? 저 좀 도와주세요! 저는 개구리 ….

21 마녀 2: 당신이 개구리라면 나는 프랑스의 왕이에요.

22 왕자: 아니요, 저는 개구리가 아니에요. 저는 개구리 왕자예요. 하지만 저를 다시 개구리로 바꿔 줘서 제가 앞으로 행복하게 살 수 있게 해 줄 마녀가 필요해요. 그렇게 해 주실 수 있나요?

23 마녀 2: 안에서 그것에 관해 이야기해 봅시다. 내가 당신에게 맛있는 점심을 대접할게요. 들어와요.

24 왕자: 저를 초대해 주셔서 감사합니다. 오, 이 집은 과자와 사탕으로 만들어져 있네요. 잠깐만요. 당신은 헨젤과 그레텔이라는 이름의 아이들을 혹시 알아요?

25 마녀 2: 그래요, 왕자님, 알고 있어요. (그녀가 군침을 흘리면서) 그 애들은 아직 충분히 살이 찌지 않았지만, 당신은 ….

26 (왕자는 도망치다가 요정을 발견한다.)

27 왕자: 만나게 되어 기쁩니다, 요정님. 저는 개구리 왕자예요. 저를 다시 개구리로 바꿔 앞으로 행복하게 살 수 있게 해 주실 수 있나요?

28 Fairy: Well, I'm _____ _____ _____ to see Cinderella, but I'll _____ _____ _____ _____. It's my first time, you know. *(Fairy _____ Prince _____ a wheel.)*

29 Fairy: Oops! Sorry, but _____ _____. Everything _____ _____ _____.

30 Prince: *(To himself)* Oh, _____ _____ _____ I've been! I want to be sitting at home with the Princess, _____ _____ ever after. But instead, I'm _____ here under this cart and I'll live _____ ever after.

31 *(The clock hits twelve, and the wheel _____ _____ Prince.)*

32 Prince: I can't believe this. Thank you for _____ _____ _____ _____ _____. Now I know _____ _____ _____ _____ my life. *(Goes out)*

33 Fairy: (_____ *her hand)* You learned a good _____. I'll _____ _____ _____ _____.

34 **Scene 3:** In the Frog _____ _____

35 *(Prince runs in, _____.)*

36 Princess: Where _____ _____ _____? I've been worried. Your _____ are a _____.

37 Prince: *(Looking at Princess)* You believed me when no one _____ in the world _____. You loved me even when I was a frog. _____ _____ _____, I will make you happier.

38 Princess: I'm glad to hear that. I'll make you _____ happier.

39 Prince: Great! I'm _____ _____ _____ our _____ _____. Ha-ha ....

40 *(They run to the pond together, _____ _____ _____ _____.)*

28 요정: 음, 저는 신데렐라를 만나러 가는 길이지만, 한번 해 볼게요. 아시다시피 이건 제가 처음으로 해 보는 거예요. (요정이 왕자를 바퀴로 바꾼다.)

29 요정: 이런! 미안하지만 걱정하지 마세요. 모든 게 잘될 거예요.

30 왕자: (혼잣말로) 오, 내가 얼마나 바보였던가! 앞으로 행복하게 살면서 집에서 공주와 함께 앉아 있고 싶구나. 하지만 대신에 여기 이 수레 아래에 붙박여 있고 앞으로 불행하게 살게 되겠구나.

31 (시계가 12시를 치자 바퀴가 왕자로 바뀐다.)

32 왕자: 믿을 수가 없네. 두 번째 기회를 주셔서 감사합니다. 이제 나는 내 인생을 어떻게 살아야 할지 알겠어요. (퇴장한다)

33 요정: (손을 흔들며) 좋은 교훈을 배웠군요. 행운을 빌어요.

34 장면 3: 개구리 왕자의 집 안에서

35 (왕자가 미소를 지으며 뛰어 들어온다.)

36 공주: 어디 있었어요? 걱정했잖아요. 옷이 엉망진창이네요.

37 왕자: (공주를 바라보며) 당신은 세상 어느 누구도 나를 믿지 않을 때 나를 믿어 주었어요. 당신은 내가 개구리일 때조차도 나를 사랑해 주었죠. 이제부터는 내가 당신을 더 행복하게 해 주겠어요.

38 공주: 그 말을 들으니 기뻐요. 제가 당신을 훨씬 더 행복하게 해 줄게요.

39 왕자: 좋아요! 난 우리의 밝은 미래를 기대할게요. 하하 ….

40 (그들은 서로 손을 잡고 함께 연못으로 뛰어간다.)

※ 다음 문장을 우리말로 쓰시오.

1 The Frog Prince Continued

➡ _____

2 Characters: Frog Prince, Princess, Witch 1, Witch 2, Fairy

➡ _____

3 Scene 1: In a room

➡ _____

4 (*Prince comes in, jumping around.*)

➡ _____

5 Princess: Stop jumping around, honey.

➡ _____

6 Prince: Well, I just can't stop.

➡ _____

7 Princess: You're not a frog anymore.

➡ _____

8 Prince: What's wrong with you? You don't go down to the pond these days.

➡ _____

9 Princess: I don't like it when you jump around in the room. Go out to kill monsters and save our people.

➡ _____

10 Prince: I don't want to go out and kill anything. I just feel like running away. (*Picking up a book*) Listen! "They lived happily ever after. The end." I'm living my life as the book says, but we're not happy. What's the problem?

➡ _____

_____

_____

11 Princess: What's the problem? There are hundreds of problems! Sometimes I think we were better off when you were still a frog.

➡ _____

12 Prince: Still a frog .... Yes! That's it! (*Goes out*)

➡ _____

13 Scene 2: On the mountain

➡ _____

14 Prince: (*To himself*) I need to find the witch, who will turn me back into a frog. (*Shouting*) Ms. Witch, Ms. Witch. Where are you? Please help me!

➡ _____

_____

15 Witch 1: (Coming out of the house) Hi, Prince. How are you feeling?

➡ _____

16 Prince: I'm glad to meet you. I'm the Frog Prince. I hope you can turn me back into a frog so I can live happily ever after.

➡ _____

_____

17 Witch 1: Frog Prince, you say? That's funny. You don't look like a frog. Well, it doesn't matter. If you're a prince, you're a prince. And I won't let you save Snow White. Here, eat the rest of this apple.

➡ _____

_____

18 Prince: No, thank you. That's not what I want! (*Runs away*)

➡ _____

19 (*Prince and Witch 2 come in.*)

➡ _____

20 Prince: Ms. Witch, Ms. Witch. Where are you? Please help me! I'm the Frog ....

➡ _____

21 Witch 2: If you're a frog, I'm the King of France.

➡ _____

22 Prince: No, I'm not a frog. I'm the Frog Prince. But I need a witch to turn me back into a frog so I can live happily ever after. Can you do it?

➡ _____

_____

23 Witch 2: Let's talk about it inside. I will serve you a delicious lunch. Come in

➡ _____

24 Prince: Thank you for inviting me. Oh, this house is made of cookies and candies. Wait a minute. Do you know any children by the name of Hansel and Gretel?

➡ _____

_____

25 Witch 2: Yes, Prince, I do. (*With her mouth watering*) They are not fat enough yet, but you are ....

➡ _____

26 (*Prince runs away and finds a fairy.*)

➡ _____

27 Prince: I'm glad to meet you, Ms. Fairy. I am the Frog Prince. Could you turn me back into a frog so I can live happily ever after?

➡ _____

_____

28 Fairy: Well, I'm on my way to see Cinderella, but I'll give it a try. It's my first time, you know. (*Fairy turns Prince into a wheel.*)

➡ _____

_____

29 Fairy: Oops! Sorry, but don't worry. Everything will be okay.

➡ _____

30 Prince: (*To himself*) Oh, what a fool I've been! I want to be sitting at home with the Princess, living happily ever after. But instead, I'm stuck here under this cart and I'll live unhappily ever after.

➡ _____

_____

31 (*The clock hits twelve, and the wheel turns into Prince.*)

➡ _____

32 Prince: I can't believe this. Thank you for giving me a second chance. Now I know how I should live my life. (*Goes out*)

➡ _____

33 Fairy: (*Waving her hand*) You learned a good lesson. I'll keep my fingers crossed.

➡ _____

34 Scene 3: In the Frog Prince's house

➡ _____

35 (*Prince runs in, smiling.*)

➡ _____

36 Princess: Where have you been? I've been worried. Your clothes are a mess.

➡ _____

37 Prince: (*Looking at Princess*) You believed me when no one else in the world did. You loved me even when I was a frog. From now on, I will make you happier.

➡ _____

_____

38 Princess: I'm glad to hear that. I'll make you even happier.

➡ _____

39 Prince: Great! I'm looking forward to our bright future. Ha-ha ....

➡ _____

40 (*They run to the pond together, jumping hand in hand.*)

➡ _____

※ 다음 괄호 안의 단어들을 우리말에 맞도록 바르게 배열하시오.

1 (Frog / The / Continued / Prince)
➡ _____

2 (Characters: / Prince, / Frog / Witch 1, / Princess, / Fairy / Witch 2,)
➡ _____

3 (Scene 1: / a / room / in)
➡ _____

4 (comes / (Prince / in, / around.) / jumping)
➡ _____

5 (Princess: / jumping / stop / honey. / around,)
➡ _____

6 (Prince: / I / well, / stop. / can't / just)
➡ _____

7 (Princess: / not / you're / a / anymore. / frog)
➡ _____

8 (Prince: / wrong / what's / you? / with // don't / you / down / go / the / to / these / pond / days.)
➡ _____

9 (Princess: / don't / I / it / like / you / when / jump / in / around / room. / the // out / go / kill / to / and / monsters / save / people. / our)
➡ _____

10 (Prince: / don't / I / to / want / out / go / and / anything. / kill // just / I / like / feel / away. / running // up / (picking / book) / a // listen! // lived / "they / ever / happily / after. // end." / the // living / I'm / life / my / the / as / says, / book / but / not / we're / happy. // the / what's / problem?)
➡ _____
_____
_____

11 (Princess: / the / what's / problem? // are / there / of / hundreds / problems! // I / sometimes / we / think / better / were / off / you / when / still / were / frog. / a)
➡ _____
_____

12 (Prince: / a / still / .... / frog // yes! // it! / that's // out) / (goes)
➡ _____

13 (Scene 2: / the / on / mountain)
➡ _____

14 (Prince: / himself) / (to // need / I / find / to / witch, / the / will / who / me / turn / back / a / frog. / into) // (shouting) // Witch, / Ms. / Witch. / Ms. // are / you? / where // help / me! / please)
➡ _____
_____

15 (Witch 1: / out / (coming / the / of / house) // Prince. / hi, // are / how / feeling? / you)
➡ _____

1 계속된 개구리 왕자

2 등장인물: 개구리 왕자, 공주, 마녀 1, 마녀 2, 요정

3 장면 1: 방 안에서

4 (왕자가 이리저리 뛰어다니며 등장한다.)

5 공주: 여보, 이리저리 뛰어다니지 마세요.

6 왕자: 저, 나는 단지 멈출 수 없을 뿐이에요.

7 공주: 당신은 이제 개구리가 아니에요.

8 왕자: 당신한테 무슨 문제가 있어요? 요즘 당신은 연못으로 내려가지도 않잖아요.

9 공주: 나는 당신이 방 안에서 이리저리 뛰어다니는 게 마음에 안 들어요. 나가서 괴물들을 죽이고 우리 백성을 구하세요.

10 왕자: 나는 밖에 나가서 아무것도 죽이고 싶지 않아요. 나는 단지 멀리 뛰어다니고 싶을 뿐이오. (책을 집어 들고) 들어 봐요! "그들은 그 후로 행복하게 살았다. 끝." 나는 책에서 말한 것처럼 내 인생을 살고 있지만, 우리는 행복하지 않아요. 뭐가 문제일까요?

11 공주: 뭐가 문제냐고요? 수백 가지 문제가 있어요! 가끔 나는 당신이 아직 개구리일 때 더 잘 살지 않았나 생각해요.

12 왕자: 아직 개구리라 …. 그래! 바로 그거요! (퇴장한다.)

13 장면 2: 산속에서

14 왕자: (혼잣말로) 나는 마녀를 찾아야 해. 그녀가 나를 다시 개구리로 바꿔 줄 거야. (소리치며) 마녀님, 마녀님. 어디 계세요? 저 좀 도와주세요!

15 마녀 1: (집 밖으로 나오며) 안녕, 왕자님. 기분이 어때요?

16 (Prince: / glad / I'm / meet / to / you. // the / I'm / Prince. / Frog // hope / I / can / you / me / turn / into / back / so / a / frog / can / I / happily / live / after. / ever)

➡ _____

_____

17 (Witch 1: / Prince, / Frog / say? / you // funny. / that's // don't / you / like / look / frog. / a // it / well, / matter. / doesn't // you're / if / prince, / a / a / you're / prince. // I / and / let / won't / save / you / White. / Snow // eat / here, / rest / of / the / apple. / this)

➡ _____

_____

_____

18 (Prince: / thank / no, / you. // not / that's / I / what / want! // away) / (runs)

➡ _____

19 (and / (Prince / come / Witch 2 / in.))

➡ _____

20 (Prince: / Witch, / Ms. / Witch. / Ms. // are / were / you? // help / please / me! // the / I'm / .... / Frog)

➡ _____

21 (Witch 2: / you're / if / frog, / a / the / I'm / of / King / France.)

➡ _____

22 (Prince: / I'm / no, / a / not / frog. // the / I'm / Prince. / Frog // I / but / a / need / to / witch / me / turn / into / back / frog / a / I / so / live / can / ever / happily / after. / you / can / it? / do)

➡ _____

_____

23 (Witch 2: / talk / let's / it / about / inside. // will / I / you / serve / a / delicious / lunch. // in. / come)

➡ _____

_____

24 (Prince: / you / thank / inviting / for / me. // this / oh, / is / house / made / of / and / cookies / candies. // a / wait / minute. // you / do / know / children / any / the / by / name / of / and / Gretel? / Hansel)

➡ _____

_____

25 (Witch 2: / Prince, / yes, / do. / I // her / (with / watering) / mouth // are / they / fat / not / yet, / enough / you / but / .... / are)

➡ _____

_____

26 (runs / (Prince / and / away / a / finds / fairy.))

➡ _____

27 (Prince: / glad / I'm / meet / to / you, / Fairy. / Ms. // am / I / Prince. / the / Frog // you / could / me / turn / back / into / frog / a / so / can / I / live / ever / happily / after?)

➡ _____

_____

16 왕자: 당신을 만나서 기뻐요. 저는 개구리 왕자예요. 저는 당신이 저를 다시 개구리로 바꿔줘서 제가 앞으로 행복하게 살 수 있게 되기를 원해요.

17 마녀 1: 개구리 왕자라고 했어요? 그거 웃기는군요. 당신은 개구리처럼 보이지 않아요. 음, 그건 중요하지 않아요. 당신이 왕자라면 왕자인 거죠. 그리고 나는 당신이 백설공주를 구하도록 놔두지 않을 거예요. 여기, 이 사과의 나머지를 먹어요.

18 왕자: 고맙지만 됐어요. 그건 제가 원하는 게 아니에요! (도망간다)

19 (왕자와 마녀 2가 등장한다.)

20 왕자: 마녀님, 마녀님. 어디 계세요? 저 좀 도와주세요! 저는 개구리 ….

21 마녀 2: 당신이 개구리라면 나는 프랑스의 왕이에요.

22 왕자: 아니요, 저는 개구리가 아니에요. 저는 개구리 왕자예요. 하지만 저를 다시 개구리로 바꿔 줘서 제가 앞으로 행복하게 살 수 있게 해 줄 마녀가 필요해요. 그렇게 해 주실 수 있나요?

23 마녀 2: 안에서 그것에 관해 이야기해 봅시다. 내가 당신에게 맛있는 점심을 대접할게요. 들어와요.

24 왕자: 저를 초대해 주셔서 감사합니다. 오, 이 집은 과자와 사탕으로 만들어져 있네요. 잠깐만요. 당신은 헨젤과 그레텔이라는 이름의 아이들을 혹시 알아요?

25 마녀 2: 그래요, 왕자님, 알고 있어요. (그녀가 군침을 흘리면서) 그 애들은 아직 충분히 살이 찌지 않았지만, 당신은 ….

26 (왕자는 도망치다가 요정을 발견한다.)

27 왕자: 만나게 되어 기쁩니다. 요정님. 저는 개구리 왕자예요. 저를 다시 개구리로 바꿔 앞으로 행복하게 살 수 있게 해 주실 수 있나요?

28 (Fairy: / I'm / well, / my / on / see / to / way / but / Cinderella, / give / I'll / a / it / try. // my / first / it's / time, / know. / you // turns / (Fairy / into / Prince / wheel.) / a)
➡ _____
_____

29 (Fairy: / oops! // but / sorry, / worry. / don't // will / everything / be / okay.)
➡ _____

30 (Prince: / himself) / (to // what / oh, / fool / a / been! / I've // want / I / to / be / sitting / home / at / the / with / Princess, / happily / living / after. / ever // instead, / but / stuck / I'm / under / here / cart / this / and / live / I'll / ever / unhappily / after.)
➡ _____
_____

31 (clock / (the / twelve, / hits // the / and / turns / wheel / Prince.) / into)
➡ _____

32 (Prince: / can't / I / this. / believe // you / thank / for / me / giving / a / chance. / second // I / now / how / know / should / I / my / live / life. // out) / (goes)
➡ _____

33 (Fairy: / her / (waving / hand) // learned / you / good / a / lesson. // keep / I'll / fingers / my / crossed.)
➡ _____
_____

34 (Scene 3: / the / in / Prince's / Frog / house)
➡ _____

35 (runs / (Prince / smiling.) / in,)
➡ _____

36 (Princess: / have / where / been? / you // been / I've / worried. // clothes / your / a / are / mess.)
➡ _____
_____

37 (Prince: / at / (looking / Princess) // belived / you / when / me / one / no / in / else / the / did. / world // loved / you / even / me / I / when / a / was / frog. // now / from / on, / will / I / you / happier. / make)
➡ _____
_____

38 (Princess: / glad / I'm / to / that. / hear // make / I'll / even / you / happier.)
➡ _____

39 (Prince: / great! / looking / I'm / to / forward / our / future. / bright // .... / ha-ha)
➡ _____

40 (run / (they / the / to / together, / pond / hand / jumping / hand. / in)
➡ _____

---

28 요정: 음, 저는 신데렐라를 만나러 가는 길이지만, 한번 해 볼게요. 아시다시피 이건 제가 처음으로 해 보는 거예요. (요정이 왕자를 바퀴로 바꾼다.)

29 요정: 이런! 미안하지만 걱정하지 마세요. 모든 게 잘될 거예요.

30 왕자: (혼잣말로) 오, 내가 얼마나 바보였던가! 앞으로 행복하게 살면서 집에서 공주와 함께 앉아 있고 싶구나. 하지만 대신에 여기 이 수레 아래에 붙박여 있고 앞으로 불행하게 살게 되겠구나.

31 (시계가 12시를 치자 바퀴가 왕자로 바뀐다.)

32 왕자: 믿을 수가 없네. 두 번째 기회를 주셔서 감사합니다. 이제 나는 내 인생을 어떻게 살아야 할지 알겠어요. (퇴장한다)

33 요정: (손을 흔들며) 좋은 교훈을 배웠군요. 행운을 빌어요.

34 장면 3: 개구리 왕자의 집 안에서

35 (왕자가 미소를 지으며 뛰어 들어온다.)

36 공주: 어디 있었어요? 걱정했잖아요. 옷이 엉망진창이네요.

37 왕자: (공주를 바라보며) 당신은 세상 어느 누구도 나를 믿지 않을 때 나를 믿어 주었어요. 당신은 내가 개구리일 때조차도 나를 사랑해 주었죠. 이제부터는 내가 당신을 더 행복하게 해 주겠어요.

38 공주: 그 말을 들으니 기뻐요. 제가 당신을 훨씬 더 행복하게 해 줄게요.

39 왕자: 좋아요! 난 우리의 밝은 미래를 기대할게요. 하하 ….

40 (그들은 서로 손을 잡고 함께 연못으로 뛰어간다.)

※ 다음 우리말을 영어로 쓰시오.

1 계속된 개구리 왕자

➡ _____

2 등장인물: 개구리 왕자, 공주, 마녀 1, 마녀 2, 요정

➡ _____

3 장면 1: 방 안에서

➡ _____

4 (왕자가 이리저리 뛰어다니며 등장한다.)

➡ _____

5 공주: 여보, 이리저리 뛰어다니지 마세요.

➡ _____

6 왕자: 저, 나는 단지 멈출 수 없을 뿐이에요.

➡ _____

7 공주: 당신은 이제 개구리가 아니에요.

➡ _____

8 왕자: 당신한테 무슨 문제가 있어요? 요즘 당신은 연못으로 내려가지도 않잖아요.

➡ _____

9 공주: 나는 당신이 방 안에서 이리저리 뛰어다니는 게 마음에 안 들어요. 나가서 괴물들을 죽이고 우리 백성을 구하세요.

➡ _____

_____

10 왕자: 나는 밖에 나가서 아무것도 죽이고 싶지 않아요. 나는 단지 멀리 뛰어다니고 싶을 뿐이오. (책을 집어 들고) 들어 봐요! "그들은 그 후로 행복하게 살았다. 끝." 나는 책에서 말한 것처럼 내 인생을 살고 있지만, 우리는 행복하지 않아요. 뭐가 문제일까요?

➡ _____

_____

_____

11 공주: 뭐가 문제냐고요? 수백 가지 문제가 있어요! 가끔 나는 당신이 아직 개구리일 때 더 잘 살지 않았나 생각해요.

➡ _____

_____

12 왕자: 아직 개구리라 …. 그래! 바로 그거요! (퇴장한다.)

➡ _____

13 장면 2: 산속에서

➡ _____

14 왕자: (혼잣말로) 나는 마녀를 찾아야 해. 그녀가 나를 다시 개구리로 바꿔 줄 거야. (소리치며) 마녀님, 마녀님. 어디 계세요? 저 좀 도와주세요!

➡ _____

15 마녀 1: (집 밖으로 나오며) 안녕, 왕자님. 기분이 어때요?

➡ _____

16 왕자: 당신을 만나서 기뻐요. 저는 개구리 왕자예요. 저는 당신이 저를 다시 개구리로 바꿔줘서 제가 앞으로 행복하게 살 수 있게 되기를 원해요.

➡ _____

17 마녀 1: 개구리 왕자라고 했어요? 그거 웃기는군요. 당신은 개구리처럼 보이지 않아요. 음, 그건 중요하지 않아요. 당신이 왕자라면 왕자인 거죠. 그리고 나는 당신이 백설공주를 구하도록 놔두지 않을 거예요. 여기, 이 사과의 나머지를 먹어요.

➡ _____

_____

18 왕자: 고맙지만 됐어요. 그건 제가 원하는 게 아니에요! (도망간다)

➡ _____

19 (왕자와 마녀 2가 등장한다.)

➡ _____

20 왕자: 마녀님, 마녀님. 어디 계세요? 저 좀 도와주세요! 저는 개구리 ….

➡ _____

21 마녀 2: 당신이 개구리라면 나는 프랑스의 왕이에요.

➡ _____

22 왕자: 아니요, 저는 개구리가 아니에요. 저는 개구리 왕자예요. 하지만 저를 다시 개구리로 바꿔 줘서 제가 앞으로 행복하게 살 수 있게 해 줄 마녀가 필요해요. 그렇게 해 주실 수 있나요?

➡ _____

_____

23 마녀 2: 안에서 그것에 관해 이야기해 봅시다. 내가 당신에게 맛있는 점심을 대접할게요. 들어와요.

➡ _____

24 왕자: 저를 초대해 주셔서 감사합니다. 오, 이 집은 과자와 사탕으로 만들어져 있네요. 잠깐만요. 당신은 헨젤과 그레텔이라는 이름의 아이들을 혹시 알아요?

➡ _____

_____

25 마녀 2: 그래요, 왕자님, 알고 있어요. (그녀가 군침을 흘리면서) 그 애들은 아직 충분히 살이 찌지 않았지만, 당신은 ….

➡ _____

26 (왕자는 도망치다가 요정을 발견한다.)

➡ _____

27 왕자: 만나게 되어 기쁩니다, 요정님. 저는 개구리 왕자예요. 저를 다시 개구리로 바꿔 앞으로
행복하게 살 수 있게 해 주실 수 있나요?

➡ _____

_____

28 요정: 음, 저는 신데렐라를 만나러 가는 길이지만, 한번 해 볼게요. 아시다시피 이건 제가 처음으로
해 보는 거예요. (요정이 왕자를 바퀴로 바꾼다.)

➡ _____

_____

29 요정: 이런! 미안하지만 걱정하지 마세요. 모든 게 잘될 거예요

➡ _____

30 왕자: (혼잣말로) 오, 내가 얼마나 바보였던가! 앞으로 행복하게 살면서 집에서 공주와 함께 앉아
있고 싶구나. 하지만 대신에 여기 이 수레 아래에 붙박여 있고 앞으로 불행하게 살게 되겠구나.

➡ _____

_____

31 (시계가 12시를 치자 바퀴가 왕자로 바뀐다.)

➡ _____

32 왕자: 믿을 수가 없네. 두 번째 기회를 주셔서 감사합니다. 이제 나는 내 인생을 어떻게 살아야
할지 알겠어요. (퇴장한다)

➡ _____

_____

33 요정: (손을 흔들며) 좋은 교훈을 배웠군요. 행운을 빌어요.

➡ _____

34 장면 3: 개구리 왕자의 집 안에서

➡ _____

35 (왕자가 미소를 지으며 뛰어 들어온다.)

➡ _____

36 공주: 어디 있었어요? 걱정했잖아요. 옷이 엉망진창이네요.

➡ _____

37 왕자: (공주를 바라보며) 당신은 세상 어느 누구도 나를 믿지 않을 때 나를 믿어 주었어요. 당신은
내가 개구리일 때조차도 나를 사랑해 주었죠. 이제부터는 내가 당신을 더 행복하게 해 주겠어요.

➡ _____

_____

38 공주: 그 말을 들으니 기뻐요. 제가 당신을 훨씬 더 행복하게 해 줄게요.

➡ _____

39 왕자: 좋아요! 난 우리의 밝은 미래를 기대할게요. 하하….

➡ _____

40 (그들은 서로 손을 잡고 함께 연못으로 뛰어간다.)

➡ _____

MEMO

적중100 plus
1학기 전과정
영어 기출 문제집

영어 기출 문제집

적중100 plus
1학기 전과정

1학기

정답 및 해설

천재 | 정사열

중 **3**

적중100

영어 기출 문제집

1학기

정답 및 해설

천재 | 정사열

중 **3**

Express Your Feelings

시험대비 실력평가
p.08

01 book   02 ④   03 ⑤   04 ①
05 stands for   06 ③   07 (f)inally   08 ④

01 '미래의 특정 시간에 좌석, 방, 공연자 등을 갖도록 준비하다'라는 의미로 'book(예약하다)'가 적절하다.

02 우리가 농담을 듣거나 우스운 것을 보거나 행복감을 느끼면 소리 내어 웃는다는 내용으로 보아 '웃음(laughter)'에 관한 것임을 알 수 있다.

03 '구입되거나 사용될 수 있는'의 뜻으로 available이 적절하다.

04 소수의 사람들 또는 단지 두 명의 사람들이 관여한 비공식적인 이야기

05 'stand for'는 '…을 상징하다'라는 뜻으로, 주어가 3인칭 단수이므로 stand에 -s를 붙인다.

06 (A) 이모티콘 XD는 우리의 행복한 감정을 하하와 LOL보다 더 시각적으로 표현한다(express). (B) 급행열차(express)는 정시에 런던을 출발했다.

07 유의어 관계다. 기회 - 마침내

08 (A) 사람들이 이모지를 사용하고 있다는 말 다음에 많은 웃는 이모지가 온라인에서 사용될 수 있다는 말이 적절하다. (B) 그래서 사람들이 다양한 방식으로 웃음을 표현한다.

서술형 시험대비
p.09

01 written, means, since
02 (1) Actually   (2) meaningful   (3) facial
03 (1) various   (2) emojis   (3) typed
04 (1) guess, 추측하다   (2) tone, 어조, 말투
    (3) human, 인간의, 인간적인
05 (t)ext

01 "하하"는 문자로 된 웃음의 한 형태이다. 모두가 그것이 무엇을 의미하는지 알고 있다. 실제로 그것은 오래전부터 사용되어 왔다. 셰익스피어조차도 "하하"를 자신의 작품에 사용하였다.

02 (1) '사실, 슬퍼. 너희 모두를 그리워할 거야.' actual은 형용사로 -ly를 붙여 부사로 만들어 주어야 한다. (2) '그에게 뭔가 의미 있는 것을 준다니 기뻐.' -thing으로 끝나는 대명사는 형용사가 뒤에서 수식한다. 동사 mean을 형용사 meaningful로 바꾸어 준다. (3) '웃음 표시는 우리의 얼굴 표정을 나타내고 우리의

목소리 어조를 전달할 수 있다.' 명사 expression을 수식하는 형용사가 필요하다. face의 형용사 형태인 facial이 적절하다.

03 (1) 다양한: various (2) 이모지: emoji (3) 타자 치다: type, 문장은 수동태로 과거분사 typed로 바꾸어야 한다.

04 (1) '모든 사실을 가지고 있지 않아서 당신이 옳은지 확신할 수 없을 때 특정 질문에 대답을 하다'라는 의미로 '추측하다 (guess)'가 적절하다. (2) '특히 특정한 감정을 표현하는 누군가의 목소리의 특질'이란 의미로 '어조, 말투(tone)'를 나타낸다. (3) '동물과는 반대로 사람 또는 사람에 관계되거나 소속되어 있는'의 뜻으로 '인간의(human)'가 적절하다.

05 text: 글, 문자 메시지

Conversation

핵심 Check
p.10~11

1 ④   2 ③

교과서 대화문 익히기

Check(√) True or False
p.12~13

1 T   2 F   3 T   4 T   5 T   6 F   7 T   8 F

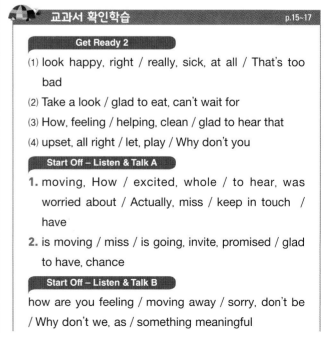

교과서 확인학습
p.15~17

Get Ready 2
(1) look happy, right / really, sick, at all / That's too bad
(2) Take a look / glad to eat, can't wait for
(3) How, feeling / helping, clean / glad to hear that
(4) upset, all right / let, play / Why don't you

Start Off – Listen & Talk A
1. moving, How / excited, whole / to hear, was worried about / Actually, miss / keep in touch / have
2. is moving / miss / is going, invite, promised / glad to have, chance

Start Off – Listen & Talk B
how are you feeling / moving away / sorry, don't be / Why don't we, as / something meaningful

---

시험대비 기본평가　　　　　　　p.18

01 How are you feeling today?

02 ⑤　　　03 ④　　　04 was worried about

---

01 How are you feeling?은 '기분이 어떠니?'라는 뜻으로 상대방의 기쁨이나 슬픔 등의 감정에 대해 물을 때 사용하는 표현이다.

02 몇몇 학생들이 학교 청소하는 것을 돕고 있어서 아침에 기분이 아주 좋다는 말에 대한 응답으로 그 말을 들으니 기쁘다는 말이 적절하다.

03 G가 정말로 슬프다고 말하고 있으므로 '닭튀김을 먹게 되어 기뻐!'라고 말하는 ④번은 자연스럽지 못하다.

04 '~에 관해 걱정하다'는 의미로 'be worried about'을 사용한다.

시험대비 실력평가　　　　　　　p.19~20

01 ②　　　02 ④　　　03 I'm sorry to hear that.

04 ①　　　05 I wonder how high it can fly.

06 ⑤　　　07 ①　　　08 ④

09 (n)ervous　10 ④　　　11 ③

---

01 G의 두 번째 말에서 '그 말을 들으니 기쁘구나.'라고 말하는 것으로 보아 Jihun은 새로운 나라로 가게 되어 슬픈 것이 아니라 기쁘거나 신나다는 것을 짐작할 수 있다. sad를 'happy' 또는 'excited'로 바꾸어야 한다.

02 B의 '좋아. 자주 화상 채팅하자.'는 마지막 말로 미루어 보아 빈칸에는 '온라인으로 계속 연락하자.'는 말이 자연스럽다.

03 상대방의 말에 대해 유감을 나타내는 표현으로 'I'm sorry to hear that.'을 사용한다. 여기서 to hear는 '~해서'의 의미를 가지는 부정사의 부사적 용법이다.

04 B가 '생일 선물을 받아서 정말 기뻐.'라고 말하는 것으로 보아 빈칸에는 B의 기분을 묻는 말이 자연스럽다.

05 동사 wonder의 목적어 자리에 사용된 간접의문문으로 'how+형용사/부사+주어+동사' 어순으로 써야 한다.

06 'I'm sorry to hear that.'은 상대방으로부터 좋지 않은 소식을 들은 후, '그것 참 안됐구나.'라고 유감이나 동정을 표현하는 말이다.

07 than이 있으면 앞 문장에는 비교급 형태가 있어야 한다. happy를 happier로 바꾸어야 한다.

08 지호가 VTS 콘서트 표를 어떻게 예매하게 되었는지는 대화에 언급되어 있지 않다.

09 '어떤 것에 대해 걱정하거나 두려워하고, 긴장을 풀지 못하는'의 뜻으로 'nervous(초조한)'가 적절하다.

10 감정을 묻는 말에 (C) 가장 좋아하는 음식을 요리하게 되어 기쁘다는 말이 오고 → (D) 그것이 무엇인지 알고 싶다는 말에 → (B) 잡채라는 답이 오고 → (A) 좀 먹어 보고 싶다는 말에 좋다며 30분 동안 기다리라는 말이 적절하다.

11 친한 친구가 외국으로 떠난다는 말에 '그 말을 들으니 기뻐.'라고 답하는 ③번은 적절하지 않다.

서술형 시험대비　　　　　　　p.21

01 She thinks they are cute.

02 I'm happier than ever

03 (A) how are you feeling?
(B) Really? I'm sorry.
(C) Why don't we make him a photo book as a goodbye gift?

04 this drone, which our grandpa sent for my birthday

05 I can't wait for lunch break.

---

01 질문: '나리는 이모지에 대해 어떻게 생각하는가?' - '나리는 그것이 귀엽다고 생각한다.'

02 '어느 때보다'라는 의미로 비교급이 적절하다. happy의 비교급 happier than ever를 사용한다.

04 계속적 용법의 관계대명사는 콤마(comma)를 관계대명사 앞에 사용한다. 목적격 관계대명사이므로 뒤에 '주어+동사'를 사용한다.

05 대화의 흐름상 '점심시간이 무척 기다려져.'라는 의미가 되도록 'can't wait for ~'를 사용한다.

3

핵심 Check   p.22~23

1 (1) who he is   (2) where he comes from
(3) how old he is
2 (1) who   (2) which   (3) who

시험대비 **기본평가**   p.24

01 (1) Tell me what the name of your school is.
(2) I'd like to know where your English teacher comes from.
(3) Can you tell me how much this bag is?
(4) I'd like to know why you are feeling sad.
02 (1) where → which   (2) that → which
(3) where did Ann spend her vacation → where Ann spent her vacation
(4) why was he → why he was
03 (1) Tell me when your birthday is.
(2) I didn't know what she majored in.
(3) Do you know what the most famous online game is these days?

01 간접의문문은 '의문사+주어+동사'의 순서로 쓴다.
02 (1) 주격 관계대명사가 계속적 용법으로 쓰인 문장이므로 which를 쓰는 것이 적절하다. (2) 관계대명사의 계속적 용법에서는 'that'은 사용되지 않는다. (3), (4) 간접의문문은 '의문사+주어+동사'의 순서로 쓴다.
03 간접의문문은 '의문사+주어+동사'의 순서로 쓰고, 반드시 의문사를 제외한 문장의 주어와 동사는 평서문의 형태로 되돌려야 한다. these days: 요즘

시험대비 **실력평가**   p.25~27

01 ②   **02** ④   **03** ②   **04** ③
05 ⑤   **06** ⑤
07 whom Amy met after a big soccer game
08 ④
09 (1) I wonder how many books you need.
(2) Tell me why he invented the machine.
10 I'm going to show you the photo, which my friend, Amy, sent to me.
11 ④   **12** (1) they (2) which (3) which
(4) which (5) which
13 how many pencils we need to bring for the next class

14 Can you tell me why you want to become a scientist?
15 I have an older sister, who is studying music in New York.
16 ④   **17** ②   **18** ②   **19** ②
20 (1) Do you know? What does the color red mean?
(2) My best friends are Ken and Mary. They are nice and smart.
(3) I wonder. How often does Mary meet Ken?
21 ③

01 'what time'이 하나의 의문사구이다. 그러므로 'Can you tell me what time it is?'로 쓰는 것이 적절하다.
02 'Can you tell me' 다음에 의문사구 'how many hours'를 함께 쓰고 나머지 부분을 평서문의 형태로 바꿔야 한다. 이 경우는 의문사를 맨 앞으로 보내지 않는다.
03 계속적 용법으로 쓰인 주격 관계대명사 자리이고 선행사가 사람이므로 'who'를 쓴다.
04 모두 관계대명사 'who'가 적절하지만 ③번은 선행사가 앞의 절 전체이므로 'which'를 쓴다.
05 첫 번째 문장에서는 그가 필통을 놓은 장소를 묻는 의문사 'where'가 적절하고, 두 번째 문장에서는 동사 got의 목적어가 필요하므로 'what'이 쓰여야 한다.
06 ①~④번은 의문사 'who'이다. ⑤는 계속적 용법으로 사용된 관계대명사이다.
07 '관계대명사+주어+동사'의 어순으로 쓴다.
08 'Do you know?'의 목적어로 간접의문문을 쓴다. 의문사가 없는 의문문은 whether+주어+동사의 어순으로 쓴다.
09 (1) 'how many books'가 하나의 의문사구이다. (2) 간접의문문이므로 '의문사+주어+동사'의 어순이 된다.
10 선행사 'the photo'를 설명하는 계속적 용법의 관계대명사 'which'를 사용하여 두 문장을 하나로 연결한다.
11 I wonder의 목적어로는 간접의문문을 쓰는 것이 자연스럽다. 의문사가 없는 간접의문문이 적절하므로 'that' 대신 'whether'를 쓴다.t to eat이 적절하다.
12 (1) 두 절을 연결하는 접속사 'and'가 있으므로 'who'를 쓰지 않는다. (2) 선행사가 'a song'이므로 who가 아닌 which가 적절하다. (3) 주어 역할을 하는 관계대명사가 필요하므로 which를 쓴다. (4) 선행사가 앞의 절 전체이므로, 'which'를 사용한 관계대명사의 계속적 용법으로 문장을 쓴다. (5) 계속적 용법의 관계대명사를 쓸 때는 'that'을 쓰지 않는다.
13 간접의문문 how many pencils(의문사구), we(주어), need to bring(동사) 순서로 쓴다.
14 Can you tell me의 목적어로 간접의문문을 '의문사+주어+동사'의 순서로 쓴다.
15 an older sister를 계속적 용법의 관계대명사를 사용하여 부연

16 관계대명사가 부연 설명하는 것이 June이 아니라 a camera이
   므로, 'who'가 아닌 'which'로 써야 한다.

17 첫 번째 문장에서는 Nancy를 설명하는 계속적 용법의 관계대
   명사 'who'를 써야 한다. 두 번째 문장에서는 your parents'
   favorite food를 질문하는 의문사 'what'을 써야 한다.

18 선행사 'Nancy'를 관계사절 'who will throw a birthday
   party tomorrow'가 꾸며 주는 형태가 자연스럽다.

19 ②에서 관계대명사가 설명하는 내용은 앞의 절 전체이므로 관계
   대명사 'which'를 써야 한다.

20 (1), (3) '의문사+주어+동사' 순서의 간접의문문을 직접의문문
   의 어순인 '의문사+동사+주어'로 바꾼다. (2) 계속적 용법의 '관
   계대명사는 접속사와 선행사의 대명사로 이루어져 있다.

21 첫 번째 빈칸은 의문사구 'how high'가 필요하고, 두 번째 빈칸
   은 this drone을 설명하는 계속적 용법의 관계대명사 'which'
   가 적절하다.

서술형 시험대비 p.28~29

01 (1) Do you know why Mira is smiling?
   (2) What do you think my dad is cooking?
   (3) How do you guess she found out the answer?
   (4) I want to know what made him happy.
   (5) I wonder how much time they spend studying.
02 (1) I wonder how you made the doll.
   (2) Do you know when the movie starts?
   (3) Can you tell me what you said to her?
03 (1) Minsu got a drone from his grandpa, who lives
       in Busan.
   (2) He is cooking *japchae*, which he likes the
       most.
04 (1) Do you know how old he is?
   (2) The girl is Amy, who enjoys cooking.
   (3) Look at this guitar, which I gave to Amy for her
       birthday.
   (4) The cute dog is Lucky, which likes catching
       balls.
   (5) Do you know when he came to Korea?
05 I want to learn what he does in his free time.
06 (1) tell me where you live
   (2) when the next bus will come
07 c. it → which / d. who → which / e. tells → tell
08 (1) She met my sister, who lives in Hawaii.
   (2) He is dancing with Nancy, who is 20 years
       old.
   (3) He is happy to get a cat, Milky, which is white
       like milk.

(4) Do you know why the boy is happy?
(5) What do you guess Mr. Lee is doing?
09 (1) When does the game start?
   (2) I want to know where she went last night.
   (3) I wonder who broke the glasses.
   (4) Can you tell me what color you like?

01 (1), (5) 주절 뒤에 간접의문문을 '의문사+주어+동사'의 어순으
   로 쓴다. (2), (3) 주절이 'Do you think[guess]'인 경우 간접
   의문문의 의문사는 문두로 보내진다. (4) 의문사가 주어인 경우
   에는 의문사 뒤에 바로 동사가 이어진다.

02 (1), (2), (3) 의문사가 있는 간접의문문은 '의문사+주어+동사'
   의 순서로 쓴다.

03 (1) 접속사 and와 대명사 he를 결합하여 선행사 his grandpa
   를 설명해 주는 관계대명사절 'who lives in Busan'으로 쓴다.
   (2) 접속사 and와 대명사 it을 결합하여 선행사 japchae를 설
   명해 주는 관계대명사절 'which he likes the most'로 쓴다.

04 (1) 의문사구 'how old'를 함께 써야 한다. (2) 관계대명사의
   계속적 용법에서는 'that'은 쓰지 않는다. (3) 목적격 관계대명
   사가 사용된 문장이므로 관계사절에 목적어 'it'은 쓰지 않는다.
   (4) 선행사가 단수 명사이므로 주격 관계대명사 뒤에 이어지는
   동사는 선행사의 수에 맞추어야 한다. (5) 간접의문문은 '의문
   사+주어+동사'의 어순으로 쓴다. 조동사 'did'는 사용하지 않는
   다.

05 직접의문문이 간접의문문이 될 때 의문사를 쓴 후 조동사
   do(does/did)를 없애고 평서문의 형태로 써야 한다.

06 (1), (2) Can you tell me 다음에 목적어로 간접의문문을 '의문
   사+주어+동사'의 어순으로 배열한다.

07 c. 한 문장에서 두 개의 절이 사용되었으므로, 두 개의 절을 연
   결하는 접속사 또는 접속사와 대명사 it을 결합한 관계대명사
   'which'를 써야 한다. d. 관계대명사가 설명하는 것이 Mary가
   아닌 Mt. Halla이므로 관계대명사 'which'를 써야 한다. e. 선
   행사가 'those guys'이므로 관계대명사 다음에 이어지는 동사
   는 'tell'로 써야 한다.

08 (1) 선행사가 my sister이므로 관계대명사 다음에 이어지는 동
   사를 'lives'로 써야 한다. (2) 한 문장에 두 개의 절이 사용될 경
   우, 두 개의 절을 연결하는 접속사 또는 접속사와 대명사를 결합
   한 관계대명사를 써야 한다. (3) 계속적 용법의 관계대명사로는
   'that'을 사용하지 않는다. (4) 간접의문문이므로 '의문사+주어
   +동사'의 어순이 되어야 한다. (5) 'Do you think[suppose,
   guess, believe]'에 뒤따르는 간접의문문은 의문사를 문두로
   보내야 한다.

09 간접의문문은 '의문사+주어+동사'의 순서로, 직접의문문은 '의
   문사+동사+주어'의 어순으로 쓴다. 이때 직접의문문에서 일반
   동사가 쓰인 경우 '의문사+조동사 do(does/did)+주어+동사원
   형'을 써야 한다. 간접의문문은 그 반대로 조동사 do(does/did)
   를 없애고 평서문의 형태로 써야 한다.

Reading

확인문제   p.30

1 T   2 F   3 F   4 T   5 F

확인문제   p.31

1 T   2 F   3 T   4 F   5 T   6 F

교과서 확인학습 A   p.32~33

01 How, Texts   02 human

03 laugh out loud

04 laugh even in our writings

05 How   06 written laughter

07 what it means   08 has been used

09 in his works   10 gentlemen, good

11 anything important   12 Act, Scene

13 written laughter   14 stands for

15 Rolling on the Floor Laughing

16 can be typed   17 Have a safe trip

18 Make sure   19 miss u

20 wishing me a safe trip   21 represents

22 with, open, closed tightly   23 a word

24 used to represent a facial expression

25 more visually   26 can't wait to

27 face with tears of joy   28 called

29 available to use, various ways

30 hit my head   31 okay

32 on the cupboard   33 okay

34 have grown, laughing sounds

35 break wind   37 just did it

39 with my earphones

40 facial expressions, voice tones

41 care for, with them 42 Laugh, and

43 cold out   44 This was

교과서 확인학습 B   p.34~35

1 How Do You "Ha-Ha" in Your Texts?

2 Laughter is human.

3 We laugh out loud when we hear a joke, see something funny, or feel happy.

4 We laugh even in our writings, such as emails or texts, as we do in our conversations.

5 How do we do that?

6 "Ha-ha" is a form of written laughter.

7 Everyone knows what it means.

8 Actually, it has been used since long ago.

9 Even Shakespeare used "ha-ha" in his works.

10 DOGBERRY: Ha, ha, ha! Well, gentlemen, good night.

11 And if anything important happens, find me and let me know.

12 (Shakespeare, Much Ado About Nothing Act 3, Scene 3, Page 4)

13 Another form of written laughter is LOL.

14 It stands for "Laughing Out Loud."

15 People also use ROFL quite often, which means "Rolling On the Floor Laughing."

16 These expressions have become popular because they can be typed quite quickly.

17 A: Have a safe trip 2mrw.

18 Make sure u don't miss me too much. LOL

19 B: OK. I'll try to make sure I don't miss u. LOL.

20 Thanks for wishing me a safe trip.

21 XD also represents laughter in text.

22 It shows a laughing face with a mouth open and eyes closed tightly.

23 XD is not a word.

24 It's an emoticon, which is a group of letters or symbols used to represent a facial expression.

25 The emoticon XD expresses our happy feelings more visually than ha-ha and LOL do.

26 I can't wait to go to Disneyland. XD

27 These days, people use 😂 — a "face with tears of joy."

28 This is a small picture called an "emoji."

29 Lots of laughing emojis are available to use online, so people can express their laughter in various ways.

30 A: I hit my head on the cupboard.

31 B: Oh, my! Are you okay?

32 A: I hit my head on the cupboard. 😂

33 B: Uh-oh! Is the cupboard okay? 😂

34 Some emojis have grown bigger, and some even move or make laughing sounds.

35 A: So yesterday, I was in a restaurant, and I really needed to break wind. 💨

36 B: And …

37 A: Well, the music was really loud, so I just did it.

38 B: And …

39 A: And then I realized I was listening to music with my earphones.

40 Laughing marks can represent our facial expressions and deliver our voice tones.

41 By using various laughing marks, we can show our friends how much we care for them or how happy we are with them.

42 Laugh, even in written forms, and your friends will laugh with you.

43 Me when it's cold out

44 This was me yesterday

시험대비 실력평가

p.36~39

01 closing → closed   02 ③   03 ④

04 ⑤   05 ④   06 ③

07 laughing emoji   08 ④

09 calling → called

10 (A) an emoji (B) Is the cupboard okay

11 be typed 12 ②   13 quite quickly

14 Everyone knows what it means.

15 "ha-ha"   16 written laughter

17 break wind 18 ⑤

19 (2) 번 ⓐ loud ⓑ his earphones

20 ④   21 ②, ⑤

22 express our happy feelings   23 ③

24 like   25 ②   26 laugh out loud

01 눈이 '감겨지는' 것이므로 closed로 고치는 것이 적절하다.

02 ⓑ와 ②, ⑤: 부사적 용법, ①, ④: 명사적 용법, ③: 형용사적 용법

03 무슨 이모티콘이 우리의 행복한 감정을 가장 효과적으로 표현할 수 있는지는 대답할 수 없다. ① It represents laughter in text. ② It shows a laughing face with a mouth open and eyes closed tightly. ③ It is a group of letters or symbols used to represent a facial expression. ⑤ XD does.

04 (A)와 ⑤: ~하는 것처럼, ~하듯이(접속사), ① ~이기 때문에 (접속사), ② (as ~ as ...로 형용사·부사 앞에서) …와 같은 정도로 (as ~ as ...에서, 앞의 as는 지시부사, 뒤의 as는 접속사), ③ ~하는 동안에(접속사), ④ ~로서(전치사)

05 앞의 내용을 추가해서 설명하고 있으므로 Actually가 가장 적절하다. ① 그러므로, ③ 대신에, ⑤ 즉, 다시 말해서

06 '우리는 이메일이나 문자 메시지 같은 글 속에서조차 대화에서 하듯이 웃는다'고 했다.

07 그것은 '웃는 이모지'이고, '기쁨의 눈물을 흘리는 얼굴'이라고 불린다.

---

08 '이모지'는 작은 그림이라고 했으므로 ④번이 적절하다.

09 '이모지'라고 불리는 작은 그림이라고 해야 하므로, 과거분사 called로 고치는 것이 적절하다.

10 이모지를 사용한 대화 (2)가 이모지를 사용하지 않은 대화 (1) 보다 더 시각적으로 웃음을 전달한다. 게다가 두 번째 대화에서 여자는 '너 괜찮니?'라는 말을 '찬장 괜찮니?'라는 말로 대체함 으로써 더 재미있게 유머러스한 분위기를 표현한다.

11 주어 they가 These expressions를 가리키므로 수동태로 쓰는 것이 적절하다.

12 위 글의 첫 문장이 '또 다른 형태의 문자로 된 웃음은 LOL이 다.'로 시작하므로, 이 글의 앞에는 '문자로 된 웃음의 형태'에 대한 소개가 있었다고 하는 것이 적절하다.

13 이 표현들은 사람들이 '상당히 빠르게' 타자 칠 수 있어서 인기를 얻었다.

14 동사 'know'의 목적어로, 의문문 "What does it mean?"을 간접의문문으로 바꿔 쓴 문장이다.

15 "하하"를 가리킨다.

16 우리는 글 속에서 "하하"와 같은 '문자로 된 웃음'의 형태를 사용 할 수 있다.

17 break wind: 방귀를 뀌다, 장에서 가스를 내보내다

18 음악이 정말 시끄러워서 그냥 방귀를 뀌었는데, 자신이 이어폰 을 끼고 음악을 듣고 있다는 걸 깨달았으므로 A의 심경으로는 '당황한'이 적절하다. ① 실망한, ② 편안한, ③ 상쾌한, ④ 기 쁜, ⑤ 당황스러운, 쑥스러운

19 그럴 수 없었다. 그가 식당 안의 음악이 정말 '시끄럽다'고 생각 하면서 방귀를 뀌었을 때, 실제로는 그가 '이어폰'을 끼고 음악을 듣고 있었기 때문이다.

20 XD는 얼굴 표정을 나타내기 위해 사용되는 이모티콘이므로, 하 하와 LOL보다 우리의 행복한 감정을 더 '시각적으로' 표현한다 고 하는 것이 적절하다. ③ 간접적으로

21 (A)와 ②, ⑤: [부대상황을 나타내는 구를 이끌어] …한 채로, …하면서, 'with+명사+형용사'가 다른 동작이나 행위를 할 때 의 상황 설명으로 쓰여서 '…(명사)가 ~(형용사)한 채로'의 의미 가 된다. ① …와 함께, ③ …을 가진, ④ …로, …을 써서[이 용하여]

22 do는 'express our happy feelings'를 받은 대동사이다.

23 can't wait to 동사원형: …하기를 몹시 바라다, 어서 빨리 … 하고 싶어 하다, look forward to ~ing: ~을 고대하다, be eager[anxious/dying] to 동사원형: ~하고 싶은 생각이 간절 하다, ③ unwilling: 꺼리는, 싫어하는

24 such as = like: ~와 같은

25 이 글은 '우리가 이메일이나 문자 메시지 같은 글 속에서조차 대 화에서 하듯이 웃는다.'는 내용의 글이므로, 제목으로는 '글에서 "하하"라고 웃을 수 있나요?'가 적절하다.

26 농담이나 우스운 광경 혹은 행복감은 우리를 '소리 내어 웃게' 만 들 수 있다.

01 (A) happy   (B) do   (C) since
02 laugh even in our writings
03 laughter
04 It stands for "Rolling On the Floor Laughing."
05 It shows a laughing face with a mouth open and eyes closed tightly.
06 LOL and ROFL are → An emoticon is 또는 a group of letters or symbols used to represent a facial expression → forms of written laughter
07 like   08 our friends
09 If you laugh, even in written forms, your friends will laugh with you.
10 (A) how much   (B) how happy
11 They can represent our facial expressions and deliver our voice tones.
12 represents
13 Have a safe trip tomorrow. Make sure you don't miss me too much.
14 (A) (the emoticon) XD   (B) ha-ha and LOL

01 (A) 감각동사 feel의 보어로 형용사를 써야 하므로 happy가 옳다. (B) laugh를 받는 대동사를 써야 하므로 do가 옳다. (C) 'long ago'는 과거의 기점을 나타내는 말이므로 since가 옳다. for+기간
02 대화에서 하듯이 '글 속에서조차 웃는다'를 가리킨다.
03 우리는 우스운 것이나 행복을 경험할 때 '웃음'을 터뜨릴 뿐만 아니라, "하하"와 같은 문자로 된 '웃음'의 형태를 사용함으로써 글 속에서도 웃음소리를 표현할 수 있다. burst into laughter: 웃음을 터뜨리다
04 ROFL은 '바닥을 구르면서 웃기'를 의미한다.
05 with를 보충하면 된다. 'with+명사+형용사'가 다른 동작이나 행위를 할 때의 상황 설명으로 쓰여서 '…(명사)가 ~(형용사)한채로'의 의미가 된다.
06 '이모티콘'은 얼굴 표정을 나타내기 위해 사용되는 한 무리의 문자나 상징이다. 또는 LOL과 ROFL은 '문자로 된 웃음의 형태들'이다.
07 care for: 좋아하다
08 '우리의 친구들'을 가리킨다.
09 명령문, and ~ = If you로 문장을 시작한 다음, 콤마 다음의 and를 생략하고 나머지 부분을 쓰면 된다.
10 다양한 웃음표시를 사용하는 것은 우리가 친구들을 '얼마나' 좋아하는지 또는 그들과 함께 있어서 '얼마나 행복한지'를 그들에게 보여 줄 수 있게 해준다.
11 웃음 표시는 '우리의 얼굴 표정을 나타내고 우리의 목소리 어조를 전달할 수' 있다.
12 stands for = represents: …을 의미하다, 상징하다, 나타내다

13 2mrw = tomorrow, u = you
14 만약 당신이 당신의 행복한 감정을 더 시각적으로 표현하기를 원한다면, '하하와 LOL'보다 '이모티콘 XD'를 사용하는 것이 낫다. It would be better for you to ~ than to …: …하는 것보다 ~하는 것이 낫다

01 whole   02 ④   03 ⑤   04 ①
05 present   06 ①   07 ②   08 ⑤
09 ③
10 I'm glad to find someone who feels the same.
11 ⑤   12 ④   13 ①
14 which → who
15 (1) He has two cats which are black.
  (2) He has two cats, which are black.
  (3) I saw a child who was wearing a yellow cap.
  (4) I saw a child, who was wearing a yellow cap.
16 ②   17 ③   18 who
19 (1) Can you tell me why you want to be a teacher?
  (2) Please tell me what your new science teacher is like.
20 ②   21 ①, ⑤   22 ③
23 because[as] they can be typed quite quickly
24 that → which   25 ③   26 ②
27 ②
28 Can you guess why Mira is smiling?
29 and, him

01 반의어 관계다. 인기 있는 : 인기 없는 = 전체의 : 일부분의
02 (a) 웃음 표시는 우리의 얼굴 표정을 나타내고 우리의 목소리 어조를 전달할 수 있다. (b) 많은 웃는 이모지가 온라인에서 사용될 수 있고, 그래서 사람들은 다양한 방식으로 자신들의 웃음을 표현할 수 있다.
03 '말하기 보다는 쓰기와 관련된'의 의미로 '쓰여진'이 적절하다.
04 '감정을 나타내기 위해 이메일 등에서 사용되는 얼굴 표정을 나타내는 일련의 짧은 키보드 기호'
05 (A) 만약 여러분이 착하게 지냈다면, 산타는 내일 멋진 선물을 줄 거예요! (B) 그룹을 이룬 학생들은 어떻게 특정 문제에 대한 그들의 결론에 이르게 되었는지를 발표할 것입니다. present는 명사로 '선물', 동사로 '발표하다, 제시하다' 등의 의미로 사용된다.
06 book은 동사로 사용될 때 '예약하다'로 사용된다.
07 엄마가 방과 후에 축구하는 것을 허락하지 않는다는 말로 기분이 언짢아 보인다가 적절하다.
08 민수의 기분을 묻는 말에 → (C) 매우 신난다고 답하고, → (D) 왜 신났는지 묻는 말에 → (B) 새로 온 학생이 그의 학교

축구팀이었고 자신의 팀에 축구 선수가 필요하다는 대답이 오고 → (A) 그 말을 들으니 기쁘다는 대답이 오는 것이 자연스럽다.

09 B가 초조하다고 말하고 있으므로 '수학 숙제 가져오는 걸 잊어버렸어.'라는 말이 가장 자연스럽다.

10 글의 흐름상 A와 B가 둘 다 초조함을 느끼고 있기 때문에 '같은 감정을 가진 사람을 찾아서 기뻐.'라는 의미가 되도록 주어진 단어를 배열한다.

11 They는 Minsu와 Yujin을 가리키고, 그들이 광선 막대기와 카메라를 가지고 온다는 말은 Nari가 이모지가 귀엽고 나는 그들의 이모지가 마음에 든다는 말 다음에 오는 것이 자연스럽다.

12 민수와 유진이는 광선 막대기와 카메라를 가지고 올 거라고 나리가 말하고 있다.

13 주절이 'Do you think'일 때 간접의문문의 의문사는 맨 앞으로 보내진다.

14 선행사 the Reds는 한국 축구팀을 응원한다는 내용으로 보아 사람을 의미한다.

16 간접의문문은 '의문사+주어+동사'의 순서로 쓰고, 반드시 의문사를 제외한 문장의 주어와 동사는 평서문의 형태로 되돌려야 한다.

17 a. 주절이 'Do you think'일 때 간접의문문의 의문사는 맨 앞으로 보내지므로 'Where do you think they will go?'로 쓴다. c. 간접의문문은 평서문의 어순이어야 하므로 'Did you ask me where he went?'로 쓴다. e. 선행사 'a watch'를 'which was broken'으로 설명해 주는 것이 자연스럽다. Minji가 선행사가 아니다.

18 첫 번째 문장은 간접의문문의 의문사 'who'가 필요하고, 두 번째 문장은 선행사 'a man'을 설명하는 계속적 용법의 관계대명사 'who'가 필요하다.

19 간접의문문의 어순인 '의문사+주어+동사'의 형태로 쓴다.

20 뒤에 such as emails or texts가 나오므로, 우리는 '글' 속에서조차 웃는다고 하는 것이 적절하다.

21 ⓑ와 ①, ⑤: 계속 용법, ②, ④: 경험 용법, ③ 완료 용법

22 이 글은 '우리가 이메일이나 문자 메시지 같은 글 속에서조차 대화에서 하듯이 웃는다.'는 내용의 글이므로, 주제로는 '우리는 글 속에서조차 웃을 수 있다.'가 적절하다. laugh: (소리 내어) 웃다

23 주어 they가 These expressions를 가리키므로, 수동태로 쓰는 것이 적절하다.

24 관계대명사 that은 계속적 용법으로 쓸 수 없기 때문에 which로 고치는 것이 적절하다.

25 XD는 알파벳 X와 D가 아니라, 입을 벌리고 눈을 질끈 감은 채 웃는 얼굴을 보여 주는 이모티콘이다.

26 이 글은 '웃음 표시의 역할'에 관한 글이다. ① pros and cons: 찬성과 반대, ③ the weak point: 약점

27 웃음 표시는 우리의 목소리 어조도 전달할 수 있다.

28 Can you guess 다음에 간접의문문 순서로 쓰는 것이 적절

하다. Why can you guess Mira is smiling?(×): 동사가 guess인 경우에도 Yes/No로 대답할 수 있으면 의문사를 guess 다음에 써야 한다.

29 계속적 용법의 관계대명사는 '접속사+대명사'로 바꿀 수 있다.

단원별 예상문제
p.48~51

01 various   **02** ②   **03** I'm glad to hear that.
04 (1) to have video chats online
    (2) to make Jihun a photo book as a goodbye gift
05 I'm glad to give him something meaningful.
06 ④   **07** ③   **08** ⑤   **09** ②
10 ③, ⑤
11 (1) Do you know where Tom worked last year?
    (2) She made chocolate cookies for me, which were very delicious.
    (3) I met Sue, who gave me a free ticket.
12 (1) Do you know what the color red means?
    (2) This is the uniform of the Reds, who cheer for the Korean soccer team.
13 written   **14** ②   **15** ⑤   **16** facial
17 and it   **18** ③   **19** the cupboard
20 ③, ④   **21** ③
22 It's a small picture which is available to use online.
23 how much we care for them or how happy we are with them
24 ④

01 유의어 관계이다. 기회 - 다양한

02 다른 무언가를 나타내기 위해 사용되는 표시, 모양 또는 물체

03 Minsu의 축구팀이 새로운 선수를 필요로 하는 상황에 새로 전학 온 친구가 이전 학교에서 축구 선수였다는 것을 알고는 Minsu가 신이 나 있다. 이 상황에서 MIso가 기쁨을 표현하는 것이 적절하다.

04 (1) Yena와 Jihun이는 온라인으로 화상 채팅을 할 것이다. (2) Yena와 Seho는 Jihun이에게 이별 선물로 사진 책을 만들어 줄 것이다.

05 '~해서 기뻐'는 'I'm glad to+동사원형'을 이용하고, something은 형용사가 뒤에서 수식하므로 meaningful이 something 뒤에 와야 한다.

06 몇몇 학생들이 학교 청소하는 것을 돕고 있다고 말하고 있기 때문에 매우 기분이 좋은 상태라는 것을 알 수 있다.

07 '~에 관해 걱정하다'는 의미로 'be worried about'을 사용한다.

08 Yunju는 Jjhun이가 이사를 가게 되어 기쁜 것이 아니라, Jihun이가 완전히 새로운 나라에 가게 되어 흥분된다는 말을 들

고서 안심이 되어 기쁘다고 말했다.

09 (A): 내 개가 아프다는 말에 대해 유감을 나타내는 표현이 적절하다. (B) '닭튀김을 먹게 되어 기뻐!'라고 말하고 있으므로 기대감을 나타내는 표현이 적절하다.

10 두 개의 절을 하나로 연결하는 접속사 'and'와 주어 'he'가 필요하고 두 단어를 하나로 합치면 'who'로 쓸 수 있다.

11 (1) 간접의문문은 '의문사+주어+동사'의 순서로 쓰고, 반드시 의문사를 제외한 문장의 주어와 동사는 평서문의 형태로 되돌려야 한다. (2) 선행사가 복수 명사 'chocolate cookies'이므로 관계대명사 뒤에 이어지는 동사도 복수형으로 써야 한다. (3) 내용상 순서대로 일어난 상황이므로 주절과 관계사절의 시제를 일치시킨다.

12 (1) Do you know의 목적어로 간접의문문을 '의문사+주어+동사'의 어순으로 쓴다. (2) 선행사 'the Reds'를 설명하는 계속적 용법의 관계대명사를 선행사 뒤에 이어 쓴다.

13 '문자로 된' 웃음이라고 해야 하므로 'written'이 적절하다.

14 ⓑ와 ②: 작품(명사), ① (어떤 직장에서) 일하다(동사), ③ 공장, 제작소(명사), 종종 works로 단수 취급함, ④ (기계 장치 등이) 작동되다(동사), ⑤ (기계의) 움직이는 부분, 장치(명사)

15 '셰익스피어조차도 "하하"를 자신의 작품에 사용하였다'고만 되어 있다.

16 face의 형용사 facial을 쓰는 것이 적절하다.

17 계속적 용법의 관계대명사는 '접속사+대명사'로 바꿀 수 있다.

18 이 글은 문자로 된 웃음 형태인 LOL, ROFL과 문자 메시지에서 웃음을 나타내는 이모티콘인 XD를 사용하여 글 속에서 웃음을 표현하는 방법들을 설명하는 글이므로, 제목으로는 '글에서 어떻게 웃음을 표현할까'가 적절하다.

19 '너 괜찮니?'라는 말 대신 '찬찬 괜찮니?'라는 말을 사용함으로써 더 유머러스한 분위기를 표현할 수 있다.

20 (A)와 ③, ④: 부사적 용법, ①, ⑤: 명사적 용법, ②: 형용사적 용법

21 a few를 various로 고치는 것이 적절하다.

22 '이모지'는 온라인에서 사용될 수 있는 작은 그림이다.

23 with를 보충하면 된다.

24 '어떤 종류의 웃음 표시를 사람들이 가장 좋아하는지'는 대답할 수 없다. ① They can represent our facial expressions. ② They can deliver our voice tones. ③ We can show our friends how much we care for them or how happy we are with them. ⑤ Yes. If we laugh even in written forms, our friends will laugh with us.

서술형 실전문제   p.52~53

01 (A) Some students are helping me clean the school.
   (B) My mom won't let me play soccer after school.

02 why are you excited?

03 (1) He booked four tickets for the VTS concert.
  (2) They sent messages with emojis.

04 (1) She wrote a poem about love. / who wrote a poem about love
  (2) The letter cheered him up. / which cheered him up

05 (1) and he   (2) and it   06 has been used

07 laugh   08 (A) writings (B) conversations

09 (A) be typed (B) open (C) used

10 quite quickly

01 (A) 'help+목적어+동사원형' 구문을 사용한다. (B) 'let+목적어+동사원형' 구문을 사용한다.

02 Minsu가 자기 반에 새 학생이 한 명 와서 정말 신난다고 말하고 있다. Miso 입장에서는 새 학생이 와서 Minsu가 신난 이유를 물어보는 것이 자연스럽다.

03 (1) 지호는 왜 행복한가? (2) 민수와 유진이는 지호에게 무엇을 보냈는가?

04 두 문장을 연결해 주는 접속사와 앞 문장의 선행사와 같은 명사를 결합하여 관계대명사로 연결한다. 선행사가 사람인 경우는 'who', 사물인 경우는 'which'를 쓴다.

05 계속적 용법으로 쓰인 관계대명사는 '접속사+대명사'로 바꾸어 쓸 수 있다.

06 현재완료 수동태로 쓰는 것이 적절하다.

07 laugh를 받는 대동사이다.

08 그것은 우리가 '글' 속에서조차 '대화'에서 하듯이 웃기 위해 사용하는 문자로 된 웃음의 한 형태이다.

09 (A) 주어 they가 These expressions를 가리키므로 수동태인 be typed가 옳다. (B) 입이 열려 있는 것이므로 open이 옳다. open: 열려 있는, with a mouth open: 입을 벌리고, (C) 얼굴 표정을 나타내기 위해 '사용되는' 한 무리의 문자나 상징이라고 해야 하므로 used가 옳다. used는 과거분사로, 뒤에서 명사를 수식하는 형용사 역할을 한다.

10 사람들은 "Laugh Out Loud"라는 전체 글자를 쓰는 대신 LOL을 사용함으로써 그들의 글에서 상당히 빠르게 웃음을 표현할 수 있다.

창의사고력 서술형 문제   p.54

|모범답안|

01 A: How are you feeling? B: I'm happy. I got a good grade. / A: How are you feeling? B: I'm angry. Someone broke my glasses. / A: How are you feeling? B: I'm sad. My brother is sick in bed.

단원별 모의고사

p.55~58

01 ④	02 bottom	03 ②	04 ④
05 ⑤	06 ③	07 ④	

08 They will bring light sticks and a nice camera.

09 happier, booked, messages, bring light sticks and a nice camera

10 How are you feeling 또는 How do you feel

11 ③	12 ④	13 ①	14 ⑤

15 who is one of the most famous artists of our time

16 ②	17 ①	18 ⑤	19 ②, ⑤

20 these expressions　　　21 which[that] are

22 ③	23 ②, ④	24 ③, ⑤

25 broke wind

01 ④번의 '어떤 것을 의미하는 것으로 받아들여지다'는 'represent'에 대한 설명이다.

02 반의어 관계이다. 일부분의 : 전체의 - 맨 위의: 밑바닥의

03 보는 것 또는 시력과 연결되는 식으로

04 B의 기분이 언짢아 보이고 괜찮은지 묻는 말에 어울리는 대답을 찾는데, 다음에 나오는 G의 '그녀에게 한 번 더 말씀드려 보지 그러니?'라는 말로 미루어 보아 ④번이 적절하다.

05 빈칸 다음의 Yunju의 대답이 그 말을 들으니 기쁘다고 했기 때문에 ⑤번이 적절하다.

06 기분을 묻는 말에 가장 좋아하는 음식을 요리해서 지루하다고 답하는 것은 어색하다.

07 주어진 문장은 '그들이 정말로 기쁘다고 말했어.'라는 내용으로 그들에게서 메시지를 받았다는 말 다음에 오는 것이 적절하다.

08 민수와 유진이는 VTS 콘서트에 무엇을 가지고 올 것인가?

10 상대방의 기쁨이나 슬픔 등의 감정에 대해 물을 때 사용하는 표현으로 'How are you feeling?'이나 'How do you feel?'을 사용한다.

11 Jihun이가 아부다비로 이사 가서 기분이 어떤지 Minsu에게 물어보고 → (B) 슬프다는 감정을 표현한 다음 지훈이가 그리울 거라는 말 다음에 → (C) 본인도 또한 슬프다고 공감하고, 하지만 아부다비를 방문할 수 있다는 기쁨의 표현에 → 마지막으로 (A) 굉장하다며 새로운 나라로 여행할 기회를 얻게 되어 기쁘다는 말이 오는 것이 적절하다.

12 이별 선물로 Jihun에게 사진 책을 만들어 주자는 제안에 좋은 생각이라고 동의하고 있으므로 빈칸에는 ④가 적절하다.

13 ② I wonder what went wrong. ③ Do you know what I mean? ④ I don't know whether he can do it. ⑤ Tell me who broke the window.

14 의문사가 주어인 경우에는 의문사 뒤에 바로 동사가 이어지며, 주절이 'Do you think'일 때 간접의문문의 의문사는 맨 앞으로 보내진다.

16 ② 간접의문문에서 의문사구 'how high'를 함께 써야 한다.

17 '~인지'의 의미를 가진 의문사가 없는 간접의문문이 들어가야 하므로 'whether'가 적절하다.

18 주어진 문장의 it에 주목한다. ⑤번 앞 문장의 "Ha-ha"를 받고 있으므로 ⑤번이 적절하다.

19 actually = in fact = as a matter of fact: 실제로, 사실, ① 아마, ③ 정확히, 꼭, 틀림없이, ④ 특히

20 '이 표현들(LOL과 ROFL)'을 가리킨다.

21 used 앞에는 '주격 관계대명사+be동사'가 생략되어 있다. used는 과거분사로, 뒤에서 명사를 수식하는 형용사 역할을 하며 'a group of letters or symbols'를 수식하고 있다.

22 이 글은 문자로 된 웃음 형태인 LOL, ROFL과 문자 메시지에서 웃음을 나타내는 이모티콘인 XD를 사용하여 글 속에서 웃음을 표현하는 방법들을 설명하는 글이므로, 주제로는 ③번 '우리는 LOL, ROFL, XD를 사용함으로써 글에서도 웃음을 표현할 수 있다'가 적절하다.

23 grow[become/get]+비교급: 더 ~해지다

24 ③과 ⑤의 내용은 언급되어 있지 않다.

25 '방귀를 꾸었다'를 가리킨다.

Let's Make Our Town Better

시험대비 실력평가   p.62

01 sneeze   02 ④   03 ③   04 ⑤
05 divided, into   06 ②
07 fix[repair]   08 ①

01 '재채기(sneeze)를 할 때, 공기와 종종 작은 액체 방울들이 갑자기 코와 입에서 여러분이 통제할 수 없는 방식으로 나온다.'

02 그 호텔은 끔찍했다! 우선, 우리 방이 너무 작았다.

03 불평하다: 무언가 잘못되었거나 만족스럽지 않다고 말하다

04 양로원: 병들고 매우 나이 든 사람들이 살고 의학 치료와 돌봄을 받는 곳

05 'A를 B로 나누다"는 'divide A into B'를 사용한다.

06 (A) 못 생긴 식품은 멋진 비주얼의 모습을 지니고 있지 않은 과일과 야채이다. (B) 중국과 미국의 친선 농구 경기가 볼썽사납게 되었다.

07 유의어 관계이다. 끈, 줄 : 수리하다

08 • 최근, Hawking이 충격적인 아이디어를 제안해서 세계를 놀라게 했습니다. • 흥미롭게도, 작은 다채로운 무지개가 하늘에 걸려 있습니다!

서술형 시험대비   p.63

01 (1) pot (2) heavy (3) hanging (4) corner
02 divide
03 leaders, set up, board, leaders, popular
04 (1) kitchen,부엌 (2) dust, 먼지
   (3) admit, 인정하다 (4) suggest, 제안하다
05 (1) (m)ess (2) (s)weaty (3) (s)neezed
   (4) (n)ewspaper

01 (1) 그 여자는 화분을 창문 옆에 두었다. (2) 무거운 상자는 꼼짝도 하지 않는다. (3) Jason은 벽에 그림을 걸고 있다. be동사 뒤에 현재분사(hanging) 형태가 적절하다. (4) 이 상자를 구석에 두자.

02 '부분 또는 그룹으로 분리하다'라는 의미로 divide가 적절하다.

03 class leader: 학급 반장, set up: 설치하다, 세우다, board: 판, popular: 인기 있는

04 (1) '음식이 보관, 준비, 조리되고, 설거지를 하는 방' (2) 건물

내부의 표면을 덮는 분말 형태의 건조한 오물 또는 매우 작은 건조한 토양, 모래 또는 기타 물질 조각 (3) 특히 내키지 않게 무언가가 사실이라는 것에 동의하다 (4) 자신이 무엇을 해야 하는지, 어디로 가야 하는지 등에 대한 당신의 생각을 누군가에게 말하다

05 (1) 내 침실이 너무 지저분해서 엄마가 나에게 방을 청소하라고 말씀하셨다. (2) 여름이 너무 덥고 땀이 많이 나기 때문에 그녀는 여름을 싫어한다. (3) 왜 재채기할 때 입을 막지 않았니? (4) 아빠는 매일 아침 신문을 읽으신다.

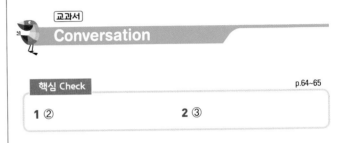

교과서 Conversation

핵심 Check   p.64~65

1 ②   2 ③

교과서 대화문 익히기

Check(√) True or False   p.66

1 T   2 F   3 F   4 T

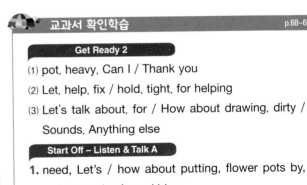

교과서 확인학습   p.68~69

Get Ready 2
(1) pot, heavy, Can I / Thank you
(2) Let, help, fix / hold, tight, for helping
(3) Let's talk about, for / How about drawing, dirty / Sounds, Anything else

Start Off – Listen & Talk A
1. need, Let's / how about putting, flower pots by, make, prettier / good idea
2. hanging / Why don't you bring, painting / Thank, for saying, bring, mine
3. about, corner, Any / How about making, corner, bring / suggesting

Start Off – Listen & Talk B
Don't / Let's talk, together / put, member, helpful for us to learn, members' / plan, school year / help, remember / suggesting

talk about, better / Let, trash / agree, Why don't we / bench / helpful, the elderly / How about putting, make, more beautiful / suggesting, shall we

Let's talk / Why don't we / Thank, for

1. coming, talk about / under, most, cleaned, planted / popular, among

2. school gate, What do you think of / leaders set up, put up, a lot, events / Let's thank

시험대비 기본평가　　　　　　　　p.70

01 Thank you for helping me.

02 ④　　　03 ⑤　　　04 ②

01 '~해서 고마워하다'라는 표현으로 'Thank you for 동명사/명사'를 사용한다. 동사 help를 동명사 helping으로 바꾸어야 한다.

02 '~하는 게 어때?'라는 제안의 표현으로 적절하지 않은 것은 ④번이다. 'Why didn't we draw ~?'는 '왜 우리가 지저분한 벽에 그림을 그리지 않았니?'라는 의미의 의문문이다.

03 깨끗한 학교 프로젝트에 대한 대화로 나무 아래의 모퉁이 주변을 청소하고 나무를 심었다는 말이 가장 자연스럽다.

04 '누가 샌드위치를 만들 것인가'에 대한 의견을 묻는 말에 '내가 하겠다.'고 말한 것으로 보아 자원해 줘서 고맙다는 대답이 가장 자연스럽다.

시험대비 실력평가　　　　　　　　p.71~72

01 ④　　　　02 (A) making　(B) suggesting

03 Let me help you fix the bench.

04 (h)elpful　05 ③　　06 ⑤　　　07 ②

08 ④　　　　09 What do you think of it?

10 set up the board　　11 Why don't you

12 my pictures　　　　13 take → bring

01 '~에 관해 이야기하자'라는 표현으로 'Let's talk about ~'을 사용한다.

02 (A)와 (B)는 모두 전치사 뒤에 오는 말로 동명사나 명사 형태가 적절하다. 동사 make와 suggest를 모두 동명사로 바꾸어 준다.

03 '…가 ~하도록 하게 하다'라는 표현으로 'Let+목적어+동사원형'을 사용한다. 그리고 '…가 ~하는 것을 도와주다'라는 표현으로 'help+목적어+동사원형'을 이용하여 영작한다.

04 '상황을 개선하거나 쉽게 만드는 데 유용한 도움을 제공하는'의 뜻으로 'helpful(유용한, 도움이 되는)'이 적절하다.

05 벽을 어떻게 꾸밀 것인지에 대해 여러 의견을 제시해 준 것에 대해 고마워한다는 표현이 적절하다.

06 'Let's talk about ~'은 '~에 대해서 말해 보자'라는 뜻으로 함께 대화하고자 하는 주제를 소개할 때 쓰는 표현이다.

07 위 대화의 내용으로 보아 마을을 더 좋게 만드는 방법에 대해 이야기 나누고 있다는 것을 알 수 있다.

08 벤치 위에 무엇을 둘 것인지는 대화에서 언급되어 있지 않다.

09 '~에 관해 어떻게 생각하니?'는 'What do you think of ~?'를 사용한다.

10 질문: 학급 반장들은 판에 포스터를 붙이기 전에 무엇을 했는가?

11 제안하는 표현으로 'Why don't you+동사원형~?'을 쓸 수 있다.

12 밑줄 친 'mine'은 소유대명사로서 앞 문장의 'my pictures'를 가리킨다.

13 take: 가져가다, 휴대하다 bring: 가져오다, (사람을) 데려오다

서술형 시험대비　　　　　　　　p.73

01 They will put some flower pots around the bench.

02 Why don't we clean the place together?

03 (A) Let's talk about it together.
(B) We also need our plan for this school year on the wall.
(C) Thank you for suggesting great ideas, everyone.

04 How about making a small library in the corner of the club room?

01 질문: '그들은 버스 정류장을 더 아름답게 만들기 위해 무엇을 할 예정인가?' - '그들은 벤치 주변에 몇 개의 화분을 놓을 것이다.'

02 '~하는 게 어때?'라는 표현은 'Why don't we+동사원형 ~?'을 이용한다.

03 (A) '~에 관해 말해 보자'라는 뜻으로 함께 대화하고자 하는 주제를 소개할 때 쓰는 표현이 적절하다. (B) 빈칸 다음에서 G가 '우리가 중요한 학교 행사를 기억하는 데 정말 도움이 될 거야'라고 말하는 것으로 보아 '이번 학년 계획도 필요하다'라는 말이 적절하다. (C) 대화의 마지막에 '좋은 의견을 내줘서 고맙다'라는 말이 적절하다.

04 '~하는 게 어때?'라는 의견을 제시할 때 사용하는 표현으로 'How about+-ing(동명사)?'를 사용한다. 동사 'make'를 동명사 'making'으로 바꾸어 준다.

Grammar

p.74~75

핵심 Check

1 (1) had (2) had left (3) turned
2 (1) much (2) a lot (3) very

시험대비 기본평가

p.76

01 (1) was much more difficult than I expected
   (2) dogs much more than cats
   (3) where you had put the box
   (4) the house had been newly painted
02 (1) My teacher was looking at the pictures that her students had drawn.
   (2) When I arrived at the station, the train had just left.
   (3) I jumped much[far, even, a lot] higher than he did.
   (4) He grew far taller than his father.
03 (1) When I entered the classroom, my friends had prepared for my birthday party.
   (2) When I got up, my husband had eaten all the sandwiches.

01 (1), (2) 비교급을 강조할 때 'much+비교급+than' 순서로 쓴다. (3), (4) 과거보다 더 이전의 일은 'had+과거분사'로 나타낸다.
02 (1) 그녀의 학생들이 그림을 그린 것은 능동이므로 과거완료 능동태(had+과거분사)로 쓴다. (2) 내가 역에 도착한 것보다 기차가 떠난 것이 그 이전의 일이므로 과거완료로 쓴다. (3) 비교급 강조할 때는 'many'를 사용하지 않는다. (4) 'far'는 비교급을 강조하는 단어이고 'than' 또한 비교급과 같이 써야 하므로 tall의 비교급 taller를 쓴다.
03 과거의 특정 시점보다 더 이전에 일어난 일이나 그 때까지 지속된 상태를 나타낼 때 과거완료시제 (had+과거분사)를 사용한다.

시험대비 실력평가

p.77~79

01 ④   **02** ⑤   **03** ③   **04** ②
05 ③   **06** ③
07 he had already fixed my bike   **08** ③
09 (1) When Jiyeon came back home, she found that her mother had already set the table for her.
   (2) He is much cooler than you think. I'm sure you will like him.
10 ⑤   **11** ④
12 (1) had (2) left (3) even (4) harder (5) a lot

13 ②
14 looks even younger than her daughter
15 She behaved much more kindly than I had expected.
16 (1) had cooked (2) had washed (3) had fixed
17 ③
18 He was surprised that he hadn't locked the door.
19 ③   **20** ⑤   **21** ③

01 비교급을 강조할 때는 'much/far/even/still/a lot+비교급'의 형태로 쓴다. 'really, very, many' 등은 쓸 수 없다.
02 선생님이 말씀하신 것보다 미국 남북전쟁이 더 이전의 일이지만 역사적 사실은 과거완료로 쓰지 않고 항상 과거로 쓴다. had been → was
03 ①, ⑤ 동사를 수식하는 부사구 'a lot' ②, ④ 비교급을 강조하는 'a lot' ③ 명사를 수식하는 'a lot of'
04 'I'가 알게 되기 전부터 'she'가 아팠기 때문에 두 문장을 합쳤을 때 그녀가 아픈 것은 과거완료로 쓰고 알게 된 것은 과거시제로 쓴다.
05 ③은 비교급을 강조하는 'much'이고, ①, ②, ④, ⑤는 셀 수 없는 명사를 수식하는 형용사 'much'이다.
06 눈사람을 만든 것이 눈사람을 파괴한 것보다 더 이전이고, 눈사람을 꾸며주는 관계대명사절이 수동이 되어야 하므로, 'destroyed - had been made'가 적절하다.
07 already는 had와 p.p 사이에 위치한다.
08 내가 소리를 지른 것보다 내 동생이 이어폰을 고장 낸 것이 더 이전의 일이므로 'had yelled'는 'yelled'로, 'broke'는 'had broken'으로 써야 한다.
09 (1) Jiyeon이 집에 온 것보다 어머니가 상을 차린 것이 더 이전의 일이므로 과거완료 'had already set'으로 써야 한다. (2) cool의 비교급은 'cooler'이므로 'much cooler'로 써야 한다.
10 빈칸에는 과거완료를 완성시킬 과거분사가 필요하므로 과거형 took은 적절하지 않다.
11 New York으로 이사 온 것보다 LA에 산 것이 더 이전의 일이므로 이사 온 것은 과거(moved)로, LA에 산 것은 과거완료 (had lived)로 쓴다. ②는 접속사 after의 쓰임이 어색하다.
12 (1) 과거완료가 적절하므로 'had'를 사용한다. 'get up'을 수동태로 쓰는 것은 적절하지 않다. (2) 과거완료를 완성해 줄 had 뒤에 과거분사가 필요하므로 'left'가 적절하다. (3) 비교급 'younger'는 'even'과 함께 쓰는 것이 적절하다. 'so'는 비교급과 쓰지 않는다. (4) 비교급을 강조하는 much가 있으므로 'harder'를 쓰는 것이 적절하다. (5) 비교급 'nicer'는 'a lot'과 쓰는 것이 적절하다.
13 'a lot'은 비교급을 강조하는 단어로 비교급 more difficult 앞에 위치하는 것이 적절하다.
14 비교급을 강조하는 'even'을 비교급 younger 앞에 넣어 문장을 완성한다. more young으로 쓰지 않도록 주의하고, 'many'는 비교급을 강조할 때 쓰지 않는다.
15 그녀가 행동한 것보다 내가 예상한 것이 더 이전이므로 과거완

료 'I had expected'로 쓴다. 행동이 훨씬 더 친절하다고 했으므로 'more kindly' 앞에 비교급을 강조하는 'much/far/even/still/a lot'을 쓴다.

16 Mr. Han이 집에 돌아오기 전에 있었던 일들을 과거완료 시제로 쓴다.

17 첫 번째 문장은 비교급을 강조하는 'much/far/even/still/a lot' 중 하나를 써야 하며, 셀 수 없는 명사 interest와 어울리는 것은 'much'이다.

18 놀란 것보다 문을 잠그지 않은 것이 더 이전이므로 놀란 것은 과거(was surprised)로, 잠그지 않은 것은 과거완료(hadn't locked)로 쓴다.

19 early의 비교급은 earlier이다. much more early → much earlier

20 비교급을 강조할 때는 'very'를 쓰지 않고 'much/far/even/still/a lot'을 쓴다.

21 a. 비교급은 그 대상이 동일한 종류이어야 한다. me → mine[my car], c. more lovely → lovelier, d. 비교급을 강조할 때 'very'는 사용하지 않고 'much/far/even/still/a lot'을 쓴다. very more handsome → much more handsome.

🦉 서술형 시험대비 p.80~81

01 (1) Did you remember where you had put the book?

(2) When I came back home, I found somebody had broken in.

(3) Did you notice the house had been newly painted?

(4) I lost my bag (that) Mom had bought for me.

(5) When I entered the classroom, I found my teacher had already left the classroom.

02 much more beautifully

03 (1) look much more comfortable than the others

(2) much cheaper than the hand bag

04 (1) Eric played the violin much better.

(2) You should work a lot harder.

05 (1) It is raining a lot harder than yesterday.

(2) Your book is even easier to read than anything else.

(3) This book looks much more difficult than that one.

06 had never visited

07 (1) Tony threw away the gift that Jack had sent to him by mistake.

(2) Yuna showed me the notebook that she had written down a poem on.

08 (1) Jack lost the umbrella that his friend had lent to him.

(2) When I called her, she had already gone to sleep.

(3) Before I got to the theater, the movie had already finished.

(4) When I arrived at the airport, the plane had already left.

(5) Did you eat the pie that Dad had baked?

09 (1) had cleaned (2) healthier (3) called

(4) had lost (5) had gone

---

01 (1) 기억한 것보다 책을 놓은 것이 더 이전이므로 간접의문문으로 두 문장을 연결하면서 'did you put'을 'had put'으로 바꾼다. (2) 집에 들어온 것보다 누군가 침입한 것이 더 이전이므로 'broke in'을 'had broken in'으로 바꾼다. (3) 집이 칠해진 것이 알아차린 것보다 더 이전이므로 'was painted'를 'had been painted'로 바꾼다. (4) 가방을 잃어버린 것보다 엄마가 사준 것이 더 이전이므로 두 문장을 관계대명사로 연결하면서 과거 'bought'를 과거완료 'had bought'로 바꾼다. (5) 교실에 들어온 것보다 선생님이 교실을 떠나신 것이 더 이전이므로 'left'를 'had left'로 바꾼다.

02 빈칸에는 부사가 필요한 자리이므로 'more beautifully'가 적절하고, 비교급을 강조하는 'much/far/even/still/a lot+비교급'의 형태로 쓴다.

03 비교급을 강조하는 문장이므로, 'much+비교급+than'의 순서로 문장을 완성한다.

04 원급을 강조할 때는 'very'를 쓸 수 있지만 비교급을 강조할 때는 'much/far/even/still/a lot+비교급'의 형태로 쓴다.

05 비교급을 강조할 때는 'much/far/even/still/a lot+비교급+than'의 형태로 쓴다.

06 그녀가 20살이 된 것(과거)보다 뉴욕에 방문한 경험이 그 이전이므로 과거완료 'had visited'를 쓴다. 'never'는 had와 과거분사 사이에 위치한다.

07 두 문장을 관계대명사를 이용하여 하나로 연결할 때 더 이전의 일은 과거완료로 쓴다.

08 (1) 우산을 잃어버린 것보다 친구가 빌려준 것이 더 이전이므로 과거완료 'had lent'로 쓴다. (2) 그녀에게 전화를 건 것보다 그녀가 잠자리에 든 것이 더 이전이므로 과거완료 'had gone'으로 쓴다, (3) 영화가 끝난 것이 과거완료이므로 극장에 도착한 것은 과거시제 'got'으로 쓴다. (4) 내가 공항에 도착한 것보다 비행기가 떠난 것이 더 이전이므로 과거완료 'had left'로 쓴다. (5) 파이를 먹은 것보다 아빠가 파이를 구운 것이 더 이전이므로 과거완료 'had baked'로 쓴다.

09 (1), (4), (5) 과거보다 더 이전의 일들은 과거완료 'had+p.p'로 쓴다. (2) 비교급을 강조하는 'much'와 비교급과 같이 쓰는 'than'이 있으므로 healthier로 쓴다. (3) 점심을 먹은 것은 과거완료 'had eaten'으로, 이후의 일은 과거시제 'called'로 쓴다.

📎 **확인문제** p.82

1 T 2 F 3 T 4 F 5 T 6 F

📎 **확인문제** p.83

1 T 2 F 3 T 4 F 5 T 6 F

교과서 확인학습 A p.84~85

01 Thumbs	02 complained
03 work, far better	
04 why we were working	05 across from
06 was full of, you can imagine	
07 I bet	08 all ages and sizes
09 this awful mess	10 where to begin
11 just to start	
12 divided, into, assigned, to	13 By lunchtime, wear
14 filled, with, were ready to	15 made us sneeze
16 At the end of	17 the toughest
18 made rows	
19 stopped complaining	20 First, the lettuce
21 so fast	22 couldn't believe
23 in size in just a few days	
24 what new flowers are ready	
25 enjoy the sights	26 hit me
27 have been a part	28 I'm in charge of
29 will go to	30 even better, that

교과서 확인학습 B p.86~87

1 Green Thumbs

2 I complained the whole day.

3 My parents were making me work on the neighborhood project, but I had far better things to do.

4 I didn't understand why we were working on this place.

5 It was just the ugly, old, empty lot across from Johnny's Shop.

6 It was full of wild plants, fast food wraps, old newspapers, broken glass, and every other kind of dirty trash you can imagine.

7 As I looked at it that first morning, I thought, "I bet there are snakes in there, too."

8 There were twenty of us — all ages and sizes — ready to work that day.

9 I didn't think that we could clean up this awful mess and turn it into a garden.

10 We were all wondering where to begin.

11 Then Mr. Hernandez said, "The only way to do it is just to start."

12 Then, he divided the lot into four parts with string and assigned five people to each part.

13 By lunchtime, I was hot, sweaty, and glad my dad had made me wear gloves.

14 We filled fifty trash bags with waste and were ready to pull wild plants.

15 As we pulled and pulled, dust filled the air and made us sneeze.

16 At the end of the day, I had to admit the lot looked much better.

17 That first day was the toughest.

18 On the weekends that followed, we made rows, planted flower and vegetable seeds, and watered them.

19 After about two weeks, I stopped complaining when I found the plants had started popping up!

20 First, the lettuce and then the beans and the tomatoes.

21 They grew so fast.

22 I couldn't believe it!

23 The bean plants grew an inch, and the tomatoes doubled in size in just a few days.

24 Now, two months later, I like to go there every day to see what new flowers are ready to pop up.

25 Lots of people in the neighborhood meet there to enjoy the sights and to talk together.

26 Tonight, it suddenly hit me — what a good thing we did!

27 I'm proud I have been a part of it.

28 I'm in charge of picking flowers for the nursing home on Fourth Street.

29 The vegetables will go to every kitchen in our town.

30 But even better, an ugly and dirty lot that people didn't like has become a pretty garden for everyone.

시험대비 실력평가 p.88~91

01 (A) complained (B) broken (C) kind 02 ③

03 filled with 04 five 05 terrific → awful

06 ②

07 (A) wondering (B) divided (C) assigned

08 ⑤   09 ②   10 ③

11 doubled in size in just a few days   12 ①

13 ④   14 good → better   15 ③

16 ④   17 ④   18 ③, ④   19 to pop

20 ⑤   21 different   22 ①, ③, ④

23 ③   24 ⑤

25 an ugly and dirty lot that people didn't like has
become a pretty garden for everyone

01 (A) the whole day는 부사구로 목적어가 아니므로 about은
불필요하다. (B) '깨진' 유리라고 해야 하므로 broken이 옳다.
(C) every 뒤에 단수 명사를 써야 하므로 kind가 옳다.

02 ③을 제외한 나머지는 모두 Johnny's Shop이 아니라, 글쓴이
가 일해야 했던 지역을 지칭한다.

03 be full of = be filled with: ~로 가득 차다

04 그 지역을 끈으로 네 구역으로 나누었기 때문에, 총 20명을 4로
나누면 한 구역 당 '5명'이라고 하는 것이 적절하다.

05 이 '끔찍하게' 더러운 곳을 청소하여 정원으로 바꾼다고 해야 하
므로 terrific을 awful이나 terrible로 고치는 것이 적절하다.
terrific: 아주 좋은, 멋진, 훌륭한, awful: 끔찍한

06 '그것을 할 유일한 방법은 그냥 시작하는 것입니다.'에 가장 잘
어울리는 속담으로는 ②번 '시작이 반이다.'가 적절하다. ① 잘
생각해 보고 행동하라[돌다리도 두드려 보고 건너라]. ③ 사공
이 많으면 배가 산으로 올라간다.(어떤 일에 관여하는 사람이 너
무 많으면 일을 망친다는 뜻.) ④ 기회를 잘 이용하라. ⑤ 안 좋
은 일은 겹쳐서 일어나기 마련이다[불운은 한꺼번에 닥친다].

07 20명의 사람들이 어디서부터 시작해야 할지 '궁금해 하고' 있을
때, Hernandez씨가 끈으로 그 지역을 네 구역으로 '나누고', 5
명을 각 구역에 '배치했다.'

08 주어진 문장의 it에 주목한다. ⑤번 앞 문장의 내용을 받고 있으
므로 ⑤번이 적절하다.

09 이 글은 불평하던 글쓴이가 자신이 재배한 식물들이 자라는
것을 보고 성취감을 느끼게 되는 경험을 얘기하고 있는 글이
므로 제목으로는 ②번 '믿을 수 없어! 나는 원예의 재능이 있
어!'가 적절하다. have a green thumb: 식물 재배를 잘하
다, 원예의 재능이 있다, green thumbs: 원예의 재능(green
fingers), ⑤ shortcut: 지름길, 손쉬운 방법

10 ⓐ와 ①, ②, ⑤: 관계대명사, ③, ④: 접속사

11 in just a few days: 며칠 만에

12 ⓐ와 ①: (사람, 일에 대한) 책임, 담당(명사), ② (상품·서비스
에 대한) 요금(명사), ③ (요금, 값을) 청구하다[주라고 하다]
(동사), ④ 비난(명사), ⑤ 돌격[공격]하다(동사)

13 'The vegetables will go to every kitchen in our town.'
이라고만 되어 있다.

14 문맥상 이웃 프로젝트에서 일하는 것보다 훨씬 더 나은 할 일들
이 있었다고 하는 것이 적절하므로, far를 very로 고치는 것보
다 good을 비교급 better로 고치는 것이 적절하다.

15 틀림없이 뱀들도 있을 것이라고 생각할 정도로 싫어하는 마음을
가지고 있는 것이므로, ③번 '꺼리는', '마지못한'이 적절하다.
① 부끄러운, ② 흥분한, ④ 기꺼이 하는, 자발적인, 열렬한, ⑤
침착한, 차분한

16 그 장소는 볼품없고, 오래되고, 텅 빈 지역이었다. ordinary: 보
통의, 평범한, ① complaint: 불평, ② have+사람+원형부정
사: ~에게 …을 하도록 시키다, ③ figure out: 이해하다

17 이 글은 불평하던 글쓴이가 자신이 재배한 식물들이 자라는 것
을 보고 성취감을 느끼게 되는 경험을 얘기하고 있는 글이므로,
주제로는 ④번 '고진감래'가 적절하다. ① 다다익선, ② 유비무
환, ③ 급할수록 돌아가라; 급히 먹는 밥이 체한다. ⑤ 안 좋은
일은 겹쳐서 일어나기 마련이다[불운은 한꺼번에 닥친다]

18 ⓐ와 ③, ④: 열[줄](명사), ①, ②: 노[배]를 젓다(동사), ⑤:
노[배]를 저어 …를 태워[데려] 주다(동사)

19 start는 목적어로 동명사와 to부정사를 쓸 수 있다.

20 ⓐ turn A into B: A를 B로 바꾸다, ⓑ assign A to B: A를
B에 배정하다

21 "모든 연령대와 몸집을 가진"은 연령과 몸집이 다 '다르다'는 뜻
이다.

22 (B)와 ②, ⑤: 명사적 용법, ①: 형용사적 용법, ③, ④: 부사적
용법

23 ③ have a light bulb go on = A light goes on in one's
head(brain): (아이디어 등이) 번득이다, 번쩍 떠오르다, ① hit
on: 불현듯 ~을 생각해 내다[떠올리다], ②와 ④: occur to =
strike: ~에게 생각이 떠오르다, ⑤ come up with: ~을 생각해
내다

24 ⓑ와 ⑤: (비교급을 강조하여) 훨씬(부사), ① …도[조차](부
사), ② (무엇의 양·득점 등이) 균등한, 동일한(형용사), ③ 짝수
[우수]의(형용사), ④ 평평한, 반반한(형용사)

25 관계대명사절인 that people didn't like가 선행사인 an ugly
and dirty lot을 수식하게 쓰는 것이 적절하다.

서술형 시험대비   p.92~93

01 I had far better things to do.

02 must / sure[certain]

03 willing → unwilling 또는 reluctant

04 (A) mess (B) wondering (C) divided

05 we should   06 assigned

07 had made   08 because of

09 (A) lot (B) lot

10 ⓐ made ⓑ planted ⓒ watered

11 the lettuce, the beans and the tomatoes

12 plants

13 an ugly and dirty lot that people didn't like has become a pretty garden for everyone

14 I'm proud of having been a part of it.

15 responsible for

16 But even better, an ugly and dirty lot people didn't like has become a pretty garden for everyone.

---

01 'far'를 비교급 앞에 써서 강조하는 것이 적절하다.

02 I bet = I'm sure[certain] that: 틀림없이 …이다, must be: ~임에 틀림없다

03 be willing to: 기꺼이 ~하다, be unwilling to: ~하는 것이 내키지 않다, be reluctant to: 마지못해 ~하다

04 (A) '더러운 곳'이라고 해야 하므로 mess가 옳다. mass: 덩어리, mess: (지저분하고) 엉망(진창)인 상태, (B) '궁금해 하다'고 해야 하므로 wondering이 옳다. wander: (이리저리 천천히) 거닐다, 헤매다, wonder: 궁금해 하다, (C) '나눴다'고 해야 하므로 divided가 옳다. decide: 결정하다, divide: 나누다

05 '의문사 to부정사'는 '의문사+주어+should'로 바꿔 쓸 수 있다.

06 assign: (일·책임 등을) 맡기다[배정하다/부과하다]

07 아버지가 나에게 장갑을 끼도록 한 것이 점심때보다 더 먼저 일어난 일이므로 과거완료로 쓰는 것이 적절하다.

08 공기를 메운 먼지 '때문에' 우리는 재채기를 했다

09 (A) lot: 지역, (B) lot 앞의 a와 합쳐서 비교급 강조(훨씬)

10 모두 과거시제로 써서 병렬구문을 만드는 것이 적절하다.

11 '상추,' '콩,' '토마토'를 가리킨다.

12 필자는 '식물들'이 자라나기 시작한 것을 발견했을 때 불평하는 것을 멈추었다.

13 '우리가 했던 좋은 일'은 '사람들이 좋아하지 않았던 볼품없고 더러운 지역이 모두를 위한 예쁜 정원이 되었다.'를 가리킨다.

14 be proud of ~ing로 고치는 것이 적절하다.

15 be in charge of: ~을 담당하다, ~을 책임지고 있다, be responsible for: ~을 책임지고[책임 맡고] 있다

16 목적격 관계대명사 that을 생략할 수 있다.

영역별 핵심문제   p.95~99

01 (a)wful	02 ⑤	03 ②	04 ①
05 green thumb		06 ④	07 ③
08 ④	09 ⑤	10 ③	11 ②

12 be helpful for us to learn the new members' names   13 ②, ③

14 Oksig is much cuter than real corn.   15 ⑤

16 (1) a lot more   (2) much better
     (3) much more popular

17 much

18 (1) Bill Gates is much richer than me[I am].
   (2) This book is even more popular than that book (is).
   (3) You dance far more gracefully than me[I do].

19 to work → work   20 ④

21 ③   22 ⑤

---

01 반의어 관계다. 채우다 : 비우다 = 멋진 : 끔찍한

02 (a) John은 파티에 초대받지 않았는데 그가 불쑥 나타나서 우리는 놀랐다. (b) 산의 풍경이 너무 아름다워서 그녀는 울었다.

03 '할 필요가 없는 일을 하겠다고 제안하다'라는 의미로 'volunteer(자원하다)'가 적절하다.

04 '서로 옆에 있는 사물이나 사람의 줄'의 의미로 'row(열, 줄)'가 적절하다. ④번의 'raw'는 형용사로 '날 것의, 요리되지 않은'의 의미이다.

05 '식물을 재배하는 데 상당한 재능이나 능력'

06 complain은 '불평하다'라는 뜻이다. '배정하다'는 'assign'이다.

07 '~하는 게 어때?'라는 제안의 표현으로 'What do you say to+V-ing(동명사)?'를 사용한다.

08 (C) 모두 와 줘서 고맙다는 말과 이야기할 주제를 소개하는 말이 오고 → (B) '깨끗한 학교 프로젝트' 중에서 나무 아래가 가장 마음에 든다는 말과 과학 동아리가 그곳을 청소하고 나무를 심었다는 말이 오고 → 마지막으로 (A) 나도 마음에 든다는 동의의 말이 오는 것이 적절하다.

09 동아리실에 관해 이야기해 보자는 대화의 주제를 소개한 후, '의견 있니?'라고 묻는 말에 좋은 생각이라고 답하는 것은 어색하다.

10 대화의 첫 문장 'Let's talk about how we can make our town better'에서 글의 제목이 언급되어 있다.

11 'Why don't we ~' 뒤에는 동사원형이 온다. 'cleaning'을 'clean'으로 바꾸어 준다.

12 주어진 단어 It'll 뒤에 동사원형 be를 사용하고 be동사 뒤에는 형용사 helpful이 온다. to부정사 앞에 의미상 주어 for us(목적격)를 사용한다.

13 ② more easy → easier ③ worse는 bad의 비교급이므로 more worse로 쓸 수 없다. more worse → much worse

14 비교급을 강조할 때에는 'even, still, far, much, a lot'을 쓴다. 'very'는 비교급 강조 역할을 하지 않는다.

15 버스를 놓친 것이 원인(더 이전의 일): because+(과거완료), 학교에 늦은 것이 결과(나중의 일): 주절 (과거)

16 비교급을 강조할 때에는 'even, still, far, much, a lot'을 비교급 앞에 쓴다.

17 두 번째 문장에서 비교급을 강조하는 'even/still/far/much/a lot' 중 하나가 필요한데, 첫 번째 문장에서 셀 수 없는 명사

'information'을 수식할 수 있는 것은 그 중에서 'much'이다. 그러므로 공통으로 들어갈 단어는 'much'가 적절하다.

18 비교급을 강조할 때에는 비교급 앞에 'even, still, far, much, a lot'을 쓴다.

19 '사역동사(making)+목적어+원형부정사'로 쓰는 것이 적절하다.

20 ⓑ와 ④: (특정 용도용) 지역[부지], ①, ③: (수양이) 많음, 다량, 다수, ② 운명, 운, ⑤ 제비뽑기, 추첨

21 very는 원급을 강조하고, 나머지는 다 비교급을 강조한다.

22 (A)와 ⑤: 쓰레기(명사), ① 낭비, 허비(명사), ② (기회 등을) 놓치다(동사), ③ 이용[활용]되고 있지 않은(형용사), ④ 낭비하다, 허비하다(동사)

23 쓰레기 봉투 50개를 쓰레기로 채운 것이 더 먼저 일어난 일이므로 과거완료로 쓰는 것이 적절하다.

24 ⓐ change A into B: A를 B로 바꾸다, ⓑ divide A into B: A를 B로 나누다

25 위 글은 '안내문'이다. notice: (보통 공공장소에 붙이는) 공고문[안내문], ① (신문·잡지의) 글, 기사, ③ (물품·책 등의) 목록, 카탈로그, ④ (책·연극·영화 등에 대한) 논평[비평], 감상문, ⑤ 광고

26 '참가 가능 연령'은 알 수 없다. ① 4월 17일, ② Johnny's Shop 건너편에 있는 텅 빈 지역, ③ 잡초들을 뽑고 그 지역을 청소함, ④ 장갑, 쓰레기 봉투

27 '약간의 꽃들'을 가리킨다.

28 글쓴이는 모두를 위한 '예쁜 정원'을 만든 것에 대해 자랑스러워한다.

단원별 예상문제
p.100~103

01 whole **02** ②
03 Thank you for volunteering. **04** ④
05 to put the club member list, for this school year
06 ③ **07** Thank you for saying that.
08 ② **09** (D) - (B) - (A) - (C) **10** ⑤
11 have → had
12 (1) after I had taken pictures of many different kinds of corn
(2) Oksig is much cuter than real corn.
13 (1) When we visited her, she said she had studied music for 5 years in Paris.
(2) It was strange that he didn't remember the movie that we had watched the other day.
(3) Walking is much more helpful for your health than running.
(4) The building is much larger than I expected.
14 ③ **15** (A) empty (B) full **16** ②

---

17 ③ **18** ① **19** A lot of, Many
20 what a good thing we did!
21 (A) a pretty garden (B) a part
22 ⓐ had drawn ⓑ had cleaned
23 (A) Art Club (B) Green Club

01 반의어 관계이다. 기억하다 - 잊다 : 부분의 - 전체의

02 어떤 것을 두 배가 되게 하다

03 감사의 표현으로 'Thank you for ~'를 사용한다. 그 다음 누가 아이들과 놀아 줄것인지 묻는 말에 B가 내가 하겠다고 말하는 것으로 보아 'volunteer'를 사용한다.

04 주어진 문장은 벽에 이번 학년의 계획이 필요하다는 내용이므로 학교 행사를 기억하는 데 도움이 된다는 말 앞인 ④번에 오는 것이 적절하다.

05 벽에 동아리 회원 목록과 이번 학년의 계획을 붙일 것이다.

06 'Don't worry about it.'은 'I'm sorry.'에 대한 대답으로 적절하다.

07 '~해서 고마워'라는 의미로 Thank you for+-ing'를 사용한다.

08 (A): 마을을 위해 무엇을 할 수 있는지에 대한 답으로 '지저분한 벽에 그림을 그리는 게 어때?'라는 제안이 적절하다. (B) '벤치를 고치는 것을 도와줄게.'라는 말에 도움을 받은 M은 감사의 말을 하는 것이 자연스럽다.

09 버스 정류장에 쓰레기가 너무 많다는 말에 → (D) 동의하고 'the place(버스 정류장)를 청소하는 게 어때?'라고 제안하는 말이 오고 → (B) '좋아'라고 말한 다음 벤치를 놓자는 말을 하고 → (A) 그것이 노인들에게 도움이 될 거라는 말 다음에, → (C) 벤치 주변에 화분을 놓자고 제안하는 말이 오는 것이 자연스럽다.

10 그들은 마을을 더 나은 장소로 만들기 위한 일을 내일 시작할 것이라고 말하고 있다. right now를 tomorrow로 바꾸어야 한다.

11 형이 집에 온 것보다 내가 설거지를 한 것이 더 이전의 일이므로 현재완료 'have done'을 과거완료로 쓰는 것이 적절하다.

12 (1) 'designed'보다 사진을 찍은 것이 더 이전의 일이기 때문에 과거완료 'had taken'을 사용하여 문장을 만든다. (2) 비교급 cuter 앞에 비교급을 강조하는 'much/still/far/even/a lot'을 '훨씬'의 의미로 사용하여 문장을 만든다.

13 (1) 그녀가 말한 것보다 그녀가 음악을 공부한 것이 더 이전에 시작된 일이므로 과거완료 'had studied'를 쓰는 것이 적절하다. (2) 주절이 과거이고 관계대명사 that절은 그 이전의 경험을 나타내는 내용이므로 과거완료 'had watched'로 쓰는 것이 적절하다. (3) Walking과 running을 비교하는 문장이므로 'helpful'을 비교급으로 써야 한다. (4) 비교급을 강조하는 어휘로 'very'를 쓸 수 없으므로 'even/still/far/much/a lot' 중에 하나를 쓴다.

14 필자는 훨씬 더 나은 할 일들이 있었는데 부모님이 이웃 프로젝

트에서 일하게 시켜서 억지로 일을 하게 된 것이라서 하루 종일 '불평했다'고 하는 것이 적절하다. ① 사과하다, ② 칭찬하다, ④ 보상하다, ⑤ 제의[제안]하다, 권하다

15 그곳은 잡초, 패스트푸드 포장지, 낡은 신문들, 깨진 유리, 그리고 상상할 수 있는 모든 다른 종류의 더러운 쓰레기로 '가득 찬' 단지 '텅 빈' 지역이었다.

16 ⓐ와 ②: 대과거 용법, ①, ④: 경험 용법, ③, ⑤: 계속 용법

17 '상추'가 제일 먼저 나왔다.

18 ①은 명사적 용법이고, 나머지는 다 부사적 용법이다.

19 A (great) number of도 가능하다. lots of = a lot of: 수와 양이 많을 때 다 사용할 수 있음.

20 '우리가 얼마나 좋은 일을 했는가!'를 가리킨다.

21 처음에 사람들은 볼품없고 더러운 그 지역을 좋아하지 않았지만 그곳이 모두를 위한 '예쁜 정원'이 되었고, 글쓴이는 그런 대단한 일을 한 것의 '일부'였다는 것에 자랑스러워한다.

22 꽃을 그린 것과 연못을 청소한 것이 날개를 그린 것과 물고기를 연못에 넣은 것보다 먼저 일어난 행동이므로 과거완료로 쓰는 것이 적절하다.

23 '미술 동아리'와 '환경 동아리' 덕분에 학교의 환경이 좋아졌다. change for the better: 좋아지다

서술형 실전문제   p.104~105

01 (A) how about putting some flower pots by the windows
   (B) Thank you for suggesting it

02 Let's talk about the volunteer work for our town.

03 (1) There is too much trash at the bus stop.
   (2) They will put a bench there for the elderly.

04 (1) ⓐthat → which (2) ⓑhave taken → had taken
   (3) ⓔthem → it

05 (1) had had (2) had told (3) had lived

06 I bet

07 why we were working on this place

08 every other kind of dirty trash that[which] you can imagine

09 to complain → complaining

10 1인치 자라났고, 토마토는 며칠 만에 크기가 두 배가 되었다

01 (A) 'How about+동명사(V-ing)?'를 사용한다. 의미상 창문 옆에 화분을 두다는 표현이 적절하므로, 'putting some flower pots by the windows'를 쓴다. (B) 감사의 표현은 'Thank you for+명사/동명사'를 이용한다. 동사 suggest는 동명사 suggesting 형태로 바꾸어 준다.

02 '~에 대해서 말해 보자'의 뜻으로 함께 대화하고자 하는 주제를

소개할 때 'Let's talk about ~'을 사용한다.

03 (1) 마을의 문제가 무엇인가? (2) 그들은 버스 정류장을 청소한 후에 무엇을 할 것인가?

04 (1) 관계대명사의 계속적 용법에서는 'that'을 사용하지 않고, 선행사가 사람이면 'who' 또는 'whom'을, 사물이면 'which'를 쓴다. (2) 주절의 동사 'designed'보다 after절의 동사가 더 이전의 일이므로 'had taken'으로 쓰는 것이 적절하다. (3) 'Oksig'을 지칭하므로 'it'으로 쓴다.

05 (1) 우리는 엄마가 집에 오시기 전에(과거) 즐거운 시간을 보냈다.(과거완료) have a good time: 즐거운 시간을 보내다 (2) 어제 나는 내 친구가 거짓말을 했다는 것을(과거완료) 알게 되었다.(과거) tell a lie: 거짓말을 하다 (3) Mark는 Irene과 결혼하기 전에(과거) 그의 가족과 함께 살았었다.(과거완료) live with one's family: 가족과 함께 살다

06 I bet = It is certain that = I'm sure[certain] that: 틀림없이 …이다

07 '의문사+주어+동사'인 간접의문문의 순서로 쓰는 것이 적절하다.

08 you can imagine 앞에 목적격 관계대명사 'that[which]'이 생략되어 있다.

09 불평하는 것을 멈춘 것이기 때문에, 동명사로 고치는 것이 적절하다. stop ~ing: ~하기를 그만두다, stop to부정사: ~하기 위해서 멈추다

10 본문의 마지막 부분을 쓰면 된다.

창의사고력 서술형문제   p.106

|모범답안|

01 (1) A: Let's talk about the class field trip. Who will take pictures of our activities?
   B: I will. I can do it well.
   A: Thank you for volunteering.
   (2) A: Let's talk about the club festival. Who will make posters?
   B: I will. I can do it well.
   A: Thank you for volunteering.
   (3) A: Let's talk about the sports day. Who will run a 100 meter race?
   B: I will. I can do it well.
   A: Thank you for volunteering.

02 (1) I had stayed up late playing games last night
   (2) he had worked out so hard
   (3) she had lost her shoes
   (4) she had already watched it before

03 (A) drew wings   (B) had drawn flowers
   (C) put some fish   (D) had cleaned

01 ①   02 (a)wful   03 ③   04 ⑤

05 ④   06 ②   07 ⑤

08 to put the club member list on the wall

09 It'll be helpful for the elderly.   10 ②

11 ②   12 ③   13 ⑤

14 (1) they had set up the board

   (2) they had cleaned the pond

   (3) they had drawn flowers

15 had never visited   16 ②

17 imaginable

18 I didn't think that we could clean up this awful mess and turn it into a garden.

19 ④   20 flower and vegetable seeds

21 ③   22 ④   23 worse → better

---

01 ①번은 '누군가에게 특정한 직업이나 일을 맡기다'라는 'assign(배정하다, 배치하다, 맡기다)'에 대한 설명이다.

02 유의어 관계이다. 불평하다 - 끔찍한

03 '다른 사람들이 고려할 아이디어, 가능한 계획 또는 행동을 언급하다'라는 의미로 suggest가 적절하다.

04 ⑤: 누가 방문객을 안내할 거니?라고 묻는 말에 '국립공원으로 가는 게 어때?'라고 답하는 것은 어색하다.

05 '그림을 좀 거는 게 어때?'라는 제안에 B의 마지막 말이 '내가 내 그림 중에서 하나를 가져올게.'라고 말하고 있으므로 빈칸에는 '그림을 가져오는 게 어때?'라는 말이 자연스럽다.

06 A의 빈칸 다음의 말이 '지저분한 벽을 누가 칠을 할 거니?'라고 묻는 것으로 보아 ②번이 가장 적절하다.

07 ⑤번은 전치사 for 뒤에 동사 suggest를 쓸 수 없다. 동명사 suggesting으로 고쳐야 한다.

08 대명사 It은 '벽에 동아리 회원들 목록을 붙이는 것'을 가리킨다.

09 인칭대명사 it(그것은)이 주어로, '도움이 될 거야'는 미래 의미로 조동사 will be helpful을 사용한다. 동사 'help'는 형용사 'helpful'로 바꾸어 준다. 마지막으로 'the+형용사'는 복수명사로 '어르신들'의 의미로 'the elderly'를 쓴다.

10 나머지는 모두 '~하자, ~하는 게 어때?'라는 의미의 제안을 할 때 사용하는 표현이다. ②번은 'let+목적어+동사원형' 구문으로 '~가 …하도록 허락하다'라는 의미이다.

11 ① much loudly → much more loudly '비교급+than'의 형태로 써야 한다. ③ much more cheap → much cheaper ④ very bigger → much bigger 비교급을 강조하는 단어로 'very' 대신 'much/still/far/even/a lot'을 써야 한다. ⑤ much wiser → much more wisely 일반 동사 'spend'를 꾸며줄 부사의 비교급이 필요하다.

12 엄마가 그의 이름을 기억한 것보다 그를 본 적이 있는 것이 더 이전이므로 과거완료 'had seen'으로 쓰는 것이 적절하다.

13 일반동사 'work' 다음에는 부사의 비교급 'more diligently'가 필요하고 그 앞에 강조의 부사 'much'를 쓴다.

14 흐름상 알맞은 내용을 과거완료시제로 변형하여 쓴다.

15 지후는 지난달에 처음으로 그 동물원에 방문했다. = 지후는 지난달 전에는 그 동물원에 가 본 적이 없었다.(과거인 지난달 보다 이전 시제인 과거완료를 쓴다.)

16 ⓐ와 ②, ③: 형용사적 용법, ①, ④: 명사적 용법, ⑤: 부사적 용법

17 imaginable: 상상할 수 있는, 생각할 수 있는(강조하기 위하여 명사의 앞이나 뒤, 형용사의 최상급, 또는 all, every, no 다음에 쓴다.)

18 turn A into B: A를 B로 바꾸다

19 Hernandez씨는 그 지역을 끈으로 '네' 구역으로 나누었다.

20 '꽃과 채소 씨앗'을 가리킨다.

21 ⓑ와 ③: 대략, 약, ① …에 대해(무엇의 '주제'나 '연관성'을 나타냄), ② [to부정사와 함께] 막 …하려고 하여, ④ 도처에, 여기저기, ⑤ …주위[둘레]에

22 자랑스러운, 앞에 what a good thing we did!라는 말이 있으므로, ④번이 적절하다. ① 부끄러운, ② 실망한, ③ 초조한, ⑤ 속상한

23 사람들이 좋아하지 않았던 볼품없고 더러운 지역이 모두를 위한 예쁜 정원이 되었으므로, '훨씬 더 좋은 것은'이라고 하는 것이 적절하다.

Laugh First and Then Think

01 discovery　02 ②　　　03 ④　　　04 ⑤
05 were eager to finish　　06 ③
07 darkness　　　　　08 ①

01 '처음으로 어떤 것을 발견하는 행위'란 뜻의 '발견 (discovery)'이 적절하다.

02 • 그 고양이와 그 개 사이의 우정은 매우 특이하다. • 몇몇 사람들은 돼지, 이구아나 심지어 뱀과 같은 특이한 애완동물을 키운다.

03 학위를 받기 위해서 공부하는 가장 높은 수준의 교육 기관

04 배에서 일하는 사람

05 '어서 ~하고 싶어 하다'는 'be eager to+동사원형'을 사용한다.

06 (A) 7월 16일에 한국어 말하기 대회가 미국 캘리포니아에서 열렸다. (B) 그 소년은 반 학생들 앞에서 연설을 했다.

07 '형용사 – 명사' 관계이다. 형용사에 '–ness'를 붙여 명사로 만들 수 있다.

08 (A) 그 대문은 사람들이 공원에 들어가는 것을 막는다. keep+목적어+from V-ing: …가 ~하지 못하게 하다 (B) Leonardo da Vinci의 그림들은 많은 돈의 가치가 있다.

01 (1) bored　(2) repeatedly　(3) A number
　　(4) received
02 award
03 (1) navy, 해군　(2) magnet, 자석
　　(3) invent, 발명하다　(4) ceremony, 의식, 식
04 not only, but also, invention, useful enough
05 (1) (a)ccept　(2) (h)umor　(3) (e)conomics
　　(4) (f)illed　(5) (i)maginative

01 (1) 지루하지 않게 기내에 게임을 가지고 와라. 사람이 지루하다는 의미로 'get bored'를 사용한다. (2) 동사 sang을 수식하는 부사(repeatedly)가 적절하다. (3) '많은 학생들'이란 의미로 a number of students를 사용한다. (4) 과거 시점인 '지난(last) 크리스마스'가 있으므로 과거동사 received가 적절하다.

02 '업적을 기리기 위해 주어지는 상이나 기타 인정의 표시'의 의미로 award가 적절하다.

03 (1) 배와 함선으로 이루어진 군대 (2) 다른 철을 끌어당기는 금속 조각 (3) 새로운 것을 만들거나 디자인하거나 생각해 내다 (4) 특별한 전통을 가진 공식적인 공개 행사

04 A뿐만 아니라 B도: not only A but also B, 발명: invention, 충분히 유용한: useful enough

05 (1) 이 회사의 직원들은 고객들로부터 어떠한 선물도 받지 않았다. (2) 나는 유머 감각이 좋다고 생각한다. (3) 나는 은행원이 되기 위해 대학에서 경제학을 공부할 것이다. (4) 큰 상자는 가난한 사람들을 위한 따뜻한 옷으로 가득 차 있다. (5) 그 동화 작가는 상상력이 매우 풍부하다.

1 I'm really looking forward to it.
2 (D) → (B) → (C) → (A)

01 '기대하다'의 의미로 forward를 포함하는 것은 'look forward to'이다.

1 T　2 F　3 T　4 F　5 F　6 T　7 T　8 T

Get Ready 2

(1) solved a lot of, I'm sure, award / think so / keep, crossed
(2) winner, award / to get, prize / I'm sure, Good luck
(3) looking forward to / make, laugh, get the prize
(4) keep my fingers crossed

Start Off – Listen & Talk A

1. can't wait for / What, going to do / practiced, for / looking forward to / Actually, a little worried, afraid, make, mistake / Don't worry, do, job, my fingers crossed
2. take part in / m going to, end / forward, seeing / sure, win / do your best, keep my fingers crossed

Start Off – Listen & Talk B

are you coming / going, for me to try / sure, do great, keep, crossed / perform, other / sounds fun, looking forward, watching, stage

Start Off – Speak Up

looking forward to, model, ready / so, nervous / do well, keep, crossed

Step Up – Real-life Scene

field trip, talent show / like, do, jokes / looking forward to it / show, sure / worry, do great, keep my fingers crossed / Let, show, Guess / sound like / show / make, laugh out loud

Fun Time

m going to / sounds great, m really looking forward to

enter, m worried about / keep my fingers crossed

Express Yourself A

1. Can you tell me, invention / a pair of special, clean, floor / win a prize, keep

2. interesting, cutting board, feeder / not only, board but also, feeder, at the same time / idea / looking forward, using

시험대비 기본평가   p.124

01 keep my fingers crossed

02 ③   03 ⑤   04 ②

01 상대가 하는 일이 잘 되기를 기원하면서 '행운을 빌어!'라고 할 때 'I'll keep my fingers crossed (for you)!'라고 한다.

02 빈칸 뒤의 말이 결과의 접속사 so로 연결되어 '그러니 네가 상을 탈 거야.'라고 말하는 것으로 보아 빈칸은 Best Joker상을 타는 이유가 나오는 것이 타당하다.

03 그 상을 받고 싶다는 G의 말에 대한 대답으로 '네가 이번에는 그 상을 탈 거라고 확신해.'라고 말하는 것이 적절하다.

04 '준비가 됐니?'라는 말에 그런 것 같다고 말한 다음 but으로 이어지는 문장으로 보아 앞 문장과 대조되는 단어가 오는 것이 적절하다.

시험대비 실력평가   p.125~126

01 (A) seeing   (B) crossed   02 ③

03 ⑤   04 ④

05 the game Kick a Shoe and perform a funny dance with some other mothers   06 ⑤

07 I'm really looking forward to using it.

08 ④   09 ⑤   10 ④

11 I'm looking forward to your game.

01 (A) 전치사 to 뒤의 동사를 동명사로 바꾸어야 한다. (B) '동사(keep)+목적어(my fingers)+목적보어'의 5형식 구문으로 목적어와 수동의 관계일 때는 과거분사(crossed)가 적절하다.

02 소윤의 엄마가 경기에 뛰기를 원한다는 내용은 언급되어 있지 않다.

03 ⑤번은 'look forward to+동명사/명사' 형태를 취한다. watch를 watching으로 바꾸어야 한다.

04 (A)는 행운을 빌어주는 표현이다. ④번은 긴장한 상대에게 긴장을 풀어주는 표현이다.

05 'Kick a Shoe' 게임에 참가하고, 다른 엄마들과 코믹 댄스를 할 것이다.

06 빈칸 다음에 '너는 동시에 두 가지를 할 수 있어.'라고 말하는 것으로 보아 도마와 새 모이통 둘 다로 사용 가능하다는 것을 알 수 있다.

07 '~을 기대한다'의 의미로 'be looking forward to -ing'를 이용한다.

08 주어진 문장은 '내가 나의 연기의 한 부분을 보여 줄게.'라는 의미로 'Guess who?' 앞에 들어가는 것이 적절하다.

09 Jimin이 몇 번이나 장기 자랑에 참가했는지는 대화에서 언급되어 있지 않다.

10 빈칸 다음의 엄마가 '그날 무엇을 할 거니?'라는 말로 보아 ④가 가장 자연스럽다.

11 '~을 기대하고 있다'는 'be looking for+명사/동명사'를 사용한다.

서술형 시험대비   p.127

01 (A) I'm (really) looking forward to it.
   (B) I'll keep my fingers crossed!

02 He talked like his English teacher.

03 It is not only a cutting board but also a bird feeder.

04 I'm afraid I'll make a mistake.

05 I can't wait for the sports day.

01 (A) 기대를 표현하는 말은 'be looking to+명사/동명사'를 사용한다. (B) 기원을 표현하는 말은 'keep one's fingers crossed'를 사용한다.

02 질문: 대화에서 Jimin은 누구처럼 말했는가?

03 'A뿐만 아니라 B도'의 의미로 'B as well as A'는 'not only A but also B'를 사용한다.

04 빈칸 앞에 '사실은, 전 조금 걱정이 돼요.'라고 말하는 것으로 보아 '실수할까봐 겁나요.'라는 말이 적절하다.

05 '~가 기다려진다'라는 표현은 'I can't wait for+명사'를 이용한다.

p.128~129

1 (1) strong enough   (2) to win   (3) for young students

2 (1) intensely   (2) but   (3) are they

시험대비 기본평가   p.130

01 (1) popular enough to win the award

(2) are easy enough to sing

(3) brave but also very nice

(4) is not only lovely but also smart

02 (1) Their music is great enough to make their fans excited.

(2) Their fans are excited enough to cry out.

(3) Pinocchio is not only popular but also very nice.

(4) I know not only the meaning of "eager" but also the meaning of "eagerness".

03 (1) The singer is tall enough to reach the shelf.

(2) The flower is big enough to cover the woman's face.

01 (1), (2) '~할 만큼 충분히 …한'의 문장은 '형용사/부사 +enough to+동사원형'의 형태로 쓴다. (3), (4) '~뿐만 아니라 …도 역시'의 문장은 'not only ~ but also ...'의 형태로 쓴다.

02 (1) 'enough'는 형용사/부사 뒤에 위치한다. (2) 'enough' 다음에 to부정사를 쓴다. (3) 'not only ~ but also ...'에 be동사의 보어로 둘 다 형용사를 써야 한다. (4) 'not only ~ but also ...' 사이에 두 어구의 형태를 일치시킨다.

03 '~할 만큼 충분히 …한'의 문장은 '형용사/부사+enough to+동사원형'의 형태로 쓴다.

시험대비 실력평가   p.131~133

01 ⑤   02 ③   03 ④   04 ⑤

05 ⑤   06 ③

07 The room is big enough to accommodate up to 100 people.   **08** ④

09 (1) He was so diligent that he could finish the work. 또는 He is so diligent that he can finish the work.

(2) Tom as well as his parents is eating chicken. 또는 His parents as well as Tom are eating chicken.

10 The puzzle was easy enough for me to solve.

11 ①

12 (1) nice enough   (2) too   (3) to fight

(4) wear it   (5) it can run   **13** ①, ④

14 This building is strong enough to survive a heavy storm.

15 The book is interesting enough to read several times.

16 ④   **17** ⑤

18 The river is deep enough for a huge ship to sail on.

19 ③   **20** (1) lovely   (2) strong

01 enough는 형용사와 부사는 뒤에서, 명사는 앞 또는 뒤에서 수식한다. 형용사 'shy'를 앞에서 수식하는 단어로 'enough'를 사용할 수 없다. ⑤에는 'too'가 적절하다.

02 의미가 올바른 것은 ②, ③, ⑤이나 어법까지 적절하게 쓰인 문장은 ③이다. ③ 나뿐만 아니라 Oliver도 독일어를 학생들에게 가르친다. ① 나와 Oliver 둘 중 한 사람이 독일어를 학생들에게 가르친다. ② 나뿐만 아니라 Oliver도 독일어를 학생들에게 가르친다.(teach → teaches) ④ 나와 Oliver 둘 다 독일어를 학생들에게 가르치지 않는다. ⑤ 나와 Oliver 둘 다 독일어를 학생들에게 가르친다.(teaches → teach)

03 형용사 'warm'을 뒤에서 수식하면서 'to부정사'와 짝을 이루는 단어로 'enough'가 적절하다.

04 'enjoy'는 동명사를 목적어로 하는 동사이므로, 'not only 동명사 but also 동명사'의 형태로 써야 한다.

05 ①~④: (원인) 날씨가 매우 추웠다. (결과) 우리는 교실에 머물렀다. ⑤는 '날씨가 너무 추워서 우리는 교실에 머물 수 없었다.'의 뜻으로 의미가 전혀 다르다.

06 첫 번째 문장에서 접속사 'that'과 함께 쓸 수 있는 것은 'so'이다. 두 번째 문장에서 형용사 'sad'를 앞에서 수식하면서 'to부정사'와 함께 쓸 수 있는 것은 'too'이다.

07 '~할 만큼 충분히 …한'의 문장은 '형용사/부사+enough to+동사원형'의 형태로 쓴다.

08 'so+형용사/부사+that+주어+(can)+동사원형'은 '형용사/부사 +enough to+동사원형'의 형태로 문장을 전환한다.

09 (1) 주절과 that절의 시제를 맞춘다. (2) 'as well as' 앞에 있는 주어의 수에 동사를 맞춘다.

10 'enough to'를 사용하여 문장을 만들 때, 문장의 주어와 'to부정사'의 주어가 다를 경우, 부정사의 의미상 주어 'for+목적격'을 부정사 앞에 넣는다. 이때 문장의 주어가 'to부정사'의 목적어 자리에 중복되어 나타나지 않도록 목적어를 쓰지 않아야 한다.

11 'Not only ~ but also ...'가 주어로 쓰일 경우 동사의 수의 일치는 'but also'와 쓰인 주어에 맞춰야 하므로 ①의 동사 'are'를 'is'로 쓰는 것이 올바르다.

12 (1), (2) 부사 'enough'는 형용사나 다른 부사를 뒤에서 수식한다. (3) '형용사/부사+enough to+동사원형'의 형태로 문장을 쓴다. (4) that절에서는 목적어를 생략하지 않는다. (5) 접속사 'that' 다음에는 '주어+동사'의 형태가 오는 것이 올바르다.

13 ② John이 아니고 Mary가 ③ Mary와 John 둘 다 아닌 ⑤ John 또는 Mary 둘 중 한 명이

14 '~할 만큼 충분히 …한'의 문장은 '형용사/부사+enough to+동사원형'의 형태로 쓴다.

15 '~할 만큼 충분히 …한'의 문장은 '형용사/부사+enough to+동사원형'의 형태로 쓴다.

16 ④ '그는 너무 힘이 세서 그 모든 책을 나를 수 없다.'는 내용상 어색하므로 'too strong' 대신 'strong enough'를 쓰는 것이 자연스럽다. (그는 그 모든 책을 나를 수 있을 만큼 충분히 힘이 세다.) ① 그는 너무 어려서 학교에 갈 수 없었다. ② 날씨가 너무 더워서 우리는 수영장에 갔다. ③ 그녀는 진실을 지지할 만큼 용감했다. ⑤ 그 상자는 어린이가 들어 올릴 수 있을 만큼 가볍다.

17 상관접속사 'both A and B'가 주어일 때. 그 주어는 복수이다. 그러므로 동사는 'were'가 적절하고, 형용사 'hungry'를 뒤에서 수식하면서 to부정사와 함께 쓸 수 있는 단어로 'enough'가 적절하다.

18 '~할 만큼 충분히 …한'의 문장은 '형용사/부사+enough to+동사원형'의 형태로 쓴다.

19 • 그는 매우 똑똑하다. • 그는 500 조각 퍼즐을 맞출 수 있다. → '그는 500 조각 퍼즐을 맞출 수 있을 정도로 똑똑하다.'에 적절한 문장은 ③이다.

20 두 단어가 짝을 이루어 하나의 접속사 역할을 하는 상관접속사에서는, 사용된 두 어구의 형태를 일치시킨다. 첫 번째 문장은 'heavy'와 같은 형용사인 'lovely'가 적절하고, 두 번째 문장은 be동사의 보어인 형용사 'strong'이 적절하다.

서술형 시험대비

p.134~135

01 (1) Eric is not only kind but also smart.
(2) Not only Jake but also you are a student.
(3) She was not only hardworking but also honest.
(4) Not only you but also he runs fast.
(5) Not only you but also he is going to join our club.

02 (1) This invention is useful enough to make your life much easier.
(2) Your smile is bright enough to light up the classroom.
(3) You not only make us happy but also help us (to) get along well.

03 (1) You can use it as a table for playing table tennis as well as as a door.

(2) She was kind enough to show me how to use chopsticks.

04 (1) Mark visited not only his mother but also his friends.
(2) This building is strong enough to survive a heavy storm.
(3) He is tall enough to touch the ceiling.
(4) They sell not only eggs but also milk.
(5) The box is too heavy for the girl to move.

05 The water is clean enough for us to drink.

06 (1) but also as a cup holder
(2) but also for storing things
(3) but also as lights

07 (A) He is a painter as well as a teacher.
(B) She looks not only friendly but also wise.

08 (1) He is tall enough to be a basketball player.
(2) Sumin ran fast enough to get there on time.
(3) The girl was brave enough to speak in front of many people.
(4) It is warm enough to play outside.
(5) He's cheerful enough to make us feel happy.

---

01 '~뿐 아니라 …도 역시'의 문장은 'not only ~ but also …'의 형태로 쓴다. 상관접속사가 주어를 연결할 때에는 but also와 함께 쓰인 주어에 동사의 수를 맞춘다.

02 (1), (2) '~할 만큼 충분히 …한'의 문장은 '형용사/부사+enough to+동사원형'의 형태로 쓴다. (3) '~뿐 아니라 …도 역시'의 문장은 'not only ~ but also …'의 형태로 쓴다.

03 (1) 'not only ~ but also …'는 '… as well as ~'로 바꾸어 쓸 수 있다. (2) 'so+형용사/부사+that+주어+(can)+동사원형'은 '형용사/부사+enough to+동사원형'의 형태로 문장을 전환한다.

04 (1) 'not only ~ but also …'의 문장에서 but은 생략하지 않는다. (2) 'enough to+동사원형'의 형태로 쓴다. (3) 'enough tall'로 형용사 'tall'을 뒤에서 수식하면서 to부정사와 같이 쓰는 것이 자연스럽다. (4) 상관접속사를 쓸 때는 두 어구의 형태가 같아야 하는데, 'They sell milk.'가 자연스러우므로, 전치사 'to'를 쓰지 않는다. (5) 'too ~ to …'에서 문장의 주어와 to부정사의 목적어가 같을 때 그 목적어는 쓰지 않는다.

05 'enough to'를 사용해서 문장을 쓸 때 문장의 주어와 to부정사의 행위자가 다르면 to부정사 앞에 의미상 주어를 'for 목적격'의 형태로 쓴다.

06 두 단어가 짝을 이루어 하나의 접속사 역할을 하는 상관접속사는 짝을 이루는 두 어구의 형태를 일치시켜야 한다. (1) 'as an umbrella'와 'as a cup holder' (2) 'for going up and down'과 'for storing things' (3) 'as shoes'와 'as lights'

07 두 단어가 짝을 이루어 하나의 접속사 역할을 하는 상관접속사

25

에서는 사용된 두 어구의 형태를 일치시킨다. 첫 번째 문장은 직업을 나타내는 'a teacher - a painter'가 적절하고, 두 번째 문장은 동사 'look'의 보어인 형용사 'wise - friendly'가 적절하다.

08 (1) 형용사 'tall'을 뒤에서 수식하면서 to부정사와 같이 쓰려면 'enough'를 쓰는 것이 자연스럽다. (2) 'enough'는 형용사/부사의 뒤에 위치한다. (3) '그 소녀는 많은 사람들 앞에서 말할 수 있을 만큼 충분히 용감하다'라고 하는 것이 문맥상 자연스러우므로 'too'를 'enough'로 바꾸어 쓴다. (4), (5) 'enough to부정사'의 형태가 올바르다.

Reading

확인문제 p.136

1 T 2 F 3 T 4 F 5 T

확인문제 p.137

1 T 2 F 3 T 4 F 5 T 6 F

교과서 확인학습 A p.138~139

01 Ig Nobel	02 happens, backward
03 did research	04 enough to
05 Maybe	06 how about
07 one	
08 are awarded for, laugh, think	
09 by honoring the unusual, the imaginative	
10 are presented by	
11 is, filled with, laughable	12 for
13 To save, instead of	14 laugh out loud
15 won an award	
16 succeeded in floating	
17 a sense of humor	18 bring, to
19 in, for	20 keeps running away
21 Not only, but also, makes	
22 a number of, keep, from getting bored	
23 two words each	
24 an eight-year-old girl called	
25 worth less than	26 Throwing, is
27 ends with, did	28 do not receive
29 great honors like	30 a lot more fun

교과서 확인학습 B p.140~141

1 The Ig Nobel Prize

2 "What happens when you walk backward while you are carrying a cup of coffee?"

3 Han Jiwon, a Korean high school student, did research on this topic in 2015.

4 Is this research project good enough to win a Nobel Prize?

5 Maybe not.

6 But how about an Ig Nobel Prize?

7 He won one in 2017 for this fun research.

8 The Ig Nobel Prizes are awarded for discoveries that "first make one laugh and then think."

9 They were started in 1991 by AIR magazine to increase people's interest in science by honoring the unusual and the imaginative.

10 The prizes are presented by real Nobel winners in Sanders Theater at Harvard University.

11 The room is usually filled with people who are eager to cheer for the brave scientists with their "laughable" research.

12 The U.K. Navy won the Ig Nobel Prize for Peace in 2000.

13 To save money, the Navy made its sailors shout, "Bang!" instead of using real bombs.

14 Is that funny enough for you to laugh out loud?

15 Andre Geim also won an award that year.

16 He succeeded in floating a live frog in the air by using magnets.

17 "In my experience, if people don't have a sense of humor, they are usually not very good scientists," he said when he accepted his award.

18 If that still does not bring a smile to your face, how about this?

19 In 2005, Gauri Nanda won the Ig Nobel Prize in Economics for inventing an alarm clock.

20 It keeps running away until the sleeper finally gets out of bed.

21 Not only the winners' fun studies but also the ceremony for the Ig Nobel Prizes makes people laugh.

22 There are a number of interesting things that keep people from getting bored.

23 The opening and closing speeches are just two words each: "Welcome. Welcome." and "Goodbye. Goodbye."

24 If someone talks for too long, an eight-year-old girl called Miss Sweetie Poo shouts repeatedly, "Please stop! I'm bored."

25 Each winner receives ten trillion Zimbabwean dollars, which is worth less than one U.S. dollar.

26 Throwing paper planes is another fun tradition.

27 The Ig Nobel Prize ceremony ends with the words, "If you didn't win a prize — and if you did — better luck next year!"

28 The winners do not receive lots of money.

29 And the awards are not great honors like the Nobel Prizes.

30 But the Ig Nobel Prizes make science a lot more fun!

시험대비 실력평가

p.142~145

01 ⑤   02 ③   03 ④   04 ⑤

05 ③   06 shouting → shout

07 funny enough for you to laugh

08 He won it in 2000.   09 ③   10 ③, ④

11 are → is   12 ③   13 ②

14 won a prize   15 ④   16 ②

17 awarded   18 ④

19 ⑤   20 running   21 using magnets

22 (A) with   (B) did   (C) like

23 Unless you won a prize

24 (A) Ig Nobel   (B) Nobel   (C) Ig Nobel

25 ③   26 The Ig Nobel Prizes

27 ⓐ unusual people   ⓓ imaginative people

01 ⓐ on: ~에 관하여, ⓑ for: (이유·원인을 나타내어) ~으로

02 ③번 다음 문장의 But에 주목한다. 주어진 문장의 내용과 상반되는 내용을 뒤이어 소개하고 있으므로 ③번이 적절하다.

03 "first make one laugh and then think"로 고치는 것이 적절하다.

04 돈을 아끼기 위해, 해군에서는 선원들에게 진짜 폭탄을 사용하는 대신에 "쾅!"이라고 소리치게 했다고 하는 것이 적절하다. ② fake: 가짜의, blow: 강타, ④ artificial: 인공적인

05 be eager[anxious/dying] to 동사원형 = be eager[anxious/dying] for 명사[동명사] = long to 동사원형 = long for 명사[동명사]: ~하고 싶은 생각이 간절하다, be anxious about: ~에 대해 염려하다

06 사역동사(made)의 목적격보어이므로 shouting을 원형부정사 shout로 고치는 것이 적절하다.

07 so ~ that ... can = enough to

08 영국 해군이 이그노벨상을 탄 것과 같은 해에 탔다고 했으므로, 2000년에 탔다.

09 ⓑ와 ③: 살아 있는(형용사), ① 살다[생존하다](동사), ② 생

방송[생중계/실황]으로(부사), ④ (공연이) 라이브의, 실황인(형용사), ⑤ (기록이나 기억에) 남다(동사)

10 ⓐ와 ①, ②, ⑤: 반복해서, ③, ④: 갑자기

11 금액을 나타내는 ten trillion Zimbabwean dollars는 단일 개념으로 생각해서 단수동사로 받는다.

12 만일 누군가가 너무 오랫동안 말을 하면 Miss Sweetie Poo가 "Please stop! I'm bored."라고 외친다고 했으므로, 수상 연설을 길게 해야만 한다는 것은 이그노벨상 시상식의 재미있는 전통에 해당하지 않는다.

13 very는 원급을 강조하는 말이고, 나머지는 다 비교급을 강조하는 말이다.

14 'did'는 'won a prize'를 대신하는 대동사이다.

15 (B)와 ④: ~와 (똑)같이[마찬가지로], …처럼(전치사), ①과 ③ (~을) 좋아하다(동사), ② 비슷한(형용사), ⑤ ~한대로[처럼](접속사)

16 돈을 아끼기 위해, 해군에서는 선원들에게 진짜 폭탄을 사용하는 대신에 "쾅!"이라고 소리치게 했다고 하는 것이 적절하다. ①과 ⑤: ~에 더하여, ~뿐 아니라, ③ ~에 덧붙여, ~와 마찬가지로, ④ ~에도 불구하고

17 present: (특히 공식적인 의식을 통해) 주다, 수여[증정]하다, award: <사람에게 상·장학금 등을> (심사하여) 수여하다, 주다

18 '시상식 시기'는 알 수 없다. ① 진짜 노벨상 수상자들, ② Sanders Theater at Harvard University, ③ '웃기는' 연구를 한 용감한 과학자들을 열렬히 격려하고자 하는 사람들, laughable: 웃기는, 터무니없는, ⑤ 영국 해군

19 '사람들이 유머 감각이 없다면, 그들은 대개 별로 훌륭한 과학자가 아니다'라는 앞 문장의 Andre Geim의 말과 어울리는 말로는 ⑤번이 적절하다. ① 안락, 편안, ② 후회, ③ 존경, ④ inner: 내면의

20 keep ~ing: 계속해서 ~하다

21 '자석을 이용해서' 그 일을 해냈다.

22 (A) '이그노벨상 시상식은 ~로 끝난다.'고 해야 하므로 with가 적절하다. end with: (…으로) 끝나다, end up: 결국 (어떤 처지에) 처하게 되다, (B) 'won a prize'를 대신하는 대동사이므로 did가 적절하다. (C) 노벨상과 '같은'이라고 해야 하므로 like가 적절하다. like: ~와 같은, alike: [형용사] (명사 앞에는 안 씀) (아주) 비슷한

23 unless = if ~ not

24 비록 '이그노벨'상의 상금이 많지 않고 수상자들이 '노벨'상 수상자들처럼 훌륭한 영광을 얻는 것도 아니지만, '이그노벨'상은 과학을 훨씬 더 재미있게 만든다.

25 ⓐ와 ③: 부사적 용법의 부사 수식 용법, 나머지도 다 부사적 용법이지만 ① 판단의 근거, ② 목적, ④ 결과, ⑤ 원인

26 '이그노벨상'을 가리킨다.

27 the+형용사 = 복수 보통명사

27

01 (A) awarded   (B) honoring

02 Is this research project good enough to win a Nobel Prize?

03 (A) Ig Nobel Prize   (B) fun

04 Real Nobel winners present the prizes in Sanders Theater at Harvard University.

05 save money

06 To save money, the Navy made its sailors shout, "Bang!" instead of using real bombs.

07 unless people have a sense of humor

08 (A) floating   (B) a sense of humor

09 The ceremony for the Ig Nobel Prizes as well as the winners' fun studies makes people laugh.

10 (1) 개회사와 폐회사는 단지 두 마디이다.

   (2) 만일 누군가가 너무 오랫동안 말을 하면, Miss Sweetie Poo라고 하는 여덟 살짜리 여자아이가 "제발 멈춰요! 지루해요."라고 계속 외친다.

   (3) 각 수상자는 미국의 1달러보다 가치가 낮은 10조의 짐바브웨 달러를 받는다.

   (4) 종이비행기를 날린다.

11 Maybe this research project is not good enough to win a Nobel Prize.

12 interest in science

---

01 (A) 이그노벨상이 '수여된다'고 해야 하므로 awarded가 적절하다. award: ~에게 〔상벌·장학금 따위를〕 주다, 수여하다, reward: 보상[보답/사례]하다, (B) '높이 평가함으로써'라고 해야 하므로 honoring이 적절하다. honor: 존경하다, ignore: 무시하다

02 enough는 형용사를 뒤에서 수식한다.

03 그는 한국의 고등학생이었고, 2015년에 그가 했던 '재미있는' 조사 때문에 2017년에 '이그노벨상'을 받았다.

04 Real Nobel winners를 주어로 하여 고치는 것이 적절하다.

05 돈을 아끼기 위해, 해군에서는 선원들에게 진짜 폭탄을 사용하는 대신에 "쾅!"이라고 소리치게 했다.

06 '돈을 아끼기 위해, 해군에서는 선원들에게 진짜 폭탄을 사용하는 대신에 "쾅!"이라고 소리치게 한 것'을 가리킨다.

07 unless = if ~ not

08 Andre Geim은 자석을 이용해서 살아 있는 개구리를 공중에 '띄우는 데' 성공했고 이그노벨상을 받았다. 그는 수상 연설에서 '유머 감각'을 좋은 과학자의 필수적인 자질로 언급했다.

09 not only A but also B = B as well as A: A뿐만 아니라 B도

10 뒤에 이어지는 내용 네 가지를 쓰면 된다.

11 'Maybe this research project is not good enough to win a Nobel Prize.'에서 'Maybe not.'만 남긴 것이다.

12 AIR 잡지는 특이하고 창의적인 사람들을 높이 평가함으로써 '과학에 대한 사람들의 흥미'를 늘리기 위해 그것들을 시작했다.

---

01 unusual   02 ③   03 worried   04 ⑤

05 ①   06 ④   07 laughing → laugh

08 ⑤   09 ③   10 ④   11 ③

12 ⑤

13 Not only Marie Curie but also her daughter was awarded the Nobel Prize.

14 ③   15 ③

16 by email as well as on the phone

17 (1) Ted was kind enough to carry my bag.

   (2) Vivian worked hard enough to save lots of money.

   (3) The yard is so big that we can ride bikes in it.

18 ②   19 who[that] is   20 ②

21 by   22 so, that, can

23 (B) ②, ④, ⑤   (C) ①, ③   24 ③, ④

25 ⑤   26 ②

27 This invention is so useful that it can make your life much easier.

28 ④

---

01 반의어 관계이다. 유용한 – 쓸모없는 : 일반적인 – 특이한

02 (a) 우리는 비가 왔기 때문에 수영장에서 나와야 했다. (b) 그 나라의 대통령은 전쟁을 끝내고 평화를 가져오기를 희망했다.

03 '일어날지도 모르는 문제나 불쾌한 일들에 관해 생각하고 있기 때문에 불행한'의 의미를 갖고 본문의 단어 worry를 활용한 형용사 'worried'가 적절하다.

04 액체의 위에 있고 가라앉지 않다

05 하기를 자랑스러워하는 어떤 것

06 imaginative는 '상상력이 풍부한'이라는 뜻이고, '가상의'는 'imaginary'를 사용한다.

07 사역동사 make는 목적보어 자리에 동사원형을 사용한다.

08 '준비됐니?'라는 말에 B가 '음, 그런 것 같아, 하지만 자신 있어'라고 말하는 것은 어색하다. '준비되었지만 긴장이 되다 또는 불안하다'라는 의미가 오는 것이 자연스럽다.

09 사역동사 let은 목적보어 자리에 동사원형을 사용한다. to show를 show로 바꾸어야 한다.

10 대화의 첫 문장 '수학여행 장기 자랑에서 무엇을 할 거니?'라는 물음에 대한 대답에서 '장기 자랑을 기대하기'라는 것을 알 수 있다.

11 수업 시간에 선생님들이 말하는 것을 흉내 내고 농담도 할 사람은 미소가 아니라 지민이다.

12 주어진 문장의 'that'은 원인과 결과를 나타내는 'that'이다. 이와 같이 쓰인 것은 ⑤이다. ①, ② 명사절을 이끄는 접속사 ③, ④ 관계대명사

13 'Not only ~ but also ...'가 주어로 쓰일 경우 수의 일치는 'but also'와 쓰인 주어에 맞춘다.

14 ③ '방은 내가 책을 읽을 수 있을 정도로 충분히 어두웠다.'의 뜻으로 어색한 문장이다.

15 a. jump → jumps, c. such → so, e. making → to make

16 'not only ~ but also ...'는 '... as well as ~'로 바꾸어 쓸 수 있다.

17 (1), (2) '~할 만큼 충분히 …한'의 문장은 '형용사/부사+enough to+동사원형'의 형태로 쓴다. (3) 'so+형용사/부사+that+주어+동사'의 형태로 '매우 ~해서 …할 수 있다'라는 의미의 문장을 쓴다.

18 turn off the light: 불을 끄다

19 주격 관계대명사와 be동사가 생략되어 있다.

20 ⓑ와 ①, ④: 동명사, ②, ③, ⑤: 현재분사

21 ⓐ 행위자를 나타내는 by, ⓑ by ~ing: ~함으로써

22 ~ enough to = so ~ that ... can

23 (B)와 ②, ④, ⑤: 'a+보통명사'를 받은 대명사, (C)와 ①, ③: 일반인을 나타내는 대명사

24 ⓐ와 ①, ②, ⑤: 마침내, 결국, ③ 무엇보다도, ④ 적어도

25 ⑤ Gauri Nanda가 발명한 자명종은 잠자는 사람을 계속 쫓아다니는 것이 아니라, 잠자는 사람이 결국 침대 밖으로 나올 때까지 계속 도망을 다닌다.

26 ⓐ와 ② (자격·기능 등이) ~으로(전치사), ① [이유·원인] ~이므로, ~이기 때문에(접속사), ③ [보통 'as ~ as ...'로 형용사·부사 앞에서] …와 같은 정도로('as ~ as ...'에서, 앞의 as가 지시부사, 뒤의 as는 접속사), ④ [때] ~일 때(접속사), ⑤ [비례] ~함에 따라, ~할수록(접속사)

27 ~ enough to = so ~ that ... can

28 not only[just/simply/merely] A but also B = B as well as A = not only[just/simply/merely] A but B as well: A뿐만 아니라 B도, not A but B: A가 아니라 B

단원별 예상문제　　　　　　　　　　p.154~157

01 float　　　02 ③　　　03 Break a leg

04 ②

05 He's going to talk like his teachers do in class and tell some jokes.

06 ③　　　07 and → or, one thing → two things

08 I'll keep my fingers crossed

09 ④　　　10 ⑤

11 not only putting → not only for putting　12 ③

13 (1) Tommy is not only strong but also wise.

(2) She has not only knowledge but also courage.

(3) I'm good at not only dancing but also singing.

(4) Not only you but also he wants to see the movie.

14 What happens when you walk backward while you are carrying a cup of coffee?

15 ②, ⑤

16 AIR magazine started them in 1991

17 ③　　　　　18 successful　　　19 ④

20 (A) laugh　(B) think　　　21 ⑤

22 ①, ②, ③　　　　　　23 to throw　24 ④

01 반의어 관계이다. 뒤로 - 앞으로 : 가라앉다 - 뜨다

02 '폭발할 물질로 만들어진 무기'란 의미로 '폭탄'이 적절하다.

03 'Break a leg!(행운을 빌어!)'라는 표현은 주로 공연이나 행사, 경기 등을 앞두고 있는 사람에게 '행운을 빌어!'라고 격려할 때 자주 쓰인다.

04 지민이 '수업 시간에 선생님들이 말하는 것을 흉내 내고 농담도 할 거야.'라는 말에 → (E) 그것이 기대된다는 말이 오고 → (A) 쇼에 대한 걱정을 말하고 → (D) 긴장을 풀어주며 행운을 비는 표현이 나오고 → (B) 감사의 대답이 온다. 그래서 네 번째 오는 대화는 (B)가 적절하다.

05 질문: 지민은 장기 자랑에서 무엇을 할 것인가? - 지민은 수업 시간에 선생님들이 말하는 것을 흉내 내고 농담도 할 것이다.

06 대화의 흐름상 긴장한 상대방에게 행운을 비는 말이나 긴장을 풀어주는 표현이 오는 것이 적절하다. ③번의 '포기하지 마!'라는 의미는 들어가기에 어색하다.

07 첫 문장은 '이것은 도마니, 아니면 새 모이통이니?'라는 의미로 and를 or로 바꾸어 준다. 그리고 도마일 뿐만 아니라 새 모이통이기도 하다고 했기 때문에 동시에 두 가지를 할 수 있다.

08 '행운을 빌어!'라고 할 때 'I'll keep my fingers crossed!'라고 한다.

09 민지의 엄마가 농구를 할 것을 기대하고 있는 것은 아니다.

10 ⑤번은 빨리 상을 받고 싶다는 의미이고, 나머지는 상대에게 행운을 빌어주는 표현이다.

11 '~뿐 아니라 …도 역시'의 문장은 'not only ~ but also ...'의 형태로 쓰고 상관접속사에 쓰인 두 어구의 형태를 일치시켜야 한다. 이때 'but also'에서 'You can use it for controlling the TV.'가 적절한 문장이므로 'not only' 부분을 for+동명사의 형태로 바꾸어 써야 한다.

12 not only 대신 not just[simply, merely]를 쓸 수 있다.

13 (1)~(3) '~뿐 아니라 …도 역시'의 문장은 'not only ~ but also …'의 형태로 쓰고 상관접속사에 쓰인 두 단어의 모양을 일치시켜야 한다. (4) 상관접속사에 주어가 쓰인 경우 'but also' 뒤의 주어에 동사의 수를 일치시킨다.

14 '커피 한 잔을 들고 가면서 뒤로 걸을 때 무슨 일이 일어날까?'를 가리킨다.

15 ⓑ와 ②, ⑤: 관계대명사, ① 지시형용사, ③ 접속사, ④ 지시대명사

16 AIR magazine을 주어로 하여 고치는 것이 적절하다.

17 ⓐ in: [성질·능력·기예 등의 분야를 한정하여] ~에서, ⓑ for: [이유·원인] ~ 때문에, ~으로 (인하여)

18 succeed in ~ing = be successful in ~ing

19 위 글은 '초청장'이다. ② 요약, 개요, ③ (신문·잡지의) 글, 기사, ⑤ 광고

20 이그노벨상을 타기 위해서는 사람들을 '웃게' 만드는 것이 사람들을 '생각하게' 만드는 것보다 더 중요하다.

21 누가 상을 수여할지는 알 수 없다. ① In 1991. ② First make one laugh and then think. ③ Thursday, September 14, 2017 6:00 PM. ④ In Sanders Theater at Harvard University.

22 keep/stop/prevent/prohibit A from ~ing: A가 ~하지 못하게 하다, ④ 허락하다, ⑤ 격려[고무]하다, 용기를 북돋우다

23 to부정사를 진주어로 해서 바꿔 쓸 수 있다.

24 개회사와 폐회사는 각각 단지 두 마디이다.

서술형 실전문제   p.158~159

01 I'm looking forward to watching you on the stage.

02 talent show, talk like, tell some jokes, looking forward to

03 I'm looking forward to seeing you at the race.

04 (a) was named (c) have (e) was awarded

05 good enough

06 the unusual and the imaginative

07 (A) laugh (B) think

08 (A) makes (B) is (C) is

09 There are a number of interesting things that[which] keep people from getting bored.

10 It is "Goodbye. Goodbye."

---

01 '~을 기대한다'의 의미로 'be looking forward to+동명사'를 사용한다.

02 지민과 미소는 장기 자랑에 대해 이야기하고 있다. 지민은 수업 시간에 선생님들이 말하는 것을 흉내 내고 농담도 할 것이다. 미소는 그의 쇼를 기대하고 있다.

03 Soyun이 100미터 달리기를 할 것이라는 말에 네가 경주에서 달리는 모습을 보는 것이 기대된다는 표현이 적절하다.

04 (1) be named after: ~의 이름을 따서 짓다 (2) 선행사가 복수 명사 people이므로 동사는 'have'로 쓰는 것이 올바르다. (3) 'Not only ~ but also ...'가 주어로 쓰일 경우 동사의 수의 일치는 'but also'와 쓰인 주어에 맞춰야 한다.

05 밑줄 친 ⓐ는 이 연구 과제가 이그노벨상을 받을 만큼 '충분히 훌륭할까?'를 의미한다.

06 the+형용사 = 복수 보통명사

07 AIR 잡지는 과학에 대한 사람들의 흥미를 늘리기 위해 1991년에 그것들을 시작했다. 만약 어떤 발견이 먼저 '웃기고' 나서 다음에 '생각하게' 만들 수 있다면, 그것은 그 상을 수상할 수 있다.

---

08 (A) not only A but also B에서는 B에 동사의 수를 일치시키고, 위 문장에서는 the ceremony가 B에 해당하므로 makes가 적절하다. (B) which의 선행사는 ten trillion Zimbabwean dollars이고, 돈은 단수 취급하므로 is가 적절하다. (C) 동명사가 주어일 때 단수 취급 하므로 is가 적절하다.

09 keep A from ~ing: A가 ~하지 못하게 하다

10 폐회사는 '안녕. 안녕'이다.

창의사고력 서술형 문제   p.160

|모범답안|

01 (A) A: I'm going to go camping with my parents.

     B: Wow! That sounds great.

     A: Yeah, I'm really looking forward to it.

   (B) A: I'm going to have a basketball game next week, but I'm worried about it.

     B: Don't worry. You'll do great. I'll keep my fingers crossed.

     A: Thank you.

02 (1) He is clever enough to understand the novel.

   (2) He is rich enough to buy the building.

   (3) He speaks not only English but also Chinese.

   (4) He is interested in not only basketball but also volleyball.

단원별 모의고사   p.161~166

01 ④   02 eagerness   03 ③

04 ②   05 ①   06 ⑤   07 ④

08 ④   09 (A) crossed (B) watching

10 (1) to talk like his teachers do in class

   (2) to tell some jokes   11 ③

12 Do I sound like our English teacher?

13 He is very popular as well as nice.

14 She is both beautiful and lovely.

15 She is neither smart nor creative.

16 ④   17 ① , ④   18 ③

19 We were brave enough to face the strong enemy.

20 Ted is so old that he can talk about the topic.

21 He has not only knowledge but also experience.

22 I must look after the children as well as feed the animals.

23 (1) cutting a pizza

   (2) but also for picking up a piece of pizza

24 (1) Not only she but also you have to leave here.

   (2) Not only I but also my brothers like to play with dogs.

   (3) Not only I but also my best friend is from Busan.

25 ⓐ an Ig Nobel Prize

   ⓑ 커피 한 잔을 들고 가면서 뒤로 걸을 때 무슨 일이 일어날까?

26 makes → make   27 ④   28 ①

29 a sense of humor

30 (A) an alarm clock   (B) gets out of bed

31 the number of → a number of / keeps → keep

32 which is worth less than one U.S. dollar

---

01 ④번은 '1,000,000,000,000'이라는 수'란 의미로 1조를 가리킨다. 'trillion'이 적절하다. 'million'은 '백만'이다.

02 '형용사-명사' 관계이다. 행복한-행복 : 열렬한-열망

03 '당신이 계획한 것을 성취하다'라는 의미로 '성공하다'가 적절하다.

04 춤 대회에 나가게 되어 걱정이 된다는 친구에게 긴장을 풀어주는 ②번의 대답이 가장 적절하다.

05 G의 말에 우리를 항상 웃게 만든다고 했기 때문에 Best Joker 상을 받기를 기대한다는 말이 자연스럽다.

06 민호는 항상 우리를 웃게 만든다는 A의 말에 B가 '걱정하지 마. 너는 잘 할 거야.'로 대답하는 것은 어색하다.

07 ④번은 대화의 흐름상 실수할까봐 겁난다고 했기 때문에 '거의 걱정이 되지 않는다.'라는 의미의 'little'을 '조금 걱정이 된다.'라는 의미의 'a little'로 바꾸는 것이 적절하다.

08 G의 마지막 말인 '무대에 선 엄마 모습을 보는 것이 기대돼요.'라는 말로 볼 때 ④에 들어가는 것이 적절하다.

09 (A)는 동사 keep의 목적보어 자리로 목적어인 my fingers의 수동 동작을 나타내는 과거분사 crossed가 적절하다. (B)는 look forward to(전치사) 뒤에 동명사 watching이 적절하다.

10 Jimin은 장기 자랑에서 수업 시간에 선생님이 말하는 것처럼 말하고, 농담을 할 것이다.

11 (A)는 대동사로 앞 문장의 동사 talk을 대신한다.

12 일반동사 의문문으로 'sound like our English teacher'와 중복되는 부분이 생략되어 있다.

13 '~뿐 아니라 …도 역시'의 문장을 'as well as'를 사용하여 쓸 때 강조하는 단어('…도 역시'에 해당하는 말)를 먼저 쓴다.

14 'both A and B'는 'A와 B 둘 다'의 뜻이다.타.나.다

16 'not only ~ but also …'의 상관접속사에 쓰인 두 단어의 모양을 일치시켜야 한다. 일반동사 'sing'은 부사와 함께 써야 하므로 형용사 happy는 부사 happily로 쓰는 것이 적절하다.

17 'too ~ to …'를 사용하여 문장을 만들 때, 문장의 주어와 'to부정사'의 주어가 다를 경우, 부정사의 의미상 주어 'for 목적격'을 to부정사 앞에 넣는다. 이때 문장의 주어가 'to부정사구'의 목적

어 자리에 중복되어 나타내지 않도록 목적어를 쓰지 않아야 한다. 'so ~ that'을 사용할 때는 목적어를 생략하지 않는다.

18 a. to put → for putting, b. dance → danced, d. could → can

19 'so+형용사/부사+that+주어+(can)+동사원형'의 문장은 '형용사/부사+enough to+동사원형'의 형태로 전환할 수 있다.

20 'so+형용사/부사+that+주어+(can)+동사원형'의 문장은 '형용사/부사+enough to+동사원형'의 형태로 전환할 수 있다.

21 'not only ~ but also …'는 '… as well as ~'로 바꾸어 쓸 수 있다.

22 'not only ~ but also …'는 '… as well as ~'로 바꾸어 쓸 수 있다.

23 (1) 전치사 다음에는 동명사구를 쓴다. (2) 'not only for 동명사'이므로 'but also for 동명사'로 쓴다.

24 'Not only ~ but also …'가 주어로 쓰일 경우 동사의 수의 일치는 'but also'와 쓰인 주어에 맞춘다. (1) you (2) my brothers (3) my best friend가 주어이고 이 주어에 동사의 수를 일치시킨다.

25 ⓐ '이그노벨상', ⓑ "What happens when you walk backward while you are carrying a cup of coffee?"를 가리킨다.

26 주격 관계대명사 that의 선행사가 복수형인 discoveries이기 때문에 make로 고치는 것이 적절하다.

27 ⓐ와 ①, ③, ④, ⑤: 부사적 용법, ②: 명사적 용법

28 상은 '진짜 노벨상 수상자들'에 의해 수여된다.

29 Andre Geim에 따르면, 매우 훌륭한 과학자가 되기 위해서는 대체로 '유머 감각'이 필요한 조건이다.

30 Gauri Nanda는 잠자는 사람이 결국 침대 밖으로 나와야만 끌 수 있는 '자명종'을 발명했기 때문에, 2005년에 이그노벨 경제학상을 받았다.

31 '많은' 재미있는 것들이라고 해야 하므로 a number of로 고치는 것이 적절하다. the number of: ~의 수, a number of: 많은, that의 선행사가 a number of interesting things이므로 keep으로 고쳐야 한다.

32 be worth: ~의 가치가 있다

Dreaming of My Future

시험대비 실력평가
p.170

01 laughed at 02 ② 03 ⑤
04 ③ 05 be afraid of 06 ③
07 allowance 08 ①

01 '당신이 누군가나 어떤 것이 어리석다고 생각하는 것을 보여주다'란 뜻의 '비웃다(laugh at)'가 적절하다.

02 명사로 '판사', 동사로 '판단하다'라는 뜻을 가진 단어는 'judge'가 적절하다. • 판사는 그에게 3년형을 선고했다. • 피부색이 다르다는 이유로 사람을 판단하는 것은 아주 잘못이다.

03 '지구의 대기 또는 태양계 너머의 지역'의 의미로 '우주(space)'가 적절하다.

04 위험하거나 어려운 상황에서 두려움을 조절하는 능력: 용기(courage)

05 '~을 두려워하다'는 'be afraid of'를 사용한다.

06 (A) 컴퓨터에 새 프로그램을 설치했니? (B) 그 무용수는 그녀의 뛰어난 춤 실력으로 선생님을 감동시켰다.

07 '동사 – 명사'의 관계다. 동사에 접미사 '-ance'를 붙여 명사로 만들 수 있다.

08 (A) 월드 디즈니는 역사상 중요한 문화계 인물이다. (B) 그 수치는 OECD 평균 6,741달러보다 낮다.

서술형 시험대비
p.171

01 (1) Thanks to (2) engineers (3) Later (4) laughter
02 disappointed
03 (1) (c)areer (2) (h)idden (3) (r)ecognizes
04 (1) face, 직면하다 (2) expert, 전문가
   (3) permission, 허락 (4) manager, 관리자
05 (1) (g)et (2) (c)olored (3) (c)ompetition

01 (1) 형의 충고 덕분에(thanks to), 민호는 의사가 될 수 있었다. (2) 'How many+복수명사'로 'engineers'가 적절하다. (3) 나중에(later), 그 가난한 소년은 대통령이 되었다. (4) 접속사 that 다음에 '주어+동사'의 문장이 와야 한다. 명사가 주어가 되어야 하므로 동사 'laugh'를 'laughter(웃음)'로 바꾸어 준다.

02 '어떤 것이 예상했던 것만큼 좋지 않거나 어떤 일이 일어나지 않았기 때문에 슬픈'의 의미로 'disappointed(실망한)'가 적절하다.

03 (1) career: 직업 (2) hidden: 숨겨진 (3) recognize: 인정하

다. 주어가 3인칭 단수이므로 동사 뒤에 '-s'를 쓴다.

04 (1) 어려운 상황을 처리하다 (2) 한 분야에서 높은 수준의 지식 또는 기술을 가진 사람 (3) 누군가에게 무엇을 하도록 허용해주는 행위 (4) 조직을 통제할 책임이 있는 사람

05 (1) 당신은 추위를 극복하기 위한 당신만의 방법을 갖고 있나요? (2) 미국 전체 인구의 8분의 1은 유색 인종의(흑인) 노예였습니다. (3) 철자 맞추기 대회는 미국의 철자 대회야.

교과서
Conversation

핵심 Check
p.172~173

1 ② 2 ⑤

교과서 대화문 익히기

Check(√) True or False
p.174

1 F 2 T 3 F 4 T

교과서 확인학습
p.176~177

Get Ready 2
(1) look down, the matter / to take, that idea, that, should / sorry to hear that
(2) disappointed / preparing, competition, record, What / keep practicing, sure, get better and better
(3) to be, cook, laughs at, give up / never give up, good at cooking, cook

Start Off – Listen & Talk A
1. look, Why, disappointed / lost, because of, mistake / makes mistakes / practice / practice makes perfect
2. are you disappointed / give, presentation / Take, easy, speech, a little, presentation / more slowly / help, understand

Start Off – Listen & Talk B
look down, disappointed / lost, competition / sorry to hear that, hard / maybe, enough, cooking tips / How about getting useful / try, for, advice / remember, dishes

시험대비 기본평가　　　　p.178

01 are, disappointed　　02 ⑤　　03 ③
04 ②

01 'disappoint'는 '실망시키다'라는 동사로 사람이 실망한 것은 과거분사 'disappointed'를 사용한다.

02 상대방이 걱정스러운 표정으로 뭔가에 불만족하거나 실망하고 있는 것을 보고 사용하는 표현으로 Why are you disappointed? = What's wrong? = What's the problem? = Is there anything wrong? = What happened? = Why the long face? 등을 사용할 수 있다.

03 '절대 포기하지 마.'라는 소녀의 대답으로 보아 빈칸에는 '내가 꿈을 포기해야 한다고 생각하니?'라고 묻는 것이 적절하다.

04 미래를 위해 롤 모델을 가져야 하는지 충고를 구하고 있는 표현이다.

시험대비 실력평가　　　　p.179~180

01 ④　　　　02 (b) / because of → because
03 ③　　04 ②　　05 ②　　06 ④
07 audition　08 ⑤　　09 ④　　10 ①
11 practice makes perfect

01 내가 실수를 해서 우리가 축구 시합에서 졌다고 말하고 나서 충

고를 구하는 말로 '더 연습을 해야 할까?'라는 ④가 적절하다.

02 (b)는 'I made'로 '주어+동사'가 있으므로 접속사 'because'가 적절하다. because of는 뒤에 명사(구)가 와야 한다.

03 상대방에게 충고를 구하는 표현으로 'Do you think I should ~?'가 적절하다.

04 충고를 명심하겠다는 표현이 적절하다.

05 요리 대회에서 떨어졌다는 말에 대해 '그것 참 안됐구나.'라는 표현이 적절하다. pleased를 sorry로 바꾸어야 한다.

06 '모든 실패는 성공으로 다가서는 한 걸음이다.'라는 조언이 가장 자연스럽다.

07 누군가가 배우, 음악가, 무용수 등으로 직업을 얻기 위해 하는 짧은 공연.

08 Ryan이 노래를 몇 곡을 만들었는지는 대화에 언급되어 있지 않다.

09 동사 'love'를 수식하는 부사가 필요하기 때문에 'how many'를 'how much'로 바꾸어야 한다.

10 ② 행함이 없는 믿음은 쓸모가 없다. ③ 충고는 해 줄 수 있으나, 행동하게 할 수는 없다. ④ 습관은 제2의 천성이다. ⑤ 어려움에 처했을 때 누가 진정한 친구인지 알게 된다.

11 '내가 더 연습해야 한다고 생각하니?'라는 말에 '음, 그래.'라고 답하고 있기 때문에 연습을 해야 한다는 의미로, 주어진 단어를 이용하여 '연습이 완벽을 만든다.'가 적절하다.

서술형 시험대비　　　　p.181

01 Because they want him to study hard and be a doctor.
02 (A) Why are you so disappointed
　　(B) Do you think I should
03 I'm sorry to hear that.
04 Are you interested in designing things?
05 it is more important to practice drawing every day

01 질문: 왜 Ryan의 부모님은 그가 슈퍼스타 101에 참가하는 걸 반대하는가?

02 (A) 'so'는 'disappointed'를 수식하는 부사로 'Why are you so disappointed'라고 쓴다. (B) 'Do you think I should ~?'는 '너는 내가 ~해야 한다고 생각하니?'라는 의미의 표현이다.

03 유감이나 동정을 나타내는 '그것 참 안됐구나.'의 의미로 'I'm sorry to hear that.'을 사용한다.

04 '~에 관심이 있다'는 표현은 'be interested in'을 이용한다. 전치사 in 다음에는 동명사 designing이 적절하다.

05 '가주어(It) ~ 진주어(to부정사)' 구문을 이용한다.

Grammar

핵심 Check p.182~183

1 (1) Having (2) Turning
2 (1) that (2) what (3) What

시험대비 기본평가 p.184

01 (1) Having no money

(2) Walking on[along] the street

(3) what you want

(4) What we need

02 (1) Feeling tired, he sat on a bench.

(2) Watching the news, she called her mom.

(3) Let me tell you what(= the thing that[which]) I heard yesterday.

(4) Show me what(= the things that[which]) you have in your pocket.

03 (1) (Being) Surprised at his test result

(2) Feeling happy with what you are doing

01 (1), (2) 때, 이유, 동시동작, 연속상황, 조건 등의 뜻을 나타내는 부사구를 현재분사(동사원형+-ing)를 써서 간략하게 나타낸다. (3), (4) '~하는 것'의 의미로 선행사를 포함한 관계대명사 what을 명사절(주어, 목적어, 보어)로 쓴다.

02 (1) 접속사와 주어가 없으므로 동사 Feel을 분사구문 Feeling 으로 쓰는 것이 적절하다. (2) 과거분사로 시작하는 분사구문은 주절의 주어와 수동 관계를 이루어야 한다. 주절의 주어인 그녀가 뉴스를 보는 것은 능동 관계이므로 Watching으로 쓰는 것이 적절하다. (3) that 앞에 선행사가 없고 동사 heard의 목적어가 없으므로 선행사를 포함한 관계대명사 'what'을 쓰거나 관계대명사 that 앞에 선행사를 넣는다. (4) 선행사 the things 가 있으므로 선행사를 포함한 관계대명사 what을 쓰는 것은 옳지 않다. 그러므로 선행사 the things를 삭제하거나 관계대명사 what을 that 또는 which로 쓰는 것이 적절하다.

03 (1), (2) 접속사를 생략하고 접속사절의 반복 주어를 생략한 다음 접속사절의 동사를 현재분사(Ving)로 바꾼다. 단, Being은 보통 생략한다.

시험대비 실력평가 p.185~187

01 ④ **02** ② **03** ①, ④ **04** ④

05 ④

06 I'm sorry, but this is not what we ordered.

07 ② **08** ⑤ **09** ④

10 (1) What he said is true.

(2) I know what you did yesterday.

11 This bag is what I want to buy.

12 (1) eating (2) Cooking (3) doing (4) Saying

(5) Get

13 cried loudly, feeling sad **14** ③

15 what you can do today **16** ②

17 (1) what I want (2) what I want **18** ①

19 They crossed the street, dancing to the music.

(Dancing to the music, they crossed the street.)

20 ④ **21** ②

01 ④는 진주어가 필요하므로 that이 적절하다. ①, ③ 선행사를 포함한 관계대명사 what ②, ⑤ 의문사 what

02 주어진 문장은 '그는 다이어트 중이기 때문에, 빵을 조금도 먹지 않는다.'라는 뜻이 적절하므로, 분사구문을 '이유(as 또는 because)'로 써야 하며, 또한 주절의 시제가 현재이므로 부사절의 시제도 현재로 쓴다.

03 주어진 문장은 '그는 산을 올라가는 중에, 회색곰과 마주쳤다.'라는 뜻이 적절하므로, 분사구문을 부사절로 쓸 때, 동시동작의 접속사 as나 while을 쓴다.

04 what은 선행사를 포함하는 관계대명사이므로 앞에 명사(선행사)가 나오면 안 된다. ④번 문장에서 선행사 all 또는 관계대명사 what 둘 중의 하나를 선택하여 쓴다. → Leaving this crowded city is all I want. (또는 what I want)

05 '접속사+주어+동사'의 부사절은 분사구문(V-ing)으로 바꾸어 쓸 수 있다. 이때, 분사구문 앞에 접속사는 생략하지 않아도 된다. 단, 주어만 생략하는 것은 올바르지 않다.

06 '이것은 우리가 주문한 것이 아니다.'라고 쓰는 것이 적절하므로 동사 is not 다음에 'what we ordered'를 보어로 쓴다.

07 첫 번째 문장의 보어절에서 선행사와 목적어 둘 다 없을 때 쓸 수 있는 것은 선행사를 포함한 관계대명사 what이다. 두 번째 문장에서는 선행사 the things가 있고 관계사절에 목적어가 없으므로 목적격 관계대명사 that 또는 which를 쓰는 것이 적절하다.

08 선행사를 포함한 관계대명사 what은 'the thing(s) that[which]'로 바꿀 수 있다. 관계대명사 that은 선행사 the book을 꾸며 줄 수 있으나 what은 선행사를 가질 수 없다.

09 주어 he가 뉴욕에 머무르는 것은 능동의 동작이므로, 'As he was staying in New York' 또는 'Staying in New York' 으로 쓴다. ⑤는 'As she was tired after the long walk' 'Being tired after the long walk' 또는 being을 생략한 'Tired after the long walk'로 쓸 수 있다.

10 (1) That he said는 선행사가 없으므로 What he said로 쓰는 것이 적절하다. (2) which를 선행사를 포함하는 관계대명사 what으로 바꾼다.

11 첫 번째 문장의 the thing과 두 번째 문장의 목적어 it을 사용하여 선행사를 포함하는 목적격 관계대명사로 문장을 만든다.

12 (1), (3). (4) 접속사가 없으므로 동사가 아닌 분사구문을 써야 한다. (2) 과거분사의 분사구문은 주절의 주어와 분사가 수동 관계일 때 사용한다. 주절의 주어 he가 요리하는 것은 능동 관계이므로 Cooking이 적절하다. (5) 접속사가 있는 문장이므로, 분사구문이 아닌 명령문을 쓰는 것이 올바르다.

13 The boy 다음에 동사 cried와 부사 loudly를 쓴 후, 분사구문에서 분사 feeling의 보어로 sad를 쓰는 것이 적절하다.

14 My brother got the thing that[which] he wanted.(선행사를 수식하는 관계사) 또는 My brother got what he wanted.(선행사를 포함한 관계사) 형태로 쓴다.

15 '오늘 할 수 있는 것'을 what을 이용하여 쓴다.

16 분사구문의 부정은 'not+분사'의 형태로 쓴다. 그러므로 'Not feeling well'로 쓰는 것이 적절하다.

17 (1)번 대화에서 Is this bed what you want?(네가 원하는 것) 에 대한 대답으로 what I want(내가 원하는 것)를 쓰는 것이 적절하고, (2)번 대화에서 질문에 대한 답을 '그것이 바로 내가 원하는 것이야.'로 할 때 'what I want'를 쓰는 것이 적절하다.

18 첫 번째 빈칸은 선행사가 없는 목적격 관계대명사가 필요하므로 'what'을 쓰고, 두 번째 빈칸은 선행사가 있는 목적격 관계대명사가 필요하므로 which 또는 that을 쓴다.

19 분사구문은 부사구로 주절의 앞이나 뒤 둘 다에 쓸 수 있다.

20 접속사를 써서 'When I opened the box, I found a gift in it.' 또는 분사구문으로 'When opening the box, I found a gift in it.', 'Opening the box, I found a gift in it.'으로 쓸 수 있다.

21 c. What you did was very brave. (what절이 주어인 경우 단수 취급) d. As the letter was written in Chinese 또는 Written in Chinese

서술형 시험대비
p.188~189

01 (1) Don't always believe what you see.
   (2) Never put off what you can do today.
   (3) What is the most important is your health.
   (4) I'm not interested in what he showed to me.
   (5) What I got used to in Korea was eating spicy food.

02 (1) Watching TV, he fell asleep.
   (2) Singing a song, she danced happily.
   (3) Working as a pilot, he travels a lot.

03 (1) She left the room, singing a song.
   (2) There being no tickets left, we couldn't go to the concert.

04 (1) She walked in the park, eating bread. 또는 Walking in the park, she ate bread.
   (2) Is this cap what you wanted?
   (3) This key is what I was looking for.
   (4) Having no money, I can't help you.
   (5) Humming a song, I vacuumed the floor.
   (6) I hope he remembers what I did for him.

05 Not knowing what to say, I just stood around like a fool.

06 Eating an apple, Amy walked her dog. / Amy walked her dog, eating an apple.

07 (1) Writing on the board
   (2) Holding a flower
   (3) Swimming in the pool

08 (1) Climbing a mountain, I fell down.
   (2) Disliking watching TV, he only listens to music.
   (3) Not having time to see the movie "Frozen", I know who the Olaf is.
   (4) Dad took me to the kitchen, showing me what he had cooked.

01 (1) Don't always believe the things that you see. (2) Never put off the things that you can do today. (3) The thing that is the most important is your health. (4) I'm not interested in the things that he showed to me. (5) The thing that I got used to in Korea was eating spicy food. 선행사 the thing 또는 the things와 관계대명사 that을 결합하여 what이 있는 문장을 쓴다.

02 (1), (2), (3) 모두 분사구문이 주어와 능동의 관계이므로 현재분사로 시작하는 문장으로 쓴다.

03 (1) 접속사를 생략하고 접속사절의 반복 주어를 생략한 다음 접속사절의 동사를 현재분사(V-ing)로 바꾼다. 단, Being은 보통 생략한다. (2) 부사절과 주절의 주어가 다를 때는 부사절의 주어를 생략하지 않고 사용한다.

04 (1) 두 절을 접속사로 연결하거나 한 절을 분사구문으로 쓴다. (2) this cap은 선행사가 아니고 문장의 주어이므로, 보어절에 선행사를 포함한 관계대명사가 필요하다. (3) 관계대명사 what이 있으므로 관계사절의 목적어는 쓰지 않는다. (4) 명령문이 올 수 없으므로, 동사가 아닌 분사구문 'Having'을 쓰는 것이 적절하다. (5) 분사구문의 주어와 주절의 주어가 일치하므로 분사구문의 주어 I를 삭제한다. (6) what이 remembers와 did의 목적어가 되도록 한다.

05 분사구문을 만들 부사절이 부정문이면 'not+현재분사'의 형태로 쓴다. 해석: 무슨 말을 해야 할지 몰라서, 나는 바보처럼 멍하니 서 있었다.

06 동시동작을 현재분사(동사원형+-ing)를 써서 문장을 완성한다.

07 (1), (2), (3) '~하면서'의 의미를 가진 동시동작의 분사구문을

쓴다. 모두 주절의 주어와 분사구문의 동작이 능동관계이므로 현재분사의 분사구문을 쓴다.

08 (1) 접속사를 생략하고 부사절의 반복 주어를 생략한 다음 부사절의 동사를 현재분사(V-ing)로 바꾼다. 단, Being은 보통 생략한다. (2) 분사구문을 만들 때 동사원형에 -ing를 붙인다. (3) 분사구문을 만들 때 부사절이 부정문이면 'not+현재분사(V-ing)'의 형태로 쓴다. (4) 연속동작의 접속사 and와 (주어) 동사를 현재분사(V-ing)'의 형태로 쓴다.

교과서 Reading

확인문제   p.190

1 T 2 F 3 T 4 T 5 F

확인문제   p.191

1 T 2 F 3 T 4 F 5 T 6 F

교과서 확인학습 A   p.192~193

01 Hidden Figures
02 last weekend
03 African-American
04 in the 1960s as
05 space experts, to get over difficulties
06 three, hidden figures
07 showed a talent in
08 got upset
09 where Katherine had been
10 bathroom
11 COLORED bathrooms
12 just to use
13 Hearing this
14 had courage to talk
15 break down
16 character
17 wasn't allowed to
18 to give her permission
19 can't change
20 have no choice but to
21 in a hundred years
22 Which one
23 impressed, what
24 stood up for
25 what impressed me most
26 first African-American woman engineer
27 the last
28 were installed, would lose
29 new programming language
30 taught it
31 was asked to
32 I'm not accepting
33 to program
34 alone
35 are ready
36 Thanks to
37 wasn't afraid of, as a chance
38 what I need to learn
39 how to face challenges
40 tears and laughter

교과서 확인학습 B   p.194~195

1 The Hidden Figures of NASA
2 I watched the movie Hidden Figures last weekend.
3 It was a movie about three African-American women who worked at NASA.
4 They began their career in the 1960s as "human computers."
5 However, they dreamed of becoming space experts at NASA and tried hard to get over difficulties.
6 Katherine Johnson was one of the three "hidden figures" in this movie.
7 She worked hard and showed a talent in math, and her manager Al Harrison recognized her ability.
8 One day, he got upset when Katherine was missing from her desk for too long.
9 Al asked where Katherine had been, and she answered.
10 Katherine: The bathroom.
11 There are no COLORED bathrooms in this building.
12 I have to run half a mile away just to use the bathroom.
13 Hearing this, I felt really sorry for her.
14 However, I was glad that she had courage to talk to the manager about the problem.
15 This made Al Harrison break down the "Colored Ladies Room" sign.
16 Mary Jackson was the character I liked the most of the three.
17 She wanted to learn more about rocket science, but she wasn't allowed to go to a white school.
18 So, she asked a judge to give her permission.
19 Mary: I can't change the color of my skin.
20 So … I have no choice but to be the first.
21 Your Honor, of all the cases you'll hear today, which one will matter in a hundred years?
22 Which one will make you the "first?"
23 The judge was impressed by what she said and finally gave her permission.
24 Mary stood up for herself and for other African-Americans.

25 That was what impressed me most in the movie.

26 Finally, she became the first African-American woman engineer at NASA.

27 Dorothy Vaughan was the last "hidden figure."

28 When IBM computers were installed at NASA in 1961, she was worried the "human computers" would lose their jobs.

29 She studied a new programming language, FORTRAN.

30 She also taught it to her team members.

31 Later, when she was asked to be the leader of a new IBM team, she made a suggestion.

32 Dorothy: I'm not accepting the offer if I can't bring my ladies with me.

33 We need a lot of people to program that machine.

34 I can't do it alone.

35 My girls are ready.

36 Thanks to Dorothy, her team members could become programmers.

37 She wasn't afraid of change and used it as a chance.

38 That's what I need to learn from her.

39 Watching this movie, I could learn how to face challenges in life.

40 I won't forget the tears and laughter of Katherine, Mary, and Dorothy.

시험대비 실력평가   p.196~199

01 ②　　02 ⑤　　03 ④　　04 ②

05 건물에 유색 인종 전용 화장실이 없어서 단지 화장실을 사용하기 위해 Katherine이 반 마일을 달려가야 했던 사실

06 ④　　　　　　07 permission

08 (A) black (B) white　09 ④

10 (A) last (B) experts (C) hard

11 three African-American women

12 ①, ③, ④　13 ②, ③　14 I should[could]

15 ③　　16 ⑤　　17 ⑤　　18 ③

19 ④　　20 ①　　21 hidden figure

22 ③　　23 to go to a white school　24 ②

01 앞에 나오는 내용과 상반되는 내용이 뒤에 이어지므로 However가 가장 적절하다. ③ 그러므로, ④ 즉[말하자면], ⑤ 게다가, 더욱이

02 (A)와 ⑤: 인물, ① (~일 거라고) 생각[판단]하다(동사), ② (특히 공식적인 자료로 제시되는) 수치, ③ (아라비아) 숫자, (숫자의) 자리, ④ 계산하다(동사)

03 그들은 NASA에서 '우주 전문가'가 되기를 꿈꾸었다. astronaut: 우주 비행사

04 ⓐ show a talent in: ~에 재능을 보이다, ⓑ feel sorry for: ~을 안쓰럽게[안됐다고] 여기다

05 앞에서 Katherine이 말한 내용을 가리킨다.

06 이 글은 'Katherine의 대답이 Al Harrison으로 하여금 '유색 여성 화장실' 표지판을 부수게 만들었다'는 내용의 글이므로, 제목으로는 ④번 ""유색 여성 화장실"은 더 이상 없다'가 적절하다. ⑤ strict: 엄격한

07 직접목적어이므로 명사 형태로 쓰는 것이 적절하다.

08 '흑인' 학생이 '백인' 학생들과 함께 수업을 받도록 허락한 최초의 판사를 의미한다.

09 finally, eventually, after all, at last, in the end, in the long run: 결국, ④ 적어도

10 (A) '지난' 주말이라고 해야 하므로 last가 적절하다. latest: 최근의, (B) 우주 '전문가'라고 해야 하므로 experts가 적절하다. experts: 전문가들, exports: 수출품, (C) '열심히' 노력했다고 해야 하므로 hard가 적절하다. hardly: 거의 ~ 아니다

11 African-American: 아프리카계 미국인

12 ⓑ와 ②, ⑤: 부사적 용법, ①, ④: 명사적 용법, ③: 형용사적 용법, relieved: 안도하는, 다행으로 여기는

13 ⓐ와 ②, ③: 현재분사, ①, ④, ⑤: 동명사

14 '의문사 to부정사'는 '의문사+주어+should[can]'를 사용하여 고치는 것이 적절하다.

15 ⓒ 다음 문장의 it에 주목한다. 주어진 문장의 a new programming language, FORTRAN을 받고 있으므로 ③번이 적절하다.

16 ⑤는 NASA의 IBM 팀을 가리키고, 나머지는 다 인간 컴퓨터(계산원)들을 가리킨다.

17 Dorothy Vaughan wasn't afraid of change and used it as a chance.

18 Katherine이 너무 오래 자리를 비웠을 때 '화가 났다'고 하는 것이 적절하다. ① 부끄러운, ④ 안도하는, 다행으로 여기는, ⑤ 쑥스러운, 어색한, 당황스러운

19 ④번 다음 문장의 This에 주목한다. 주어진 문장에서 언급한 내용(그 문제에 대해 그녀가 상사에게 말한 것)을 받고 있으므로 ④번이 적절하다.

20 그 영화의 세 명의 '숨겨진 인물들'이 누구인지는 알 수 없다. ② She showed a talent in math. ③ He was Katherine's manager. ④ Because Katherine was missing from her desk for too long. ⑤ Because there were no COLORED bathrooms in the building and she had to run half a mile away just to use the bathroom.

21 Katherine Johnson은 Al Harrison으로 하여금 '유색 여성 화장실' 표지판을 부수게 만든 '숨겨진 인물'이었다.

22 ⓐ와 ③: 중요하다(동사), ① (고려하거나 처리해야 할) 문제[일/사안], ② (세상의 모든 것들을 구성하는 일반적인) 물

질, properties: 속성, ④ (특정한 종류의) 물질[물건/성분], reading matter: 읽을거리, ⑤ (걱정·고민 등의 원인이 되는) 문제[일]

23 ⓑ의 permission은 '(흑인 학생이) 백인 학교에 다닐 수 있는' 허락을 가리킨다.

24 위 글은 '일화(逸話, 에피소드, 세상에 널리 알려지지 아니한 흥미 있는 이야기)'이다. ① 수필, ③ (책·연극·영화 등에 대한) 논평[비평], 감상문, ④ (신문·잡지의) 글, 기사, ⑤ 독후감

서술형 시험대비
p.200~201

01 the movie *Hidden Figures*

02 nineteen sixties　　03 overcome

04 Because there were no colored bathrooms in the building.

05 When[As] I heard this　　06 to break → break

07 same　　08 being, be

09 That was what impressed me most in the movie.

10 (A) rocket science　(B) engineer

11 unless I can bring my ladies with me

12 She wasn't afraid of change and used it as a chance.

13 (A) new programming language
　　(B) programmers

01 '영화 히든 피겨스'를 가리킨다.

02 연대는 두 자리씩 끊어 읽는 것이 적절하다.

03 get over = overcome: ~을 극복하다

04 건물에 유색 인종 전용 화장실이 없었기 때문이다.

05 'Hearing this'는 '이것을 듣고서'라는 의미의 분사구문으로, 부사절로 고칠 때는 접속사 When이나 As를 사용하는 것이 적절하다.

06 사역동사 made의 목적격보어이므로 동사원형인 'break'로 고치는 것이 적절하다.

07 과거에 유색 인종들은 인종차별에 직면했다. 예를 들어 심지어 Katherine 같이 똑똑한 여성도 백인들과 '같은' 화장실을 사용할 수 없었고, 별도의 다른 화장실을 사용하도록 강요받았다.

08 have no choice but to = cannot help ~ing = cannot but 원형: ~할 수밖에 없다

09 선행사를 포함하는 관계대명사 what을 사용하는 것이 적절하다.

10 Mary Jackson은 백인 학교에서 '로켓 공학'에 대해 더 많이 배웠고, NASA에서 최초의 아프리카계 미국인 여성 '공학자'가 되었다.

11 if ~ not = unless

12 앞 문장의 내용을 가리킨다.

13 Dorothy Vaughan은 '새로운 프로그래밍 언어'인 포트란을 공부했고, 그녀의 팀원들에게 그것을 가르침으로써 그들이 '프로그래머'가 될 수 있도록 도와준 히든 피겨였다.

영역별 핵심문제
p.203~207

01 expert　　02 ③　　03 ⑤　　04 ①

05 against　　06 ②　　07 cooker → cook

08 ②　　09 ⑤　　10 ②　　11 ④

12 ②　　13 ②

14 Left alone in the room, the baby began to cry.

15 ②　　16 ③　　17 ④

18 (1) David는 그녀가 말한 것을 기억하고 있다.
　　(2) 그것이 네가 배워야만 하는 것이다.
　　(3) 중요한 것은 네가 최선을 다했다는 것이다.

19 ③

20 Al asked where Katherine had been　21 ③

22 ②　　23 ④

24 (A) the permission (B) stood up　　25 ②

26 by myself　　27 change

28 while he was decorating some cupcakes

29 ②, ⑤

01 반의어 관계다. 용기 : 비겁함 - 초보자 : 전문가

02 (a) 분노는 당신이 부당하게 대우를 받았을 때 스스로를 옹호할 수 있도록 도와주기 때문에 좋은 것일 수도 있습니다. (b) 교사들, 기자들, 그리고 공무원들은 값비싼 선물을 받을 수 없다.

03 법정에서 범죄자들이 어떻게 처벌 받아야 하는지를 결정하는 사람

04 매우 빠르게 이동하며 우주 여행에 사용되는 큰 원통 형태의 물체

05 '계획이나 활동에 동의하지 않는'의 의미를 가지는 'against(반대하여)'가 적절하다.

06 'audition'은 '오디션'이고, '관객'은 'audience'이다.

07 cooker: 요리 기구, cook: 요리사

08 실망한 이유를 묻는 말에 → (B) 이유를 설명하고 → (D) 위로하는 말을 한 후, 발표 때의 문제점을 말해 주고 → (C) 충고를 구하는 말을 한다. 마지막으로 (A) 충고를 구하는 말에 대한 대답이 오는 것이 적절하다.

09 '내 미래를 위해 롤 모델을 가져야 한다고 생각하니?'라는 물음에 '모형 비행기를 만드는 것은 쉽지 않다.'고 말하는 것은 어색하다.

10 부모님이 경연대회에 참석하는 것을 반대한다는 내용이기 때문에 'for'를 'against'로 바꾸어야 한다.

11 위 대화는 가수가 되고 싶은 자신의 꿈을 부모님에게 어떻게 보여 줄 것인가에 관한 내용이다.

12 Ryan의 부모님은 그의 성적에 대해 걱정을 한다.

13 주어진 문장과 ②: 선행사를 포함한 관계대명사 what, ①, ③, ④, ⑤: 의문사 what

14 동사 leave는 '남기고 가다'라는 뜻이며, 아기는 홀로 '남겨진' 상태이므로 수동의 분사구문으로 쓴다.

15 As it rained, we didn't play soccer outside. 또는 분사구문을 사용하여 It raining, we didn't play soccer outside.

16 a. Walking along the street, I saw a big cat. b. Living in America, he speaks English very well. d. They sat on the beach, looking at the rising sun.

17 ④는 의문사 what ①, ②, ③, ⑤는 선행사를 포함한 관계대명사 what.

18 (1), (2), (3) 선행사를 포함한 관계대명사는 '~하는 것'으로 해석되며 문장의 목적어, 보어, 주어로 쓰인다.

19 선행사와 목적어가 없으므로 선행사와 목적어 둘 다로 쓰일 수 있는 것을 써야 한다. that은 선행사가 없으므로 적절하지 않고, ①, ④는 목적격 관계대명사가 생략된 것으로 볼 수 있다.

20 'where Katherine had been'은 동사 'asked'의 목적어이므로 간접의문문 순서로 쓰는 것이 적절하다.

21 Al Harrison은 그녀의 능력을 '알아차렸다.' envy: 부러워하다

22 ⓐ와 ②: (소송) 사건, ①, ⑤: (특정한 상황의) 경우, ③ (질병, 부상) 사례[환자], ④ 용기, 통, 상자

23 이 글은 '"최초"가 되는 것 이외에는 선택이 없었던 Mary Jackson이 마침내 NASA 최초의 아프리카계 미국인 여성 공학자가 된' 내용의 글이므로, 제목으로는 ④번 '최초가 되는 것 이외에는 선택이 없었던 여성'이 적절하다.

24 Mary Jackson은 백인 학교에 다니도록 '허락'을 받았고, 그곳에서 로켓 공학에 대해 더 많이 배웠다. 그리고 그녀는 자신과 다른 아프리카계 미국인들의 '편에 섰다.'

25 Dorothy '덕분에', 그녀의 팀원들은 프로그래머가 될 수 있었다고 하는 것이 적절하다. Thanks to: ~ 덕분에, ① ~에도 불구하고, ③ ~보다는[대신에], ④ ~ 면에서[~에 관하여], ⑤ ~ 대신에

26 alone = by oneself: 혼자

27 '변화'를 가리킨다.

28 'decorating some cupcakes'는 '컵케이크에 장식하며'라는 의미의 동시동작을 나타내는 분사구문으로, 부사절로 고칠 때는 접속사 While을 사용하여 진행형으로 고치는 것이 적절하다.

29 ⓑ와 ②, ⑤: 관계대명사, ① 의문형용사, ③ 의문대명사, ④ [감탄사적] 의문형용사

단원별 예상문제
p.208~211

01 competition
02 ③
03 Why the long face?
04 (A) – (C) – (B)
05 He should practice drawing every day and read design magazines.
06 ③   07 ⑤   08 ④   09 ②
10 (1) 감기에 걸려서, 그는 일찍 잠자리에 들었다.
　(2) 공항에 도착해서, 그녀는 그녀의 부모님에게 전화를 걸었다.
　(3) 물을 많이 마시면, 너는 더 건강해 질 거야.
11 ③, ④

12 (1) Make what[the things that] your family will love.
　(2) Design what you dream of.
　(3) I will not forget what he said.
　(4) She told me about her job, drawing some product designs.
　(5) You can be what you act.
13 (1) That's what I want to read.
　(2) That's what I was looking for.
　(3) That's not what I have in mind.
14 career   15 ③   16 missed → missing
17 ②   18 answer   19 ⑤
20 The judge was impressed by what she said and finally gave her permission.
21 ③

01 '동사-명사'의 관계다. 받아들이다 - 수용 : 경쟁하다 – 시합, 대회

02 '직장 생활 동안 하는 일련의 직업' 의미로 'career(경력, 직장 생활)'가 적절하다.

03 상대방의 걱정, 슬픔이나 불만족, 실망의 원인에 대해 물을 때 사용되는 일반적인 표현으로 'Why are you disappointed?' = What's the problem? = Is there anything wrong? = What happened? = Why the long face? 등이 있다.

04 (A) 물건 디자인하는 데 관심 있는지 묻는 말에 → (C) 긍정의 대답과 제품 디자이너가 되고 싶다고 말하고, 디자인 학교에 가야 하는지 조언을 구하는 질문에 대해 → (B) 가는 것이 도움이 되고, 매일 그림을 연습하는 것이 중요하다고 말하고 디자인 잡지를 읽는 것도 또한 도움이 된다는 말이 이어지는 것이 자연스럽다.

05 질문: 소년은 제품 디자이너가 되기 위해 무엇을 해야 할까?

06 빈칸 다음에 '여자'의 대답이 '아뇨. 매일 열심히 연습하면 점점 더 나아질 거예요.'인 것으로 보아 마술 대회에서 떨어졌다는 말 다음에 부정적인 말이 오는 것이 자연스럽다.

07 주어진 문장은 '온라인 요리 영상에서 유용한 조언들을 얻는 게 어때?'라는 의미로 '알았어. 시도해 볼게.'라는 대답 앞인 ⑤에 들어가는 것이 적절하다.

08 오늘 우울해 보인다는 말 다음에 상대방의 걱정, 슬픔이나 불만족, 실망의 원인에 대해 물어보는 것이 자연스럽다.

09 실수로 경기에 진 사람이 상대방에게 충고를 구하는 내용으로 ②번의 질문이 가장 적절하다.

10 (1) As[Because] he had a cold, he went to bed early. (2) When[As] she arrived at the airport, she called her parents. (3) If you drink a lot of water, you will be healthier.

11 접속사 while 대신 as를 쓸 수 있다. 분사구문에서 접속사는 생략하지 않고 사용할 수 있다.

12 (1) what은 선행사를 포함하고 있으므로 선행사 'the things'

39

또는 관계사 what 둘 중 하나만 쓴다. (2) that은 선행사가 필요한 관계대명사이나 그 앞에 선행사가 없으므로, 선행사를 포함한 관계대명사 what으로 쓴다. (3) what이 선행사와 목적격 관계대명사의 역할을 하고 있으므로, 관계사절의 목적어 it을 쓰지 않는다. (4) 주어진 문장에 접속사 and가 있으므로, 분사구문이 아닌 동사 drew 또는 and를 없애고 분사 drawing만 쓴다. (5) which는 선행사가 필요한 관계대명사이나 그 앞에 선행사가 없으므로, 선행사를 포함한 관계대명사 what으로 쓴다.

13 선행사를 포함한 관계대명사는 '~한 것'으로 해석되며 명사절 역할을 하여 문장의 보어로 쓸 수 있다.

14 career: 직업, 직장 생활, 어떤 사람이 삶의 오랜 기간 동안 하는 일, 직업

15 ⓑ와 ③: (자격·기능 등이) ~로(서)(전치사), ① ~한 대로(접속사), ② [보통 as ~ as ...로 형용사·부사 앞에서] …와 같은 정도로(앞의 as는 지시부사, 뒤의 as는 접속사), ④ ~이기 때문에(접속사), ⑤ 가령 ~와 같은(전치사)

16 missing: (제자리나 집에 있지 않고) 없어진[실종된]

17 ⓑ와 ②, ④: 형용사적 용법, ①: 부사적 용법, ③, ⑤: 명사적 용법

18 그의 질문에 대한 Katherine의 '대답'이 그로 하여금 '유색 여성 화장실' 표지판을 부수게 했다.

19 선행사를 포함하는 관계대명사 'what'을 쓰는 것이 적절하다.

20 be impressed by: ~에 의해 깊은 인상을 받다, what: 선행사를 포함하는 관계대명사

21 Mary Jackson은 최초가 될 수밖에 없었다. Mary Jackson couldn't but be the first. stand up for = support: ~을 지지하다

선행사가 없으므로 선행사를 포함한 관계대명사 what을 쓴다.
(3) ⓜ 주절 이후에 접속사가 없으므로 '~하면서'의 의미로 분사구문 seeing을 쓰는 것이 적절하다.

04 (1), (2) 주절이 뒤에 있으므로, 분사구문을 사용하여 문장을 쓴다. (3), (4) 분사구문이 앞에 있으므로, 주절을 과거시제를 사용하여 쓴다.

05 be allowed to 부정사: ~하는 것이 허용되다

06 Mary Jackson은 NASA에서 최초의 '아프리카계 미국인' 여성 공학자가 되었다.

07 Mary Jackson은 판사로 하여금 흑인 학생이 백인 학생들과 함께 수업을 받도록 허락한 최초의 인물이 되도록 만든 숨겨진 인물이었다. 그녀는 또한 자신뿐만 아니라 다른 아프리카계 미국인들의 편에 섰다. stand up for = support: ~을 지지하다

08 NASA에 IBM 컴퓨터가 '설치되었을' 때라고 해야 하므로, 수동태로 고치는 것이 적절하다.

09 be afraid of: ~을 두려워하다, use A as B: A를 B로 사용하다, 대명사 it: 앞에서 언급된 'change'를 가리킨다.

10 'Watching this movie'는 '이 영화를 보면서'라는 의미의 동시동작을 나타내는 분사구문으로, 부사절로 고칠 때는 접속사 While을 사용하여 진행형으로 고치는 것이 적절하다.

창의사고력 서술형 문제 p.214

|모범답안|

01 (1) A: Why are you disappointed?
    B: I lost the dance competition. Do you think I should practice harder?
    A: Yes, I think so.(Sure. Don't give up.)
   (2) A: Why are you disappointed?
    B: I fought with my friend. Do you think I should talk to my friend about it?
    A: Yes, I think so.

02 (A) designer   (B) what you dream of
   (C) magician   (D) what you see

서술형 실전문제 p.212~213

01 Do you think I should practice more?

02 dream, enter, against, doctor, disappointed, advises, show, how much, thanks, advice

03 (1) ㉠ →to do (2) ㉣ →what (3) ㉤ →seeing

04 (1) Singing a song   (2) Drinking milk
   (3) Lucy read a book   (4) David kicked a ball

05 to go

06 first woman → first African-American woman

07 (A) first   (B) supported

08 installed → were installed

09 She wasn't afraid of change and used it as a chance.

10 While I was watching this movie

01 'Do you think I should ~?'는 '너는 내가 ~해야 한다고 생각하니?'라는 의미이다.

03 (1) ㉠ '~해야 할'의 의미로 things을 꾸미는 to부정사의 형용사적 용법을 쓰는 것이 적절하다. (2) ㉣ 목적격 관계대명사에

단원별 모의고사 p.215~220

01 ④   02 hidden   03 ③   04 ⑤

05 How about getting useful tips

06 ⑤   07 ①   08 ②

09 (C) – (A) – (D) – (B)   10 ④   11 keep

12 ⑤

13 Because his parents won't let him enter Superstar 101.

14 ③   15 ①, ③   16 ④   17 ②

18 (1) decorating some cupcakes
   (2) saying his famous lines

(3) doing some magic tricks

(4) showing me his news reports

(5) controlling robots

19 (1) what you see　(2) what is true

(3) what you cannot do

20 새 IBM 팀의 리더가 되어달라는 요청　　　21 ④

22 It was a new programming language.　　23 ⑤

24 courageous / courageous　　25 ③

26 ②　　27 ①　　28 ④　　29 ③

30 ⑤

---

01 ④번은 '무언가를 하기 위해 필요한 기술이나 자질'을 의미하는 'ability'에 대한 설명이다. 'courage'는 'the ability to control your fear in a dangerous or difficult situation'이다.

02 유의어 관계이다. 용기 : 숨겨진

03 '기계나 장비를 제자리에 놓고 사용할 준비가 되도록 하다'는 의미로 'install(설치하다)'이 적절하다.

04 ⑤ '마술 수업을 들어야 한다고 생각하니?'라고 충고를 구하는 말에 '당신과 같은 마술사가 되고 싶어.'라고 대답하는 것은 어색하다.

05 'how about'은 뒤에 동명사를 취한다. get을 getting으로 바꾸어 준다.

06 우울해 보인다는 말 다음에 상대방의 걱정, 슬픔이나 불만족, 실망의 원인에 대해 물어보는 말이 자연스럽다.

07 대화의 첫 문장에 '왜 실망하고 있나요?'라고 묻는 것으로 보아 '슬퍼 보이지 않는다.'는 말은 어색하다. 'sad'를 'happy'로 바꾸어야 한다.

08 발표가 약간 빨랐다는 말에 대해 더 천천히 말해야 한다고 생각하는지 묻는 것이 자연스럽다.

09 실망한 이유를 묻는 질문에 → (C) 오디션에서 떨어졌다는 대답을 하고 → (A) 그 말에 유감을 표현한다. → (D) 계속 노력해야 하는지 충고를 구하는 질문을 하고 → 마지막으로 (B) 충고에 대한 긍정의 답을 하는 것이 자연스럽다.

10 주어진 문장에 'also(또한)'라는 첨가의 부사가 사용되었기 때문에 앞 문장에도 도움이 되는 내용이 오는 것이 적절하다.

11 'in mind'와 함께 사용이 되어 '~을 명심하다'라는 의미로 'keep'이 적절하다.

12 빈칸 다음에 Ryan의 부모님이 그의 성적에 대해 걱정한다고 말하는 것으로 보아 ⑤가 적절하다.

13 'Ryan은 왜 실망하고 있는가?'라는 물음에 대한 답은 '그의 부모님이 슈퍼스타 101에 참가하는 것을 허락하지 않아서.'이다.

14 (A)는 '~에 반대하여'의 의미이다. ③ 1959년, 티베트 사람들은 중국 통치에 반대하는 운동을 일으켰습니다. ① 나는 마하트마 간디의 동상에 기대어 서 있었습니다. ② 그들은 화재에 대비하여 예방책을 취했다. ④ 그의 빨간 옷이 눈과 대비를 이루며 선명히 두드러져 보였다. ⑤ 당신은 비용 대비 이득을 따져 봐야 한다.

15 ① This is the thing that she likes. 또는 This is what she

---

likes. ③ He read a newspaper, and drank[as he was drinking] coffee. 또는 He read a newspaper, drinking coffee.

16 '비록 나는 운동을 많이 하지만, 여전히 살이 찌고 있다.'라는 뜻이 가장 적절하므로 접속사 Though를 쓴 문장이 가장 가까운 뜻이다.

17 주절과 접속사가 있는 부사절의 형태 또는 주절과 분사구문의 형태로 쓰는 것이 적절하다. He said good-bye as he waved his hand. 또는 He said good-bye, waving his hand.

18 글의 흐름상 적절한 구절을 골라 분사구문의 형태로 쓴다. (1) 그는 컵케이크에 장식하며 그의 직업에 대해 말해 주었습니다. (2) 그는 자신의 유명한 대사를 말하면서 그의 직업에 대해 말해 주었습니다. (3) 그녀는 몇 가지 마술을 보여 주며 그녀의 직업에 대해 말해 주었습니다. (4) 그는 그의 뉴스 보도를 저에게 보여 주면서 그의 직업에 대해 말해 주었습니다. (5) 그녀는 로봇을 조종하면서 그녀의 직업에 대해 말해 주었습니다.

19 선행사를 포함한 관계대명사 what을 '~하는 것'의 의미로 명사절(목적어)로 쓴다.

20 'to be the leader of a new IBM team'을 가리킨다.

21 ④ 못 보고 지나치다, 빠뜨리고 못 보다, ⓑ 직면하다, ① 직면하다, 맞서다, ② ~에 대처하다, ③ 다루다, ⑤ ~을 다루다, 상대하다

22 포트란은 '새로운 프로그래밍 언어'였다.

23 앞에 나오는 내용과 상반되는 내용이 뒤에 이어지므로 However가 가장 적절하다. ① 게다가, 더욱이, ② 따라서, 그러므로, ③ 비슷하게, 마찬가지로, ④ 그 결과

24 'be 형용사 enough to부정사'는 'be so 형용사 as to부정사' 구문으로 고치는 것이 적절하다. 참고: 'have the 추상명사 to 부정사' 구문은 'be 형용사 enough to부정사' 구문이나 'be so 형용사 as to부정사' 구문으로 고칠 수 있다.

25 전반부의 'he got upset'을 통해 'unpleasant'를, 본문 끝의 'This made Al Harrison break down the "Colored Ladies Room" sign.'을 통해 'sympathetic'을 찾을 수 있다. unpleasant: 불쾌한, sympathetic: 동정적인, 동조하는, 공감하는, ① upset: 속상한, disappointed: 실망한, ② nervous: 초조한, ④ bored: 지루한

26 ⓐ in: (시간의 경과를 나타내어) ~ 후에[~ 만에/~ 있으면], ⓑ stand up for: ~을 지지하다

27 ①번 다음 문장의 So에 주목한다. 주어진 문장의 결과를 나타내고 있으므로 ①번이 적절하다.

28 (A)와 ④: (소설 등의) 등장인물, ① 성격, 기질, ② 개성, ③ 문자(letter), ⑤ 인격, 품성

29 위 글은 Dorothy가 새로운 변화를 두려워하지 않고 도전하여 목적을 이루는 이야기이므로 ③이 적절하다.

30 Dorothy 덕분에 몇 명의 팀원들이 프로그래머가 될 수 있었는지는 대답할 수 없다. ① In 1961. ② She was worried the "human computers" would lose their jobs. ③ No. ④ She suggested bringing her team members with her.

The Frog Prince Continued

교과서
Reading

교과서 확인학습 A
p.226~228

01 Frog Prince	02 Characters
03 Scene	04 jumping
05 Stop jumping	06 can't stop
07 anymore	08 What's wrong with
09 I don't like it when	10 feel like running, as
11 hundreds of, were better off	
12 That's it	13 Scene
14 To himself, into	15 How
16 turn me back into, ever after	
17 look like, let you save	18 want
19 come in	20 Where
21 If	
22 turn me back into, live happily	
23 serve	
24 is made of cookies, by the name of	
25 I do	26 runs away
27 Could you, so	
28 on my way, give it a try	29 will be okay
30 what a fool, stuck, unhappily	
31 turns into	
32 giving me a second chance, how I should live	
33 keep my fingers crossed	35 smiling
36 have you been	37 else, did
38 even	39 looking forward to
40 hand in hand	

교과서 확인학습 B
p.229~231

1 The Frog Prince Continued

2 Characters: Frog Prince, Princess, Witch 1, Witch 2, Fairy

3 Scene 1: In a room

4 (*Prince comes in, jumping around.*)

5 Princess: Stop jumping around, honey.

6 Prince: Well, I just can't stop.

7 Princess: You're not a frog anymore.

8 Prince: What's wrong with you? You don't go down to the pond these days.

9 Princess: I don't like it when you jump around in the room. Go out to kill monsters and save our people.

10 Prince: I don't want to go out and kill anything. I just feel like running away. (*Picking up a book*) Listen! "They lived happily ever after. The end." I'm living my life as the book says, but we're not happy. What's the problem?

11 Princess: What's the problem? There are hundreds of problems! Sometimes I think we were better off when you were still a frog.

12 Prince: Still a frog .... Yes! That's it! (*Goes out*)

13 Scene 2: On the mountain

14 Prince: (*To himself*) I need to find the witch, who will turn me back into a frog. (*Shouting*) Ms. Witch, Ms. Witch. Where are you? Please help me!

15 Witch 1: (*Coming out of the house*) Hi, Prince. How are you feeling?

16 Prince: I'm glad to meet you. I'm the Frog Prince. I hope you can turn me back into a frog so I can live happily ever after.

17 Witch 1: Frog Prince, you say? That's funny. You don't look like a frog. Well, it doesn't matter. If you're a prince, you're a prince. And I won't let you save Snow White. Here, eat the rest of this apple.

18 Prince: No, thank you. That's not what I want! (*Runs away*)

19 (*Prince and Witch 2 come in.*)

20 Prince: Ms. Witch, Ms. Witch. Where are you? Please help me! I'm the Frog ....

21 Witch 2: If you're a frog, I'm the King of France.

22 Prince: No, I'm not a frog. I'm the Frog Prince. But I need a witch to turn me back into a frog so I can live happily ever after. Can you do it?

23 Witch 2: Let's talk about it inside. I will serve you a delicious lunch. Come in.

24 Prince: Thank you for inviting me. Oh, this house is made of cookies and candies. Wait a minute. Do you know any children by the name of Hansel and Gretel?

25 Witch 2: Yes, Prince, I do. (*With her mouth watering*) They are not fat enough yet, but you are ....

26 (*Prince runs away and finds a fairy.*)

27 Prince: I'm glad to meet you, Ms. Fairy. I am the Frog Prince. Could you turn me back into a frog so I can live happily ever after?

28 Fairy: Well, I'm on my way to see Cinderella, but I'll give it a try. It's my first time, you know. (*Fairy turns Prince into a wheel.*)

29 Fairy: Oops! Sorry, but don't worry. Everything will be okay.

30 Prince: (*To himself*) Oh, what a fool I've been! I want to be sitting at home with the Princess, living happily ever after. But instead, I'm stuck here under this cart and I'll live unhappily ever after.

31 (*The clock hits twelve, and the wheel turns into Prince.*)

32 Prince: I can't believe this. Thank you for giving me a second chance. Now I know how I should live my life. (*Goes out*)

33 Fairy: (*Waving her hand*) You learned a good lesson. I'll keep my fingers crossed.

34 Scene 3: In the Frog Prince's house

35 (*Prince runs in, smiling.*)

36 Princess: Where have you been? I've been worried. Your clothes are a mess.

37 Prince: (*Looking at Princess*) You believed me when no one else in the world did. You loved me even when I was a frog. From now on, I will make you happier.

38 Princess: I'm glad to hear that. I'll make you even happier.

39 Prince: Great! I'm looking forward to our bright future. Ha-ha ....

40 (*They run to the pond together, jumping hand in hand.*)

🐺 서술형 실전문제
p.232~233

01 (1) feel like (2) feel like

02 (1) wheel, 바퀴 (2) frog, 개구리 (3) princess, 공주
   (4) fairy, 요정

03 (1) (c)art (2) (s)erved (3) (I)nstead

04 (1) Listening to music, she wiped the window.
   (2) Hearing the news, she began to cry.
   (3) Leaving now, you won't be late.

05 which → what   06 running

07 to jump → jumping

08 (A) jumps around (B) doesn't want

09 (A) *himself* (B) How (C) look like

10 to save

11 Because he thinks he can live happily ever after (if he becomes a frog again).

01 (1) 해석: 여러분은 종종 더운 여름날에 아이스크림을 먹고 싶어 한다. (2) 해석: 너무 추워서 나는 우리가 마치 북극에 있는 것처럼 느껴져!

02 (1) 지면 위로 차량이 부드럽게 움직이도록 차량 아래에 고정되어 있는 원형 물체 (2) 물속이나 물가에 사는, 점프하기 위한 긴 뒷다리를 가진 작은 녹색의 동물 (3) 왕이나 왕비의 딸, 또는 그들의 가까운 여성 친척 중 한 명 (4) 마법의 힘을 가진 날개가 있는 작은 사람같은 상상 속의 생명체

05 목적격 관계대명사 which의 선행사가 없고, 선생님이 말씀하신 것으로 해석하면 자연스럽기 때문에 선행사를 포함한 관계대명사 what을 쓰는 것이 적절하다.

06 feel like -ing: ~하고 싶다, ~하고 싶은 기분이다

07 '주변을 뛰어다니지 마세요.'라고 해야 하므로, to jump를 jumping으로 고치는 것이 적절하다. stop+to부정사: ~하기 위해 멈추다, stop+~ing: ~을 그만두다

08 공주는 왕자가 방 안에서 '이리저리 뛰어다니는 게' 마음에 안 들어 왕자더러 나가서 괴물들을 죽이고 백성을 구하라고 말하지만, 왕자는 밖에 나가서 아무것도 죽이고 '싶지 않다.'

09 (A) '혼잣말로'라고 해야 하므로 himself가 적절하다. to oneself: 혼잣말로, (B) How are you feeling?: 기분이 어때요? (C) look+형용사, look like+명사: ~처럼 보이다

10 let+목적어+원형부정사 = allow+목적어+to부정사

11 앞으로 행복하게 살 수 있을 것이라고 생각하기 때문이다.

🐺 단원별 예상문제
p.234~237

01 ②   02 shout   03 ①

04 water, water

05 am looking forward to watching

06 ④   07 ④   08 rest, rest

09 (1) better off (2) run away (3) From now on

10 ⑤   11 ④

12 (1) which was closed because it was Sunday
   (2) which is located near my school
   (3) who is good at kung fu

13 ⑤

14 My dad will not let me stay up all night.

15 ③   16 ⑤   17 ⑤   18 ③

19 ⑤   20 ②   21 ④   22 ④

23 ②　　　　24 ③　　　　25 ⑤　　　　26 ②

27 Do you know any children by the name of Hansel and Gretel?

28 ④　　　　　　　29 how foolish I've been!　　　30 ③

---

01 ②번은 '크고, 추하고, 무서운 상상 속의 생명체'의 뜻을 가지고 있는 'monster'에 대한 설명이다. 'dinosaur'에 관한 설명은 'a very large type of animal that used to live millions of years ago'가 적절하다.

02 유의어 관계다. 구하다 : 외치다, 소리치다

03 '대개 무언가를 다치게 하거나 손상시키기 위해 물건이나 사람을 힘을 가해 빠르게 손을 대다'

04 • 부엌에서 나는 냄새에 우리 입 안에 군침이 돌았다. • 비는 자연에서 물의 순환에 의한 결과이다.

05 앞으로 다가올 일에 대한 기대감을 표현하는 말로 'I'm looking forward to+명사/동명사'를 사용한다.

06 • hand in hand: 손에 손을 잡고. • turn ... into ~: …을 ~로 바꾸다 • by the name of: ~라는 이름의

07 모두 반의어 관계이고, ④번은 '외치다'라는 뜻의 유의어 관계이다.

08 take a rest: 휴식을 취하다 the rest: 나머지. • 휴식을 취하는 것은 좀더 활기차고 활동적이게 해 줄 것이다. • 남은 휴가 동안, 우리는 디즈니랜드에 갈 거야!

09 (1) 그는 3년 전보다 훨씬 잘 살고 있다. than이 있기 때문에 'good'의 비교급을 사용해야 한다. (2) 만약 낯선 어른이 여러분에게 오거나 부른다면, 도망치세요. (3) 이제부터, 우리는 어떠한 일본 제품도 판매하지 않을 것입니다.

10 보기와 ⑤번의 'as'는 '~하듯이'의 뜻으로 쓰인 접속사이다. ① ~함에 따라, ② ~이기 때문에, ③, ④ ~할 때

11 ④번은 분사구문이므로 현재분사이다. ①, ②, ⑤ 전치사의 목적어로 쓰인 동명사 ③ 보어로 쓰인 동명사

12 접속사와 대명사를 관계대명사의 계속적 용법을 사용하여 같은 의미로 바꿀 수 있다.

13 'What (a) 형용사+명사+주어+동사!' 어순으로 감탄문을 쓴다.

14 'let+목적어+원형부정사'는 'allow+목적어+to부정사'로 쓸 수 있다. 주어진 단어 중 'to'가 없기 때문에 let을 이용하여 문장을 완성한다.

15 stop 동명사: ~하기를 멈추다, stop to부정사: ~하기 위해 멈추다. • 나는 복통이 있다. 나는 먹는 것을 멈추어야 한다. • 한 소년이 장난감을 찾고 있었다. 그래서 나는 그를 돕기 위해 멈추었다.

16 ⑤ 관계대명사의 계속적 용법은 관계사 앞에 쉼표(,)를 쓰고 that은 사용하지 않는다.

17 ⑤의 by는 of로 쓰는 것이 적절하다. be made by: ~에 의해 만들어지다, be made of: ~로 만들어지다

18 보기에 쓰인 'did'는 앞선 'tell the truth'를 대신하는 대동사이다. ③의 'did'는 앞선 'moved slowly'를 대신하는 대동사이다. ①. ②, ④, ⑤: 일반동사 'did'

19 선행사를 포함하는 관계대명사 what이 적절하다.

20 ②는 Ms. Witch를 가리키고, 나머지는 다 Prince를 가리킨다.

21 '자신을 다시 개구리로 바꿔주는 것에 대한 대가로 왕자가 마녀 1에게 무엇을 지불할지'는 대답할 수 없다. ① It is on the mountain. ② He wants to meet a witch. ③ He wants her to turn him back into a frog. ⑤ Because he doesn't look like a frog.

22 ⓐ와 ④: ~하는 것처럼(접속사), ① ~이기 때문에(접속사), ② (자격·기능 등이) ~로(서)(전치사), ③ [보통 'as ~ as ...'로 형용사·부사 앞에서] …와 같은 정도로, 마찬가지로('as ~ as ...' 에서, 앞의 as는 지시부사, 뒤의 as는 접속사), ⑤ ~하는 동안에(접속사)

23 위 글은 '희곡'이다. ① (신문·잡지의) 글, 기사, ③ 전기, ④ 수필, ⑤ (책·연극·영화 등에 대한) 논평[비평], 감상문

24 ③ 'Princess' doesn't go down to the pond these days.

25 ⓐ turn A into B: A를 B로 바꾸다, ⓑ be made of: ~으로 만들어지다(물리적 변화), be made from: (화학적 변화)

26 '당신이 개구리라면 나는 프랑스의 왕이라는 말'은 왕자의 말을 '믿지 않는다.'는 의미이다. 'doubtful: 의심을 품은, ① 흥분한, ③ 지루한, ④ 우울한, ⑤ 만족한

27 by the name of: ~라는 이름의

28 시계가 12시를 치자 바퀴가 왕자로 바뀐 것이므로, '두 번째 기회'를 주셔서 감사하다고 하는 것이 적절하다. ③ identity: 신원, 신분, 정체, ⑤ an attractive personality: 매력적인 성격

29 'what+a+형용사+명사'는 'how+형용사[부사]'로 고칠 수 있다.

30 요정은 왕자를 바퀴로 바꿨다.

교과서 파헤치기

Lesson 1

단어 TEST Step 1
p.02

01 건강에 좋은	02 농담	03 예매하다, 예약하다
04 전달하다	05 그리워하다	
06 구할 수 있는, 이용할 수 있는		07 초조한
08 표현	09 글로 쓴, 글로 표현된	
10 신사	11 실제로	12 추측하다, 짐작하다
13 선물	14 인간적인, 인간의	15 다양한
16 어조, 말투	17 방귀를 뀌다	18 시각적으로
19 인기 있는	20 완전한, 전체의, 전부의	
21 기회, 가능성	22 얼굴의	23 점심시간
24 ~부터, ~ 이후	25 궁금해 하다	
26 드디어, 마침내, 마지막으로		27 약속하다; 약속
28 웃음	29 나타내다, 대표하다	
30 심지어, ~조차	31 문자, 편지	32 의미 있는
33 눈물	34 이사하다	35 계속해서 연락하다
36 ~와 같은	37 ~을 좋아하다	
38 ~을 의미하다, 상징하다		39 큰 소리로 웃다
40 점점 ~해지다	41 ~와 같은 …	
42 ~을 몹시 기다리다		
43 … (명사)가 ~(형용사)한 채로		

단어 TEST Step 2
p.03

01 joke	02 actually	03 stick
04 meaningful	05 deliver	06 expression
07 laughter	08 gentleman	09 finally
10 available	11 book	12 healthy
13 whole	14 human	15 promise
16 tone	17 miss	18 facial
19 written	20 visually	21 nervous
22 popular	23 present	24 quite
25 represent	26 move	27 guess
28 wonder	29 chance	30 tear
31 various	32 letter	33 cupboard
34 fried	35 laugh out loud	36 can't wait for
37 stand for	38 the same ~ as	39 care for
40 keep in touch	41 happier than ever	
42 take a look at	43 be worried about	

단어 TEST Step 3
p.04

1 various, 다양한   2 form, 형식, 방식
3 written, 글로 쓴   4 available, 구할 수 있는
5 visually, 시각적으로   6 since, ~ 이후
7 type, 타자 치다, 입력하다   8 deliver, 전달하다
9 gentleman, 신사   10 represent, 나타내다, 대표하다
11 conversation, 대화   12 symbol, 상징
13 book, 예약[예매]하다   14 emoticon, 이모티콘
15 human, 인간의, 인간적인   16 guess, 추측하다

대화문 TEST Step 1
p.05~07

Get Ready 2

(1) look happy, right / really sad, sick, at all / That's too bad
(2) be, good day, Take a look / glad to eat, can't wait for lunch break
(3) How, feeling, helping, clean / glad to hear that
(4) upset, all right / let, play, after school / Why don't you

Start Off – Listen & Talk A

1. moving, another country, How, feeling / excited to, whole / to hear, was worried about / Actually, miss, a lot / keep in touch / Let's have
2. is moving, How, feeling / going to miss / is going, invite, promised / glad to have, chance, travel

Start Off – Listen & Talk B

how are you feeling / feeling, sad, moving away / sorry, don't be, video chats / Why don't we, as, goodbye gift / something meaningful

Start Off – Speak Up – Mission

How are you / feeling / glad to hear that

Step Up – Real-life Scene

How, feeling / happier, ever / why, didn't you / booked / about / got messages / How cute, emojis, bring, light sticks / I'm glad to hear that, lots of fun

Fun Time

How, feeling / nervous, forgot to bring, How are / nervous, too, glad to find, who feels / too / How / happy, got, grade / angry, broke

Express Yourself A 1

How are / glad to get a present / present / which, sent for / wonder how high, can fly / Let me show

Express Yourself A 2

How, feeling / to cook, favorite / to know what it is / which, delicious, healthy / to try / Wait for, minutes

Check Yourself – Listen & Speak 1

how are you feeling / excited, have, in our class / why, excited / on, team, As you know, needs / I'm glad to hear, hope, joins

Get Ready 2

(1) B: You don't look happy. Are you all right?

G: No, I'm really sad. My dog is sick. He won't eat.

B: That's too bad.

(2) B: It'll be a good day today! Take a look at today's lunch menu.

G: Wow! I'm glad to eat fried chicken! I can't wait for lunch break.

(3) W: Good morning, Mr. Lee. How are you feeling?

M: I'm feeling very happy this morning. Some students are helping me clean the school.

W: I'm glad to hear that.

(4) G: You look upset. Are you all right?

B: My mom won't let me play soccer after school.

G: Why don't you ask her one more time?

Start Off – Listen & Talk A

1. G: Jihun, you're moving to another country next week. How are you feeling?

B: I'm excited to go to a whole new world, Yunju.

G: I'm glad to hear that. I was worried about you.

B: Actually, I'm sad, too. I'll miss all of you a lot.

G: Let's keep in touch online.

B: Okay. Let's have video chats often.

2. G: Minsu, Jihun is moving to Abu Dhabi in the UAE next week. How are you feeling?

B: I'm sad. I'm going to miss him a lot.

G: I'm sad, too, but I'm also happy. We can visit Abu Dhabi. He is going to invite us. He promised.

B: That's great! I'm glad to have a chance to travel to a new country.

Start Off – Listen & Talk B

B: Yena, how are you feeling?

G: I'm feeling very sad, Seho. My best friend Jihun is moving away.

B: Really? I'm sorry. But don't be so sad. You two can have video chats online.

G: You're right.

B: Why don't we make him a photo book as a goodbye gift?

G: Great idea. I'm glad to give him something meaningful.

Start Off – Speak Up – Mission

A: How are you feeling today?

B: I'm feeling happy. Today's lunch is great.

A: I'm glad to hear that.

Step Up – Real-life Scene

Nari: Hi, Jiho. How are you feeling?

Jiho: I'm happier than ever, Nari.

Nari: I know why. You did it, didn't you?

Jiho: Yes. I finally booked four tickets for the VTS concert!

Nari: Good job. Did you tell Minsu and Yujin about that?

Jiho: Sure. Oh, I just got messages from them. They said they are really happy. Look.

Nari: How cute! I like their emojis. They will bring light sticks and a nice camera.

Jiho: I'm glad to hear that. We're going to have lots of fun!

Fun Time

A: How are you feeling?

B: I'm nervous. I forgot to bring my math homework. How are you feeling?

A: I'm nervous, too. I have a math test tomorrow. I'm glad to find someone who feels the same.

B: Me, too.

A: How are you feeling?

B: I'm happy. I got a good grade. How are you feeling?

A: I'm angry. Someone broke my glasses.

Express Yourself A 1

G: How are you feeling today?

B: I'm really glad to get a present for my birthday.

G: What is the present?

B: It's this drone, which our grandpa sent for my birthday.

G: Wow! I wonder how high it can fly.

B: Let me show you.

G: Thanks.

Express Yourself A 2

G: How are you feeling?

M: I'm really glad to cook my favorite food.

G: I want to know what it is.

M: It's *japchae*, which is delicious and healthy.

G: I want to try some.

M: Okay. Wait for 30 minutes!

Check Yourself – Listen & Speak 1

G: Minsu, how are you feeling?

B: I'm really excited, Miso. We have a new student in our class. His name is Kim Kihun.

G: So why are you excited?

B: He was a soccer player on his school team. As you know, my team needs a player.

G: I'm glad to hear that. I hope he joins your team.

B: Thanks a lot.

01 How, in, Texts　　　02 Laughter, human

03 laugh out loud, joke

04 even, writings, as, conversations

05 How, we, that　　　06 form, written laughter

07 what it means　　　08 has been used since

09 Even, in, works

10 gentlemen, good night

11 anything important happens, let

12 *Much*, Act, Scene

13 Another, written laughter

14 stands for, Out Loud

15 quite, Rolling on, Laughing

16 expressions, popular, be typed

17 Have, safe trip

18 Make sure, don't miss　　　19 try, sure, miss

20 for wishing, safe trip

21 represents laughter, text

22 with, open, closed tightly　　23 not a word

24 used, represent, facial expression

25 emotion, expresses, feelings, visually

26 can't wait to

27 with tears of joy　　　28 small, called, emoji

29 laughing, available, laughter, various

30 hit, head, cupboard　　　31 Are, okay

32 hit, head, cupboard　　　33 Is, cupboard, okay

34 have grown, laughing sounds

35 needed to break wind　　　37 loud, so, just did

39 realized, listening, with, earphones

40 facial expressions, voice tones

41 By, care for, with

42 Laugh, written forms, and

43 when, cold out　　　44 was me yesterday

01 How, Texts　　　02 Laughter, human

03 laugh out loud, somthing funny

04 laugh even in our writings, as

05 How, that　　　06 form, written laughter

07 what it means

08 has been used since

09 in his works　　　10 gentlemen, good

11 anything important　　　12 Act, Scene

13 Another, written laughter

14 stands for Laughing, Loud

15 Rolling on the Floor Laughing

16 expressions, because, can be typed

17 Have a safe trip

18 Make sure, miss　　　19 miss u

20 wishing me a safe trip　　　21 represents laughter

22 laughing face with, open, closed tightly

23 a word

24 which, used to represent a facial expression

25 expresses, more visually　　　26 can't wait to

27 These days, face with tears of joy

28 called

29 available to use, various ways

30 hit my head　　　31 okay

32 hit, on the cupboard　　　33 okay

34 have grown bigger, even move, laughing sounds

35 needed to break wind　　　37 loud, so, just did it

39 realized, listening to, with my earphones

40 represent, facial expressions, deliver, voice tones

41 By using, care for, with them

42 Laugh, written forms, and, laugh

43 cold out　　　44 This was

1 글에서는 어떻게 "하하"라고 웃나요?

2 웃음은 인간 고유의 것이다.

3 우리는 농담을 듣거나 우스운 것을 보거나 행복감을 느끼면 소리 내어 웃는다.

4 우리는 이메일이나 문자 메시지 같은 글 속에서조차 대화에서 하듯이 웃는다.

5 어떻게 그렇게 하는가?

6 "하하"는 문자로 된 웃음의 한 형태이다.

7 모두가 그것이 무엇을 의미하는지 안다.

8 실제로 그것은 오래전부터 사용되어 왔다.

9 셰익스피어조차도 "하하"를 자신의 작품에 사용하였다.

10 DOGBERRY: 하하하! 자, 신사분들, 좋은 밤 보내시오.

11 그리고 만일 뭔가 중요한 일이 일어난다면 나를 찾아서 알려 주시오.

12 (셰익스피어. 헛소동. 3막 3장 4쪽)

13 또 다른 형태의 문자로 된 웃음은 LOL이다.

14 그것은 '크게 소리 내어 웃기'를 상징한다.

15 사람들은 또한 ROFL도 꽤 자주 사용하는데, 그것은 '바닥을 구르면서 웃기'를 의미한다.

16 이 표현들은 상당히 빠르게 타자를 칠 수 있어서 인기를 얻었다.

17 A: 내일 안전한 여행을 해.

18 나를 너무 많이 그리워하지 않도록 해. LOL

19 B: 좋아. 너를 그리워하지 않도록 할게. LOL.

20 안전한 여행을 기원해 줘서 고마워.

21 XD 또한 문자 메시지에서 웃음을 나타낸다.

22 그것은 입을 벌리고 눈을 질끈 감은 채 웃는 얼굴을 보여 준다.

23 XD는 단어가 아니다.

24 그것은 이모티콘이고, 얼굴 표정을 나타내기 위해 사용되는 한 무리의 문자나 상징이다.

25 이모티콘 XD는 우리의 행복한 감정을 하하와 LOL보다 더 시각적으로 표현한다.

26 나는 디즈니랜드에 가는 게 몹시 기다려져. XD

27 요즘 사람들은 '기쁨의 눈물을 흘리는 얼굴'인 😂를 사용한다.

28 이것은 '이모지'라고 불리는 작은 그림이다.

29 많은 웃는 이모지가 온라인에서 사용될 수 있고, 그래서 사람들은 다양한 방식으로 자신들의 웃음을 표현할 수 있다.

30 A: 찬장에 머리를 부딪쳤어.

31 B: 오, 이런! 너 괜찮니?

32 A: 찬장에 머리를 부딪쳤어.😂

33 B: 어 어! 천장 괜찮니?😂

34 어떤 이모지들은 크기가 커졌고, 또 어떤 것들은 심지어 움직이거나 웃음소리를 내기까지 한다.

35 A: 그래서 어제 나는 식당에 있었는데 정말 방귀를 뀌어야 했어.. 🐰

36 B: 그리고 …

37 A: 음, 음악이 정말 시끄럽길래 나는 그냥 뀌어 버렸어.

38 B: 그리고 …

39 A: 그리고 그때 나는 내가 이어폰을 끼고 음악을 듣고 있다는 걸 깨달았지.

40 웃음 표시는 우리의 얼굴 표정을 나타내고 우리의 목소리 어조를 전달할 수 있다.

41 다양한 웃음 표시를 사용함으로써, 우리는 친구들을 얼마나 좋아하는지 또는 그들과 함께 있어서 얼마나 행복한지를 그들에게 보여 줄 수 있다.

42 웃어라, 문자로 된 형태로라도. 그러면 친구들도 여러분과 함께 웃을 것이다.

43 추울 때 내 모습이네.

44 이건 어제의 나야.

1 How Do You "Ha-Ha" in Your Texts?

2 Laughter is human.

3 We laugh out loud when we hear a joke, see something funny, or feel happy.

4 We laugh even in our writings, such as emails or texts, as we do in our conversations.

5 How do we do that?

6 "Ha-ha" is a form of written laughter.

7 Everyone knows what it means.

8 Actually, it has been used since long ago.

9 Even Shakespeare used "ha-ha" in his works.

10 DOGBERRY: Ha, ha, ha! Well, gentlemen, good night.

11 And if anything important happens, find me and let me know.

12 (Shakespeare, Much Ado About Nothing Act 3, Scene 3, Page 4)

13 Another form of written laughter is LOL.

14 It stands for "Laughing Out Loud."

15 People also use ROFL quite often, which means "Rolling on the Floor Laughing."

16 These expressions have become popular because they can be typed quite quickly.

17 A: Have a safe trip 2mrw.

18 Make sure u don't miss me too much. LOL

19 B: OK. I'll try to make sure I don't miss u. LOL

20 Thanks for wishing me a safe trip.

21 XD also represents laughter in text.

22 It shows a laughing face with a mouth open and eyes closed tightly.

23 XD is not a word.

24 It's an emoticon, which is a group of letters or symbols used to represent a facial expression.

25 The emoticon XD expresses our happy feelings more visually than ha-ha and LOL do.

26 I can't wait to go to Disneyland. XD

27 These days, people use 😂 — a "face with tears of joy."

28 This is a small picture called an "emoji."

29 Lots of laughing emojis are available to use online, so people can express their laughter in various ways.

30 A: I hit my head on the cupboard.

31 B: Oh, my! Are you okay?

32 A: I hit my head on the cupboard. 😂

33 B: Uh-oh! Is the cupboard okay? 😂

34 Some emojis have grown bigger, and some even move or make laughing sounds.

35 A: So yesterday, I was in a restaurant, and I really needed to break wind. 🐰

36 B: And …

37 A: Well, the music was really loud, so I just did it.

38 B: And …

39 A: And then I realized I was listening to music with my earphones.

40 Laughing marks can represent our facial expressions and deliver our voice tones.

41 By using various laughing marks, we can show our friends how much we care for them or how happy we are with them.

42 Laugh, even in written forms, and your friends will laugh with you.

43 Me when it's cold out

44 This was me yesterday

구석구석지문 TEST Step 1   p.24

Self-study Guide
1. when you live
2. live in
3. Could you, when the next bus will come
4. in ten minutes

Link to the World
1. what the color red means
2. who cheer for, means
3. traffic light
4. Of all the meanings, never fails

Express Yourself C
1. guess what my brother got
2. got, from, who lives in

단어 TEST Step 1   p.26

01 끔찍한, 지독한   02 땀투성이의, 땀에 젖은
03 반장   04 더러운   05 두 배가 되다
06 활동   07 다른, 그 밖의   08 텅 빈, 비어 있는
09 제안하다   10 재채기하다   11 기쁨
12 쓰레기 봉투   13 걸다. 매달다   14 끈, 줄
15 힘든   16 채우다
17 불평하다, 투덜거리다   18 수리하다
19 인정하다, 시인하다   20 먼지
21 상추   22 이웃, 인근 주민   23 ~ 중에, ~ 사이에
24 쓰레기   25 포장지   26 상상하다
27 콩   28 도움이 되는, 유용한
29 궁금해 하다, ~할까 생각하다
30 쓰레기 더미, 지저분함, 엉망진창
31 배정하다, 배치하다, 맡기다   32 광경
33 단단히, 꽉   34 인기 있는
35 ~에 공들이다[애쓰다]
36 ~을 맡아, ~을 담당하여
37 설치하다, 마련하다   38 ~을 돌보다
39 A를 B로 채우다   40 A를 B로 나누다   41 A를 B로 바꾸다
42 ~할 준비가 되다   43 갑자기 나오다, 불쑥 나타나다

구석구석지문 TEST Step 2   p.25

Self-study Guide
1. A: Can you tell me where you live?
2. B: Sure. I live in Mokpo.
3. A: Could you tell me when the next bus will come?
4. B: Sure. It will come in ten minutes.

Link to the World
1. Do you know what the color red means.
2. • This is the uniform of the Reds, who cheer for the Korean soccer team. Red means "power" on this uniform.
3. • Red on a traffic light means "stop."
4. • Of all the meanings of red, "love" is my favorite. "Love never fails."

Express Yourself C
1. Yeji: Can you guess what my brother got for his birthday?
2. He got a drone from our grandpa, who lives in Busan.

단어 TEST Step 2   p.27

01 awful   02 dirty   03 suggest
04 double   05 fill   06 complain
07 fix   08 trash bag   09 dust
10 helpful   11 hit   12 string
13 assign   14 imagine   15 tight
16 empty   17 pleasure   18 admit
19 among   20 wrap   21 sweaty
22 bean   23 sneeze   24 hang
25 tough   26 popular   27 row
28 sight   29 trash   30 lettuce
31 mess   32 neighborhood   33 nursing home
34 heavy   35 be full of   36 take care of
37 set up   38 turn A into B   39 work on
40 be ready to-V   41 divide A into B   42 across from
43 in charge of

1 lot, 부지, 구획   2 fix, 고치다   3 fill, 채우다

4 awful, 끔찍한   5 tough, 힘든   6 sweaty, 땀에 젖은

7 empty, 텅 빈, 비어 있는   8 volunteer, 자원하다

9 complain, 불평하다   10 double, 두 배가 되다

11 admit, 인정[시인]하다   12 assign, 배치하다, 맡기다

13 suggest, 제안하다   14 dust, 먼지

15 nursing home, 양로원   16 hang, 매달다

Get Ready 2

(1) flower pot, heavy, Can I / kind, Thank you

(2) Let me help, fix / hold, tight, for helping

(3) Let's talk about, for / How about drawing, dirty / Sounds, Anything else

Start Off – Listen & Talk A

1. need, Let's / how about putting, flower pots by, make, prettier / good idea

2. How about hanging / Why don't you bring, good at painting / Thank, for saying, bring, mine

3. about, corner, Any / How about making, corner, bring / for suggesting

Start Off – Listen & Talk B

Don't / right, Let's talk, together / need to put, member, helpful for us to learn, members' / also need, plan, school year / help, remember / suggesting

Step Up – Real-life Scene

talk about, better / Let me tell, trash, bus stop / agree, Why don't we / cam put, bench, too / helpful, the elderly / How about putting, around, make, more beautiful / for suggesting, shall we / problem

Fun Time

Let's talk, town party / Why don't we cook / Thank, for

Express Yourself A

1. for coming, talk about / under, most, cleaned around, planted / popular place among

2. Let's talk, school gate, What do you think of / leaders set up, put up, a lot more, events / Let's thank, class leaders

Get Ready 2

(1) B: The flower pot looks heavy. Can I help you, Ms. Min?

W: You're so kind. Thank you very much.

(2) G: Let me help you fix the bench.

M: Please hold this tight. Thank you for helping me.

(3) B: Let's talk about what we can do for our town.

G: How about drawing pictures on the dirty walls?

B: Sounds good. Anything else?

Start Off – Listen & Talk A

1. B: What do we need in our club room? Let's talk about it.

G: Sure. Well, how about putting some flower pots by the windows? They'll make our room prettier.

B: That's a good idea. Thank you, Jiu.

2. B: How about hanging some pictures?

G: Good. Why don't you bring one of your pictures? You're good at painting, Seho.

B: Thank you for saying that. I'll bring one of mine.

3. B: Let's talk about the corner this time. Any ideas?

G: How about making a small library in the corner of the club room? I will bring some books tomorrow.

B: Great idea! Thank you for suggesting it, Minju.

Start Off – Listen & Talk B

G: Seho, we need something on the wall, too. Don't you think so?

B1: You're right. Let's talk about it together.

G: I think we need to put the club member list there. It'll be helpful for us to learn the new members' names.

B2: That's a good idea. We also need our plan for this school year on the wall.

G: Right! That'll really help us remember important school events.

B1: Thank you for suggesting great ideas, everyone. We are a good team.

Step Up – Real-life Scene

G1: Let's talk about how we can make our town better.

B: Let me tell you first. There's too much trash at the bus stop.

G2: I agree. Why don't we clean the place together?

B: Good. We can put a bench there, too.

G1: Great idea. It'll be helpful for the elderly.

G2: How about putting some flower pots around the

bench? They'll make thebus stop more beautiful.

G1: Thank you for suggesting great ideas, everyone. Then, shall we start tomorrow?

G2, B: No problem.

Fun Time

A: Let's talk about the town party.

B: Okay. Why don't we cook *bibimbap*?

A: Wonderful. Thank you for your idea.

Express Yourself A

1. M1: Thank you for coming, everyone. Let's talk about the Clean School Project.

   W: I like the corner under the tree most. The Science Club cleaned around the corner and planted the tree.

   M2: I like it, too. It is a very popular place among the students.

2. M1: Let's talk about the school gate this time. What do you think of it?

   W: The class leaders set up the board and put up some posters. We can know a lot more about school events.

   M2: Right! They did a good job. Let's thank the class leaders.

본문 TEST Step 1 p.33~34

01 Green Thumbs

02 complained, whole day

03 work, neighborhood, far better

04 why we were working

05 ugly, empty, across from

06 full, wraps, other, imagine   07 at, bet, there, too

08 ages, sizes, ready, work

09 up, awful mess, into   10 where to begin

11 only way, just, start

12 divided, into, assigned, to

13 By lunchtime, sweaty, wear

14 filled, with, ready, pull

15 filled, made us sneeze

16 end, admit, much better   17 first, the toughest

18 followed, rows, seeds, watered

19 about, stopped complaining, up

20 First, lettuce, then, beans   21 grew so fast

22 couldn't believe   23 doubled, size, few

24 later, every, what, ready

25 Lots, there, enjoy, sights

26 suddenly hit, what, thing

27 proud, have been, part

---

28 charge, picking, nursing home

29 will go to, in

30 even better, that, become

본문 TEST Step 2 p.35~36

01 Thumbs

02 complained, whole day

03 making, work, far better, to do

04 why we were working

05 ugly, empty, across from

06 was full of, wraps, broken, every other kind, you can imagine

07 I bet, bet there are, too

08 all ages and sizes, ready to work

09 clean up this awful mess, turn, into

10 where to begin

11 only way to do, just to start

12 divided, into, with string, assigned, to

13 By lunchtime, sweaty, wear gloves

14 filled, with waste, were ready to pull

15 As, dust filled, made us sneeze

16 At the end of, had to admit, much better

17 the toughest

18 made rows, watered

19 stopped complaining, popping up

20 First, the lettuce   21 grew so fast

22 couldn't believe

23 in size in just a few days

24 later, what new flowers are ready

25 Lots of, to enjoy the sights   26 suddenly hit me

27 proud, have been a part

28 I'm in charge of picking, nursing home

29 will go to

30 even better, that, has become

본문 TEST Step 3 p.37~38

1 식물을 잘 키우는 사람들

2 나는 온종일 불평했다.

3 우리 부모님은 나를 이웃 프로젝트에서 일하게 하셨지만, 나에게는 훨씬 더 나은 할 일들이 있었다.

4 나는 우리가 왜 이곳에서 일하고 있어야 하는지 이해하지 못했다.

5 그곳은 그저 Johnny's Shop 건너편에 있는 볼품없고, 오래되고, 텅 빈 지역이었다.

6 그곳은 잡초와 패스트푸드 포장지와 낡은 신문, 깨진 유리,

그리고 상상할 수 있는 모든 다른 종류의 더러운 쓰레기로 가득 차 있었다.

7 그 첫날 아침에 그곳을 보았을 때, 나는 "틀림없이 저 안에는 뱀들도 있을 거야."라고 생각했다.

8 그날 일할 준비가 된 — 모든 연령대와 몸집을 가진 — 우리 20명이 있었다.

9 나는 이 끔찍하게 더러운 곳을 청소하여 정원으로 바꿀 수 있다고 생각하지 않았다.

10 우리는 모두 어디서부터 시작해야 할지 궁금해 하고 있었다

11 그때 Hernandez 씨가 "그것을 할 유일한 방법은 그냥 시작하는 것입니다."라고 말했다.

12 그리고 나서, 그는 그 지역을 끈으로 네 구역으로 나누고, 5명을 각 구역에 배치했다.

13 점심 무렵, 나는 덥고, 땀이 났으며, 아버지가 나에게 장갑을 끼도록 한 것이 기뻤다.

14 우리는 쓰레기 봉투 50개를 쓰레기로 채웠고, 잡초를 뽑을 준비가 되어 있었다.

15 우리가 뽑으면 뽑을수록, 먼지가 공기를 가득 메워서 재채기가 나왔다.

16 그날이 끝날 무렵, 나는 그 지역이 훨씬 더 나아 보인다는 것을 인정해야 했다.

17 그 첫날이 가장 힘들었다.

18 그다음 주말에 우리는 열을 만들고, 꽃과 채소 씨앗을 심고, 물을 주었다.

19 약 2주 뒤, 나는 식물들이 자라나기 시작한 것을 발견했을 때 불평하는 것을 멈추었다!

20 처음에는 상추, 그리고 나서, 콩과 토마토.

21 그것들은 아주 빨리 자랐다.

22 나는 믿을 수가 없었다!

23 콩 식물은 1인치 자라났고, 토마토는 며칠 만에 크기가 두 배가 되었다.

24 두 달이 지난 지금, 나는 매일 어떤 새로운 꽃들이 피어날 준비가 되었는지 보러 그곳에 가는 것을 좋아한다.

25 이웃의 많은 사람이 그곳에서 만나 풍경을 즐기고 함께 이야기를 나눈다.

26 오늘 밤, 갑자기 생각났다 — 우리가 얼마나 좋은 일을 했는가!

27 나는 내가 그 일의 일부였다는 것이 자랑스럽다.

28 나는 'Fourth Street'에 있는 양로원을 위해 꽃을 따는 일을 맡았다.

29 채소들은 우리 마을의 모든 부엌으로 갈 것이다.

30 하지만 훨씬 더 좋은 것은, 사람들이 좋아하지 않았던 볼품없고 더러운 지역이 모두를 위한 예쁜 정원이 되었다는 것이다.

1 Green Thumbs

2 I complained the whole day.

3 My parents were making me work on the neighborhood project, but I had far better things to do.

4 I didn't understand why we were working on this place.

5 It was just the ugly, old, empty lot across from Johnny's Shop.

6 It was full of wild plants, fast food wraps, old newspapers, broken glass, and every other kind of dirty trash you can imagine.

7 As I looked at it that first morning, I thought, "I bet there are snakes in there, too."

8 There were twenty of us — all ages and sizes — ready to work that day.

9 I didn't think that we could clean up this awful mess and turn it into a garden.

10 We were all wondering where to begin.

11 Then Mr. Hernandez said, "The only way to do it is just to start."

12 Then, he divided the lot into four parts with string and assigned five people to each part.

13 By lunchtime, I was hot, sweaty, and glad my dad had made me wear gloves.

14 We filled fifty trash bags with waste and were ready to pull wild plants.

15 As we pulled and pulled, dust filled the air and made us sneeze.

16 At the end of the day, I had to admit the lot looked much better.

17 That first day was the toughest.

18 On the weekends that followed, we made rows, planted flower and vegetable seeds, and watered them.

19 After about two weeks, I stopped complaining when I found the plants had started popping up!

20 First, the lettuce and then the beans and the tomatoes.

21 They grew so fast.

22 I couldn't believe it!

23 The bean plants grew an inch, and the tomatoes doubled in size in just a few days.

24 Now, two months later, I like to go there every day to see what new flowers are ready to pop up.

25 Lots of people in the neighborhood meet there to enjoy the sights and to talk together.

26 Tonight, it suddenly hit me — what a good thing we did!

27 I'm proud I have been a part of it.

28 I'm in charge of picking flowers for the nursing home on Fourth Street.

29 The vegetables will go to every kitchen in our town.

30 But even better, an ugly and dirty lot that people didn't like has become a pretty garden for everyone.

5. I hope everybody likes it.

Link to the World

1. • Kampong Ayer is the largest "water village" in the world.

2. It is made up of about 40 small villages.

3. • All the houses are built over the water.

4. • There are schools, police stations, gas stations, and post offices.

5. It is much more beautiful than you think.

6. It is called the Venice of Asia.

구석구석지문 TEST Step 1
p.43

After You Read A

1. visited, after school

2. while, were looking

3. picked, flowers, took, to, nursing home

4. proud that, mad, for everyone

Do It Yourself

1. Our, Symbol

2. which, drew as, my town

3. designed, had taken, many different kinds of corn

4. much cuter than

5. everybody likes it

Link to the World

1. the largest, in the world

2. is made up of

3. are built over

4. There are, police stations, post offices

5. much more, than

6. is called

구석구석지문 TEST Step 2
p.44

After You Read A

1. I visited the town garden after school.

2. Some people were talking while they were looking at the beautiful garden.

3. I picked some flowers and took them to the nursing home.

4. I'm proud that we made a pretty garden for everyone.

Do It Yourself

1. Our Town Symbol

2. This is Oksig, which I drew as a symbol of my town.

3. I designed this after I had taken pictures of many different kinds of corn.

4. Oksig is much cuter than real corn.

단어 TEST Step 1   p.45

01 용감한	02 발견	03 대학, 대학교
04 뒤로	05 폭탄	06 뜨다
07 실수	08 존중하다; 명예	
09 창의적인, 상상력이 풍부한		10 아마도
11 수여하다; 상	12 개막	13 발명, 발명품
14 웃기는	15 의식, 식	16 저장하다
17 가치; ~의 가치가 있는		18 받아들이다
19 자석	20 열렬한, 간절히 바라는	
21 반복적으로	22 응원하다	23 전통
24 공연하다	25 실제로, 사실은	26 경제학
27 해군	28 수여하다	29 관심
30 연구, 조사; 조사하다		31 선원
32 유용한	33 1조	34 드문, 특이한
35 ~ 대신에	36 계속 ~하다	37 ~에 성공하다
38 큰 소리로 웃다	39 ~에 참여하다	
40 A가 ~하지 못하게 하다		
41 ~을 (열렬히) 하고 싶어 하다		
42 ~에서 떠나다, 나가다		43 행운을 빌다

단어 TEST Step 2   p.46

01 accept	02 opening	03 backward
04 discovery	05 eager	06 repeatedly
07 perform	08 economics	09 float
10 peace	11 honor	12 bomb
13 brave	14 award	15 ceremony
16 invention	17 while	18 laughable
19 actually	20 unusual	21 navy
22 magnet	23 maybe	24 mistake
25 sailor	26 tradition	27 research
28 trillion	29 useful	30 worth
31 imaginative	32 interest	33 university
34 receive	35 less than	36 instead of
37 succeed in	38 take part in	39 laugh out loud
40 keep -ing	41 get out of	42 be eager to
43 keep A from -ing		

단어 TEST Step 3   p.47

1 live, 살아 있는　2 award, 수여하다　3 sailor, 선원

4 trillion, 1조　5 accept, 받아들이다　6 magnet, 자석

7 navy, 해군　8 backward, 뒤의　9 discovery, 발견

10 float, 뜨다, 띄우다　11 research, 연구, 조사

12 invent, 발명하다　13 eager, 열렬한, 간절히 바라는

14 honor, • 명예 • 존경하다

15 imaginative, 창의적인, 상상력이 풍부한

16 university, 대학

대화문 TEST Step 1   p.48~50

Get Ready 2

(1) solved a lot of, I'm sure, win, award / think so / keep, crossed

(2) winner, award / to get, prize / I'm sure, get, prize, Good luck

(3) looking forward to / make, laugh out loud, get the prize

(4) get, award, keep my fingers crossed

Start Off – Listen & Talk A

1. can't wait for / What, going to do / practiced, for a few weeks / looking forward to / Actually, a little worried, afraid, make, mistake / Don't worry, do, job, my fingers crossed

2. take part in / m going to run, end / looking forward, seeing / sure, win / do your best, keep my fingers crossed

Start Off – Listen & Talk B

are you coming / going to play, for me to try / sure, do great, keep, fingers crossed / going to perform, other mothers / sounds fun, looking forward, watching, stage

Start Off – Speak Up

looking forward to, model, ready / so, nervous / do well, keep my fingers crossed

Step Up – Real-life Scene

field trip, talent show / going to, like, do in class, jokes / looking forward to it / show, sure / worry, do great, keep my fingers crossed / Let me show, act, Guess / sound like / going to show / make, laugh out loud

Fun Time

m going to travel / sounds great, m really looking forward to

going to enter, m worried about / Don't worry, keep my fingers crossed

Express Yourself A

1. Can you tell me, invention / a pair of special, clean, floor / win a prize, keep, crossed

2. looks interesting, cutting board, feeder / not only, board but also, feeder, at the same time / idea / really think so / looking forward, using

Get Ready 2

(1) G: You solved a lot of problems in class. I'm sure you'll win the Class Brain award.

B: Do you really think so?

G: Of course. I'll keep my fingers crossed for you, Sangjun!

(2) B: The winner of the Oh So Sweet award will get some candies.

G: Oh, I want to get the prize.

B: I'm sure you'll get the prize this time. Good luck, Jiu!

(3) B: I'm looking forward to the Best Joker award this time.

G: Ha-ha. You always make us laugh out loud. So you'll get the prize, Yunki. Good luck.

B: Thank you.

(4) B: Minji, you're a happy girl. I think you'll get the Ms. Cheerful award. I'll keep my fingers crossed!

G: Oh, thank you, Jiho.

Start Off – Listen & Talk A

1. G: Mom, I can't wait for the sports day.

W: What are you going to do on that day, Minji?

G: I'm going to play basketball for my class. We've practiced hard for a few weeks.

W: Oh, I'm looking forward to your game.

G: Actually, I'm a little worried. I'm afraid I'll make a mistake.

W: Don't worry. You'll do a good job. I'll keep my fingers crossed!

2. W: Soyun, are you going to take part in any races on the sports day?

G: Sure. I'm going to run a 100 meter race at the end of the day.

W: Wow, I'm looking forward to seeing you at the race.

G: But, Mom, I'm not sure I'll win the race.

W: Just do your best. I'll keep my fingers crossed!

Start Off – Listen & Talk B

G: Mom, are you coming to the sports day?

W: Sure. I'm going to play the game Kick a Shoe. This will be the first time for me to try it.

G: Don't worry. I'm sure you'll do great. I'll keep my fingers crossed for you!

W: Thank you. I'm also going to perform a funny dance with some other mothers.

G: That sounds fun. I'm looking forward to watching

you on the stage.

Start Off – Speak Up

A: I'm looking forward to the model airplane contest tomorrow. Are you ready?

B: Well, I think so, but I'm nervous.

A: You will do well. I'll keep my fingers crossed!

Step Up – Real-life Scene

Miso: We're going on a field trip next Tuesday. What are you going to do in the talent show, Jimin?

Jimin: I'm going to talk like our teachers do in class and tell some jokes.

Miso: Wow! I'm really looking forward to it.

Jimin: Will everyone like my show? I'm not sure.

Miso: Don't worry. I'm sure you'll do great. I'll keep my fingers crossed!

Jimin: Thank you, Miso. Let me show you one part of my act. Guess who? "Goood Jooob!"

Miso: Ha-ha, you sound like our English teacher.

Jimin: Do I? I'm going to show you more at the show.

Miso: Great! You always make us laugh out loud.

Fun Time

A: I'm going to travel to Jejudo next week.

B: Wow! That sounds great.

A: Yeah, I'm really looking forward to it.

A: I'm going to enter the dance contest next week, but I'm worried about it.

B: Don't worry. You'll do great. I'll keep my fingers crossed.

A: Thank you.

Express Yourself A

1. G: Can you tell me something about your invention?

B: They are a pair of special shoes. You can also clean the floor with them.

G: Great! I'm sure you'll win a prize. I'll keep my fingers crossed!

2. B: This looks interesting. Is this a cutting board or a bird feeder?

G: It is not only a cutting board but also a bird feeder. You can do two things at the same time.

B: That's a great idea!

G: Do you really think so?

B: Yes. I'm really looking forward to using it.

01 Ig Nobel Prize

02 happens, backward while, carrying

03 did research on, topic

04 research, enough to win

05 Maybe not   06 how about

07 won, fun research

08 awarded for, laugh, think

09 interest, honoring, unusual, imaginative

10 are presented by, winners

11 filled with, cheer, laughable

12 won, for, in   13 To save, instead of

14 enough, laugh out loud   15 also won, award

16 succeeded in floating, using

17 sense, humor, accepted, award

18 bring, to, face, how

19 in, for inventing, alarm

20 keeps running away, out   21 Not only, but, makes

22 number, keep, from, bored

23 opening, closing, words each

24 called, shouts repeatedly, bored

25 trillion, which, worth less

26 Throwing, is another, tradition

27 ends with, win, did

28 winners, receive lots of

29 awards, great honors like   30 a lot more fun

20 keeps running away, gets out of

21 Not only, but also, makes, laugh

22 a number of, keep, from getting bored

23 opening, closing speeches, two words each

24 an eight-year-old girl called, repeatedly

25 ten trillion, which, worth less than

26 Throwing, is, tradition

27 ends with, win, prize, did   28 do not receive

29 great honors like   30 a lot more fun

01 Ig Nobel Prize

02 happens, backward while, carrying

03 did research, topic   04 good enough to win

05 Maybe   06 how about

07 won one, fun reserch

08 are awarded for discoveries, laugh, think

09 to increase, interest, by honoring the unusual, the imaginative

10 are presented by real Nobel winners

11 is, filled with, eager to cheer, laughable

12 won, for

13 To save, made, shout, instead of using

14 funny enough, laugh out loud

15 won an award

16 succeeded in floating, by using magnets

17 a sense of humor, when, accepted, award

18 bring, to, how about

19 in, for inventing

1 이그노벨상

2 "당신이 커피 한 잔을 들고 가면서 뒤로 걸을 때 무슨 일이 일어날까?"

3 한국의 한 고등학생인 한지원은 2015년에 이 주제에 관해 연구했다.

4 이 연구 과제는 노벨상을 받을 정도로 훌륭할까?

5 아마도 아닐 것이다.

6 하지만 이그노벨상은 어떤가?

7 그는 이 재미있는 연구로 2017년에 상을 탔다.

8 이그노벨상은 '먼저 웃기고 나서 다음에 생각하게 하는' 발견에 수여된다.

9 그것은 특이하고 창의적인 사람들을 높이 평가함으로써 과학에 대한 사람들의 흥미를 늘리기 위해 AIR 잡지에 의해 1991년에 시작되었다.

10 그 상들은 하버드 대학의 Sanders 극장에서 진짜 노벨상 수상자들에 의해 수여된다.

11 그 방은 대개 '웃기는' 연구를 한 용감한 과학자들을 열렬히 격려하고자 하는 사람들로 가득 찬다.

12 영국 해군은 2000년에 이그노벨 평화상을 탔다.

13 돈을 아끼기 위해, 해군에서는 선원들에게 진짜 폭탄을 사용하는 대신에 "쾅!"이라고 소리치게 했다.

14 그것이 당신이 큰 소리로 웃을 정도로 우스운가?

15 Andre Geim도 그해에 상을 탔다.

16 그는 자석을 이용해서 살아 있는 개구리를 공중에 띄우는 데 성공했다.

17 그는 상을 받을 때, "내 경험상, 사람들이 유머 감각이 없다면, 그들은 대개 별로 훌륭한 과학자가 아니다."라고 말했다.

18 그것이 아직도 당신의 얼굴에 미소를 띠게 하지 않는다면, 이것은 어떤가?

19 2005년에 Gauri Nanda는 자명종을 발명해서 이그노벨 경제학상을 받았다.

20 그것은 잠자는 사람이 결국 침대 밖으로 나올 때까지 계속 도망을 다닌다.

21 수상자들의 재미있는 연구뿐만 아니라 이그노벨상 시상식도 또한 사람들을 웃게 만든다.

22 사람들이 지루해하지 않도록 하는 재미있는 것들이 많이 있다.

23 개회사와 폐회사는 단지 두 마디이다: "환영합니다. 환영합니다."와 "안녕. 안녕."

24 만일 누군가가 너무 오랫동안 말을 하면, Miss Sweetie Poo라고 하는 여덟 살짜리 여자아이가 "제발 멈춰요! 지루해요."라고 계속 외친다.

25 각 수상자는 10조의 짐바브웨 달러를 받는데, 그것은 미국의 1달러보다 가치가 낮다.

26 종이비행기를 날리는 것은 또 다른 재미있는 전통이다.

27 이그노벨상 시상식은 "만일 당신이 상을 타지 못했다면 — 그리고 만일 탔다면 — 내년에는 좀 더 많은 행운이 있기를!"이라는 말로 끝이 난다.

28 수상자들은 많은 상금을 받지 않는다.

29 그리고 그 상은 노벨상같이 훌륭한 영광은 아니다.

30 하지만 이그노벨상은 과학을 훨씬 더 재미있게 만든다!

본문 TEST Step 4~Step 5 p.62~66

1 The Ig Nobel Prize

2 "What happens when you walk backward while you are carrying a cup of coffee?"

3 Han Jiwon, a Korean high school student, did research on this topic in 2015.

4 Is this research project good enough to win a Nobel Prize?

5 Maybe not.

6 But how about an Ig Nobel Prize?

7 He won one in 2017 for this fun research.

8 The Ig Nobel Prizes are awarded for discoveries that "first make one laugh and then think."

9 They were started in 1991 by *AIR* magazine to increase people's interest in science by honoring the unusual and the imaginative.

10 The prizes are presented by real Nobel winners in Sanders Theater at Harvard University.

11 The room is usually filled with people who are eager to cheer for the brave scientists with their "laughable" research.

12 The U.K. Navy won the Ig Nobel Prize for Peace in 2000.

13 To save money, the Navy made its sailors shout, "Bang!" instead of using real bombs.

14 Is that funny enough for you to laugh out loud?

15 Andre Geim also won an award that year.

16 He succeeded in floating a live frog in the air by using magnets.

17 "In my experience, if people don't have a sense of humor, they are usually not very good scientists,"

18 he said when he accepted his award.

18 If that still does not bring a smile to your face, how about this?

19 In 2005, Gauri Nanda won the Ig Nobel Prize in Economics for inventing an alarm clock.

20 It keeps running away until the sleeper finally gets out of bed.

21 Not only the winners' fun studies but also the ceremony for the Ig Nobel Prizes makes people laugh.

22 There are a number of interesting things that keep people from getting bored.

23 The opening and closing speeches are just two words each: "Welcome. Welcome." and "Goodbye. Goodbye."

24 If someone talks for too long, an eight-year-old girl called Miss Sweetie Poo shouts repeatedly, "Please stop! I'm bored."

25 Each winner receives ten trillion Zimbabwean dollars, which is worth less than one U.S. dollar.

26 Throwing paper planes is another fun tradition.

27 The Ig Nobel Prize ceremony ends with the words, "If you didn't win a prize — and if you did — better luck next year!"

28 The winners do not receive lots of money.

29 And the awards are not great honors like the Nobel Prizes.

30 But the Ig Nobel Prizes make science a lot more fun!

구석구석지문 TEST Step 1 p.67

Self-study Guide

1. words
2. showed, eagerness to learn
3. get, meaning
4. not only, but also

Express Yourself C

1. Stairs
2. These, Magic
3. not only, going, but also, storing
4. useful enough to make, much easier

Link to the World

1. Nobel Prize
2. named after, Swedish scientist
3. is awarded to, who, great work
4. all the winners, the youngest
5. at the age of, had fought, children's rights

6. received, three times
7. Not only, but also, was awarded

구석구석지문 TEST Step 2 p.68

Self-study Guide

1. New words again!
2. He showed great eagerness to learn new things.
3. Oh, I get the meaning of "-ness."
4. Now I know not only the meaning of "eager" but also the meaning of "eagerness."

Express Yourself C

1. Magic Stairs
2. These are Magic Stairs.
3. You can use them not only for going up and down but also for storing things.
4. This invention is useful enough to make your life much easier.

Link to the World

1. The Nobel Prize
2. The Nobel Prize was named after Alfred Nobel, a Swedish scientist.
3. It is awarded to people who have done great work for the world.
4. Of all the winners, Malala Yousafzai is the youngest.
5. She won the Nobel Prize at the age of 17 because she had fought for women's and children's rights.
6. The Curie family received the Nobel Prize three times.
7. Not only Marie Curie but also her daughter was awarded the Nobel Prize.

단어 TEST Step 1 p.69

01 알아보다, 인정하다　02 직업, 직장 생활
03 대회, 시합　04 숨겨진, 비밀의　05 능력
06 감명을 주다, 깊은 인상을 주다　07 소송 사건
08 (상황에) 직면하다　09 판사　10 마술사
11 전문가　12 허락　13 조종하다
14 (중요한) 인물, 숫자　15 웃음(소리)
16 시합, 경기　17 (연극, 영화 등의) 대사
18 발표　19 유용한　20 받아들이다
21 중요하다, 문제가 되다　22 용기
23 기록　24 색깔이 있는, 유색 인종의
25 관리자, 경영자　26 제의, 제안　27 장식하다
28 등장인물　29 옷걸이　30 실망한
31 설치하다　32 ~에 반대하여, ~에 맞서
33 허락하다　34 나중에, 후에　35 기분이 상하다
36 ~을 옹호하다, 지지하다　37 포기하다
38 ~을 부수다　39 ~을 극복하다　40 ~ 덕분에
41 ~을 준비하다　42 ~을 비웃다　43 ~할 수밖에 없다

단어 TEST Step 2 p.70

01 ability	02 hidden	03 impress
04 courage	05 accept	06 decorate
07 colored	08 career	09 against
10 character	11 disappointed	12 presentation
13 case	14 record	15 magician
16 figure	17 permission	18 recognize
19 control	20 install	21 judge
22 later	23 matter	24 offer
25 lose	26 expert	27 face
28 match	29 line	30 competition
31 useful	32 speech	33 manager
34 laughter	35 give up	36 thanks to
37 stand up for	38 look down	39 keep ~ in mind
40 get over	41 keep -ing	42 laugh at
43 break down		

단어 TEST Step 3 p.71

1 colored, 유색 인종의　2 hidden, 숨겨진, 비밀의
3 figure, (중요한) 인물, 거물　4 baker, 제빵사
5 face, (상황에) 직면하다　6 allow, 허락하다
7 laughter, 웃음(소리)　8 career, 직업, 직장 생활

9 engineer, 기술자, 엔지니어   10 courage, 용기

11 permission, 허락   12 expert, 전문가

13 judge, 판사   14 manager, 관리자, 경영자

15 space, 우주   16 record, 기록

대화문 TEST Step 1
p.72~73

Get Ready 2

(1) look down, the matter / to take dance classes, that idea, that, should / sorry to hear that

(2) disappointed / preparing for, competition, record, What / keep practicing, sure, get better and better

(3) to be, cook, laughs at, give up / never give up, good at cooking, cook

Start Off – Listen & Talk A

1. look, Why, disappointed / lost, because of, mistake / makes mistakes / should practice more / practice makes perfect

2. are you disappointed / give, presentation / Take, easy, speech, a little, presentation / more slowly / help, understand, better

Start Off – Listen & Talk B

look down, disappointed / lost, cooking competition / sorry to hear that, tried hard / maybe, enough, learn more cooking tips / How about getting useful, from, online / try, for, advice / welcome, remember, dishes

Start Off – Speak Up

Why, disappointed / failed, audition, keep trying / Don't give up, better

Start Up – Real-life Scene

disappointed / won't let, enter, singing competition / sorry to hear, against / to study hard, worried about my grades / parents, to be / Not yet, talk with / how much, Why don't you sing, in front of / Thank you for

Express Yourself A

1. look happy, disappointed / magician like, failed, competition, give up / Practice hard, get better, better, it's, to keep trying / your advice

2. come in, Are, interested in designing things / product designer, design / it's, to practice drawing, Reading, magazines will also help / keep that in mind

Learning Diary– Listen & Speak 1

look down, Why are you disappointed / lost, because, made, mistake / Don't be, happen, anyone / practice more / if, You know

대화문 TEST Step 2
p.74~75

Get Ready 2

(1) G: You look down today. What's the matter?

B: I want to take dance classes, but my father doesn't like that idea. He thinks that boys should play sports.

G: I'm sorry to hear that.

(2) G: Why are you disappointed?

B: I'm preparing for the ski jumping competition, but my record is not good. What should I do?

G: I think you should keep practicing more. I'm sure you'll get better and better.

(3) B: I want to be a cook, but everybody laughs at me. Do you think I should give up my dream?

G: No, never give up. I think you're really good at cooking. You'll be a great cook!

B: Thank you.

Start Off – Listen & Talk A

1. B: You don't look happy. Why are you disappointed?

G: We lost the basketball game because of my mistake.

B: Come on. Everyone makes mistakes.

G: Do you think I should practice more?

B: Well, yes. You know, practice makes perfect.

2. G: Why are you disappointed?

B: I didn't give a good presentation.

G: Take it easy. Your speech was a little fast, but I liked your presentation.

B: Do you think I should speak more slowly?

G: Yes. It will help your classmates understand you better.

Start Off – Listen & Talk B

G: Junsu, you look down today. Why are you disappointed?

B: I lost the cooking competition.

G: I'm sorry to hear that. I know you tried hard.

B: Yeah, but maybe that wasn't enough. Do you think I should learn more cooking tips?

G: Yes. I think they will help. How about getting useful tips from cooking shows online?

B: Okay. I'll try. Thank you for your advice, Mina.

G: You're welcome. Just remember I'm a fan of your dishes.

Start Off – Speak Up

B: Why are you disappointed?

G: I failed the audition for the Mapo Youth Band. Do you think I should keep trying?

B: Sure. Don't give up. You'll do better next time.

G: Thank you.

59

Jisu: Why are you so disappointed, Ryan?

Ryan: My parents won't let me enter Superstar 101, a singing competition.

Jisu: I'm sorry to hear that. Why are they against it?

Ryan: They want me to study hard and be a doctor. They're always worried about my grades.

Jisu: Did you tell your parents you really want to be a singer?

Ryan: Not yet. Do you think I should talk with them about it?

Jisu: Yes. Just show them how much you love singing. Why don't you sing the songs you made in front of them?

Ryan: Okay. I'll try. Thank you for your advice, Jisu.

Express Yourself A

1. W: You don't look happy. Why are you disappointed?

B: I want to be a wonderful magician like you, but I failed the magic competition. Do you think I should give up?

W: No. Practice hard every day and you'll get better and better. It's important to keep trying.

B: Okay, I'll try. Thank you for your advice.

2. W: Please come in. Are you interested in designing things?

B: Yes, I want to be a product designer. Do you think I should go to design school?

W: I think that will help, but it's more important to practice drawing every day. Reading design magazines will also help you.

B: Thank you. I'll keep that in mind.

Learning Diary– Listen & Speak 1

B: You look down today, Minji. Why are you disappointed?

G: We lost the soccer game because I made a mistake.

B: Don't be so sad. It can happen to anyone.

G: Do you think I should practice more?

B: Well, yes. I can help you if you want. You know, I'm a good soccer player.

G: Really? Thank you, Seho.

본문 TEST Step 1   p.76~78

01 Hidden Figures, NASA

02 watched, movie, last weekend

03 African-American women who worked

04 career in, as human

05 experts, get over difficulties

06 one, hidden figures, movie

07 hard, talent, recognized, ability

08 got upset, missing, for

09 where Katherine had been 10 The bathroom

11 There are, COLORED bathrooms

12 have, half, away, use

13 Hearing, felt, sorry   14 had courage to talk

15 made, break down, sign

16 character, most, three

17 learn, wasn't allowed to

18 judge, give her permission

19 can't change, color, skin   20 no choice but to

21 cases, which, matter, years

22 Which one, make

23 impressed, what, finally, permission

24 stood up, herself, other

25 what impressed me most

26 first African-American woman engineer

27 the last, hidden figure

28 installed, worried, would lose

29 new programming language

30 taught it, members

31 asked to, made, suggestion

32 accepting, offer, bring, with

33 need, lot, to program   34 can't do, alone

35 are ready

36 Thanks to, become programmers

37 afraid of, as, chance   38 what, need to learn

39 how to face challenges

40 won't forget, tears, laughter

본문 TEST Step 2   p.79~80

01 Hidden Figures

02 watched, last weekend

03 African-American women, worked at

04 in the 1960s as

05 of becoming space experts, to get over difficulties

06 three, hidden figures

07 showed a talent in, recognized her ability

08 got upset, was missing

09 where Katherine had been 10 bathroom

11 There, COLORED bathrooms

12 half a mile, just to use

13 Hearing this, felt, sorry

14 However, had courage to talk

15 break down   16 character

17 wasn't allowed to, white school

18 to give her permission   19 can't change, skin

20 have no choice but to

21 cases, in a hundred years   22 Which one

23 impressed, what, finally gave, permission

24 stood up for herself, other

25 what impressed me most

26 first African-American woman engineer

27 the last

28 were installed, would lose

29 new programming language

30 taught it

31 was asked to, made, suggestion

32 I'm not accepting, offer   33 lot, to program

34 alone   35 are ready

36 Thanks to

37 wasn't afraid of, as a chance

38 what I need to learn

39 Watching, how to face challenges

40 tears and laughter

1 NASA의 숨겨진 인물들

2 나는 지난 주말에 〈히든 피겨스〉라는 영화를 보았다.

3 그것은 NASA에서 일했던 세 명의 아프리카계 미국인 여성들에 대한 영화였다.

4 그들은 1960년대에 '인간 컴퓨터(계산원)'로 일을 시작했다.

5 하지만 그들은 NASA에서 우주 전문가가 되기를 꿈꾸었고 어려움을 극복하기 위해 열심히 노력했다.

6 Katherine Johnson은 이 영화에서 세 명의 '숨겨진 인물들' 중 한 명이었다.

7 그녀는 열심히 일했고 수학에서 재능을 보였으며, 그녀의 상사인 Al Harrison은 그녀의 능력을 알아차렸다.

8 어느 날, 그는 Katherine이 너무 오래 자리를 비웠을 때 화가 났다.

9 Al은 Katherine에게 어디에 갔었는지 물었고 그녀는 대답했다.

10 Katherine: 화장실요.

11 이 건물에는 유색 인종 전용 화장실이 없어요.

12 저는 단지 화장실을 사용하기 위해 반 마일을 달려가야 해요.

13 이 말을 듣고서, 나는 그녀가 정말로 안됐다고 느꼈다.

14 그러나 나는 그 문제에 대해 상사에게 말한 그녀의 용기를 보고 기뻤다.

15 이것은 Al Harrison으로 하여금 '유색 여성 화장실' 표지판을 부수게 만들었다.

16 Mary Jackson은 셋 중에 가장 나의 마음에 드는 인물이었다.

17 그녀는 로켓 공학에 대해 더 많이 배우고 싶었지만 백인 학교에 다니는 것이 허락되지 않았다.

18 그래서 그녀는 판사에게 허락해 달라고 요청했다.

19 Mary: 저는 제 피부색을 바꿀 수 없어요.

20 그래서… 저는 '최초'가 되는 것 이외에는 선택이 없어요.

21 판사님, 당신이 오늘 들을 모든 사건 중에서, 백 년 뒤에 어느 것이 중요할까요?

22 어느 것이 판사님을 '최초'로 만들까요?

23 판사는 그녀가 말한 것에 감명을 받고 마침내 그녀에게 허락해 주었다.

24 Mary는 그녀 자신과 다른 아프리카계 미국인들의 편에 섰다.

25 그것은 영화에서 나를 가장 감동하게 한 점이었다.

26 마침내 그녀는 NASA에서 최초의 아프리카계 미국인 여성 공학자가 되었다.

27 Dorothy Vaughan은 마지막 '히든 피겨(숨은 인물)'였다.

28 1961년 NASA에 IBM 컴퓨터가 설치되었을 때, 그녀는 '인간 컴퓨터(계산원)'들이 직업을 잃을까봐 걱정했다.

29 그녀는 새로운 프로그래밍 언어인 포트란을 공부했다.

30 그녀는 또한 그것을 그녀의 팀원들에게 가르쳤다.

31 나중에 그녀가 새 IBM 팀의 리더가 되도록 요청받았을 때, 그녀는 제안했다.

32 Dorothy: 저는 저의 여성 팀원들을 데려올 수 없다면 그 제안을 받아들이지 않겠습니다.

33 그 기계의 프로그램을 짜기 위해서는 많은 사람이 필요합니다.

34 저는 그것을 혼자 할 수 없습니다.

35 제 여성 팀원들은 준비가 되어 있습니다.

36 Dorothy 덕분에, 그녀의 팀원들은 프로그래머가 될 수 있었다.

37 그녀는 변화를 두려워하지 않고 그것을 기회로 이용했다.

38 그것이 내가 그녀에게서 배울 필요가 있는 점이다.

39 이 영화를 보면서, 나는 삶에서 어떻게 도전에 직면해야 하는지 배울 수 있었다.

40 나는 Katherine, Mary, 그리고 Dorothy의 눈물과 웃음을 잊지 않을 것이다.

1 The Hidden Figures of NASA

2 I watched the movie *Hidden Figures* last weekend.

3 It was a movie about three African-American women who worked at NASA.

4 They began their career in the 1960s as "human computers."

5 However, they dreamed of becoming space experts at NASA and tried hard to get over difficulties.

6 Katherine Johnson was one of the three "hidden figures" in this movie.

7 She worked hard and showed a talent in math, and her manager Al Harrison recognized her ability.

8 One day, he got upset when Katherine was missing from her desk for too long.

9 Al asked where Katherine had been, and she answered.

10 Katherine: The bathroom.

11 There are no COLORED bathrooms in this building.

12 I have to run half a mile away just to use the bathroom.

13 Hearing this, I felt really sorry for her.

14 However, I was glad that she had courage to talk to the manager about the problem.

15 This made Al Harrison break down the "Colored Ladies Room" sign.

16 Mary Jackson was the character I liked the most of the three.

17 She wanted to learn more about rocket science, but she wasn't allowed to go to a white school.

18 So, she asked a judge to give her permission.

19 Mary: I can't change the color of my skin.

20 So … I have no choice but to be the first.

21 Your Honor, of all the cases you'll hear today, which one will matter in a hundred years?

22 Which one will make you the "first?"

23 The judge was impressed by what she said and finally gave her permission.

24 Mary stood up for herself and for other African-Americans.

25 That was what impressed me most in the movie.

26 Finally, she became the first African-American woman engineer at NASA.

27 Dorothy Vaughan was the last "hidden figure."

28 When IBM computers were installed at NASA in 1961, she was worried the "human computers" would lose their jobs.

29 She studied a new programming language, FORTRAN.

30 She also taught it to her team members.

31 Later, when she was asked to be the leader of a new IBM team, she made a suggestion.

32 Dorothy: I'm not accepting the offer if I can't bring my ladies with me.

33 We need a lot of people to program that machine.

34 I can't do it alone.

35 My girls are ready.

36 Thanks to Dorothy, her team members could become programmers.

37 She wasn't afraid of change and used it as a chance.

38 That's what I need to learn from her.

39 Watching this movie, I could learn how to face challenges in life.

40 I won't forget the tears and laughter of Katherine, Mary, and Dorothy.

구석구석지문 TEST Step 1   p.88

Express Yourself C

1. had a good time with
2. told me, decorating
3. what he said, what your family love
4. had a good time with
5. told me about, saying his famous lines
6. what he said, what you act

After You Read A

1. made my manager break down, sign
2. asked the judge to allow, to study
3. to prepare for change

Link to the World

1. What, at this restaurant
2. make various Italian dishes
3. is difficult, your job
4. many things to do other
5. have to buy fresh meet, every day
6. wash the dishes, keep my kitchen clean
7. Are, happy with
8. tough job, what I do
9. feel proud, seeing people enjoy

구석구석지문 TEST Step 2   p.89

Express Yourself C

1. 1. I had a good time with the baker.
2. He told me about his job, decorating some cupcakes.
3. I will not forget what he said, "Make what your family love."
4. 2. I had a good time with the actor.
5. He told me about his job, saying his famous lines.
6. I will not forget what he said, "You can be what you act."

After You Read A

1. Katherine Johnson: I made my manager break down the "Colored Ladies Room" sign.

2. Mary Jackson: I asked the judge to allow me to study at a white school.

3. Dorothy Vaughan: I studied a new programming language to prepare for change.

Link to the World

1. Q1 What do you do at this restaurant?

2. A1 I make various Italian dishes and desserts.

3. Q2 What is difficult about your job?

4. A2 I have so many things to do other than cooking.

5. I have to buy fresh meet and vegetables every day.

6. I also wash the dishes and keep my kitchen clean.

7. Q3 Are you happy with your job?

8. A3 Yes, I am. It's a tough job, but I love what I do.

9. I feel proud, seeing people enjoy my dishes.

 Lesson S

단어 TEST Step 1   p.90

01 아무것도, 어떤 일도		02 믿다
03 수레	04 (손을) 흔들다	05 맛있는
06 충분히	07 요정	08 통통한, 살찐
09 백성, 국민	10 밝은, 눈부신	11 찾다
12 바보, 멍청이	13 기회	14 괴물
15 침이 고이다, 침을 흘리다		16 옷, 의복
17 치다, 때리다	18 안에, 안으로	19 대신에
20 구하다	21 죽이다	22 교훈, 단원
23 중요하다, 문제되다		24 바퀴
25 대접하다	26 마녀	27 엉망진창
28 공주	29 개구리	30 나머지
31 외치다	32 꼼짝 못 하는, 움직일 수 없는	
33 불행하게	34 걱정하다	35 지금부터 죽
36 손에 손을 잡고	37 혼잣말로	38 줍다, 집어 들다
39 도망가다, 달아나다		
40 ~에 가는 길(도중)에		41 더 잘 살다
42 ~라는 이름의	43 한번 해 보다, 시도하다	

단어 TEST Step 2   p.91

01 cart	02 monster	03 delicious
04 enough	05 believe	06 fairy
07 fat	08 witch	09 mess
10 save	11 stuck	12 bright
13 fool	14 people	15 serve
16 hit	17 inside	18 still
19 instead	20 clothes	21 kill
22 wave	23 matter	24 chance
25 even	26 rest	27 shout
28 pond	29 unhappily	30 water
31 lesson	32 princess	33 worry
34 funny	35 hand in hand	36 not ~ anymore
37 on one's way to		38 be better off
39 hundreds of	40 from now on	41 run away
42 jump around	43 to oneself	

단어 TEST Step 3   p.92

1 rest, 나머지　2 shout, 외치다　3 delicious, 맛있는

4 stuck, 꼼짝 못하는　5 lesson, 교훈　6 witch, 마녀

7 cart, 수레　8 invite, 초대하다　9 monster, 괴물

10 pond, 연못　11 princess, 공주　12 frog, 개구리

13 wheel, 바퀴   14 fairy, 요정   15 wave, (손을) 흔들다
16 hit, 치다, 때리다

01 Frog Prince Continued
02 Characters, Princess, Fairy
03 Scene, in, room   04 in, jumping around
05 Stop jumping around   06 just can't stop
07 a frog anymore
08 wrong, down, pond these
09 around, kill monster, save
10 feel, away, after, as
11 hundreds of, better off
12 Still, it, out
13 Scene, On, mountain
14 himself, witch, turn, back
15 out of, How, feeling
16 meet, into, ever after
17 like, matter, let, save   18 what, want, away
19 come in
20 Where, Please, help   21 If, frog, France
22 turn, back, live happily
23 Let's, inside, serve, delicious
24 made of, by, name
25 With, watering, fat enough 26 runs away, finds
27 Could, turn, so, after
28 on, way, try, into   29 worry, will be okay
30 what, fool, stuck, unhappily
31 hits, turns into
32 chance, how, should live
33 Waving, lesson, keep, crossed
34 In, Prince's house   35 runs in, smiling
36 been, worried, clothes, mess
37 believed, else, did, on
38 glad, hear, make, even
39 looking forward, bright future
40 to, jumping, in hand

01 Frog Prince Continued
02 Characters, Princess, Fairy
03 Scene, In   04 jumping around
05 Stop jumping   06 can't stop
07 anymore
08 What's wrong with, these days

09 I don't like it when, kill monsters, save
10 feel like running away, Picking up, as
11 hundreds of, were better off when, were still
12 That's it   13 Scene, On
14 To himself, turn, into   15 out of, How
16 turn me back into, so, live happily ever after
17 look like, doesn't matter, let you save, rest
18 want   19 come in
20 Where   21 If
22 turn me back into, live happily
23 Let's, serve, delicious
24 for inviting, is made of cookies, by the name of
25 I do, fat enough   26 runs away
27 Could you, so
28 on my way, give it a try, turns, into
29 don't worry, will be okay
30 what a fool, living happily, stuck, unhappily
31 turns into
32 giving me a second chance, how I should live
33 Waving, lesson, keep my fingers crossed
34 Prince's house   35 smiling
36 have you been, clothes, mess
37 else, did, From now on
38 even
39 looking forward to, bright future
40 jumping hand in hand

1 계속된 개구리 왕자
2 등장인물: 개구리 왕자, 공주, 마녀 1, 마녀 2, 요정
3 장면 1: 방 안에서
4 (왕자가 이리저리 뛰어다니며 등장한다.)
5 공주: 여보, 이리저리 뛰어다니지 마세요.
6 왕자: 저, 나는 단지 멈출 수 없을 뿐이에요.
7 공주: 당신은 이제 개구리가 아니에요.
8 왕자: 당신한테 무슨 문제가 있어요? 요즘 당신은 연못으로
   내려가지도 않잖아요.
9 공주: 나는 당신이 방 안에서 이리저리 뛰어다니는 게 마음에
   안 들어요. 나가서 괴물들을 죽이고 우리 백성을 구하세요.
10 왕자: 나는 밖에 나가서 아무것도 죽이고 싶지 않아요. 나는
   단지 멀리 뛰어다니고 싶을 뿐이오. (책을 집어 들고) 들어 봐요!
   "그들은 그 후로 행복하게 살았다. 끝." 나는 책에서 말한
   것처럼 내 인생을 살고 있지만, 우리는 행복하지 않아요. 뭐가
   문제일까요?
11 공주: 뭐가 문제냐고요? 수백 가지 문제가 있어요! 가끔 나는
   당신이 아직 개구리일 때 더 잘 살지 않았나 생각해요.
12 왕자: 아직 개구리라 …. 그래! 바로 그거요! (퇴장한다.)

64 정답 및 해설

13 장면 2: 산속에서

14 왕자: (혼잣말로) 나는 마녀를 찾아야 해. 그녀가 나를 다시 개구리로 바꿔 줄 거야. (소리치며) 마녀님, 마녀님. 어디 계세요? 저 좀 도와주세요!

15 마녀 1: (집 밖으로 나오며) 안녕, 왕자님. 기분이 어때요?

16 왕자: 당신을 만나서 기뻐요. 저는 개구리 왕자예요. 저는 당신이 저를 다시 개구리로 바꿔줘서 제가 앞으로 행복하게 살 수 있게 되기를 원해요.

17 마녀 1: 개구리 왕자라고 했어요? 그거 웃기는군요. 당신은 개구리처럼 보이지 않아요. 음, 그건 중요하지 않아요. 당신이 왕자라면 왕자인 거죠. 그리고 나는 당신이 백설공주를 구하도록 놔두지 않을 거예요. 여기, 이 사과의 나머지를 먹어요.

18 왕자: 고맙지만 됐어요. 그건 제가 원하는 게 아니에요! (도망간다)

19 (왕자와 마녀 2가 등장한다.)

20 왕자: 마녀님, 마녀님. 어디 계세요? 저 좀 도와주세요! 저는 개구리 ….

21 마녀 2: 당신이 개구리라면 나는 프랑스의 왕이에요.

22 왕자: 아니요, 저는 개구리가 아니에요. 저는 개구리 왕자예요. 하지만 저를 다시 개구리로 바꿔 줘서 제가 앞으로 행복하게 살 수 있게 해 줄 마녀가 필요해요. 그렇게 해 주실 수 있나요?

23 마녀 2: 안에서 그것에 관해 이야기해 봅시다. 내가 당신에게 맛있는 점심을 대접할게요. 들어와요.

24 왕자: 저를 초대해 주셔서 감사합니다. 오, 이 집은 과자와 사탕으로 만들어져 있네요. 잠깐만요. 당신은 헨젤과 그레텔이라는 이름의 아이들을 혹시 알아요?

25 마녀 2: 그래요, 왕자님, 알고 있어요. (그녀가 군침을 흘리면서) 그 애들은 아직 충분히 살이 찌지 않았지만, 당신은 ….

26 (왕자는 도망치다가 요정을 발견한다.)

27 왕자: 만나게 되어 기쁩니다, 요정님. 저는 개구리 왕자예요. 저를 다시 개구리로 바꿔 앞으로 행복하게 살 수 있게 해 주실 수 있나요?

28 요정: 음, 저는 신데렐라를 만나러 가는 길이지만, 한번 해 볼게요. 아시다시피 이건 제가 처음으로 해 보는 거예요. (요정이 왕자를 바퀴로 바꾼다.)

29 요정: 이런! 미안하지만 걱정하지 마세요. 모든 게 잘될 거예요.

30 왕자: (혼잣말로) 오, 내가 얼마나 바보였던가! 앞으로 행복하게 살면서 집에서 공주와 함께 앉아 있고 싶구나. 하지만 대신에 여기 이 수레 아래에 붙박여 있고 앞으로 불행하게 살게 되겠구나.

31 (시계가 12시를 치자 바퀴가 왕자로 바뀐다.)

32 왕자: 믿을 수가 없네. 두 번째 기회를 주셔서 감사합니다. 이제 나는 내 인생을 어떻게 살아야 할지 알겠어요. (퇴장한다)

33 요정: (손을 흔들며) 좋은 교훈을 배웠군요. 행운을 빌어요.

34 장면 3: 개구리 왕자의 집 안에서

35 (왕자가 미소를 지으며 뛰어 들어온다.)

36 공주: 어디 있었어요? 걱정했잖아요. 옷이 엉망진창이네요.

37 왕자: (공주를 바라보며) 당신은 세상 어느 누구도 나를 믿지 않을 때 나를 믿어 주었어요. 당신은 내가 개구리일 때 조차도 나를 사랑해 주었죠. 이제부터는 내가 당신을 더 행복하게 해 주겠어요.

38 공주: 그 말을 들으니 기뻐요. 제가 당신을 훨씬 더 행복하게 해 줄게요.

39 왕자: 좋아요! 난 우리의 밝은 미래를 기대할게요. 하하….

40 (그들은 서로 손을 잡고 함께 연못으로 뛰어간다.)

---

1 The Frog Prince Continued

2 Characters: Frog Prince, Princess, Witch 1, Witch 2, Fairy

3 Scene 1: In a room

4 (*Prince comes in, jumping around.*)

5 Princess: Stop jumping around, honey.

6 Prince: Well, I just can't stop.

7 Princess: You're not a frog anymore.

8 Prince: What's wrong with you? You don't go down to the pond these days.

9 Princess: I don't like it when you jump around in the room. Go out to kill monsters and save our people.

10 Prince: I don't want to go out and kill anything. I just feel like running away. (*Picking up a book*) Listen! "They lived happily ever after. The end." I'm living my life as the book says, but we're not happy. What's the problem?

11 Princess: What's the problem? There are hundreds of problems! Sometimes I think we were better off when you were still a frog.

12 Prince: Still a frog …. Yes! That's it! (*Goes out*)

13 Scene 2: On the mountain

14 Prince: (*To himself*) I need to find the witch, who will turn me back into a frog. (*Shouting*) Ms. Witch, Ms. Witch. Where are you? Please help me!

15 Witch 1: (*Coming out of the house*) Hi, Prince. How are you feeling?

16 Prince: I'm glad to meet you. I'm the Frog Prince. I hope you can turn me back into a frog so I can live happily ever after.

17 Witch 1: Frog Prince, you say? That's funny. You don't look like a frog. Well, it doesn't matter. If you're a prince, you're a prince. And I won't let

65

you save Snow White. Here, eat the rest of this apple.

18 Prince: No, thank you. That's not what I want! (*Runs away*)

19 (*Prince and Witch 2 come in.*)

20 Prince: Ms. Witch, Ms. Witch. Where are you? Please help me! I'm the Frog ....

21 Witch 2: If you're a frog, I'm the King of France.

22 Prince: No, I'm not a frog. I'm the Frog Prince. But I need a witch to turn me back into a frog so I can live happily ever after. Can you do it?

23 Witch 2: Let's talk about it inside. I will serve you a delicious lunch. Come in

24 Prince: Thank you for inviting me. Oh, this house is made of cookies and candies. Wait a minute. Do you know any children by the name of Hansel and Gretel?

25 Witch 2: Yes, Prince, I do. (*With her mouth watering*) They are not fat enough yet, but you are ....

26 (*Prince runs away and finds a fairy.*)

27 Prince: I'm glad to meet you, Ms. Fairy. I am the Frog Prince. Could you turn me back into a frog so I can live happily ever after?

28 Fairy: Well, I'm on my way to see Cinderella, but I'll give it a try. It's my first time, you know. (*Fairy turns Prince into a wheel.*)

29 Fairy: Oops! Sorry, but don't worry. Everything will be okay.

30 Prince: (*To himself*) Oh, what a fool I've been! I want to be sitting at home with the Princess, living happily ever after. But instead, I'm stuck here under this cart and I'll live unhappily ever after.

31 (*The clock hits twelve, and the wheel turns into Prince.*)

32 Prince: I can't believe this. Thank you for giving me a second chance. Now I know how I should live my life. (*Goes out*)

33 Fairy: (*Waving her hand*) You learned a good lesson. I'll keep my fingers crossed.

34 Scene 3: In the Frog Prince's house

35 (*Prince runs in, smiling.*)

36 Princess: Where have you been? I've been worried. Your clothes are a mess.

37 Prince: (*Looking at Princess*) You believed me when no one else in the world did. You loved me even when I was a frog. From now on, I will make you happier.

38 Princess: I'm glad to hear that. I'll make you even happier.

39 Prince: Great! I'm looking forward to our bright future. Ha-ha ....

40 (*They run to the pond together, jumping hand in hand.*)

MEMO

MEMO

적중 1◐◐ + 특별부록

Plan B

우리학교
최신기출

천재 · 정사열 교과서를 배우는

학교 시험문제 분석 · 모음 · 해설집

전국단위 학교 시험문제 수집 및 분석
출제 빈도가 높은 문제 위주로 선별
문제 풀이에 필요한 상세한 해설

중3-1
영어

천재 · 정사열

3학년 영어 1학기 중간고사(1과) 1회

문항수 : 선택형(27문항) 서술형(4문항) 20 . . .

◎ 선택형 문항의 답안은 컴퓨터용 수정 싸인펜을 사용하여 OMR 답안지에 바르게 표기하시오.
◎ 서술형 문제는 답을 답안지에 반드시 검정 볼펜으로 쓰시오.
◎ 총 31문항 100점 만점입니다. 문항별 배점은 각 문항에 표시되어 있습니다.

[광주 ○○중]

1. 다음 빈칸에 공통으로 들어갈 말로 가장 알맞은 것을 고르시오. (2점)

• I will _____ four tickets for the VTS concert.
• She wrote a _____ about space.

① report
② roll
③ type
④ scale
⑤ book

[충북 ○○중]

2. 다음 대화의 빈칸에 들어갈 말로 가장 잘 짝지어진 것은? (3점)

W: Jihun, you're moving to another country next week. (A)_____
M: I'm excited to go to a whole new world, Yunju.
W: I'm glad to hear that. I was worried about you.
M: Actually, (B)_____. I'll miss all of you a lot.
W: Let's keep in touch online.
M: Okay. Let's have video chats often.

　　　(A)　　　　　　　　(B)
① What's wrong with you? - I am so sad, too
② What's wrong with you? - I feel happy, too.
③ How are you feeling? - I am so sad, too.
④ How are you feeling? - I feel happy, too.
⑤ How are you feeling? - I am pleased, too.

[광주 ○○중]

3. 다음 대화의 흐름에 맞도록 빈칸에 들어갈 단어가 순서대로 알맞게 짝지어진 것은? (3점)

A: Finally, you became a member of the writing club. How are you feeling?
B: I'm very _____ but _____. I'm not sure I will do well.
A: Come on. You've practiced writing for a long time. You'll be the best soon.
B: Thanks. I'm _____ to hear that.

① worried – sad – glad
② excited – worried – nervous
③ happy – worried – glad
④ nervous – bored – happy
⑤ relieved – happy – worried

[부산 ○○중]

4. 다음 Seho의 말에 이어질 (A)~(E)를 가장 자연스럽게 순서대로 배열한 것은? (4점)

Seho: Yena, how are you feeling?

(A) Why don't we make him a photo book as a goodbye gift?
(B) I'm feeling very sad, Seho. My best friend Jihun is moving away.
(C) Really? I'm sorry. But don't be so sad. You two can have video chats online.
(D) Great idea. I'm glad to give him something meaningful.
(E) You're right. Is there anything we can do for him?

① (A)-(D)-(B)-(C)-(E)   ② (A)-(E)-(C)-(B)-(E)
③ (B)-(A)-(E)-(D)-(C)   ④ (B)-(C)-(E)-(A)-(D)
⑤ (B)-(C)-(D)-(A)-(E)

[5~6] 다음 대화를 읽고 물음에 답하시오.

Andriam: Hey, Lidrew. I heard you are moving to Abu Dhabi next week! ⓐHow are you feeling?

Lidrew: Well, I am (A)_____ to go to a whole new world. ⓑI really want to experience new things there!

Andriam: ⓒI'm glad to hear that. I was worried about you.

Lidrew: Actually, I'm sad, too. I will miss all of you a lot.

Andriam: ⓓLet's keep in touch online. We could share our Instabook IDs!

Lidrew: Instabook? LOL. That sounds great.

Andriam: Will you invite me to Abu Dhabi?

Lidrew: ⓔNo, I won't.

Andriam: Thank you. I'll wait for your invitation. Until then, let's have video chats often!

5. 위 대화의 빈칸 (A)에 들어갈 말로 가장 적절한 것은?

(2점)

① excited　　② touched　　③ irritated

④ terrified　　⑤ doubtful

6. 위 대화의 밑줄 친 ⓐ~ⓔ 중 흐름상 적절하지 않은 것은?

(3점)

① ⓐ　② ⓑ　③ ⓒ　④ ⓓ　⑤ ⓔ

7. 다음 두 문장을 합친 문장이 어법상 옳지 않은 것은?

(3점)

① I don't know. + Is she happy?

　→ I don't know if she is happy.

② Can you tell me? + Where did you go?

　→ Can you tell me where you go?

③ Do you know? + What is my hobby?

　→ Do you know what my hobby is?

④ I want to know. + How old is Heajin?

　→ I want to know how old Heajin is.

⑤ Can you tell me? + Who ate my sandwich?

　→ Can you tell me who ate my sandwich?

8. 어법상 가장 어색한 것은?

(4점)

① Can you tell me where you were?

② I wonder who stole my book.

③ Tell me how old you are.

④ I don't know how many friends you have.

⑤ Can you guess how long did she stay here?

9. 주어진 우리말을 영어로 바르게 옮긴 것은?　(3점)

• 나는 그가 일주일에 몇 권의 책을 읽는지 궁금하다.

① I wonder how he reads many books a week.

② I wonder how many he reads books a week.

③ I wonder how many books he reads a week.

④ I wonder how many books does he read a week.

⑤ I wonder how many does he read books a week.

10. 빈칸에 들어갈 말이 <u>다른</u> 하나는? (4점)

① This girl is Amy, _____ enjoys cooking.

② Tom was late, _____ surprised me.

③ I bought a new book, _____ had some dirty pages.

④ My grandfather passed away, _____ makes me sad.

⑤ Sarah tried to please her sister, _____ was really hard.

11. 다음 문장 중 어법상 가장 <u>어색한</u> 것을 고르시오. (3점)

① Do you think what they will do next?

② I wonder who broke the glasses.

③ Do you know how old she is?

④ I don't know where she went last night.

⑤ Can you tell me what you do in your free time?

12. 괄호 안의 의문문을 이용하여 간접의문문으로 바꾸시오. (4점)

• Do you know _____?
(Where does he come from?)

1. 대/소문자 구분 안 하면 1점 감점.
2. 주어진 말을 포함하여 완전한 문장으로 쓸 것.

답: _____

13. 우리말에 맞도록 빈칸에 3 단어로 쓰시오. (4점)

• 그는 딸이 한 명 있는데, 그녀는 울산에서 공부하고 있다.

답: He has a daughter, _____ _____ _____ in Ulsan.

14. 보기의 문장을 활용하여 우리말과 같은 뜻의 완전한 영어 문장으로 서술하시오. (5점)

(보기: It had lots of photos of my mother.)
• I opened the box _____.
(12 단어) (나는 그 상자를 열었다, 그리고 그것에는 나의 엄마의 많은 사진이 있었다.)

1. 대/소문자 구분 안 하면 1점 감점.
2. 주어진 말을 포함하여 완전한 문장으로 쓸 것.

답: _____

15. 다음 글의 흐름으로 보아, 주어진 문장이 들어가기에 가장 적절한 곳은? (4점)

Actually, it has been used since long ago.

Laughter is human. (A) We laugh out loud when we hear a joke, see something funny or feel happy. (B) We laugh even in our writings, such as emails or texts, as we do in our conversations. (C) How do we do that? "Ha-ha" is a form of written laughter. Everyone knows what it means. (D) Even Shakespeare used "ha-ha" in his works. (E)

① (A) ② (B) ③ (C) ④ (D) ⑤ (E)

[16~18] 다음 글을 읽고 물음에 답하시오.

How Do You "Ha-Ha" in Your Texts?
Laughter is human. We laugh out loud when we hear a joke, see ⓐsomething funny or feel happy. We laugh even in our writings, such as emails or texts, as we do in our conversation. How do we do that?
"Ha-ha" is a form of ⓑwritten laughter. Everyone knows ⓒwhat means it. Actually, it has been used since long ago. Even Shakespeare used "ha-ha" in his works.
Another form of written laughter is LOL. It stands for "Laughing Out Loud." People also use ROFL quite often, (A)_____ means "Rolling On the Floor Laughing." These expressions have become popular because they can ⓓbe typed quite quickly.
XD also represents laughter in text. It shows a ⓔlaughing face with a mouth open and eyes closed tightly. XD is not a word. It's an emoticon, (B)_____ is a group of letters or symbols used to represent a facial expression. The emoticon XD expresses our happy feelings more visually than ha-ha and LOL do.

16. 위 글의 빈칸 (A), (B)에 공통으로 들어갈 말로 가장 적절한 것은? (3점)

① who   ② that   ③ whom
④ which   ⑤ whose

17. 위 글의 밑줄 친 ⓐ~ⓔ 중 어법상 옳지 않은 것은? (3점)

① ⓐ   ② ⓑ   ③ ⓒ   ④ ⓓ   ⑤ ⓔ

18. 위 글의 내용과 일치하지 <u>않는</u> 것은? (3점)

① We can laugh in our writings.
② "Ha-ha" has been used for a long time.
③ LOL has become popular because it is cute.
④ XD is an emoticon.
⑤ XD shows our happy feelings visually.

[19~20] 다음 글을 읽고 물음에 답하시오.

These days, people use ― a "face with tears of joy." This is a small picture called an "emoji." Lots of laughing emojis are available to use online, ⓐ_____ people can express their laughter in various ways. Some emojis have grown bigger, and some even move or make laughing sounds.

19. 위 글의 빈칸 ⓐ에 들어갈 가장 알맞은 말을 고르시오. (3점)

① if   ② after
③ but   ④ so
⑤ until

20. 위 글의 내용으로 알맞지 <u>않은</u> 것을 고르시오. (3점)

① Emojis are small pictures.
② Emojis don't move or make sounds.
③ Emojis are available to use online.
④ Some emojis are getting bigger and bigger.
⑤ Emojis help people express their laughter in various ways.

[21~24] 다음 글을 읽고 물음에 답하시오.

Another form of written laughter is LOL. It stands ⓐ_____ "Laughing Out Loud." People also use ROFL quite often, which means "Rolling on the Floor Laughing." These expressions have become popular ⓑ_____ they can be typed quite quickly.

XD also represents laughter in text. It shows a laughing face ⓒ_____ a mouth open and eyes closed tightly. XD is not a word. It's an emoticon, ⓓ_____ is a group of letters or symbols used to represent a facial expression. The emoticon XD expresses our happy feelings more visually than ha-ha and LOL do.

21. 위 글의 ⓐ, ⓒ에 들어갈 가장 알맞은 것을 고르시오. (3점)
① with — of
② by — for
③ for — with
④ on — with
⑤ for — in

22. 위 글의 내용으로 알맞지 <u>않은</u> 것을 고르시오. (4점)
① XD는 단어가 아니고 이모티콘이다.
② ROFL은 XD보다 행복한 감정을 시각적으로 나타낸다.
③ XD는 입을 벌리고 눈은 감고 웃는 모습이다.
④ LOL과 ROFL은 문자로 된 웃음이다.
⑤ ROFL은 바닥에 구르며 웃기를 의미한다.

23. 위 글의 ⓑ, ⓓ에 들어갈 알맞은 말로 짝지어진 것을 고르시오. (3점)

	ⓑ	ⓓ
①	because	which
②	when	that
③	so	which
④	because	who
⑤	though	what

24. 위 글을 읽고 다음 질문에 대한 답을 완전한 영어 문장으로 서술하시오. (5점)

Q: What is an emoticon?
A: _____.

1. 대/소문자 구분 안 하면 1점 감점.
2. 완전한 문장으로 쓸 것.

답: _____

25. Which is NOT proper for the blank? (3점)

Laughter is human. We laugh out loud when we hear a joke, see something funny, or feel happy. We laugh even in our writings, such as _____ or _____, as we do in our conversations.

① emails
② texts
③ articles
④ letters
⑤ voice messages

- 5 -

[26~27] 다음 글을 읽고 물음에 답하시오.

ⓐ By using various laughing ①marks, we can show our friends how much we ②care for them or how happy we are with them. ⓑ Laughing marks can ③represent our ④facial expressions and ⑤deliver our voice tones. ⓒ Laugh, even in written forms, and your friends will laugh with you.

26. 문맥상 글의 순서가 가장 알맞은 것은? (3점)

① ⓐ-ⓑ-ⓒ   ② ⓒ-ⓐ-ⓑ   ③ ⓑ-ⓐ-ⓒ

④ ⓒ-ⓑ-ⓐ   ⑤ ⓑ-ⓒ-ⓐ

27. 위 글에 쓰인 단어와 뜻이 제대로 연결되지 않은 것은? (3점)

① mark: 표시

② care for: 좋아하다

③ represent: 나타내다

④ facial expression: 얼굴

⑤ deliver: 전달하다

28. Which is proper for the blank Ⓐ? (2점)

Another form of written laughter is LOL. It stands for "Laughing Out Loud." People also use Ⓐ_____ quite often, which means "Rolling on the Floor Laughing." These expressions have become popular because they can be typed quite quickly.

① ;)   ② XD   ③ LOL

④ OTL   ⑤ ROFL

[29~31] 다음 글을 읽고 물음에 답하시오.

Laughter is human. We laugh out loud when we hear a joke, see something funny or feel happy. We laugh even in our writings, such ⓐ_____ emails or texts, ⓑ_____ we do in our conversations. How do we do that? "Ha-ha" is a form of written laughter. Everyone knows what ⓒit means. Actually, it has been used since long ago. Even Shakespeare used "ha-ha" in his works.

DOGBERRY - Ha, ha, ha! Well, gentlemen, good night. And if anything important happens, find me and let me know.

(Shakespeare, *Much Ado About Nothing* (Act 3, Scene 3, Page 4) William shakespeare

29. 위 글의 ⓐ, ⓑ에 공통으로 들어갈 말로 가장 알맞은 것을 고르시오. (3점)

① after   ② as   ③ before

④ when   ⑤ like

30. 위 글의 내용으로 알맞지 않은 것을 고르시오. (3점)

① We don't laugh in our writings.

② Shakespeare used "ha-ha" in his writings.

③ Written laughter has been used since long ago.

④ We laugh when we hear a joke, see something funny, or feel happy.

⑤ Emails and texts are examples of writings.

31. 위 글의 ⓒ가 의미하는 것을 고르시오. (2점)

① human   ② Shakespeare

③ conversation   ④ everyone

⑤ ha-ha

◎ 선택형 문항의 답안은 컴퓨터용 수정 싸인펜을 사용하여 OMR 답안지에 바르게 표기하시오.
◎ 서술형 문제는 답을 답안지에 반드시 검정 볼펜으로 쓰시오.
◎ 총 29문항 100점 만점입니다. 문항별 배점은 각 문항에 표시되어 있습니다.

① When is the VTS concert?
② How is Jiho feeling now?
③ Is Jiho eager to go to the VTS concert?
④ How many tickets did Jiho book?
⑤ Will Minsu and Yujin go to the concert?

[부산 ○○중]

1. 우리말과 같은 뜻이 되도록 빈칸을 채울 때, 쓰이지 않는 표현은? (3점)

[보기]
• A white bird is a _____ of peace.
  하얀 새는 평화의 상징이다.
• Her facial _____ changed to happiness.
  그녀의 얼굴 표정은 행복으로 바뀌었다.
• Ha-ha is the sound of _____.
  하하는 웃음소리이다.
• TBH _____ "To Be Honest."
  TBH는 "To Be Honest"를 나타낸다.

① expression   ② laughter   ③ realizes
④ stands for   ⑤ symbol

[충북 ○○중]

3. 다음 대화에서 여자의 마지막 말에 대한 남자의 응답으로 가장 적절한 것은? (3점)

M: You don't look happy. Are you all right?
W: No, I'm really sad. My dog is sick. He won't eat at all.
M: _____

① Sounds great!
② That's too bad.
③ That sounds good.
④ I am feeling happy.
⑤ I am delighted to hear that.

[광주 ○○중]

2. 다음 대화의 내용으로 미루어 보아 답할 수 없는 질문은? (3점)

A: Hi, Jiho. How are you feeling?
B: I'm happier than ever, Nari.
A: I know why. You did it, didn't you?
B: Yes. I finally booked four tickets for the VTS concert.
A: Good job. Did you tell Minsu and Yujin about that?
B: Sure. Oh, I just got messages from them. They said they are really happy. Look.
A: How cute! I like their emojis. They will bring light sticks and a nice camera.
B: I'm glad to hear that. We're going to have lots of fun.

[부산 ○○중]

4. 다음 대화의 내용과 일치하는 것은? (4점)

Yunju: You're moving to another country next week. How are you feeling?
Jihun: I'm excited to go to a whole new world.
Yunju: I'm glad to hear that. I was worried about you.
Jihun: Actually, I'm sad, too. I'll miss all of you a lot.
Yunju: Let's keep in touch online.
Jihun: Okay. Let's have video chats often.

① Yunju wants to meet Jihun face to face.
② Jihun will be able to talk with Yunju online.
③ Yunju doesn't want to contact with Jihun.
④ Jihun feels sad because he can't go to a new country.
⑤ Yunju and Jihun are going to move to another country.

5. 다음 문장의 빈칸 (A), (B), (C)에 들어갈 말로 가장
바르게 짝지어진 것은?　　　　　　　　(4점)

- I am going to show you this photo,
(A)_____ my friend Amy sent to me.
- The soccer ball is from Messi, (B)_____
Amy met after a big soccer game.
- The cute son is Michael, (C)_____ likes
catching balls.

	(A)	(B)	(C)
①	which	who	who
②	which	that	who
③	which	which	which
④	who	who	which
⑤	who	which	who

6. 두 문장을 간접의문문을 이용하여 5단어의 한 문장
으로 쓰세요.　　　　　　　　　　　(4점)

1. I wonder.
2. What did he do?

답: _____ _____ _____ _____ _____

7. 어법상 가장 옳은 문장은?　　　　　　(4점)

① I wonder that you can help me.
② Do you know whose is this book?
③ I don't know what brought her here.
④ Do you think who broke the window?
⑤ I can't remember how much does it cost.

8. 다음 두 문장을 밑줄 친 부분에 유의하여 우리말로
해석하고, 두 문장의 의미의 차이를 비교하여 우리말
로 쓰시오.　　　　　　　　　　　(6점)

A. He has a son who is a lawyer.
B. He has a son, who is a lawyer.

(1) 우리말로 해석하시오.
A: _____
B: _____
(2) 의미의 차이 _____
* 반드시 두 문장의 차이를 비교하여 서술하시오.

9. 어법상 가장 바르게 쓴 것은?　　　　　(3점)

① He has two children, that go to middle
school.
② She has three friends, who they all live in
New York.
③ Look at this violin, Jenny gave me for my
birthday.
④ Jimin is wearing a hair band, which her
aunt bought for her.
⑤ I'm going to show you this photo, which
my friend Amy sent it to me.

10. 다음 빈칸에 들어갈 알맞은 것을 고르시오.　(3점)

- She has an office, _____ is located on
Temple Street.

① which　　② whose　　③ who
④ whom　　⑤ that

11. 다음 우리말을 영어로 바르게 옮긴 것은?   (3점)

> • 나는 네가 어떻게 그 인형을 만들었는지 궁금하다.

① I wonder what you made the doll.
② I wonder how do you make the doll.
③ I wonder how did I make the doll.
④ I wonder how did you make the doll.
⑤ I wonder how you made the doll.

12. 두 문장의 의미가 같도록 빈칸에 들어갈 알맞은 말을 고르시오.   (2점)

> • This girl is Amy, and she enjoys cooking.
> → This girl is Amy, _____ enjoys cooking.

① whom   ② that
③ who   ④ which
⑤ whose

[13~14] 다음 글을 읽고 물음에 답하시오.

> These days, people use — a "face with tears of joy." This is a small picture called an (A)"emoji." Lots of laughing emojis are available to use online, so people can express their laughter in various ways. Some emojis have grown bigger and some even move or make laughing sounds.
> Laughing marks can represent our facial expressions and deliver our voice tones. By using various laughing marks, we can show our friends (B)우리가 친구들에게 얼마나 관심을 갖는지 or how happy we are with them. Laugh, even in written forms, and your friends will laugh with you.

13. 위 글의 밑줄 친 (A)에 대한 설명으로 옳은 것은?   (4점)

① It is a group of small texts.
② It is not available online.
③ People can't express their emotions using this.
④ Some emojis are bigger than before.
⑤ Emojis cannot move or make laughing sounds.

14. 위 글의 밑줄 친 (B)를 영어로 바꾼 것으로 옳은 것은?   (3점)

① we care how much for them
② we care for them how much
③ how much care we for them
④ how much we for them care
⑤ how much we care for them

15. 다음 글의 빈칸에 주어진 철자로 시작하는 적절한 단어를 쓰고 그 이유를 쓰시오.   (5점)

> XD also represents laughter in text. It shows a laughing face with a mouth open and eyes closed tightly. XD is not a word. It's an emotion, which is a group of letters or symbols used to represent a facial expression. The emotion XD expresses our happy feelings more v_____ than ha-ha and LOL do.

(1) v_____
(2) 이유 _____

[16~17] 다음 글을 읽고 물음에 답하시오.

Another form of written laughter is LOL. It stands for "Laughing Out Loud." People also use ROFL quite often, @which means "Rolling On the Floor Laughing." These expressions have become popular because they can be typed quite quickly.

Have a safe trip 2mrw. Make sure u don't miss me too much. LOL
Okay. I'll try to make sure I don't miss u. LOL.
Thanks for wishing me a safe trip.

XD also represents laughter in text. It shows a laughing face with a mouth open and eyes closed tightly. XD is not a word. It's an emoticon, which is a group of letters or symbols used to represent a facial expression. The emoticon XD expresses our happy feelings more visually than ha-ha and LOL do.
I can't wait to go to Disneyland. XD

16. 위 글의 내용과 가장 일치하는 것은? (3점)

① XD는 음성 메시지에서 웃음을 나타낸다.
② ha-ha는 우리의 행복한 감정을 표현한다.
③ ROFL은 입을 벌린 채 웃는 얼굴을 보여준다.
④ ROFL은 느리게 타자를 치면서 인기를 얻었다.
⑤ LOL은 우리의 행복한 감정을 XD보다 더 잘 표현한다.

17. 위 글의 밑줄 친 @which가 가리키는 것은? (2점)

① XD   ② LOL   ③ ROFL
④ ha-ha   ⑤ People

18. 다음 글을 읽고, (A), (B) 두 문장을 바르게 영작한 문장을 짝지은 것을 고르면? (3점)

Laughing marks can represent our facial expressions and deliver our voice tones. By using various laughing marks, we can show our friends (A)우리가 친구들을 얼마나 좋아하는지 or (B)그들과 함께 있어서 얼마나 행복한지. Laugh, even in written forms, and your friends will laugh with you.

① (A) how much we care for them
   (B) how happy we are with them
② (A) how much we worry for them
   (B) how happy we are with them
③ (A) how we care for them much
   (B) how we are with them happy
④ (A) how much we care for them
   (B) how was we are with them
⑤ (A) how care for we them much
   (B) how happy them with we

19. 다음 글의 내용과 일치하지 않는 것은? (4점)

These days, people use — a "face with tears of joy." This is a small picture called an "emoji." Lots of laughing emojis are available to use online, so people can express their laughter in various ways.
Some emojis have grown bigger and some even move or make laughing sounds.

① 사람들은 기쁨의 눈물을 흘리는 emoji를 사용한다.
② emoji는 작은 그림이다.
③ 사람들은 온라인상에서 우는 emoji를 많이 사용한다.
④ 사람들은 다양한 방법으로 웃음을 표현할 수 있다.
⑤ 어떤 emoji는 움직이기도 한다.

[20~21] 다음 글을 읽고 물음에 답하시오.

Laughter is human. We laugh out loud when we hear a joke, see ⓐ<u>funny something</u> or feel happy. We laugh even in our writings, such as emails or texts, as we do in our conversations. How do we do that?

"Ha-ha" is a form of written laughter. Everyone knows what it means. Actually, it ⓑ<u>has used</u> since long ago. Even Shakespeare used "ha-ha" in his works.

Another form of written laughter is LOL. It stands for "Laughing Out Loud." People also use ROFL quite often, which means "Rolling On the Floor Laughing." These expressions ⓒ<u>had become</u> popular because they can ⓓ<u>be typed</u> quite quickly.

XD also represents laughter in text. It shows a laughing face with a mouth open and eyes ⓔ<u>closing</u> tightly. XD is not a word. It's an emoticon, which is a group of letters or symbols used to represent a facial expression. The emoticon XD expresses our happy feelings more visually than ha-ha and LOL do.

20. 밑줄 친 ⓐ~ⓔ 중 어법상 가장 바르게 쓴 것은?

(3점)

① ⓐ 　② ⓑ 　③ ⓒ 　④ ⓓ 　⑤ ⓔ

21. 위 글의 내용과 가장 일치하는 것은? (4점)

① There's no way to express our feelings in the writing.

② Written laughter was recently created by a modern writer.

③ LOL and ROFL are popular because they are the type of letters that sound funny.

④ XD is a shortened word that represents the sound of laughing.

⑤ XD is the most visual way to show our emotions among the above three examples of written laughter.

22. 다음 글의 괄호 (A), (B), (C) 안에서 어법상 알맞은 표현을 골라 옳게 나열한 것은? (4점)

These days, people use 😂 – a "face with tears of joy." This is a small picture called an "emoji." Lots of laughing emojis are available to use online, so people can express their laughter in various ways.

Some emojis (A)[grow / have grown] bigger, and some even move or make laughing sounds.

Laughing marks can represent our facial expressions and deliver our voice tones. By using various laughing marks, we can show our friends how (B)[many / much] we care for them or how happy we are with them. Laugh, even in written forms, (C)[or / and] your friends will laugh with you.

	(A)	(B)	(C)
①	grow	many	or
②	grow	much	and
③	have grown	many	or
④	have grown	much	or
⑤	have grown	much	and

[23~26] 다음 글을 읽고 물음에 답하시오.

Laughter is human. We laugh out loud when we hear a joke, see ⓐsomething funny, of feel happy.

We laugh even in our writings, ⓑsuch as emails or texts, ⓒas we do in our conversations. How do we do that?

"Ha-ha" is a form of written laughter. Everyone knows ⓓwhat does it mean. Actually, ⓔit has been used since long ago. Even Shakespeare used "ha-ha" in his works. Another form of written laughter is LOL. It stands for "(A)_____." People also use ROFL quite often, (B)_____ means "Rolling On the Floor Laughing." These expressions have become popular because they can be typed quite quickly.

23. 위 글의 내용과 일치하지 <u>않는</u> 것은?　　(3점)

① 웃음은 인간적인 것이다.

② 농담을 들을 때 우리는 크게 웃는다.

③ 우리는 이메일 같은 글 속에서는 웃지 않는다.

④ "Ha-ha"는 글로 된 웃음이다.

⑤ Shakespeare도 자신의 작품에서 "ha-ha"를 썼다.

24. 밑줄 친 ⓐ~ⓔ 중에 어법상 잘못 쓰인 것은?　(3점)

① ⓐ　　② ⓑ　　③ ⓒ　　④ ⓓ　　⑤ ⓔ

25. 빈칸 (A)에 들어갈 알맞은 말을 3단어로 쓰세요.

　　　　　　　　　　　　　　　　　　(4점)

답: _____ _____ _____

26. 빈칸 (B)에 들어갈 것으로 가장 알맞은 것은? (3점)

① what　　　② which　　　③ that

④ who　　　⑤ where

[27~28] 다음 글을 읽고 물음에 답하시오.

XD also represents laughter in text. ⓐIt shows a laughing face with a mouth open and eyes closed tightly. ⓑXD is not a word. ⓒIt's an emoticon, which is a group of letters or symbols used to represent a facial expression. ⓓThe cute dog is Lucky, which likes catching balls. ⓔThe emoticon XD expresses our happy feelings more visually than ha-ha and LOL do.

27. 위 글의 흐름상 어색한 문장은?　　　　(3점)

① ⓐ　　② ⓑ　　③ ⓒ　　④ ⓓ　　⑤ ⓔ

28. 'emoticon'의 정의를 볼 때, 'emoticon'은 무엇인가?　　　　　　　　　　　　　　　(4점)

① :-)　　　　　② ha-ha　　　　③ LOL

④ ROFL　　　⑤

29. 다음 Ⓐ~Ⓔ 중 어법상 옳지 <u>않은</u> 것은?　(3점)

ⒶLaughing marks can represent our facial expressions and deliver our voice tones. Ⓑ<u>By using various laughing marks</u>, we can show our friends Ⓒ<u>how we care for them much</u> or Ⓓ<u>how happy we are with them.</u> Laugh, even in Ⓔ<u>written forms,</u> and your friends will laugh with you.

① Ⓐ　　② Ⓑ　　③ Ⓒ　　④ Ⓓ　　⑤ Ⓔ

3학년 영어 1학기 중간고사(2과) 1회

반		점수	
이름			

문항수 : 선택형(31문항) 서술형(1문항) 20 . . .

◎ 선택형 문항의 답안은 컴퓨터용 수정 싸인펜을 사용하여 OMR 답안지에 바르게 표기하시오.
◎ 서술형 문제는 답을 답안지에 반드시 검정 볼펜으로 쓰시오.
◎ 총 32문항 100점 만점입니다. 문항별 배점은 각 문항에 표시되어 있습니다.

[충북 ○○중]

1. 다음 중 단어와 그 뜻의 연결이 적절하지 <u>않은</u> 것은? (2점)

① dirty - 더러운
② admit - 거절하다
③ fix - 고치다
④ bet - 확신하다
⑤ suggest - 제안하다

[충북 ○○중]

2. 다음 대화에서 빈칸에 들어갈 말로 알맞지 <u>않은</u> 것은? (2점)

B: What do we need in our club room?
_____
G: Sure. Well, how about putting some flower pots by the windows? They'll make our room prettier.
B: That's a good idea. Thank you, Jiu.

① Let's talk about it.
② Shall we talk about it?
③ I am taking care of it.
④ I'd like to talk about it.
⑤ Why don't we talk about it?

[광주 ○○중]

[3~4] 다음 대화를 읽고 질문에 답하시오.

A: Let's talk about how we can make our town better.
B: Let me tell you first. There's too much trash at the bus stop.
C: I agree. Why don't we clean the place together?
B: Good. We can put a bench there, too.
A: Great idea. It'll be helpful ___A___ the elderly.
C: How about putting some flower pots around the bench? They'll make the bus stop more beautiful.
A: Thank you ___B___ suggesting great ideas. Then, shall we start tomorrow?
B, C: No Problem!

3. 버스 정류장에 놓기로 한 것 2가지는? (3점)

① 쓰레기통   ② 벤치   ③ 노선표
④ 신문가판대   ⑤ 화분

4. 위 글의 빈칸에 공통으로 들어갈 단어는? (3점)

① for   ② about   ③ to
④ on   ⑤ at

[경기 ○○중]

5. 다음 문장의 빈칸 (A), (B)에 들어갈 말로 옳은 것은? (4점)

• When Anne came home, she found that somebody (A)_____ dinner for her.
• Yesterday, Heajin's teacher (B)_____ the handouts that she had made last week.

	(A)	(B)
①	prepared	give out
②	prepared	has given out
③	had prepared	gave out
④	had prepared	gives out
⑤	has prepared	gave out

- 13 -

6. 주어진 문장 다음에 이어질 글의 순서로 가장 적절한 것은? (4점)

> A: We need something on the wall. Don't you think so?

> (A) That's a good idea. We also need our plan for this year on the wall.
> (B) You're right. Let's talk about it together.
> (C) Thank you for your idea. We are a good team.
> (D) I think we need to put the club member list there. It'll be helpful for us to learn the new members' names.
> (E) Right! That'll really help us remember important school events.

① (A)-(B)-(D)-(E)-(C)
② (A)-(C)-(D)-(B)-(E)
③ (B)-(A)-(E)-(C)-(D)
④ (B)-(D)-(A)-(E)-(C)
⑤ (D)-(E)-(A)-(C)-(B)

7. 다음 빈칸에 들어갈 내용으로 가장 알맞은 것은? (3점)

> • Yuna was late for school. Later, she told it to me.
> → Yuna told me that she _____.

① was late for school
② had late for school
③ had been late for school
④ has been late for school
⑤ has late for school

8. 빈칸에 들어갈 말로 알맞지 <u>않은</u> 것은? (3점)

> My friend likes fall _____ better than summer.

① very
② much
③ even
④ a lot
⑤ still

9. 우리말과 같은 뜻이 되도록 빈칸에 들어갈 가장 알맞은 말을 고르시오. (3점)

> • He couldn't open the door because he _____ his key. (그는 열쇠를 잃어버려서 문을 열 수가 없었다.)

① had lost
② lost
③ was losing
④ loses
⑤ have lost

10. 다음 글의 밑줄 친 부분 중, 어법상 <u>어색한</u> 것은? (4점)

> I complained the whole day. My parents were making me ⓐ<u>work</u> on the neighborhood project, but I had ⓑ<u>the very</u> better things to do. I didn't understand ⓒ<u>why we were working</u> on this place. It was just the ugly, old, empty lot across from Johnny's Shop. It was full of wild plants, fast food wraps, old newspapers, broken glass, and ⓓ<u>every other kind</u> of dirty trash you can imagine. As I looked at it that first morning. I thought, "I bet there ⓔ<u>are</u> snakes in there, too."

① ⓐ ② ⓑ ③ ⓒ ④ ⓓ ⑤ ⓔ

[11~12] 다음 글을 읽고 물음에 답하시오.

2020. 7. 1. Anne's Diary

Yesterday, I had a big fight with my mom. I couldn't understand why she didn't let me use my phone at night. This morning, I woke up and I was still angry. I took online classes in my room and when I finished, I went to the kitchen. Mom wasn't there but I saw that she (A)_____ a delicious sandwich for me. (B)I felt sorry and wished that I hadn't yelled at her last night.

---

11. 위 글의 (A)에 들어갈 말로 행위의 시간차를 나타내기 위한 단어로 가장 알맞은 것은? (3점)

① made
② making
③ had made
④ has made
⑤ will have made

12. 위 글의 (B)에 드러난 'I'의 심경으로 가장 알맞은 것은? (3점)

① terrified
② regretful
③ delighted
④ optimistic
⑤ doubtful

[13~14] 다음 글을 읽고 물음에 답하시오.

ⓐThat first day was the toughest. On the weekends that followed, we made rows, planted flower and vegetable seeds, and ⓑwatered them. After about two weeks, I stopped complaining when I found the plants ⓒhave started popping up! First, the lettuce and then the beans and the tomatoes. They grew so fast. I couldn't believe it! The bean plants grew an inch, and the tomatoes

doubled in size in just a few days.

Now, two months later, I like to go there every day ⓓto see what new flowers are ready to pop up. ⓔLots of people in the neighborhood meet there to enjoy the sights and to talk together.

---

13. 위 글에 대한 설명으로 옳은 것은? (3점)

① 첫날이 가장 수월했다.
② 글쓴이는 주말에 줄을 만들고, 씨앗을 심고 물주는 일을 했다.
③ 상추가 가장 늦게 자랐다.
④ 토마토는 며칠 만에 3배 커졌다.
⑤ 글쓴이는 요즘 매일 정원을 방문해 꽃을 딴다.

14. 위 글의 밑줄 친 ⓐ~ⓔ 중 어법상 옳지 않은 것은? (2점)

① ⓐ ② ⓑ ③ ⓒ ④ ⓓ ⑤ ⓔ

15. 다음 빈칸 (A), (B)에 들어갈 말로 가장 알맞은 것은? (4점)

By lunchtime, I was hot, sweaty, and glad my dad (A)_____ me wear gloves. We filled fifty trash bags with waste and were ready to pull wild plants. As we pulled and pulled, dust filled the air and made us sneeze. At the end of the day, I had to admit the lot looked (B)_____ better.

	(A)	(B)
①	made	far
②	made	much
③	had made	very
④	had made	even
⑤	has made	much

[16~19] 다음 글을 읽고 물음에 답하시오.

[Sunday, April 5, 2020]
I complained the whole day. My parents were making me (A)work on the neighborhood project, but I had @far better things to do. I didn't understand why we were working on this place. It was the ugly, old, empty lot across from Johnny's Shop. There were twenty of us — all ages and sizes — ready to work that day. I didn't think that we could clean up this awful mess and turn it into a garden. We filled fifty trash bags with waste and pulled wild plants. At the end of the day, the lot looked better.

[Saturday, June 20, 2020]
Two weeks ago we made rows, planted flower and vegetable seeds, and watered them. And today I stopped (B)complain when I found the plants had started to pop up! First, the lettuce and then the beans and the tomatoes. They grew so fast. I couldn't believe it! The bean plants grew an inch and the tomatoes doubled in size in just a few days.

[Tuesday, August 15, 2020]
Tonight, it suddenly hit me — what a good thing we did! I'm in charge of picking flowers for the nursing home on Fourth Street. The vegetables will go to every kitchen in our town.

16. 위 글의 (A)work와 (B)complain의 올바른 형태는? (4점)

	(A)	(B)
①	work	complaining
②	work	to complain
③	work	complain
④	to work	complaining
⑤	to work	to complain

17. 위 글의 밑줄 친 @far 대신에 쓸 수 있는 말로 적절하지 않은 것은? (2점)

① very　　　② much　　　③ even
④ a lot　　　⑤ still

18. 위 글에 나타난 글쓴이의 심경 변화로 가장 적절한 것은? (4점)

① happy → sad
② excited → disappointed
③ sad → excited
④ irritated → proud
⑤ embarrassed → worried

19. 위 글의 내용과 일치하는 것은? (3점)

① 나는 친구의 권유로 이웃 프로젝트에서 일하게 되었다.
② 백 명이 넘는 사람들이 그 프로젝트에서 함께 일했다.
③ 우리는 많은 양의 쓰레기를 줍고 잡초를 뽑았다.
④ 지역의 농부들이 그 땅에 야채와 과일을 심었다.
⑤ 나는 병원에 보낼 꽃을 따는 일을 맡았다.

20. 빈칸 (A)에 들어갈 말로 적절한 것은? (3점)

Tonight, it suddenly hit me – what a good thing we did! I'm (A)_____ I have been a part of it. I'm in charge of picking flowers for the nursing home on Fourth Street. The vegetables will go to every kitchen in our town. But even better, an ugly and dirty lot that people didn't like has become a pretty garden for everyone.

① sad　　　② modest　　　③ angry
④ proud　　　⑤ polite

- 16 -

[21~24] 다음 글을 읽고 물음에 답하시오.

There were twenty of us – all ages and sizes – ready ①to work that day. I didn't think that we could ②mess up this awful place and turn (A)it into a garden. We were all wondering where to start. Then Mr. Hernandez said, "The only way to do it is just to ③start." Then, he ④divided the lot into four parts with string and ⑤assigned five people to each part.
ⓐBy lunchtime, I was hot, sweaty, and glad my dad ⓑhas made me wear gloves. We filled fifty trash bags with waste and were ready to pull wild plants. ⓒAs we pulled and pulled, dust ⓓfilled with the air and made us sneeze. At the end of the day, I had to admit the lot ⓔlooked even better.

21. 밑줄 친 ①~⑤ 중, 문맥상 가장 어색한 것은? (3점)

① ② ③ ④ ⑤

22. 밑줄 친 (A)it이 가리키는 것을 위 글에서 찾아 3 단어로 쓰시오. (3점)

답: _____

23. 밑줄 친 ⓐ~ⓔ 중, 어법상 어색한 것을 모두 고르면? (4점)

① ⓐ, ⓑ ② ⓑ, ⓒ ③ ⓑ, ⓓ
④ ⓒ, ⓓ ⑤ ⓓ, ⓔ

24. 글쓴이가 한 일을 순서대로 나열한 것은? (3점)

① 구역 배정 받기 – 쓰레기 줍기 – 잡초 뽑기
② 잡초 뽑기 – 쓰레기 줍기 – 구역 나누기
③ 역할 정하기 – 구역 나누기 – 잡초 뽑기
④ 구역 나누기 – 쓰레기 분리수거하기 – 역할 정하기
⑤ 쓰레기 분리수거하기 – 잡초 뽑기 – 역할 정하기

[25~27] 다음 글을 읽고 물음에 답하시오.

I complained the whole day. My parents were making me work on the neighborhood project, but I had ⓐfar better things to do. I didn't understand why we were working on ⓑthis place. ⓒIt was just the ugly, old, empty lot across from ⓓJohnny's Shop. ⓔIt was full of wild plants, fast food wraps, old newspapers, broken glass, and every other kind of dirty trash you can imagine. As I looked at it that first morning, I thought, "I bet there are snakes in ⓕthere, too."

25. 위 글에서 'I'의 심정으로 가장 알맞은 것을 고르시오. (3점)

① proud ② satisfied ③ bored
④ unpleased ⑤ excited

26. 위 글에서 ⓐ와 바꿔 쓸 수 없는 것을 고르시오. (3점)

① very ② much ③ still
④ even ⑤ a lot

27. 위 글의 ⓑ~ⓕ 중에서 가리키는 것이 다른 것을 고르시오. (3점)

① ⓑ ② ⓒ ③ ⓓ ④ ⓔ ⑤ ⓕ

[28~30] 다음 글을 읽고 물음에 답하시오.

There were twenty of us – all ages and sizes – ready to work that day. I didn't think that we could clean up this awful mess and turn it ⓐ_____ a garden. We were all wondering where to begin. The Mr. Hernandez said, "The only way to do it is just to start." Then, he divided the lot ⓑ_____ four parts with string and assigned ⓒ_____ people to each part.

28. 위 글의 ⓐ, ⓑ에 공통으로 들어갈 알맞은 말을 고르시오. (3점)

① on   ② of
③ into   ④ to
⑤ off

29. 위 글의 ⓒ에 들어갈 알맞은 말을 고르시오. (3점)

① two   ② three
③ four   ④ five
⑤ six

30. 위 글의 내용과 일치하지 <u>않는</u> 것을 고르시오. (3점)

① 모두 20명이 모였다.
② 사람들의 연령대와 몸집이 다양했다.
③ 사람들은 매우 더러운 곳을 청소해야 했다.
④ Hernandez씨는 각 구역에 사람들을 배치했다.
⑤ 글쓴이는 어디서부터 일을 해야 할지 잘 알고 있었다.

[31~32] 다음 글을 읽고 질문에 답하시오.

That first day was the toughest. On the weekends that followed, we made rows, planted flower and vegetable seeds, and watered them in the lot. After about two weeks, I stopped complaining when I found the plants _____ popping up! First, the lettuce and then the beans and the tomatoes. They grew so fast. I couldn't believe it! The bean plants grew an inch, and the tomatoes doubled in size in just a few days.
Now, two months later, I like to go there every day to see what new flowers are ready to pop up. Lots of people in the neighborhood meet there to enjoy the sights and to talk together.

31. 위 글을 읽고 답할 수 <u>없는</u> 질문은? (4점)

① Why does the writer go to the place every day?
② What did the people do on the weekends that followed?
③ What happened to the lot after about two weeks?
④ How many kinds of plants are there in the lot?
⑤ When did the write stop complaining?

32. 위 글의 빈칸에 들어갈 말로 가장 알맞은 것은? (3점)

① have started   ② had started
③ is started   ④ are started
⑤ were started

3학년 영어 1학기 중간고사(2과) 2회

문항수 : 선택형(24문항) 서술형(4문항)   20 . . .

◎ 선택형 문항의 답안은 컴퓨터용 수정 싸인펜을
 사용하여 OMR 답안지에 바르게 표기하시오.
◎ 서술형 문제는 답을 답안지에 반드시 검정
 볼펜으로 쓰시오.
◎ 총 28문항 100점 만점입니다. 문항별 배점
 은 각 문항에 표시되어 있습니다.

[광주 ○○중]

1. 영영 풀이로 올바르지 <u>않은</u> 것을 고르시오.   (4점)

① wrap: to cover something completely to protect it

② mess: a place or thing that is dirty or untidy

③ lot: a small area of land that belongs to a person or company

④ assign: to give someone a piece of work to do

⑤ complain: to say that you are satisfied with something.

[충북 ○○중]

2. 다음 대화의 빈칸에 들어갈 말로 가장 적절한 것은?   (3점)

B: Let's talk about the corner this time. Any ideas?
G: How about making a small library in the corner of the club room? I will bring some books tomorrow.
B: Great idea! _____, Minju.

① I am glad to help you

② I do not like your idea

③ I am so pleased to see you

④ Thank you for suggesting it

⑤ I am so grateful for giving you a hand

[충북 ○○중]

[3~4] 다음 대화를 읽고 물음에 답하시오.

Minsu: What do we need in our club room? Let's talk about it.
Jisu: Sure. Well, how about (A)put some flower pots by the windows? They'll make our room prettier.
Sera: That's a good idea. Thank you, Jisu. Shall we hang some pictures on the wall?
Jisu: Good. Why don't you bring one of your pictures? You're good at painting, Seho.
Seho: Thank you for (B)say that. I'll bring one of mine. Let's talk about the corner this time. Any ideas?
Minsu: Let's put some books in the corner of the club room. I will bring the books tomorrow.
Sera: Great idea! Thank you for your idea, Minsu.

3. 위 대화의 내용과 일치하지 <u>않는</u> 것은?   (4점)

	flower pots	some pictures	some books
whose idea	Jisu	ⓐSera	Minsu
where	ⓑby the windows	on the wall	ⓒin the corner
who will bring	-	ⓓJisu	ⓔMinsu

① ⓐ   ② ⓑ   ③ ⓒ   ④ ⓓ   ⑤ ⓔ

4. 위 대화의 밑줄 친 (A)put과 (B)say의 올바른 형태는?   (3점)

	(A)	(B)
①	put	to say
②	put	say
③	put	saying
④	putting	saying
⑤	putting	to say

- 19 -

5. 두 문장을 한 문장으로 만들 때 빈칸에 알맞은 말을 조건에 맞춰 쓰시오. (4점)

> 조건: 반드시 과거완료를 사용하여 6단어로 쓸 것.
> • Mike told me a lie, so I got angry.

답: I got angry because _____ _____

_____ _____ _____ _____.

6. 우리말과 같은 뜻이 되도록 밑줄 친 부분에 유의하여 빈칸에 알맞은 말을 쓰고, 그 이유를 우리말로 쓰시오. (4점)

> • 수학 시험은 내가 예상한 것보다 훨씬 더 어려웠다.
> → The math test was _____ _____ difficult than I expected.

(1) _____ _____

(2) 이유: _____

7. 괄호 안의 단어를 알맞게 이용하여 우리말과 같은 뜻의 완전한 영어 문장으로 서술하시오. (3점)

> • Playing baseball is _____ _____ _____ watching baseball games. (even, good, than)
> (야구를 하는 것은 야구 경기를 보는 것보다 훨씬 더 낫다.)

> 1. 대/소문자 구분 안 하면 1점 감점.
> 2. 주어진 말을 포함한 완전한 문장으로 쓸 것. (9단어)

답: _____

8. 주어진 문장 다음에 이어질 글의 순서로 가장 적절한 것은? (3점)

> There were twenty of us — all ages and sizes — ready to work that day.

> (A) By lunchtime, I was hot, sweaty, and glad my dad had made me wear gloves. We filled fifty trash bags with waste and were ready to pull wild plants.
> (B) I didn't think that we could clean up this awful mess and turn it into a garden. We were all wondering where to begin.
> (C) Then Mr. Hernandez said, "The only way to do it is just to start." Then, he divided the lot into four parts with string and assigned five people to each part.

① (A) - (C) - (B) ② (B) - (A) - (C)
③ (B) - (C) - (A) ④ (C) - (A) - (B)
⑤ (C) - (B) - (A)

9. 다음 글을 읽고 어법상 가장 어색한 문장을 고르면? (4점)

> When Mr. Han came back home, ⓐhe was surprised that he hadn't locked the door. ⓑHe had found that somebody cooked rice for him. ⓒHe was surprised because somebody had washed his T-shirt. ⓓHe was happy that somebody had cleaned his house. ⓔHe found somebody had fixed his chair.

① ⓐ ② ⓑ ③ ⓒ ④ ⓓ ⑤ ⓔ

[10～11] 다음 글을 읽고 물음에 답하시오.

Green Thumbs

I complained the whole day. My parents were making me work on the neighborhood project, but I had (A)훨씬 better things to do. I didn't understand why we were working on this place. It was just the ugly, old, empty lot across from Johnny's Shop. It was full of wild plants, fast food wraps, old newspapers, broken glass, and every other kind of dirty trash you can imagine. As I looked at it that first morning, I thought, "I bet there are snakes in there, too."

There were twenty of us — all ages and sizes — ready to work that day. I didn't think that we could clean up this awful mess and turn it into a garden. We were all wondering where to begin. Then Mr. Hernandez said, "The only way to do it is just to start." Then, he divided the lot into four parts with string and assigned five people to each part.

By lunchtime, I was hot, sweaty, and glad my dad had made me wear gloves. We filled fifty trash bags with waste and were ready to pull wild plants. As we pulled and pulled, dust filled the air and made us sneeze. At the end of the day, I had to admit the lot looked much better.

10. 위 글을 읽고 답할 수 <u>없는</u> 질문은? (3점)

① Why did the writer complain the whole day?

② Where is the lot located? (*be located: ~에 위치하다)

③ How many people were there to work on the lot?

④ How many parts did Mr. Hernandez divide the lot into?

⑤ How many wild plants did they pull?

11. 위 글의 빈칸 (A)에 들어갈 수 <u>없는</u> 것은? (3점)

① far ② still ③ very

④ even ⑤ a lot

12. 다음 글을 읽고 글의 내용과 일치하지 <u>않는</u> 것을 고르면? (4점)

That first day was the toughest. On the weekends that followed, we made rows, planted flower and vegetable seeds, and watered them. After about two weeks, I stopped complaining when I found the plants had started popping up! First, the lettuce and then the beans and the tomatoes. They grew so fast. I couldn't believe it! The bean plants grew an inch, and the tomatoes doubled in size in just a few days.

① 첫날이 가장 힘들었다.

② 꽃과 채소의 씨앗을 심고, 물을 주었다.

③ 약 2주가 지나고 필자는 불평하는 것을 멈추었다.

④ 상추가 제일 먼저 자랐고 콩과 토마토가 자랐다.

⑤ 콩은 1인치가 자랐고, 토마토는 몇 주 만에 크기가 두 배가 되었다.

13. 다음 글의 흐름에 맞도록 빈칸에 ①～⑤를 알맞은 순서로 배열할 때 ◆자리에 올 수 있는 것은? (4점)

Tonight, it suddenly hit me – what _____ _____◆_____ _____ _____ _____! I'm proud I have been a part of it. I'm in charge of picking flowers for the nursing home on Fourth Street. The vegetables will go to every kitchen in our town. But even better, an ugly and dirty lot that people didn't like has become a pretty garden for everyone.

① we ② did ③ a

④ thing ⑤ good

14. 다음 글에 드러난 'I'의 심경으로 가장 적절한 것은? (3점)

Tonight, it suddenly hit me — what a good thing we did! I'm proud I have been a part of it. I'm in charge of picking flowers for the nursing home on Fourth Street. The vegetables will go to every kitchen in our town. But even better, an ugly and dirty lot that people didn't like has become a pretty garden for everyone.

① 뿌듯함　　② 서러움　　③ 우울함
④ 지루함　　⑤ 당황함

[15~16] 다음 글을 읽고 물음에 답하시오.

I complained the whole day. My parents were making me work on the neighborhood project, but I had far better things to do. I didn't understand why we were working on this place. It was just the ugly, old, empty lot across (A)_____ Johnny's Shop.

15. 글쓴이의 심정으로 가장 알맞은 것은? (3점)

① glad　　　　② irritated
③ pleased　　　④ excited
⑤ worried

16. 빈칸 (A)에 들어갈 알맞은 전치사는? (3점)

① in　　　　② of
③ from　　　④ with
⑤ without

[17~18] 다음 글을 읽고, 물음에 답하시오.

That first day was the toughest. (A) On the weekends that followed, the town people made rows, planted flower and vegetable seeds, and watered them. (B) After about two weeks, I stopped complaining when I found the plants had started popping up! First, the lettuce and then the beans and the tomatoes. (C) I couldn't believe it! The bean plants grew an inch, and the tomatoes doubled in size in just a few days.

Now, two months later, I like to go there every day to see what new flowers are ready to pop up. (D) Lots of people in the neighborhood meet there to enjoy the sights and to talk together. (E)

17. 위 글의 (A)~(E) 중 다음의 문장이 들어갈 곳으로 가장 알맞은 것은? (4점)

They grew so fast.

① (A)　② (B)　③ (C)　④ (D)　⑤ (E)

18. 위 글을 읽고 답할 수 <u>없는</u> 질문은? (4점)

① What does the writer do for the town now?
② What happened to the lot after about two weeks?
③ What kinds of plants were there in the garden?
④ What did the town people do after the first day?
⑤ When did the writer stop complaining?

[19~20] 다음 글을 읽고, 물음에 답하시오.

A(그 첫날이 가장 힘들었다.) ⓐOn the weekends that followed, we made rows, planted flower and vegetable seeds, and watered them. ⓑAfter about two weeks, I stopped complaining when I found the plants had started popping up! ⓒFirst, the lettuce and then the beans and the tomatoes. ⓓThey grew so fast. I couldn't believe it! ⓔThe bean plants grew an inch, and the tomatoes doubled in size in just a few days.

19. 괄호 A의 우리말과 같은 뜻이 되도록 〈보기〉의 영어 단어를 어법에 맞게 6 단어로 쓰세요. (4점)

〈보기〉
that, was, toughest, the, first, day

답: _____ _____ _____ _____ _____

_____

20. 밑줄 친 ⓐ~ⓔ 중 글쓴이의 심경 변화가 일어나기 시작한 것은? (4점)

① ⓐ　② ⓑ　③ ⓒ　④ ⓓ　⑤ ⓔ

[21~22] 다음 글을 읽고 물음에 답하시오.

Now, two months later, I like to go there every day to see what new flowers are ready to pop up. Lots of people in the neighborhood meet there to enjoy the sights and A(to talk / talking) together.
Tonight, it suddenly hit me – what a good thing we did! I'm proud I B(have been / had been) a part of it. I'm in charge of C(to pick / picking) flowers for the nursing home on Fourth Street. The vegetables will go to every kitchen in our town. But even better, an ugly and dirty lot that people didn't like D(had become / has become) a pretty garden for everyone.

21. 괄호 A~D에 들어갈 말로 알맞은 것끼리 짝지은 것은? (4점)

　A　-　B　-　C　-　D

① talking - have been - to pick - had become
② talking - have been - picking - has become
③ to talk - have been - to pick - had become
④ to talk - have been - picking - has become
⑤ to talk - had been - to pick - had become

22. 글쓴이가 요즘 담당하고 있는 일은? (3점)

① 공터에서 분리수거하기
② 각 가정으로 야채 배달하기
③ 정원에서 이웃 만나기
④ 다양한 종류의 꽃 심기
⑤ 양로원에 가져갈 꽃 따기

[23~24] 다음 글을 읽고 물음에 답하시오.

By lunchtime, I was hot, sweaty, and glad my dad ⓐhad made me wear gloves. We ⓑfilled fifty trash bags with waste and were ready to pull wild plants. ⓒAs we pulled and pulled, dust filled the air and ⓓmade us to sneeze. At the end of the day, I ⓔhad to admit the lot looked much better.

23. 위 글의 밑줄 친 ⓐ~ⓔ 중에서 어법상 어색한 것을 고르시오. (4점)

① ⓐ　② ⓑ　③ ⓒ　④ ⓓ　⑤ ⓔ

24. 위 글의 내용과 일치하는 것을 고르시오. (4점)

① 점심시간에 아버지는 나에게 장갑을 가져다 주셨다.
② 쓰레기 봉투 15개를 쓰레기로 채웠다.
③ 쓰레기를 아무리 치워도 줄어들지 않았다.
④ 글쓴이는 쓰레기만 치웠고 잡초는 뽑지 않았다.
⑤ 먼지로 인해 재채기를 했다.

26. 위 글을 읽고 답할 수 없는 질문은 무엇인가? (3점)

① What happened to the lot after two weeks?
② What did the writer do on the first day?
③ What kinds of plants were there in the garden?
④ Why do the town people meet there?
⑤ Is the boy still complaining about the project?

[광주 ㅇㅇ중]

[27~28] 다음 글을 읽고 질문에 답하시오.

I complained the whole day. My parents were making me work on the neighborhood project, but I had far better things to do. I didn't understand why we were working on Ⓐthis place. It was just the ugly, old, empty Ⓑlot across from Johnny's Shop. It was full of wild plants, fast food wraps, old newspapers, broken glass, and every other kind of dirty Ⓒtrash you can imagine. As I looked at Ⓓit that first morning, I thought, "I bet there are snakes in Ⓔthere, too."

[광주 ㅇㅇ중]

[25~26] 다음 글을 읽고 물음에 답하시오.

That first day was the toughest. (①) On the weekends that followed, we made rows, planted flower and vegetable seeds, and watered them. (②) After about two weeks, I stopped complaining when I found the plants had started popping up!
(③) They grew so fast. (④) I couldn't believe it! (⑤) The bean plants grew an inch, and the tomatoes doubled in size in just a few days. Now, two months later, I like to go there every day to see what new flowers are ready to pop up. Lots of people in the neighborhood meet there to enjoy the sights and to talk together.

27. 위 글의 "I"의 심정으로 가장 적절한 것은? (3점)

① upset   ② disappointed
③ fascinated   ④ surprised
⑤ excited

25. 위 글에서 주어진 문장이 들어갈 위치로 가장 알맞은 곳을 고르시오. (4점)

First, the lettuce and then the beans and the tomatoes.

①   ②   ③   ④   ⑤

28. 위 글의 밑줄 친 Ⓐ~Ⓔ 중 지칭하는 것이 같은 것끼리 짝지어진 것은? (4점)

① Ⓑ, Ⓒ — Ⓓ
② Ⓒ, Ⓓ — Ⓔ
③ Ⓐ, Ⓑ — Ⓒ
④ Ⓐ, Ⓑ, Ⓓ — Ⓒ
⑤ Ⓐ, Ⓑ, Ⓒ — Ⓓ, Ⓔ

◎ 선택형 문항의 답안은 컴퓨터용 수정 싸인펜을 사용하여 OMR 답안지에 바르게 표기하시오.
◎ 서술형 문제는 답을 답안지에 반드시 검정 볼펜으로 쓰시오.
◎ 총 26문항 100점 만점입니다. 문항별 배점은 각 문항에 표시되어 있습니다.

[충북 ○○중]

1. 다음 주어진 단어의 영영 풀이로 잘못된 것은? (4점)

① bet: hope or expect that something will happen
② realize: become aware of a fact or understand it
③ conversation: talking with someone, usually in an informal situation
④ award: a prize or certificate that a person is given for doing something well
⑤ unusual: interesting and normal to people

[충북 ○○중]

2. 다음 대화의 빈칸에 가장 알맞지 않은 것을 고르면? (3점)

W: Soyun, are you going to take part in any races on the sports day?
G: Sure. I'm going to run a 100 meter race at the end of the day.
W: Wow, I'm looking forward to seeing you at the race.
G: But, Mom, I'm not sure I'll win the race.
W: Just do your best.
_____

① Good luck!
② I wish you good luck!
③ I'll keep my fingers crossed!
④ I hope you will do a great job.
⑤ I am afraid that you will win the race.

[인천 ○○중]

3. 다음 중 어법상 어색한 것은? (4점)

① I'm good at singing as well as dancing.
② Their fans are excited enough to cry out.
③ He speaks not only English but also Chinese.
④ Not only you but also him is going to join our club.
⑤ The flower is big enough to cover the woman's face.

[인천 ○○중]

4. 다음 대화의 내용과 가장 일치하는 것은? (4점)

Miso: We're going on a field trip next Tuesday. What are you going to do in the talent show, Jimin?
Jimin: I'm going to talk like our teachers do in class and tell some jokes.
Miso: Wow! I'm really looking forward to it.
Jimin: Will everyone like my show? I'm not sure.
Miso: Don't worry. I'm sure you'll do great.
Jimin: Thanks. Let me show you one part of my act. Guess who? "Goood Jooob!"
Miso: Ha-ha, you sound like our English teacher.
Jimin: Do I? I'm going to show you more at the show.
Miso: Great! You always make us laugh out loud.

① Miso talked like her English teacher.
② Jimin always makes Miso laugh out loud.
③ Jimin's teacher wants Jimin to talk like Miso.
④ Miso and Jimin are talking about their English class.
⑤ Miso and Jimin are going to the show this Tuesday.

5. 다음 대화를 읽고 빈칸에 들어갈 적절한 말을 조건에 맞는 한 문장으로 완성하고, 그 이유를 쓰시오.

(6점)

A: We're going on a field trip next Tuesday. What are you going to do in the talent show, Jimin?
B: I'm going to talk like our teachers do in class and tell some jokes.
A: Wow! I'm really looking forward to it.
B: Will everyone like my show? I'm not sure.
A: Don't worry. I'm sure you'll do great. I'll _____.
B: Thank you, Miso.

(1) I'll _____.

조건 1. 4단어로 완성할 것.
조건 2. fingers, keep을 사용할 것.

(2) 이유 _____

6. 올해 생일에도 가족을 만날 수 없는 Nick에게 생일 카드를 만들어 줄 경우, 수동태를 써서 영작하시오.

(6점)

(1) 생일카드가 나에 의해 Nick을 위하여 만들어졌다.

→ _____

(2) Nick은 그 생일카드에 의해 행복해졌다.

→ _____

7. 다음 대화의 빈칸에 들어갈 말로 가장 적절하지 않은 것은?

(3점)

A: I'm going to enter the dance contest tomorrow.
B: Are you? _____.
A: Thank you.

① Good luck to you.
② I wish you good luck.
③ I'm sure you will do well.
④ I also want to enter the contest.
⑤ I'll keep my fingers crossed for you.

8. 다음 우리말과 일치하도록 바르게 배열한 것은? (4점)

• 그녀는 매일 연습을 할 정도로 충분히 열정적이었다.
(every day / she / enough / was / to / passionate / practice)

① She was enough to practice passionate every day.
② She was enough passionate to practice every day.
③ She was to practice every day passionate enough.
④ She was passionate enough to practice every day.
⑤ She was passionate to practice enough every day.

9. 다음 해석에 맞게, 주어진 단어를 활용하여 문장을 완성하시오. (5점)

<조건>
• to부정사 구문을 사용할 것.

(1) 그녀는 애완용 고양이를 찾아서 매우 기뻤다.

→ She _____.

(find, her pet cat, happy)

(2) 그는 재미 삼아 읽을 책을 몇 권 빌렸다.

→ He _____.

(read, some, for fun, borrow)

[10~11] 다음 글을 읽고 물음에 답하시오.

Examples of the Ig Nobel Prize
The U.K. Navy won the Ig Nobel Prize for Peace in 2000. To save money, the Navy made its sailors shout, "Bang!" instead of using real bombs. Is that funny enough for you to laugh out loud?
Andre Geim also won an award that year. He succeeded in floating a live frog in the air by using magnets. "In my experience, if people don't have a sense of humor, they are usually not very good scientists," he said when he accepted his award.
If that still does not bring smile to your face, how about this? In 2005, Gauri Nanda won the Ig Nobel Prize in Economics for inventing an alarm clock. It keeps running away until the sleeper finally gets out of bed.
The Ig Nobel Prize Ceremony
(A)수상자들의 재미있는 연구뿐 아니라 시상식도 for the Ig Nobel Prizes makes people laugh. There are a number of interesting things that keep people from getting bored.

10. 위 글에 대한 설명으로 옳은 것은? (3점)

① 영국 해군은 2000년도에 경제학 부문 이그노벨상을 수상했다.
② 영국 해군은 비용을 절약하기 위해 실제 폭탄 대신 선원들에게 "뱅!" 소리를 외치도록 했다.
③ Andre Geim은 2005년도에 이그노벨상을 수상했다.
④ Andre Geim이 생각하는 훌륭한 과학자의 자질은 호기심이다.
⑤ Gauri Nanda는 손에 쉽게 잡히는 자명종을 발명하였다.

11. 위 글의 밑줄 친 (A)를 영어로 바꾼 것으로 옳은 것은? (3점)

① The winners' fun studies enough to ceremony
② The winners' so fun studies that the ceremony
③ The ceremony so well as the winners' fun studies
④ Not only the winners' fun studies but also the ceremony
⑤ Not only but also the winners' fun studies and ceremony

12. 다음 글의 흐름상 주어진 문장이 들어갈 가장 알맞은 곳은? (4점)

And the awards are not great honors like the Nobel Prizes.

(A) The Ig Nobel Prize ceremony ends with the words, "If you didn't win a prize — and if you did — better luck next year!" (B) The winners do not receive lots of money. (C) But the Ig Nobel Prizes make science a lot more fun! (D) So it is famous now. (E)

① (A)　② (B)　③ (C)　④ (D)　⑤ (E)

[13~14] 다음 글을 읽고 물음에 답하시오.

Andre Geim also won an award that year. He succeeded in ⓐ<u>floating</u> a live frog in the air by ⓑ<u>using</u> magnets. "In my experience, if people don't have a sense of humor, they are usually not very good scientists," he said when he accepted his award.

If that still does not ⓒ<u>bringing</u> a smile to your face, how about this? In 2005, Gauri Nanda won the Ig Nobel Prize in Economics for ⓓ<u>inventing</u> an alarm clock. It keeps ⓔ<u>running</u> away (A)_____ the sleeper finally gets out of bed.

13. 위 글의 밑줄 친 ⓐ~ⓔ 중에서 올바르게 쓰이지 않은 것은? **(3점)**

① ⓐ   ② ⓑ   ③ ⓒ   ④ ⓓ   ⑤ ⓔ

14. 위 글의 빈칸 (A)에 들어갈 알맞은 말을 쓰시오.

(4점)

→ _____

[15~16] 다음 글을 읽고 질문에 답하시오.

The Ig Novel Prizes are awarded for discoveries that "first make one laugh and then think." They were started in 1991 by *AIR* magazine to increase people's interest in science by honoring the unusual and the imaginative.

The prizes are presented by real Nobel winners in Sanders Theater at Harvard University. The room is usually filled with people who are eager to cheer for the brave scientists with their "___ⓐ___" research.

15. 위 글의 내용과 일치하는 것은? **(3점)**

① 이그노벨상은 개그맨에게 수여된다.

② 이그노벨상은 1991년 한 신문사에 의해서 시작되었다.

③ 이그노벨상은 대학생의 학구열을 높이기 위해서 시작되었다.

④ 이그노벨상 수상자들은 진짜 노벨상 수상자들에 의해 상이 수여된다.

⑤ 이그노벨상은 하버드 대학 출신의 창의적인 사람들을 위해 만든 상이다.

16. 위 글의 빈칸에 들어갈 단어로 가장 적절한 것은?

(4점)

① smart   ② laughable

③ tiring   ④ disappointing

⑤ useless

17. 다음 글의 빈칸 (A), (B)에 들어갈 연결사로 가장 바르게 짝지어진 것은? **(4점)**

The Ig Nobel Prize ceremony ends with the words, "If you didn't win a prize — and if you did — better luck next year!" The winners do not receive lots of money. (A)_____ the awards are not great honors like the Nobel Prizes. (B)_____ the Ig Nobel Prizes make science a lot more fun!

	(A)	(B)
①	And	But
②	And	So
③	And	Or
④	But	And
⑤	But	Or

[18~20] 다음 글을 읽고 물음에 답하시오.

(A)

The U.K. Navy won the Ig Nobel Prize for Peace in 2000. To save money, the Navy made its sailors ⓐuse real bombs instead of shouting, "Bang". Is that funny enough for you to laugh out loud?

(B)

Andre Geim also won an award that year. He ⓑsucceeded in floating a live frog in the air by using magnets. "In my experience, if people don't have a sense of _____, they are usually not very good scientists," he said when he accepted his award.

(C)

If that still does not bring a smile to your face, how about this? In 2005, Gauri Nanda won the Ig Nobel Prize in Economics for inventing an alarm clock. It keeps ⓒrunning away until the sleeper finally gets out of bed.

(D)

There are a number of interesting things. The opening and closing speeches are just two words each: "Welcome. Welcome." and "Goodbye. Goodbye." If someone talks for too long, an eight-year-old girl called Miss Sweetie Poo shouts repeatedly, "Please stop!, I'm bored." Each winner receives 10 trillion Zimbabwean dollars, which is worth less than one U.S. dollar. Throwing paper planes is another fun tradition.

(E)

The Ig Nobel Prize ceremony ends with the words, "if you didn't win a prize — and if you did — better luck next year!" ⓓThe winners do not receive lots of money. ⓔAnd the awards are not great honors like the Nobel prizes. But the Ig Nobel Prizes make science more fun!

18. 위 글의 밑줄 친 ⓐ~ⓔ 중, 글의 흐름상 어색한 것은? (4점)

① ⓐ ② ⓑ ③ ⓒ ④ ⓓ ⑤ ⓔ

19. 위 글의 흐름상 (B) 부분의 빈칸에 들어갈 어휘로 가장 적절한 것은? (3점)

① wonder ② thrill ③ humor

④ achievement ⑤ sight

20. 위 글을 읽고 알 수 없는 사실은? (4점)

① Ig Nobel상의 수상자들

② Ig Nobel상의 수상 이유

③ Ig Nobel상의 상금

④ Ig Nobel시상식에서의 전통

⑤ Ig Nobel상의 기원

21. 다음 글의 밑줄 친 ⓐ와 어법상 같은 것은? (3점)

The Ig Nobel Prizes are awarded for discoveries that "first ⓐmake one laugh and then think." They were started in 1991 by *AIR* magazine to increase people's interest in science by honoring the unusual and the imaginative.

① They made me go home.

② He made her a new dress.

③ The boy made a noise late at night.

④ We need to think of ways to make money.

⑤ She's a person who always makes mistakes.

[22~23] 다음 글을 읽고 물음에 답하시오.

Not only the winners' fun studies but also the ceremony for the Ig Nobel Prizes ⓐmakes people laugh. There are a number of interesting things that ⓑkeep people from getting bored. The opening and closing speeches ⓒare just two words each: "Welcome. Welcome." and "Goodbye. Goodbye." If someone talks for too long, an eight-year-old girl called Miss Sweetie Poo shouts repeatedly, "Please stop! I'm bored." Each winner ⓓreceives ten trillion Zimbabwean dollars, _____ worth less than one U.S. dollar. Throwing paper planes ⓔare another fun tradition.

---

22. 위 글의 ⓐ~ⓔ 중에서 동사의 어형이 바르지 않은 것은? (3점)

① ⓐ　　② ⓑ　　③ ⓒ　　④ ⓓ　　⑤ ⓔ

23. 위 글의 빈칸에 들어갈 알맞은 것은? (4점)

① which is　　② which are
③ that is　　④ who is
⑤ who are

[24~25] 다음 글을 읽고 질문에 답하시오.

The U.K. Navy won the Ig Novel Prize for Peace in 2000. To save money, the Navy made its sailors shout, "Bang!" instead of using real bombs. Is that funny enough for you to laugh out loud?

Andre Geim also won an award that year. He succeeded in floating a live frog in the air by using magnets. "In my experience, if people don't have a sense of ___Ⓐ___, they are usually not very good scientists," he said when he accepted his award.

If that still does not bring a smile to your face, how about this?

---

24. 위 글의 다음에 이어질 내용으로 가장 적절한 것은? (4점)

① 이그노벨상의 기원
② 한국인 이그노벨상 수상자들
③ 영군 해군의 생활 모습
④ 공중 부양 개구리의 생태 환경
⑤ 이그노벨상의 또 다른 수상 이야기

25. 위 글의 흐름으로 보아, Ⓐ에 가장 적절한 것은? (4점)

① humor　　② emotion
③ taste　　④ touch
⑤ hearing

26. 다음 글의 흐름상 밑줄 친 부분이 의도하는 것으로 가장 알맞은 것은? (4점)

"What happens when you walk backward while you are carrying a cup of coffee?" Han Jiwon, a Korean high school student, did research on this topic in 2015. Is this research project good enough to win a Nobel Prize? Maybe not. But how about an Ig Nobel Prize? He won one in 2017 for this fun research.

---

① 이 연구 과제는 노벨상의 가치를 퇴색시킨다.
② 이 연구 과제는 노벨상을 받을 만큼 훌륭하다.
③ 이 연구 과제는 이그노벨상을 받을 자격이 없다.
④ 이 연구 과제는 이그노벨상을 받을 가치가 있다.
⑤ 이 연구 과제는 노벨상을 받을 정도까지는 아니다.

◎ 선택형 문항의 답안은 컴퓨터용 수정 싸인펜을
사용하여 OMR 답안지에 바르게 표기하시오.
◎ 서술형 문제는 답을 답안지에 반드시 검정
볼펜으로 쓰시오.
◎ 총 26문항 100점 만점입니다. 문항별 배점
은 각 문항에 표시되어 있습니다.

[충북 ○○중]

1. 다음 대화의 밑줄 친 부분과 바꾸어 쓸 때, 가장 어
색한 문장을 고르면? (3점)

> G: Mom, I can't wait for the sports day.
> W: What are you going to do on that day,
> Minji?
> G: I'm going to play basketball for my class.
> We've practiced hard for a few weeks.
> W: Oh, I'm looking forward to your game.
> G: Actually, I'm a little worried. I'm afraid
> I'll make a mistake.
> W: Don't worry. You'll do a good job. I'll
> keep my fingers crossed!

① I hope to see your game.

② I can wait for your game.

③ I wish to see your game.

④ I am eager to see your game.

⑤ It will be nice to see your game.

[인천 ○○중]

2. 다음 밑줄 친 부분에서 소윤의 심정으로 가장 알맞
은 것은? (3점)

> Mom: Soyun, are you going to take part in
> any races on the sports day?
> Soyun: Sure. I'm going to run a 100 meter
> race at the end of the day.
> Mom: Wow, I'm looking forward to seeing
> you at the race.
> Soyun: But, Mom. I'm not sure I'll win the
> race.
> Mom: Just do your best.

① 화남　　　② 즐거움　　　③ 불안함

④ 놀라움　　　⑤ 기대감

[충북 ○○중]

3. 다음 대화의 내용과 일치하지 <u>않는</u> 것은? (4점)

> Miso: We're going on a field trip next
> Tuesday. What are you going to do in
> the talent show, Jimin?
> Jimin: I'm going to talk like our teachers do
> in class and tell some jokes.
> Miso: Wow! I'm really looking forward to
> it.
> Jimin: Will everyone like my show? I'm not
> sure.
> Miso: Don't worry. I'm sure you'll do great.
> I'll keep my fingers crossed!
> Jimin: Thank you, Miso. Let me show you
> one part that I'll act in the talent
> show. Guess who? "Goood Jooob!"
> Miso: You sound like our English teacher.
> Jimin: Do I? I'm going to show you more
> at the show.
> Miso: Great! You always make us laugh out
> loud.

① The talent show will be held on the day of a
field trip.

② Jimin will talk like his teachers in the talent
show.

③ Miso is cheering up Jimin for the show.

④ Miso is expecting Jimin's show because he
always makes her laugh out loud.

⑤ Miso and Jimin are talking about their
English teacher's show.

[강원 ○○중]

4. 다음 우리말에 맞도록 어휘를 재배열하여 영어로
쓰시오. (5점)

> • 폴킴의 노래들은 부르기에 충분히 쉽다.
> (the / Paul Kim / of / songs / easy / are /
> to / enough / sing)

→ _____

5. 다음 대화를 읽고 빈칸에 들어갈 말로 가장 알맞은 것은? (3점)

> A: Nami, I can't wait for the sports day.
> B: What are you going to do on that day, Minji?
> A: _____.
>   We've practiced hard for a few weeks.

① I'm going to stay at home.
② I'm going to study math hard.
③ I'm going to play basketball for my class.
④ I'm going to go to church with my family.
⑤ I'm going to read the book for my homework.

6. 다음 중 어법상 올바른 것은? (4점)

① I lost not only my bag but also my wallet.
② She is studying science not only but also history.
③ Not only Andrew but also Liam love Korean food.
④ I enjoy not only watching movies but also read books.
⑤ Not only my friends but also my teacher study very hard.

7. 다음 중 어법상 올바른 것은? (4점)

① The boy was kind enough to help the poor.
② The box is enough small to put in the car.
③ The prince was brave enough to fighting the monster.
④ This coat is warm to wear enough in winter.
⑤ The computer is enough fast running the program.

8. 다음 대화에 이어지는 우리말을 영어로 표현하시오. (4점)

> A: I think Nick is very smart. What do you think?
> B: (그는 명석할 뿐만 아니라 친절합니다.)
>   (smart, only 이용, 8 words)

→ _____

9. 내 친구가 원격 수업 기간 동안에 다음 두 가지를 해낸 경우, 그 내용을 to부정사를 넣어서 영어로 바르게 표현하시오. (6점)

> <조건>
> • 주어진 단어를 모두 사용할 것.

(1) he / not / too much TV / promised / to watch

→ _____

(2) he / to / exercise more / tried / eat less / and

→ _____

10. 우리말과 같은 뜻이 되도록 빈칸에 들어갈 말로 알맞은 것은? (3점)

• 그녀는 노래를 잘했을 뿐만 아니라 춤도 완벽하게 추었다.
→ She _____ but also danced perfectly.

① didn't sing well
② not only sang well
③ sang well not only
④ didn't sing well only
⑤ sang not only well

[11~13] 다음 글을 읽고 물음에 답하시오.

The Ig Nobel Prize
"What happens when you walk backward while you are carrying a cup of coffee?" Han Jiwon, a Korean high school student, did research on this topic (A)[in / at] 2015. Is this research project ⓐgood enough to win a Nobel Prize? Maybe not. But how about an Ig Nobel Prize? He won ⓑone in 2017 for this fun research.
The Ig Nobel Prizes are awarded for discoveries that "first make one laugh and then think." They were started in 1991 by *AIR* magazine ⓒto increase people's interest (B)[in / from] science by honoring ⓓthe unusual and the imaginative.
The prizes are presented by real Nobel winners in Sanders Theater at Harvard University. The room is usually filled (C)[in / with] people ⓔwho are eager to cheer for the brave scientists with their "laughable" research.

11. 위 글의 이그노벨상에 대한 설명으로 옳지 않은 것은? (3점)

① 한국 고등학생이 2017년에 이그노벨상을 수상한 적이 있다.
② 웃기지만 생각하게 만드는 발견들을 높이 평가한다.
③ 1991년에 시작되었다.
④ Sanders Theater에서 수상자에게 상을 수여한다.
⑤ 하버드 졸업생들이 수상자에게 상을 수여한다.

12. 위 글의 괄호 (A), (B), (C) 안에 들어갈 말로 알맞은 것은? (4점)

	(A)	(B)	(C)
①	in	in	with
②	in	in	in
③	in	from	with
④	at	from	in
⑤	at	from	with

13. 위 글의 ⓐ~ⓔ에 대한 설명으로 옳지 않은 것은? (4점)

① ⓐ: '노벨상을 받을 정도로 충분히 좋은'으로 해석한다.
② ⓑ: 부정대명사로 앞에 언급된 Han Jiwon을 가리킨다.
③ ⓒ: to부정사의 부사적 용법으로 '높이기 위해'로 해석한다.
④ ⓓ: 'unusual and imaginative people'로 해석할 수 있다.
⑤ ⓔ: 선행사 people을 수식하는 관계대명사절이다.

[14~16] 다음 글을 읽고 질문에 답하시오.

ⒶNot only the winners' fun studies but also the ceremony for the Ig Novel Prizes (ⓐmake) people laugh. ⒷThere are a number of interesting things (㉠) keep people from getting bored. ⒸThe opening and closing speeches are just two words each: "Welcome. Welcome." and "Goodbye. Goodbye." ⒹIf someone talks for too long, an eight-year-old girl called Miss Sweetie Poo shouts repeatedly, "Please stop! I'm bored." Each winner receives ten trillion Zimbabwean dollars, (㉡) is worth less than one U.S. dollar. ⒺThrowing paper planes is another fun tradition.

14. 위 글의 Ⓐ~Ⓔ 중 주제가 되는 문장으로 가장 알맞은 것은? (4점)

① Ⓐ   ② Ⓑ   ③ Ⓒ   ④ Ⓓ   ⑤ Ⓔ

15. 위 글의 빈칸 ㉠과 ㉡에 공통으로 들어갈 수 있는 것은? (4점)

① that
② who
③ what
④ which
⑤ whose

16. 위 글의 빈칸 ⓐ에 주어진 동사의 적절한 형태는? (3점)

① make
② to make
③ makes
④ making
⑤ made

17. 다음 글의 흐름으로 보아, 주어진 문장이 들어가기에 가장 적절한 곳은? (4점)

Is this research project good enough to win a Nobel Prize?

"What happens when you walk backward while you are carrying a cup of coffee?" (A) Han Jiwon, a Korean high school student, did research on this topic in 2015. (B) Maybe not. (C) But how about an Ig Nobel Prize? (D) He won one in 2017 for this fun research. (E)

① (A)   ② (B)   ③ (C)   ④ (D)   ⑤ (E)

18. 다음 글의 밑줄 친 ⓐ~ⓔ 중 동사의 형태가 알맞지 않은 것은? (4점)

The Ig Nobel Prizes ⓐare awarded for discoveries that "first make one laugh and then think." They ⓑwere started in 1991 by *AIR* magazine to increase people's interest in science by honoring the unusual and the imaginative.

The prizes ⓒare presented by real Nobel winners in Sanders Theater at Harvard University. The room ⓓis filled with people who are eager to cheer for the brave scientists with their "laughable" research.

The U.K. Navy won the Ig Nobel Prize for Peace in 2000. To save money, the Navy ⓔwas made its sailors shout, "Bang!" instead of using real bombs.

① ⓐ   ② ⓑ   ③ ⓒ   ④ ⓓ   ⑤ ⓔ

- 34 -

[19~21] 다음 글을 읽고 물음에 답하시오.

"What happens when you walk backward ⓐwhile you are carrying a cup of coffee?" Han Jiwon, a Korean high school student, did research on this topic in 2015. Is this research project good enough to win a Nobel Prize? Maybe not. But how about an Ig Nobel Prize? He won one in 2017 for this fun research.

The Ig Nobel Prizes ⓑare awarded for discoveries that "first make one laugh and then ⓒthink." They were started in 1991 by *AIR* magazine to increase people's interest in science by honoring ⓓthe unusual and the imaginative.

The prizes are presented by real Nobel winners in Sanders Theater at Harvard University. The room ⓔis usually filled of people who are eager to cheer for the brave scientists with their "laughable" research.

19. 위 글의 밑줄 친 ⓐ~ⓔ 중, 어법상 어색한 것은?

(4점)

① ⓐ   ② ⓑ   ③ ⓒ   ④ ⓓ   ⑤ ⓔ

20. 위 글을 읽고 답할 수 없는 질문은? (4점)

① Who presents the Ig Nobel Prizes?
② When were the Ig Nobel Prizes started?
③ Why were the Ig Nobel Prizes started?
④ Where are the Ig Nobel Prizes presented?
⑤ How much money do the winners get?

21. 위 글을 바탕으로 아래의 이그노벨 시상식의 초청장을 만들려고 한다. 다음 중, 초청장의 빈칸에 사용되지 <u>않을</u> 어휘는? (4점)

The 27th Ig Nobel Prize Ceremony
Since _____
First make one _____ and then _____

Thursday, September 14, 2017 6:00 PM
in Sanders Theater at Harvard University

[Join us for this ceremony]

Winners of 2017: _____, Korea
"How to Carry Your _____"

① 2015   ② Coffee   ③ laugh
④ Han Jiwon   ⑤ think

22. 다음 글의 흐름상 제시된 문장이 들어갈 곳으로 가장 알맞은 것은? (4점)

There are a number of interesting things that keep people from getting bored.

Not only the winners' fun studies but also the ceremony for the Ig Nobel Prizes makes people laugh. (A) The opening and closing speeches are just two words each: "Welcome. Welcome." and "Goodbye. Goodbye." (B) If someone talks for too long, an eight-year-old girl called Miss Sweetie Poo shouts repeatedly, "Please stop!, I'm bored." (C) Each winner receives ten trillion Zimbabwean dollars, which is worth less than one U.S. dollar. (D) Throwing paper planes is another fun tradition. (E)

① (A)   ② (B)   ③ (C)   ④ (D)   ⑤ (E)

23. 다음 글의 밑줄 친 부분 중, 문맥상 낱말의 쓰임이 적절하지 <u>않은</u> 것은? (4점)

The U.K. Navy won the Ig Nobel Prize for Peace in 2000. To save money, the Navy made its sailors shout, "Bang!" instead of using ⓐ<u>real</u> bombs. Is that ⓑ<u>gloomy</u> enough for you to laugh out loud?
Andre Geim also won an award that year. He ⓒ<u>succeeded</u> in floating a live frog in the air by using magnets. "In my experience, if people don't have a sense of ⓓ<u>humor</u>, they are usually not very good scientists," he said when he ⓔ<u>accepted</u> his award.

① ⓐ　② ⓑ　③ ⓒ　④ ⓓ　⑤ ⓔ

25. 다음 글의 빈칸 (A)와 (B)에 들어갈 말이 순서대로 알맞은 것은? (3점)

"What happens when you walk backward while you are carrying a cup of coffee?" Han Jiwon, a Korean high school student, did research (A)_____ this topic in 2015. Is this research project good enough to win a Nobel Prize? Maybe not. But how about an Ig Nobel Prize? He won one (B)_____ 2017 for this fun research.

① in - on　　② on - in
③ of - in　　④ of - for
⑤ to - with

24. 다음 글에서 전체 흐름과 관계 <u>없는</u> 문장은? (4점)

Not only the winners' fun studies but also the ceremony for the Ig Nobel Prizes makes people laugh. ⓐThere are a number of interesting things that keep people from getting bored. ⓑThe opening and closing speeches are just two words each: "Welcome. Welcome." and "Goodbye. Goodbye." ⓒMost people want to listen to the nice words when they attend the graduation ceremony. ⓓIf someone talks for too long, an eight-year-old girl called Miss Sweetie Poo shouts repeatedly, "Please stop!, I'm bored." ⓔEach winner receives 10 trillion Zimbabwean dollars, which is worth less than one U.S. dollar. Throwing paper planes is another fun tradition.

① ⓐ　② ⓑ　③ ⓒ　④ ⓓ　⑤ ⓔ

26. 다음 글의 빈칸에 들어갈 말로 가장 적절한 것은? (4점)

The Ig Nobel Prizes are awarded for discoveries that "first make one laugh and then think." They were started in 1991 by *AIR* magazine _____ by honoring the unusual and the imaginative. The prizes are presented by real Nobel winners in Sanders Theater at Harvard University. The room is usually filled with people who are eager to encourage the brave scientists with their 'laughable' research.

① to laugh at the brave scientists
② to increase people's interest in science
③ to decrease people's interest in science
④ to discourage good investment in science
⑤ to get a reward for the dishonest scientists' effort

3학년 영어 1학기 기말고사(4과) 1회

문항수 : 선택형(23문항) 서술형(1문항)   20 . . .

◎ 선택형 문항의 답안은 컴퓨터용 수정 싸인펜을 사용하여 OMR 답안지에 바르게 표기하시오.
◎ 서술형 문제는 답을 답안지에 반드시 검정 볼펜으로 쓰시오.
◎ 총 24문항 100점 만점입니다. 문항별 배점은 각 문항에 표시되어 있습니다.

[충북 ○○중]

1. 다음 대화 내용을 읽고 가장 자연스럽지 <u>않은</u> 것을 고르면? (4점)

① A: You look down today. What's the matter?
  B: My father doesn't allow me to take a dance class.
  A: I'm sorry to hear that.

② A: Why are you disappointed?
  B: My record is not good. What should I do?
  A: I think you should keep practicing more.

③ A: I want to be a teacher, but everybody laughs at me. Do you think I should give up my dream?
  B: Yes, you should. I think you're really good at teaching. You'll be a great teacher!
  A: Thank you.

④ A: Junsu, you look down today. Why are you disappointed?
  B: I lost the soccer competition.
  A: I'm sorry to hear that. I know you tried hard.

⑤ A: Why are you disappointed?
  B: I failed the audition for the Dae-sung Youth Band. Do you think I should keep trying?
  A: Sure. Don't give up. You'll do better next time.

[충북 ○○중]

2. 다음 문장이 자연스러운 대화가 되도록 가장 바르게 배열한 것을 고르면? (4점)

G: Why are you disappointed?
(A) Yes. It will help your classmates understand you better.
(B) Take it easy. Your speech was a little fast, but I liked your presentation.
(C) Do you think I should speak more slowly?
(D) I didn't give a good presentation.

① (A)-(B)-(D)-(C)   ② (A)-(D)-(B)-(C)
③ (B)-(C)-(D)-(A)   ④ (D)-(C)-(B)-(A)
⑤ (D)-(B)-(C)-(A)

[광주 ○○중]

3. 다음 Ⓐ~Ⓓ를 주어진 문장 다음에 자연스러운 흐름이 되도록 알맞게 배열한 것은? (4점)

A: Why are you disappointed?
B: _____
A: _____
B: _____
A: _____

Ⓐ: I'm sorry to hear that.
Ⓑ: Sure. You'll do better next time.
Ⓒ: I failed the audition for the band.
Ⓓ: Do you think I should keep trying?

① Ⓒ-Ⓓ-Ⓑ-Ⓐ   ② Ⓒ-Ⓐ-Ⓓ-Ⓑ
③ Ⓐ-Ⓓ-Ⓒ-Ⓑ   ④ Ⓒ-Ⓓ-Ⓐ-Ⓑ
⑤ Ⓐ-Ⓓ-Ⓑ-Ⓒ

4. 다음 대화의 내용과 일치하는 것은? (5점)

A: Why are you so disappointed, Ryan?

B: My parents won't let me enter Superstar 101, a singing competition.

A: I'm sorry to hear that. Why are they against it?

B: They want me to study hard and be a doctor. They're always worried about my grades.

A: Did you tell your parents you really want to be a singer?

B: Not yet. Do you think I should talk with them about it?

A: Yes. Just show them how much you love singing. Why don't you sing the songs you made in front of them?

B: Okay. I'll try. Thank you for your advice, Jisu.

① 슈퍼스타 101은 댄스 경연 대회이다.

② 지수는 가수가 되고 싶은 꿈을 갖고 있다.

③ Ryan은 열심히 공부해서 의사가 되고 싶어 한다.

④ 지수는 부모님 앞에서 자신이 만든 노래를 부르려고 한다.

⑤ Ryan은 부모님께 슈퍼스타 101 참가 허락을 받지 못해 실망하고 있다.

Mina: Yes. I think they will help. How about getting useful tips from cooking shows online?

Junsu: Okay. I'll try. Thank you for your advice, Mina.

Mina: You're welcome. Just remember I'm a fan of your dishes.

5. 위 대화의 빈칸 (A)에 들어갈 말로 가장 알맞은 것은? (5점)

① Why are you angry?

② Why are you excited?

③ Why are you so hungry?

④ Why are you so pleased?

⑤ Why are you disappointed?

6. 위 대화의 밑줄 친 ⓐ의 목적으로 알맞은 것은? (3점)

① 조언 구하기

② 관심사 묻기

③ 도움 제안하기

④ 사과 요청하기

⑤ 알고 있는지 묻기

[5~6] 다음 대화를 읽고 물음에 답하시오.

Mina: Junsu, you look down today.

(A)_____

Junsu: I lost the cooking competition.

Mina: I'm sorry to hear that. I know you tried hard.

Junsu: Yeah, but maybe that wasn't enough. ⓐDo you think I should learn more cooking tips?

7. 다음 대화의 흐름상 어색한 것은? (4점)

Boy: ⓐYou look happy today. What's the matter?

Girl: ⓑWe lost the basketball game because of my mistake.

Boy: Come on. ⓒEveryone makes mistakes.

Girl: ⓓDo you think I should practice more?

Boy: Well, yes. ⓔYou know, practice makes perfect.

① ⓐ　② ⓑ　③ ⓒ　④ ⓓ　⑤ ⓔ

[8~9] 다음 대화를 읽고 물음에 답하시오.

Girl: Why are you so disappointed, Ryan?

Boy: My parents won't let me enter Superstar 101, a singing competition.

Girl: I'm sorry to hear that. Why are they (A)[against / for] it?

Boy: They want me to study hard and be a doctor. They're always worried about my grades.

Girl: Did you tell your parents you really want to be a singer?

Boy: Not yet. Do you think I should talk with them about it?

Girl: Yes, just show them how (B)[many / much] you love singing. Why don't you sing the songs you made in front of them?

Boy: Okay, I'll try. Thank you for you (C)[advise / advice], Jisu.

8. 위 대화의 괄호 (A), (B), (C) 안에서 문맥에 맞는 낱말로 가장 적절한 것은?　　　(4점)

	(A)	(B)	(C)
①	against	many	advise
②	against	much	advise
③	against	much	advice
④	for	much	advice
⑤	for	many	advise

9. 위 대화를 읽고 대답할 수 없는 것은?　　　(4점)

① What does the boy want to be?

② Why is the boy disappointed?

③ What is Superstar 101?

④ What should the boy do?

⑤ When will the boy sing the songs he made in front of his parents?

10. 다음 문장을 읽고 가장 알맞게 작문한 것으로 잘 짝지어진 것은?　　　(4점)

• 그는 지도를 보면서 길을 걸었다.
→ (A)_____, he walked along the street.

• 피곤해서 그는 벤치에 앉았다.
→ (B)_____, he sat on a bench.

	(A)	(B)
①	Looking at the map	Feeling tired
②	Looking at the map	Feeling tiring
③	Looked at the map	Feeling tired
④	Looked at the map	Being tired
⑤	Look at the map	Being tiring

11. 다음 짝지어진 두 문장의 의미가 일치하지 않는 것은?　　　(5점)

① This math problem is so easy that you can solve it.
= This math problem is easy enough for you to solve.

② He as well as you wants to see the movie.
= Not only you but also he wants to see the movie.

③ We're looking forward to joining the club.
= We can't wait to join the club.

④ We've practiced hard for a few weeks.
= We started to practice a few weeks ago, and still practice hard.

⑤ The play keeps people from getting bored.
= The play makes people get bored.

[12~14] 다음 글을 읽고 물음에 답하시오.

I watched the movie *Hidden Figures* last weekend. It was a movie about three African-American women ⓐwho worked at NASA. They began their career ⓑin the 1960s as "human computers." However, they dreamed of becoming space experts at NASA and tried hard ⓒto get over difficulties.

Katherine Johnson was one of the three "hidden figures" in this movie. She worked hard and ⓓshowed a talent in math, and her manager Al Harrison recognized her ability. One day, he got upset when Katherine was missing from her desk for too long. Al asked "Where have you been so far?" And then Katherine answered. The bathroom. There ⓔis no COLORED bathrooms in this building. I have to run half a mile away just to use the bathroom.

(A)When I heard this, I felt really sorry for her. However, I was glad that she had courage to talk to the manager about the problem. This made Al Harrison break down the "Colored Ladies Room" sign.

12. 밑줄 친 ⓐ~ⓔ 중, 어법상 어색한 것은? (3점)

① ⓐ ② ⓑ ③ ⓒ ④ ⓓ ⑤ ⓔ

13. 위 글의 내용과 일치하는 것은? (5점)

① "Hidden Figures"는 NASA에서 일했던 한 명의 아프리카 여성에 대한 영화였다.

② Katherine Johnson의 상사는 그녀의 재능을 알아차렸다.

③ 영화 속 주인공들은 모두 수학에서 재능을 보였다.

④ Al Harrison은 Katherine Johnson의 용기에 화가 났다.

⑤ Katherine Johnson은 유색인종 여성 화장실 표지판을 부셨다.

14. 위 글의 밑줄 친 (A)를 바꾸어 쓴 것으로 적절한 것은? (5점)

① Heard this ② To hear this
③ Hear this ④ Hearing this
⑤ When I hear this

[15~16] 다음 글을 읽고 물음에 답하시오.

Mary Jackson was the character I liked the most of the three. She wanted to learn more about rocket science, but she wasn't allowed to go to a white school. So, she asked a judge to give her permission. She said, "I can't change the color of my skin. So ... I have no choice but to be the first. Your Honor, of all the cases you'll hear today, which one will matter in a hundred years? Which one will make you the "first"?"

The judge was impressed by ⓐwhat she said and finally gave her permission. Mary stood up for herself and for other African-Americans. That was what impressed me most in the movie. Finally, she became the first African-American woman engineer at NASA.

15. 위 글의 내용과 일치하는 것은? (4점)

① The writer's favorite character of the three was Mary Jackson.

② Mary didn't want to ask the judge to give her permission to go to a white school.

③ Mary couldn't become the first African-American woman engineer at NASA.

④ Mary stood up only for herself.

⑤ Thanks to other African-Americans, Mary could learn more about rocket science.

16. 위 글의 ⓐwhat과 쓰임이 같은 것은?　　(4점)

① What car do you have?
② That is what I want to read.
③ What a lucky boy he is!
④ He asked me what time he should come.
⑤ What shall we have for lunch?

18. 위 글의 빈칸 (A)에 들어갈 말로 가장 알맞은 것은?　　(4점)

① And　　② Because　　③ When
④ However　　⑤ Therefore

[인천 ○○중]

[17~18] 다음 글을 읽고 물음에 답하시오.

I watched the movie *Hidden Figures* last weekend. It was a movie about three African-American women who worked at NASA. They began their career in the 1960s as "human computers." (A)_____, they dreamed of becoming space experts at NASA and tried hard to get over difficulties.

Katherine Johnson was one of the three "hidden figures" in this movie. She worked hard and showed a talent in math, and her manager Al Harrison recognized her ability. One day, he got upset when Katherine was missing from her desk for too long. Al asked where Katherine had been, and she answered. The bathroom. There are no COLORED bathrooms in this building. I have to run half a mile away just to use the bathroom.

17. 위 글의 내용과 일치하는 것은?　　(3점)

① Katherine은 수학과 과학을 잘했다.
② Katherine은 화장실을 가려고 1마일을 달렸다.
③ Al Harrison은 Katherine의 과학적 재능을 알았다.
④ Katherine은 1960년대 인간 컴퓨터 일을 그만두었다.
⑤ Katherine은 유색 인종 전용 화장실만을 사용할 수 있었다.

[인천 ○○중]

19. 다음 Mary Jackson에 관한 설명으로 가장 옳은 것은?　　(5점)

Mary Jackson was the character I liked the most of the three. She wanted to learn more about rocket science, but she wasn't allowed to go to a white school. So, she asked a judge to give her permission.

I can't change the color of my skin. So... I have no choice but to be the first. Your Honor, of all the cases you'll hear today, which one will matter in a hundred years? Which one will make you the "first?"

The judge was impressed by what she said and finally gave her permission. Mary stood up for herself and for other African-Americans. That was what impressed me most in the movie. Finally, she became the first African-American woman engineer at NASA.

① She wasn't interested in rocket science.
② She stood up for herself and for other Africans.
③ She was the writer's favorite character out of the three.
④ She became the first African woman manager at NASA.
⑤ She asked the judge to give her permission to go to a black school.

[20~22] 다음 글을 읽고 질문에 답하시오.

Ⓐ I watched the movie *Hidden Figures* last weekend. Ⓑ It was a movie about three African-American women who worked at NASA. Ⓒ They began their career in the 1960s as "human computers." Ⓓ Katherine Johnson was one of the three "hidden figures" in this movie. Ⓔ She worked hard and showed a talent in math, and her manager Al Harrison recognized her ability. (가)One day, he got upset when Katherine was missed from her desk for too long. Al asked where Katherine had been, and she answered.

Katherine Johnson: The bathroom. There are no COLORED bathrooms in this building. I have to run half a mile away just to use the bathroom.

20. 위 글의 Ⓐ~Ⓔ 중 다음 문장이 들어갈 가장 알맞은 곳은? (3점)

However, they dreamed of becoming space experts at NASA and tried hard to get over difficulties.

① Ⓐ　② Ⓑ　③ Ⓒ　④ Ⓓ　⑤ Ⓔ

21. 위 글의 밑줄 친 (가)에서 어색한 것을 고치시오. (5점)

→ _____

22. 위 글의 내용과 일치하는 것은? (4점)

① Katherine은 Al Harrison의 상사이다.
② 영화 속 세 여성들은 모두 백인이었다.
③ 글쓴이는 지난 주말에 NASA를 방문했다.
④ Katherine은 매일 반마일을 걸어서 출근했다.
⑤ Al Harrison은 Katherine의 재능을 알아차렸다.

23. 다음 글의 밑줄 친 단어의 뜻과 선택지에 있는 뜻이 가장 동일하게 해석되는 것은? (4점)

Thanks to Dorothy, her team members could become programmers. She wasn't afraid of ⓐchange and used it ⓑas a ⓒchance. That's what I need to learn from her. Watching this movie, I could learn how to ⓓface challenges in life. I won't forget the ⓔtears and laughter of Katherine, Mary, and Dorothy.

① ⓐ: The ticket machine gives change.
② ⓑ: You can use that glass as a vase.
③ ⓒ: I met her by chance at the airport.
④ ⓓ: How can you have the face to say such a thing?
⑤ ⓔ: He often tears his jeans on the fence.

24. 다음 글의 밑줄 친 부분 중, 문맥상 낱말의 쓰임이 적절하지 <u>않은</u> 것은? (5점)

Mary Jackson was the character I liked the most of the three. She wanted to learn ⓐmore about rocket science, but she wasn't ⓑallowed to go to a white school. So, she asked a judge to give her permission. The judge was ⓒdepressed by what she said and finally gave her permission. Mary ⓓstood up for herself and for other African-Americans. That was what ⓔimpressed me most in the movie. Finally, she became the first African-American woman engineer at NASA.

① ⓐ　② ⓑ　③ ⓒ　④ ⓓ　⑤ ⓔ

정답 및 해설

Lesson 1 (중간) 1회

1회

01 ⑤	**02** ③	**03** ③	**04** ④	**05** ①	**06** ⑤	**07** ②

08 ⑤ **09** ③ **10** ① **11** ①

12 Do you know where he comes from?

13 who is studying

14 I opened the box, which had lots of photos of my mother.

15 ④ **16** ④ **17** ③ **18** ③ **19** ④ **20** ② **21** ③

22 ② **23** ①

24 It is a group of letters or symbols used to represent a facial expression.

25 ⑤ **26** ③ **27** ④ **28** ⑤ **29** ② **30** ① **31** ⑤

---

01 book은 동사로 '예약하다', 명사로 '책'의 뜻을 갖는다.

02 (A) 뒤에서 'I'm excited to go to a whole new world, Yunju.'라고 했으므로 상대방의 감정을 묻는 'How are you feeling?(기분이 어때?)'이 적절하다. (B) 뒤에서 'I'll miss all of you a lot.'이라고 했으므로 슬픔을 표현하는 'I am so sad, too.(슬프기도 해.)'가 적절하다.

03 마침내 회원이 됐으므로 excited나 happy, but으로 상반되는 내용이므로 sad나 worried, 격려를 받았으므로 glad나 happy가 적절하다.

04 기분이 어떤지 묻자 (B) 슬프다며 친한 친구인 지훈이가 멀리 이사 간다고 답하고 (C) 유감이라며 온라인으로 화상 채팅을 할 수 있으니 너무 슬퍼하지 말라며 위로하자 (E) 맞다며 뭘 해 줄 수 있을지 묻고 (A) 사진책을 만들어 주는 게 어떤지 제안하자 (D) 좋은 생각이라고 하는 순서가 적절하다.

05 뒤에서 'I really want to experience new things there!'라고 했으므로 'excited(신이 난)'가 적절하다.

06 뒤에서 'Thank you. I'll wait for your invitation.'이라고 했으므로 'No, I won't.'는 어색하고 'Yes, I will.'이 적절하다.

07 간접의문문으로 '의문사+주어+동사'의 어순은 맞지만, 과거시제(Where did you go?)이므로 go가 아닌 went가 되어야 한다.

08 간접의문문은 '의문사+주어+동사'의 어순이다. 'Can you guess how long she stayed here?'로 써야 한다.

09 간접의문문은 '의문사+주어+동사'의 어순이다. 'how often, how much, how many books, what color'처럼 하나의 의미 단위로 쓰이는 의문사구는 하나의 의문사처럼 취급한다.

10 ①번은 Amy를 선행사로 하는 계속적 용법의 관계대명사 who가 들어간다. ②, ④, ⑤번은 앞 절 전체를 선행사로 하는 계속적 용법의 관계대명사 which가 들어간다. ③번은 a new book을 선행사로 하는 계속적 용법의 관계대명사 which가 들어간다.

11 간접의문문은 '의문사+주어+동사'의 어순이지만 주절의 동사가 believe, imagine, soppose, consider, think, guess 등의 동사일 경우 의문사가 문장의 맨 앞으로 나간다. ①번은 What do you think they will do next?가 적절하다.

12 간접의문문은 '의문사+주어+동사'의 어순이다.

13 계속적 용법의 관계대명사로 사람이 선행사이므로 who를 이용한다.

14 사물을 선행사로 하는 계속적 용법의 관계대명사 which를 이용한다.

15 주어진 문장의 it이 (D) 앞의 Ha-ha를 가리키므로 (D)가 적절하다.

16 계속적 용법으로 선행사가 사물이므로 which가 적절하다.

17 간접의문문이므로 '의문사+주어+동사'의 어순이 적절하다.

18 'These expressions have become popular because they can be typed quite quickly.'라고 했다.

19 앞의 내용에 대한 결과가 이어지므로 so가 적절하다.

20 'Some emojis have grown bigger, and some even move or make laughing sounds.'라고 했다.

21 ⓐ stand for: ~을 의미하다, 상징하다 ⓒ 'with+명사+형용사'가 다른 동작이나 행위를 할 때의 상황 설명으로 쓰여서 '…(명사)가 ~(형용사) 한 채로'의 의미가 된다.

22 'The emoticon XD expresses our happy feelings more visually than ha-ha and LOL do.'라고 했다.

23 ⓑ 이유가 이어지므로 because가 적절하다. ⓓ 계속적 용법의 관계대명사로 사물이 선행사이므로 which가 적절하다.

24 'It's an emoticon, which is a group of letters or symbols used to represent a facial expression.'이라고 했다.

25 'such as'는 '~와 같은'이라는 뜻으로 'for example'로 쓸 수도 있다. 그러므로 앞에서 언급한 'our writings'에

해당되지 않는 것은 ⑤번 'voice messages(음성 메시지)'이다.

26 ⓑ 'Laughing marks가 우리의 얼굴 표정을 나타내고 우리의 목소리 어조를 전달할 수 있다.'는 말에 이어 ⓐ 'Laughing marks를 사용하여 친구들을 얼마나 좋아하는지 또는 그들과 함께 있어서 얼마나 행복한지를 그들에게 보여 줄 수 있다.'고 앞에서 한 말에 대해 추가로 진술하고 ⓒ '웃어라, 문자로 된 형태로라도. 그러면 친구들도 여러분과 함께 웃을 것이다.'로 마무리 하는 순서가 적절하다.

27 facial expression: 얼굴 표정

28 ROFL은 'Rolling on the Floor Laughing'의 첫 글자들을 따서 만든 말이다.

29 ⓐ such as: ~와 같은, 예를 들어 ⓑ as: [양태] ~한[하는] 것과 같이, ~하는 대로(접속사)

30 'We laugh even in our writings'라고 했다.

31 ⓒ의 it은 앞에 나온 "Ha-ha"를 의미한다.

Lesson 1 (중간)

> **01** ③　**02** ①　**03** ②　**04** ②　**05** ①
> **06** I wonder what he did.　　**07** ③
> **08** (1) 해석 A: 그는 변호사인 아들이 하나 있다. B: 그는 아들이 하나 있는데, 그 아들은 변호사다. (2) 의미의 차이: A는 변호사인 아들이 하나 있다고 했으므로 다른 아들이 또 있을 가능성이 있는 반면, B는 아들이 하나 인데, 그가 변호사라고 했으므로 아들이 한 명이라는 의미상의 차이가 있다.
> **09** ④　**10** ①　**11** ⑤　**12** ④　**13** ④　**14** ⑤
> **15** (1) visually
> 　(2) 이유: 입을 벌리고 눈을 질끈 감은 채 웃는 얼굴을 보여주기 때문에 더 시각적이다.
> **16** ②　**17** ③　**18** ①　**19** ③　**20** ④　**21** ⑤　**22** ⑤
> **23** ③　**24** ④　**25** Laughing Out Loud
> **26** ②　**27** ④　**28** ①　**29** ③

01 순서대로 • symbol • expression • laughter • stands for가 들어간다.

02 VTS 콘서트가 언제인지는 알 수 없다.

03 앞에서 'My dog is sick. He won't eat at all.'이라고 했으므로 'That's too bad.(정말 안됐구나.)'가 적절하다.

04 'Let's have video chats often.'이라고 했다.

05 모두 계속적 용법이므로 that은 쓸 수 없고 (A) 선행사가 사물이므로 which, (B) 선행사가 사람이고 목적격이므로

who나 whom, (C) 선행사가 사람이고 주격이므로 who가 적절하다.

06 간접의문문은 '의문사+주어+동사'의 어순이다. 'I wonder what he did.'로 써야 한다.

07 ① wonder that → wonder if[whether] ② whose is this book → whose book this is ④ Do you think who → Who do you think ⑤ does it cost → it costs

08 관계대명사의 한정적 용법과 계속적 용법의 차이를 잘 알아두어야 한다.

09 ① that → who ② they → 삭제
③ Jenny → which Jenny ⑤ it → 삭제

10 계속적 용법의 관계대명사로 사물이 선행사이므로 which가 적절하다.

11 간접의문문은 '의문사+주어+동사'의 어순이다.

12 계속적 용법의 관계대명사로 사람이 선행사이므로 who가 적절하다. 계속적 용법의 관계대명사는 '접속사+대명사'의 역할을 하며 여기서는 'and she'의 역할을 한다.

13 'Some emojis have grown bigger and some even move or make laughing sounds.'라고 했다.

14 간접의문문이므로 '의문사(how much)+주어(we)+동사(care for them)'의 어순이 적절하다. 'how often, how much, how many books, what color'처럼 하나의 의미 단위로 쓰이는 의문사구는 하나의 의문사처럼 취급한다.

15 'It shows a laughing face with a mouth open and eyes closed tightly.'라고 했다. visually: 시각적으로, (눈에) 보이도록

16 'The emoticon XD expresses our happy feelings more visually than ha-ha and LOL do.'에서 ha-ha가 우리의 행복한 감정을 표현한다는 것을 알 수 있다.

17 People also use ROFL quite often. ROFL means "Rolling On the Floor Laughing."를 관계대명사로 연결한 문장이다. 그러므로 which가 가리키는 것은 선행사인 ROFL이다.

18 간접의문문이므로 '의문사(how much, how happy)+주어(we)+동사(care for them, are with them)'의 어순이 적절하다. 하나의 의미 단위로 쓰이는 의문사구는 하나의 의문사처럼 취급한다.

19 'Lots of laughing emojis are available to use online'이라고 했다.

20 ⓐ funny something → something funny ⓑ has used → has been used ⓒ had become → have

become ⓔ closing → closed

21 'The emoticon XD expresses our happy feelings more visually than ha-ha and LOL do.'라고 했다.

22 (A) grow를 쓸 경우 현재만을 나타내므로 'have grown'으로 과거부터 현재까지를 나타내는 것이 적절하다. (B) 좋아하는 것을 숫자가 아닌 양으로 나타내므로 much (C) 명령문,+and ...: ~해라, 그러면 …

23 'We laugh even in our writings, such as emails or texts'라고 했다.

24 간접의문문은 '의문사+주어+동사'의 어순이다. 'what it means'로 써야 한다.

25 LOL은 'Laughing Out Loud'의 첫 글자만을 쓴 것이다.

26 ROFL을 선행사로 하는 계속적 용법의 관계대명사 which가 적절하다.

27 emoticon을 언급하는 글에서 '공잡기를 좋아하는 귀여운 개 Lucky'에 대한 언급은 어색하다.

28 'It's an emoticon, which is a group of letters or symbols used to represent a facial expression'이라고 했다.

29 간접의문문이므로 '의문사(how much)+주어(we)+동사(care for them)'의 어순이 적절하다. 'how often, how much, how many books, what color'처럼 하나의 의미 단위로 쓰이는 의문사구는 하나의 의문사처럼 취급한다.

Lesson 2 (중간)

01 ②	02 ③	03 ②, ⑤	04 ①	05 ③	06 ④
07 ③	08 ①	09 ①	10 ②	11 ③	12 ②	13 ②
14 ③	15 ④	16 ①	17 ①	18 ④	19 ③	20 ④
21 ②	22 this awful place	23 ③	24 ①	25 ④
26 ①	27 ③	28 ②	29 ④	30 ⑤	31 ④	32 ②

01 admit: ~에게 입장[입회·입학·입국]을 허가하다, 인정하다, 허용하다

02 ③번은 '그것을 돌보고 있다'는 뜻으로 어색하지만 나머지는 모두 '주제 소개하기'로 쓰일 수 있다.

03 'We can put a bench there, too.', 'How about putting some flower pots around the bench?'라고 했다.

04 be helpful for: ~에게 도움이 되다, thank A for B: B에 대하여 A에게 감사하다

05 (A) Anne이 발견한 시점(found: 과거)보다 앞서는 시점

이므로 과거완료로 나타내는 것이 적절하다. (B) 어제 (Yesterday)의 일이므로 과거시제가 적절하다.

06 '벽에 뭔가 필요'하다는 주어진 글에 이어, 맞다며 그것에 대해서 함께 이야기 해 보자는 (B)가 나오고, 회원 목록을 붙일 필요가 있다는 (D)가 이어지고, 좋은 생각이라며 이번 학년도의 우리 계획도 벽에 필요하다는 (A)가 나오고, 맞다며 우리가 중요한 학교 행사를 기억하는 데 도움이 될 거라는 (E)가 이어지고, 좋은 의견을 내줘서 고맙다는 (C)가 나오는 순서가 자연스럽다.

07 Yuna가 말한 시점(told: 과거)보다 앞서는 시점이므로 과거완료로 나타내는 것이 적절하다.

08 even, much, far, a lot, still 등은 비교급을 수식하지만, very는 비교급을 수식하지 못한다.

09 과거완료 'had lost'로 열려고 하는 시점보다 앞서는 시점임을 나타내도록 쓴다.

10 'the very'로 비교급을 수식할 수 없다.

11 Anne이 본 시점(saw: 과거)보다 앞서는 시점이므로 과거완료로 나타내는 것이 적절하다.

12 ① terrified: (몹시) 무서워[두려워]하는 ② regretful: 후회하는 ③ delighted: 아주 기뻐[즐거워]하는 ④ optimistic: 낙관적인, 낙관하는 ⑤ doubtful: 확신이 없는, 의심[의문]을 품은

13 'On the weekends that followed, we made rows, planted flower and vegetable seeds, and watered them.'이라고 했다.

14 내가 발견한 시점(found: 과거)보다 앞서는 시점이므로 과거완료로 나타내는 것이 적절하다.

15 (A) 내가 기뻐한 시점(was: 과거)보다 앞서는 시점이므로 과거완료로 나타내는 것이 적절하다. (B) 비교급 (better)을 강조할 수 있는 even, much, far, a lot, still 등이 적절하다.

16 (A) 사역동사 make의 목적격보어로 동사원형 work, (B) stopped의 목적어로 동명사 'complaining'이 적절하다.

17 even, much, far, a lot, still 등으로 비교급을 강조할 수 있으나 very는 쓸 수 없다.

18 도입부의 'I complained'로 보아 'irritated'가 적절하고 'what a good thing we did!'로 보아 'proud'가 적절하다.

19 'We filled fifty trash bags with waste and pulled wild plants.'라고 했다.

20 'what a good thing we did!'로 보아 'proud(자랑스러운)'가 적절하다.

21 mess up을 clean up으로 고쳐야 한다.

22 (A)의 it은 앞에 나온 this awful place를 가리킨다.

23 ⓑ has made → had made ⓓ filled with → filled

24 'he divided the lot into four parts with string and assigned five people to each part.'라고 한 후 'We filled fifty trash bags with waste and were ready to pull wild plants.'라고 한 다음에 'we pulled and pulled'라고 했으므로 ①번이 적절하다.

25 'I complained the whole day.', 'I didn't understand why we were working on this place.' 등으로 보아 'unpleased(기뻐하지 않는, 불만인)'가 적절하다.

26 even, much, far, a lot, still 등으로 비교급을 수식하지만 very는 비교급을 수식하지 못한다.

27 ⓓ는 'Johnny's Shop'이지만 나머지는 'this place'를 가리킨다.

28 turn ... into ~: …를 ~로 바꾸다
divide ... into ~: …를 ~로 나누다

29 20명을 4로 나누면 5명이다.

30 'We were all wondering where to begin.'이라고 했다.

31 그 지역에 얼마나 많은 종류의 식물이 있는지는 알 수 없다.

32 내가 발견한 시점(found: 과거)보다 앞서는 시점이므로 과거완료로 나타내는 것이 적절하다.

Lesson 2 (중간)

```
01 ⑤  02 ④  03 ④  04 ④
05 Mike had told me a lie
06 (1) even/much/far/still more
   (2) 이유: 비교급인 more를 강조해 '훨씬'이라는 의미
   를 나타내는 부사는 even, much, far, still 등이 있다.
07 Playing baseball is even better than watching
   baseball games.
08 ③  09 ②  10 ⑤  11 ③  12 ⑤  13 ⑤  14 ①
15 ②  16 ③  17 ③  18 ①
19 That first day was the toughest.
20 ②  21 ④  22 ⑤  23 ④  24 ⑤  25 ③  26 ②
27 ①  28 ④
```

01 complain: to say that you are not satisfied with something: 불평하다

02 앞에서 '좋은 생각이야!'라고 했으므로 'Thank you for

suggesting it(제안해 줘서 고마워.)'이 적절하다.

03 Seho가 'I'll bring one of mine.'이라고 했다.

04 (A)는 전치사 about의 목적어이고, (B)는 전치사 for의 목적어이므로 동명사가 나와야 한다.

05 'got angry'보다 'told me a lie'가 먼저 일어난 일이므로 told me a lie를 과거완료를 이용하여 'had told me a lie'로 나타낸다.

06 비교급은 even, much, far, a lot, still 등으로 강조한다.

07 비교급 better를 even으로 강조한다.

08 '일할 준비가 되었다'는 주어진 글에 이어, 어디서부터 시작해야 할지 궁금해하는 (B)가 나오고, 그때 Hernandez 씨가 일을 분배하고 (C)가 이어지며, 점심 무렵, 쓰레기봉투 50개를 쓰레기로 채웠고, 잡초를 뽑을 준비가 된 (A)가 이어지는 것이 적절하다.

09 'He found that somebody had cooked rice for him.'으로 써야 한다.

10 그들이 얼마나 많은 잡초를 뽑았는지는 알 수 없다.

11 very는 비교급을 수식할 수 없다.

12 'the tomatoes doubled in size in just a few days'라고 했다.

13 what으로 시작하는 감탄문이다. what a good thing we did!

14 'what a good thing we did!' 'I'm proud ~' 등에서 '뿌듯함'이 적절함을 알 수 있다.

15 'I complained the whole day.', 'I didn't understand why we were working on this place.' 등으로 보아 'irritated(짜증이 난)'가 적절하다.

16 across from: ~ 건너편[맞은편]에

17 주어진 문장의 They가 가리키는 것이 (C) 앞의 'the plants'이므로 (C)가 적절하다.

18 필자가 마을을 위해 지금 무슨 일을 하는지는 알 수 없다.

19 the를 'first day' 앞에 쓰지 않고 'toughest' 앞에 써야 하는 것에 주의한다.

20 ⓑ에서 'stopped complaining'이라고 했다.

21 A: to enjoy와 병렬 관계로 to talk, B: 지금도 이어지고 있으므로 have been, C: of의 목적어로 동명사 picking, D: 현재 바뀐 상태를 나타내므로 has become 이 적절하다.

22 'I'm in charge of picking flowers for the nursing home on Fourth Street.'라고 했다.

23 ⓓ에서 사역동사 made의 목적격보어로 원형부정사 sneeze가 나와야 한다.

24 'As we pulled and pulled, dust filled the air and

25 'the plants had started popping up'의 내용을 설명하는 문장들이 이어지는데 주어진 문장의 First로 보아 맨 처음에 나와야 하므로 ③이 적절하다.

26 글쓴이가 첫날에 무엇을 했는지는 알 수 없다.

27 'I complained the whole day.', 'I didn't understand why we were working on this place.' 등으로 보아 'upset(화가 난)'이 적절하다.

28 Ⓐ, Ⓑ, Ⓓ, Ⓔ: the ugly, old, empty lot Ⓒ: trash

Lesson 3 (기말)

01 unusual: different from what is usual or normal 특이한, 색다른

02 ⑤번은 '나는 네가 경주에서 이기는 것이 두렵다'라는 말로 어색하다.

03 'not only A but also B'에서 A와 B에는 문법적으로 동등한 것이 와야 한다. 주어이므로 him을 he로 고쳐야 한다.

04 'You always make us laugh out loud.'라고 했다.

05 keep one's fingers crossed: 행운을 빌다

06 (1) 'made to Nick'이 아니라 'made for Nick'으로 쓰는 것에 주의한다.
    (2) 'Nick was made happy'로 쓰는 것에 주의한다.

07 모두 '격려'하거나 '행운'을 비는 말로 다음의 '고맙다'는 말에 자연스럽게 이어지는데 ④번은 '나도 참가하고 싶다'는 말로 자연스럽지 않다.

08 '형용사/부사+enough to부정사'는 '…할 정도로 충분히 ~한/하게'라는 뜻이다.

09 (1) 'to find her pet cat'이 happy를 수식하도록 한다 (부사적 용법).
    (2) 'to read for fun'이 some books를 수식하도록 한다(형용사적 용법).

10 'To save money, the Navy made its sailors shout, "Bang!" instead of using real bombs.'라고 했다.

11 not only A but also B = B as well as A: A뿐만 아니라 B도

12 주어진 문장의 'And'로 (C) 앞의 내용에 동등한 것을 추가하므로 (C)가 적절하다.

13 부정문을 만드는 조동사 'does not' 다음에 나오는 동사이므로 동사원형 bring이 적절하다.

14 until[till]이 적절하다.

15 'The prizes are presented by real Nobel winners'라고 했다.

16 'The Ig Novel Prizes are awarded for discoveries that "first make one laugh and then think."'라고 했으므로 'laughable'이 적절하다.

17 (A) 앞의 내용과 동등한 것이 추가적으로 연결되므로 And가 적절하다. (B) 앞의 내용과 상반되는 것이 연결되므로 But이 적절하다.

18 'To save money'라고 했으므로 'shout, "Bang!" instead of using real bombs'가 적절하다.

19 'funny enough for you to laugh out loud', 'bring a smile to your face' 등으로 보아 ③번 'humor'가 적절하다.

20 'Ig Nobel 상의 기원'에 대한 언급은 없다.

21 ⓐ와 ①: 사역동사 ② 수여동사 ③, ④, ⑤ 일반동사

22 동명사 Throwing이 주어이므로 is가 적절하다.

23 'ten trillion Zimbabwean dollars(10조의 짐바브웨 달러)'를 하나의 단위처럼 생각하여 단수로 받는 것에 주의한다.

24 마지막에 'If that still does not bring a smile to your face, how about this?'라고 했으므로 ⑤번이 적절하다.

25 뒤에서 'If that still does not bring a smile to your face'라고 했으므로 'humor'가 적절하다.

26 이어서 나오는 'Maybe not.'에서도 알 수 있듯이 '이 연구 과제는 노벨상을 받을 정도까지는 아니다.'라는 의미이다.

Lesson 3 (기말) 2회

01 ② **02** ③ **03** ⑤

04 The songs of Paul Kim are easy enough to sing.

05 ③ **06** ① **07** ①

08 He is not only smart but also kind.

09 (1) He promised not to watch too much TV.
(2) He tried to exercise more and eat less. 혹은 He tried to eat less and exercise more.

10 ② **11** ⑤ **12** ① **13** ② **14** ① **15** ④ **16** ③
17 ② **18** ⑤ **19** ⑤ **20** ⑤ **21** ① **22** ① **23** ②
24 ③ **25** ② **26** ②

01 'I can't wait for your game.'이 되어야 한다.

02 '하지만 엄마, 전 경주에서 이길지 잘 모르겠어요.'라는 뜻이므로 ③번 '불안함'이 적절하다.

03 Miso가 'You sound like our English teacher.'라고 한 것으로 보아 Jimin이 영어 선생님이 말하는 것을 흉내냈음을 알 수 있다. 영어 선생님의 쇼에 대해 말한 것이 아니다.

04 형용사/부사+enough to부정사: …할 정도로 충분히 ~한/하게

05 '체육 대회가 정말 기다려진다.'라는 말에 어울리는 것은 '학급을 대표해서 농구를 할 거야'라는 말이다.

06 'not only A but also B'는 'A뿐만 아니라 B도'라는 뜻으로 A와 B에는 문법적으로 동등한 것이 와야 하며 주어로 쓰일 때는 B에 동사를 일치시킨다.
② science not only but also history → not only science but also history
③ love → loves
④ read → reading
⑤ study → studies

07 ② enough small → small enough
③ fighting → fight
④ to wear enough → enough to wear
⑤ enough fast running → fast enough to run

08 not only A but also B: A뿐만 아니라 B도

09 (1) to부정사의 부정은 not을 to부정사 앞에 쓴다.
(2) try to부정사: ~하려고 노력하다

10 not only A but also B: A뿐만 아니라 B도

11 'The prizes are presented by real Nobel winners' 라고 했다.

12 (A) 년도 앞에는 in을 쓴다. (B) interest in: ~에 대한 흥미 (C) be filled with: ~로 가득 차다

13 ⓑ의 one은 부정대명사로 an Ig Nobel Prize를 가리킨다.

14 사람들을 웃게 만드는 시상식에 관한 이야기가 이어지므로 Ⓐ가 적절하다.

15 ㉠ things를 수식하는 주격 관계대명사 that 또는 which, ㉡ ten trillion Zimbabwean dollars를 수식하는 계속적 용법의 주격 관계대명사 which가 적절하다.

16 the ceremony가 주어이므로 makes가 적절하다.

17 주어진 문장이 (B) 뒤의 대답 'Maybe not.'에 대한 질문이므로 (B)가 적절하다.

18 해군이 선원들에게 '~하도록 시킨' 것이므로 능동태가 적절하다.

19 be filled with: ~로 가득 차다

20 수상자들이 얼마나 많은 돈을 받는지는 나와 있지 않다.

21 빈칸에는 차례대로 1991, laugh, think, Han Jiwon, Coffee가 들어간다.

22 '이그노벨상 시상식도 또한 사람들을 웃게 만든다.'는 말에 이어 '사람들이 지루해하지 않도록 하는 재미있는 것들이 많이 있다.'는 제시된 문장이 온 후 다양한 사례들이 이어지는 것이 자연스러우므로 (A)가 적절하다.

23 뒤에서 'to laugh out loud'라고 했으므로 ⓑ의 gloomy를 funny 정도로 고치는 것이 적절하다. gloomy: 울적한, 침울한, 우울한

24 Ig Nobel Prizes의 개회사와 폐회사에 대한 언급 이후에 갑자기 '졸업식'을 언급하는 ⓒ는 어색하다.

25 (A) research on: ~에 대한 연구 (B) 년도 앞에는 in을 쓴다.

26 문맥상 '과학에 대한 사람들의 흥미를 늘리기 위해'가 적절하다.

Lesson 4 (기말) 1회

01 ③ **02** ⑤ **03** ② **04** ⑤ **05** ⑤ **06** ① **07** ①
08 ③ **09** ⑤ **10** ① **11** ⑤ **12** ⑤ **13** ② **14** ④
15 ① **16** ② **17** ⑤ **18** ④ **19** ③ **20** ④
21 missed → missing **22** ⑤ **23** ② **24** ③

01 '너는 내가 꿈을 포기해야 한다고 생각하니?'라는 질문에 '네가 가르치기를 잘한다고 생각해.'라는 대답이 이어지는 것으로 보아 'No, never give up.(아니, 절대 포기하지 마.)'이 나오는 것이 적절하다.

02 '왜 실망하고 있는지' 묻는 주어진 글에 이어, (D) 발표를 잘하지 못했다고 이유를 언급하고 (B) '괜찮다며 발표가

약간 빨랐지만, 마음에 들었다'라고 위로하자 (C) 더 천천히 말해야 한다고 생각하는지 의견을 묻고 (A) 그렇다고 답하는 순서가 적절하다.

03 왜 실망했는지 묻자, ⓒ 오디션에 떨어졌다고 답하고 Ⓐ 유감을 표명하고 Ⓓ 계속 노력해야 할지 의견을 묻자 Ⓑ 물론이라며 다음에는 더 잘할 것이라고 답하는 순서가 적절하다.

04 'Why are you so disappointed, Ryan?'이라는 질문에 'My parents won't let me enter Superstar 101, a singing competition.'이라고 답했다.

05 앞에서 'you look down today'라고 한 것으로 보아 'Why are you disappointed?(왜 실망하고 있니?)'가 적절하다.

06 밑줄 친 ⓐ는 '조언'을 구하는 말이다.

07 뒤에 나오는 'We lost the basketball game because of my mistake.(내 실수 때문에 우리가 농구 시합에서 졌어.)' 등으로 보아 'You look down today.'나 'You don't look happy.' 정도가 적절하다.

08 (A) against: ~에 반대하여 for: ~에 찬성하여 (B) '노래를 좋아하는 것'은 '수'가 아닌 '양'으로 나타낼 수 있다. (C) advise: 충고하다(동사) advice: 충고(명사)

09 Ryan이 언제 자기가 만든 노래를 부모님 앞에서 부를지는 알 수 없다.

10 (A) 'While he was looking at the map'을 분사구문으로 고치면 'Looking at the map'이 된다. (B) 그가 피곤해진 것이므로 'Being tired' 또는 'Feeling tired'로 써야 한다.

11 keep A from ~ing: A가 ~하는 것을 막다, 방해하다 make people get bored: 사람들을 지루하게 하다

12 'bathrooms'라는 복수 명사가 나오므로 is가 아니라 are 가 되어야 한다.

13 'her manager Al Harrison recognized her ability' 라고 했다.

14 분사구문은 부사절의 주어와 주절의 주어가 같을 때 부사절의 접속사와 주어를 없애고 동사를 현재분사형으로 바꾸는 것이다.

15 'Mary Jackson was the character I liked the most of the three.'라고 했다.

16 ⓐ와 ②: 관계대명사 ①, ④ 의문형용사 ③ 감탄문에 쓰이는 형용사 ⑤ 의문대명사

17 'There are no COLORED bathrooms in this building. I have to run half a mile away just to use the bathroom.'이라고 했다.

18 앞 문장의 내용과 상반되는 내용이 나오므로 'However' 가 적절하다.

19 'Mary Jackson was the character I liked the most of the three.'라고 했다.

20 주어진 문장의 However로 Ⓓ 앞의 내용과 상반되는 내용이 이어지므로 Ⓓ가 적절하다.

21 missing: 없어진, 행방불명된

22 'her manager Al Harrison recognized her ability' 라고 했다.

23 ⓐ 변화 ① 거스름 돈 ⓑ, ②: ~로서 ⓒ 기회 ③ 우연 ⓓ ~에 용감하게 맞서다 ④ 뻔뻔스러움 ⓔ 눈물 ⑤ 찢다

24 뒤에서 'finally gave her permission'이라고 하고 있으므로 ⓒ는 'depressed(우울한)'가 아닌 'impressed (감명을 받은)'가 적절하다.

MEMO